Ferghana Valley

The Heart of Central Asia

With some twelve million inhabitants, the Ferghana Valley is one of the most densely populated places in the world. It is also the most volatile region of Central Asia. Not only is the area ethnically and linguistically diverse, it is politically divided, with parts ruled by three different states—Uzbekistan, Tajikistan, and the Kyrgyz Republic—whose distant capital cities all relegate Ferghana to their respective peripheries.

These complexities make a comprehensive, multidimensional understanding of the Ferghana region all the more elusive. In order to construct such an analysis, the Central Asia–Caucasus Institute assembled an international, interdisciplinary team of thirty scholars with the requisite expertise. Their carefully planned, collaboratively authored chapters cover the historical and topical terrain with unmatched depth and breadth and balance.

STUDIES OF CENTRAL ASIA
AND THE CAUCASUS

Books in this series are published in association with the Central Asia–Caucasus Institute and Silk Road Studies Program Joint Center at the Johns Hopkins University's Paul H. Nitze School of Advanced International Studies in Washington, DC, and the Institute for Security and Development Policy in Stockholm, under the editorship of Svante Cornell.

Ferghana Valley

The Heart of Central Asia

EDITED BY

S. FREDERICK STARR
WITH BAKTYBEK BESHIMOV,
INOMJON I. BOBOKULOV,
AND PULAT SHOZIMOV

M.E.Sharpe
Armonk, New York
London, England

The EuroSlavic and Transroman fonts used to create this work are © 1986–2011
Payne Loving Trust. EuroSlavic and Transroman are available
from Linguist's Software, Inc., www.linguistsoftware.
com, P.O. Box 580, Edmonds, WA 98020-0580 USA, tel (425) 775-1130.

Library of Congress Cataloging-in-Publication Data

Starr, S. Frederick.
  Ferghana Valley : the heart of Central Asia / edited by S. Frederick Starr with Baktybek
Beshimov, Inomjon I. Bobokulov, and Pulat Shozimov.
  p. cm. — (Studies of Central Asia and the Caucasus)
  Includes bibliographical references and index.
  ISBN 978-0-7656-2998-2 (cloth : alk. paper) — ISBN 978-0-7656-2999-9 (pbk. : alk. paper)
  1. Fergana Valley—History. 2. Fergana Valley—Geography. 3. Fergana Valley—Social
conditions. I. Beshimov, Baktybek. II. Bobokulov, Inomjon I. III. Shozimov, P.D. IV. Title.

DK919.F47S73 2011
958—dc22   2010044468

Printed in the United States of America

The paper used in this publication meets the minimum requirements of
American National Standard for Information Sciences
Permanence of Paper for Printed Library Materials,
ANSI Z 39.48-1984.

∞

| EB (c) | 10 | 9 | 8 | 7 | 6 | 5 | 4 | 3 | 2 | 1 |
| EB (p) | 10 | 9 | 8 | 7 | 6 | 5 | 4 | 3 | 2 | 1 |

Contents

Acknowledgments

This book was conceived by Drs. Pulat Shozimov of Dushanbe, Tajikistan, and Dr. Inomjon Bobokulov of Tashkent, Uzbekistan. Shozimov, having achieved early fame as a chess master and athlete, was already one of the most broadly gauged and internationally acclaimed anthropologists and ethnographers from Central Asia. Bobokulov, with his mild manner and fast-rising fame in the field of international relations, brought an encyclopedic knowledge of the region's best social scientists, historians, and economists. At the time, both were fellows of the Central Asia–Caucasus Institute at Johns Hopkins School of Advanced International Studies (SAIS) in Washington, DC. They burst into my office, carefully closed the door and, not even bothering to seat themselves, announced the plan.

Now, in the context of the early twenty-first century, it is nothing short of amazing that scholars from two countries that maintain rocky relations with each other might conceive a joint study on one of the most sensitive topics that divides them. So much the better, we agreed. But we immediately realized that the project would be incomplete without participation from the third country into which the Ferghana Valley has been divided since 1991, the Kyrgyz Republic. Dr. Bakty-bek Beshimov was the obvious choice. A native of Osh and former rector of the university in that city, Beshimov had coordinated the United Nations' program of research and assistance in the Ferghana Valley in the early 1990s. To our delight, Beshimov agreed to join us.

This book is the product of a remarkable team effort involving Shozimov, Bobo-kulov, and Beshimov, a feat of cooperation that should be the envy of, and model for, political leaders in all three Ferghana countries. As the book's editor, I know better than anyone else the generous yet rigorous spirit in which all three went about their assignments. It has been an honor to collaborate with them.

Once the general issues and topics had been laid out, the four of us began seeking qualified scholars to contribute to the project of which we dreamed. Our plan was to have a "lead author" for each chapter, with the key people coming from the three Ferghana states. They were to be assisted by "contributing authors" for each chapter, who would be drawn from the other two countries. In selecting authors and contributors, we faced an abundance of riches and difficult choices had to be made. The resulting team proved remarkable in every respect. Little did we imagine when we began that the Ferghana book would include the best study ever written on the Kokand Khanate or that it would present astonishingly new material on recent religious groups. The editors join me in thanking all the authors for their generous contributions.

Even though the "Ferghana Project" was conceived in the Internet age, it nonetheless posed complex problems of coordination. These were ably handled by Katarina Lesandric and Roman Muzalevsky at the Central Asia–Caucasus Institute. Their task was as thankless—until now—as it was endless, with drafts to be elicited from several dozen very busy scholars, comments to be shared, corrections to be made, and then more drafts to be sent out for more comments and more corrections, ad nauseam. And so, on behalf of all the editors, I want to send warm thanks to these two heroes of virtual labor. Without them this book would never have seen the light of day.

All the members of the Ferghana team join me in expressing our deep gratitude to M.E. Sharpe's Irina Burns, whose meticulous and highly professional editing brought unity to the work of authors from six countries and as many scholarly traditions.

The Ferghana Project was made possible through a generous grant to the Central Asia–Caucasus Institute from the Sasakawa Peace Foundation. Its Washington director, Mr. Keiji Iwatake, had to endure the multiple delays that were inevitable in so complex a project, and he did so with patience and understanding.

Finally, warm thanks to Anna Starr Townsend for her splendid design of the cover. Selected by the editors from a bouquet of half a dozen alternatives she offered, this one appealed because it suggested that Ferghana was somehow still the center of Central Asia and also a bright and colorful place, rather than the grim and conflicted zone we imagine based on all too many recent events.

S. Frederick Starr
Chairman, Central Asia–Caucasus Institute, SAIS

Introducing the Ferghana Valley

S. Frederick Starr

Besides its beauty and abundant natural endowments, nothing about the Ferghana Valley is simple. For one thing, it is not a linear valley defined by rivers, although it roughly corresponds to the basins of the lower Naryn and Kara Darya rivers and their confluence to form the Syr Darya River. Rather, it is a large and roughly oblong flatland defined by no fewer than five chains of surrounding mountains, the Kuramin, Chatkal, Alai, Ferghana, and Turkestan ranges. The distance from north to south is about 100 kilometers, while east to west it measures approximately 300 kilometers at its widest. On a very clear day between late October and April one can stand in the middle of this valley and see snow-capped mountains on the horizon in every direction. Another distinctive feature of the valley is that its name is not really Ferghana, or Fergana (forms that date from Russian colonial rule), but Farghona. However, given that the term Ferghana or Fergana has gained common usage we will use it, while acknowledging that a different name prevails locally. Either way, the single name suggests a degree of uniformity or unity that does not exist. This non-valley with a name imposed from without is divided both linguistically and politically, with parts ruled by three states: Uzbekistan, Tajikistan, and the Kyrgyz Republic. Yet, as if to emphasize the theme of complexity, the three national zones have as much or more in common with each other than they do with the rest of the states of which each is a part.

It is worth pausing further on the geography of this peculiar place. Though seemingly flat, Ferghana rises to broad terraces in the north and long, sloping terraces in the south, on which one finds the Kyrgyz town of Batken. Nature made Ferghana a high semi-desert, ranging from 400 to 500 meters in altitude. But like the Fertile Crescent in the Middle East and the Indus Valley in Pakistan, it was the site of ancient but highly efficient irrigation systems. Thanks to irrigation, this naturally dry zone supports a major cotton industry. Much of the rest of the land is devoted to water-consuming crops, including *devzira*, the widely available local rice, hot peppers, and *husaini*, the tasty finger-like grapes. The Syr Darya and other rivers are home to the large and abundant *sazan* fish, and the roads and avenues around the ancient silk-producing center at Margilan are lined with lush mulberries. Besides these "signature" crops, numerous other forms of agricultural produce thrive throughout the valley.

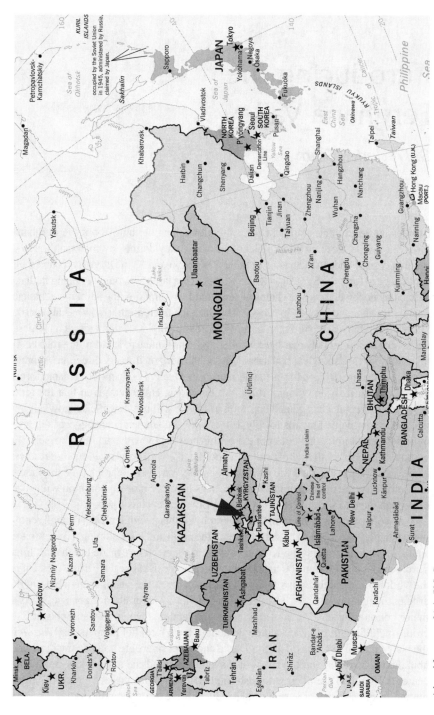

Adapted from map of Asia (U.S. Government sources).

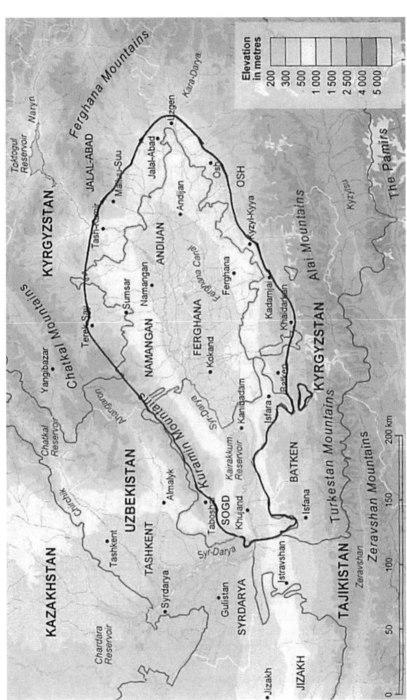

Adapted from map of Ferghana Valley topography and hydrography by Viktor Novikov and Philippe Rekacewicz (UNEP/GRID-Arendal).

Further paradoxes abound. If the valley is broad, it is also surprisingly intimate. The central city of Namangan in Uzbekistan is a mere 60 kilometers from the eastern Uzbek city of Andijan, which in turn is only 50 kilometers from Osh in Kyrgyzstan. From Kokand in Uzbekistan to Khujand in Tajikistan is also a mere 125 kilometers. Demographers identify the Ferghana Valley as one of the most densely inhabited areas on earth. Yet in the lush countryside one encounters empty vistas of green, and hay set out to dry on little-traveled trunk highways, while in the cities a leisurely and spacious life prevails, with no sense of teeming masses.

Life may be leisurely but, for many, it is not prosperous. Poverty exists amid natural wealth. And even though irrigation has been practiced in the valley for two millennia, the present system is one of the least efficient anywhere.

In a world of pressing global issues and a myriad of crises, what claim can the distant and paradoxical Ferghana Valley make on our attention? To start, the region can reasonably be said to lie in the heart of Central Asia. As such, the Valley has made an inordinate contribution to the history and culture of the region as a whole. Today, with a population of nearly twelve million, it accounts for approximately one-fifth of the total population of formerly Soviet Central Asia. Its population density on average is 360 persons per square kilometer and reaches 550 in some places. This compares with a density for all central Asia of a mere fourteen persons per square kilometer. Beyond this, residents of the valley comprise nearly one-third of the population of Tajikistan and of Kyrgyzstan, and close to one-quarter of the population of Uzbekistan. As such, whatever happens in the valley significantly affects all three of these countries in their economic, political, and religious spheres.

The valley's economic contribution to each of the three countries is enormous. Until the collapse of the USSR, powerful figures from Leninabad (now Khujand) in the Ferghana Valley ruled Tajikistan; and. today's president of Kyrgyzstan, who hails originally from Jalalabad, served earlier in the Ferghana city of Osh. Religious movements in the Ferghana Valley clearly impact the surrounding regions and countries; indeed, it is no exaggeration to say that many of the most important religious, and hence social, currents in all three countries began in the Ferghana Valley.

Heightening these factors is the fact that the Ferghana region as a whole constitutes the largest and most concentrated market in all Central Asia. Even though this market has yet to be developed in the context of a post-socialist economy it is there, an attractive opportunity for investors from the region and elsewhere. Through it passes one of the most ancient east-to-west roads connecting China and India to Europe, a route to which a rail line and a gas pipeline may soon be added. It is already home to an oil refinery and an international automobile plant, and it is the heart of the Central Asian cotton industry, the world's second largest. These factors alone should warrant the world's attention. However, the Ferghana Valley recently has come to the world's notice for an entirely different reason, namely, as a major source of instability now extending over more than two decades. It is true that the Ferghana region was always prone to disasters. A powerful earthquake and resulting floods in the seventeenth century forced Namangan and other cities to move, while a powerful earthquake in 1920 obliterated scores of settlements, killing thousands. But beginning in late Soviet times, the main source of instability became social and cultural conflict, not geology.

Even before the USSR imploded, violence erupted between forcibly resettled Meskhetian Turks and their neighbors in several Ferghana cities in 1989. Then, in 1990 ethnic Uzbeks and Kyrgyz fought bitterly in Osh, Kyrgyzstan's second largest city, situated at the eastern entrance to the valley. In 1992 the Uzbek city of Namangan witnessed an outbreak of religious-based violence that presaged the founding of the radical Islamic Movement of Uzbekistan. In 1999 a Tajik colonel, Mahmud Khudoiberdiev, took control of large areas of the Tajik sector of the valley in an attempt to oust President Emomali Rakhmonov. That same year, and again in 2000, bands of Muslim extremists intent on moving into the valley as a whole invaded the Kyrgyz province of Batken, on the valley's south side adjoining Tajikistan. Later, on March 18, 2005, demonstrators took over the governor's offices in Jalalabad in southern Kyrgyzstan. President Askar Akaev had just been pushed from office, and the Jalalabad events figured centrally in what later became known as Kyrgyzstan's Tulip Revolution. Only two months later, on May 13, 2005, heavily armed religious extremists attacked city offices and a maximum security prison in the nearby Uzbek city of Andijan, taking and killing scores of hostages and giving rise to reprisals from government forces that left large numbers of people dead.

The Kyrgyz sector of the valley once more exploded in conflict in April 2010, this time in the wake of a coup in Bishkek against the corrupt rule of President Kurmanbek Bakiyev, an ethnic Kyrgyz from the country's south, specifically Ferghana. Impoverished locals, stirred up by Bakiyev holdouts, lashed out in frustration at the steady decline of their region's fortunes since the demise of the USSR, with Kyrgyz killing up to a thousand Uzbeks and the latter responding in kind.

Individually and collectively, these and other incidents have given rise to the notion that the Ferghana Valley is fundamentally unstable. The image is one of a zone of crisis, with a generalized state of turmoil lying just beneath the surface which can at any time burst into the light of day. An ample literature on the Ferghana Valley has emerged, much of it the product of freshly coined experts who have read ten articles in order to write the eleventh. Most of these writings can be characterized as "catastrophizing," in that they regard the various explosions of instability as intimately linked with one another causally and arising from supposedly age-old ethnic hostilities across the Ferghana territory. Thus, one study speaks of the valley as an ethnic tinderbox that somehow must be "calmed,"[1] while many others, accepting this hypothesis, confidently trace the source of all recent conflicts to specific governmental policies.[2]

Such speculations—and they are only that—have in common a failure to consider these various incidents in any kind of broader context. Admittedly this is no simple matter, for to do so demands an understanding of very diverse aspects of human activity, including economics, social relations, politics, culture, religion, and a myriad of sub-elements within each of these spheres. This in turn calls for an array of skills that cannot be found in any one analyst or scholar, or even a small group of them. Only a team of social scientists, historians, and linguists could sketch for us the full context of Ferghana life in a manner that would enable us better to understand not only worrisome past events but also future developments, be they positive or negative. Equally important, such a three-dimensional picture of the Ferghana Valley might help policymakers, business leaders, and members of the active public to appreciate the area's full potential and design programs and policies that will allow the region to flower while minimizing existing forces of instability.

To this end, the Central Asia–Caucasus Institute undertook to assemble such a group of scholars. The initiative for this ambitious undertaking came from Dr. Pulat Shozimov of the Tajik Academy of Sciences in Dushanbe, and Dr. Inomjon Bobokulov of the University of World Economy and Diplomacy in Tashkent. Both were Fellows at the Institute in Washington. In the spring of 2005 they asked the Central Asia–Caucasus Institute to mount the project, and for me to serve as general editor, to which I eagerly consented. From the outset, Drs. Shozimov and Bobokulov conceived the "Ferghana Project" as a regional undertaking, involving scholars from all three Ferghana countries. Accordingly, they added to their directorate Dr. Baktybek Beshimov, then provost at the American University of Central Asia, Bishkek, and subsequently a distinguished member of the Kyrgyz Parliament. All three had conducted previous research on the Ferghana region in their respective disciplines. Thus was born the Ferghana Project.

The first task was to map out the parameters of a three-dimensional study of the Ferghana Valley. Members of the core group at once agreed that it would be essential to view the region over time, from its early history to the present. A second axiom to which all assented was that the study must embrace not just the obvious fields of politics, economics and religion, but also ethnography, sociology, and culture. The Ferghana Project's third underlying principle was that it had to include the insights of leading scholars from all three Ferghana countries. The idea was for each scholar to focus on his or her own national territory within the Ferghana region, while also offering insights on the whole.

But how to do this? One approach would have been to commission parallel essays for each chapter heading. But besides rendering the book unreadable, such an approach would have implied greater degrees of disagreement throughout than may in fact exist. Worse, it would have robbed participating scholars of the possibility of comparing their various insights, identifying common elements, and of appreciating legitimate differences where they exist. A better alternative soon presented itself. We decided to commission three "national" essays for each topic, and then designate a "principal author" who would combine and synthesize the various contributions into a single chapter for publication. These "principal authors" would work with the "contributing authors" to assure that all national territories were adequately covered, while also faithfully identifying areas of agreement and disagreement. In the end, however, the published chapters would be the work of the principal authors alone. To assure overall balance, it was agreed that we would impose a rough balance in the number of principal authors from each country.

Two chapters presented a special challenge: Chapter 4 on the delineation of borders during the Soviet period and Chapter 11 on water. These topics are of such great political sensitivity that it was agreed that the principal authors should be drawn from outside the Ferghana countries. In both cases the final choice was obvious. Not only is Dr. Sergey Abashin of the Institute of Ethnography and Anthropology in Moscow an expert on the historical archives in which records pertaining to the delineation of borders are preserved, he also could bring to bear his deep understanding of Soviet policymaking in the 1920s and 1930s. Regarding Ferghana water issues, Dr. Christine Bichsel's recent dissertation for the University of Bern, Switzerland, came immediately to attention, as did her about-to-be-published major monograph on the subject. Each of these principal authors has benefited from the research of the national contributing authors.

This, then, is the process that informed the preparation of this book. Note that it involved the close collaboration of no fewer than twenty-seven scholars from Uzbekistan, Tajikistan, and the Kyrgyz Republic, and one each from the Russian Federation, Switzerland, and the United States. Drafting involved constant and intense interchange among contributing authors, between contributing authors and principal authors, among principal authors, and between principal authors and the four editors. This culminated in a two-day conference in Almaty in August 2008. Had the goal of the Ferghana Project merely been to produce a series of unconnected essays, such close collaboration would have been unnecessary. But the editors and authors aspired to an overall synthesis that simultaneously would be respectful of legitimate differences of fact and interpretation wherever they exist. Considering the number of contentious issues the three Ferghana countries must address as they coexist in the great valley, the Ferghana Project stands as a noble model of collaboration and mutual respect.

As work on the project got underway, the authors immediately faced a perplexing question: what is reality? As is normal in human affairs, the same situation can give rise to very different answers. Thus, to take one example, mention was made of the bloody political and religious conflict that exploded in the Uzbek city of Namangan in 1992. This culminated in a frontal confrontation between a band of militants and newly independent Uzbekistan's new president Islam Karimov. Some argue that this had been the work mainly of a former Soviet Army soldier named Jumabai Khojiyev (nom de guerre, "Namangani"), and did not reflect the local public's sentiments. Others argue to the contrary, and assert that such tensions still simmer just beneath the surface of daily life.

Today there are some 400 madrassas in the Namangan district, but the area is peaceful. At the same time, the city boasts of modern foreign enterprises including Nestle, Tip Top, and others from the Netherlands, Turkey, and Oman. The priests of three churches maintain cordial links with local Muslim leaders at the Khuja

Amin Kabri Mosque. When evening falls, young couples sip juice or locally made cognac at open-air restaurants, the women fashionably adorned in stylish scarves that expose their necks. Back in their family homes, elders still prefer to use the more formal plural "you" as a mark of politeness, reflecting the region's traditional civility.

Which of these images represents the "true" Namangan? In the end, the authors concluded that their task is not to choose between alternative perspectives, each of which may reflect different elements of reality, but rather to present all aspects of the picture, accurately and fairly.

This affirmation has important corollaries. For one, it required that the insights of many disciplines be brought to bear on one and the same situation. The reader will therefore notice that many important subjects appear in more than one chapter, often in quite different lights. Another corollary is that it was important to identify a few fundamental questions that would be addressed again and again throughout the book. In the end, the authors framed nine such questions, each of which will be outlined here.

First, the Project has asked what parts of the valley's long past are relevant to the present. This question lends itself to both simple and complex answers. One might argue, for example, that the collapse of the USSR and subsequent division of the valley into national sovereignties largely shaped what we see today. Or that the last decades of Soviet rule so fundamentally transformed the region that everything that came before was merely a preparation. Does not the forced-march (forty-day) construction of the enormous Ferghana Canal and the unbounded expansion of cotton culture thereafter dwarf all that came before it, and go far toward defining the present? Or maybe the watershed occurred with the delineation of Soviet borders in 1924, which produced a map with all the madcap complexity of a jigsaw puzzle? Yet soon we find ourselves immersed in much earlier events: the brief Turkestan autonomous republic, the tsarist imperial era, the age of the Kokand Khanate . . . or clear back to dim antiquity, recalling how Stalin countered Hitler's boastful claims about Neanderthal Man with his own Ferghana Man. The appearance of those fossil fragments in Ferghana earned their discoverer, a Jew, the Stalin Prize!

Second, the Project has sought to determine whether the Ferghana Valley is in some sense a center—or is it merely a peripheral zone to other centers? This question, too, can be approached in many ways. One might cite the many great trading centers and capitals that once existed there: Kasansai near the Qaratogh Mountains in the east; Ershi near Batken; Babur's birthplace at Aksikent; Andijan in the post-Mongol period; the emirate controlled from Kokand; Novyi Margilan (now Ferghana City) in the tsarist era; and Khujand through the centuries. Surely, one might argue, these suggest that Ferghana's being a central place in politics and economics was long the rule, not the exception. And yet a more present-minded observer might stress the opposite, that the inevitable consequence of the establishment of Soviet national republics was to subordinate all three parts of the Ferghana Valley to distant power centers and to marginalize it.

Third, is there in some sense a "Ferghana" history and culture, and if so what is the role of localism *within* the Ferghana Valley? The case for localism is strong. Most men wear black caps called *do'ppi,* whose design signifies their town of origin. Most Valley residents live within an hour of where they were born, each region prepares the traditional rice and lamb dish in a distinctive manner, and local accents are strong. Going back in time, one encounters the high-wheeled Kokand wagons, distinctive local pottery types, and even special designs stamped in the center of loaves of bread.

Against this is a welter of Ferghana-wide customs. Ferghanans lustily sing a capella at weddings and teahouses (*chaikhanas*), and the Tajiks and Uzbeks share a common instrumental tradition in their variant of the classical *shashmakom.* Unlike their neighbors, they endlessly concoct *askiya,* short poems rich with word play and double meanings on such immortal themes as politics, food, gossip, sex, and the good life. Which of these trends—regional or local—is waxing and which waning? And what meaning does this evolution have for the valley as a whole?

Fourth, what is the interplay between isolation and contact in the life of Ferghana, past and present? One scarcely has to look to find examples of Ferghana's rich involvement with the outer world. As early as the eighth century the region's greatest thinker lived within a few meters of the Silk Road as it passed through the center of Margilan. For centuries, artisans in Aksikent fashioned razor-sharp sabers for the immense Chinese market, while other locals surpassed most of China in their silk exports to the West. The cars rolling off the Korean-American assembly line in Andijan are today's equivalent. And, when the pious elders of Kokand built their new Friday mosque in the eighteenth century, to do so they hauled ninety huge wooden columns all the way from India.

In this connection it is also worth noting that the population of the Ferghana Valley has always been in flux. Waves of migrants have swept in from every direction, including not only Turkic and Iranian peoples but also Russians and other Slavs, Armenians, Germans, and Crimean Tatars. More recently, male laborers from the valley have left to find work elsewhere, whether in Kazakhstan, Russia, Ukraine, or the Persian Gulf states.

But such examples must be balanced against inescapable signs of inward-looking withdrawal. How else could the local population withstand onslaughts from abroad, whether from Alexander the Great, who supped on chicken and bread (*murgh va nan*) in Margilan and found a wife in Khujand, or Russian and then Soviet conquerors, or the goods that flood in from China today?

Fifth, what has been role of religion and of secularism in the Ferghana Valley— and what is that role today? On this crucial subject no less than four alternative narratives compete with one another. One holds that the Ferghana region always has been a land of religious diversity and hence, of necessity, one of tolerance. Until the twelfth century one could find Zoroastrian temples, Buddhist stupas, Syrian Christian churches, Jewish synagogues, and Muslim mosques in close proximity to one another in most Ferghana cities. In the early twenty-first century, governments still defend this pluralism as the norm. That concept competes with the notion of Ferghana as part of the Muslim heartland, the land where the worldly Hanafi school of Sunni jurisprudence was codified, then spread to Afghanistan, Pakistan, and on to India.[3]

Yet another notion stresses the role of secular education in the valley, and in particular the so-called Jadid tradition of the early twentieth century. While the Jadids were themselves pious Muslims, many of the reforms they advocated fed into the Soviet policy of secularism until 1992. And finally one must speak of Muslim fundamentalism, which appeared under tsarist rule and rose to prominence in recent years, with its venomous hostility not only to secularism but to more orthodox traditions of Sunni Islam. An important challenge facing our scholars was to determine how these various strains interact and what the sources of their respective strengths are today.

Sixth, one must ask whether change in the Ferghana Valley characteristically has been driven from within or without, and what prevails in this regard today? Closely related to several of the questions posed above, this demands that we consider different levels of culture. Clearly many changes, from the introduction of sericulture to cell phones to the Olympic tennis center in Andijan, have come from without. Indeed, all the religions that flourished there, with the exception of ancient local deities and Zoroastrianism, came from without as well, as did the transformations wrought by Russian and Soviet rule. But the Ferghana Valley is not a cultural blank slate on which any outsider can write at will. We are obliged to weigh the importance of local responses in many spheres. Specifically, this requires that we consider not only the manner in which foreign ways have been *adopted* in the valley but also the process by which they have been reworked and *adapted* by the forces of local culture to meet local circumstances.

Seventh, have tensions in recent decades arisen from stagnation or from too rapid change? The very process of framing this question poses an intellectual challenge. Surely, one may object, it is possible for each of these seeming opposites to arise out of the other. Is this not precisely what occurred through the process of collectivization after 1929, when age-old patterns of local life were ruthlessly uprooted, but as a result of which whole extended families or local communities moved smoothly into the collective farms, thus transforming them from agents of revolution into breeding-grounds of social stagnation? This possibility creates one of the most elusive questions before us, yet also one of the most important.

Eighth, has the Ferghana Valley characteristically been "over-governed" or "under-governed"— and what is the balance today? This issue, too, calls for fresh thinking from the outset. In all three of the countries that meet in the Ferghana Valley it is customary to speak of authoritarian rule. But the habit of governments imposing decisions from the top down does not necessarily mean that the affected region is over-governed. On the contrary, pretenses of authoritarian rule may coexist with a situation in which decisions are implemented poorly at the community level, or not at all. This in turn raises important questions about the actual interplay over the years between centralized administration and local civic initiatives.

Moreover, both pre- and post-colonial elites in the three distant capitals may be preoccupied with issues far removed from the realities of daily life in the Ferghana Valley. This can lead to a steady breakdown of services, even as the claims of a nominally strong government increase. Such a hypothesis may at first seem highly speculative. But the rise of such figures as the late Ahmadjon Adilov (Odilov in Uzbek), who in late Soviet times ran a virtual state within the state in large parts of the Ferghana Valley, forces us to consider that possibility seriously.

Finally, what is the balance between centripetal and centrifugal forces across the expanse of the Ferghana Valley, that is, between the forces of coordination and un-coordination, integration and disintegration? This is an absolutely central issue, not merely for the Ferghana Valley but for all three of the states that rule there. To a significant degree, developments in the Ferghana Valley not only affect but do much to define the polities of Uzbekistan, Tajikistan, and Kyrgyzstan, and frame the terms in which leaders in Tashkent, Dushanbe, and Bishkek address their countries' various challenges. For this reason, the task of correctly describing the interplay between integration and disintegration both within the Ferghana Valley and in the three new sovereign states assumes particular importance in our enquiry.

These, then, are nine of the key questions to which the authors of this volume sought answers. Taken together, the questions all pertain to issues of identity. What does it mean to be a citizen of Batken, Khujand, or Ferghana City? Is this compatible with being a citizen of the Ferghana Valley as a whole? And how does that identity, if it even exists, relate to the emerging national identities of the three post-colonial states that are still gradually emerging from the demise of the Soviet Union? Our distinguished scholars mulled these questions both individually and collectively, through numerous conversations, e-mail exchanges, sub-group meetings, and at our overall editorial meeting held in Almaty in August 2008. As they considered them, the authors also bore in mind comparable situations elsewhere in the world, both present and past.

Whenever twenty-seven experts come together, one can expect at least twenty-seven perspectives to emerge, if not many more. When they are drawn from three such different countries as comprise the Ferghana Valley, these divergent points of view will be all the more evident. Throughout the volume that follows, such differences have been respectfully acknowledged, and indeed have been treated as alternative sources of insight. In the end, the scholarly values of open-mindedness, genuine curiosity, rigor, and fairness led to more common ground than anyone might have expected at the outset. In the course of the Ferghana Project far more bridges were constructed than demolished.

If the reader finds himself or herself drawn into these debates, and if that reader is moved beyond clichés and stereotypes to embrace some of the universal questions posed by the life-story of this beautiful, complex, vexed, but in the end promising region, the twenty-seven authors will rest contented with their work. All of us have come to realize that to understand the Ferghana Valley is to begin to understand Central Asia itself.

Notes

1. Council on Foreign Relations and Century Foundation, *Calming the Ferghana Valley: Development and Dialogue in the Heart of Central Asia,* Preventive Action Reports, Vol. 4, New York, 1999.

2. The literature on the 2005 Andijan events largely applies this hypothesis. See *Saving Its Secrets: Government Repression in Andijan,* Human Rights Watch, New York, 2005; and International Crisis Group, *The Andijan Uprising,* Asia Briefing no. 38, Brussels and Washington, DC, 2005.

3. The key figure in this development was Burhan al-Din al-Marghinani, 1152–1197 and his seminal code, *Al Hidayah* (The Guidance).

Ferghana Valley

1

The Ferghana Valley: The Pre-Colonial Legacy

*Abdukakhor Saidov (Tajikistan), with
Abdulkhamid Anarbaev (Uzbekistan) and
Valentina Goriyacheva (Kyrgyz Republic)*

The Ferghana Valley, surrounded by mountains on all sides, is one of nature's unique regions. The intermountain plain—the Ferghana Valley itself—was formed a million years ago by a lifting of the earth's crust. It is bounded on the south by the Alai and Turkestan mountain ranges, on the east by the Ferghana range, and on the north and west by the Chatkal and Kuramin mountains. A natural route to the west provides the sole link between the Ferghana Valley and the rest of Central Asia, which is why the Mughal emperor Babur, himself a native of the valley, wrote that the Ferghana Valley is wide open to attack from that direction throughout the year.

Here almost all types of natural landscapes are found, from the sand dunes of central Ferghana to alpine meadows. The valley is distinctive for its dry, continental climate. The high mountain ranges form a natural barrier for water-saturated air masses, which inhibits rain from reaching fields in the heart of the valley. Despite this, the region is able to sustain both agriculture and cattle raising.

The valley is defined by the basins of the Syr Darya, Amu Darya, and Naryn rivers, with the Syr Darya being the valley's largest. Formed at the junction of the Naryn and Kara Darya rivers, its waters flow from east to west across the entire valley, separating it into uneven northern and southern areas. Many run-off channels flow into the Syr Darya from the surrounding mountains, creating in their deltas favorable conditions for human life. The mountains are rich in juniper, hazelnut, hawthorn, and other fruit and berries, as well as diverse fauna.

The Ferghana Valley was initially an agricultural region separated from the nomadic tribes by the encircling mountains. Over time the cultures of farmers and nomads melded together into a single, inseparable history. The Davan kingdom was but one of many societies created there through such symbiosis. These processes led gradually to the mutual enrichment of cultures, values, and traditions among the peoples living on this territory. This imparted to them a common identity that was preserved through the centuries and came to define the Ferghana Valley as a whole.

The first signs of irrigated agriculture in Ferghana date to no later than the fifteenth and sixteenth centuries BCE, that is, during the late Bronze Age. At the time two cultures coexisted there: one agricultural—the Chust—identified by its painted ceramics; and the other cattle breeding—the so-called Kairakkum—with its ceramics drawn from the steppes. In the middle of the second century BCE, a new pastoral culture from the steppes made its appearance in the southern foothills of the Ferghana range and the north of the Alai ridges. This formed part of the Andronovo culture that was widespread in Eurasia.

The remains of more than 80 settlements of the agrarian Chust culture have been discovered. These were situated along rivers on the large, isolated oases at a typical distance of 20–30 kilometers from one another. Thus, in the Uzgen the largest late Bronze Age remains in the Ferghana Valley is the site at Dalverzin, which consists of three parts surrounded by separate defensive walls. The citadel comprises 2 hectares. Its 2.5-meter thick fortification wall is built on the occupation layer and reaches up to 2.6 meters in height. The inner city, with an area of eighteen hectares, is surrounded by a 6-meter defensive wall built on a special platform from adobe bricks (*pahsa*) and rammed earth. Under this base have been discovered occupational layers up to 0.8-meters thick. Inside the fortification, three types of habitations corresponding to the three periods of settlement have been found: frame houses, wattle-and-daub houses, and dugouts. The outer city, with an area of about 5 hectares, was used as a shelter for cattle.

Iurii A. Zadneprovskii delineated three long periods in the history of the site. The first witnessed an unfortified agricultural settlement; in the second period, fortifications were constructed; during the third period, the fortifications were no longer functional and occupational layers appear above them. Carbon 14 analyses indicate that Dalverzin existed for about 800 years, that is, from the fourteenth or fifteenth to the eighth or seventh centuries BCE. Diverse types of cultural materials were found there, including ceramics, copper, bronze, stone, and bone.

Sometimes fragments of ceramic pottery were also found. Tableware painted with a black-gray glaze is one of the most significant signs of the Chust culture. These were adorned with geometrical designs, painted with black paint over a bright red background. The motifs of these ornaments were made up of triangles and rhombuses; there were various ribbons filled with diamond-shaped drawings, circles with dots in the center, and the like. The entire array of ornaments was crafted with such deliberation that one can safely assume that even the most simplified variants of these ornaments carry certain semantic meanings.

The remains of a foundry workshop, a crucible, a clay nozzle, slag, a series of casting moulds, and a variety of metal tools indicate the development of metallurgy using copper and bronze. Researchers attribute the wide development of bronze metallurgy to two factors: the presence of copper mines in the Ferghana Valley and the influence of the Andronovo steppe tribes, among whom metallurgical manufacturing was widespread.[1] On archaeological digs more than a thousand stone tools have been found, including crescent knives, graters, burnishes, and various seed grinders. Bone products are of equal interest: notably bone combs for nailing down the wefts on a weaving loom, various parts of horse harnesses, and a number of astragals were found.[2]

The Chust settlement at Burnamozor, with a walled area of about five hectares, was located in the northern Ferghana on a terrace of the Gavasay. Recent research shows that the Chust culture cultivated the most favorable lands in the valleys of such rivers as the Karasu, Kara Darya, Ak-Bura, Margilansai, Gavasay, Kasansai, and others.[3] Here, as in Dalverzin, three types of dwellings were discovered: frame houses, wattle-and-daub houses, and dugouts. The ceramics, metal, stone and bone products excavated there all are very similar to the findings at Dalverzin. It is important to note that, unlike in Dalverzin, in Chust there is no black-gray glazed tableware, nor are there any iron artifacts.[4]

Among the Chust monuments, the Osh (Sulaiman-Too Mountain) settlement stands out.[5] It consists of dwellings with in-house pits, fireplaces, production complexes, and a sanctuary, and is located on the terraces around the mountain peak, covering an area of more than 2,000 square meters. Fifteen inhabited terraces were unearthed, cut out of rock, with the foundation pits of the semi-dugouts at a different depth, along with earthen wattle-and-daub houses and wooden constructions of rush-and-clay covers.

Most of the constructions of the Osh settlement had not been inhabited, but were used instead as industrial facilities, with more than 200 storage pits for grain and other supplies having been discovered. According to Zadneprovskii, this part of the Osh settlement was considered a highland sanctuary and its terraces were places for performing rituals related to the worship of the mountain, or perhaps to a proto-Zoroastrian cult of the sun, fire, and water. A considerable quantity of painted ceramics and about 76.3 percent of the total number of structures on the Sulaiman-Too Mountain warrant the conclusion that it was the original cultural-ideological center of all the Chust culture of Ferghana.[6]

Archeologists assume that in the eighth and seventh centuries BCE some hundreds—and in other places, thousands—of hectares of fertile land were devoted to agriculture. This led to an increase in food production, greater social differentiation, and the start of urbanization. Probably in this period the first political associations or rudiments of statehood occupying the territory of one, two, and sometimes even three irrigational regions—oases—began to emerge. Dalverzin and Chust were the centers of these political developments. Later, perhaps in the tenth and ninth centuries bce, "centralized" and considerably large state-type entities appeared.[7] This was supported by an agricultural system that produced wheat, rye, and millet and had domesticated cattle, horses, donkeys, dogs, and camels.[8] It was probably at this time that the first iron tools appeared.

The agricultural tribes of the south and the southwest also played a role in the formation of the Chust culture in Ferghana. Some findings are testaments to this, such as stone images of snakes with Elamite origins found in the Sokh region,[9] the Haksky treasures,[10] and bronze relics from Aflatuna.[11] The remains of a cattle raising culture were found in the foothill zones of western and southern Ferghana. The nomadic culture of Ferghana is more similar to the culture of the peoples from Semireche (Seven Rivers) and the Central Syr Darya regions. The intersection of these two cultures is reflected in the appearance of the nomads' earthenware in various towns.[12]

The early Iron Age began in the eighth century BCE and lasted to the third century BCE,[13] an era known to archeologists as the Eilatan or Eilatan-Aktam period. There were no written records from this era in Ferghana but the archeological finds suggest how closely the excavated settlements conform to descriptions in the Zoroastrians' holy book, the *Avesta*. One commonly finds in the *Avesta* such concepts as a "house-dwelling family" and a "generational-patrimonial settlement," which are similar to the Chust groups and with the social structure of ancient Iranians generally, with its three carefully delineated estates: soldiers, priests, and farmers-cattlemen.

The site of ancient Eilatan is a good example of the urban growth in the early Iron Age.[14] A planned area, it is an irregular quadrangle of defensive walls with towers. The area of the inner building is twenty hectares. The fortifications have a thickness of four meters. At a distance of 500 meters from it, there is a second external wall protecting the city's arable lands and a shelter for cattle measuring 200 hectares. Another urban settlement of the same type—Nurtepe—was excavated in the Ura-Tyube region.[15]

In southern Ferghana, the remains of monumental architecture were excavated at the urbanized settlement Symtepe, which was founded in the fourth century BCE. Natalia G. Gorbunova[16] and others have uncovered nearly a dozen major burial grounds from the sixth to the fourth centuries BCE; nearly all of them were earthen graves with the bodies oriented to the west and accompanied by niches with ritual food. This further strengthens the conclusion that by the Early Iron Age in the Ferghana Valley a unique agricultural and cattle-raising culture existed, with comprehensive social and religious institutions.[17]

By 800–400 BCE an integrated system of trade put the people of Ferghana into cultural contact not only with neighboring cattle-raising peoples but also with the more developed civilizations of the Asian Near East, but both Greek and Persian and Greek sources are silent on whether Ferghana actually became part of the Achaemenid Empire. Conversely, they were in close contact with the Saka tribes,[18] who founded the Davan kingdom of which the Chinese chronicles have much to say.[19]

Antiquity (Fourth Century BCE–Fourth Century CE)

The first written information on Ferghana appeared in the second and first centuries BCE in the Chinese chronicles, written as an account of the westward travels of the famous diplomat Chang Ch'ien in 138 year BCE. The fundamental sources of our knowledge about the population of Ferghana are the *Shih Chi* (Records of the Grand Historian) and *Han Shu* (Book of Han).

Shih Chi contains information about events from 138 to the 90s BCE. The author writes that: "the Davan people lead a settled life, engage in agriculture, sowing rice and wheat. They have grape wine. Their horses have bloody sweat and come from the breed of heavenly horses. There are up to 70 large and small cities in Davan, with populations reaching up to several hundred thousand. Their weapons consist of bows with arrows and spears. They are skillful with the horse bow."[20]

The Han army, led by the commander Li Guang, twice visited Ferghana. The first time they reached Yucheng City (Yu); the second time Li Guang attacked Ershi—the capital of Ferghana—with a large force and, after a forty-day siege, the inhabitants agreed to surrender horses to the Han court. Here, only two large capital cities—Ershi and Yucheng—are mentioned.

The *Shih Chi* is not free of inaccuracies. For example, its statement that the Ferghanans and their neighbors learned how to produce (to cast) weapons from a Chinese refugee is contradicted by much archaeological evidence. Moreover, the Chinese source claims that when the people of Ferghana received gold and silver from the Chinese they used it to make tableware instead of coins, when actually they had been minting coins for centuries.

The first-century source, *Han Shu,* describes events from 138 BCE until the year 23 CE. The author of *Han Shu,* Ban Gu, used the *Shih Chi* information, and enriched it with some new facts. In particular, he reported that the Davan emperor resided at Guishuang City and that the Ferghanans used silk and varnish.[21]

The next historical source, the *Hou Hanshu* (fifth century CE), covers events from 25 to 221 CE, when there were clashes for leadership across East Turkestan. From 23 CE Davan paid tribute to Yarkant but still recognized the supreme power of the Han dynasty. Later, in 130 CE the Kashgar emperor seized power and thereafter sent his ambassador, along with envoys from Yarkant and Davan, to the Han court.[22]

In the *Bei Shi* (400–600 CE), Davan is referred to as "Lona, the ancient province of Davan, with its imperial residence in Guishuang city."[23] The Chinese chronicles mention only three large cities in Ferghana: Ershi, Yucheng, and Guishuang. Some scholars place Ershi City at Ura-Tyube; others put it at Kokand[24] and still others at Osh,[25] but most accept Alexander Bernshtam's placement at the Markhamat ruins in Ming-Tepa. Similarly, some scholars place Yucheng City somewhere in Uzgen,[26] others on the site of the ancient settlement of Shurabashat,[27] and the rest near Osh or Uzgen.[28] Bernshtam puts Guishuang at the ancient settlement of Mug-Tepe (Kasan);[29] Edwin G. Pulleyblank notes that the Guishuang or Kushan tribes renamed the capital of Davan as Guishuang.[30] Chinese sources provide only standardized figures on population; for Davan, as an example, "the population consists of 60,000 families, 300,000 heads; 60,000 soldiers."

Excavations at Eski Ahsi (Ahsiket, Ahsikent, Akhikent) and Eilatan lead us to propose that Ershi, the ancient capital of Ferghana, was in fact Eski Ahsi.[31] The large area of the inner city, which includes two *shakhristans*; the 40-hectare citadel; the 10-hectare suburb as well as its 20-meter high walls,[32] exceed all other remains in

Ferghana.[33] By the third and fourth centuries CE the thickness of Eski Ahsi's walls at the base had reached 7.5 meters.[34] Thus, during and after the two main Chinese incursions into Ferghana, the local populace strongly reinforced its capital, working for nearly 100 years to construct the two large walls and smaller double ditches. The resulting defenses were formidable indeed, reaching a thickness of 20 meters with an overall appearance of a collection of towers.

The author of the *Shih Chi* notes that the second city of Ferghana, Yucheng, was located at 200 lee (50–60 km) to the east of the main city of Ershi. The best candidate for this site is the ancient settlement of Eilatan. It was probably destroyed during the second Chinese campaign against Ferghana, losing its big-city status after 90 BCE. Kasan was apparently the summer residence of the kings of Ferghana and was called by the same name as the main capital, Guishuang.[35]

Irrigation-based farming served as the main economic activity of the Ferghana-Davan people. The deep channel of the Uzgen-Aryk, which still exists today, dates to this time. Large underground storage pits attest to the productivity of their farming.

The gracefully shaped and thin-walled ceramics of ancient Ferghana reveal some interesting features. On the one hand, there is a big difference between the elegant products of the urban centers and rural towns.[36] On the other hand, while the new technologies of the best urban ceramics reveal influences from the Middle East, the traditional regional decorations of the Chust culture (harrowed ornaments and red-engobed color) were continued from the first to fourth centuries CE, suggesting a strong capacity to assimilate new influences from abroad.

Mention has been made of the highly developed Ferghana art of viniculture. Because it was new to them, the Chinese wrote of it in detail:

> In Davan, the wine is made from grapes. The rich store up to 10 000 *dan* (1 *dan* is more than 80 kg). The old wine can be kept for decades without deterioration. Residents enjoy wine the way their horses enjoy the *Moussa* (alfalfa) grass. Chinese envoys exported the seeds, and the Son of Heaven issued orders for his subjects to plant both *Moussa* and grapes in rich soil.[37]

Ferghana's interactions across Eurasia intensified in ancient times. Finds of *u-shu* coins, Chinese mirrors, basketry, bronze items, and fabric[38] testify to relations with China. A famous mirror handle in the form of an Indian dancer[39] and two bronze pendants from burials at Kara-Bulak and Tour-tash[40] attest to links with India. Red-decorated vessels from the second to the fourth centuries BC[41] reflect Ferghana's trade relations with the Middle East. Meanwhile, wooden utensils and bronze cosmetic devices found in graves in Talas, Tian Shan, and Alai mountains[42] attest that the people of Ferghana had constant contact with the nomadic tribes living in nearby mountain valleys and on the steppes.

A fourth to sixth century CE estate excavated at Kayragach in western Ferghana shed light on both the art and religion of these early Ferghanans.[43] Here were found small groups of painted alabaster statuettes—local idols and gods, which are very specific to this historical and cultural region. All have sharply beveled foreheads, large convex eyes, straight noses with a crook, straight eyebrows converging in the bridge of the nose, and small mouths. The sculptures of idols and local deities from the Kayragach estate stood in a special niche in a building of the fifth and sixth centuries CE that served as a sanctuary as well as a place of worship for the tenants. Twelve sculptures from 16 to 67 centimeters were found, all of alabaster, with disproportionately large heads and narrow shoulders. The Kayragach sculptures are likely portraits representing specific people, apparently respected ancestors.

N.G. Gorbunova wrote of ethnic assimilation of such diverse tribes as Sakas, Usuni, and Kangju[44] and the gradual emergence of a specific Ferghana people by the fifth to seventh centuries CE, with its own eastern Iranian language. The King of Ferghana bore an Iranian title *ishhid,* and was connected to all the main landowners in the villages and city-states. Starting from the time of Alexander the Great Sogdians had colonized Ferghana, bringing with them the Sogdian spoken and written language, based on which there could also have been a Ferghanan writing system before the penetration of the Aramaic and then the Arabic in the early Middle Ages.

The Early Middle Ages (Fifth to Eighth Centuries CE)

During the early medieval period, Sogdian-Turkic traders reached China, Korea and Japan; as well as the Mediterranean, Iran, India, and Ceylon. The Sogdian language became the language of international trade and communication. Using the Great Silk Road, people transported silk, precious stones, gold and silver jewelry, ornaments of colored glass, pharmaceuticals and paint, thoroughbred horses, and various fruits. Along these routes there also passed religious missionaries, master craftsmen, musicians, actors, and artists. The palace feasts of Chinese emperors were accompanied by performances of dancers and singers from Ferghana, Sogdiana, and Chach (Tashkent), while Central Asians judged their wealth by the quantity of Chinese silk they owned.[45] By the sixth and seventh centuries CE, Ferghana also practiced sericulture, fragments of which have turned up in various European treasuries.[46] But silk was only one among many valuables exported from Ferghana. In 479 Ferghanans reciprocated a visit by Chinese ambassadors by sending to that realm an embassy that brought their famous horses as gifts.[47]

The Ferghana Valley became increasingly Turkicized during the late Kushan period between the late 500s through the 650s CE, as the Western Turk state extended its authority there.[48] The Turks successfully played off the various city-states against each other. They met strong resistance but eventually established new Turkic dynasties at Kasan and Ahsiket, called Gesay and Sigyan by Chinese sources.[49] Shortly afterward, the Arab conqueror Kutaiba attacked the country, leading punitive raids against Turks in alliance with the Tibetans. It looked briefly as if a Ferghana-Chinese alliance might lead both the anti-Turk and anti-Arab resistance. The Ferghanans entered into an alliance with China, which repelled the Western Turkic Kaganat and subdued Ferghana, renaming it Ninyuan. But in 739 CE the Turkic prince Arslan Tarkhan took control of Ferghana away from China, and thenceforth headed the anti-Arabic movement.

By the seventh century CE, Sigyan (Ahsiket) had again become the major city of the Ferghana Valley,[50] with only two other Ferghanan cities—Gesay at Mug-tepe and Humyn—figuring in the Chinese chronicles.[51] In the first quarter of the eighth century CE, the Arab writer al Taraba mentions five Ferghana cities.[52] The eighth century "Sogdian Documents from the Mug Mountain" report the existence of a king of Ferghana and a Ferghana *tutuk* (representative). Foreign sources of the 500–700 period refer to Ferghana as Faihani, Bohan, Pahana,[53] with its capital at Ferghana which, as argued earlier, must be the same as the Eski Ahsi settlement at Ahsiket.[54]

The other capital city of Ferghana at that time was the city of Kasan, now Kasansai, where the *tutuk* of the Western Turkic Kaganate lived. This trapezoidal-shaped city occupied several high hills on the Uzbek side of the Uzbek-Kyrgyz border. This strongly fortified town, with six towers, had arisen in the first century BCE and was now one of the most defensible places in the entire region.[55] A third urban center of the early Middle Ages was Kuva, a classic three-part Central Asian settlement with citadel (*ark*), inner city (*shakhristan*), suburbs (*rabad*), and a major Buddhist temple that functioned as late as the eighth century CE.[56] The regional governor resided here.[57]

All these cities gradually evolved from being mere castles with settlements attached to being the economic and social centers of entire oases. They drew the entire life of their respective oases into their well-developed markets, streets, and buildings.[58] Religious life in this last pre-Muslim era centered at the Sulaiman-Too Mountain near Osh, dubbed by Chinese chronicles the "city of the saints, or highly sacred Mountain."[59]

The Turkic conquest of the valley led to a new phase of its development. Numerous examples of Turkic runic writing have recently been found in cemeteries and elsewhere, suggesting that Turks' role expanded from politics into culture during the early Middle Ages.[60] Their rule also fostered improvements in animal husbandry, creating more effective animal power for farming and manufacturing.[61] The Turks' arrival did not disrupt the continuity of Ferghana's royal dynasty. Continuity helped Ferghana rulers grow more powerful and to oppose any form of mutual subordination.[62] Thus, on the eve of the Arab conquest, Ferghana thrived as a powerful and self-confident land based on economically prosperous city-states but without a powerfully centralized administration and with inter-city competition the order of the day.

The first campaign of Arabian conquest took place in 712 CE, headed by Kutteiba ibn Muslim. Citizens of the Ferghana strongly resisted. In 715 CE Kutteiba attacked Ferghana for the second time and also rebelled against his own caliph, Suleiman (715–717 CE). But his troops did not support him and he was soon killed. Locals still point out his grave in the village of Jalal Kuduk near Andijan.

The Arabs left governors in Ferghana and other places to lead local troops and collect taxes; however, the people of Ferghana remained independent, relying on the strength of the Turkic tribes. Around 720 CE Ferghana was ruled by a strong king named Alutar. In 723 CE, he linked up with other Turkic forces from Chach (Tashkent) to strike a blow against the Arabs, chasing them the entire way to Samarkand. A few years later another Turkic leader, Arslan Tarkhan,[63] ruled all Ferghana and developed friendly relations with the Chinese.[64] Mansur (754–775) forced the king of Ferghana to live in Kashgar and levied an annual payment on him. However, the Ferghanans still resisted politically and militarily, and they refused to meet the Arabs' major demand—to embrace Islam. Under Caliph Mamun (813–833) the Arabs sent troops once more against the population of Ferghana. In the end Mamun granted governance over Ferghana and certain other provinces to the Samanid dynasty of Samarkand, but even this did not mark the Arabs' last effort to subdue the region.

The Political Situation in Ferghana from the Ninth to the Seventeenth Centuries

From 819 to the tenth century CE, Ferghana was part of the Samanids' kingdom and Ahsiket remained its capital. In 992 CE, Ilias ibn Ishak started an uprising against the caliphate in Ferghana, enlisting in his project, among others, the Qarluq Turks. The Tahirid dynasty that eventually stifled this rebellion by "the enemies of the Faith," (the Qarluq Turks) would build a new capital for the valley, which they named Nasrabod and surrounded with gardens.[65] After the death of Asad, the ruler of Ferghana, the caliph appointed Asad's son, Ahmed, to rule the territory. At that time Ferghana was an economic and cultural center, later to become a political center as well. Coins were minted at both Ferghana and Nasrobod in the name of the local leaders and their Samanid overlords.

Starting from the middle of the tenth century CE, Ferghana was ruled by high local dignitaries who remained independent of their nominal masters in Samarkand. The local copper coinage did not bother to mention the Samanids. All the traditional leaders of principalities within Ferghana had the status of emirs and starting from the middle of the tenth century CE they acquired the further title of "Client of the Master over the Faithful."[66]

At the end of the tenth century Ferghana fell to the invading Karakhanid Turks. Since ancient times Turks had wielded military and political power in Ferghana. Now the Karakhanids made the city of Uzgen their capital, sustaining the prosperity that had prevailed under the Samanids. In 999 they consolidated regional power by seizing the Samanids' capital of Bukhara.[67] Prosperity led to a proliferation of mints, which were maintained at Ahsiket, Margilan, Osh, and Kuba, as well as Uzgen. In 1001 an alliance was struck with another rising Turkic ruler, Mahmud of Ghazni, who already ruled Afghanistan and was soon to conquer India.[68]

The eleventh century witnessed various feudal wars among rival Karakhanids, the stakes including not only control over Ferghana but of the other Karakhanid holdings as far west as Bukhara and as far east as Kashgar. Each shift in power brought about a move of the mint, which was based at various times in Ahsiket, Uzgen, and elsewhere.[69]

In the twelfth century Uzgen continued strengthening and protecting its position as the capital of Ferghana. The results of this are the beautiful ornamented brick tombs and minarets that survive there today. Uzgen maintained its status as a mint until 1178.[70] Soon after 1212 CE the entire southern part of Ferghana was conquered, ruled, and at times decimated by yet other Turkic groups, one from Khorezm in the western part of Central Asia and the others, the Karakitai, from East Turkestan. This was a prelude to the Mongol conquest after 1219. Ismail, the ruler of Ahsiket and Kasan, quickly expressed his obedience to Genghis Khan's military commander and thereby saved his cities. But not everyone did the same. Khujand, the western gateway to Ferghana, resisted bitterly and was destroyed. Not breaking with tradition, Mongols eventually situated their local capital at Uzgen and placed their treasury there.

The Mongol conquerors devastated Ferghana along with other provinces of Central Asia. Only at the start of the thirteenth century did the process of economic revival take hold. Before the Mongol conquest, silver-covered copper dirhems minted in Ferghana, Uzgen, Merv, and elsewhere had been the main currency circulating in Central Asia. At the end of the twelfth century CE, however, a deep currency crisis began in Ferghana, exacerbated by the economic blow the Mongol conquest had inflicted on Ferghana and other parts of Central Asia. The crisis of silver-covered copper dirhem went so far that Mahmud Yalavach, the merchant-ruler of Ferghana, made no effort to restore the monetary trade and did not even try to return to the use of dirhems.[71]

By now Ferghana had become thoroughly Muslim, and the Mongols had reason to fear that, as non-Muslims, they might have trouble sustaining their rule there. What most weakened the Mongols was infighting between successors to the far-off throne. Timur the Lame (also known as Tamerlane) capitalized on this situation by conquering Ferghana in 1370–71. After the conclusion of his eastern campaigns in 1404 CE Timur delegated control over East Turkestan (now Xinjiang in China) to his governor in Ferghana.[72] But the division of large Turkic empires into principalities continued after Timur, when a unified Ferghana left to one of Timur's sons began to break apart.[73] By the fifteen century competing coins were being minted in Andijan, Margilan, Osh, and Khujand, with economic interests clearly ascendant over any aspirations for political independence.

In 1479 the local throne in Andijan fell to an ambitious eighteen-year-old, Sultan Ahmed, the son of Abu Said, who promptly began launching attacks on the Mongol's suzerain, Omar Sheikh, who in turn allied himself with the Mongol ruler Yunus Khan. After several years of exceedingly complex maneuvers, in which the point at issue was who would attack Samarkand and who would remain in control in Ferghana, Timur's heir in Ferghana had managed to bargain away province after province in order obtain for himself a secure rule in Andijan. Eventually this pitiful ruler was sending his neighbors to attack his enemies[74] while he himself stayed home and amused himself on the roof of his pigeon house. When he unexpectedly fell to his death, much of Ferghana became a theater of feudal war.[75] Eventually a mere twelve-year-old, Babur of Ahsiket, became ruler of the principality of Ferghana. Rulers from as far afield as Kashgar in Xinjiang also vied for the various parts of Ferghana. When Babur's father emerged victorious he distributed lands, titles and money to his loyal *beks* according to their status.[76]

The Ferghana Civil War and Its Legacy

The minute Babur's rule began, these local emirs initiated a bitter, multi-sided civil war among themselves. Babur lost Samarkand but was eventually reinstated there in 1497, at which time the emir who ruled Ahsiket rebelled against him and gained the support of one of Babur's own military commanders, Sultan Ahmed Tenbel, the ruler of Osh. The rebel emirs entered Andijan and surrounded the city. The nobility of the city sought help from Babur, but he arrived too late to save them.

The ruler of Margilan city, Ali Dust Tagai, sent his ambassador to Babur and promised to give the city to him. After strengthening his positions in Margilan, Babur directed his forces to overthrow Uzun, Khasan, and Tenbel. The latter ones, after receiving this news about Babur's arrival to Margilan, left Andijan and engaged Babur's troops. After a brief peace, the war for the throne of Andijan between Babur and his former general Tenbel, a Mongol officer, reignited. In 1500 Babur and Tenbel finally made a deal dividing Ferghana along the Syr Darya, but with the understanding that if both sides joined in a successful attack on Samarkand, Babur would leave Ferghana.[77] This promptly broke down when Tenbel reconquered Ferghana for himself. In 1503–4 Babur entered Ferghana with the Mongolian Khan Sultan Mahmud and 30,000 troops.[78] Soon the whole of Ferghana territory except two capital cities, Andijan and Aksu, submitted to the Mongols. Just when Babur seemed on the verge of success, yet another Turkic force, that of Shaybani Khan, appeared on the scene from the west. Ever more intricate alignments of forces ensued, with Babur fighting Tenbel, who aligned with the Shaybani Khan, until the latter achieved a final victory, after which Shaybani Khan, for tactical reasons, rewarded none other than Babur's enemy, Tenbel.[79]

This multi-year intra-Turkic war over the Ferghana Valley had profound consequences. First, it drove Babur out of his native land to Afghanistan and eventually to India, where he launched the renowned Mughal dynasty, in effect exporting a political and cultural ideal from the Ferghana Valley to the Indian sub-continent. Second, it left Ferghana politically divided, so that outsiders, the Kazakh sultans, could take control of a major part of the valley in the seventeenth century. Worst of all, it shattered the economy and social cohesion of the valley, inflicting a blow from which it would not recover for many centuries. As a result the valley faced the challenges of the modern world in the nineteenth century divided and in a greatly weakened condition.

Even the name of Ferghana fell out of use and was replaced with Andijan. By the end of the seventeenth century, local *hojas,* the descendants of earlier Arab conquerors, took control.[80] The temporary capital of Ferghana became an insignificant village named Chadak ("close to the hojas") located on northern side of the Syr Darya River 60 kilometers northwest of Ahsiket. Only in 1709 was their power destroyed when they were driven from power and an independent Uzbek Turkic state established in Ferghana, with its capital at Kokand.

Cities, Trade Routes, and Raw Materials

The Ferghana Valley, as noted, is comprised of distinctive inter-mountain hollows, bordered by the Kuramin and Chatkal ridges to the north, the Ferghana ridge of the Tian Shan Mountains to the east, and the Alai and Turkestan ridges of Pamir Mountains to the south. In the western part of the valley there is a narrow pass called the "Khujand Gates" through which the valley merges with the Turan lowlands.[81]

Throughout its early history Ferghana was one of the more economically developed regions of all Central Asia. Almost all lands on the western side of the Ferghana Valley through Ak-Bura (one of the tributary of Syr Darya, also called the Osh River) and on the east up to the Syr Darya had been divided into two districts: Upper Nesya including Kokand, Rishton, Vankent, and Sokh; and the Lower Nesya including Margilan, Andijan, Isfara, Zenderamsh, Nookat, Jidgil, and Urest.

That part of Ferghana located between the Kara Darya (Upper Syr Darya) and Haylam (riverhead of the Naryn River), was known as Miyan-i Rudan (between two rivers). Bordering it were Biskend and Selat, as well as the Haftdeh area (seven settlements), which was conquered by Muslims only in the tenth century. The main city in this sub-region was Haylam, which had a beautiful mosque.[82]

From medieval written sources we see that the number of Ferghana cities varied from twenty-four to forty. Typical of the broader region, all of them were comprised of three parts named *kuhandiz* (old fortress), *shakhristan* (inner city), and the *rabad* (external town). Important centers within these sectors included the palace of the ruler, the Friday mosque, bazaars, and the prison.

The cities of Kend (Kanibadam), Sokh, Rishtan, Zenderamsh, and Kuva (Kuba) stood on the main road from Khujand through Osh. Kuva was the second city in Ferghana because of its abundant amount of water and gardens, exceeding even Ahsiket in wealth and outnumbering in population the city of Osh. The mosque was in the citadel while the bazaars, palaces, and prison were all located in the rabad.[83] Each main city, like Kuva, was the business center of its entire region. Near Sokh, with its two gates, were up to sixty villages and towns, including the cities of Kokand and Vankent.[84] This comprised the most densely settled area of Upper Nesya.

Of the Lower Nesya cities, the largest one was Margilan. During the Samanid period Margilan remained small, with only the single trade road leading through it to southern Ferghana. But during the Karakhanid period, Margilan became one of the important cities of Ferghana on the strength of its mint. The Silk Road passed through Khujand, where it split into a northern and southern route. The southern route passed through Kanibadam to the mining district of Solh, then from Haydarken to Ohna, Kadamjai, and finally reaching Margilan. The northern route split routes beyond Ahsiket, with one route passing through Mion Rudan to Uzgen and the other running to Margilan.[85]

Andijan (also called Andujan, Andugan, Andikan, and Andigan in medieval sources) was among the Lower Nesya cities. The Mongol conquest devastated the city and left it desolate for many years. Only by the end of the thirteenth century was Andijan rebuilt and resettled.[86] In the fourteenth century a defensive wall was erected around the city and remained functional until the eighteenth century. From the end of the fourteenth century, during the Timurid dynasty and up to the eighteenth century, the rulers of Ferghana, with independent authority granted them by the reigning supreme powers, had their seat at Andijan, to which the capital was moved from Ahsiket. During that period, the city of Andijan became so dominant in the region that people came to call the inhabitants of Ferghana and East Turkestan "Andijanians."[87]

The mountainous part of Ferghana, the third row of towns on the caravan route from Kuva to Margilan and Andijan, encompassed the following districts:

a. Isfara, located to the north of the present-day village of Isfara, was in a mixed mountain and valley area five *farsahs*[88] from Sokh, and known for its coal fields.

b. Aval, which still exits south of Margilan, the capital of the district of Aval, was situated within ten *farsahs* from Osh and bordered by Margilan to the south and ten *farsahs* from Solh en route to Uzgen.

c. Nookat was seven *farsahs* from Kuva. And included as part of its region the town of Miskan.[89]

Osh, approached by Urest to the east and Urshab on the way from Uzgen,[90] was the Turkish-ruled border city of Ferghana and the third city by size after Ahsiket and Kuva. It had a mountain gate, a river gate, and a Mugkede, or "gate of the fire-worshippers." The mosque was situated between the bazaars.[91] The city of Uzgen was smaller in size than Osh, and distinctive in that the citadel made up part of the *shakhristan* in Uzgen. This city had four gates. Trade with the Turks brought major income to the city, especially under the Karakhanids. The city was located on the important route connecting Ferghana with the Tian Shan Mountains, in particular, the town of Atbashi (present-day Kyrgyzstan) through the Yassi and Gugart passes. Atbashi briefly served as the capital of Ferghana in the seventh century CE.

Ahsiket, the center of Ferghana in the ninth and tenth centuries, was located in the north of Ferghana on the right bank of the Syr Darya and on a crossroads of the Great Silk Road. The city's mint issued embossing coining dies for the Samanid state in the ninth and tenth centuries CE.[92] The palace, prison, main bazaar, and mosque were all located in the *shakhristan* near the citadel. The city was surrounded by five gates and was irrigated by a multitude of canals that fed beautiful bricked reservoirs (*hauzes*), traces of which remain on the site. The banks of the canals were also bricked and a unique system of underground water pipes fed public baths and residential dwellings.[93] In addition, the city *moats* located by the fortified walls served as reservoirs. Archeologists have found fence constructions that served as dams, and water-lifting engines known as *chigir* that obtained water from mountain streams flowing into the rivers. Archeologists have also often found millstones that prove the presence of water mills along the streams.

During the eleventh century the Ahsiket mint produced coining dies for the Karakhanid dynasty.[94] By 1075, however, the production of coins had declined, even though the city remained a major metallurgical center, exporting expensive ironware and particularly swords. The blacksmiths of Ahsiket learned the secret of making Damascus steel and would create wonderful swords as subtle in design as they were sharp.[95]

In the south, Ahsiket was linked by a straight route to Kokand. The route from Ahsiket to Khujand in the west passed through Bab, Turmukan, Hajistan, Samgar, and Khujand.[96] Five *farsahs* north of Ahsiket was the city of Kasan, the capital of Ferghana emirs from the end of the eighth century CE through the beginning of the ninth century CE. There also resided several renowned religious figures (*seyids*), whose essays were long known to all Muslims.[97] Along the north of Ferghana near Kasan could be found such towns as Nejm, Karvan, Jidgil, Ardlanket, Nedm, Kervan, and Ardlanket.[98] Every town had its specific role. Raielnt became known for its rich agriculture, while Karak acquired fame for its rice. Agriculture was also important for the Syr Darya River city of Farab, though it is best known for its renowned medieval philosopher, al Farabi.[99]

In early times the countryside was secured by military settlements, with the safety of traders protected by well-defended caravanserais. Over time Ferghana's dense population rendered the military settlements (*ribats*) and caravanserais unnecessary. Ferghana cities were largely built on elevated land and promontories, with deep channels on each side that divided the cities into several *shakhristans*. This was the situation, for example, in Osh, Uzgen, and Ferghana, among others.[100] These centers survived the fall of the Samanids and continued to thrive through Karakhanid times, as can be seen by the continued minting of coins in Uzgen, Ahsiket, Kasan, Margilan, and Osh.[101] This enabled a place like Uzgen to have an extensive fresh-water system as well as a sewage system with galleries of baked brick. The security and prosperity of the area is evident in the medieval city of Bab, where archeologists have found a giant unfortified settlement of craftsmen, along with ample raw materials, semi-prepared and final pottery, and blacksmith-made products.[102]

After the Mongol conquest and civil wars in Babur's time, Ferghana as a whole, and all its cities, lost importance as a center of craftsmanship. Now rough unglazed household ceramics came into general use, irrigation systems fell to ruin, and many cities had to relocate. Uzgen long disappeared from the historical written resources.

Cities of the Upper Nesya such as Nookat, Miskan, and Aval also ceased to exist. The famous Kuva was no longer. Ferghana lost its political significance and could not compete as an industrial economy against the craftsmen workshops of the rest of Central Asia.

Ferghana's decline came as a result of its internal fighting, civil war, and political divisions, as well as the absence of a centralized power. Henceforth there was only one trade route leading to the south of the country and continuing eastward beyond the mountain ridges to Kashgar.

Trade Routes

Medieval geographers paid copious attention to the trade routes of Ferghana. The eastward international route started in Kuva and passed through southern Ferghana from Urest to Osh and further to Kurshab and Uzgen. From Uzgen the route went up the Yassi River toward the Yassi Pass. The route traveled to Tian Shan and Kadzhingarbashi, passing by Atbashi through Jaman-davan, and through the Turgat passages to Kashgar.

Ferghana's internal routes branched on the way southward through the Tegizbai pass. One of the routes headed through Arslanbob to the Haylama region (Ketmen-Tyube), reaching Naryn, where it merged with the right tributary of Uzun-Ahmat.

In the area of modern Uch-Kurgan a pass existed heading to the right bank of the Naryn-Syr Darya. Ferghana was also crossed by several branches of a trade route that passed through the territory of Kyrgyzstan in two directions: to the Chui Valley on the north through Yassi and Kochkor, and to the south through the territory of southern Ferghana.[103]

A degree of political stability prevailed in Central Asia by the seventh century, leading to economic and cultural development. During that period, the Great Silk Road passed through Kashgar, the Issyk Kul region in the south, and the Talas Valley. However, the more ancient route that passed through Ferghana did not lose its importance. Until the early eighth century Sogdian merchants traded on the Great Silk Road that connected Japan in the east with the Mediterranean Sea in the west, and Vietnam and Ceylon in the south. The rise of the Turkic powers enabled the indigenous Sogdians to become the chief traders on the Great Silk Road. The Arab authors Al-Mujaddasi, Istahri, and Ibn Haukal wrote about a route that connected the west and the east. During that period, trade caravans coming from India, Iran, and Middle Eastern countries would pass through Samarkand and reach Khujand, whence the route would head East via two different directions. One route went from Khujand through Kanibadam, Sokh, Rishtan, Margilan, Kuva, Osh, Uzgen, Atbashi, and the Terekdavan Pass to China. The other route headed to Ahsiket and thence either to Uzgen or south through Kuva, where it merged with the southern route. In the eleventh and twelfth centuries CE, caravan routes through the Ferghana Valley shifted, thanks to the emergence of mining in the region of Sokh-Haydarkan.

Minerals

The Ferghana Valley, rich in minerals, had a highly developed mining industry. Silver, gold, and iron were mined in the mountain areas of northern Ferghana but the greatest mineral deposits were found in southern Ferghana, which therefore drew trade routes to and through this area. Sokh was rich in mercury, still mined there today;[104] Isfara had coal deposits;[105] while oil and iron came from the northern parts of Sokh and Isfara. The Isfara Valley had a large smelting center that used ore from Sokh and coal from Isfara for the production of various steel products. The region yielded such minerals and gems as turquoise, copper, tin, ammoniac salt, flint, zinc, resin, asbestos, lead, and others. Written sources confirm that in the ninth century 1,330 iron bars from Isfara were paid annually to the caliph's treasury.[106] Ferghana's metal products, particularly weaponry, were sold even in Baghdad.[107]

Irrigation

Boris A. Latinin identifies three stages in the development of irrigation and farming in Ferghana.[108] The earliest phase, from the early Bronze Age through the beginning of the Iron Age,[109] focused on cultivating flood lands and the lower deltas of mountain rivers as they faded into the plains. Modest irrigation systems developed to regulate natural flooding, artificial estuaries were created, and irrigation canals dug alongside the dwindling river channels.

The inhabitants of the Chust settlements and of eastern Ferghana apparently also used underground spring water to irrigate their fields, especially on the terraces of the Kara Darya, Kurshab, Yassi, Taldyk, Ak-Bura, Kugart, and Kara-Unkur rivers. Each spring could irrigate nearly ten hectares of land. Water was regulated by setting small ditches in the right direction. Even today rice fields are watered by the springs located in the flood-lands of the aforementioned rivers, which have the advantage of not fluctuating.[110]

Ancient Chust farmers of the late Bronze Age at Kizil-Zengir village in the Kurshab Valley left an early irrigation system explored in 1971. The main irrigation canal could be traced for some distance. Along its banks were found evidence of man-made rollers of a type that later became widespread on major channels.

In the second phase, ancient settlements during the Chust period transitioned to more developed irrigation systems in order to protect their larger settlements from drought.[111] Canals were deepened and large, fan-shaped irrigation systems were developed. Still later, in the historic period, humans even shifted the course of major rivers to accommodate their needs.[112] Once they had turned the lower courses of rivers into canals it was possible to cultivate virgin lands far from water sources. For example, at the Ahsiket oasis a canal replaced of an old right bank stream of the Kasansai River, providing water to fields many kilometers distant.

The Chinese began writing about irrigation in the Ferghana Valley during the second century BCE,[113] while Arab geographers later recorded that water for irrigation was still drawn exclusively from the Syr Darya tributaries, with no large canals in evidence.[114] The hydraulic system at the capitals of Ahsiket and Kasansai have been mentioned, with both drawing on the waters of the Kasansai River. At Ahsiket, by the tenth century there existed canals and reservoirs lined with baked brick and canals spreading as much as two *farsahs* from the city.[115] Babur records that the high right bank was gracefully stepped and landscaped, obviously with the help of irrigation.[116]

The city of Osh was irrigated by the Ak-Bura River and several other major streams. The Ak-Bura was also Andijan's source of irrigation, with nine canals bringing water to the city from the south.[117] Babur organized the irrigation of the whole Ak-Bura Valley, including Osh. A mosque in Osh (now west of the modern city) had three ponds and trees where any traveler could rest. Abundantly irrigated gardens full of tulips, roses, and violets lay along both banks of the Ak-Bura.[118]

Cultural and Linguistic Diversity in Ferghana

The geographical location of the Ferghana Valley all but invited an influx of various ethnic elements. From ancient times the Ferghana Valley was populated by Iranian-speaking tribes, with the Sakas and other settled tribes of western Ferghana significantly prevailing from 600 to about 100 BCE.[119] The population of Ferghana was always mixed, but with a dominant Europoid component. The Turkic or Mongoloid element came to play an ever-growing role in the anthropologic composition of the area even before 100 CE, but starting from the sixth and seventh centuries CE, the role of ethnically Mongoloid tribes in Ferghana and surrounding territories drastically increased. Already between the fifth and seventh centuries a Ferghana nation had come into being, with its ethnicity and language combining Eastern-Iranian and Turkic elements.[120]

In the fifth and sixth centuries CE the Hephthalites or Huns entered the territory in great numbers. Linguists argue whether their language was east Iranian or Turkic,[121] or perhaps some combination of the two.[122] Only one of the two groups of Huns, the Red Huns, has pertinence to Ferghana. Between the fifth and seventh centuries CE, Ferghana retained a large number of people speaking an east Iranian language, although in general during the first half of the first millennium CE Turkic-speakers came to form the linguistic foundation of Ferghana and Central Asia as a whole. In the sixth century CE, Central Asia became a part of the Turkic Khaganate; the share of Turkic tribes on its territory significantly increased, an important moment in its ethnic history. Starting from this time the so-called Turkization of the local Iranian tribes began in earnest.[123] In the process the formerly ubiquitous Sogdians merged into the new population. Many fled from the Arabs to Ferghana and were taken in by a king in the area of Isfara, while a majority were exterminated by the Arab conquerors.[124]

Under Karakhanid rule the number of settled Turkic-language speaking residents of Ferghana sharply increased, partly as a result of assimilation but also by mutual interaction with East Turkestan. The subsequent conquest of Ferghana by Karakitai nomads after 1125 did not drastically change Ferghana's ethnicity, as their rule was thin and brief. The Mongols conquered Ferghana in the early thirteenth century using large number of Turkic troops, who subsequently figured in the ethnic makeup of the Ferghana Valley.

In the fourteenth and fifteenth centuries CE, the process of mass Turkization of settled groups occurred across the region. Literary sources refer to these settled groups as Sarts,[125] a term which, as Babur writes,[126] was applied equally to both Turkic and Tajik peoples, indicating that for most purposes they had become a single people.[127]

The inflow of Turkic people continued through the early sixteenth century. It was then that Kyrgyz tribes first attempted to enter Ferghana from the Tian Shan Mountains. Under pressure from the Kalmyks, two more large groups of Kyrgyz arrived in the seventeenth and eighteenth centuries, with many of them settling in the valley.[128]

Religious Beliefs

The most dramatic evidence of early spiritual life in the ancient Ferghana are the monumental temples of fire-worshippers in Sultanabad[129] and Kizlartepe, consisting of a central hall and surrounding corridors.[130] The former has been dated to the third to the first century BCE.[131] The Kizlartepe temple on the edge of an ancient town near Margilan was built in the second century CE, functioned for two centuries thereafter, and was apparently destroyed by invading steppe tribes in the early Middle Ages.[132]

The earlier worship of forces of nature lived on into this era. Designs found on first-century vases depict stylized mountains, rain, and the sun, all of which residents worshiped as holy forces. In the south of Ferghana stood the holy mountain of Ulugtog (Great Mountain), while the Suleiman-Too near Osh has been a place of worship since earliest times. As recently as the 1960s locals were conducting ritual immolations at a mountain in the Arayan region, where ancient images of horses are also to be found. All of these may attest to the beliefs of early Turkic peoples, among whom reverence for mountains was widespread. Popular images of grape vines, spirals, and circles are most likely linked to a vegetable cult of the early Ferghanans. Also appearing are a triangular-shaped figure and stylized images of the sun. A downward-pointing triangle symbolized fertility and was common in the region since Neolithic times.[133] As we have seen from the Kayragach sculpture, the ancient peoples of Ferghana also worshipped the spirits of their ancestors and considered them their patrons.

Zoroastrianism was the most ancient religion in Ferghana and all Central Asia, preceding the main world religions. The spread of Zoroastrianism in the northern and eastern territories of Central Asia was stimulated by the growth of long-distance trade, which bloomed especially in the period 500–900 CE. Thus, we find the early acceptance of Zoroastrian burial practices far beyond the original focus of Zoroastrianism in Bactria to the south. In Ferghana as elsewhere the bones of the dead were now separated from flesh, and instead of using underground catacomb graves they were preserved in above-ground structures, called *dahma, ustadan, tanbar,* and *kaftarhona.* Long after the arrival of Islam, Zoroastrianism remained a major religion in Ferghana. Near the ancient town of Sari-Kurgan in Sokh region there is a large and famous Zoroastrian cemetery that continued to receive burials long into the Muslim era. Reports of "magicians" (i.e., magi) and fire-worshippers still abound at many sites in Ferghana. Thus, the ruins of Kasan are called Mug-tepe or the "Magis' Hill."

Almost no information exists about the proselytizing of religions in Ferghana until the times of the Arabic conquest. However, since Buddhism was so wide-spread from Balkh and Termez to Merv, Samarkand, and even the Seven Rivers area, one may assume there were Buddhist adherents in Ferghana. Evidence from elsewhere in the region suggests further that it was likely to have been of the Vajrayana school—a later path of Buddhism in Central Asia as compared to the earlier Hinayana and Mahayana.[134] Evidence also exists of at least one Christian church in Ferghana, and one can safely assume that there many others, mostly of the Nestorian Syrian theology.

Islam spread quickly from its source in Arabia. Social discontent among the lower levels of the Arab tribal elites was easily directed by the leadership toward non-believers and heretics in faraway places. For the Arabic aristocracy, the Islamic notion of jihad, or holy war against non-believers, provided a convenient screen to disguise the true goals of their campaigns of conquest. When the Arab forces arrived in Central Asia, they found a rich region in a state of political uncertainty, with many independent and semi-independent principalities competing against each other.[135] But when Caliph Osman sent his troops to Ferghana they faced staunch resistance at Ispid-Bulan (now Safed-Bulon in Jalalabad province), as a result of which 2,700 "Companions of the Prophet" died in battle and were buried there.[136]

The inhabitants of Ferghana gradually embraced Islam, and by the mid-eighth century Muslim shrines started appearing there. They are still considered sacred places. The tomb of the saintly Ayuba was established near Jalalabad, the tomb of Abdullah, grandson of Imam Khussein, was in Kokand, and the tomb of the Arab conqueror Nasr ibn Ali is in Uzgen.[137] There were also two holy places in Andijan, one of them close to the Rushnabi Mosque, where the famous sheikh al-Marvazi was buried, and the other in Ilamish, where the famous sheikh Jamal ad'din al-Ilamishi had lived. And at Osh was the tomb of Asaf, the vizier of Sulayman ibn Daud, from the early eighth century.[138]

Muslim teachers and clerics gradually came to play an important part in the social and political life of the country. Thus, from earliest times Sheikh Sultan Said and his son Sheikh Burhan ad'din Klich al-Uzgendi came to be acknowledged as figures of impeccable authority. In every part of the country and in any city, the authority of religious leaders among the local population grew rapidly. Special authority was extended to the author of a famous religious tract titled Al-Hidayah fi-l-fikh (*Guidelines of the Muslim Law*), Sheikh Burhan al-Din al-Marghinani. Emirs and other feudals often based their decisions on the opinion of the clergy. In the thirteenth and fourteenth centuries CE, the most influential figures among the clergy in Ferghana included Nusrat ad-din, the son of Sheikh Burhan ad'din Klich al-Uzgendi, Munir ibn Abu-l-Kasim al-Oshi, Shams ad'din Muhammad ibn Muhammad al-Kubavi, Taj ad'din Razi Birdi ash-Sharistani al-Andijani, and Jamal ad'din al-Hiravi al-Ilamishi.[139] Their names reveal them as natives of Uzgen, Osh, Kuba, Andijan, and Ilamish, respectively.

During Babur's short reign in Ferghana in the fifteenth century, the head of the Muslim clergy, Hodja Kazi, played an important role in the affairs of state. In the next century a similarly notable role was played by a famous sheikh from the Naqshbandia order of Sufis, Mahdumi A'zam from the city of Kasan, and his successor, Mavlana Lutfullah Chusti from Chodak in the Ferghana Valley.[140]

In the sixteenth and seventeenth centuries the status of religious leaders grew even greater, and they came to play direct roles in governance. It is no exaggeration to conclude that by the end of seventeenth century the *hojas* and mullahs had become a dominant force in the social and political life of Ferghana.

Science and Literature

The period of the ninth and tenth centuries witnessed a time of cultural flourishing in Ferghana, as can be judged by the great scientists who came from there. Among them, the most famous one was the acclaimed astronomer and mathematician of the ninth century, Abu-al-Abbas Ahmed ibn Muhammad ibn Kasir al-Ferghani. In the East, Ferghani was known simply as "the Mathematician," and in the West as Alfraganus, meaning, "From Ferghana." He participated in the constructions of observatories in Baghdad and Basra and the reconstruction of a nilometer on the island of Rauda, close to Cairo. He wrote a number of works on astronomy, mathematics, and other sciences, such as *Kitab fi usul ilm an-nujum* (A Book About Elements of the Science of the Stars), *Kitab fi-harakat as-samaviya va javami' ilm an-nujum* (A Book About Cosmic Movements and the Astronomical Science), *Kitab al-haya al-fusul as-salasin* (A Book of Astronomy in Thirty Chapters"), *al fusul madhal fi Majisti va huva salasuna faslan* (Chapters Introducing the Almagest), *'Ilal al-aflak* (Reasons of the Cosmic Spheres), *Tarkib al-aflak* (*The Construction of the Cosmic Spheres*), *al-Majisti* (Almagest), *Ilm al-haya* (The Science of Astronomy), *Madhal an-nujum* (Introduction to Astronomy), and *Kitab ul-amal-ir-ruhumot* (A Book About Marble Processing). His *Kitab fi-harakat as-samaviya va javami' ilm an-nujum* is among the first Arabic writings in astronomy, and became one of the most popular works in this field in Europe during the Middle Ages. Besides the brief basics of astronomy, the volume also contains a table of geographic locations in seven climatic zones, and descriptions of astronomic instruments and sun dials.[141]

Abu al-Abbas Ahmed ibn Muhammad ibn Kasir al-Ferghani, a student of the historian Tabari, and his son Ahmed ibn Abdullo al-Ferghani, were famous historians of the tenth century who worked mainly in Egypt and Baghdad. Both of them continued to write *A History of Prophets and Kings,* which was originally created by Tabari, who continued it up until 915 CE. Besides that, Ahmed al-Ferghani wrote two works on the history of Egypt.[142] Another famous Ferghana historian was Saif ad'din Ahsikendi who in the sixteenth century wrote *Majma'at at-tavarih* (The Composition of Histories) in Tajik.[143]

A highly regarded Ferghani poet of the seventh century was Abu-l-Fazl Muhammad ibn Tahir Asir ad'din Ahsikati. His *divan* of poems written in Tajik consisted of 5,756 couplets. Another famous poet of that epoch was Saifi Isfarangi, of the town of Isfara, whose poetic works in Tajik include more than 12, 000 couplets.[144]

During the Karakhanid period, the formation of a Turkic literature was very intensive, with the parallel development of literature in Persian (Dari, or Tajik). The connection between the two was very close, given the prevalence of bilingualism. Good examples of this is the *Kutadgu Bilig* by Yusuf of Balasagun or Mahmud al-Kashgari's great work on Turkic ethnography and linguistics, as well as comparable works in Persian. Another Ferghanan, Ahmed Yugnaki, wrote the poem *Gift of Virtues* in Turkic.

Valuable data on ancient Muslim scholars, readers, oracles and poets can be gleaned from the posthumous epitaphs in Arabic or Persian on their gravestones, or *kayraks.* One reads, for example, about Ali ibn Osman, the author of legal works and court orders who died in 1173 CE in Osh. He was also the author of 1,000 essays on the sayings and stories of the Prophet Muhammad, and *Kasidi* (poetic descriptions of the foundations of Islam). Muhammad ibn Ahmad ibn Ali abu Abdullah, also buried in Osh (d. 1125 CE), receives mention in the literature as a scholar-lecturer in Baghdad.[145]

A group of epitaphs adorned with sayings from Omar Khayam and Abdilkhasan Rudaki have been found in Uzgen, Nookat, and Safed-Bulon; these are dedicated to the highly educated clergy who were professional readers of the *Sayings* of Mohammed and other core religious works. From these texts on graves it is clear that the best-known religious leaders not only bore such titles as imam, sheikh, al-islam, and mufti, but often acted as civil and judicial authorities (*rais* and *qadis*).[146]

One of the giants of fifteenth-century history and literature is Zahir ad'din Muhammad Babur, from the city of Ahsiket. He founded the vast Mughal Empire which existed for 300 years in India, and created many poetic works in which he showed himself to be a master of his native Chagatai Uzbek language. One of the most notable literary monuments of this period is his autobiography, the *Baburname,* which is rich with sharply observed details of his personal life and experience.[147] Another famous voice in Ferghana, at the close of the seventeenth century, was Mashrab Boborahim from Andijan. In his poems, many of them written in Uzbek, he criticized the nobility and thereby became much beloved by the common people.[148]

Notes

1. V.I. Sarianidi, *Khram i nekropol Tilliatepe*, Moscow, 1989, p. 42; K.I. Tashbaeva, *Oshskii oazis v epokhu bronzy*, Osh and Bishkek, 2000, p. 10.

2. Ia.A. Zadneprovskii, "Drevnezemledelcheskaia kultura Fergany," *Materialy i issledovaniia po arkheologii SSSR*, vol. 118, pp. 35–36.

3. A.A. Anarbaev, *Uzbekistonda ilk sugorma dekh.krnchilikning shakllanishi va antropogen landshaftni tashkil topishi//Uzbekiston khududida dekhkhonchilik madaniyatining tarikhiy ildizlari va zamonaviy zharayenlar*, Tashkent, 2006, pp. 9–10; A.A. Anarbaev and F.A. Maksudov, *Drevnii Margilan*, Tashkent, 2007, p. 145.

4. V.I. Sprishevskii, "Chustskoe poselenie epokhi bronzy (iz raskopok 1954 goda)," *Kratkie soobshcheniia Insntituta istorii materialnoi kultury AN SSSR*, no. 69, Moscow and Leningrad, 1957 pp. 40–49; Ia.A. Zadneprovskii, "1962 raskopki Chustskogo poseleniia v 1956 g.," *Sovetskaia arkheologiia*, no. 3, 1958, pp. 185–89.

5. Ia.A. Zadneprovskii, "Osnovnye etapy istorii kultury Iuzhnogo Kyrgyzstana v svete novykh dannykh (1976–1984)," *Drevni i srednevekovyi Kyrgyzstan*, Bishkek, 1996, pp. 15–32.

6. Ia.A. Zadneprovskii, "Oshskoe poselenie epokhi bronzy," *Pamiatniki Kirgizii*, vol. 5, Frunze, 1992, p. 28; idem, *Oshskoe poselenie: K istorii Fergany v epokhu pozdnei bronzy*, Bishkek, 1997, p. 103.

7. A.A. Anarbaev, "Uzbekistonda ilk davlatchilik va uning urganilish tarihidagi ba'zibir muammolar," *O'zbekiston tarixi*, no. 4, Tashkent, 2004, p. 13.

8. Zadneprovskii, "Drevnezemledelcheskaia kultura Fergany," pp. 75–77.

9. M.E. Voronets, "Kamennoe izobrazhenie zmei iz kishlaka Sokh Ferganskoi oblasti," *KSIIMK*, no. 61, 1956, pp. 48–56.

10. S.S. Sorokin, "Khakskii klad," *Soobshcheniia Gosudarstvennogo Ermitazha*, vol. 19, Leningrad, 1966, pp. 28–32.

11. Zadneprovskii, "Drevnezemledelcheskaia kultura Fergany," p. 52.

12. N.G. Gorbunova, "Nekotorye osobennosti formirovaniia drevnikh kultur Fergany," *Arkheologicheskii sbornik Gosudarstvennogo Ermitazha*, Leningrad, vol. 25, 1984, p. 104.

13. N.G. Gorbunova, "The Culture of Ancient Ferghana, VI Century BC–VI Century AD," *BAR International Series*, no. 281, 1986, p. 48.

14. Zadneprovskii, "Drevnezemledelcheskaia kultura Fergany," pp. 108–15.

15. H.H. Negmatov, "K otkrytiiu goroda epokhi bronzy i rannego zheleza—Nur-Tepa," in *Kultura pervobytnoi epokhi Tadzhikistana (ot mezolita do bronzy)*, Dushanbe, 1982, pp. 89–111.

16. N.G. Gorbunova, "Kultura Fergany v epokhu rannego zheleza," *Arkheologicheskii sbornik Gosudarstvennogo Ermitazha*, vol. 5, 1962, p. 94.

17. Gorbunova, "Nekotorye osobennosti formirovaniia drevnikh kultur Fergany," pp. 101–2; idem, "The Culture of Ancient Ferghana," pp. 58–68.

18. B.A. Litvinskii, "Saki, kotorye za Sogdom," *Trudy Akademii Nauk Tadzhiksogo SSR*, vol. 120, 1960, pp. 26–28.

19. Gorbunova, "Nekotorye osobennosti formirovaniia drevnikh kultur Fergany," p. 102.

20. N.Ia. Bichurin, *Sobranie svedenii o narodakh, obitavshikh v Srednei Azii v drevnie vremena*, Moscow and Leningrad, 1950, vol. 2, pp. 161–62.

21. Ibid., p. 188.

22. Ibid., pp. 232, 235.

23. Ibid., p. 260.

24. L.A. Borovkova, *Zapad Tsentralnoi Azii vo II v. do n.e.*, Moscow, 1989, p. 260.

25. Kh.I. Tashbaeva, "K probleme lokalizatsii gorodov gosudarstva Davan," in *Tsivili-*

zatsii skotovodov i zemledeltsev Tsentralnoi Azii, Samarkand and Bishkek, 2005, pp. 155–64; A. Khodzhaev, "Svedeniia drevnikh kitaiskikh istochnikov o gorodakh-gosudarstvakh Fergany (Dyuiiuan)," in *Materialy respublikanskoi nauchno-prakticheskoi konferentsii na temu "Velikii shelkovyi put" i Ferganskaia dolina,"* Tashkent, 2004, p. 62.

26. A.N. Bernshtam, *Drevniaia Fergana,* Tashkent, 1951, p. 11.

27. Ia.A. Zadneprovskii and B.I. Matbabaev, "Gorodishche Markhamat (nekotorye itogi izucheniia)," in *Istoriia materialnoi kultury Uzbekistana (IMKU),* vol. 25, Tashkent, 1991, pp. 62–72.

28. Gorbunova, "The Culture of Ancient Ferghana," pp. 66–67.

29. Bernshtam, *Drevniaia Fergana,* p. 19.

30. E.G. Pulleyblank, "Chinese and Indo-European," *Journal of the Royal Asiatic Society of Great Britain and Ireland,* nos. 1–2, 1966, p. 26.

31. A.A. Anarbaev, "Kadimgi va urta asrlarda Akhsikent," in *Uzbekiston tarikhida kadimgi Fargona,* Tashkent, 2001, p. 11; idem, "The Capitals of the Ferghana Valley and Their Localization (Antiquity and Early Middle Ages)," in *Civilizations of Nomadic and Sedentary People of Central Asia,* Samarkand and Bishkek, 2005, p. 51.

32. A.A. Anarbaev, "Uzbekistonda ilk davlatchilik va uning urganilish tarihidagi ba'zi-bir muammolar," *O'zbekiston tarixi,* no. 4, Tashkent, 2004, pp. 21–24; Anarbaev, "The Capitals of the Ferghana Valley and Their Localization," pp. 51–52.

33. Zadneprovskii and B.I. Matbabaev, "Gorodishche Markhamat," *IMKU,* vol. 25, Tashkent, 1991, pp. 64, 67.

34. B.M. Abdullaev, "K izucheniiu oboronitelnykh sil Ferganskoi doliny antichnogo perioda," *IMKU,* vol. 34, Samarkand and Tashkent, 2004, p. 45.

35. Anarbaev, "The Capitals of the Ferghana Valley and Their Localization," p. 53.

36. A.A. Anarbaev, N. Bababekov et al., *Margilan: A Pearl in the Necklace of Ancient History,* Tashkent, 2007, p. 23.

37. Bichurin, *Sobranie svedenii o narodakh,* p. 161.

38. B.I. Lubo-Lesnichenko, "Shelkovyi put v period shesti dinastii (III–V vv.) (po novym materialam)," *Trudy Gosudarstvennogo Ermitazha,* vol. 19, Leningrad, 1978, pp. 15–24.

39. B.A. Litvinskii, *Ukrasheniia iz mogilnikov Zapadnoi Fergany,* Moscow, 1973, p. 124.

40. Iu.D. Baruzdin and G.A. Brykina, *Arkheologicheskie pamiatniki Batkena i Lailiaka (Iugo-zapadnaia Kirgiziia),* Frunze, 1962, p. 22.

41. G. Sharma, J. Negi, "The Saka-Kushans in the Central Ganga Valley," in *Tsentralnaia Aziia v Kushanskuiu epokhu,* Moscow, 1975, pp. 15–41.

42. N.G. Gorbunova, "O tipakh ferganskikh pogrebalnykh pamiatnikov pervoi poloviny tysiacheletiia n.e.," *ASGE,* vol. 22, Leningrad, 1981, pp. 178–83; A.N. Bernshtam, "Istoriko-arkheologicheskie ocherki Tsentralnogo Tian-Shania i Pamiro-Altaia," *Materialy i issledovaniia po arkheologii SSSR,* no. 26, Moscow, 1952, pp. 86–87, 202.

43. G.A. Brykina, *Iugo-Zapadnaia Fergana v I tysiacheletie n.e.,* Moscow, 1982.

44. Gorbunova, "Nekotorye osobennosti formirovaniia drevnikh kultur Fergany," p. 104.

45. E. Shefer, *Zolotye persiki Samarkanda: Kniga o chuzhezemnykh dikovinakh v imperii Tan,* Moscow, 1951, pp. 83–85, 89–91, 161; Etienne Vaissiere, *Sogdian Traders: A History,* Boston, 2005, pp. 102–14, 208–11, 227–22.

46. A.A. Anarbaev and B. Matbabaev, "An Early Medieval Urban Necropolis in Fergana," *Silk Road Art and Archaeology,* Kamakura, no. 3, 1993/94, pp. 231–32.

47. Bernshtam, *Drevniaia Fergana,* pp. 22–23.

48. Ibid.

49. V. Bartold, "Fergana," in *Sochineniia,* vol. 3, Moscow, 1965, p. 529.

50. Ibid.

51. Bernshtam, *Drevniaia Fergana,* p. 23; idem, "Istoriko-arkheologicheskie ocherki," pp. 244–45.

52. *Istoriia at-Tabari,* trans. V.I. Beliaeva, Tashkent, 1987, pp. 143, 159, 251, 269.

53. V.A. Livshits, "Iuridicheskie dokumenty i pisma (chtenie, perevod i kommentarii)," in *Sogdiiskie dokumenty s gory Mug,* Mocow, 1962, pp. 78–79, 85, 117.

54. Ibn Khordadbekh, *Kniga putei i stran,* Baku, 1986, pp. 65–66; A.A. Anarbaev, "Srednevekovye goroda Fergany po pismennym istochnikam," in *Mezhdunarodnaia nauchnaia konferentsiia "Istoriia, kultura, i ekonomika iuga Kyrgyzstana,"* Osh, 2000, pp. 110–11.

55. Bernshtam, "Istoriko-arkheologicheskie ocherki," pp. 233–44.

56. V.A. Bulatova, *Drevniaia Kuva,* Tashkent, 1972, pp. 18–59.

57. A.R. Gibb, *The Arab Conquest of Central Asia,* London, 1923, p. 91.

58. Bernshtam, *Drevniaia Fergana,* p. 24.

59. B. Amanbaeva and D. Abdullaev, "Doarabskii Osh," in *Osh-3000,* Bishkek 2000, pp. 33–40.

60. Ibid., p. 295.

61. Bernshtam, *Drevniaia Fergana,* p. 24.

62. B.G. Gafurov *Tadzhiki,* Dushanbe 1972, p. 293.

63. Ibid.

64. Bernshtam, *Drevniaia Fergana,* p. 25.

65. Bartold, "Geograficheskii ocherk Maverannahra," in *Sochineniia,* vol. 1, p. 220.

66. E.A. Davidovich, "Monety Fergany kak istochnik dlia kharakteristiki instituta feodalnykh pozhalovanii za sluzhbu v Tsentralnoi Azii X veka," in *Pismennie pamiatniki Vostoka,* Moscow, 1972, p. 141.

67. Bernshtam, *Drevniaia Fergana,* p. 35.

68. Bartold, "Tsentralnaia Aziia do XII veka," in *Sochineniia,* vol. 1, p. 333.

69. Bernshtam, *Drevniaia Fergana,* p. 36.

70. Bartold, "Kara-Kitai i Khorezm-shah," in *Sochineniia,* vol. 1, p. 418.

71. E.A. Davidovich, *Monetnaia sistema v Tsentralnoi Azii XIII veka,* Moscow. 1972, p. 129.

72. Bernshtam, *Drevniaia Fergana,* pp. 40–41.

73. "Abdurazzak Samarkandi, Matla' as-Sa'dain va majma' al-bahrain," in *Trudy,* vol. 157, St. Petersburg State University, 2005, p. 349.

74. Babur, *Baburname,* St. Petersburg, 1900, p. 23.

75. Ibid., p. 16.

76. Ibid., p. 28.

77. Ibid., p. 90.

78. Ibid., p. 122.

79. Ibid., pp. 128–30.

80. Bartold, "Fergana," p. 536.

81. Anarbaev and Maksudov, *Drevnii Margilan,* p. 9.

82. D.M.J. de Goeje, ed., *Desciptio ditionis moslemicae auctore Abu Ishak al-Farisi Al-Istakhri,* Leiden, 1870, pp. 346–48.

83. Ibid.

84. D.M.J. de Goeje, ed., *Descriptio ditionis moslemicae auctore Abu'l-Kasim Ibn Haukal,* Leiden, 1873 pp. 395–96; D.M.J. de Goeje, ed., *Descriptio imperii moslemici auctore Schmas'd-din Abu Abdallah Mohammad ibn Ahmed ibn Abi Bekr al-Banna al-Basschari al-Mokaddasi,* Leiden, 1877, p. 272.

85. Anarbaev and Maksudov, *Drevnii Margilan,* p. 148.

86. Bartold, "Andijan," in *Sochineniia,* vol. 3, p. 326.

87. Ibid.

88. The *ah* is a length measurement that equals 6 kilometers.

89. de Goeje, ed., *Descriptio ditionis moslemicae auctore Abu'l-Kasim Ibn Haukal*, p. 396.

90. de Goeje, ed., *Desciptio ditionis moslemicae auctore Abu Ishak al-Farisi Al-Istakhri*, p. 347; de Goeje, ed., *Descriptio ditionis moslemicae auctore Abu'l-Kasim Ibn Haukal*, p. 396.

91. Bartold, "Geograficheskii ocherk Maverannahra," p. 213.

92. E.A. Davidovich, "Monety Fergany kak istochnik instituta feodalnykh pozhalovanii za sluzhbu v Tsentralnoi Azii X veka," in *Pismennye pamiatniki Vostoka*, Moscow, 1972, pp. 110–41.

93. A.A. Anarbaev, "Ahsikent v drevnosti i srednevekove (itogi i prespektivy issledovaniia)," *Sovetskaia Arkheologiia*, no. 1, Moscow, 1988, pp. 184–86.

94. B.D. Kochnev, "Istoriia monetnogo obrashcheniia v Tsentralnoi Azii XI i XII veka," *IMKUz*, vol. 12, 1975, pp. 129–30; B.D. Kochnev, "Zametki o srednevekovoi numizmatike v Tsentralnoi Azii (Karakhanidy)," *IMKUz*, no. 15, 1979, pp. 128–29.

95. Anarbaev, "Ahsikent v drevnosti i srednevekove,"p. 185.

96. de Goeje, ed., *Descriptio imperii moslemici auctore Schmas'd-din Abu Abdallah Mohammad ibn Ahmed ibn Abi Bekr al-Banna al-Basschari al-Mokaddasi*, pp. 165, 345; de Goeje, ed., *Desciptio ditionis moslemicae auctore Abu Ishak al-Farisi Al-Istakhri*, pp. 335–36.

97. Bartold, "Geograficheskii ocherk Maverannahra," p. 219.

98. Bernshtam, *Drevniaia Fergana*, p. 32.

99. Ibid., pp. 32–33.

100. Ibid., p. 34.

101. B.D. Kochnev, "Monety, novye dannye o monetnom dvore Karakhanidov v Fergane," *Otchet Gosudarstvennogo Ermitazha*, vol. 49, Leningrad, 1984, p. 63.

102. Ibid., p. 38.

103. O. Kagaev, *Arabskie i persidskie istochniki o kirgizakh i Kirgizii*, Frunze, 1968, p. 60.

104. M.E. Mason, *Gornoe delo: istoriia gornogo dela na territorii Uzbekistana*, Tashkent, 1953, pp. 27–29.

105. de Goeje, ed., *Desciptio ditionis moslemicae auctore Abu Ishak al-Farisi Al-Istakhri*, p. 334.

106. *Arkheologicheskie raboty v Tadzhikistane*, vol. 19, Dushanbe, 1979, pp. 430–31.

107. Bernshtam, *Drevniaia Fergana*, p. 29.

108. B.A. Latinin, "Nekotorye voprosy metodologii izucheniia irrigatsii v Tsentralnoi Azii," *Sovetskaia Arkheologiia*, no. 3, 1959, pp. 19–27.

109. O. Berenaliev, "Vozniknovenie iskusstvennogo orosheniia v Fergane," in *Istoriia dorevoliutsionnoi Kirgizii*, Frunze, 1985, p. 282.

110. Ibid., pp. 284–85.

111. Ibid., pp. 286–88.

112. *Istoriia Uzbekskoi SSR*, vol. 1, bk. 1, Tashkent, 1955, pp. 36–37.

113. V.V. Bartold, "Istoriia irrigatsii v Turkestane," in *Sochineniia*, vol. 3, Moscow, 1965, p. 211.

114. Ibid.

115. Ibid.

116. Babur, *Baburname*, p. 15.

117. Ibid., p. 126.

118. Ibid., p. 13.

119. B.A. Litvinskii, "Problemy etnicheskoi istorii drevnei i rannesrednevekovoi Fergany," in *Istoriia i kultura narodov Tsentralnoi Azii*, Moscow, 1976, p. 54; N.G. Gorbunova, "Fergana soglasno antichnym avtoram," in ibid., p. 29.

120. Litvinskii, "Problemy etnicheskoi istorii," p. 59.

121. Gafurov, *Tadzhiki*, Dushanbe, 1972, p. 210; S.P. Tolstov, *Po drevnim deltam Oxa i Yaxarta*, Moscow, 1962, pp. 244–45.

122. F. Aktheim, *Geschichte der Hunnen*, vol. 1, Berlin, 1959, pp. 41–54; E.G. Pulley-blank, "The Consonantal System of Old Chinese," *AMNS*, vol. 9, pt. 1, 1962, pp. 259–60.

123. S.S. Gubaeva, *Etnicheskaia kompozitsiia Fergany v kontse XIX–nachale XX veka*, Tashkent, 1983, pp. 43–44.

124. Ibid., p. 44.

125. S.S. Abashin, *Naselenie Ferganskoi doliny/Ferganskaia dolina*, Moscow, 2004, pp. 38–101.

126. Babur, *Baburname*, p. 13.

127. Gafurov, p. 547.

128. S.S. Gubaeva, *Etnicheskaia kompozitsiia Fergany v kontse XIX–nachale XX veka*, pp. 44–45.

129. G. Abdulgazieva, "Stratigraficheskie issledovaniia pamiatnikov Shurabashatskoi kultury," in *Fergana v drevnem i rannem srednevekove*, Samarkand, 1994, pp. 26–29.

130. Anarabaev and Maksudov, *Drevnii Margilan*, pp. 44–49.

131. Abdulgazieva, "Stratigraficheskie issledovaniia pamiatnikov Shurabashatskoi kultury," p. 27.

132. Anarbaev and Maksudov, *Drevnii Margilan*, pp. 5–49.

133. V.M. Masson et al., "Period neolita v Tsentralnoi Azii," in *Period neolita v SSSR*, Moscow, 1982, p. 60.

134. T.K. Mkrtichev, *Buddistskoe iskusstvo v Tsentralnoi Azii (I–X veka)*, Moscow, 2002, pp. 162–72.

135. Bartold, "Fergana," p. 529.

136. Jemal al-Karshi, *Mulhakat as-Surah*, Dushanbe, 2006, p. 83. The accuracy of these historical designations is far from clear. The name of Muhammad ibn Jarir is historically unknown. The several tombs or *mazars* (sacred sites) in Safed-Bulon are said to honor Arabs killed during their prayers by the Turkic commander Karvan-Bash, but this is not verifiable. According to local legend, the main holy site of the village relates to the events of the Arab conquest, but it is the burial site of Muhammad ibn Nasir, known as Shah-Fazil, who died a martyr ca. 1056–57 during the feudal wars of Ferghana rulers—some 300 years after the conquest.

137. de Goeje, ed., *Descriptio imperii moslemici auctore Schmas'd-din Abu Abdallah Mohammad ibn Ahmed ibn Abi Bekr al-Banna al-Basschari al-Mokaddasi*, p. 36.

138. V.D. Goriacheva and *Safed Bulon, Istoricheskii i arkheologicheskii zapovednik Fergany*, Bishkek, 2002; V.D. Goriacheva and V.N. Nastich, "Epigraficheskie pamiatniki Safid-Bulana v XII–XIV vekakh," *Epigrafiia Vostoka*, vol. 22, Leningrad, 1984, pp. 61–72.

139. Jemal al-Karshi, *Mulhakat as-Surah*, pp. 84–86.

140. L. Ismoilov, *Manakib kak istoricheskii istochnik XVI veka*, Tashkent, 1991, p. 9.

141. D.P. Matvievskaia and B.A. Rozenfeld, *Matematiki i astronomy musulmanskogo srednevekovia i ikh trudy VIII–XVII veka*, Moscow, 1983, pp. 55–58.

142. V.I. Beliaev, *Arabskie istochniki istorii turkmen i Turkmenii v IX–XIII veke*, Moscow, vol. 1, 1939, p. 39.

143. A.T. Tagirzhanovim, ed., "Majma'at-tavarih," in *Iranskaia filologiia*, vol. 2, Leningrad, 1960, pp. 97–103.

144. *Adabiyoti forsu Tochik dar asrhoi XII–XIV*, vol. 1, Dushanbe, 1976, pp. 70–80.

145. V.Y. Galitskii and V.M. Ploskikh, *Vo vremena Kara-Khanidov*, Osh and Bishkek, 2000, p. 58.

146. V.N. Nastich, *Pogrebalnaia epigrafika arabskogo pisma kak istochnik po srednevekovoi istorii Kirgizii i Iuzhnogo Kazahstana*, Moscow, 1984, pp. 161–77.

147. Babur, *Baburname*, pp. 5–8.

148. *Tadzhikskaia sovetskaia entsiklopediia*, vol. 4, Dushanbe, 1983, p. 276.

2

The Rise and Fall of the Kokand Khanate

Victor Dubovitskii (Tajikistan), with
Khaydarbek Bababekov (Uzbekistan)

At first glance it would appear that nearly all aspects of the history of Central Asia in the eighteenth and nineteenth centuries have been studied and described in hundreds of books worldwide. The names of rulers, commanders, leaders of uprisings, poets, and court physicians are all well known. Starting from the mid-nineteenth century, there are photographs of many of the great figures of the day. There even exist eyewitness accounts, written not in the mysterious old *shikasta* and *sarvi* scripts but in accessible editions by publishers in St. Petersburg, Tashkent, London, and New Delhi. Yet lurking behind the apparent openness and simplicity of the prevailing narrative are intrigues that make those of Cardinal Richelieu or Talleyrand pale by comparison. Moreover, there exist huge gaps in our knowledge, where even the most elemental information is lacking.

This is precisely the situation with our understanding of the Kokand Khanate, a small state in the heart of the Ferghana Valley. It occupied the historical stage for only 167 years, from 1709 to 1876 CE, or from 1087 to 1254 according to the Muslim calendar by which the khanate lived. The khanate existed at the point of junction of three world civilizations: the Muslim world to which it belonged, the Orthodox Christian Russian Empire, and Buddhist-Confucian China of the Qin Empire.

Given the abundance of information on Central Asia, it astonishes one all the more that major research has never been done on the Kokand Khanate. This is largely because the entire state archives were destroyed after the last ruler, Khudayar Khan, escaped from Kokand to Tashkent in 1876. The task of rediscovering this fading past will take decades, but the following account summarizes the state of our knowledge to date.

The Dynasty over Time

When the nomadic Uzbeks conquered Central Asia in the sixteenth century and laid the foundations of the Shaybanid state, they delivered a shattering blow to the heirs of Timur (Tamerlane) and their feudal leadership. The country was increasingly divided thereafter, and bloody feudal wars prevailed between Bukhara and Khiva. In the early eighteenth century the Ferghana Valley area separated itself from Bukhara and an independent Kokand Khanate appeared.

The Kokand khans were said to be linked through the figure of one Altun-Bishik to the great Babur and to Tamerlane himself. Most contemporary Muslims, as well as European scholars, accepted this mythological genealogy and the legitimization of the Kokand dynasty it implied. According to this legend, Babur did not retreat from Samarkand directly south to Afghanistan, but instead diverted through Ferghana. One of Babur's wives had just given birth to his son, but the dangers threatening the fugitives forced them to leave the newborn to the mercy of fate. They placed him in a richly decorated cradle, along with much jewelry, and left behind a faithful servant who was to report on the baby's fate to Babur. Nearby were some Turkic villages where Kyrk, Kipchak, Ming, and Kyrgyz lived near each other as one society. These people found the child and gave him the name Altun-Bishik, or "Golden Cradle." He was raised in one of the villages, and when he reached adulthood received a wife from each of the villages. In due course the eldest of his wives gave birth to Khudayar or Ilik-Sultan, progenitor of the Kokand dynasty.

Neither Babur nor his contemporary biographers so much as mention Altun-Bishik. It is likely that the rulers of Kokand concocted the entire legend in order to link their dynasty with the descendants of Genghis Khan and thus consolidate their power. According to legend, Altun-Bishik died in 1545, and his son Tangriyar became the ruler of Ferghana, but with the title of bey instead of khan. The same title was given his descendants up to and including Alim Khan. When finally the first khan, Shah Rukh, ascended the throne he constructed a new citadel at Kokand, while his son Abd al-Kerim built a second one.[1]

The events of 1709 are interestingly described in *Tarixi Turkestoni* (History of Turkestan), written by Mullah Alim Makhdum-Hajji. An assembly of elders and the nobles from Jankat, Pilahkan, Tufantip, Partak, Tepa-Kurgan, Kainar, and other towns elected the intelligent and generous Shah Rukh Khan. No sooner had he been elected than he instructed them to find a convenient place to build a castle. The notables decided on a spot between two rivers, constructed there a citadel surrounded by buildings and yards, and immediately enthroned the new Shah Rukh there. Mullah Alim believed that Shah Rukh ruled for twelve years and died in 1721.[2] By that year his state included the territories of Kokand, Isfara, and Margilan.

The eldest of Shah Rukh's three sons, Abdu-Raim, succeeded his father. Abdu-Raim's permanent residence was at the village of Dikan-Toda until 1732, when he began reconstructing the city of Kokand.[3] At this time the ruler of Khujand, the leader of the Yuz tribe named Ak-Buta Bey, decided to put an end to Abdu-Raim's rule. However, Abdu-Raim chased down and beheaded his enemy, then proclaiming himself Abdu-Raim, ruler of both Khujand and its new territorial acquisition, Kokand. In due course Abdu-Raim also gained control of Andijan. But Abdu-Raim eventually became severely ill, which brought on madness. Seizing on their ruler's mental instability, his officials killed the khan in 1733.[4] Abdu-Raim left behind a son, Irdana, and several daughters, but the conspirators chose as ruler his brother Abdu Karim Bey, who promptly moved to Kokand and again rebuilt it.

For the first quarter-century of its existence, the Kokand Khanate displayed all the typical features of a medieval Central Asian state. These included feuds between the oppressed farming people and the politically dominant nomadic populations, palace revolutions, and continuous warfaring with all its neighbors. However, geographical location, the structure of its population, and its climate gave the new Kokand Khanate marked advantages. The core of the state was the largest oasis in the region, framed by the Kuramin and Alai mountain ranges, as well as several smaller ranges. A huge valley irrigated by one of the two great inner Asian rivers, Syr Darya, stretches from east to west and is open on the east via mountain passes to Kashgar in Xinjiang, and to the west to the plains of Transoxiana, the region between Syr Darya and Amu Darya—the point of contact and competition between the Muslim and Buddhist-Confucian worlds. Thus, its geography made the khanate a natural transit route in every direction.

With regard to its cultural and political influence on the various ethnic groups of Central Asia, the Kokand Khanate was particularly important for the Kara-Kyrgyz (Kyrgyz) and Kyrgyz-Kaysak (Kazakhs). By contrast, the Khanate of Bukhara influenced the Sarts and Tajiks, as well as the nomadic Uzbeks, while it was natural for the major Turkmen tribes—the Teke, Yomud, and Salar peoples—to be drawn toward the Khanate of Khiva.

In 1746, the Chinese conquered Kashgar and defeated the Buddhist Kalmyks in Dzungaria. On the giant steppe that stretches from Mongolia to Hungary, such events pushed hordes of nomads into new regions, where they formed new nations. Kalmyk nomads, having lost their state, shifted westward and invaded the Ferghana Valley.

Abdu-Karim sent a detachment against the Kalmyks under the command of Kipchak-bachi, but the latter was killed and his troops fled, opening the road to Kokand for the Kalmyks. Pazyl Bey, the khan of Ura-Tyube, learned of this situation and brought his army to help. After a bloody battle, the Kalmyks retreated from Kokand and the Buddhists' aspirations in Muslim Central Asia came to nothing.

After the death in 1750 of Khan Abdu-Karim, his son Abdurakhman ruled for approximately a year before being deposed. Power then passed into the hands of Irdana who, after further intrigues, ended up as the ruler of Kokand. Irdana Bey continued to expand the territory of his state, acquiring the city of Isfara and treacherously killing its ruler, Abdurakhman-Batir, whose son Narbut Bey survived only because he had gone to stay with his grandmother. Irdana Bey also organized a campaign against Ura-Tyube, but failed and retreated toward Khujand. Taking advantage of a dust storm, Pazyl Bey and his allies attacked the retreating Irdana and captured the soldiers from Kokand, many of whom they executed and from whose heads was built a *kala-minar*, or pyramid of heads. Irdana himself managed to escape to Kokand.

Irdana succeeded in his next campaign against Ura-Tyube. He killed all his prisoners from Ura-Tyube and from their heads Irdana built a new *kala-minar*—Mullah Avazmat wrote that in 1859 he saw this tower.[5] In 1758, weakened by constant wars with his neighbors, Irdana Bey had to accept the suzerainty of China. In 1762, the Chinese ambassador declared to the khan of the Middle Horde of Kazakhs that the Chinese would launch a spring campaign against Turkestan and Samarkand, for which they demanded people, horses, bulls, and rams. Learning of this plan, Irdana and the rulers of Ura-Tyube and Khujand, along with the Kyrgyz sultans, sent a letter to the Afghan monarch, Ahmad Shah, the region's most powerful ruler at the time, asking him to save the Muslim world from the invading infidels.[6]

It was a rare event in the history of Central Asia when leaders of various regions united under the founder of the new Durrani dynasty in Afghanistan, Ahmed Shah, to resist the Chinese. According to Ch.Ch. Valikhanov, "this alliance did not last but it is important that it stopped China's plans to extend its borders to Tashkent, Sairam, Suzaka and Turkestan."[7]

Irdana ruled for more than a decade, but his successor did so for only three months before plotters killed him. His murderers and several other representatives of the Kokand nobility persuaded one Narbuta to take over, and they proclaimed him ruler. From the start of his reign Narbuta Bey worked to suppress separatist moves by the rulers of Chust and Namangan, and he devoted much effort to subjugating Khujand. The death of the ruler of Ura-Tyube and Dzhizak enabled Narbuta to add those areas to Kokand, as well. These tasks completed, Narbuta then had to manage his domain. He had eleven children, five of them daughters and six of the total from enslaved women. Narbuta appointed his brothers as governors in Namangan and Khujand, his eldest son as governor of Margilan, and another son to Tura-Kurgan.

The early years of Narbuta's reign are described in the book of a Russian traveler, Philip Efremov, who was captured by Kyrgyz in 1774, sold as a slave to Bukharans, and returned to Russia through India and England only in 1782. According to Efremov, Narbuta had hostile relations with Bukhara but was recognized as khan by the Chinese, with whom he maintained an alliance. This stability enabled Narbuta Bey to govern for a long time and for his lands in the Ferghana Valley to achieve relative prosperity. New irrigation canals were built and the area of irrigated land increased. Commerce expanded and the quality of urban craftsmanship rose. The city of Kokand itself thrived. Kokand's chroniclers of the day reported on the low cost of goods and favorable conditions for merchants during Narbuta Bey's rule. Eastern chroniclers, it should be said, took low prices and order as the main indicators of social welfare.[8] The highly valued tanga served as the main currency in Kokand, but at the time of Narbuta Bey's accession there existed no smaller coins for change. He therefore introduced into circulation a very small coin, the *pulus*. This suggests that during Narbuta Bey's reign there was no inflation and the standard of living significantly improved. Indeed, over the more than thirty years of Narbuta Bey's rule no popular uprisings surfaced against the government.

Narbuta died in 1801 and was succeeded by his son, Alim. He continued to expand the territory of Kokand by conquering the valley of Angren, Chimkent (now Shymkent), Sairam, and the entire Tashkent region, a key area along the caravan route to Russia. Seeing that his state was strong enough to resist Bukhara, Alim accepted the title of khan, and the state he ruled became known officially as the Kokand Khanate, with its capital at Kokand.

Kokand's political significance grew during Alim Khan's reign. He created a mercenary army consisting mostly of Tajik mountaineers from Karategin, Shugnan, and Badakhshan, as well as Iranians. This force supported him in the struggle to centralize power and later became the core of his new and much larger army. He also opened trade relations with Russia, although these did not develop further inasmuch as safe passage for caravans could not be guaranteed owing to the absence of diplomatic ties.

Alim Khan also took several steps to reorganize religious life. Thus, he abolished the religious title *ishan,* and gave land and livestock to the poor and so-called *kalandars* (hermits) in order to engage them in socially useful work. To assure the accuracy and correctness of prayers in the mosques, he required that religious leaders take examinations, and he punished those who deviated from the true faith. This was too much for the reactionary clergy. In 1810 they took advantage of the population's discontent with Alim Khan's frequent military operations and current presence in Tashkent to disseminate the false rumor that he had been killed. His brother Umar ascended to the throne, but Alim Khan soon learned of the treason and rushed back to Kokand by the shortest route. However, the conspirators lay in ambush and one of them, one Kambar Mirza from Andijan, shot Alim Khan.

During the reign of Umar Khan that followed, Kokand continued to expand its territory. Umar also attempted to establish diplomatic ties with Russia, but on the return trip from St. Petersburg one of the ambassadors died of disease, a second member of the embassy was killed by a Russian soldier, and a third was exiled to the settlement of Petropavlovsk.

Literature and the arts flourished at the time of Umar, but he also restored the clergy's status and benefits and concentrated nearly all power in their hands. Under the guise of sharia law, they suppressed every manifestation of discontent. Nonetheless, Umar's lavish reconstruction of the Friday Mosque in Kokand earned him the title of *amir-ul-muslimin* (captain of the faithful). And indeed, many local historians described Umar Khan as "pious," though he was brutal in his wars of conquest. Dishod, a famous poetess of the nineteenth century, described his actions in Ura-Tyube in 1817 in her *Tarih-i-muhajiron* (History of Settlers):

> All the prisoners were herded into the square of Chor-su. People whispered that on that day 13,400 people had been taken prisoner. The amir of Ferghana himself, Amir Umar Khan, despite being a scholar and great poet, had mercy neither on the scholars nor poets of this oppressed people.[9]

In the fall of 1822 Umar Khan fell ill, and he died a year later. On the day of his death his sixteen-year-old son, Muhammad Ali (Madali), was proclaimed khan. V.P.

Nalivkin describes him as "a willful boy, spoiled, capricious, evil, and morally and physically depraved thanks to the flatteries of courters, wine, women, and the bad examples that abounded in his court."[10] This did not, however, prevent his using the army to expand the Kokand Khanate to include the southern foothills of the Alai range inhabited by Tajiks, as well as Karategin, Darwaz, Shugnan, Rushan, and Vakhan in the Pamirs. Between 1826 and 1831 he organized expeditions against Kashgar, as a result of which the Chinese were forced to allow Muhammad Ali Khan to collect duty on that territory. For this coup, Muhammad Ali Khan was honored with the religious title of "Defender of the Faith" or *Ghazi.* But such rejoicing proved premature, for during the reign of Muhammad Ali Khan, relations between Kokand and Bukhara steadily worsened. As a result of repeated wars between the khanates, the Emir of Bukhara Nasrullah Khan succeeded in seizing Khujand and adding it to his own realm. Worse, Muhammad Ali Khan himself had to acknowledge himself a vassal of the emir of Bukhara.

Realizing his precarious political position, Muhammad Ali Khan tried in 1842 to forge an alliance with Russia. For this purpose he sent an ambassador to St. Petersburg with a letter stating that "the genuine friendship between the high court of Russia and the kingdom of Kokand was reflected in the steady exchange of ambassadors which, for reasons entirely unknown, ceased completely. We do not know if this unpleasant development was caused by officials of our government or of your Imperial Majesty. But in order to rekindle the old friendship, I am sending to you a true well-wisher of noble origin—the deserving Naqib-Gale-Ashraf."[11] Tsar Nicholas I addressed his letter of response to "the Kokand landowner Seyid Muhammad Ali Khan Bahadur." He indicated that We were very pleased to hear . . . of your wish to maintain friendly relations with the powerful Russian State, and we, for our part, express absolute readiness to meet your good intentions. . . . Your subjects that come to Russia are being protected and receive our patronage. We want Russian citizens to find equal security and justice in your land. . . . Only then can the foundations of reciprocal relations between us become solid."[12]

The Kokand government also requested permission for its subjects to travel to Mecca via Russia, help for Kokand and Tashkent traders traveling to Siberia, and medals and diplomas for various Kokand luminaries and mullahs.[13] The Russian side promised to examine these requests and to meet them if possible.

All this ended without the slightest effect when the ambassador from Kokand reached Semipalatinsk and discovered that internecine fighting had again broken out in his land.[14] Moreover, relations between Kokand and Bukhara soon degenerated into war, and eventually Muhammad Ali Khan's was forced to abdicate in favor of his younger brother, Sultan Mahmud. In April 1842, the Emir of Bukhara Nasrullah, conquered Kokand and executed Sultan Mahmud Khan, his elder brother and former khan Muhammad Ali, and their mother Nadira, a famous poet.

A Russian participant of these events, Vasilii Pshenichnikov, later wrote that "After the capture of Kokand, the city and its surrounding villages were left to be plundered by the Bukharan cavalry, and the khan's palace was given to the people of Sarbaz, who immediately seized sixteen chests of gowns and thirty of the khan's wives. The emir of Bukhara took the treasury. Meanwhile, the khan of Kokand escaped to Margilan, but was captured and brought in a cart to the capital, where he was slaughtered along with his people."[15]

In June 1842, Sher Ali was proclaimed khan, and shortly thereafter arrived in Kokand with his 3,000–4,000-man army. Learning of their approach, Ibrahim-Dadhoh, the leader whom the khan of Bukhara had installed, escaped to Khujand. The people of Kokand, knowing that Nasrullah would mount another campaign against them, set about fortifying the city and erecting a new city wall. As soon as he heard about this, the emir of Bukhara set out with a large army to Kokand, reaching the city on July 29. Nasrullah set up headquarters in the village of Muy-Muborak, where he stayed for more than two months. Encircling Kokand on four sides, he thought the people would soon be starved into surrendering.[16] Meanwhile, one of his prominent commanders, Musulmankul, asked the emir's permission to enter Kokand to persuade the inhabitants to surrender. After Nasrullah gave his assent, Musulmankul entered the city and began at once to call on the people to come together and defend themselves, explaining that the Bukharan forces were so weak that Emir Nasrullah would soon have to lift the siege and return to Bukhara. Surviving archival sources confirm that the armed Kokandis immediately rallied around their khan and mounted a heroic defenses, repelling all attacks by the Bukharan forces. Meanwhile, an army from the Emirate of Khiva invaded Bukhara on September 26. Upon receiving this news, Nasrullah left Kokand for Bukhara on October 9.[17]

Thus, even though the Kokandis failed to defeat the emir of Bukhara's forces, they still kept themselves free from his potential yoke. In spite of this achievement, Sherali's rule proved extremely onerous for the population, which reacted to his extortions with uprisings across the entire khanate. One such uprising broke out in Osh in 1845. Meanwhile, Musulmankul had decided to take advantage of the political situation to get rid of Sherali Khan. To do so, Musulmankul planned to move the entire Kokand army to Osh to quell the uprising. Not knowing of the plot, Murad, son of Ali Khan, who had been dethroned in 1841, decided to take advantage of Musulmankul's absence from Kokand and seized the throne himself. Proclaiming himself monarch, he also announced he would be a vassal of the emir of Bukhara. The now-dethroned Sherali Khan was killed the next night. But the people of Kokand hated the khan of Bukhara and therefore opposed Murad Khan as well. Musulmankul arrived in Namangan, gave his twelve-year-old daughter in marriage to the young Khudayar, Sherali Khan's son. Arriving in Kokand, he executed Khan Murad and all those who supported him.

To seize the throne for himself, Musulmankul then manipulated the aspirations of several other potential claimants. He knew that one of them, the nomadic leader Sarymsak, dreamed of becoming khan, and therefore invited him from Tashkent to Kokand to be crowned. But Musulmankul then gave orders for Sarymsak to be killed, which was done. After this, Musulmankul arranged for the under-aged Khudayar to be proclaimed khan, and for himself to be his regent.

This began a period in which the Kipchak party dominated Kokand. Taking advantage of the khan's youth, Musulmankul managed the khanate with near-total authority. Yet, according to the Russian orientalist and diplomat, N.F. Petrovskii, Musulmankul's reign "was not bad for the people, because the strict and harsh Musulmankul was in his own way a fair ruler and a good head of the khanate."[18]

The author of the contemporary study "Seyid Mohammad Khudayar Khan from Kokand" has observed that Musulmankul always acted in the name of either the khan or someone else within the khan's immediate circle.[19] He treated Khudayar Khan the way Alexander Menshikov treated Peter II, keeping the young khan locked up, giving him no money, and forbidding him from issuing orders independently. The Kipchaks reigned supreme in these years, under the guidance of Musulmankul. Opposition to them arose among other segments of the population, however, and in 1853 a massive wave of violence exploded against Kipchaks. Before it subsided 20,000 of them had been killed, among them Musulmankul.

With these events Khudayar Khan began his reign, which lasted from 1853 to 1858. He continued the dismal policies of his predecessors by oppressing the populace and totally disregarding its needs. Out of the northern provinces of the khanate he formed a special region ruled by a governor-general. Khudayar Khan entrusted its management to Mirza Akhmad, who proceeded to arouse the nomads' indignation with his outrageous behavior. As a result, the entire northern part of the khanate rebelled in 1858.

Meanwhile, the khan, having had no news from Mirza Akhmad and assuming he was in danger, dispatched his older brother, Mallya Bek, to Tashkent and granted his request for control over all the forces in the northern province. Mallya Bek saw an opportunity in this and immediately pardoned all those involved in the uprising; he also decreased their taxes. With the support of Tashkent and the entire northern part of the khanate, Mallya assembled an army, routed his brother at Samanchi, occupied Kokand, and named himself khan. Soon coins were being minted with the name Mallya Khan.

From this time forward the role of the Kipchaks in the political life of the khanate steadily increased. All the land taken away from them by Khudayar Khan was returned to its former owners. Such actions increased Mallya Khan's credibility among large parts of the population. Less successful were his efforts to open diplomatic relations with China and to place the Karategin region under the jurisdiction of Kokand.

During Mallya Khan's reign the Russian Empire intensified its military operations against the Khanate of Kokand, seizing Tokmak, Pishpek (later Frunze, now Bishkek) and a number of other fortresses in their vicinities. Mallya Khan made several attempts to retrieve the lost settlements, but without success. Resentment against him increased and was fanned by unbearable taxes and duties, as well as the government's harsh retaliations against those who failed to pay. Finally, in March 1862 Mallya Khan was assassinated and his nephew, the seventeen-year-old Shakhmurad, was declared khan.

The new khan immediately executed everyone who had been close to his uncle. Kanaat, the ruler of Tashkent, feared for his life. Reinforcing the defenses of Tashkent, he then invited Khudayar to join him, promising to return the former khan to his throne. Khudayar arrived in Tashkent in March. Upon hearing this, Shakhmurad besieged Tashkent with a 14,000-man army. However, Khudayar Khan's supporters managed to kidnap Shakhmurad. At the same time the emir of Bukhara, Muzaffar, marched on Kokand. What was left of Shakhmurad's forces lifted the siege of Tashkent and retreated to the Alatau Mountains. As a result, Khudayar Khan reclaimed the throne of Kokand.

At that time there were three descendants of former Kokand khans living in Kokand: Sadykbek, Hodjibek, and Shakhrukh. These were all young (around twenty years of age), and all of them unexpectedly declared their intention of claiming their rightful throne. The Kokand elite were divided, with some supporting the young claimants and others, who remained loyal to Alimkul, moving to crush their forces. Alimkul himself, watching the machinations of the ambitious youths, resolved to eliminate them. He called each of the young claimants, promising each in turn that he would have him named as khan. When the young men, believing this, arrived in Osh, Alimkul gave orders for all of them to be killed. All three unlucky hopefuls were buried on the cemetery at Osh, where their graves can still be found on the northern slope of the Solomon's Mountain (Takht-Suleiman).

After that, on July 9, 1863, Alimkul named as khan the son of Mallya Khan, Sultan Murad, and immediately launched an attack on Khudayar Khan's forces. At the same time the Emir of Bukhara Muzaffar had to return to his capital because a rebellion had broken out in Shakhrisabz. Learning of this, the Kipchaks, together with some Kyrgyz tribes, assembled their troops and simultaneously besieged Kokand and Tashkent.[20] The next phase of this drama was recounted by a Russian corps commander stationed in Orenburg. According to Adjutant General Bezak, "the emir reconciled with the Kipchaks and agreed to remove Khudayar Khan and to elect the son of the deceased Mallya instead of Sultan Murad, who was a mere boy of thirteen–fourteen years."[21] Mullah Alimkul would be regent with the power to appoint all officials.

As regent, Alimkul's goal was to consolidate the Kipchaks' control of the khanate. This was to be accomplished by "concentrating around Kokand those Kyrgyz tribes that had been most helpful to the Kipchaks during their uprising against Khudayar Khan."[22] It also meant strengthening the Kokand government by recruiting more troops, amassing weapons, and reinforcing Kokand's defenses. Influential people were sent to rule Tashkent and other distant cities.[23] All this was costly and burdened the populace with heavy taxes. The people of Kokand had little sympathy for the new khan. Fearing a sudden attack, Alimkul destroyed the old palace in the center of Kokand and began to build a new one in the suburbs.[24]

Khudayar in the Shadow of the "Great Game"

The 1850s were a time of trouble for Kokand-Russian relations. The main cause of this was Kokand's active expansion northeast of the Syr Darya River. Over the previous thirty years many of the Kyrgyz-Kaysaks (Kazakh) nomads in that territory had taken Russian citizenship, and did not now welcome Kokand's interference in their affairs. As a result, in 1864 Russian troops seized Chimkent, and in 1865, Tashkent as well. Mullah Alimkul was killed in the fighting. The Kipchaks and Kyrgyz then declared Hudaykul Bey (later called Belbakchi Khan) as their khan, but he ruled only fourteen days before gathering his treasures and fleeing to Kashgar. Shortly afterward, Khudayar seized Kokand without any resistance.

Khudayar's reign was even harsher than those of his predecessors. As one observer noted, "He unleashed a ten-year robbery of his own people, replete with all kinds of plundering and murder."[25] In 1870 groups in Kokand who opposed Khudayar Khan invited Seyid Khan, Mallya Khan's son, to come to Kokand from Bukhara. When Khudayar learned of this he ordered that Seyid be captured and killed, which was done in a village called Yakkatut. The emir of Bukhara knew that it looked as though he had tried to organize a coup against his neighbor. He therefore tried to make light of it, claiming Seyid had left Bukhara without his knowledge. As proof of his good intentions he turned over to Khudayar the names of all of Seyid's allies, as well as the actual signed and stamped invitation that had been sent to Bukhara from Kokand. With the list of the conspirators in hand, the khan of course proceeded to eliminate them in his usual way. Between 1866 and 1871 Khudayar Khan secretly executed some 3,000 people.[26]

The populace endured relentless extortions from Khudayar Khan's tax collectors. As the tsarist-era historian M.A. Terentev put it, "new taxes were imposed on all newly planted trees except fruit trees, on coal burned in the mountain forests, on every weed, thorn, reed, and thistle collected for fuel, on hay brought to the capital, and on every purchase and sale at the bazaar. These levies, along with earlier taxes on metals and pack animals, were an inexhaustible source of wealth for the greedy khan."[27] In 1873 Khudayar Khan went so far as to tax wild fruit trees in the mountains, and sent his minions to Osh to collect these fees. The locals refused to pay and beat up the tax collectors. Upon hearing this, Khudayar Khan sent forces to quell the rebellion. A "bloody fight" ensued and the khan's forces had to withdraw without victory.[28]

Again the opposition tried to take advantage of the people's discontent and seize power. This time they turned to a distant relative of the khan, Pulat Bek, who lived in Samarkand; however, he refused to cooperate. They next enlisted the mullah Ishaq Hassan Ogly to lead, with Pulat Bek as a figurehead.[29] This gambit, known to history as "Pulat Khan's Revolution," proved no more successful.

Kokand as a State

The Khanate of Kokand was a typical oriental feudal state, at the head of which stood the biggest feudal lord, the khan, who resided in the city of Kokand. Under him was a hierarchy of offices consisting of no few than nine different levels. All members of the clergy, military officers, court officials and administrators carried honorific titles under the Khanate of Kokand.

The right to no fewer than six titles belonged exclusively to men who could claim to be descended either from Mohammed or from the first four caliphs.[30] These officials received an annual salary ranging from 120 to 1,200 tanga, as well as between 50 to 70 tubs of grain.[31] Eleven more offices, including all those pertaining to religion, went exclusively to people who had been educated in Muslim schools and madrassas. However, a scholarly record did not suffice to obtain the rank of *shaykh-ul-islam*; for this it was necessary also to be descended from someone who had made the pilgrimage to Mecca (*hajj*). Clergy were supported by foundations (*waqfs*) or taxes, and they received gifts or bonuses from the khan in the form of money, grain, or rich robes. Those who administered the religious duties of Muslims and oversaw the sharia, called *mukhtasibs,* had the additional requirement of demonstrating certain positive moral traits.[32]

The khan's fiscal affairs were managed by a senior official called *mirza-i-daftar*; he kept special accounts of the treasury. Another official was the custodian of payments in kind to the khan. This officer provisioned the palace and the khan's numerous bodyguards and servants. A treasurer received all payments in cash, and also managed the khan's jewels.[33]

The most influential people of the dominant party usually cornered the best positions in the khanate. At the peak of the system was the khan's permanent council, to which the occupants of all the main posts were appointed ex officio, as well as others named by the khan and his closest advisers. The clergy also played a significant role in urban life, and exercised judicial power even in civil issues. All litigation in Kokand was based on the sharia and adat, as were the punishments administered. For the theft of more than ten tenga a person would have one hand chopped off; for murder the offender's head would be cut off; apostates and women guilty of adultery would be stoned to death.[34] In 1814 F. Nazarov watched as a sword was used to chop off the right hand of an offender for the theft of thirty sheep. He also witnessed the killing of a seventeen-year-old girl in Kokand, whose sole crime was that she had refused to marry anyone but her beloved.

The highest judicial authority was the *qazi* or judge, who served as the clergy's weapon in sentencing often-innocent people to death. Citizens were allowed to appeal the *qazi*'s sentence, but rarely dared to do so. An unwary applicant appealing the decisions of the *qazi* to the khan would turn all the judicial class against himself. If he could not prove the *qazi*'s alleged abuse, he was accused of defaming the holy law, for which he could pay with his life.[35]

Slavery and the slave trade existed in the Khanate of Kokand, and their vestiges endured to the end of the khanate. In the city of Kokand, a young male slave was worth 30 tillya, and a young slave-girl, 40 tillya.[36] Slaves were treated as objects. For example, on March 1, 1871, the khan's brother, Sultan Murad, organized a horse race in honor of Khudayar Khan. The first prize consisted of one male slave (*gulyam*) and one young female slave (*churi*), plus a fabric yurt, an Arabian carpet, two Kipchak carpets, three blankets, nine porcelain plates, nine cups, two horses with a golden harness and a horse cloth sewed with silver, and other items.[37] Sultan Murad owned twenty slaves who performed heavy work in his fields and gardens, repaired equipment, and served as gatekeepers and stablemen.[38] Acknowledging all this, there were far fewer slaves in Kokand than in either Bukhara or Khiva—and they received better treatment in Kokand. Most slaves were former soldiers who had been taken captive during raids on neighboring states.

The top military rank in the Khanate of Kokand was the *mingbashi* (commander of thousand horsemen), which was usually combined with the post of vizier or prime minister. During the reigns of Sherali Khan and Khudayar Khan, the *mingbashi* also served as commander-in-chief in times of hostility. Beneath him were *ponsadbashis* (leaders of five hundred men) and *yuzbashis* (leaders of one hundred men). Upon admission to the service each soldier received a horse and a harness, and before each campaign he received a fixed sum according to his rank. Otherwise, soldiers were paid in cash and provisions.[39]

There were no class or ethnic distinctions in the designation of military ranks, although in ranks 1 to 7 Uzbeks predominated.[40] The problems that steadily accumulated were less in the officer corps than in the rank and file. By 1860, Kokand had nothing resembling a regular army. In order to maintain tranquility in the khanate, mercenaries had to be hired to man the fortress garrisons. During wartime, all males able to bear arms were recruited into the service.

Each fall the government announced the recruitment of people to serve in the garrisons. The lower ranks received monthly payments of one tillya and a year's supply of two bags of flour and seven to ten sacks of barley for their horse. In addition, in the spring they received four summer garments, boots, a turban, sash, and a skullcap; and for the winter a warm garment, a sheepskin coat, boots, a warm hat and a horse. Their weapons included a saber, lance, and rifle, all generally of poor quality.

When a military campaign was planned, the khan sent out a decree for troops to assemble at a given place and in certain numbers. The *mingbashi* carried out these orders and became the corps commanders. Following this, the khan himself took the field with his bodyguards, gathering fortress garrisons on his way and leaving behind only a minimum number of soldiers. Citizen-soldiers also joined the khan.

In addition to large copper cannons, the army had small cast-iron cannons, including short ones that were like falconets, and longer ones similar to Russian fortress guns. They were transported on special carts with large wheels (*Kokand arba*). Traders were warned in advance and were ready with food whenever the army pitched camp. Fortress garrisons were paid in advance, but line troops received no money for food, nor did the citizen-soldiers. Worse, merchants frequently failed to arrive in time, leaving the army without essentials. Indeed, there were cases when campaigns had to be interrupted owing to a lack of food supplies.

It is difficult to determine the number of Kokand's forces. Some reports in the

1850s claim that the khan could gather up and put in the field some 40,000 men in twenty days. However, internecine wars undermined the khanate's forces. For example, in spite of an all-out effort in 1860 the khan could assemble only some 25,000 men.[41]

Kokand, Bukhara, Khiva, and East Turkestan

At the beginning of the eighteenth century, Ferghana separated from the khanate of Bukhara and formed an independent state at Kokand. Relations between Kokand and Bukhara became highly unstable thereafter. The emirs of Bukhara systematically tried to regain their lost territories, while Kokand khans sought to be independent and even expand their territory at the expense of Bukhara. These considerations assured continual conflict between them. The foci of contention usually included the cities of Khujand and Ura-Tyube. However, at some moments the two state became allies. For example, in 1823 I. Chekalin wrote that "Thirty years ago the Kokandis allied themselves with Bukhara against the Kabul Shah, Tamir, who tried to conquer Bukhara for the Afghans."[42] In this instance the Central Asian khanates united against a foreign conqueror. Similar cooperation had taken place in the mid-eighteenth century when China tried to capture Samarkand, at which time the Central Asian khans united under the leadership of the Afghan ruler, Ahmed Shah.[43]

In the second half of the nineteenth century, the relationship between Kokand and Bukhara turned on the policies of tsarist Russia. A. Glukhovskii reported in detail on the conflict between Bukhara and Kokand in 1865, at which time each tried to conquer the other.[44] Subsequently, the emir of Bukhara wrote to Alexander II, "at the request of the Kokand people we fought against Kokand, at which time your troops conquered Tashkent. Our people advised us to go to Tashkent to help the Muslims against the Russian forces. But recalling our old friendship, we did not bend to their will and instead returned to our capital at Bukhara."[45]

The emir of Bukhara was obviously being deceptive. He would have gained no benefit from joining Kokand in fighting the Russians, for if the latter were defeated the Kokandis would get the credit. At the same time, the emir, being a patron of the Muslim religion, could not fail to support Muslims against the infidels; moreover, the Uzbeks in Bukhara insisted that he act. For the Bukharans to had waged war on Kokand at that point would have assisted the Russians, for the Kokandis would then have had to fight on two fronts. As it was, the Bukharans returned to their capital, giving Kokand the opportunity to redeploy its troops against Russia at Tashkent, and the emir made excuses to his Muslims for not going to Tashkent himself.

Due to the destruction of archival materials from Khiva, the relationship between Kokand and the Khanate of Khiva has scarcely been explored. According to Russian Major-General Ladyzhinskii, as of 1853 "Kokand and Khiva maintain the best relationships, sending each other envoys, but for unknown purposes. Both know that the Russians will come from two directions, and both the Kokandis and Khivans are waiting, but no one has heard of them acting together."[46] Friendly relations were established as early as 1842, when the khan of Khiva attacked Bukhara and forced Emir Nasrullah to lift his siege of the city of Kokand and hastily return home. An important motive for the friendship between Kokand and Khiva was that both were face-to-face with Russian forces, which sought to seize their territories.

Nevertheless, disagreements and conflicts flared up between the two khanates over border issues. For example, at the remote Kuyn Darya the Khivans had built a fortification to mark the border both with Russia and with Kokand.[47] Kokand did not acknowledge Khiva's ownership of this territory, and over the twenty years of the fort's existence seized it twice and drove away the Khivans. In order to return, the Khivans eventually made a significant payment in livestock to Kokand's representative.[48]

In connection with the worsening of Kokand-Russian relations in 1858, a Kokand envoy came to the khan of Khiva to ask for assistance against the Russians; however, the Khivan leader absolutely refused.[49] The fact that a year later the khan of Khiva sent an ambassador to Kokand testifies to their renewal of diplomatic relations. However, the emir of Bukhara did not welcome the development of friendly relations between Khiva and Kokand; indeed he did everything to impede them. To that end, he tried unsuccessfully to capture and seize the documents of a Khivan envoy who was returning from Kokand.[50] Within the year the emir of Bukhara learned from a spy in Khiva that the Kokandis and Khivans had agreed to join forces in attacking the Russians as soon as the rivers had frozen over.[51] However, this plan remained unfulfilled. Further consultations at Kokand in 1860[52] and at the end of 1861, with the latter including ambassadors from Afghanistan as well as Khiva, may have sought to revive this plan, but surviving documents shed no light on what occurred.[53] In December 1861, and again in either June or July 1862, Said Muhammad, Kokand's ambassador to Khiva, proposed that the khan of Khiva end his offensive and defensive alliance with the Russians. The Khivan khan not only rejected this proposal, but also advised Kokand's ambassador to abandon all hostile plots and actions against the Russians.[54]

In the fall of 1863, the Khan of Kokand sent yet another ambassador to Khiva with an offer to unite against the Russians. The results of the visit are unknown, but it can be assumed that the Khan of Khiva, given the difficult situation he faced at home, was in no position to agree to such a step. Moreover, all of Said Muhammad Khan's previous actions had showed him very reluctant to oppose the Russians. Thus, the attempts of the Kokand khans to make an alliance with Khiva against Russia did not succeed, notwithstanding the generally friendly relations between them.

The relationship of the Kokand Khanate with East Turkestan was closely intertwined Kokand-China relations. In the mid-eighteenth century, the Chinese had conquered East Turkestan and defeated the Kalmyk state of Dzungaria. According to M. Gorchakov, the descendants of the Kashgar *hodjas*, who had been exiled by the Chinese, lived at the Kokand court under close supervision as political exiles. The Chinese paid the khan a large annual sum in silver to prevent the Kashgarians from reclaiming their former lands.[55] Nevertheless, some descendants of the Kashgar rulers managed to travel to Kashgar to restore their authority. Whether the khans knew of this or even facilitated it, these visits soured Kokand's relations with China.

In the end the Chinese decided to buy tranquility through the 1831 treaty, signed in Beijing by the ambassador of the Kokand Khanate, Alim Bek. At issue was the status of a series of cities in East Turkestan that had been conquered earlier by the Chinese. The agreement transferred authority over Aksu, Uch-Turfan, Kashgar, Yangi-Ghissar, Yarkant, and Khotan[56] from China to the khan of Kokand, Muhammad Ali. Henceforth a representative of the khan would collect duties from the merchants in these places. This treaty achieved its end, and Kokand-Chinese trade through East Turkestan began to revive. Not only did this trade enable the khanate to meet its populations' expectations for Chinese goods, but taxes on the resulting trade helped replenish the khan's treasury.

In 1857 rioting broke out in East Turkestan and developed into a general uprising against the Chinese government. Kokand broke the terms of its agreement and assisted the rebellion by releasing the descendants of the *hodjas*. The uprising was suppressed in the most ruthless manner. The Chinese government, believing that Kokand had contributed to the turmoil when it released the offspring of the *hodj*as, severed all relations with the khanate. All attempts of the latter to restore friendly ties came to nothing. In 1860 Kokand's ambassador was killed in Yarkant by order of the Chinese.[57] Severe exploitation, poverty, lawlessness, and harsh treatment of the local populace by Chinese officials led to another uprising in 1864.

A manuscript account titled "Ansab al-salatin va tavarihiand al-havakin" states that representatives from Kashgar arrived in Tashkent with a message signed by dignitaries and beks. They related how they had rebelled against Chinese rule, won many battles and gained control of several towns. They now asked Kokand to send an intelligent, sensitive man who could take over the country's administration. The khan chose a little-known but curious figure, Yaqub Bek, and one of the exiled *hodjas*, Buzruk-Hodja. Once in Kashgar they placed themselves at the head of the uprising and promptly gained the respect of the people of East Turkestan by capturing many cities. Local leaders looked on in envy and several of them, Kyrgyz and Kipchaks, decided to kill Yaqub Bek and take power themselves. Yaqub Bek tried to calm the situation, but the rebels amassed troops, only to be defeated by Yaqub Bek.

The Kyrgyz and Kipchaks then complained about Yaqub Bek to the top military officer of the land, *mingbashi* Mullah Alimkul; he however rebuffed them. Yaqub Bek then sent Mullah Alimkul expensive gifts and reported on the true state of affairs in Kashgar. The *mingbashi* gladly accepted them, arranged a feast for the envoys from Kashgar, and sent them home with costly robes.[58] In due course all power in Kashgar passed into the hands of Yaqub Bek, who dispatched Buzruk-Hodja back into exile in Kokand.

Kokand and Russia

Neither Turkey, Iran, Afghanistan, nor India played a significant role in the political life of the Kokand Khanate. The archives contain only a few mentions of Kokand-Turkish diplomatic releations,[59] and in general Kokand's links with these states came mainly through trade. By contrast, Kokand had both diverse and intense relations with Russia.

Alim Khan had made the first attempt to establish formal relations with Russia. Responding to the khan's invitation, the tsar sent an ambassador with a message addressed to Alim Khan. When the Russian ambassador arrived in Turkestan, he learned that Alim Khan had been murdered and his place taken by Umar Khan. In 1810 the Russian ambassador finally arrived in Kokand with the goal of establishing friendly relations. Umar Khan reciprocated in 1812 by sending envoys to St. Petersburg. On the return journey one ambassador died of disease and a second was killed at Petropavlovsk. Eager to repair relations, the Russian government sent Philip Nazarov to Kokand the following year.

During the reign of Muhammad Ali Khan (1822–1841), ambassadors from Kokand made several trips to Russia. In 1825 we find Kokand's governor in Tashkent complaining to the governor-general of Western Siberia that the khanate's ambassador had not been let through. More successful exchanges occurred in 1828[60] and 1830.[61] In 1831, the khanate's governor in Tashkent advised the khan to send an ambassador to St. Petersburg[62] to seek engineers to inspect the khanate's mines. Significantly, he also proposed that the Russians be asked for both ordnance and experienced military officers whom Kokand could "use them against the Chinese, with whom the Kokand khan is at war."[63] The Russians rejected the latter request, because they did not want "to give the Chinese government cause for displeasure (with Russia)."[64]

Further complications arose. In the spring of 1834 the Tashkent governor attacked some Kazakhs who were Russian subjects. In response the Russian government organized a punitive squad under the command of the chief of staff of the Siberian corps. This detachment marched to the Kokandi fortress of Ulutau, surrounded it, made off with a herd of 110 horses, and captured five soldiers from Tashkent. One of the prisoners was sent to the fortress with a demand of unconditional surrender. When no reply came the Russians opened fire. Two hours later the garrison surrendered, captives were exchanged,[65] and there was every hope that Russian-Kokand relations would settle down once more.

Muhammad Ali Khan, realizing the need to establish friendly relations with Russia, sent another ambassador to St. Petersburg in 1841. When Muhammad Ali abdicated, his younger brother, Sultan Mahmud, also reached out to St. Petersburg.[66] But in April 1842, Nasrullah, the emir of Bukhara, captured Kokand and executed Sultan Mahmud Khan, Muhammad Ali, various dignitaries, and other members of the royal family. Upon receiving this news, Kokand's ambassador to Russia feared for his life and approached no closer to Kokand than Semipalatinsk.

Russia now seized the opportunity to take advantage of Kokand's misfortunes. In 1852 General Lev Perovskii stormed the Kokand fortress of Ak-Mechet but failed. A year later the Russians returned, having secretly planned a fresh campaign. Archival documents record that after a twenty-day siege Russian forces successfully stormed the fortress of Ak-Mechet on July 28, 1953. The Russians lost only nine soldiers, with forty-six wounded. According to a Russian participant, "the Kokand people, claiming to be fully justified, defended desperately: out of 400 people located in the fortress garrison, only 74 people were taken as prisoners and even they were seriously wounded." Some "326 others," a Russian participant wrote, "were killed by the activities of our cannonballs, grenades and missiles . . . , and some of them were buried alive under the exploded walls, defending the fortress to the end."[67] After a further confrontation,[68] the Russians settled into Ak-Mechet and renamed it Fort Perovskii.

After these events, the Kokand-Russian relationship became outwardly tranquil. However, even as the Russian foreign ministry was proclaiming the onset of friendly relations, Russia's army officers were making quite different plans. Striking proof of this can be found in a secret letter sent to the Siberian corps commander on October 12, 1856, which stated: "first of all, we need to consolidate our Cossack settlements in the Zailiiskii area and bind to us the various tribes of mountain Kyrgyz by supporting their dissatisfaction and hostility toward Kokand."[69] In another letter the same officer noted that the hostility to Kokand of one of the Kyrgyz sultans was helpful to the tsar's government; because he never refused to help the Russians, he was rewarded with a gold medal and an honorary sultan's robe.[70]

A January 19, 1859 "Note" from G. Gosford, the Siberian corps commander and governor-general of Western Siberia, titled "On the need to occupy the upper areas of the Chui River and related preliminary instructions," mentioned that Tsar Nicholas I had already considered this issue and accepted it before he died. The former minister of war Prince Dolgorukii, Count Perovskii, and General of the Infantry G., Gosford had all participated in the discussion of this note. They unanimously concluded that Tokmak, Pishpek, Aulie-Ata, Suzak, and Turkestan, with the lands adjoining them up to Syr Darya, should all be occupied. This would connect the southern flank of Western Siberia with the Orenburg flank.

This same "Note" noted the accession to power of the new Kokand khan, Mallya. Given that he "enjoys the trust of the people and has the reputation of a person experienced in governmental affairs, it is important not to postpone for long the aforementioned actions." It therefore set 1861 as the absolute deadline for seizing the territories in the upper Chui River Valley, at the same time expressing the hope that this task would be accomplished "no later than 1860."[71]

Tsar Alexander participated in an advisory meeting on the Orenburg territory and Western Siberia on January 24, 1859, and approved Gosford's Note, which stated that "the occupation of upper areas of the Chui River can take place no later than in 1860, provided the forthcoming reconnaissance turns up no insuperable obstacles and that the mission itself will not require excessive expenditures."[72]

Sensing trouble, Mallya Khan tried to avoid all border conflicts with Russia. He strictly forbade forays beyond the Russian border and ordered violators to be put to death.[73] He also planned to send an ambassador to St. Petersburg in the spring of 1859, but the tsar's generals impeded this in every way, even seizing the ambassador when he arrived at Fort Perovskii.[74]

Finally, armed fighting broke out. On July 8, 1860, 3,000 Kokand troops tried to attack the fortress at Kastek. However, the Russians had been alerted and killed many of the attackers, who then withdrew.[75] A month later a detachment of Russian troops advanced on Tokmak in two columns. When they reached the fortress the Russian commander demanded that the Kokandis surrender. Receiving no response, he poured fifty cannonballs into the fort, pounding the defenders into submission.[76] Days late the Russian troops besieged Pishpek. After undergoing bombardment of their fortress for two days, the 665 defenders, including 38 young children, surrendered.[77] The fortress was then leveled and the Russian commander was promoted to the rank of major-general.[78]

On June 21, 1861, Tsar Alexander II convened a meeting to examine Russia's actions in Central Asia. With regard to the Kokand Khanate, it was agreed that Russia, for strategic and political reasons, should advance across the border into Kokand's territory in order to secure a natural boundary. Since it was an inopportune time to move Russian troops deep into the khanate, it was decided to seek more amicable relations with Kokand, at the same time recognizing that "peaceful relations with the people of Kokand were [merely] a truce, not positively limiting us to the Chui River as a border, and without constraining our plans for the future."[79] Notwithstanding these cautious sentiments, on January 20, 1862, after a fifteen-hour blockade and stubborn battle, Russian troops captured and destroyed the Kokand fortress of Din-Kurgan.[80] Four months later Russian forces troops occupied, without a fight, the fortresses of Aq-Su, Pish-Tyube, and Chaldovar.[81] Taking advantage of internal strife in the Kokand Khanate, they next moved on the towns of Turkestan, Suzak and Chulak-Kurgan. At the same time the Beshtamgalinskii tribe of Kazakhs surrendered,[82] leaving Russia in control of a vast swath of former Kokand territory. A historian once noted that eight centuries earlier Hodja Ahmad Yassavi had written that the Russians would seize the city of Turkestan in the year 1281 of the Hijri, or 1864 CE.[83] As further described in the historian's manuscript, Kokand would try to recapture Turkestan, but would not succeed. Now Russia had fulfilled this prophesy. In the same year Russian troops conquered Chimkent and came close to Tashkent.

The Russian general M.G. Cherniaev reported on December 28, 1864 that people in Chimkent had grown displeased with the Kokand military leadership, as well as with one of the most important Kokandi officials in Tashkent, Abdurakhman Bek, who governed half the city. Clearly the level of dissatisfaction in Tashkent was rising, as the Tashkent "Kyrgyz" (i.e., Kazakhs) began to place themselves under the Russians' protection. As they did this, Cherniaev asked the minister of war what he should do if a revolution were to break out and residents were to ask for help.[84]

To this the minister replied that Cherniaev should do nothing until reinforcements arrived, but that he also should "not deprive them of hope for help in time."[85]

Events, however, unfolded more quickly than the minister anticipated, with Cherniaev moving almost immediately "to constrain Tashkent, and put it in direct and immediate dependence on us."[86] He accomplished this by first draining the two main rivers that supplied Tashkent and surrounding environs with water. Then he moved his forces closer to the city, while awaiting word that pro-Russian forces from within the city had disarmed the Kokand garrison and opened the city gates to Russian troops. But on the same day Alimkul arrived in Tashkent from Kokand with 6,000 troops and 40 guns, thus preventing the planned treason. On May 9 the tsar's forces engaged the Kokand army in battle, leading to the deaths of 300 Kokandis as well as their leader, Ali Kuli. The Russians suffered only ten wounded.[87]

A month later (July 14–15) Cherniaev's forces again attacked Tashkent, this time successfully storming the city and its citadel while losing only 135 soldiers in the fighting.[88] When the shooting died down, the elders came out to surrender and promised to bring leading citizens to meet with the Russians on the next day. However, that same evening the populace of Tashkent began shooting again, throwing up barricades on streets and intersections and mounting a desperate resistance. Cherniaev later reported that "There were cases when one or two men with *oyboltas* (long-handled axes) threw themselves on an entire company, dying on the bayonets without seeking mercy. . . . Each hut had to be taken with bayonets, and was cleared only when everyone within had been killed."[89] By the evening of June 16 the streets finally had been cleared, and the next day the elders (*aksakals*) and local dignitaries met with Cherniaev to express their obedience to Russia.

Cherniaev's memoirs are of particular value, as they help to reveal aspects of the Kokand-Russian relations in the 1860s, and the personal attitudes of the tsar's generals that cannot be found in official documents.

Thus, Cherniaev for instance narrates that he petitioned Minister of War Vasilchikov to assign him to Orenburg, which was granted. At just this time N.A. Kryzhanovskii had just been appointed governor-general of Orenburg.

As Cherniaev recalls:

> He [Kryzhanovskii] badly wanted to seize Tashkent. To this end he wrote me very kind letters, asked me to wait until he arrived, and so on. But this was impossible because the forces from Bukhara were certain to move toward Tashkent. For two months I walked around the walls of the city, my plan being to force [the Tashkent forces] to scatter their forces along the entire length of the walls. In this I succeeded. Finally, leaving the lanterns burning at our camp site, we wrapped the wheels of our cannon with felt and travelled ten *versts* to the gates we intended to assault. At dawn the next day we stumbled upon a guard detachment outside the fortress. They were asleep and we killed them all, not allowing them to utter a sound. Then we put in place the scaling ladders and immediately climbed the walls to the left and right of the gates. I sent Colonel Kraevskii to attack the citadel, and Abramov opened the gates for him. The people of Tashkent mounted a defense on their curving streets. I realized that there was no alternative but to

set fire to the streets along the route to the market. The Kokand garrison fled to the gates opposite, where 15,000 people had assembled. I instructed Abramov, as he moved along the fortification wall, to waste no time over the rivets [holding them in place] and to throw the defensive cannon outside the wall. Later we gathered them all, and got back our two our two cannons as well.

As generally is the case in Asian cities, Tashkent had an elected municipal government. These people are in general very intelligent, and are not cowards. Beyond the walls they are brave, but carefree. They had a sultan, the son of the Kyrgyz (Kazakh) Batyr Kenisary Kasymov, whom they had designated commander in chief. He is a dashing horseman. They succeeded in mounting a few raids but Kasymov did not have a sound strategy. Instead of arranging a single chain of troops along the city's wall and keeping a reserve in the interior, he placed all his forces on the wall.

Kryzhanovskii wanted to seize Tashkent immediately and all by himself, and this is why he was so greatly annoyed with me. He had visited us September on his way to Tashkent from Orenburg. While inspecting the troops he yelled to them that, "You need brooms, not guns!" Kryzhanovskii wanted to mark his arrival with some fresh act of heroism and therefore proposed to march at once against Kokand. Indeed, Kokand had indeed been weakened after the emir of Bukhara captured and ransacked it, killing many people. After naming a relative to be khan, he returned to Bukhara. But the fact of the matter is that I had at hand an army of only 1,100. How could I leave the city of Tashkent, which had just been conquered, to the mercy of fate?

Moreover, our forces were tired and in need of rest to consolidate their strength. It was under these circumstances that Kryzhanovskii sent Romanovskii to ask me if we could mount an expedition to Kokand. I told him "Do as you wish, but in this case, I will ask for permission to leave. You will doubtless achieve success there but you will win and leave. How am I to remain here until summer without any reinforcements?"[90]

For his capture of Tashkent, General Cherniaev was assigned a lifetime pension of 3,000 rubles.[91]

In 1867 a general-governorship was created for the conquered territories, and in the following year a team of experts was assembled from various departments of the Russian government to gather all available information on the Khanate of Kokand.

The new governor-general of Turkestan, K.P. Kaufman, was very pleased, noting that "the heterogeneous information and data collected by these individuals significantly enriches our lean supply of knowledge about this province."[92] According to this study, the people of Kokand were divided into pro- and anti-Russian parties. The khan himself led the pro-Russian faction, although he did not say so publicly for fear of antagonizing his opponents. Opposing the Russians was the general public, which feared that their khan would yield to a bribe from General Kaufman and sell the khanate to the Russian government.[93]

A treaty concluded in 1868 established "friendly relations" between Kokand and Russia, with an exchange of ambassadors and a growth in trade. But one analyst, N. Raevskii, considered these "friendly relations" nothing more than misleading rhetoric:

Without even mentioning Muslim fanaticism, which the Central Asian leaders are full of, and which the Muslim clergy feeds to the nation, let us not forget that in the last eight or nine years we [Russians] seized most of their territories and reduced them from the status of powerful and independent rulers to that of vassals. Can one really expect their defeated and humiliated leaders to harbor "friendly" feelings toward those to whom they owe their humiliation? Let us not delude ourselves: the rulers and their subjects hate us equally, and even if the former sometimes pretend to be our friends, it is only because they are forced by circumstances to do so, but the insincerity of their assurances is proven by much evidence.[94]

In 1873 the Khanate of Kokand was rocked by a massive rebellion against the khan and his brutal exploitations. Khudayar Khan, increasingly desperate as the revolt dragged on, finally requested military assistance from Russia. When the rebels approached the capital in the company of Pulat Khan, a pretender of Kyrgyz ethnicity, Khudayar Khan grew fearful that the Russian troops would not arrive in time to save him; accordingly, on July 22, 1875, he fled to Tashkent.

Khudayar's son Nasreddin Bek was immediately proclaimed khan, but the resentful pretender Pulat Khan gathered an army of Kyrgyz to seize the throne. This put Kokand under the rule of a highly unstable diarchy, with civil war a possibility at any time unless the warring factions could somehow be brought together under a single banner. That unifying cause turned out to be a jihad against the Russian colonizers. Just such a jihad was declared in the name of Nasreddin Khan, and the united Kokandis called all Muslims to raise a holy war to liberate the Khanate of Kokand from the Russians and restore the old borders.

As a Muslim, Pulat Khan had no choice but to support this appeal, although he tried not to involve himself in fighting with Russian troops. On August 7, 1875, some 10,000 Kokand forces arrived in the southern outskirts of Tashkent. General Kaufman immediately sent an infantry battalion, cavalry, and 400 Kazaks into the field against them.[95] He also gave orders to distribute weapons to the Russian residents of Tashkent.[96]

That same day, Kaufman sent a telegram to the minister seeking authorization to pursue the enemy, plus a line of credit for 100,000 rubles to pay for the campaign.[97] The tsar himself approved the requests, and soon a large force of heavily armed and rigorously trained Russian troops set out in pursuit of the hastily formed militia of the popular liberation movement. On August 22, 1875 a major battle occurred near the town of Makhram. Several thousand Kokandis were killed, as the Muslim army suffered a major defeat. General Kaufman later wrote the minister of war that the "Makhram Massacre" had determined the fate of the Khanate of Kokand.

Russian forces then occupied Margilan and Kokand itself, in the process meeting only sporadic resistance. Arriving in Margilan, Kaufman received a delegation of citizens and imposed on them a formidable retribution sum of half a million rubles. Days later he commanded Nasreddin Khan to Margilan and levied a staggering retribution on the entire khanate, a sum so large that it virtually enslaved the population, particularly the poor farmers and townspeople. Learning of this, the entire region exploded in rebellion. A new phase of the uprising, this time a classic national liberation movement, now began.

The main rebel forces, led by Pulat Khan and strongly supported by the populace, were concentrated in Andijan, against which the Russian command promptly organized a punitive expedition. The Russian major-general in charge of this campaign boasted, "If they propose to receive us with hospitality I will not accept it. I plan instead to fire a few grenades." And if, as he hoped, they should capture a figure who had rebelled against the Russians, "I think it would be useful to hang him in Andijan."[98] In contrast to this highly personalized view of the conflict, another officer, A. Kuhn, reported that "the factors that caused the unrest, I am deeply convinced, were unrelated to us."[99]

On October 1, 1875, Russian troops took Andijan by storm. During the defense of the city several thousand rebels died, many of them women, children, and the elderly. The tsar's forces suffered 66 dead and wounded.[100] Nine days later in Kokand a huge band of residents of Kokand attacked the khan's palace, although Nasreddin Khan himself managed to escape.[101]

Meanwhile a seasoned Central Asia hand, M.D. Skobelev, had been elevated to the rank of major general. He eagerly sought to celebrate his promotion by launching a raid to regain the right bank of the Syr Darya from the rebels. Hoping to lure the rebel forces to the city of Namangan and crush them, he withdrew his troops from the city and retired to the nearby mountains. The rebels thereupon entered Namangan. Then on October 26 Skobelev bombarded the city with sixteen cannons, killing several thousand, and retook Namangan. Two weeks later Russian troops defeated another rebel force at nearby Balikchi. Then, on November 8 the people of Matcho decided to join the Kokand rebellion, but a punitive detachment under Staff Captain Arandarenko ruthlessly suppressed their rebellion.

The rebels fought desperately. Ten days after the fighting at Matcho a Russian squadron approaching the village of Ashaba encountered shooting from behind the village's walls. After a hard exchange of fire, the infantry stormed the settlement. Residents died with guns in their hands; women armed with knives threw themselves at the soldiers and hurled stones at them. In the end, the entire population was killed and the village burned down.

Meanwhile, General M.D. Skobelev received permission to conduct a winter expedition to Ikki Su-Arasi in the eastern Ferghana. The insurgents found out about this and prepared to confront Skobelev at Andijan. On January 8, 1876, Skobelev overwhelmed the rebels. Documents from the time record that Russian forces killed some 20,000 insurgents and residents of the city.[102] Yet the rebels continued to mount armed resistance. Meanwhile, on January 16, 1876 the minister of war sent Kaufman a confidential letter that determined the fate of the Kokand Khanate: "His Majesty," Miliutin related, "deigned to allow the occupation of the rest of the Kokand Khanate whenever you consider it inevitable."[103] K.P. Kaufman, the governor-general of Turkestan, was at the time in St. Petersburg. As soon as the tsar approved it, Kaufman set out to conquer the Khanate of Kokand.

Meanwhile, on January 18 Russian forces destroyed detachments of rebels near the village of Asaka, after which one of the leaders of the rebellion, Abdurakhman Bek, and his subordinates surrendered to Skobelev and disbanded their militia. This freed the Russians to hunt down and defeat Pulat Khan, which they accomplished at the village of Uch-Kurgan. Official documents confirm that the rebels suffered overwhelming damage. All the infantry protecting Pulat Khan were killed, part of his cavalry was destroyed, and the rest put to flight. Pulat Khan himself escaped. Russian losses were negligible.[104]

On January 30, 1876 Nasreddin Bek arrived in Kokand and was proclaimed khan before a disapproving public. Days later Kaufman telegraphed from St. Petersburg to the commander of the troops in Turkestan, Major-General Kolpakovskii: "at the request of the people of Kokand for Russian citizenship, and seeing no other way to calm the population, the Sovereign Emperor deigns to order you to receive the khanate into His Majesty's realm, thus allowing you to occupy the khanate with troops . . . The former Khanate of Kokand will be renamed 'the Ferghana region' and I appoint Skobelev as its head. Nasreddin is to be sent to Tashkent."[105]

Thus, on February 19, 1876 General Kaufman presented the Kokand Khanate to Alexander II as a gift honoring the tenth anniversary of his reign. However, by now few Kokandis were willing to take Russian citizenship. As Skobelev reported, "In the Kokand Khanate there are three factions: the merchants, who have long constituted the pro-Russian party and certainly wish to join Russia; the powerful clergy and general public, both of which oppose doing so; and Nasreddin's supporters, who also oppose doing so."[106]

The proclamation of Nasreddin as khan caused confusion among the Russians. Baron Nolde, head of the Khujand region, asked permission "to send a small native delegation to Nasreddin to congratulate him."[107] Skobelev, who had not yet received the order to occupy the khanate, urged instead "to immediately set up government that is under our direct supervision, or to occupy the khanate with our troops."[108] But for his part, Kaufman telegrammed back that "There is no guarantee that the accession of Nasreddin to the throne in Kokand will appease the khanate, which is why no changes are to be made."[109]

Kolpakovskii received repeated instructions from Kaufman on the need to occupy the Kokand Khanate. He in turn told Skobelev to approach Kokand from the southwest and inform the public that "the Great Sovereign has accepted them into Russian citizenship."[110] Otherwise however he did not take action. Sensing Kolpakovskii's hesitation, Kaufman telegraphed General Skobelev on February 5 to move his squadron immediately to Kokand. At a meeting two days later Nasreddin Khan acceded to Alexander's will, and the next day the Russian army entered Kokand. According to General Kolpakovskii, "the people of Kokand on the streets met the news about Kokand's accession to Russia without enthusiasm."[111] Within two weeks the other leaders of the rebellion, including Pulat Khan, had all been arrested.

On February 19, 1876, the minister of war announced that the tsar had ordered:

1. That former territories of the Kokand Khanate occupied by Russian troops were now incorporated into the Russian Empire as a new "Ferghana region."
2. That management of this new region will be entrusted to the governor general of Turkestan.
3. That all levies against the region's population are to be devoted to offsetting the cost of administering the new territories.[112]

Following the conquest and abolition of the Khanate of Kokand, the Russian generals focused on suppressing the remaining resistance. By March they had captured and hanged Pulat Khan at Margilan. But the Kyrgyz continued to offer serious resistance. Fighting broke out again between the Russians and rebels, most of whom were Kyrgyz from the Alai Mountains and the remainder Uzbeks, Tajiks, and Kipchaks. The Russian generals engaged turncoat Kyrgyz and Kazakh horsemen on their side, sending them out in squads from Margilan and elsewhere to engage the rebels. But the rebels succeeded in killing or capturing large numbers of these *jigits.*

On April 25, up to 1,500 troops of the rebel forces engaged General Skobelev's army in a fierce battle in the canyon of Yangi-Aryk, twenty-five *versts* away from Gulcha.[113] On this occasion the rebels suffered heavy losses, but that did not cut short the Alai War or make it any less difficult for the Russians. Similar other such clashes continued for several months. In the end, General Skobelev had to meet personally with one of the leading rebels, a woman named Kurbanjan-Dadhah; Skobelev agreed not to prosecute the rebels, to release Alai Kyrgyz prisoners, and to allow her sons free return. Only then, in January 1877, was General Kaufman able to telegraph St. Petersburg and report that victory had been achieved.

Describing these events in his memoirs, Kaufman observed that had the Russians been fighting only the khan, who was of no significance to the people of Kokand, they would have achieved victory immediately after the battle at Makhram and the occupation of the city of Kokand. But the fight was not with the khan, whose forces left the field after the Russians occupied Tashkent and Kurama.[114] Instead, the Russians faced a committed national movement, which was by no means so easily crushed. Never before in Central Asia had the tsar's troops been forced to endure so long and arduous a struggle.

Nor did the struggle end with the crushing of the 1873–76 revolt. Individual members of the uprising remained committed to their cause and prepared to continue their active and armed battle through other means. They succeeded in raising uprisings against the Russian occupation in 1882, 1885, 1892, and 1898. In each case the colonial power itself generated support for the rebel cause through its ruthless exploitation of the local population. Archival documents suggest that for the first years after the conquest most residents of the Ferghana region respected and honored the Russians. But after 1884 taxes in the Syr Darya district rose by 100 percent. Small farmers went bankrupt, leading to a dramatic reduction in their standard of living. Moreover, colonial administrators increasingly abused their powers over the local populace, cruelly suppressing the slightest manifestations of discontent. As this went on, indignation and resistance spread among the population.[115]

At the same time, significant advances occurred in a number of areas. For one thing, the fratricidal wars that had claimed hundreds of thousands of innocent lives were permanently discontinued. Slavery was abolished and large numbers of the nomadic population adopted a sedentary mode of life.

Local people also gained the opportunity to familiarize themselves with European and world culture. Typical of this was the French Corsican M. Aloise, who in 1882 taught five students in Ferghana how to use the microscope. Under Aloise's leadership, a science textbook on *How to Utilize the Breeding Method of Silkworms* was published in the Uzbek language. Aloise also opened a school for silkworm breeders in Kokand. At the same time Russian doctors began to develop health care in the region, setting up small hospitals and clinics that began to institute preventive care and provide medical assistance to the local population. Postal and telegraph communications also were introduced, with telephone, radio, and electricity soon to follow. Newly constructed railways played a positive role in the development of industry and the regional economy. Cotton gins, creameries and other enterprises also opened. Wide-ranging geological explorations were carried out, leading to the development of mineral resources. As the local population began to take jobs in factories and other enterprises, a working class began to emerge.

Anglo-Russian Rivalry in Central Asia

Given the existence of a broader problem of Anglo-Russian rivalry in Central Asia in the nineteenth century, it is inevitable that the conquest of Kokand would be interpreted in some quarters as but one element among many in that larger competition. And indeed, some Russian academic historians have blamed the English for all sins committed during Russia's conquest of the region, as a means of justifying Russia's aggressive policy in Central Asia. These scholars frightened their readers with the fear that England could have conquered Central Asia and imposed worse suffering on it, and that the local populations should consider themselves fortunate to have "joined" with the great Russia; in short, to have chosen the lesser of two evils.

The most amazing thing was that the vast majority of Russian generals and officers wrote in their reports and memoirs that they had "conquered" the Central Asian states, an assertion that has been repeated by Russian historians. But Asian historians, including Uzbeks, have objected, claiming that "No, Russia did not 'conquer' us, it 'annexed' us!" History shows that invaders who enslaved others to enrich their own treasuries are neither good nor kind; indeed, otherwise there is no logic or sense in their military campaigns.

For example, as A. Aminov and A. Babakhodzhaev wrote: "English-Russian conflict in Central Asia was at times acute . . . the desire of England to conquer the entire East, including Central Asia, as well as its hope of using the local khanates to fight against Russia, played a significant role in these controversies." Since the 1820s the foreign historiography, particularly English, has strenuously advanced exaggerated claim about Russia's expansionist designs and its alleged plans to send Russian troops clear to India. In making this claim, British scholars have attempted to prove that England sought only to defend "its Indian dominions," while Russia was aggressively seeking to acquire new territories. Aminov and Babakhodzhaev conclude that "in general, a long-lasting English-Russian rivalry in Central Asia did not conclude in a way that benefited England, and Central Asia, once it became a part of the Russian Empire, was protected from the imperialist expansion of England."

The historian T. Tukhtametov, in his monograph *Russia and Khiva in the Late 19th–Early 20th Centuries,* wrote that Central Asia attracted the attention not only of imperial Russia but also of Great Britain. "The plans of the English ruling circles in this regard were far-reaching: after seizing Central Asia and consolidating their position there, the entertained the idea of attacking the southern and southeastern regions of the Russian Empire, using Central Asia as a springboard. The English ruling circles covered up their own expansionist plans with slogans about providing for India's security."

Many other studies in Russian have dwelled on these issues from diverse perspectives. Documents studied by the present authors suggest that England tried by every means to oust the Russians from Central Asian markets and prevent their political expansion there. The British wanted the Central Asian states to be a kind of "neutral zone" between Russia and the British colonies in India. The British government clearly foresaw that Russia would try to seize the Central Asian khanates, and that they would begin with Kokand Khanate on account of the frequency of palace revolutions there.

Terentev wrote that in 1853 that rumors abounded in the Central Asian khanates about Russia's intention to eradicate Islam, destroy the Turkish state, seize Christ's tomb, and enslave all the people of the khanates. The rumors alleged that Allah had opened the hearts of the "Ingliz," who opposed Russia's schemes, and that it was now time for the khanates to ally with one another into a single powerful union and defeat the Russians on the Syr Darya. The movement to which this gave rise collapsed at the end of 1853 when Kokand's forces failed to dislodge the Russians from their former fortress at Ak-Mechet (Fort Perovskii). Following this, the khanates lost all interest in the British and their plans.[116] The British nonetheless used all means at their disposal to prevent Russian forces from advancing further into Central Asia. They helped the khanates strengthen their defenses by sending a certain Mustafa to help the khan of Kokand cast cannons in 1853[117] and by sending other agents to Kokand in 1856.[118] Moreover, in 1855 England signed an agreement with the khan of Kokand that enabled sepoys "of native origin" to join Kokand's forces in fighting against Russia. Indian newspapers confirm that such mercenaries were successfully recruited in the Punjab.[119] The Anglo-Russian agreement of March 19, 1856, could have ameliorated relations in Central Asia but failed to do so, leaving observers on the spot expecting a full-blown war there.[120] At least one Russian officer on the scene argued that this left England, in the name of defending the region against Russian encroachments, free to operate freely in the Khanate of Kokand and, indeed, up to the Aral and Caspian seas.[121] The same officer, General S.A. Khrulev, proposed in a note that the command at Orenburg in Russia should be given a free hand to protect Kokand in the event of a Chinese invasion provoked by England.[122] The "Note" written in October 1857 to the Ministry of Affairs mentioned that an enhanced Russian role in those countries separating the dominions of Russia and Britain, as opposed to the maintenance there of the largest army in Europe, would serve as an important guarantor of peace.[123]

In March 1858, the British Parliament appointed a special committee to raise funds for the colonization of India and the expansion of trade relations with Central Asia. In 1859 the British used Afghan merchants armed with large sums of cash to make trial purchases in Central Asian markets of silk and opium.

In 1861 the commander of Russia's Orenburg corps, Adjutant General Bezak, submitted a memorandum on what he thought were British plans to weaken the Bukhara Khanate. To do this it would build a strong Central Asian state tied to Britain by combining Afghanistan with some areas of Bukhara, Khiva, and Kokand. If they accomplished this before the Russians took Tashkent, then the British would become the absolute rulers of Central Asia, and its commerce, as well as the Kashgar trade, would remain in their hands indefinitely.[124]

Western governments, especially in England, were unhappy with Russia's actions against the Central Asian khanates. So as to reassure Western diplomats, the tsarist government temporarily halted attacks against the Kokand Khanate. Minister of War Nikolai Sukhozanet spelled out this tactical step in a secret letter to the commander of the Siberian corps on November 7, 1859. But while playing to Western opinion, Sukhozanet acknowledged laconically that "It may happen that the Kokandis might begin hostile actions against us, and so will thereby give us reason to punish them; in this case, your Excellency is allowed to use the prepared means, and without waiting for a special command to occupy Pishpek, notwithstanding what was said above on this subject."[125]

A letter by the Kokand's Mallya Khan to the Tsar of Russia at the same time says much about the state of Kokand-British relations. He explains that while his predecessor, Khudayar Khan, had "grown close to the rulers of England and Europe," he himself had terminated ties to London, opened relations with China, and, "wishing to follow in the footsteps of former rulers of my country, wished to re-open the blocked path to relations with your Imperial Majesty . . . and to strengthen the old ties of friendship even more."[126]

When a Tatar businessman visited Kokand-ruled Tashkent in 1860, he saw twenty large-caliber copper cannon being loaded on gun carriages. He learned that they were the work of French and British experts who were casting European-type cannons in Kokand.[127] The Russian military gathered all such information and rumors, and also strictly monitored the actions of the Kokand khan, and especially of his armed forces, which is how they confirmed that Europeans were casting cannons in Kokand.[128] In early 1862 Mallya Khan and Kanaat returned from Ura-Tyube to Kokand, where they found the ambassador of Bukhara and Kabul, the latter purportedly an English agent. The reasons for the ambassador's presence remain unknown to this day.[129] However, we may assume that an English agent was trying to ally the Central Asian khanates against Russia, as well as to collect intelligence of Kokand-Russian relations and on prospects for Kokand-English trade.

The Russians were not insensitive to the fact that their moves in Central Asia could arouse England's hostility. An 1862 "Note on Settlement of the Syr Darya Line" preserved in the archives warns that any significant expansion of Russia's presence in Central Asia could "bring the envy and grudge" of Western powers, especially England, and could lead to an unpleasant diplomatic exchange.[130] In December 1863, Adjutant General Bezak reported to the Ministry of War that some English agents in Kokand who had long had relations with the Kokandis had asked to be allotted land near Kokand, but had been told that the only land available to the British was at a great distance from the capital.[131] Despite all of England's efforts to prevent Russians from moving deeper into Central Asia, Russia conquered the cities of Turkestan, Chimkent, Tashkent and the surrounding territories, along with their garrisons and adjacent villages.

Anglo-Russian rivalry was acute not only in the area of politics, but also of trade. British manufactured goods barely entered the Kyrgyz steppe, but could be found almost everywhere in the regions of Tashkent and the town of Turkestan. However, Russian goods prevailed in the markets; they did so first, because they were superior in quality and also cheaper, and second, because they were manufactured nearer to Central Asian markets than the British goods, which had to be transported overland either from ships landing at ports on the Indus to Bukhara and Tashkent, or via Persia to Mashad and then Bukhara. Besides this, Russian caravans enjoyed an exemption from taxes while the British caravans had to pay them.

In July 1869 the British ambassador at St. Petersburg complained to the minister of finances that Indian exports to Kokand were being charged 25 percent duty. Further, Russian authorities had warned that in four months all imports from India to Kokand would be banned, except for indigo and cheese cloth, which would be taxed at 50 percent.[132] The minister did not respond, observing only that even the khanate had levied a 2.5 percent tax on imports, so the current taxes could not be considered new.[133] It was such disagreements as this that had prompted the two governments to agree to establish a neutral zone between them. The idea had been England's. Russia agreed to accept Afghanistan as a neutral territory and to respect its independence. The British Cabinet did not accept this, believing that Afghanistan could not fulfill this role and implying that the neutral territory therefore had to be further north, which Russia would not accept. A few years later the minister of war wrote to Alexander II that "your Imperial Highness is aware of the jealousy with which a suspicious England watches our every step in Central Asia." Even with an agreement on Afghanistan as a neutral zone and Russia's assurance not to cross the Afghan border, the British "cannot easily watch our success outside the assigned intermediate zone."[134] Meanwhile, a British general noted dryly that if the capital cities of the Bukharan and Kokand khanates were still independent, "there was no guarantee that this would last for long."[135]

In the end, the British had to yield in their rivalry with the Russians over the Kokand Khanate. In 1873 General Kaufman and British diplomat Douglas Forsyth held a secret meeting in the khanate, during which the British agreed to pose no objections as Russia conquered all of Kokand, but that Bukhara would remain independent. Russia and England also agreed that each would exert pressure from its side to assure that neither Afghanistan nor Bukhara attacked the other.

Thus, the fate of the Kokand Khanate was sealed in 1873, with the final conquest depending only on just when Russia found it convenient to do so and found a plausible excuse. When Pulat Khan rose up against Kokand the Russian army rolled in under the pretext of suppressing the rebellion and soon conquered the entire state.

Civil Administration

In the first half of the nineteenth century, the Kokand Khanate was bordered on the north by a band of barren steppes, beyond which lay Siberia; on the west by the khanates of Khiva and Bukhara; in the south by Karategin, Darvaz, and Kuliab; and in the east by Kashgaria (East Turkestan). The Kokand Khanate therefore included the current territory of the Ferghana, Andijan, Namangan, Tashkent, a part of the Syr Darya River regions of Uzbekistan, the Khujand area of Tajikistan, the Osh region of Kyrgyzstan, and southern Kazakhstan. The fortress Ak-Mechet, now the city of Kyzyl-Orda, was considered its northern boundary. A. Kuhn, writing in 1871, included within the Kokand Khanate Margilan, Shakhrikhan, Andijan, Namangan, Sokh, Makhram, Bulak-Bashi, Araban, Balikchi, Chartak, Nookat, Kasan, Chust, Babadarkhan, and Kokand itself.[136]

The Kokand Khanate was a typical feudal state with remnants of slavery still evident. At the head of state was the khan, wielding unlimited power through his leadership of a permanent council of secular and spiritual dignitaries including the military leader, the *mingbashi*. Some of these personages ruled provinces (*vilaets*) and cities, where they directed their own lower officials. The regional heads were called *hakims*, the heads of smaller towns *beks,* and village heads a*ksakals*—elders or "white beards," who also exercised judicial functions, referring as necessary to the authority of the *hakims*. The khan himself appointed the heads of the larger towns, including Kokand itself.

The highest judicial authority was the *qazi*, whom the khan appointed from among the theologians and jurists, with the army having its own judge, the *qazi-askar.*[137] High judicial officials included the *sheikh al-islam* and *sheikh al-mashoih*, who focused on religious affairs and not only had to have been educated at a madrassa but also had to have made the pilgrimage to Mecca. As noted earlier, half a dozen other religious offices were limited to those who could claim descent either from Mohammed or from the first four caliphs.[138]

We have noted that the top commanders of the army were the *mingbashi* and *amir-lyashkar,* the former functioning both as minister of war and also minister of foreign affairs. Second in command was the *kushbegi,* who served concurrently as head of a major city, usually Tashkent, and advised the khan. Beneath him were arrayed nearly two- dozen ranks of lower officers.[139]

At the top of this structure was the *atalyk* or vizier, who was always older than the khan, and whose stamp of office was considered of equal authority to his.[140]

Population and Employment

At its height the Kokand Khanate had a population of about three million people. However, after the first wave of Russian conquest it was reduced to the one million inhabitants of the Ferghana Valley. The population consisted mostly of Uzbeks, Tajiks, Kazakhs, and Kyrgyz, all of whom belonged to numerous different tribes and families. In the Kokand Khanate there also lived a small number of Russians, Afghanis, Uyghurs, Iranians, Indians, Turks, Arabs, Jews, and other ethnic groups. The urban population was mainly Uzbek, but also included some Kipchaks, Tajiks, Kyrgyz, Kazakhs, and other nationalities. Both the Uzbeks and Tajiks were sedentary peoples, but the Kipchaks, Kyrgyz, and a small portion of Kazakhs remained mainly nomadic.

The nineteenth-century scholar A. Middendorf wrote that none of Ferghana's natural potential would have been reaped had the inhabitants not been an industrious and settled people. He wrote that over thousands of years the populace had constructed huge water channels, carried out large-scale fertilization, and planted whole forests of shade-giving trees for fruits and wood, with "each individual tree being in need of life-giving water."[141] The Kokandis planted fields of wheat, barley, millet, sorghum, corn, rice, beans, sesame, flax, hemp, cotton, and alfalfa, while their gardens included melons, watermelons, cucumbers, pumpkins, grapes, apricots, peaches, apples, pears, quinces, nuts, plums, cherries, not to mention onions, carrots, beets, and other produce. The main grain crop was wheat, which Kyrgyz cattle ranchers raised on the lower slopes of the Alai range as a kind of side business. Nomads provided the sedentary populations with meat, fat, wool, and leather, and wild furs, as well as such finished products as sheepskin coats, rugs, carpets, and shoes. The expansion of irrigation after the early eighteenth century increased the number of villages and reduced the area available for grazing.

Cotton growing always had held a special place throughout the Kokand Khanate, but in the nineteenth century farmers also began cultivating American long-fibred hybrids. Sericulture was also of ancient origin, but the highest-quality silks came from the areas of Namangan, Andijan, Margilan, and Kokand—with declining yields as one approached Semireche (Seven Rivers) area. The northern boundary of sericulture in Khujand-Kokand region was considered to be the Namangan ridge and its southwest branch, the Kurama ridge. Silk from more northern towns like Tashkent, Chimkent, and Turkestan was not considered marketable.

Land ownership in the irrigated areas of the Kokand Khanate differed little from the neighboring Bukhara Emirate. Most of the land was the property of the government, and as such was called state land (*zamin mamlaka*). Most of the income from it went to the khan and *beks* in the form of rents or taxes, the *haraj* or *tanabana*. The khan had full control over the land, and could give its income as a reward to civil servants, religious figures, or to a theological foundation (*waqf*). By the end of the khanate, though, such grants were few and limited in size. More and more land was concentrated in the hands of the central government, and as this occurred the area of irrigated land increased.[142] By contrast, landownership among the nomads came to be determined by the structure of society and justified by tradition. Poorer nomads, who lacked sufficient herds to produce for the market, concentrated on meeting their own food needs.[143]

Resources and Crafts

Archival evidence attests to the existence of more than a hundred crafts in the Khanate of Kokand. The choice of domestic crafts in the khanate evolved in part according to the availability of such metals and gemstones as gold, silver, copper, iron, lead, turquoise, emeralds, rubies, lapis lazuli, and carnelian. During the khanate many miners worked the rich mineral deposits in the Kuramin Mountains,[144] where saltpeter, sulfur, salt, and coal were also extracted. Locally raised larkspur mallow and cochineal provided dyes. But research by M. Veniukov has shown that a poor knowledge of chemistry, metallurgy, and mechanics meant that the area's mineral wealth came to be much less well-developed than its agricultural potential.[145]

Oil had been known and exploited since ancient times in Kokand, where it served primarily as a medicine for rashes. In addition, local manufacturers produced tar from it, which they used in making shoes. The mines of the khanate also yielded a mineral wax (*saryq mum*), which was otherwise known only on the shores and islands of the Caspian Sea, and in Galicia and Moldova.[146] There were up to twenty copper mines in the Kuramin Mountains,[147] while the residents of Aykent "engaged in the smelting of excellent iron ore, which they mined in the Temura Mountains"; as a result they also made excellent steel and became very skilled gunsmiths.[148] In Kokand and Tashkent were foundries and armament plants, where guns and cannons were made.[149] In 1872 the Russian photographer Krivtsov also inspected a large armaments plant in Andijan.[150] The shotguns produced in the khanate were mostly smoothbore and rarely grooved, while bullets were round and made of lead.[151] Mention has been made of the European-type cannons and mortars being cast in Kokand.[152] Gunpowder was produced by various one-man enterprises.

There was a high degree of specialization in the crafts of the khanate. Thus, the most highly valued thread was produced in Kokand, while Tashkent excelled at weaving.[153] Central Asian fabrics found a large market locally but also in Russia, which led to the expansion of that industry. According to the British ambassador in Kashgar, the silk from the factories in Kokand was much better than that produced in Kokand's East Turkestan fabric center, Khotan.[154] Similar regional specialization existed in the manufacture of paper, ceramics, exquisite bronze water jugs, enamelware, and silver bracelets, which were made—as in medieval times—without locks.[155]

An important technical skill practiced across the territory of Kokand was bridge building. The enormous irrigation system called for many canals and *aryks* that had to cross roads and paths. Each crossing required a bridge, which constantly had to be constructed, maintained, and replaced. These same skills were applied to the construction of buildings of every type, which gave rise to a large group of professional builders and designers.

A significant number of rural dwellers engaged in domestic crafts. In particular villagers spun yarn from cotton, wove cloth, sewed clothes, wove carpets, and embroidered scarves, caps and other articles of clothing. They also produced large quantities of woven bands (*jiyak*), baskets, hanging stands for dishware (*charkha*) made of twigs, shovel handles, hoes, and so forth. Many of these products were sold in the markets. In addition, nomads and semi-nomads brought raw leather, sheep coats and jackets, wool shawls, and carpets to the region's bazaars.

Domestic and Foreign Trade

Domestic trade in the Kokand Khanate was based on the long-standing division of labor between sedentary artisans in towns and villages, and nomadic herders. Internal trade was conducted at the many city markets, the best of which in the nineteenth century was considered to be at Kokand. Every town and village had market day, when people from nearby places came to trade. The important markets at Kokand and Tashkent opened twice weekly. On those days, the Kazakhs and Kyrgyz brought their horses and sheep, and sedentary people brought corn, cotton and silk fabrics, as well as various household products. Tashkent also was the main distribution point for supplying Russian goods to Kokand, Margilan, Andijan, Namangan, Khujand, Osh, and other cities.

Foreign trade played a major role in the economy, especially with Bukhara and Kashgar, but also with Khiva, Afghanistan, Iran, India, China, Turkey, and especially Russia. Caravan traffic with Bukhara was especially heavy in the early summer and late fall, and consisted mainly of plants for dyes, cotton fabrics, and English cheesecloth. Kokandis also benefited from such Chinese transit goods as tea, porcelain tablewear, and silk.

Because all trade between Kokand and Khiva had to traverse the hostile territory of the Emirate of Bukhara, few caravans made the trip, with trade consisting mainly of Khivan gowns and English printed cotton. Trade links with East Turkestan were much closer. The Kokand-China treaty of 1831 had given the Kokand khan the right to collect fees on trade in Kashgar, which reaped great profits. Among the exports from

Kokand to Kashgar were silk, paint, and especially printed cotton, while the Kokandis imported sal ammoniac, carpets, tea, and felt mats.

Kokand-Russian trade relations occupied an important place in the economic life of the khanate. For example, from 1758 to 1853 the value of Russian exports to Kokand increased from 174,000 to 2,171,000 rubles, while imports increased from 37,000 to 676,000 rubles. Russians mainly exported iron, copper, and steel factory products, faience, dishes, mirrors, treated and finished leather, calico, woven cotton, velvet, sugar, faience dishes, and mirrors. Kokand merchants brought silk and cotton fabrics, carpets, dried fruits, and rice to Russia. Even in the nineteenth century the Ferghana's main export to Russia was cotton. On this basis, the Kokand Khanate and Russia developed a mutual interest in trade, especially after the proprietors of Russian cotton mills discovered that the khanate could become a major market for their finished goods.

Education and Culture

Education in nineteenth-century Kokand developed solely along traditional Muslim lines, with three basic types of schools: *madrassa, maktab,* and *qarihana.* Madrassa was the highest school, with each one serving a large area. The lower schools or *maktabs* were maintained either at mosques or in private homes. All but the latter were supported by the income from endowments or *waqfs* donated by philanthropists. The largest endowments were connected with mosques, and it was there that the largest number of schools was formed.[156]

In 1841 Kokand boasted a madrassa with one thousand students, who flocked there to study under the well-regarded teachers Yishan Mavlyavi and Mahzumi-Bukhari. Smaller madrassas existed in other cities, as well. The course of study consisted mainly of theology and Qur'anic studies, but also the Arabic, Persian and Turkic (Uzbek) languages, grammar (*nakhu*); mathematics, astronomy, philosophy, history and geography taught from ancient Arab, and Persian and Turkish historical and geographical manuscripts. The curriculum in *maktabs* focused on memorization of the Quran, but also included mathematics, literature and the basic rules of grammar. *Qarihanas*, or special schools, taught mainly blind children, who were encouraged to learn the Qur'an and major poems by heart. There were separate schools for boys and girls.

Statistics on Ferghana region schools compiled in 1875–76, and other data from 1878 on[157] indicate that in the provinces of Margilan, Kokand, and Andijan there also were six Jewish schools that enrolled 220 students.[158] Some individuals maintained schools, among them the poetess Dilshad. She wrote of her teaching that "My students and friends were intelligent girls and talented poetesses. For fifty-one years I maintained a school and had on average twenty to thirty students annually. In all, I taught 890 girls to read and write, with nearly a quarter of them gaining recognition for their poetic talents."[159]

The dominant literary environment of the Kokand Khanate in the nineteenth century consisted of two opposed tendencies. Many clerical writers and poets penned works praising the khan and other officials. Other poets and writers devoted their talents to exposing such lies; they wrote openly about the plight of the poor, and criticized the bloody wars, tyranny, ruthlessness and greed of the rulers. The latter group included poets Akmal, Bokikhan-ture, Gulkhany, Ery Hukandy, Zavky, Zory, Makhmour, Mahjoub, Mukimov, Muntazib, Muhayr, Muhammad Yunus Tayyib, Muhsin, Nasim, Nizam Hukandy, Nodir, Nozil, Pisandy, Rozhy, Sado, Umid, Furcat, Shahdi, Shukurov, and Ferghani.

During the era of the Khanate of Kokand, a revival of historiographical writing occurred. A number of ancient historical works were translated into Uzbek, and new ones were written about the Kokand Khanate. Many historians, such as Niaz Muhammad bin Ashour Muhammad Khukan-dy, Mullah Shams Namangani, penned their works using both poetry and prose.

Some remarkably progressive actors of the nineteenth century played a great role in raising the cultural level of the populace. With their performances these actors not only aesthetically pleased the audience, but also scathingly criticized in small plays and pantomimes the vices of feudal life. Zakir Eshan Rustam Mekhtar Ogly, Sadi Makhsum, Matkholik Qiziq, Ismail-naychi, Ashurali-makhram, and many others were particularly popular actors of that time.

The rich popular culture of Kokand Khanate deserves more attention than it can receive here. For example, in 1871 a visitor to Kokand wrote about the tradition there of dancing boys in small boats. He asked the Sultan's brother, the Sultan Murad, "How did the people of Kokand adopt this dance in boats, which is unknown elsewhere in Central Asia?" In reply, he was told that "this occurred at the order of Khudayar Khan, in imitation of a Chinese dance, only replacing the [female] dancers with boys."[160] Later they moved the dance from boats to horseback, which became very popular in the Ferghana Valley on account of its closeness to the region's many other games and sports involving horses. Another popular entertainment was the carousel in Kokand featuring musicians in rows one above the other, all turning furiously. The people of Kokand also adeptly organized magnificent feasts with fireworks. In many folk festivals they created statues of mythic heroes like Rustam, while puppet theaters also drew large crowds during holidays.

Particularly popular were tightrope walkers (*darbaz*), who walked, jumped, ran, walked and even did handsprings on ropes up to fifty meters above the ground. The *darbaz*, who included children as well as adults, performed with their eyes closed, blindfolded, or with copper trays or knives tied to their feet. The performances of ropewalkers invariably included entertainment by musicians, clowns, singers, or even comedians. Interestingly, musicians and singers always accompanied the Kokand army on its campaigns, with drummers and *karnai* (long brass horns) announcing the beginning and the end of each battle. *Ulak* (horse racing) was immensely popular in the khanate, with races organized to celebrate folk holidays, family celebrations, and even weddings. Expensive prizes went to all winners, adding still more to the excitement.

Calligraphers gained great renown in the Khanate of Kokand, as they copied and beautifully ornamented the works of eminent poets and historians, as well as mystical literature. Some of the calligraphers were themselves poets who could beautifully decorate their own verse. The names of many of these calligraphers are known to every educated person in Ferghana even today, and their works are still treasured. The first photograph appeared in the Kokand Khanate in 1872. In that year the newspaper *Turkestan Vedomosti* announced that "here in the center of Muslim Asia, in the Kokand Khanate, there exist two photographers."[161]

On Taxes and Discontent

The main tax in Kokand and the other khanates was levied on the product of the land (*haraj*). From land used for rice, wheat, sorghum, and other cereal crops, the government collected a fifth of the harvest, and from land used for vineyards, vegetables, and cotton the size of the *haraj* was determined by the specific crop. In addition, cash payments in the form of *tanabana* were demanded for garden plots devoted to melons, watermelons, cucumbers, clover, onions, and carrots, vineyards or orchards.[162]

The *haraj* supported the army and local administration, and enabled local *beks* to respond to calls from Kokand for troops in wartime. A tax-collector (*sarkor*) and his assistants down to the level of *aksakals* managed the actual collection.[163]

The tax on cattle, manufactures, and property in general was known as the *zakat*. As was typical in Muslim countries, the *zakat* was set at one fortieth of the cost of sale, although in practice it was often more. The growth of urban enterprises and the increased levies at the borders increased the khan's revenues over time. In addition, there were a lot of special fees, duties, and levies on everything from dairy cows to fodder for horses.[164] And, finally, the population was burdened with many other obligations and demands that left the labor force in a very precarious condition. Independent of the amount of taxes they had paid, residents had to supply horses, wagons, and manpower for the renovation or construction of fortresses, irrigation canals, the cleaning of stables, and so forth. Those not paying in labor were obliged to pay in cash.

A review of the socio-economic and political conditions in the khanate over its entire existence suggests that the preconditions for popular rebellions against the khans, feudal lords, and their surrogates were always present, and that such uprisings in the name of freedom nearly always focused on economic and tax issues. Such uprisings occurred in the suburbs of major cities and across the central regions of the khanate, and were deftly manipulated by feudal lords who drew the lower classes into their own political conflicts. Many such uprisings looked backwards, but some looked forward as well.

The backward-looking rebellions that merit mention include the revolt by Hodja Bek in 1799, the Chust mutiny in 1800, and the uprising of the Kipchaks in 1843. Others that appear to belong to this group but cannot firmly be ascribed to it because of the paucity of archival materials are, the Andijan uprising at the time of Abdu-Raim Bey, the Kabul revolt, the Karategin rebellions in Karategin and Issyk Kul, the Osh revolt of 1849, the 1850 and 1854 revolts in Tashkent, the 1957 rebellion of Rustam Khan and Mirza Munavvar, and the 1858 insurrection in Khujand.

More forward-looking were the revolt of Chadak *hodjas* in 1709, the Kipchaks uprising in 1748–49, the Tashkent revolt of 1808, a rebellion under the leadership of Tentak-Ture in 1821, Kalandar's revolt in 1841, the Kokand national uprising of 1842, the Tashkent national uprising in 1847, the Kipchaks' movement in 1853, the uprising in Ura-Tyube in 1858, a Kazakh rebellion in 1858, the Kyrgyz uprising in the 1860s, the Sokh revolt of 1871, and the Pulat Khan rebellion of 1873–76. The goal of many of these, including the Kazakh and Kyrgyz revolts, was national liberation. Similar uprisings at various times were initiated by Uzbeks and Tajiks. Such Uzbek uprisings included the Andijan revolt of 1721, the Kalandar revolt in 1841, the Kokand popular uprising of 1841, the national uprisings in Tashkent in 1847 and 1850, the uprising of Rustam Khan and Mirza Munavvar. Nearly all these rebellions broke out spontaneously and without preparation. Whatever the objects of the rebels' wrath, the driving force of their uprisings were the poorer segments of the population.

The uprisings of 1858–60 on the territory of southern Kazakhstan were directed against the tax policies and general despotism of the Kokand khans, with the Kazakhs seeking Russian protection or citizenship. To the east, Kyrgyz uprisings included the revolt of the Sary-bagysh, Taylak, and Issyk Kul Kyrgyz, and also the Osh rebellion, the revolt of Alim bek, and the Sokh uprising. Kyrgyz revolts were also directed against the tax policies of the Kokand khan, but they were usually accompanied by a parallel struggle with the Kipchaks over key positions in the khanate's government locally. It is notable that few, if any, rebellions of the Kazakhs, Kyrgyz, or Kipchaks had as their primary aim to secede from the Kokand state and establish an independent government.

Tajik uprisings included the Chust revolt and uprisings in Karategin, Ura-Tyube, and Khujand. Unlike the Kazakhs and Kyrgyz, the Tajiks generally appealed to independence, while also opposing the khanate's tax system. Among the Kipchak rebellions can be included: the uprisings of 1748–49, 1843, 1853, 1854, and 1857–58. The Kipchaks largely fought for the survival of their people, and hence tended to act together, regardless of position and class. The Uzbeks, Kipchaks, Tajiks, and Kyrgyz participated together in a number of revolts, specifically the Kokand national uprising of 1842 and the most ambitious movement of 1873–76, which involved almost the entire population of the Kokand Khanate. Such revolts prepared the soil for the larger acts of rebellion that were to occur later and, indirectly, for the numerous acts of sedition that were committed during Soviet times.

Thus, the liquidation of the Kokand Khanate and its inclusion into the territory of the Russian Empire stopped the many conflicts and wars, including those among the elites, that had long inflicted suffering on the local population.

Notes

1. V.V. Bartold, *Sochineniia,* Moscow, 1965, vol. 3, p. 462.
2. Mullah Alim Makhdum khodzha, *Tarikh-i Turkiston,* Tashkent, 1915, pp. 8–11. See also *Turkestanskii sbornik,* vol. 88, pp. 5–7.
3. V.P. Nalivkin, *Kratkaia istoriia Kokandskogo khanstva,* Kazan, 1886, p.16.
4. Mullah Alim Makhdum khodzha, *Tarikh-i Turkiston,* p. 15.
5. Nalivkin, *Kratkaia istoriia Kokandskogo khanstva,* p. 66.
6. Ch.Ch. Valikhanov, *Sobranie sochinenii v piati tomakh,* vol. 2, Alma-Ata, 1962, p. 316.
7. Ibid.
8. F. Nazarov, *Zapiski o nekotorykh narodakh i zemliakh Srednei chasti Azii,* Moscow, 1968, p. 43.
9. A. Mukhtarov, *Dilshod i ee mesto v obshchestvennoi zhizni tadzhikskogo naroda v 19–nachale 20 veka,* Dushanbe, 1969, pp. 296–97.
10. Nalivkin, *Kratkaia istoriia,* p. 122.
11. TsGA RUz, I-715, on. 1, ed. khr. 4. 6–9.
12. TsGA RUz, I-715, on. 1, ed. khr. 4, 1. 15–16.
13. TsGA RUz, I-715, on. 1, ed. khr. 4, 1. 18–20.
14. TsGA RUz, I-715, on. 1, ed. khr. 4, 1. 273.
15. M.N. Galkin, *Etnograficheskie i istoricheskie materialy po Srednei Azii i Orenburgskomu kraiu,* St. Petersburg, 1869, pp. 238–39.
16. TsGA RUz, f. I-715, op. 1, ed. khr. 4, 1. 113–14.
17. TsGA RUz, f. I-715, op. 1, ed. khr. 4, 1. 115.
18. N. F. Petrovskii, "Ocherki Kokandskogo khanstva," in *Turkestanskii sbornik,* vol. 76, p. 9b.
19. *Turkestanskii sbornik,* vol. 89, pp. 332–35.
20. TsGA RUz, f. I-715, on. 1, ed. khr. 26, 1. 374–75.
21. TsGA RUz, f. I-715, on. 1, ed. khr. 26 a, 1. 117.
22. TsGA RUz, f. I-715, on. 1, ed. khr. 26 b, 1. 27
23. TsGA RUz, f. I-715, on. 1, ed. khr. 26 b, 1. 168–69.
24. TsGA RUz, f. I-715, on. 1, ed. khr. 27, 1. 22.
25. Iu. Rossel, "Sredneaziatskaia kultura i nasha politika na Vostoke," *Turkestanskii sbornik,* vol. 22, 1873, pp. 28–29.
26. A.P. Fedchenko, *Puteshestvie v Turkestan,* vol. 1, pt. 2, St. Petersburg and Moscow, 1875, pp. 95–96.
27. M.A. Terentev, *Istoriia zavoevaniia Srednei Azii,* vol. 2, St. Petersburg, 1906, p. 327.
28. Rossel, "Sredneaziatskaia kultura," p. 29.
29. Kh.N. Bababekov, *Narodnye dvizheniia v Kokandskom khanstve i ikh sotsialno-ekonomicheskie i politicheskie predposylki,* Tashkent, 1990, pp. 83–109.
30. A.L. Kun, "Nekotorye svedeniia o Ferganskoi doline," *Voennyi sbornik,* 1876, p. 52.
31. A.I. Khoroshkhin, *Sbornik statei, kasaiushchikhsia do Turkestanskogo kraia,* St. Petersburg, 1876, p. 52.
32. N.P. Ostroumov, *Sarty,* Tashkent, 1890, p. 38.
33. *Obozrenie Kokandskogo khanstva v nyneshnem ego sostoianii/Zapiski IRGO,* Vol. 3, St. Petersburg, 1849, pp. 207–8.
34. L.F. Kostenko, *Sredniaia Aziia i vodvorenie v nei russkoi grazhdanstvennosti,* St. Petersburg, 1871, p. 64.
35. I.D. Gorchakov, "Obozrenie Kokandskogo khanstva v nyneshnem ego sostoianii," *Zapiski IRGO,* vol. 3,1847, pp. 199–200.

36. Khoroshkhin, *Sbornik statei, kasaiushchikhsia do Turkestanskogo kraia,* p. 43.
37. *Turkestanskie vedomosti,* no. 45, 1871.
38. "Zapadno-kitaiskaia narodnost v Fergane," *Russkii mir,* no. 158, 1876.
39. "Veroispovedanie i obrazovanie," *Voenno-statisticheskii sbornik,* St. Petersburg, 1868, pp. 142–43.
40. Nalivkin, *Kratkaia istoriia Kokandskogo khanstva,* p. 209.
41. TsGA RUz, f. I-715, op. 1, ed. khr. 24, 1. 244–47.
42. GPB im. M.E. Saltykova-Shchedrina, otdel rukopisei, f. 3, ed. khr. 14, 1. 39 ob.
43. Ch.Ch. Valikhanov, *Sobranie sochinenii v 5 tomakh,* Alma-Ata, vol. 2, 1962, p. 316.
44. Archive of the Russian Geographic Society, f. 89, on. 1, ed. khr. 2, p. 12.
45. GPB im. Lenina, otdel rukopisei, f. 169, op. 65, ed. khr. 23, 1, 9–9 ob.
46. TsGA RUz, f. I-715, op. 1, ed. khr. 14, 1. 226.
47. TsGA RUz, f. I-715, op. 1, ed. khr. 17, 1. 30.
48. TsGA RUz, f. I-715, op. 1, ed. khr. 4, 1. 135.
49. TsGA RUz, f. I-715, op. 1, ed. khr. 19, 1. 212.
50. TsGA RUz, f. I-715, op. 1, ed. khr.22, 1. 442.
51. TsGA RUz, f. I-715, op. 1, ed. khr. 22, 1. 443.
52. TsGA RUz, f. I-715, op. 1, ed. khr. 23, 1. 297.
53. TsGA RUz, f. I-715, op. 1, ed. khr. 25, 1. 202.
54. TsGA RUz, f. I-715, op. 1, ed. khr. 26b, 1. 167.
55. *Zapiski IRGO,* St. Petersburg, vol. 3, 1849, p. 195.
56. *Turkestanskii sbornik,* vol. 22, 1875, p. 602.
57. TsGA RUz, F. I-715, op. 1, ed. khr. 25, 11. 474–75.
58. Institute of Oriental Studies of ANRUz, Manuscript, inv. no. 3753, pp. 146–47.
59. TsGVIA RF, f. 483, op. 1, ed. khr. 11, 11. 4–4 ob.
60. TsGVIA RF, f. 483, op. 1, ed. khr. 11, 1. 4 ob.
61. *Vestnik IRGO,* St. Petersburg, vol. 2, 1856, p. 6.
62. TsGIA RF, f. 1264, op. 1, ed. khr. 348, 1. 202.
63. TsGVIA RF, f. 483, op. 1, ed. khr. 11, 1. 4 ob.
64. TsGIA RF, f. 1264, op. 1, ed. khr. 348, 1. 202.
65. TsGIA RF, f. 1264, op. 1, ed. khr. 348, 11. 189–90.
66. TsGA RUz, f. I-715, op. 1, ed. khr. 4, 11. 145–47.
67. TsGIA RF, f. 853, op. 2, ed. khr. 57, 11. 2–2 ob.
68. TsGIA RF, f. 1021, op. 1, ed. khr. 102, 1. 80.
69. TsGA RUz,f. I-715, op. 1, ed. khr. 17, 1. 225.
70. TsGA RUz,f. I-715, op. 1, ed. khr. 17, 1. 57.
71. TsGARUz, f. I-715, op. 1, ed. khr. 21, 11. 89–92.
72. TsGA RUz,f. I-715, op. 1, ed. khr. 17, 11. 101–3.
73. TsGA RUz, f. I-715, op. 1, ed. khr. 22, 1. 354.
74. TsGA RUz, f. I-715, op. 1, ed. khr. 22, 1. 193.
75. TsGA RUz, f. I-715, op. 1, ed. khr. 23, 1. p. 209.
76. TsGA RUz, f. I-715, op. 1, ed. khr. 23, 11. 340–43.
77. TsGA RUz, f. I-715, op. 1, ed. khr. 24, 11. 14–19.
78. TsGA RUz, f. I-715, op. 1, ed. khr. 24, 1. 75.
79. TsGA RUz, f. I-715, op. 1, ed. khr. 24, 1. 75.
80. TsGA RUz, f. I-715, op. 1, ed. khr. 26, 1, p. 52.
81. TsGA RUz, f. I-715, op. 1, ed. khr. 26, 1. 208.
82. TsGA RUz, f. I-715, op. 1, ed. khr. 26b, 1. 168.
83. Institute of Oriental Studies of AN RUz., Manuscript, inv. no. 1011178, pp. 63–67.
84. TsGVIA RF, f. 1442, op. 1, ed. khr. 10, 1. 5.
85. TsGVIA RF, f. 1442, op. 1, ed. khr. 10, 1. 7.

86. TsGVIA RF, f. 1442, op. 1, ed. khr. 10, 11. 10–10 ob.
87. TsGVIA RF, f. 1442, op. 1, ed. khr. 10, 11. 10 ob.-13 ob.
88. TsGVIA RF, f. 483, op. 1, ed. khr. 83, 11. 43, 70 ob.
89. TsGVIA RF, f. 483, op. 1, ed. khr. 83, 1. 66 ob.
90. St. Petersburg, GPB im. Saltykova-Shchedrina, otdel rukopisei, f. 1008, ed. khr. 4, 11. 10 ob.-12.
91. St.-Petersburg, GPB im. Saltykova-Shchedrina, otdel rukopisei, f. 1009, ed. khr. 6, 1. 4.
92. TsGVIA RF, f. 1396, op. 2, ed. khr. 44, 1. 43.
93. TsGVIA RF, f. 1396, op. 2, ed. khr. 44, 1. 43–43 ob.
94. TsGADA RF, f. 1274, op. 1, ed. khr. 931a, 11. 1–1 ob.
95. TsGA RUz, f. I-715, op. 1, ed. khr. 63, 1. 137.
96. TsGIA RF, f. 560, op. 21, ed. khr. 335, 1. 1.
97. TsGA RUz, f. I-715, op. 1, ed. khr. 63, 1.136.
98. TsGA RUz, f. I-715, op. 1, ed. khr. 63, 11. 625–26.
99. "Otdelnyi ottisk," Izvestiia IRGO, St. Petersburg, vol. 12, 1876, p. 3.
100. TsGVIA RF, f. 1396, op. 2, ed. khr. 91, 11. 362–362 ob.
101. TsGA RUz, f. I-715, op. 1, ed. khr. 64, 11. 93–94.
102. TsGA RUz, f. I-715, op. 1, ed.khr. 66, 1. 292.
103. TsGA RUz, f. I-715, op. 1, ed.khr. 66, 1. 133.
104. TsGVIA RF, f. 1393, op. 1, ed. khr. 80, 11. 95–104.
105. TsGA RUz, f. I-715, op. 1, ed. khr. 66, 1. 254.
106. TsGA RUz, f. I-715, op. 1, ed. khr. 66, 1.285.
107. TsGA RUz, f. I-715, op. 1, ed. khr. 66, 1. 261.
108. TsGA RUz, f. I-715, op. 1, ed. khr. 66, 1. 255.
109. TsGA RUz, f. I-715, op. 1, ed. khr. 66, 1. 270.
110. TsGA RUz, f. I-715, op. 1, ed. khr. 66, 1. 271.
111. TsGA RUz, f. I-715, op. 1, ed. khr. 66, 1. 311.
112. TsGIA RF, f. 1291, op. 82, 11. 1–2.
113. A.G. Serebrennikov, K istorii Kokandskogo pokhoda. See also Kh.N. Bababekov, Narodnye dvizheniia v Kokandskom khanstve i ikh sotsialno-ekonomicheskie i politicheskie predposylki Tashkent, 1990, p. 104.
114. TsGA RUz, f. I-715, op. 1, ed. khr. 67, 11. 319–323.
115. TsGIA RF, f. 933, op. 1, ed. khr. 38, 1. 98 ob.
116. M.A. Terentev, Rossiia i Angliia v Srednei Azii, St. Petersburg, 1875, pp. 217–18.
117. Turkestanskii sbornik, vol. 6. p. 303.
118. TsGA RUz, f. I-715, op. 1, ed. khr. 17, 1. 203.
119. TsGIA RF, f. 1101, op. 1, ed. khr. 587, 11. 68–68 ob.
120. TsGIA RF, f. 1687, op. 1, ed. khr. 279, 1. 6.
121. TsGIA RF, f. 1687, op. 1, ed. khr. 279, 11. 6 ob–7.
122. TsGIA RF, f. 1687, op. 1, ed. khr. 279, 11. 7 ob.–8.
123. TsGIA RF, f. 1561, op. 1, ed. khr. 31, 11. 33–33 ob.
124. TsGA RUz, f. I-715, op. 1, ed. khr. 25, 1. 477.
125. TsGA RUz, f. I-715, op. 1, ed. khr. 22, 1. 371.
126. TsGA RUz, f. I-715, op. 1, ed. khr. 22, 11. 455–56.
127. TsGA RUz, f. I-715, op. 1, ed. khr. 22, 1. 105.
128. TsGA RUz, f. I-715, op. 1, ed. khr. 24, 1. 207.
129. TsGA RUz, f. I-715, op. 1, ed. khr. 26, 11. 95, 113.
130. TsGA RUz, f. I-715, op. 1, ed. khr. 26b, 11. 37–38.
131. TsGA RUz, f. I-715, op. 1, ed. khr. 26b, 11. 159–60.
132. TsGIA RF, f. 20, op. 5, ed. khr. 191, 11. 96–96 ob.
133. TsGIA RF, f. 20, op. 5, ed. khr. 191, 11. 97–98.

134. TsGVIA RF, f. 1393, op. 1, ed. khr. 78, 11. 17–17 ob.
135. TsGVIA RF, f. 431, op. 1, ed. khr. 45, 11. 33–36 ob.
136. *Turkestanskii sbornik,* vol. 149.
137. *Zapiski Russkogo geograficheskogo obshchestva,* St. Petersburg, vol. 2, 1849, p. 200.
138. *Voennyi sbornik,* St. Petersburg, 1876, p. 52.
139. *Tarikh-i Turkestan,* Tashkent, 1915, pp. 169–70.
140. Institute of Oriental Studies of AN RUz., Manuscript, inv. no. 10117, p. 56.
141. A. Middendorf, *Ocherki Ferganskoi doliny,* St. Petersburg, 1882, pp. 11–12.
142. R.N. Nabiev, *Iz istorii Kokandskogo khanstva,* Tashkent, 1973, p. 131.
143. TsGIA Rossii, f. 1291, op. 82, d. 3, 1. 11–13.
144. M.A. Terentev, *Statisticheskie ocherki Sredne-Aziatskoi Rossii,* St. Petersburg, 1874, p. 24.
145. M.I. Veniukov, *Opyt voennogo obozreniia russkikh granits v Azii,* St. Petersburg, 1874, pp. 345–46.
146. *Turkestanskii sbornik,* vol. 52, 1881, p. 442.
147. Russian Geographical Society, f. razr. 74, op. 1, d. 1, 1. 1 ob.
148. Russian Geographical Society, f. razr. 87, op. 1, d. 1, 1.32.
149. TsGA RUz, f. I-715, op. 1, d. 11, 1. 249.
150. *Turkestanskie vedomosti,* 1872, no. 30.
151. TsGA RUz f. I-715, op. 1, d. 65, 1. 449–50.
152. TsGA RUz f. I-715, op. 1, d. 22, 1. 113.
153. *Vestnik IRGO,* vol. 18, St. Petersburg, 1885, p. 276.
154. A. Belliu, *Kashmir i Kashgar,* St. Petersburg, 1877, p. 20.
155. *Turkestanskii sbornik,* vol. 402, 1892, pp. 98–99.
156. TsGIA RF, f. 954, op. 1, ed. khr. 134, 1.1. pp. 9–10.
157. A. Kun, *Nekotorye svedeniia o Ferganskoi doline,* pp. 161–70.
158. Kokand Local History Museum, archive, inv. no. 995 N.V., p. 116.
159. Mukhtarov, *Dilshod i ee mesto v istorii obshchestvennoi mysli Tadzhikskogo naroda v XIX nachale XX vv.,* p. 301.
160. *Turkestanskie vedomosti,* no. 95, 1871.
161. *Turkestanskie vedomosti,* nos. 29–30, 1872; no. 9, 1873.
162. *Turkestanskii sbornik,* vol. 5,1872, pp. 130–31.
163. Russian Geographical Society, f. raz. 74, op. 1, d. 1, 1.Z.
164. TsGVIA RF, f. 1393, op. 1, d. 81, 1. 553–553 ob.

3

Colonial Rule and Indigenous Responses, 1860–1917

Ravshan Abdullaev (Uzbekistan), with
Namoz Khotamov (Tajikistan) and
Tashmanbet Kenensariev (Kyrgyz Republic)

Process of Conquest and Post–Conquest Organization

As it gained political and economic power, the Russian Empire showed a clear interest in Central Asia, beginning in the late 1830s and early 1840s. Russia's incursion into the region occurred at a time when the Central Asian khanates themselves were in a state of permanent confrontation with one another. Thus, the emirs of Bukhara undertook military campaigns against the Kokand Khanate in 1840, 1842, 1862, and 1865. As a result, the areas located between the two states (e.g., Ura-Tyube or Istaravshan, Khujand, Nau, Dzhizak) suffered heavily. These constant wars among the khanates drove down living standards and weakened the states themselves, thus facilitating Russia's conquests of Central Asia and of the Ferghana Valley itself.

Just before mid-century, Russia undertook a broad study of the military, political, and economic capacities of the Central Asian khanates and of regional trade routes. At the same time Russian factory owners who were interested in new sources of cotton and other resources and new markets demanded that the Russian government pursue an active policy toward the khanates. The desire to preempt any possible British moves into the region further prompted Russia to act militarily.[1]

By 1847 Russian troops had conquered the Syr Darya estuary and constructed a fort at what is now Aralskoe, paving the way for an invasion of the Kokand Khanate, then ruled by Khudayar Khan. In 1851 General Lev Perovskii, an advocate of decisive actions against the khanates, was appointed governor-general of Orenburg and Samara. In 1853 he took control of Ak-Mechet, a strategic Kokandi fort located on the right bank of the Syr Darya River, renaming it Fort Perovskii. He then strengthened it and incorporated it into Russia's Syr Darya military line. Another "Siberian" line of forts was built from Semipalatinsk to Vernii (Almaty). Clearly, the Russian Empire was readying a major invasion of the khanates.

The Crimean War (1853–56) and subsequent period of urgent internal reforms stalled Russia's advance into the region until the early 1860s, at which time the tsar's armies inflicted a decisive defeat on the weakened and ethnically divided Kokand Khanate.[2] In the fall of 1862 they conquered Kokand's dominions of Pishpek (later Frunze, and now Bishkek) and Tokmak, the fort of Suzak in 1863, and the towns of Turkestan, Aulie-Ata, and Chimkent (Shymkent) over the course of 1864. Forts built during these campaigns created a new Kokand line that integrated all the existing forts into a continuous front line.[3]

Having secured Chimkent, General M.G. Cherniaev moved on Tashkent in the fall of 1864. As shown in the preceding chapter, the city offered significant resistance with the help of Kokand's people headed by the famous commander Alikuli Amirlashkar. The Russians had to retreat with substantial losses.

By spring 1865, Cherniaev had taken control of Tashkent, in the process killing significant numbers of the indigenous population for whom he felt no sympathy. For him, the Uzbeks, Tajiks, Kyrgyz, Kazakhs, Kipchaks, and other peoples of the Kokand Khanate were not people but *khalatniki* (robe-wearers) "who should be beaten for their robes alone."[4]

Meanwhile, Russia's invasion of the Kokand Khanate aroused indignation in the British government, which filed a note of protest to Russia. The country's Minister of Foreign Affairs A.M. Gorchakov laconically replied that Russia, like any other great power, had its own interests in the region and that its actions in Central Asia were no different from England's activities in India and Afghanistan.[5]

During Russia's campaign against Tashkent, the rulers of Bukhara and Khiva rendered no support to the city and even rejoiced at its defeat. General D.I. Romanovskii, writing in 1866, explained how Russia could exploit these local enmities: "They [Bukharans and Kokandis] do not conceal their mutual hatred. On many occasions their respective envoys have expressed their readiness to assist us, the Kokandis for an attack on Bukhara and the Bukharans for an offensive against Kokand."[6]

In 1865 Russia renamed the conquered Kokand territories as Turkestan and moved the capital to Tashkent, which it placed under the governor-general of Orenburg. Two years later it elevated Tashkent to the status of a separate governor-generalship and folded into it all the parts of the Kazakh steppes, the Kokand Khanate, and the Emirate of Bukhara that had been conquered since 1847. It consisted of two sub-regions: the Syr Darya province based in Tashkent and the Semireche (Seven Rivers) province based in Vernii. K.P. Kaufman was appointed governor-general and vested with independent authority to undertake military campaigns and diplomatic negotiations with the neighboring states.[7]

In 1868 Kaufman proposed a deal to the ruler of Kokand, Khudayar Khan, consisting of several provisions: Khudayar Khan would grant Russian merchants the right to visit all cities of the khanate and to establish representatives in each city, equalize taxes for Russian and Muslim merchants, and allow Russian caravans free passage into other areas of Kokand.[8] By signing this agreement Khudayar

Khan became a vassal of the Russian Empire. After settling issues with Khudayar Khan and inflicting military defeats on the neighboring khanates, Kaufman forced Bukhara and Khiva to sign similar treaties in 1868 and 1873 respectively, making them protectorates of the Russian Empire as well.

These military campaigns significantly shrank the territories of the Kokand Khanate and forced its economy into decline. To pay the large indemnity to Russia, Khudayar Khan had to increase taxes, which led to protests both in the periphery and in central districts of the ethnically diverse khanate. Many blamed Khudayar Khan for betraying Kokand's interests and for becoming dependent on Russia. Heavy taxes, especially on cattle, led to revolt in the summer of 1873. The uprising erupted in the villages of Kasan and Nanaia near Namangan and soon consumed the whole Ferghana Valley, raging unchecked until February 1876. Kyrgyz nomads and cattle breeders refused to pay the increased tax and retreated to inaccessible mountain areas. As noted in the previous chapter, Ishak Mulla Hasan-ogly (Iskak Asan uulu), an ethnic Kyrgyz known as Pulat Khan, led an armed rebellion against the khan in July 1873.[9] Various ethnic groups of the Ferghana Valley participated in the revolt, but it was the Kyrgyz who constituted the military core of Pulat Khan's rebellion.

This uprising alarmed not only Khudayar Khan but also the Russians, who sent special punitive detachments against the rebels, crushing them by February 1876. Losses among the rebels were enormous. Speaking of only one day, Lieutenant General Golovachev indicated in his report to the minister of war that "up to 20,000 residents of Andijan perished on January 8 as a result of our artillery."[10] Russian forces also suffered heavy losses at Andijan. "The battle was dreadful, unprecedented; lots of Russians were killed, some troops simply fled," wrote General Kuropatkin in his diary.[11] Following the suppression of the military revolt, Ishak Mulla (Pulat Khan) and some of his confidants were hanged in Margilan in March, 1876, while his followers were physically punished, jailed, or sent into exile. In spite of this, the Alai Kyrgyz from the mountains adjoining the Ferghana Valley continued to offer resistance.

Khudayar Khan fled Kokand for Tashkent in July 1875, whence the Russians sent him to Orenburg.[12] The khan's abdication opened the fight for his throne. With Kipchak backing against the Kyrgyz, Khudayar Khan's eldest son, Nasreddin Bek, emerged as the successor. But neither the rebels nor the Russian army trusted Nasreddin Bek, which prompted Tsar Alexander II on February 19, 1876 to disband the Kokand Khanate and rename it Ferghana province. A new governor-generalship was established under M.D. Skobelev at Novyi Margilan (now Ferghana). To kill all thoughts of reestablishing the khanate, the Russians sent Nasreddin Bek to the remote Russian city of Vladimir. Only after four years were the last khan and his wife allowed to return to Tashkent, where Nasreddin Khan died in 1882, at the age of thirty-two.[13]

Russia's military conquest forced upon the peoples of Central Asia a new system of law, politics, and socio-economic relations that from the very beginning redefined Central Asia as a periphery and made it utterly dependent on the Russian center. Imposed on local traditions by force, the new system weakened the region's traditional patterns of life and further undermined national development there.[14]

By 1886 the Russians imposed new administrative borders, dividing the governor-generalship into provinces, districts, and sub-districts, along with coterminous military units on the same territories. Thus, the Ferghana province included the districts of Andijan, Kokand, Margilan, Namangan, Osh, Chust, and Chemion district (renamed Isfara in 1879).

The administrative and territorial divisions which the Russian Empire created in Turkestan bore little relation to the geographical, historical, economic, or ethnocultural realities of the region. Instead, they reflected the same imperial principles of rule that prevailed throughout the Russian Empire. Both the territorial divisions and the administrative apparatus and procedures were defined and set in motion by a complex bureaucratic machinery based in the capital of St. Petersburg.

The key link to the imperial capital was the Chancellery of the governor-general of Turkestan, created in 1867 and based in Tashkent. This executive organ existed under the minister of war. It was responsible for staffing, inspections, taxes and work duties, road construction, mining, and all dealings with Russia's protectorates of Khiva and Bukhara, as well as relations with the neighboring countries of the Orient. The Chancellery and its special commissions participated in the drafting of all laws relating to Turkestan. These were then reviewed by the ministries and State Council in St. Petersburg. In practice, the Chancellery's powers over all political, administrative, and military issues were practically unlimited. Hence, it was the Russian Ministry of War that controlled the region.

Military governors headed provincial offices and also commanded the troops,[15] wielding dictatorial powers over every aspect of life in the Ferghana Valley. They designated places where both settled and nomadic populations were allowed to meet, confirmed elected district administrators and appointed all others, confirmed candidates standing for election as judges, and appointed and dismissed at will all district administrators and their staffs. The governor- general appointed district heads, but the military governors reported on their activities to the governor-general and passed on complaints from the local populace concerning taxes they levied.[16]

The governor-general of the Ferghana province was also vested with police and judicial powers. He could fine indigenous persons up to 100 rubles and hold them in custody for up to one month. His powers also included control over judicial bodies and prisons and the confirmation of sentences in criminal cases.[17]

The most important governmental institution was the Ferghana province administration, a collegial body chaired by an assistant to the military governor. This group performed administrative, judicial, law enforcement, financial and economic functions.[18] Its economic department carried out a series of important duties, among them allocating land to settled and nomadic populations, superintending religious endowments (*waqfs*), managing water resources, imposing levies on the indigenous population, compiling budgets for land and peasant-related duties, handling expenditures, supervising the collection of customs duties and settling disputes, approving contracts, issuing licenses for mining, and establishing private industrial enterprises.[19]

The head of the district administration also commanded the district's troops. The governor-general appointed and dismissed district chiefs on the recommendation of the provincial military governors. The district chief also served as the chief of police, land captain, city mayor, and chairman of the body overseeing taxes on land.

The district administration was also charged with the difficult tasks of managing taxes paid in labor, peacekeeping, settling disputes over water and land, and overseeing the work of the provincial and district administrations. It is no exaggeration to say that the provincial head had a monopoly of power in almost all spheres of social and economic life as he applied the logic and spirit of the tsarist colonial policy locally. The provincial administration was in effect all-powerful, but nonetheless worked tirelessly in the pursuit of its own interests tirelessly to strengthen and expand its authority all the more.

The Ferghana administration divided both the nomadic and settled populations into districts (*volosts*) and each district into villages (*auls*). District and village elders, who exercised administrative and police authority, were elected to three-year terms and were confirmed by the military governor. To weaken the power of the traditional Kyrgyz elites, the Russian administration based the district and village units on territorial rather than clan principles. The clan elites resisted this, recognizing it as an attack on the clan structure itself. The colonial administration defended its actions as part of an effort to remove the "inconveniencies inherent in the [traditional] administrative system."[20] It made the same claim when it abolished the clan chiefs' authority and introduced instead elected elders, explicitly defending the move in terms of "maintaining stability" and achieving the more efficient collection of taxes.

A two-step process was introduced for electing district chiefs. First, each fifty households elected a delegate to a village assembly, which met in the presence of the Russian administrators. As a rule, the Russians would keep order but not interfere in the electoral process. A quorum of two-thirds was required for an assembly's votes to be considered valid. Then second, the district assembly elected the district chief and judges, set pay scales for local officials, and oversaw all roads, bridges, and irrigation systems, as well as domestic construction. The district head maintained order with the help of the police, conducted criminal investigations, communicated the laws and decrees of the colonial administration to the populace, and could—with the concurrence of the provincial head—convene and dissolve district assemblies.

If for any reason the Russian administration did not like a district head, the military governor could call for new elections or temporarily replace the person. Lower level administrators frequently abused their offices by illegally exacting payments, embezzling tax funds, and punishing anyone considered undesirable. Elections for local officials were frequently accompanied by fierce fights among the contending factions. Judicial bodies also protected the interests of the tsarist regime, leading to abusive practices by judges that engendered discontent among people. The authorities set up "criteria of allegiance" for all judicial candidates, hoping over time that such men would become reliable tools for protecting the social and political order that the Russians hoped to establish in Turkestan.

The tsarist police were the colonial rulers' most reliable weapons and the guardians of monarchical interests in the Ferghana region. In larger cities like Kokand and Novyi Margilan, police chiefs wielded extensive executive powers and could call on the Russian military to reinforce their actions. Inevitably, the indigenous population was subject to fines and arrest for even minor offenses and acts of disobedience. To assist the police, tsarist officials deputized citizens who would unquestioningly apply all police measures and take steps on their own to keep order. Such minor offenses as rudeness, disrespect, and disobedience warranting large fines and punishments were set at the sole discretion of the colonial administrators and based on their own interests.

Tsarist authorities considered prisons as an important tool for controlling movements that threatened the established order. Four jails in the Ferghana Valley (in Novyi Margilan, Kokand, Namangan, and Osh) were supplemented by a large number of lockup houses, military detention centers and similar facilities. All together, Russian government regarded these assemblies, local heads, police, and the prison system as the backbone of imperial authority in Ferghana and the best tools for suppressing rebellion even before it started.

Initially, people from the old khanate system continued to carry out their duties, but over time these "indigenous administrators" were reduced to a supporting role in the colonial system. Meanwhile, following the usual imperial practice, migrants from Central Russia settled in separate villages in rural areas, and enjoyed a high degree of self-rule under their elders. Neither the old nor the new administrators were particularly qualified. A minimum age of twenty-five was set for members of the local governments, but there were no educational requirements except for judges, who had to have completed a Russian middle school. Low salaries fostered a climate of corruption.[21]

During Russia's colonization of Central Asia, the imperial authorities paid close attention to ethnic and political relations within the region. Of course, they took full advantage of the prevailing conflicts between ethnic groups and between political elites. As one Russian scholar put it, "The tsarist regime used their mutual hostilities to weaken the regional peoples and prevent them from uniting to resist their colonial masters."[22]

As part of its colonial policy, Russia imposed territorial divisions on Turkestan and other parts of Central Asia that would assure its continued political, military, and economic control of the region. Actively drawing on the experience of other colonial powers, Russia's political elite actively and effectively applied the famous principle of "divide and rule." From the very beginning the colonial administration based in Tashkent worked to sow seeds of distrust and hostility among the conquered peoples, so as to prevent the consolidation of any nationalist movement.

Forms of Acceptance and Resistance

Even so, the conquest of the Kokand Khanate and its loss of sovereignty laid the ground for popular discontent. Further contributing to a new wave of anti-Russian protests were the arbitrary ways of Russian and local officials, the Russian immigrants' expropriation of lands from both settled and nomadic peoples, increased taxes, and a disregard for national traditions and Muslim values. Colonization and the prevailing style of colonial rule united local peoples against Russia. A consistent pattern emerged, with each new colonial abuse giving rise to new and more radical modes of resistance.

Anti-colonial rebellions broke out in various parts of Turkestan throughout the second half of the nineteenth century. In the Ferghana province alone, there were more than 200 anti-colonial protests during the three decades after 1870. In 1885 alone the Andijan, Osh, and Margilan districts witnessed mass protests led by one Dervish Khan. Another rebellion led by the Kyrgyz woman Kurmanjan Datka took place during the same period. Kurmanjan Datka was one of the first Kyrgyz females to use lethal force against the colonial regime. Even General Skobelev, the military governor of Ferghana province, was forced to negotiate with this courageous woman.

The largest rebellion of the late-nineteenth century occurred in 1898 in Andijan, and was led by Ishan Muhammad-Ali Halpha Sabir Sufiev (also known as Madali Dukchi Ishan). Beginning in May in the district of Ming-Tepe, the uprising quickly spread throughout the whole Ferghana Valley and other parts of the Turkestan governor-generalship. It was well organized and encompassed more than 2,000 people of all national and social groups. The rebels divided themselves into separate units called *bairaks* (banners), numbering up to 400 people each. Although *bairaks* even attacked military posts in the Ferghana province, they were no match for the well-equipped and trained tsarist army, and within a month the revolt had been crushed. Five hundred and fifty people were arrested in connection with the uprising in Andijan, while Madali Dukchi Ishan and all his immediate associates were executed.

Many villages that had become centers of resistance were all but wiped out. In the Ming-Tepe district alone the settlements of Tajik, Koshgar, and Kutchi, where most of the population took part in the revolt, were razed. These territories were then repopulated by immigrants from southern Russia, who came there via Namangan.[23] Altogether, the Russian command intended to destroy twenty-nine additional settlements whose population had participated in the revolt. Only fear of still more popular revolts stopped the Russians from implementing this plan.

On June 20, 1899, new uprisings engulfed almost the entire Ferghana Valley. The gravity of this outbreak forced the Russian government to analyze its causes and implications in order to improve its colonial policy in the region. Russian officials assembled twenty volumes of information on the issue. However, this did not lead them to draw the correct conclusions, with the result that the local population's living standards continued to fall, with the result that discontent mounted further.

Social and economic conditions plummeted in the wake of Russia's entry into World War I, when the tsarist policy of predatory exploitation of the colony turned into direct plunder. At the start of war officials in Turkestan and Ferghana were ordered to provide raw materials, foodstuffs, and fuel for the army and industry. Together, 668,000 tons of cotton, 9,617,000 tons of cottonseed, 3,206,000 tons of oilseed residues, as well as dehydrated fruit and millions of sheep and cattle were taken away from Turkestan between 1914 and 1916.[24] Grain deliveries from Russia, however, were sharply reduced. As a result, famine broke out across Central Asia and especially in the cotton-producing regions of the Ferghana Valley. Tens of thousands died of starvation.

This situation was exacerbated by the 100 percent tax increase, instituted in December 1914, on irrigated land in the Ferghana province. When the tsarist government established a low standardized price for requisitioned cotton in the summer of 1915, cotton producers lost about 60 million rubles in the first year alone.[25] Not only did the price fall short of the producers' personal needs, it did not even cover the cost of planting and harvesting. Rising prices, especially on essentials, further worsened the situation. For example, between 1915 and 1916 grain prices in Turkestan rose by 300 percent, rice and sugar by 250 percent, cloth and shoes by 200 percent to 350 percent, and the price of bread quadrupled.[26] Prices on food and basic goods rose most precipitously in the Ferghana, forcing the entire population of the Ferghana Valley into abject misery. Skyrocketing prices and the forced requisitioning of horses, carts, and other items led to large-scale unrest in the region.

The 1916 Revolt, occurring on the eve of the collapse of tsarism, was the pinnacle of the national liberation movement. It was triggered by the imperial decree of June 25, 1916, "On the Recruitment of Alien Males for Work Behind the Lines," which mobilized more than 200,000 men between the ages of nineteen and thirty-one. Most of these involuntary recruits came from the most populous part of the region, the Ferghana Valley. The Khujand area was told to mobilize 8,948 men, including 2,708 from Khujand city alone.[27] This probably explains why the first wave of the revolt arose in that Ferghana Valley city, on July 3 and 4, 1916. As news of the events in Khujand fanned quickly across Turkestan, the revolt engulfed other provinces as well. Both urban and rural populations joined the resistance, as did workers, craftsmen, members of the local intelligentsia, and clergymen.[28]

On July 9 the rebels killed a district chief and his clerk in Gazy-Yaglyk village near Kokand. Authorities sent a police squad and twenty-five soldiers to crush the revolt. The same day, young people in the old quarter of Andijan loudly protested when a county chief assembled the people and read the tsarist draft call. The rebels swept into the new section of the city, where they were met by armed police and Cossacks. The Cossacks opened fire, as the rebels began throwing stones, sticks, and *ketmens*, a local form of pickaxe. Three rebels were killed, 22 wounded, and

119 participants put on trial. On the morning of July 10 a large crowd in Margilan prevented the local official from reading the imperial decree. The police attempted to seal off the crowd, but the people attacked the police with sticks and stones. One town elder (*aksakal*), three irrigation managers (*mirabs*), and a city police-man were killed.

Almost all areas of the Namangan district were engulfed by unrest. In nineteen villages the rebels beat local administrators and destroyed lists of those being drafted into the army. The public supported the rebels. A famous Tajik writer, Sadriddin Aini, wrote of this period: "I spent the summer of 1916 traveling. I visited numer-ous villages in Bukhara, traveled to Samarkand, Khujand, and to the outskirts of Ferghana . . . everywhere the population was in sympathy with the rebels. People prayed for a rebel victory. When the revolt was crushed, they hid the rebels in their houses and protected them in remote places."[29]

A wave of repressions swept across the Ferghana Valley and the entire region. Three thousand people were arrested and 347 sentenced to death, of whom 51 were actually executed. Others were imprisoned or sent into exile.[30] The imperial forces' military and material supremacy, and the rebels' lack of an effective plan and centralized leadership, led to the defeat of the 1916 Revolt. However, the revolt prepared the ground for further struggle by the local peoples against the colonial authorities.

Continuity and Change in the Economy and Society

Once the governor-generalship of Turkestan was established, the Russian Empire undertook a program of large-scale colonial exploitation in the region. The goals of this effort were to weaken both the settled and nomadic aristocracies, to expro-priate land from the indigenous population, to exploit agriculture to the maximum extent possible, and to foster colonization. In 1871, on instructions from the em-peror, Kaufman and his colleagues drafted a decree on the administration of the Turkestan region. In the form reviewed two years later, Kaufman's commission proposed to nationalize all family farms (*dehkan*), leaving their former owners with limited rights to their permanent use. All other forms of land tenure could be terminated if the land had to be used for land or water-based communications, for public buildings, for irrigation canals, or, significantly, for Russian coloniza-tion. The only exceptions were some land belonging to foundations (*waqf*), land designated for constructing cities, and urban lands purchased by Russian officers, merchants, and clerics. Foundation lands leased to family farmers were also to become state-owned.[31]

The agrarian program of 1871–73 made it easy to expropriate family farms in the Ferghana Valley. However, some Russians were not interested in doing so, because they realized the family farms were producing a lot of cotton. In 1882 a commission headed by Senator F.K. Giers was sent out to "identify and conclu-sively determine land ownership rights in the Turkestan region." This commission succeeded in limiting the ambitions of those Russian landowners who wanted to treat the irrigated lands of Turkestan as a kind of colonization fund.

The Giers Commission also decided against allocating large plots of irrigated land for the construction of Cossack villages. The commission noted that the Cossacks followed the usual Russian practice of extensive farming, which involved low yields on very large plots. This was incompatible with the Central Asian practice of intensive farming, leading to high yields on small plots. Giers concluded that "It would be almost impossible to allot large plots from the well-irrigated lands, while the Cossacks will be unable to pursue intensive farming, which alone is profitable in Central Asia."[32]

Thanks to Giers, as noted above, an 1886 decree reestablished the local populace's right to own land. Article 255 of this decree affirmed that "The settled population is entitled to lands it has owned, used, and disposed of on a permanent and hereditary basis and in accordance with local customs." Meanwhile, Article 256 established that "The local population is entitled to use the water in irrigation canals, streams and lakes in accordance with local customs."[33] Article 259 stated that land could be used by a community or by households or neighborhoods, depending on local customs.

Finally, Article 270 affirmed that "Public lands occupied by nomad camps are granted to nomads for their indefinite use [but not ownership], on the basis of custom and the provisions of this Regulation."[34] Even Russian authors have acknowledged that this article treated nomadic peoples unjustly. One wrote that "The settled and nomadic populations in Ferghana have dissimilar land rights. Settled residents have vested rights to both cultivated and uncultivated lands they have owned, used and disposed of on a hereditary basis, but nomads do not enjoy such a right. Article 270 of the 'Regulation' states that the lands they occupy are considered to be public and granted to them for use only. Even if they took up settled lives the nomads would not possess the same rights, and would be entitled only to lands already under cultivation."[35]

Senator K.K. Palen, who examined the region in 1909-1910, reported that Russia had abolished tax privileges relating to land, equalized access to land, and confirmed that people who owned and used land they had inherited could continue to do so. By contrast, he noted that "Lands occupied by the nomadic population were considered public property."[36] The decision to treat the nomads' lands this way, which further divided nomadic and settled peoples from one another, flowed naturally from the Russian Empire's policy on settlement. A contemporary wrote frankly that "to recognize land as belonging to the Kyrgyz people would make it impossible . . . to expand Russian settlements."[37] At the same time, the Kyrgyz *biis* and *beks* were not able freely to dispose of pastures and wintering areas as they had done before. By binding nomads to specific lands, Russia restricted their mobility and to a certain extent expedited the process of their settlement.

Russia's leaders, well aware of Central Asia's military-strategic significance and its abundant resources, intended to establish a firm colonial dominion over the region. They were not content to rely solely on a strong army and administration. In addition, they enlisted Russian immigrants to help create a firm foothold in the region. The masterminds and leaders of the colonization movement concluded that this task required special attention in Turkestan, where the indigenous population of about 5 million people exhibited a demonstrably hostile attitude toward the new authorities.

If the colonial goals of tsarism shaped Russian imperial policy on settlements, so did its internal concerns. Declining access to land and the rise of commercial agriculture within Russia were driving many Russian peasants into poverty and despair. Tsarist officials hoped to resolve this acute economic and social problem by resettling restive peasants to Central Asia. Count K.K. Palen openly stated this strategic purpose of Russian colonial policy. Beyond the purely political motives for conquering Turkestan, he noted, St. Petersburg annexed Central Asia because "it would be a source of revenue for the government, and a new market for its domestic products, and the resulting colonies could become a new area for resettling surplus population from the internal provinces."[38]

New colonization rules for Turkestan introduced in 1883 allowed for the free resettlement of Slavic peoples (Russians, Belarusians, and Ukrainians) who were Orthodox Christians. All others needed to obtain special permission from the imperial institutions and the Ministry of Internal Affairs. Subsequent "Rules of Resettlement" introduced in 1886 and supplemented in 1889 and 1903 explicitly fostered Russian migration into the region's richest agricultural and commercial areas. The 1903 law was candidly titled "Rules for the voluntary resettlement of rural inhabitants and peasants into public lands of the Syr Darya, Ferghana, and Samarkand provinces."[39]

Despite continual resistance from the indigenous population, colonial administrators utilized these acts to pursue a targeted policy to increase the number of Russian immigrants and use them to exploit as much as possible the natural and human resources of Central Asia. In the Ferghana region alone, more than twenty Russian settlements were established between 1882 and 1900, increasing to more than sixty by World War I.[40] According to survey data presented by Count Palen, a quarter of the Russian peasants who arrived in the Ferghana Valley in 1907 had been landless back home.

Colonists often arbitrarily seized indigenous lands, especially those used by nomads and semi-nomads. Thus, a document of the era reports that as soon as the Kyrgyz shepherds made their annual springtime trek to high mountain grazing lands, the settlers "set out to build housing on the irrigated lands belonging to the indigenous Kyrgyz. In some places they even seized the Kyrgyz winter huts, destroying the Kyrgyz structures and using the lumber for their own construction, and burning whatever was left as fuel for cooking."[41]

What particularly infuriated the local population was that the Russian settlers, after destroying their winter huts and stealing their irrigated fields, took advantage of the Kyrgyz departure to high pastures by "seizing the Kyrgyz crops for their own use and feeding their cattle on the Kyrgyz seed corn."[42] Colonial administrators did nothing to impede the colonists' arbitrary seizure of native lands and even encouraged the practice. One method of seizing land from the Kyrgyz nomads was to dispatch a few settlers, who quietly leased large tracts and built houses on them. Once established, the settlers would then petition the authorities to confirm their ownership of the land.[43] There were many such cases where Kyrgyz leased land to Russian settlers "for a period of one year only," but the settlers then sought to "settle down permanently on both the temporarily allotted land and the land they had arbitrarily seized."[44]

The bulk of the colonists moved to cities. By 1907 there were 24,346 people of east Slavic ethnicity in the Ferghana province, 14,722 of whom resided in cities.[45] In spite of the migration law's emphasis on Slavic and Orthodox migration, colonial administrators from the 1890s on noted that Turkestan's new Russian colonial population was "created out of the most heterogeneous elements."[46] A Russian official in Ferghana province, writing in 1908, observed wryly that the new settlers in the Ferghana Valley "did not include the best representatives of the Russian people, and indeed included all but the very worst."[47]

By 1910 the European population of the Ferghana Valley, primarily Russian and Ukrainian, constituted slightly more than 2 percent of the total.[48] In spite of the relatively small numbers involved, colonial resettlement policies had led to the expropriation of hundreds of thousands of acres of irrigated lands, a decrease in the number of *waqfs*, and a sharp reduction in the amount of land available to nomads for cattle-breeding. Meanwhile, the urban population faced similar changes, above all in the division of the larger and mid-size cities into a Russian "new city" with improved services and a native "old city," whose residents were subject to serious discrimination.

In spite of some well-known positive aspects of Russian policies, the Russian Empire's approach to colonization and land-use left a deeply negative mark on the social and economic conditions of the indigenous peoples. It led to sharp increases in the numbers of both landowners and landless natives, and it impoverished most of the nomadic population, whose members were forced to leave their pastures and encampments in search of subsistence in the cities, which further exacerbated social and interethnic tensions in the region.

Prior to the conquest, food crops were dominant in Central Asia as a whole and in the Ferghana Valley, with cotton being a secondary product. But Russian traders and investors demanded an increase in cotton production, as this would enable them to reduce their import of expensive raw cotton from abroad. The government, too, supported this because it would improve its balance of payments. Thus, between 1869 and 1893 Russia imported—mainly from the United States—1,133,980,925 pounds of cotton at a cost of 1,568,931,000 rubles.[49] The rise of production in Central Asia and especially the Ferghana Valley enabled Russia to reduce this figure sharply. In 1916 the Director of the Bukhara railway issued a report on "The need for measures to sustain the cotton crop in Central Asia in 1916," which noted that if this were not done Russia would have to import a corresponding amount from abroad at a whopping price of 525 million rubles. The report concluded by noting that the saving to Russia from growing cotton in Central Asia, and above all in the Ferghana Valley, had exceeded two billion rubles in the past decade alone.[50]

By the start of the twentieth century cotton growing already dominated the economy of the Ferghana Valley. The region's General Manager of Land-Use and Animal Husbandry, A.V. Krivoshein, acknowledged bluntly that cotton was "the central nerve and main point of interest and concern of the local population. At the same time it is also the link connecting Turkestan with Moscow and the rest of Russia."[51] The major area for cotton production in all Central Asia and over-whelmingly the source of increased production after the Russian conquest was the Ferghana Valley. From earliest times farmers there had planted an indigenous strain of cotton called *guza*. The fibers of *guza* were short and of low quality, which was made into a coarse local fabric (*karbos*) used mainly for clothing sold locally. Because *guza* did not meet the demands of the Russian cotton trade, Russian cotton manufacturers introduced the longer-fibred American strain of cotton. They employed various incentives to accomplish this: they distributed free American seeds to local growers; provided interest-free loans to whomever would switch to the American strain of cotton; offered twice the price for U.S. cotton as for the local *guza*; and gave bonuses to growers who succeeded in producing large crops of the American cotton.

These measures succeeded to such an extent that, while in the 1860s Central Asia supplied only an insignificant 4 to 7 percent of raw cotton used by Russian mills, by 1914–15 that figure had risen to 70 percent.[52] Russian officials quickly realized that the very continued existence of their cotton industry depended on the welfare of Ferghana farmers and households. But these *dehkans* could not survive between planting and harvest without loans, and local money-lenders charged high interest rates. Cheap credit somehow had to be extended to the *dehkans*. This was accomplished by expanding the operations of the existing county loan offices (called "people's loan institutions") into Turkestan and the Ferghana Valley. Local authorities organized the region's first such loan office in 1876 at Namangan city in the Ferghana Valley. By 1909 twenty-one such loan offices were operating across Turkestan, five of them located in the Ferghana province.

Russian trading companies and banks also contributed significantly to the extension of credit to small farms and households in the Turkestan region, including in the Ferghana Valley. The Russian State Bank established the first banking office in the region in 1875 in Tashkent. It subsequently opened six more offices in Central Asia, including ones in both Kokand and Andijan in the Ferghana Valley. Russian commercial banks entered the region in the 1890s, reaching a total of forty-five offices across Central Asia by 1917. Meanwhile, eighteen local banks were formed. Overall, the total number of banking institutions in Central Asia reached 72 by 1917, with twenty of them in the Ferghana province. Kokand alone boasted branches of ten different banks. All of these offices provided short-term loans for periods of three months to a year. In addition, a Russian land bank also operated in the Ferghana Valley, providing loans backed by the value of the borrower's real estate.

The rise of cotton cultivation facilitated the emergence of allied industries. Nearly all the main growers financed by banks owned their own gins, and some also operated oil-pressing enterprises. The first two cotton gins in the Ferghana Valley appeared under the Kokand Khanate in 1847. By the 1880s Russian trading companies were opening gins all over the valley, soon to be joined by merchant-owned gins. By 1914 no fewer than 378 cotton gins were operating in Turkestan, two thirds of them in the Ferghana province.[53] The Ferghana province also boasted fifteen oil-pressing factories and several breweries.[54]

Russians also exploited the oil and coal resources of the Ferghana province, with six oilfields and twenty-eight coalmines operating there by 1913–14. The largest of these coal mines were near the towns of Kizilkie and Sulukta.[55]

A network of railways facilitated the regular transport of raw materials and goods between the colony and the metropolis to the north. From 1872 to 1915 some 5,000 kilometers of railways were built in Central Asia. Since rail lines were focused on strategic and economically important regions, it is noteworthy that one traversed the Ferghana Valley.

Having found its way into Turkestan and taken full political and economic control there, Russia quickly turned the region into an agrarian and raw materials-producing appendage of the metropolis. With the help of loans, *dehkans* were forced to produce the raw materials necessary for maintaining the Russian Empire. Local industrial enterprises were small and confined the primary processing of raw materials, chiefly cotton. There were no textile factories in the colony, because Russian tycoons did not want competitors to their own mills at Ivanovo, Moscow, and Vladimir.[56]

From the outset, the Russian government paid special attention to trade in Turkestan, and as it learned more about the region it introduced Russian trade practices there. As early as 1884 the military governor of the Ferghana province petitioned the governor-general of Turkestan to abolish the traditional Muslim tax or *zakat* and introduce general rules on trade there.[57] In response, an 1885 State Council decree extended imperial business and trade rules to the region of Turkestan, and a year later the *zakat* system was abolished in the Ferghana province.[58] By 1889 the new rules and taxes were imposed on all traders, including traditional steppe merchants.

Further measures streamlined local trade. In 1894 the State Council abolished traditional measures, scales, and trademarks, calling instead for the introduction of imperial Russian ones within five years.[59] The same decree introduced Russian currency into the region and withdrew all local coinage by 1895.[60] Thus, by 1900 Russian trade practices and currency prevailed across Turkestan and in the Ferghana Valley. But in spite of the law, these new measures and procedures were put into practice mainly in cities and large towns, while more remote and nomadic areas of the Ferghana province continued to rely on traditional barter with scant concern for the Russians' regulations.

With the development of an economy based on commodities and money, the old steppe trade gradually lost its significance, and parts of the Kyrgyz population abandoned nomadism for a settled existence. Among the emerging hubs of trade in the Ferghana Valley were Andijan, Namangan, Kokand, Margilan (Ferghana), Osh, and Uzgen. The new centers of trade and industry became magnets for people from neighboring nomadic regions. As the expanded markets of cities and villages took over the steppe trade, former steppe merchants became sales clerks in the new, larger enterprises, and they survived on goods and credit extended to them by the owners. The numbers of people directly involved in trade soared. By some estimates, more than two million people were living in the Ferghana Valley by 1914,[61] and a significant percent of these were directly or indirectly in trade.

Cultural Responses, Jadidism, and Religious Revival

Russia's conquest of the Ferghana Valley led to a loss of independence and fundamental changes in the social political, economic, and cultural life of the region. Members of the general public and the national intelligentsias perceived these changes in different ways. Some considered the colonial regime to be a standing humiliation to the national and religious feelings of their people. During the second half of the nineteenth century and early twentieth century, many with such views departed Central Asia with their families and relatives and emigrated to various lands of the East, mainly such Muslim countries as Afghanistan, Iran, and Turkey.

Others, however, viewed tsarist Russia's colonial domination as a temporary phenomenon. These people neither left the region nor accommodated themselves to the colonial rulers. They expected to regain the region's political independence and therefore participated actively in movements of national liberation organized throughout the Ferghana Valley.

But there were still others who neither left their homeland nor confronted the powerful Russian Empire with force of arms. They instead chose another way, one that called for the gradual enlightenment and reform of traditional society so as to adapt it to modern life. Epitomizing this approach were the local enlighteners and their disciples known as Jadids, from the Arabic word for "new." The Jadids acutely realized that a main reason for the fall of the Kokand Khanate and the loss of sovereignty in the region was the comprehensive backwardness of Central Asian society. They identified the sources of this backwardness as equally existing in the political, social, economic, and cultural spheres of their lives.

Many prominent writers and champions of enlightenment played an active role in the campaign for regional revival during the second half of the nineteenth century. They included Ahmad Donish (1826–1897), a Bukharan by origin, as well as such Ferghana Valley natives as Muhammadjan Mukimi (1851–1903), Zakirdjan Furkat

(1858–1909), Toshhodja Asiri (1864–1915), Hodja Yusuf Mirfaiazov (1842–1924). It was no easy matter to grasp in all its dimensions the nature and consequences of Russia's colonization of the region. Yet these writers strove relentlessly to do so and were always sincere and consistent patriots.

The ideology they professed can be seen as a precursor of Jadidism, in that they supported social, economic, and political reforms. Particularly notable was the prominent Tajik thinker and publicist Ahmad Donish, who drafted a package of reforms for the Bukharan Khanate. He invoked the best national and world practices when shaping his plans, which were grounded on the principle of a just and progressive system of government. He also insisted that a country's development required education, and called upon his contemporaries to study modern science and to master various trades.

Furkat's life's work was suffused with a desire to find a way for his people to achieve progress. He equated ignorance with Hell, where no ray of light is visible, and advised the young to study the secular sciences and both Eastern and European culture. He directed his poetry against backwardness and stagnation, and offered a vivid image of reality. In his essays Furkat attempted to appraise the colonial policies of different European states and the struggles of oppressed peoples for freedom and independence.

Mukimi, a contemporary of Furkat, used his writings to criticize sharply the oppression, violence, and arbitrariness of both local administrators and Russian officials. Like other enlighteners of the day, he hoped to live in a society where people could receive a modern education, develop trades and industries, enrich their spiritual world, and deepen the general culture.

A devout supporter of these ideas was the educator and poet Toshhodja Asiri, who blamed people's hardship and suffering squarely on the powers that be. In his works he propagated the ideal of friendship among the Tajiks, Uzbeks, Kyrgyz, and other local people. A practical reformer, Asiri proposed to relieve misery by extending irrigation canals and thereby bring new land under cultivation. His vision encompassed the utilization of natural resources.[62]

An outstanding literary and scientific figure of the Ferghana Valley was the explorer, geographer, and educator Hodja Yusuf Mirfaiazov. A native of Khujand, he had traveled to Russia, Italy, Spain, France and a number of countries in the Middle East. During his travels Hodja Yusuf had frequented libraries and studied various cultures, seeing at first hand the degree of progress achieved in each of those lands. A polymath, he studied medicine, wrote verses, cultivated many types of cocoons, was interested in irrigation, and wrote a book titled *Cosmography*. His house became a favored place for meetings, convocations, and discussions among scientists, artists, and writers.[63]

Donish, Mukimi, Asiri, Hodja Yusuf, and other leading Central Asian writers of the late nineteenth and early twentieth centuries held Russian literature in high respect and championed it among their contemporaries. They realized that a close understanding of the humanistic and democratic features of that culture could help people of the region integrate themselves into modern world culture and facilitate their mastery of the highest achievements of human thought. At the same time, they knew full well that the Russian conquest of their region, far from improving the lives of indigenous people, had extinguished their political and economic independence and caused a serious spiritual and moral disorientation among many strata of their own population.

The Jadid movement arose across Turkestan at the end of the nineteenth century. It united within its ranks the most educated, patriotic, and progressive intellectuals among the young followers of the famed regional educators discussed above. Over time, their agenda came to include a far broader range of social, economic, political, and culturological issues than their teachers had pursued. However, they followed their predecessors in devoting special attention to education. Prominent Jadids like Mahmudhodja Behbudi, Abdulla Avloni, Abdurauf Fitrat, Munavvar qori Abdurashidkhonov, Ishakhan Ibrat, Ashurali Zahiri, Obidzhon Mahmud, and others all knew that their traditional education had failed to keep up with the times. All of them called for the creation of New Method (*usuli-dzhadi*) schools that would provide education along totally modern lines.

The new Jadid schools used the efficient audio-lingual method to teach reading and writing, as opposed to the slow pedagogy based on composition that still prevailed in traditional schools. The Jadid schools also introduced new subjects, including the natural and social sciences, which they combined under the name "intellectual sciences" (*aklli ilmlar*). The new schools were set up in the European manner, with desks, maps, globes, blackboards, abacuses, and other such classroom materials.

These new *maktabs* or schools organically blended the best of European and Central Asian educational thought. Their appearance coincided with the infiltration into Central Asia of bold new ideas on liberation that came from other Muslim regions of the Russian Empire and from nearby countries of the East. This aroused concern among the colonial administrators, who began to check very carefully on the activities of these schools. Wherever possible, Russian officials tried to divert the Jadid schools into instruments of Russification. One such official noted: "*maktabs* that employ the new methods can and should serve as a transfer points to more purely Russian schools, but they can also develop into centers of opposition to Russian culture."[64]

Russian policy in the sphere of education and culture gave overwhelming priority to the interests of the metropolis, that is Russia, as opposed to the Muslims' natural right to a liberal type of cultural development. In this respect Russian policy was clearly imperial in nature. Naturally, Russian administrators rebuffed any efforts not clearly aligned with official edicts. They staunchly opposed what they took to be the Jadids' efforts to change the status quo, and few Russians made any effort to understand those efforts.

One who did try was an official of the tsarist police, who penned a remarkable report on Jadid schools:

Evidence from the Police Department confirms the existence of a completely new trend [in Central Asian education], which threatens to shatter the centuries-old way of life of the more than fourteen million Muslims living within the Russian state, and to mark a turning point in their existence. The adherents of this new trend . . . point to the need to purge the faith of the mullahs' superstitions and ignorant expositions, and to strengthen the national character by expanding the use of native languages in the literary, scientific, and religious spheres, and generally working toward progress on the basis of Islam and Turkic national identity.

The police officer then got to the heart of the matter:

Whether these progressive forces will confine themselves to the above-mentioned aspirations and goals or will, once they defeat those who support the old traditions, proceed further cannot yet be determined. Similarly, there is no way to predict the implications [of the Jadid movement] for the interests of the Russian state.[65]

In 1908 Count Palen designated a special commission to examine the new schools in various cities across Turkestan, including fourteen in Kokand and five in Andijan. All followed the principles of such famous Ferghana advocates of progressive education as Ishakhan Ibrat, Ashurali Zahiri, Ibrohim Davron, Abdulvahhob Ibodii, and Muhammad Sufizoda. The commission found that the local reformers

wish to return Islam to its previous position of power by developing new ways of life. They seek to assure its progress and to revive the faded idea of religious and political unity and solidarity. They are perfectly aware that to achieve these goals they must bring the Muslim peoples out of their present state of ignorance. Therefore, these reformers of Muslim life want to take a firm hold of the schools and other appropriate educational institutions and turn them into strong and enlightened champions of such ideals.[66]

The inspectors also wrote with alarm that the Jadid schools were already using textbooks from Kazan and Constantinople that had not been reviewed by official censors. The commission declared that the textbooks in question propagated "dangerous" pan-Islamic and pan-Turkic ideas. All this provided a political and ideological pretext for closing down numerous Jadid schools and prosecuting activists who supported the new methods of schooling.

One way to fight the Jadid movement was to expand the network of Russian schools in the region. The authorities viewed this as a means of Russifying the indigenous people and preparing a new generation of Muslim youths who would be more loyal to Russia. Yet despite some initial successes, this campaign did not produce the expected results, and most indigenous families continued sending their children to either traditional or Jadid schools.

That said, the process by which Jadidism evolved from being a new philosophy of education the status of an influential political movement was difficult. The wretched condition of the indigenous population and the stagnation of social and political life guaranteed that Turkestan, Bukhara, and Khiva would continue to lag far behind the developed countries. This reality prompted the Jadids to search for more effective means of accelerating social progress on their soil.

The Jadids, including those from Ferghana, pointed to the fact that the Muslim Orient had experienced a period of vital spiritual and cultural flowering in the ninth to the fifteenth centuries, but which by the nineteenth century had become stagnant. They attributed this to the slow intellectual adaptation by Muslim peoples and states to changing conditions in the world. The Jadids concluded that "frozen" forms of religious thinking retarded the process of modernization within Muslim society and its adaptation to present-day realities. By liberating religious thinking from that prevailing "ossification," the Jadids hoped to revive the humanitarian values and universal appeal of Islam. One Jadid intellectual, Sherzod Ahmadi, wrote insightfully that:

> The reason for our decline and our inability to follow the example of more advanced peoples is that our eyes have been covered by a "fog" of superstitions. Some people try to shift the blame for our current decline on our sacred religion. They think that the sharia law impedes progress and promotes setbacks. This is not so. Once upon a time this religion enabled Arabs to triumph over ignorance . . . and gave birth to a prominent culture. . . .
>
> At the end of the day, religion cannot initially be a cause of flowering and then a cause of decline. Islam is not against chemistry, philosophy and other sciences . . . It is not the religion that estranged us from modern sciences and universal literacy, but the myths, legends and superstitions we accepted in the name of religion . . .
>
> Why can't we see that those who repeat these superstitions are blind to modern science and culture? . . . Such a religious life, preoccupied as it is with mutual strife, leads to our subjugation. If this continues longer, we will not have a future.[67]

The local Jadids opposed the "ossification" and ignorance of some members of the Muslim clergy, who misinterpreted sharia norms and distorted the meaning of many of the most important tents of the faith. Regarding the topic of the day, namely the revival of forgotten or ignored national and spiritual values, the Jadids underscored to their compatriots the importance of strictly observing ethical standards. They believed this to be the sole path to social progress. They also sincerely supported the cleansing from Islam of the many destructive layers, distortions, superstitions, and dogmatic postulates that had infiltrated it over the years.

Many progressive figures from the Ferghana Valley worked to convince their compatriots of the need for profound structural, social, and ideological reforms, without which the Muslim world would be destined, they believed, to trudge along in the rear guard of civilization. Accordingly they directed all their activities toward achieving this goal. Thus, one of the most prominent Ferghana Valley Jadids, Ishakhan Ibrat (1862–1937), inspired by enlightened ideas, opened new schools, bookstores, libraries, and even print shops in Namangan and other towns and villages of the Ferghana Valley. Conscious of the importance of national history as a component of identity, Ibrat set about writing a number of works concerning regional history and culture.

Abdulvahhob Ibodii (1877–1942) was one of the first to open an innovative school in Kokand. In 1912–13 he issued popular textbooks on contemporary affairs (*Tashil ul-alifbo* and *Etikodoti Islomia*) that these schools came to use extensively. Ashurali Zahirii (1885–1938), Obidzhon Mahmud (1858–1936), and Nosirhontura Kamolhon-turaev (1871–1938) also engaged in substantial educational and political work during this period, as did many other Jadids of the Ferghana Valley. Some of them launched the first newspapers and later formed national, social, and political organizations.

This active phase of the Jadid movement coincided with a new stage in the liberation struggles of the colonial and semi-colonial peoples of the Muslim world. Thus, the constitutional movement arose in Iran (1905–11), anti-colonial demonstrations occurred in India (1905–8), and the Young Turk Revolution (1908–9) emerged in the Ottoman Empire. Despite all obstacles and constrains, information continued to flow into the region from these restless and rebellious lands. Clearly, Russian authorities had failed to isolate Turkestan from the rest of the world. News of these events elsewhere in the Muslim world stimulated the efforts of the Jadids in the Ferghana Valley and in Turkestan as a whole.

Despite censorship, the Jadids continued to subscribe to various newspapers and journals both from the eastern regions of the Russian Empire, including *Tarjimon* from Bahchisarai, *Vakt* and *Yulduz* from Kazan, and *Mulla Nasriddin* from Tiflis. The Jadids also read such periodicals from abroad as *Sirotil mustakim* from Turkey, *Sirodj-ul'-Akhbar* from Afghanistan, *Habul'-Vatan* from India, and others. Accessible materials in these publications gave readers a general idea of modern economics, international law, parliamentary and municipality institutions, and of the significance of joint stock companies. They introduced Turkestani readers to many heretofore unknown developments, and prompted them to reflect on human progress, European political and social institutions, national development, and the evolution of eastern societies under colonial and semi-colonial regimes. Articles and books by leaders of liberation movements went further, calling on dependent peoples to fight in the name of freedom and justice.

The massive influx of progressive literature from "awakened" parts of Asia inspired the Jadids to develop their own periodical press. They issued scores of newspapers and journals in almost all of the large regional cities, among them *Sadoi-Fargona* and *El-bairogi* in Kokand; *Tarakki, Shuhrat, Hurshid*, and *Sadoi-Turkiston* in Tashkent; *Samarkand* and *Oina* in Samarkand; and *Turon, Buhoro-i-Sharif* in Bukhara. This national press did much to activate political life in the region. A Russian paper correctly observed that such publications had "agitated the stagnant waters of social life."[68]

The new press published articles by Jadids and other prominent writers that explicitly criticized the colonial practices thwarting the national development of the indigenous peoples. But these progressive writers did not stop at criticizing the colonial administration. Acknowledging their own responsibilities before the nation, they attempted to join forces for the common cause. The first decade of the twentieth century witnessed a significant expansion of direct contacts between Jadids in Ferghana and those elsewhere in Turkestan, including the "Young Bukharans" and "Young Khivans," as well as with reform-oriented groups like the Young Turks, who generated an enormous resonance throughout the Muslim world. Local activists wasted no time in sending their most prominent leaders to Turkey, where the Young Turks helped them form a "Constantinople" association to spread useful knowledge from that city.[69] The leaders of this and similar associations viewed education as the chief means of bringing about comprehensive reform. No sooner did they return from Turkey, Afghanistan and other countries than these young reformers launched a massive recruiting campaign to enlist hundreds of new people in their ranks. In the process they created yet more associations and organizations, including Tarbiaii-atfol, Padarkush, Umid, Nashri-Maorif, Barakat, Heirat, and Tarakki-parvar. Notable among them was the Shamsinur association, created in 1908 by a group of madrassa students from Kokand who sought to foster cultural and political education among local Muslims.

World War I unleashed revolutionary activity within Russia, and powerful anti-colonial currents in Central Asia. Local associations multiplied. Within the Ferghana Valley, the Padarkush and Tarakki-parvar groups played so active a role in 1915-1916 that they aroused the attention of the Turkestani regional police. A police agent reported that "Members of Tarakki-parvar party [*sic*] confuse the population and spread rumors about Russia's weakness. By purposefully misinterpreting newspaper reports [about the progress of the war] they point to the possible separation of Muslims from Russia and the creation of an independent [Muslim] state."[70]

Such reports led authorities to conduct searches and interrogations of alleged nationalists, confiscate their property, and deport their leaders. Thus, following a search and interrogation in early 1917, the governor-general of Turkestan banned a leader of both the Padarkush and Tarakki-parvar groups, Ubaidulla Hodjaev, from Andijan and Tashkent.[71] Members of the Kokand association Heirat faced similar measures.

An association headed by Islam Shoahmedov, editor and publisher of the Russian-language newspaper *Turkestanskii krai*, wanted to issue a local-language journal and newspaper. He operated a bookstore in the old part of the city and had 45,000 rubles in assets.[72] Shoahmedov planned to use the profits from his new publications to assist wartime Turkey, which stood as "The guardian of Islam . . . , under whose banner all Muslims should unite."[73] From all cities and towns of the region, authorities received reports on the collection of funds, travel by nationalist activists to Turkey, and the arrival in Central Asia of "emissaries" from Turkey and elsewhere. All this prompted the authorities to circulate to local authorities such instructions as the following, dated December 27, 1916:

> Based on available evidence from the police, the Turkish committee of the "Solidarity and Progress" party plans to send its agents to organize strikes locally. The Department . . . therefore asks that you undertake measures to identify, within the

jurisdiction entrusted to you, all persons of Turkish origin and put them under surveillance in order to prevent them from agitating or triggering strikes. Report on this work to the Department.[74]

Despite of such measures, progressive reformers in the Ferghana Valley and elsewhere continued to maintain contact with one another while the national resistance gained momentum. The Jadids had no intention of abandoning their goal of modernizing Central Asian society, and remained true to their dream of overcoming cultural isolation and familiarizing Muslims with recent advances in human thought.

They also supported a democratic system of governance that would guarantee civil liberties and political rights. Immediately after the February Revolution in Russia, such new political organizations as Shuroi-Islomiia and Tyurk Odami Markaziat Firkasi arose to champion these goals. Set up by Jadids and others, they all maintained active branches throughout the Ferghana Valley. Their idea was not to imitate in a perfunctory way or mechanically to adopt the externals of European civilization. Rather, they sought to create the conditions necessary for national revival by harmoniously blending useful European elements into the rich spiritual culture of the region.

In all this the Jadids' ideology was substantially shaped by currents of thought flowing into the Ferghana Valley and the region as a whole from adjacent Muslim countries. But even here they did not simply embrace the alien ideas from abroad. Instead, they allowed the new ideas to pass through the prism of national beliefs and traditions. Indeed, some radical Muslims from abroad already were propagating the notion of a hard-line opposition to the Christian West and a revival of the universal caliphate. However, such ideas did not find widespread sympathy in either the Ferghana Valley or Turkestan as a whole.

Progressive thinkers in Ferghana and elsewhere in Central Asia were deeply aware of the huge role Islam had played over the centuries in the life of their traditional society. Yet they did not exaggerate its potential as an integrative force for the future. Most could not reconcile the concept a universal Islamic state or a Turkic commonwealth with the reality of other countries undergoing development, and as such had no desire to abandon their affirmation of national sovereignties and identities.

The Jadids viewed the pan-Islamic trends in the early twentieth century not in terms of political integration, but as an opportunity to establish closer connections among diverse Muslim peoples. Indeed, they even advanced the idea of uniting Muslims with the more tolerant European democrats in a joint struggle for freedom and human rights.

The outbreak of World War I and the subsequent wave of national liberation movements that swept the Ferghana Valley and other parts of Central Asia in 1916 provoked deep concern among Russian officials and elites over the fate of their "one and undivided" empire. Soon bankruptcy loomed over Russia, and the failure of its domestic policy became evident to all.

As this happened, numerous oppressed peoples within Russia's imperial borders appealed to European and American leaders to support their independence from that empire.[75] One such appeal arose in May 1916 in the name of the "League of Non-Russians in Russia" (*Liga russkikh inorodtsev*). Addressed to U.S. president Woodrow Wilson, it was signed by representatives of Muslims in Russia.[76]

The advance of political, economic, and social breakdown in the Ferghana Valley and in the Central Asian region overall strongly politicized local reformers. They now realized that national revival in Turkestan would become possible only when despotism and colonialism were abolished, parliaments (*majlisi*) established, effective governments built, and—when the doors were opened to modern civilization—new knowledge, social justice, and national unity were affirmed.

Following the fall of tsarism and the Kerensky Revolution in February 1917, Ferghana Jadids continued to fight for socio-economic and political liberty, and for the agenda of the national movement. Thinking that the Bolsheviks supported their goals, they also supported the October Bolshevik Revolution later in 1917. But once the Bolsheviks seized power in October 1917, they quickly accused Jadid leaders of a reactionary "Pan-Islamism" and "bourgeois nationalism." Notwithstanding the Jadids' clear rejection of those positions, which they had repeated in numerous publications, Lenin and the Bolsheviks began at once to subject them to brutal repressions. Under such conditions, the best the Jadids could do was to continue to stand up for what they had affirmed all along.

Notes

1. Referring to the Anglo-Afghan war of 1838–42.
2. See Z.D. Kastelskaia, *Iz istorii Turkestanskogo kraia,* Moscow, 1980, pp. 15–16.
3. *Istoriia Uzbekistana,* Tashkent, 2002, p. 91.
4. M.A. Terentev, *Istoriia zavoevania Srednei Azii,* vol. 3, Saint Petersburg, 1906, appendix, p. 3.
5. *Istoriia Uzbekistana,* p. 91.
6. Kastelskaia, *Iz istorii Turkestanskogo kraia,* p. 16.
7. *Istoriia Uzbekskoi SSR,* vol. 2, Tashkent, 1968, p. 25.
8. Kastelskaia, *Iz istorii Turkestanskogo kraia,* p. 18.
9. *Istoriia Uzbekskoi SSR,* p. 30.
10. Ibid., p. 36.
11. Ibid.
12. After two years Khudayar Khan escaped from Orenburg. He lived several years in Afghanistan, Iran, India, and visited Mecca and Medina. Following a prolonged illness in 1882 he passed away at the age of fifty-one in the city of Karruh (Afghanistan, Herat province).
13. A. Egamberdiev and A. Amirsaidov, *Istoriia Kokandskogo khanstva (Bibliograficheskii ukazatel, XVIII vek–1876 g.),* Tashkent, 2007, p. 87.
14. N. Abdurahimova and G. Rustamova, *Kolonialnaia sistema vlasti v Turkestane vo vtoroi polovine XIX–pervoi chetverti XX vv.,* Tashkent, 1999, p. 19.
15. Ibid., p. 30.
16. *Proekt polozheniia ob upravlenii v Semirechenskoi i Syrdarinskoi oblastiakh,* Saint Petersburg, 1867, pp. 109–26.
17. Ibid.
18. Ibid., pp. 11–12, 41.

19. TsGARUz, f. I-1, op. 27, d. 659, pp. 27–28.

20. *Otchet po revizii Turkestanskogo kraiia proizvedennyi po vysochaishemu poveleniiu senatorom grafom K.K. Palenom. Selskoe upravlenie: russkoe i tuzemnoe*, Saint Petersburg, 1910, p. 9.

21. S.B. Tillabaev, *Sistema administrativno–territorialnogo upravleniia v Turkestanskom krae v kontse XIX–nachale XX veka i uchastie v nei predstavitelei mestnogo naselenia (na primere Ferganskoi oblasti)*, Tashkent, 2006, pp. 17–18.

22. Kastelskaia, *Iz istorii Turkestanskogo kraia*, p. 33.

23. *Istoriia narodov Uzbekistana*, vol. 2, Tashkent, 1947, p. 370.

24. J. Ismailova, *Natsionalno–osvoboditelnoe dvizhenie v Turkestane v nachale XX veka (na primere vosstania 1916 goda v Ferganskoi doline)*, Tashkent, 2002, p. 26.

25. Ibid.

26. Ibid.

27. N.B. Khotamov, *Tarihi halki tojik. (az solnon 60-umi asri XIX to soli 1924)*, Dushanbe, 2007, pp. 94–95.

28. *Istoriia Uzbekistana*, p. 104.

29. S. Aini, *O moei zhizni (Kratkaia avtobiografia), Sobranie sochinenii*, vol. 1, Moscow, 1971, pp. 90–91.

30. *Istoriia Uzbekistana*, p. 105.

31. Kastelkaia, *Iz istorii Turkestanskogo kraia*, p. 41.

32. Ibid., p. 45.

33. *Polozhenie ob upravlenii Turkestanskim kraem (12 iunia 1886 g.)*, Saint Petersburg, 1886, p. 32.

34. Ibid., p. 34.

35. G. Loganov, "Rossia v Srednei Azii," in *Voprosy kolonizatsii*, Saint Petersburg, no. 4, 1909, p. 16.

36. Cited in *Istoriia Uzbekskoi SSR*, p. 51.

37. TsGARUz, f. 1, op. 1, d. 56, pp. 21–98.

38. K.K. Palen, *Prilozhenie k otchetu revizii Turkestanskogo kraia*, Saint Petersburg, 1911, p. 496.

39. Sh. Gofforov, *Pereselencheskaia politika Rossiiskoi imperii v Turkestane (vtoraia polovina XIX–nachalo XX vekov)*, Tashkent, 2003, p. 29.

40. Ibid., p. 30.

41. K.K. Palen, *Pereselencheskoe delo v Turkestane*, Saint Petersbrug, 1910, p. 225.

42. TsGARUz, f. I.-1, op. 12, d. 382, l. 123.

43. O.A. Shkapskii, *Pereselentsy–samovoltsy i agrarnyi vopros v Semerechenskoi oblasti*, Saint Petersburg, 1906, p. 40.

44. TsGARUz, f. I.-1. op. 12. d. 382. l. 124.

45. O. Ata-Mirzaev et al., *Uzbekistan mnogonatsyonalnyi: istoriko–demograficheskii aspect*, Tashkent, 1998, p. 49.

46. TsGARUz, f. I-1.-717, op. 1, d. 8, l. 23.

47. TsGARUz, f. I.-1, op. 31, d. 466, ll. 4-4 ob.

48. S.S. Gubaeva, *Naselenie Ferganskoi doliny v kontse XIX–nachale XX vv. (etnokulturnye voprosy)*, Tashkent, 1991, p. 104.

49. A. Niallo, N. Halfin, "Turkestanskii khlopok i amerikanskie milliony (Iz istorii amerikanskoi ekspansii v Srednei Azii)," *Zvezda Vostoka*, no. 3, 1953, p. 106.

50. Cited in A.M. Aminov, *Ekonomicheskoe razvitie Srednei Azii (so vtoroi poloviny XIX stoletiia do pervoi mirovoi voiny)*, Tashkent, 1959, p. 100.

51. See A.V. Krivoshein, *Zapiski glavnoupravliaiushchego zemleustroistvom i zemledeliem o poezdke v Turkestanskii krai v 1912 godu*, Poltava, 1912, p. 5.

52. See N.B. Khotamov, *Rol bankovskogo kapitala v sotsialno-ekonomicheskom razvitii Srednei Azii (nachalo 90-gg. XIX v.–1917 g.)*, Dushanbe, 1990, pp. 6, 292.

53. N.B. Khotamov, *Iz istorii pervykh promyshlennykh predpriatii Srednei Azii (fabrichno–zavodskie predpriatiia Srednei Azii v kolonialnyi period),* Dushanbe, 2005, pp. 20–82.

54. Ibid., pp. 20–56.

55. N.U. Musaev, *Formirovanie i razvitie promyshlennogo proizvodstva v Turkestane (konets XIX–nachalo XX vv.),* Tashkent, 1999, p. 36.

56. Kastelskaia, *Iz istorii Turkestanskogo kraia,* pp. 60, 62.

57. TsGARUz, f. 19, op. 1, d. 23311, l. 2.

58. TsGARUz, f. 19, op. 1, d. 23311, l. 23.

59. TsGVIAR, f. 400, op. 1, d. 1402, l. 19.

60. TsGVIAR, f. 400, op. 1, d. 1361, l. 48.

61. N.A. Abdurakhimova and V.G. Kiselev, "Demograficheskaia statistika v kolonialnom Turkestane v nachale XX veka," in *Uzbekistonda tarih fani: yutuklar va rivojlanish muammolari,* vol. 2, Tashkent, 2006, p. 46.

62. Z.Sh. Radzhabov, *Poet-prosvetitel tadzhikskogo naroda Asiri,* Dushanbe, 1974, p. 44; *Istoriia Leninabada,* Dushanbe, 1986, pp. 187–88.

63. See S. Marofiev, "Huland va baze guzashtagoni marufi on," *Uch. zap. LGPI im. S.M. Kirova,* issue 20, Leninabad, 1964, p. 135; *Istoria Leninabada,* p. 188.

64. *Nauka i prosveschenie,* no. 2, Tashkent, 1922, p. 19.

65. Cited in G. Safarov, *Problemy Vostoka,* Petrograd, 1922, pp. 146–47.

66. Cited in K.E. Bendrikov, *Ocherki po istorii narodnogo obrazovaniia v Turkestane,* Moscow, 1960, p. 63.

67. Cited in B.M. Babadzhanov, *Zhurnal HAQIQAT kak zerkalo religioznogo aspekta v ideologii dzhadidov,* Tokyo: University of Tokyo, 2007, pp. 24–25.

68. *Russkii Turkestan,* 1906, July 19.

69. TsGARUz, f. I-461, op. 1, d. 2115, l. 19.

70. TsGARUz, f. I-461, op. 1, d. 1968, l. 31.

71. Ibid.

72. TsGARUz, f. I-461, op. 1, d. 2115, l. 91.

73. TsGARUz, f. I-461, op. 1, d. 1919, l. 9.

74. TsGARUz, f. I-461, op. 1, d. 1919, l. 14.

75. See P.N. Miliukov, *Natsionalnyi vopros (Proiskozhdenie natsionalnosti i natsionalnogo voprosa v Rossii),* Prague, 1925, p. 180.

76. Ibid., p. 181.

4

Soviet Rule and the Delineation of Borders in the Ferghana Valley, 1917–1930

Sergey Abashin (Russia), with Kamoludin Abdullaev (Tajikistan), Ravshan Abdullaev (Uzbekistan), and Arslan Koichiev (Kyrgyz Republic)

Overview of the Soviet Takeover

In early March 1917, reports about the change of power in Petrograd[1] reached Turkestan. This led to the rapid reconfiguration of the former colonial relations and a transformation of the region's political life. Three parallel seats of local authority emerged, appearing first in Tashkent, where the tsarist governor-generalship had been based, and spreading from there throughout the region.

First, the legal successor of the former governor-general was the Turkestan Committee of the Provisional Government, headed by a member of the Constitutional Democrats or Cadet Party, Nikolai Shchepkin. After July Shchepkin was succeeded by a famous public figure and socialist from Turkestan, Vladimir Nalivkin. The second body that aspired to wield power was the Soviet of Workers' and Soldiers' Deputies. It consisted of several regional soviets, with the one in Tashkent being the most influential. From the outset it included both the Bolshevik and Menshevik factions of the Social Democrats, Socialist Revolutionaries, and other parties. The third power base was the National Center of the Turkestan Muslims (Turkistan millii shurasi), comprised of various organizations representing the Muslim population. Among these were a reformist Islamic Council (Shurosi-islamia) and a conservative Association of Ulamas (Djamiati-ulamo). The National Center was headed by a Kazakh by the name of Mustafa Chokaev,[2] who previously had worked closely with the Russian Cadet Party.

Both the soviets, which drew mainly on the Russian-speaking population, and the Muslim organizations extended their loyalty to the Provisional Government that Alexander Kerensky had formed in Petrograd. Both also sent delegates to the Turkestan committee. In addition to these organizations, many other national, professional, and political associations also sprang up, from time to time entering into coalitions and even influencing the course of events.

The alliance among this diverse array of forces that emerged following the February Revolution was based upon the Kerensky government's recognition that all citizens of Russia enjoyed equal rights, and its commitment to hold general elections for a Constitutional Assembly based on proportional representation. This satisfied the liberal parties, which viewed democracy as their political goal, and also the various socialist forces that sought to increase the representation of the lowest classes. This also pleased non-Russian elites, particularly Muslims, since it could significantly enhance their influence in the capital and possibly gain a degree of control over the former colonial territories on the periphery.

At the same time, a tough struggle broke out among and within the parties over leadership, the future organization of Turkestan, and related societal reforms. This continued throughout 1917. Some Muslim leaders leaned toward socialism, others supported the type of modernization promoted by the Young Turks in the waning Ottoman Empire, and still others sought to institute rule based on sharia law. As ideological and factional clashes sharpened in Petrograd, the struggle intensified in Turkestan as well. It was also fed by social tensions that arose from cutbacks in the delivery of the wheat on which Turkestan depended, and the subsequent spread of hunger. All of this reinforced mutual suspicions, accusations, and hostility.

At the beginning of October 1917, reports reached Turkestan that Bolsheviks and Left Socialist Revolutionaries had organized an armed uprising. This called to action the Tashkent-based Soviet of Workers' and Soldiers' Deputies. Using its influence among the troops, the Soviet expelled the Turkestan Committee, which had lost its legitimacy, and proclaimed a new authority comprised of leftist radicals but including no representative from among the Muslims. On November 15, 1917 the left-wing parties from Tashkent held a Third Regional Congress of the Soviet of Workers' and Soldiers' Deputies. This assembly explicitly declared that "Muslim participation in the highest revolutionary bodies is for now unacceptable due to the complete uncertainty that exists regarding the attitude of the indigenous population toward the Soviet of Workers' and Peasants' Deputies. It is also ruled out because the indigenous population has no proletarian class organizations of the kind that the Bolsheviks would be prepared to welcome into the highest regional authority."[3] In November the soviets created a new administrative body called the Turkestan Council of People's Commissars, with a Russian Bolshevik named Fedor Kolesov as its chairman.

The Turkestan Autonomous Government

Throughout 1917 it seemed that these political tempests would not penetrate into the Ferghana province. The centralized and semi-military structures of Russia's colonial administration had only recently been introduced there and were now gradually losing control over the situation in the valley. Their efforts were increasingly concentrated on the protection of the city of Tashkent and especially its Russian-speaking residents. In the Muslim quarters of cities and especially in the rural areas where the majority of the indigenous population lived, district and rural institutions gained in importance, thanks both to the formal and informal authority vested in them, and to their many informal connections with the local society. Particularly important were the *kurbashi*s, who served as police chiefs in Muslim urban quarters and were the only figures with legal access to weapons and the right to use force. All this helped split society into numerous antagonistic yet simultaneously compromise-seeking groups and factions.

Deteriorating economic conditions also caused mounting tensions in the Ferghana Valley. Cotton producers faced the collapse of commodity prices and the disappearance of buyers. The area of land under cotton cultivation shrank by 54.4 percent between 1915 and 1916.[4] However, the peasants could not replace the land with corn because they had no access to credit with which to buy seeds. Therefore, corn acreage shrank by 41 percent in the same period.[5] Even before the war Ferghana had grown only half of the corn it needed, and now corn deliveries from other regions fell, spreading hunger among significant parts of an already jobless populace.

Crucial developments in the winter of 1917–18 harshly destabilized conditions throughout the region, and made the Ferghana Valley the center of Turkestan's political life. Turkestan On November 26, 1917 a Fourth Extraordinary Regional Congress of Muslims convened at Kokand, formerly the capital of the Kokand Khanate and still one of the major economic centers of the valley. The Congress consisted of some 200 delegates, more than half of whom came from the Ferghana Valley itself. At the top of the agenda was the issue of Turkestan's independence. Ubaidulla Hodjaev made a report justifying the need for a declaration of independence. He noted that "There is no hope now for convoking an All-Russia Constituent Assembly since most of the nations that formerly were part of Russia have left in opposition to the Bolshevik usurpers."[6] In the end the delegates adopted the following resolution:

> The Fourth Extraordinary All-Muslim Regional Congress, expressing the will of the peoples of Turkestan to attain self-determination on the basis of principles annunciated by the great Russian revolution [of February, 1917], declares Turkestan's autonomy within a union with the Russian Federal Republic. [The form of the new autonomous government] will be decided by a Constituent Assembly of Turkestan, which should be convened at the earliest possible date. This Congress solemnly affirms that the rights of all national minorities inhabiting Turkestan will be protected in every possible way.[7]

A more radical proposal to announce an independence from Russia did not receive a majority of the votes. Finally, the congress elected a Provisional Government of Autonomous Turkestan, initially headed by a Kazakh named Muhammadjan

Tynyshpaev, a former member of the Second Russian State Duma. He was later succeeded by Chokai. Both were former members of the Turkestan Committee. Also elected was the Provisional People's Council, which exercised parliamentary powers. The future parliament, the People's Assembly, was supposed to have fifty-four members, with fully a third of its places reserved for the "European" part of the population.

The Bolsheviks called the self-proclaimed Muslim government the "Kokand Autonomy." It was an attempt by various anti-Bolshevik forces to forge a legitimate authority that could counterbalance the Soviets. This attempt was in many respects involuntary, and had been provoked by the Bolsheviks' unwillingness to share power with Muslims. The anti-Bolshevik forces enjoyed the support of the local population, but their leaders were divided sharply between moderate socialists, nationalist reformers, and conservative Islamists. Such ideological divisions probably doomed them from the start. They tried to deflect the accusation that they were anti-Russian. At the same time they addressed an appeal to the Petrograd Bolsheviks, reminding them that the Petrograd Soviet, in its "Declaration of the Rights of the Peoples of Russia," had promised autonomy to Muslims. At the same time they appealed to the Bolsheviks' adversaries, particularly to General Alexander Dutov,[8] in whom they saw a real military force that could be mobilized against the usurpers in Tashkent.

This "project" was relevant to the Ferghana Valley, albeit indirectly. Kokand was chosen as a meeting place merely because it was sufficiently distant from Tashkent as to avoid an immediately reprisal. Even so, Kokand immediately became an important symbol of the anti-Bolshevik opposition. The interests of the Muslim opposition extended beyond the Ferghana Valley to Tashkent, where major resources were concentrated, and many of its leaders looked even further—to Orenburg and Ufa, where Kazakhs, Bashkirs, and other Muslim peoples were busily organizing governments. However, the Kokand "autonomists" in the end failed to enlist the support of Muslims elsewhere in Turkestan and even in Tashkent. The emir of Bukhara withheld his support. They did not identify their movement as a successor to the Kokand Khanate. Instead, they mainly invoked values that were intelligible mainly to Muslim reformers and Russians, and which would be understood in Petrograd and in the European capitals to which they appealed for support.

Even the population of the Ferghana Valley was by and large indifferent to calls by the new government for Turkestani autonomy, unsupported as they were by military and economic power. The Cadet Party member Chokaev and the Bolshevik Kolesov were equally alien to them.[9] The "autonomists" attempted to create their own armed-squads headed by the Russian Tatar and Muslim, Mahdi Chanyshev. However, an irreconcilably fractious officer of the "Kokand People's Police" named Ergashbai promptly seized control and escalated the conflict among the various factions, effectively preventing them from rallying together in opposition to the Bolsheviks and making them easy prey to their enemies.

While leaders of the Turkestan autonomy were nursing their internal antagonisms and waiting on developments in Petrograd, where the situation remained uncertain until the Constituent Assembly was convoked, Russian army soldiers based in Tashkent and the Ferghana region took decisive action. A small band of soldiers seized a fortress in Kokand and proclaimed the creation of a Revolutionary Committee (Revkom) headed by a Bolshevik named Efim Babushkin. Similar revkoms were set up in Skobelev (now Ferghana City), the new administrative center of Ferghana province, and in Namangan and Andijan. This meant that, in effect, all units of the former tsarist army still based in the Ferghana Valley had gone over to the Bolsheviks.

In late January 1918, the Fourth Congress of Soviets of the Turkestan Region outlawed the Kokand autonomous government and ordered the arrest of all its leaders. It confiscated the autonomous government's monetary assets in Tashkent and Kokand banks. Artillery squadrons were sent from Tashkent and other cities in the Ferghana Valley to support the beleaguered post in Kokand. Among members of the armed squads of Red Guard who arrived at Kokand were resident local Armenians. Seeing the growing strength of the Muslims and fearing a repeat of the anti-Armenian pogroms that recently had occurred in the Ottoman Empire, they joined with the Dashnaktsyutun party as part of the Red Guards.[10] They violently suppressed every attempt by the Turkestan autonomists and Ergashbai's forces to maintain control over Kokand, resulting in large-scale destruction and numerous casualties among the city's civilian population. The newspaper *Ulug Turkiston* (Great Turkestan) reported that:

> One-third of the old city was reduced to ruins. Piles of corpses, many of them completely burned, are everywhere . . . Thousands of Kokand people have been left without a roof over their head . . . It is worse than after a war . . . The exact number of the casualties has not been reported but estimates put the number at no less than ten thousand.[11]

Ergashbai set up base in his native village of Bachkir, 20 kilometers from Kokand, and began assembling fighters there. Increasingly, the struggle of Muslim volunteer detachments against the Red Guards and Armenians assumed a religious character. As violence spread throughout the Muslim "old towns" and the villages, initiative on the Muslim side passed from leaders of the "autonomy" movement to local leaders. Chokaev and other autonomist leaders fled Ferghana and Turkestan.

In this manner, what began as a confrontation between the Soviets and the "Turkestan Autonomy" turned into a general open conflict among diverse forces that spread across the Ferghana Valley. The universal resort to force was of paramount importance, because it had the effect of delegitimizing all major governing institutions. The conflict between the Bolsheviks and Muslims resulted in the former having no reliable allies for negotiations and no permanent contacts with the local population, which only strengthened the hand of local radicals who had no interest in dialogue. The defeat of the autonomist reformers removed the last leaders with an interest in, or experience at, compromise. Now the Turkestan region was left in the hands of those advocating active resistance, with the Ferghana Valley in particular becoming one of its main centers.

The Anti-Soviet War in the Ferghana Valley

The new Bolshevik government achieved a major success by defeating the Turkestan Autonomy at the start of 1918. But even this demonstrated the Bolsheviks' military power, it did not leave them in full political and military control over the Ferghana Valley. The Soviet government had stripped Turkestan of autonomy and declared it part of the Russian Socialist Republic, but the region remained in the hands of a variety of factions and local forces that often acted on their own authority and understood the revolutionary goals in their own way. Most Russian-speaking units of the tsarist army deployed in Ferghana came over to the Bolsheviks' side. They were joined by Austro-Hungarian prisoners of war who had been sent to the areas during World War I and whom the Bolsheviks had managed to draw to their side. Also exercising significant influence were well-organized and heavily armed Armenian units, which distinguished themselves in combat by their notable ferocity and determination. A representative of these Armenian brotherhoods was appointed chairman of the Kokand Soviet, while other members assumed important positions in Andijan. The Soviets also enjoyed the support of railway, mining and oil workers, as well as the small Russian population in the cities of the Ferghana Valley, above all the city of Skobelev. Also, a considerable number of local Muslims supported the Bolsheviks, which gave the conflict the character of a civil war.

Resistance against the Soviet government was no less fragmented. It included groups of the most diverse backgrounds, political interests, and power. Although this resistance was complex and comprised many different streams, it was and is commonly referred to under the single name of *basmachestvo*.[12] This movement emerged less as a political resistance to the Bolshevik regime, although that factor was present, than as a reaction to the breakdown of local authority and the collapse of the area's economy. The violence of the radically inclined Bolsheviks and Armenian militants also played an important causal role, especially in the early phase of fighting, giving rise to widespread discontent and a desire for revenge against them.

At first the majority of *kurbashis*, the local police who led rebel squads in the Ferghana Valley, were neither politicians nor ideologues. They did not develop a clear political program, but instead stood up for the interests of local communities and clans. Their horizons were defined by their Muslim identity and sense of belonging to an Islamic community, and it was this which served as a significant factor in mobilizing and uniting the resistance. Closely integrated with their very local environments, *kurbashis* entered into complex alliances with and against the Bolsheviks, fiercely fought against each other, and readily made and broke alliances.

Scores of resistance fighters operated in Ferghana. Among the largest and most famous were the squads of Mullah Ergash in the Kokand district (replacing Ergash-bai, who perished in the spring of 1918), Madaminbek (Muhammad-Amin Bek) and Kurshirmat (Sher-Muhammad Bek) in the district of Margilan, Aman-Pahlavon, Kabul, Rahmankul in Namangan county, Hol-Hodja in Osh county, and Ahunjon, Parpi, and Mahkam-Hodja in Andijan district. At one time or another each of these groups numbered several thousand men, with smaller detachments active in many villages. Only nominally subordinated to "large" *kurbashi* squadrons, they acted mainly on their own authority. The total number of these military alignments in various years ranged from twenty to sixty.[13]

Some squads hid in mountains and foothills, where regular Bolshevik units could not easily reach them, and from time to time carried out attacks on the Red Army home bases and garrisons. This backbone was well armed, had seen active service, and had been trained by a number of Russian military officers, as well as by Ottoman-Turkish and Afghan prisoners of war. Regular peasants made up a significant part of the rebel bands. Most lived at home and led simple lives, ready when needed to mobilize rapidly to participate in large-scale campaigns in suburban areas, towns, and railway stations. There were also many *basmachi* informers and adherents who collected fodder and food supplies. Such semi-partisans significantly complicated the Bolsheviks' operations, and in the end made their military victory impossible.

Kurbashis, in an effort to coordinate their activities, occasionally held conferences (*kurultai*) to try to formulate some kind of common platform. As early as the spring of 1918 the *kurbashi* council elected Mullah Ergash as the single "leader of the Muslims" (*amir-al-muslimin*). In the spring of the same year another influential *kurbashi* by the name of Madaminbek assumed this honorary title. Despite clashes and hostilities among rebel leaders, Ergash managed to unite most of the *kurbashis* under his leadership. In the spring of 1919 these strengthened and united squads carried out a number of large-scale operations and attacks on the cities of Skobelev, Chust, Andijan, and Namangan.

Other forces opposing the Bolsheviks tried to establish relations with the *kurbashis* of the Ferghana Valley. Among them were *kurbashis* from Djamiati-ulamo and Shurosi-islamia, Turkic nationalists from among the Tatar-Bashkirs and Kazakhs, members of the White Guard, Englishmen, and various authority figures from Bukhara and even from Afghanistan. All of them provided organizational and military support to the resistance forces, offering ideological programs and slogans as well.

Russian settlers and Cossacks, concentrated mainly on the eastern part of the Ferghana Valley, tried valiantly to defend themselves both from the Muslims and from the "Soviet workers." In the summer of 1918 they created a Peasant Army under the leadership of Konstantin Monstrov. By September 1919 Monstrov reached an agreement with Madaminbek to carry out joint operations against the Red Army. In the fall of the same year the rebels temporarily occupied Osh, boldly attacked Old Margilan, and laid siege to Andijan. At this moment it seemed that the united forces of the *basmachi* and peasant settlers could turn the tide and take full control of the valley. During the same fall they proclaimed the creation of a Provisional Autonomous Government of the Ferghana Valley.

However, by this time the military initiative wash passing into the Bolsheviks' hands. Their forces were now much better equipped than formerly, thanks to their ability to run the blockade between central Russia and Turkestan. Active combat units deployed to the Ferghana Valley, including a Volga Tatar Rifle Brigade, enabled them to conduct a series of large-scale operations against the *kurbashis* and the Peasant Army. In January 1920, Mullah Ergash's faction met its Waterloo in the vicinity of the Bachkir fort in western Ferghana. At the same time, the seizure of the fort at Gulcha led to the capture not only of the leadership of the Peasant Army but of Monstrov himself. In February and March the Red Army attacked the squads of Madaminbek, Kurshirmat, and Hol-Hodja in the central region of the Ferghana Valley. The Reds went on to occupy major settlements in the foothills, driving the *basmachi* into the mountains and cutting off their communications with the flatlands, on which they had depended for food and equipment.

Following up on their successes in the field, the Bolsheviks approached selected *kurbashis* with proposals to surrender and join the victors. This was part of a new strategy which the Turkestan Commission had brought from Moscow and which the Bolsheviks' new leaders in Tashkent announced in 1919.[14] The core of this strategy was to enlist local forces in the Bolsheviks' ranks. Within the Communist Party they created a Regional Muslim Bureau headed by Turar Ryskulov, and Party cells that included many Muslim public figures and supporters of reforms. They adopted resolutions condemning the actions of the "Armenian instigators," and orders were given to disarm the Armenian units. The Muslim Bureau branded *basmachi* as "desperate peasants" but offered amnesty to members of the resistance. In the fall of 1919 a Muslim Communist named Nizamiddin Hodjaev was appointed head of the Ferghana Revcom. He actively supported negotiating with the rebels and ending the confiscation of corn, which were main sources of rural animosity toward the authorities. He also advocated that sharia courts be legalized. Influential Muslim clergymen were invited to participate in the negotiations with the *kurbashis*.

The new policy gained even more momentum with the election of Ryskulov, in January 1920, to the post of chairman of the authoritative Central Executive Committee of the Communist Party in Turkestan. This culminated in the signing on March 6, 1920 in Old Margilan of a treaty with Madaminbek, who bound himself "to defend the Soviet government from its enemies in every possible way." In return, the Bolsheviks promised to preserve the people's right to live under the laws of Islam. Indeed, the treaty states explicitly that "The Soviet government will preserve the principles of sharia law while protecting the interests of working people in Turkestan. It grants the Muslim population the right to live according to this sharia law as it relates to the local conditions and traditions of the population."[15] Finally, the *kurbashi* cavalry were incorporated as combat units of the red Army.

Madaminbek was killed in May 1920, while negotiating to surrender. In the wake of this, Kurshirmat and Hol-Hodja, who also had thought of surrender, now declared the creation of an Islamic state of Turkestan and vowed to continue the struggle against the Bolsheviks. The rebels elected Kurshirmat as their head. At the same time Mikhail Frunze and Valerian Kuibyshev, the most powerful members of the Turkestan Commission, sidelined Ryskulov and his supporters on the Muslim Bureau and rewrote many of the agreements with the *kurbashis*. This caused a number of former *kurbashis* to quit the Red Army and rejoin the resistance movement. Frunze ordered severe measures against all who opposed the Soviets. The Reds should "cease all negotiations with the gang leaders. . . . All members of the *basmachi* gangs should be considered robbers and enemies of the people and must be executed on the spot. And persons or groups found guilty of aiding the *basmachi* will be subject to the most severe punishment under the laws of war."[16]

Fighting flared up once again during the summer of 1920, although by now the rebel forces were much weaker and numbered not more than 6,000 fighters in total. Attacks on the *kurbashis* gained new momentum during the fall. Newly reinforced Red Army regulars, now backed by artillery and even aircraft, defeated the *kurbashis* in central and eastern Ferghana, which left practically the entire valley under the Soviets' control. Operations continued against separate large detachments late in 1921 and early in 1922, but these were purely local affairs.

In conclusion, let us ask about the loss of lives in this war and the "price" that society paid during this period of transition. The Ferghana Valley suffered more heavily than practically any other area of Central Asia. Obviously, nobody at the time was tallying the exact number of victims. Various documents of the time offer their versions of the totals; these figures cannot be substantiated, but we can arrive at tentative numbers on the losses by comparing relatively reliable data on the population of the Ferghana province in 1914 and again in 1926. The two extant census figures for 1914 are 2,190,424 and 2,130,700, the difference between them a modest 60,000.[17] If we assume an annual natural increase in population of 1.4 percent, then the population of the Ferghana province by 1926 should have been on the order of 2,588,116 or 2,482,788. However, the actual census for 1926 reported a total of only 2,037,484.[18] Over the intervening twelve-year-period, the missing number somewhere between 550,632 and 445,304 people. This figure includes all the unborn for the period, as well as those who died prematurely as a result of starvation, disease, or in combat operations, as well as those who simply left the area. Between 1916 and 1922 the birth rate almost certainly declined. So, if we reduce the annual rate of increase from 1.4 percent to 1 percent, then the shortfall falls to somewhere between 430,740 and 339,670 people. Thus, one may reasonably conclude that between a third and a half million people perished in the war.

Policies of the 1920s

At the beginning of the 1920s the Bolsheviks substantially modified their policies, moving away from confrontation and entering into tactical and strategic alliances with various forces and factions within the society. This was epitomized by the New Economic Policy (NEP), which allowed non-proletarian organizations to operate in the economic, administrative, and cultural realms. In the culturally alien periphery, including Turkestan, the Bolsheviks pursued a similar strategy of multi-sided alliances.

The combination of more active military operations and tactical collaborations with various local factions enabled the Soviet government to establish firm control over the Ferghana Valley. By abandoning its brutal approach, adopting more flexible tactics, and utilizing reformist and anti-imperial rhetoric, the Bolsheviks managed rather quickly to restore relations with the Central Asian elite. They engaged its members as intermediaries with the Muslim community, as partners in the process of reform and modernization, and as assistants in the imposition of new systems of governance and control. While each side pursued its own interests, they both wanted an end to hostilities and the restoration of stability.

The Soviet government signaled its willingness to cooperate with the most diverse groups, including Jadids from Bukhara and Turkestan, members of the Kazakh intelligentsia who had received Russian educations, Muslim reformers, nationalists, and others. With the help of a few timely concessions, the Soviet government co-opted members of these elites by giving them positions in government agencies and party institutions, and by granting them power in the local administrations. In return, the Party demanded that the elites be loyal and parrot the Bolsheviks' class rhetoric.

This new approach consisted not only of deals and agreements but of deliberate efforts to set various groups against each other. This resulted in direct clashes, which in turn enabled the Soviet authorities to impose themselves as arbitrators. A principal feature of the more conciliatory side of the policy was to recognize Islam and incorporate it into the legal domain. Religious schools, sharia courts, and *waqfs* were all legalized, and Muslim institutions were granted the inalienable right to land and immovable property.[19] By legalizing and preserving key Muslim institutions in exchange for the Muslims' loyalty, the government drew Muslim conservatives to its side. In doing this the Soviet government pursued a policy similar to that of the Russian empire, which also preserved and even legalized Muslim institutions in return for the loyalty of Muslim elites.

According to 1927 data on the Uzbekistan part of the Ferghana Valley, there were 99 schools and 11 madrassas in the Khujand district, 162 schools and 37 madrassas in Kokand district, 461 schools and 23 madrassas in the Andijan district, and 78 schools in the two southernmost cantons of Kyrgyzia.[20] Data from the *waqf* departments of the People's Commissariat of Education indicate that *waqf* revenues for the same year (excluding hidden costs) totaled 367 rubles for Khujand, 1,995 rubles for Kokand, 258 rubles for Andijan, 255 rubles for Namangan, 212 for Margilan, and 75 rubles for Kanibadam.[21] The actual assets of Muslim institutions were much higher than these figures suggest, since mosques and madrassas maintained many "off the books" *waqfs* with tens of thousands of rubles in revenues.

An important Soviet initiative in the Ferghana Valley was the establishment of "clerical administrations" (*mahkama-i-shariat*) in the major cities and then in the villages as well. The task of these bodies was to control the activities of the mosques. They generally worked through proxies, a clerical fifth column in mosque organizations who, according to one observer, "pushed through resolutions in support of countries and peoples oppressed by the imperialists" and endlessly expressed their allegiance to the Soviet government in order to gain its support.[22] A Communist Party official wrote sarcastically that "For the greatest possible show, at a large public meeting in Margilan they followed a reactionary speech by a Muslim cleric with the playing of the *Internationale*."[23]

The government helped these clerical stooges deal with the conservative religious elites, particularly the hereditary holy men or *ishans*. Yet at the same time it restrained them, preventing them from forming independent clerical administrations and from communicating with Muslim clerics in central Russia. Soviet authorities were particularly careful to observe the activities of reformers among them.

The Bolsheviks gradually managed to restore the Ferghana Valley's economic life. In order to restore the central Russian textile industry, the government became interested in resuming large-scale cotton deliveries from the region. On its side, the people of Ferghana needed grain and manufactured goods which they could not obtain on their own. The resulting exchange contributed to social stability and strengthened the authority of the Soviets, making them all the more resolute in their efforts to reform society along the lines of their communist project.

The Bolsheviks aimed to create groups and forces through which they could exercise control over the region, pursue reforms, and weaken unreliable and potentially dangerous forces. Their approach combined administrative changes, attempts to reform water-management, financial subsidies, and efforts to "emancipate" women. To the same end they also took up the redistribution of land. The chief tool which the Soviets used to mobilize support for redistributing land along class lines was the Union of Paupers and Day Laborers, or Koshchi. In 1921 branches of this Union were set up in all counties and districts of the Ferghana Valley. Its head was Yuldash Akhunbabaev, who hailed from the outskirts of Margilan.

The first attempt at land and water reform in the Ferghana Valley was undertaken in 1921 in the Kanibadam district of Kokand, the Jalalabad district of Andijan, and in some areas of Osh County. One thousand six hundred and eighteen households were exiled, most of them wealthy Russian and Ukrainian settlers (*kulaks*), and more than 45,000 hectares or 110,000 acres of land were confiscated and distributed among members of Koshchi.[24]

A still larger-scale land and water reform was attempted in 1925–26. The goal was to transfer land from non-working households to farmers and paupers. In total, about 136,000 hectares or 337,000 acres in the Ferghana Valley were transferred to a land fund. The land was then distributed among 42,000 poor households.[25] These economic reforms were not sweeping and did not fundamentally change conditions within society, the status of its major groups, or system of governance. However, they served a critical function of creating loyal factions and classes within the population, advancing new leaders, and reallocating resources and power—all to the benefit of the Soviet government.

The Process of Administrative and National Delineation

An important dimension of the Bolsheviks' policy of strengthening their position in the non-Russian areas of the former Russian empire was to redraw or re-delineate national and administrative borders. This was seen as an essential step toward efficient control and modernization in the region. As early as 1920, following Ryskulov's promulgation of the plan to create a "Turkic Republic," Moscow began discussing the possibility of dividing Turkestan along ethnic or national lines. Vladimir Lenin himself set out the procedure for doing so:

1. Authorize the creation of maps (ethnographic and other ones) of Turkestan showing its division into Uzbekia, Kyrgyzia,[26] and Turkmenia.
2. Then determine the possibility of merging or dividing these three areas.[27]

Lenin proposed this as a response to what he saw as a dangerous process of consolidation occurring among the Muslim elite. Even though the Soviet government did not yet reach a decision to redraw the borders, the Uzbeks and Turkmen were henceforth accepted as national groups and would be treated as such within major official institutions at all levels.

The effort to find an effective balance between the "rights of peoples to national self-determination" and the organization of administrative and economic life continued. In 1922 the government developed a general plan for the administrative division of the Republic of Turkestan. That same year a group of Soviet and Communist Party activists from the Semireche (Seven Rivers) and Syr Darya provinces declared that the Kara-Kyrgyz, or "Black" Kyrgyz, should enjoy the rights of a separate people. A new project thus emerged, with the goal of creating a separate administrative unit for these people, the "Mountainous Province." Following stormy discussions, however, this plan was dropped.[28] In 1923 communists from the Ferghana Valley sent Tashkent a draft proposal calling for the creation of a separate and autonomous Ferghana province within the Republic of Turkestan. Officials in Tashkent promptly rejected this proposal, labeling it a "political mistake." In doing so they indicated that local authorities did not yet consider the issue of territorial administration from the perspective of ethnic or national distinctions. All such proposals to redraw boundaries arose from a struggle between Tashkent and local elites on how to redistribute powers, resources, and authority among them.

The idea of redrawing the borders along ethnic or national lines did not originate in Central Asia, but had been brought to the region from without, namely Moscow. It first appeared on the agenda at the end of 1923. This time it was decided to incorporate into the discussion the "Bukhara Republic" and the "Khorezm Republic," along with the "Turkestan Republic."[29] In the spring of 1924 the central government managed to persuade local elites of the need to pursue these reforms. Then, on June 12, 1924, the Politburo of the Central Committee of the Russian Communist Party adopted a resolution "On the National Delineation of the Central Asian Republics." This document laid the foundations of the delineation process that followed.

The original plan for delineating the borders sought to merge most of Central Asia into a single powerful Republic of Uzbekistan that would become a "union republic" of the USSR as a whole. Parts of the regional territory were also designated for inclusion into a Republic of Turkmenistan, which would also become a "union republic" of the USSR, while still other areas were to be incorporated into Kazakhstan, which since 1920 had existed as an autonomous national republic within the Russian Soviet Federated Socialist Republic (RSFSR). It was also planned to create three "autonomous regions," with the Tajiks to acquire such a status within Uzbekistan, Kara-Kalpakia to become an autonomous region within Kazakhstan, and Kara-Kyrgyzia to become part of either Kazakhstan or of the RSFSR.

Responsibility for working out the borders of the proposed new republics was assigned to the Central Asian Bureau of the Central Committee of the Russian Community Party. Chairing the Bureau's "territorial committee" was Isaac Zelenskii, although the work was administered by his deputy, a Latvian named Otto Karklin. Supervising the project as a whole was Josef Stalin.

Membership of Zelenskii's "territorial committee" included Uzbeks (e.g., Rakhimbaev, Islamov, Khodjaev, Segizbaev, Homuthanov, Maksumov, Manzhara, Sultan-Kary), Turkmen (e.g., Naitakov, Atabaev, Nazarov, Paskutskii), Kazakhs (e.g., Hodzhanov, Asfendiiarov, Kuchukovskii, Ambekov), and Kyrgyz (e.g., Tokbaev, Aidarbekov, Abdrakhmanov, Khudaikulov, Sulembaev, Lipatov), as well as Tajiks (Khadzhibaev, Imanov) and Kara-Kalpaks. The planning process proved difficult. All officials participating in the discussions were forbidden to travel until the process was completed. Any public mention of the discussions and especially of the antagonisms emerging in the process was also strictly outlawed until such time as the leaders had reached a common decision.

In essence, the delineation process turned on the balancing of contradictory alliances between the Bolsheviks and the diverse elites of Central Asia. Within the region itself the process of drawing new borders consolidated a new distribution of power and resources at both the practical and symbolic levels. Jadids, Young Bukharans, and Turkestan Muslim reformers had long wished to see the creation of a "united Turkestan." The creation of "Uzbekistan" on the territory of the earlier provinces of Bukhara and Turkestan (Khorezm was added later) represented a particular concession to them.[30] As the capital of this new state the drafters rejected Tashkent, with its Russian "imperial" connotations, and instead chose the ancient city of Samarkand. This underscored the element of historical continuity with pre-Russian times and celebrated the settled, Muslim, and bilingual (Turco-Persian) culture of the population of that city. At the same time, by separating from Uzbekistan the Kazakh and Turkmen lands populated by former or current nomads, the drafters limited any possible pan-Turkic ambitions the Uzbek leaders may have harbored, and created political and symbolic "counterbalances" to them. This administrative separation of nomadic cultures from settled ones arose directly from the previous imperial tradition, which assumed the nomadic peoples to be more open to modernization and Russification than the oasis dwellers. In this connection, it is worth noting that the commission seriously considered the possibility of transferring "Russian" Tashkent to Kazakhstan.

Viewed in the context of these discussions, the Ferghana Valley was on the periphery of the main transformations taking place, and far removed from the main symbolic centers. The one important intrigue in the valley concerned the borders of the proposed Kara-Kyrgyz Autonomous Region. In the end it was decided to assign the region, with its nomadic population, either to the RFSFR or to the new republic of Kazakhstan.[31] This issue had been hotly disputed since 1922. The reason the issue was decided as it was is because Kyrgyz activists who were lobbying for their own administrative unit succeeded in gaining ideological and personal support from within the central government.

The Uzbek side put forward its own vision for the national borders. It did not object to the plan to create a Kara-Kyrgyz Autonomous Region and easily consented to the transfer of parts of the Ferghana Valley to the RSFSR. It assumed this stance as part of the play over the more complex and urgent issue of Tashkent, to which Kazakhstan also laid claim. By sacrificing the economically insignificant piedmont areas of the Tian Shan Mountains and Alai Valley, the Uzbek side gained a powerful bargaining chip in advancing its claims in other areas. By volunteering to give up these marginal areas of the Ferghana Valley, Uzbek leaders absolved themselves of the charge that they were uncompromising and wanted to keep territories everywhere under their control.

The process of dividing the Ferghana Valley into "Uzbek" and "Kara-Kyrgyz" parts involved a variety of issues that related directly to the borders themselves. The first of these concerned the characteristics by which a person qualified as being "Uzbek" or "Kara-Kyrgyz," and how to handle groups whose linguistic and cultural identity was unclear. The second issue concerned the process of territorial division in areas where "Uzbeks" and "Kara-Kyrgyz" lived discretely or in close proximity, and at the same time-shared pastures, roads, and irrigation systems. The third issue concerned the manner in which a Kara-Kyrgyz Autonomous Region could develop its economy to the point that it could exist as an independent administrative unit. Members of the Uzbek and Kara-Kyrgyz commissions held robust debates on these issues over the summer of 1924, in the course of which both sides sought to strike a balance between the various arguments, interests, and lobbying efforts.

Any effort to create a separate administrative entity for nomadic and mountainous peoples who were not urban dwellers was bound to come up against the problem of economic viability. Without cities that could serve as centers of trade, administration, and culture, an independent "national" life for Kara-Kyrgyzia was inconceivable. The cities of the Ferghana Valley were inhabited mainly by "Uzbeks"[32] and other groups who were clearly part of the settled population, and by no stretch of the imagination could be recast as "Kara-Kyrgyz" nomads. The one way to solve this was to shift one of the Ferghana cities populated mainly by Uzbeks into the Kara-Kyrgyz Autonomous Region. Members of the commission who represented the future Uzbekistan had to accept this change. The choice fell on the easternmost center of the valley, namely Osh, around which many nomads were living. Although the city was small, it adjoined the sacred mountain known as Tahti-Sulaiman (Solomon Throne), which attracted many pilgrims and gave Osh a significant reputation.

In spite of this, the Kara-Kyrgyz negotiators insisted on the transfer to Kara-Kyrgyzia of Andijan, one of the largest administrative and business centers of the valley. Its supporters underlined the city's importance to those Kara-Kyrgyz who inhabited the eastern part of the Ferghana Valley, and argued that it had to be incorporated into the autonomous region for the area to fulfill its economic potential. The Uzbek side responded by pointing out that ethnic Uzbeks constituted a substantial majority of the population of Osh, and that they had every right to national self-determination. In this case, the ethnic or national argument appeared more convincing than the economic one.

On August 20, 1924 these and other contentious issues were submitted for discussion to the Territorial Committee. This body decided to transfer the formerly nomadic districts of Kokand, Namangan, and Margilan counties and some separate rural communities to the Kara-Kyrgyz Autonomous Region, while keeping the primarily settled districts within Uzbekistan. The district of Osh, excluding certain territories, was transferred whole to Kara-Kyrgyzia. Both sides eventually agreed with this decision, and so the issue of borders between the two republics was resolved. The outcome was duly reported by Stalin. It was then decided that the remaining issues in contention could be considered later.

In October 1924, the highest authorities in Moscow decided in favor of the plan to create new national republics and regions in Central Asia. At the close of that year, representatives of Kara-Kyrgyzia moved from Tashkent to Pishpek (later Frunze, now Bishkek), which became the capital of the newly formed region.[33] Throughout the winter and summer of 1925, new governing structures and institutions were being created and elections held to fill administrative positions. In May 1925 the Kara-Kyrgyz Autonomous Region was renamed Kyrgyzia.

No sooner were the major new institutions constituted than the question of adjusting the boundaries between Uzbekistan and Kyrgyzia arose. Kyrgyz officials presented an entire list of new territorial claims. The provincial Commission on Delineation, which included T. Divnogorskii, L. Zulfibaev, L. Defe, and others, set forth these claims in November 1925. At stake were uninhabited territories, separate settlements, and entire districts. The Kyrgyz authorities insisted that all these territories be transferred to the autonomous region. The leaders of Kyrgyzia also raised the question of settlements in a number of areas of the former Margilan and Osh districts that had been transferred to Uzbekistan, among them Bulakbashi, Kulinsk, and Markhamat. Beyond this, they proposed a new boundary in the former Andijan and Namangan districts. Finally, they put forward some claims affecting the modified boundaries of the former Kokand district, including proposals that certain settlements in the Sokh River Valley be transferred to Kyrgyzia.

Kyrgyz lobbyists actively used ethnographic arguments whenever the opportunity presented itself. Specifically, they pointed to the fact that the population of many settlements in Ferghana's east, former Andijan, Margilan, and certain districts of Osh were of "non-Uzbek" ethnicity. The exchanges on these matters were replete with references to the populations as "Turks," "Kipchaks," "Kashgaris," and "Tajiks." The "Turks," while close to the Uzbeks by language and traits of every-day life, led a nomadic way of life and therefore had close ties with the Kyrgyz. For purposes of delineation they could well be classified as people from the "nomadic" part of the valley. The Kipchaks were former nomads who also had close links with the Kyrgyz. Further, the Kyrgyz argued that the Kashgaris, many of whom registered under the new name of "Uyghur,"[34] and the Tajiks were distinct nationalities and should not automatically be counted on the Uzbek side when determining the national majority in a given district.

Viewing all of these claims as a breach of the previously reached balance of interests, the Uzbek authorities responded by again raising the issue of the Uzbek-populated city of Osh and the Osh district, which they proposed to annex to Uzbekistan. Also, Uzbekistan laid claim to Margilan's former Aravan district, which had been transferred to Kyrgyzia, and part of the Aim district that had been removed from Andijan. In these and other cases the Uzbek side alleged that partition would disrupt the integrity of irrigation systems, and that river heads that had long been used to irrigate "Uzbek" land had ended up as part of the Kyrgyzia region. To compensate for this, the Uzbeks proposed to transfer certain piedmont districts (Kashgar-kishlak and Khanabad) to Uzbekistan.

Objections and petitions sent by local people to the authorities exerted pressure on decision-makers both in 1924 and during the discussions of 1925–27. The archives attest that most of them arose from the unwillingness of many residents to become a part of the Kyrgyz region, and their aspirations to remain within Uzbekistan. One of the numerous appeals put it this way:

> From citizens of the Osh region we have heard rumors that a delineation of Central Asian borders is about to be carried out, and that separate Uzbek and Tajik republics and provinces are to be established. We, the 2,250 citizens of the Ichkilik district who signed this appeal, ask the Turkestan Central Executive Committee, in the delineation process, to keep us in the district of Margilan, that is, within the Uzbek republic. For decades we have been engaged in agriculture. There are no divisions among us and the Uzbeks and we live as one family. Our economic life is in every way connected with the Uzbeks. Taking all this into consideration, we hope that the Turkestan Committee will honor our request that we be left as part of the Margilan district of the Uzbek republic.[35]

Similar letters sent by residents of Andijan, Margilan, and Osh districts all mentioned that the local Kyrgyz were on friendly terms with Uzbeks, had long been engaged in agriculture rather than lives of nomadism, and would like to remain within Uzbekistan. "We are now more Uzbek even than those Uzbeks in the city," wrote Osh residents in one such petition.[36] Other reasons cited by those who did not want to be part of Kyrgyzia were its weak economic conditions and the requirement in Kyrgyz schools to study the Kyrgyz language. It is hard to determine whether such appeals were generated by the Uzbeks or genuinely reflect the population's concern over its future. It appears that both motives existed.

Throughout 1926 a series of special commissions on the regulation of frontiers between the Central Asian republics considered all of these mutual claims. The commissions were set up by the Central Executive Committee of the Communist Party of the USSR. Special delegations, sent to the region from Moscow, examined border disputes and adduced arguments on the ground. In 1926 Kyrgyzia received the status of an autonomous republic within the Russian Federated Soviet Republic, buts its lobbying capabilities were no match for those of Uzbekistan. In addition to having received the status of a separate "union republic," Uzbekistan enjoyed strong support from statisticians and economists and had the ability to exert influence in the capital. Notwithstanding this, Moscow sought to strike a compromise while also taking into account the arguments of the weaker side. Various commissions made decisions one after another, each new position being subjected to a barrage of claims, counterclaims, and outright rejection, a pattern repeated over and over. The resulting uncertainty caused a recurring escalation of claims and fresh demands for the government to reconsider the entire issue.[37] But in May 1927, the Presidium of the All-Russian Central Executive Committee decided not to consider any petitions relating to delineation of borders for a period of three years.

The debate over the border between Uzbekistan and the RSFSR, of which the Kyrgyz Autonomous Region was a part until it became a republic, was not the only issue in dispute. Within each "national territory" a complex process of administrative delineation was under way throughout the mid-1920s, and especially between 1925 and 1927. This process also gave rise to clashes over economic and ethnic issues, with the stakes in their outcome being no less important than in the inter-republic conflicts.

With respect to two important areas of the former Ferghana province that remained within Uzbekistan, two options were under consideration: either to preserve Andijan's and Kokand's previous status as two separate jurisdictions, or to merge them into a single administrative district.[38] The choice fell on the second. This in turn led to two further and very different options: either, first, to automatically incorporate the former Andijan and Margilan districts into the Andijan region and merge the Kokand and Namangan districts into the Kokand region, or, second, to incorporate the predominantly agricultural eastern areas of Ferghana into the Andijan region and move the more industrialized central and western parts of the valley into the region of Kokand.[39] The government eventually chose the first of these options. In a parallel move, Kyrgyzia created two new districts in its sector of the Ferghana Valley—Osh and Jalalabad—and proceeded in 1926 to classify them as provinces.

As the Bolsheviks conceived it, new internal borders were delineated in such a way not only to meet the needs of agriculture, but also to respond to the ethnographic composition of the population and to the various groups claiming the status of national minorities. True, the old regions were reorganized into something akin to counties, and these in turn were reorganized into districts, then rural communities, and then rural soviets. But overall, the borders of the new units were fixed on the basis of the national composition of each area. As a member of the Andijan revolutionary committee mentioned in a 1923 report: "When carrying out the delineation the best we can do is strive to avoid situations in which a given minority, unable to form an independent district of its own, is divided among several jurisdictions. But even if members of a given minority constitute only part of the population of a district, they will still have the opportunity of uniting within a single rural community."[40]

The allocation of territories was to be based on the settlement patterns and the population mix. Working on the delineation of borders in 1924–1925, officials made use of existing statistics and the inaccurate 1917 census data. In 1926 the government carried out an All-Union Census. This gave rise to a complex discussion among scholars and officials about the ethnic and national composition of the Central Asian population, and this debate in turn influenced the reconfiguration of administrative borders in the region.[41] The census symbolically fixed the results of the national delineation. Titular names such as "Kazakhs," "Kara-Kalpaks," "Kyrgyz," "Tajiks," "Uzbeks," and "Turkmens" were given to the majority populations of each of the corresponding republics and provinces. In this connection, the most radical change occurred in Uzbekistan. There the term Uzbek was used to designate not only the people formerly known as Sarts,[42] but also significant numbers of Persian speakers residing in Samarkand, Bukhara and specific settlements in the Ferghana Valley.

The 1926 Ferghana Valley census identified a small number of groups that had the potential of becoming officially recognized minorities and of being classified as such. Among these were the Kara-Kalpaks, Turks, Kurama, Kipchaks, Uyghurs (Kashgaris), and others. Each of these groups produced its own activists who demanded their share of representation and resources at the local level.

The Persian-speaking people of the Ferghana Valley, namely the Tajiks—who had been placed in the redrawn boundaries in Uzbekistan—were soon engulfed by a rising tide of demands for some degree of national autonomy. Thus, when residents of Kanibadam held a meeting in their town with the Chairman of the All-Russian Central Executive Committee Mikhail Kalinin, in February 1925, they declared their readiness to proclaim Kanibadam an autonomous Tajik district. The government accepted their demand, and on April 15 the Central Executive

Committee of Uzbekistan declared the Kanibadam an autonomous Tajik district. From then on both official business and education in Kanibadam were conducted in the Tajik language.[43]

The Khujand region was formed by combining territories of the former Samarkand province (Khujand city) and some areas of the former Ferghana province (the cities of Isfara, Kanibadam, and the village of Asht). This precinct brought together areas that the 1926 Census reported as having a Tajik majority.

As in the case of Osh and Kyrgyzia, by no means all of the population welcomed these changes. One declaration stated that:

> Based on existing evidence, the Babadarkhan district (*volost*) Executive Committee hereby notes that it has allegedly been decided that the process of delineation will result in the transfer of our district to the Khujand region. Such a decision by the higher and pertinent authorities surely contradicts local conditions on the following grounds: first, our district is situated far from Khujand, which naturally presents some difficulties for the farming population to get from the district to the regional center in Khujand; second, the people of our district without exception are displeased with this authorities' decision. Surely the discontent of the people of the district and of farmers, along with the problems that will face the latter, certainly provide grounds for reconsidering and revoking the proposed decision, which is unacceptable from the standpoint of the geography and conditions of the locality. Concurrent with this, and in conformity with the proposals and demands of the people of the district, our district should be annexed to the Kokand region.[44]

Because the delineation occurred within the boundaries of Uzbekistan and did not concern relations between the republics, all of the conflicts and disputes regarding the administrative boundaries of the Khujand district failed to gain a hearing at the national political level. Thus, they remained merely an internal affair of the republic.

The "Tajik issue" already had surfaced in the course of delineation in 1924. It was originally intended to create a Tajik Autonomous Region within Uzbekistan that would include areas of the former eastern Bukhara and some settlements and cities of the former Samarkand province of the Turkestan republic. This resulted in the creation of a Tajik Autonomous Region that also included a Badakhshan Autonomous Region in the Pamirs. Areas in the western Ferghana Valley were also mentioned in the delineation debates, since various censuses had reported that they were also inhabited by Tajiks. But in the end it was decided that to avoid disrupting established economic links the Ferghana territories should be left within Uzbekistan, as the Tajiks there had closely intermingled with Uzbeks and other peoples.

This decision embodied the emphasis on economics that predominated at the time among the national leadership. It also reflected the tendency to stress above all the juxtaposition of settled and nomadic peoples, according to which any differences between the Uzbeks and Tajiks, since both were settled, were by definition inconsequential.

A Tajik sub-committee was formed within the Territorial Committee, but its members were quite passive, tending to accept policies developed by the Uzbek side. However, once the delineation of 1924 was announced, conflicts between the Uzbeks and Tajiks began to intensify. By 1926 the Tajik elite and the champions of Tajik autonomy were constantly raising questions about Uzbekistan's policy toward their autonomous region, with issues concerning Tajik ethnicity and the Tajik language growing especially strong. To assure healthy regional development and true cultural independence, the Tajik autonomists demanded that their region be elevated to the status of a "union republic" and then incorporated directly into the USSR, leaving out Uzbekistan. Following on this demand, they also called for the annexation of new territories to the future republic in order to strength its economic base. An alternate approach that was considered would have created a "Central Asian federation," in which all republics would enjoy equal status and would then be incorporated into the USSR as a whole.

Moved by both domestic and international circumstances, the Soviet higher authorities acceded to the Tajiks' demand and made Tajikistan a union republic in its own right. On the domestic side, Soviet officials quite explicitly feared Uzbek hegemony in the region, and had plans to limit further the Uzbeks' power. On the international side, Soviet authorities were eager to use the creation of a "Tajik national state" within their borders as a point of leverage over the civil war that had flared up in neighboring Afghanistan, and which centrally involved the Tajik or Persian-speaking population of that country.

Why had the original plan made Tajiks a part of Uzbekistan and given them the status of an autonomous region rather than of a union republic? Lobbying by such Tajik leaders as Abdukadyr Mukhitdinov, who had good connections in Moscow, played a part in that decision. Mukhitdinov, who had chaired the Revolutionary Committee of the Bukhara Republic and then the Council of People's Commissars of the Tajik Autonomous Soviet Socialist Republic, wrote in 1929 about his earlier belief that all groups speaking Turkic languages constituted a "single free nation," and that Tajiks were "in fact Uzbeks" who "had forgotten their language and national identity and should be made Turks again."[45] "This is how the national delineation occurred," wrote Mukhitdinov. Now, he concluded, "We, who started this criminal affair, acknowledge our mistake and want to correct it."[46]

In 1929 a commission on the territorial delineation of Tajikistan and Uzbekistan began its work.[47] The Uzbek leadership quickly agreed on the transfer of the entire Khujand region to the newly created Tajik republic. Thereafter the discussion focused solely on the issues of Samarkand, Bukhara, and Surkhandarya province. Uzbek members of the commission based their arguments on economic considerations, and especially on the economic links between the western Ferghana areas and the Uzbek city of Kokand. The Tajiks easily refuted this argument by referring to the priority of "national principles," the need for Khujand to emerge as an integral administrative unit, and the transfers to Tajikistan, noted above, to which the Uzbeks had already agreed.

In the fall of 1929 an independent Tajik Soviet Socialist Republic was established. The country's leadership attempted, and nearly succeeded, to gain new territories from Uzbekistan from Surkhandarya province. But at the beginning of 1930 Moscow arbitrarily decided to put an end to all these disputes.

The last major changes occurred in 1936, when the Kyrgyz Autonomous Region was removed from the RSFSR, and received the status of a "union republic," becoming the Kyrgyz Soviet Socialist Republic.[48] This change took place as a result of an arbitrary decision taken in Moscow, in the absence of any claims, counterclaims, or discussions.

Reviewing the territorial issues, during the 1920s the Ferghana Valley remained outside the core debates over the delineation of Central Asian borders. Neither Moscow nor leaders of the national republics considered it a zone of problems or conflicts. Indeed, differences among the various elites over border issues appeared insignificant within the context of the hard struggles within the Bolshevik party in which they were engaged.

In general, the population responded calmly to the delineation of borders. Being transferred to another administrative unit did not produce immediate changes in people's everyday lives, nor did it seriously affect their interests. Because borders were open and local institutions weak, the revised boundary lines had little or no immediate effect on familiar economic practices, personal relations, or transport routes. Under any circumstances, Moscow still had the last word and easily could reconcile disputers through persuasion or force, and punish anyone deemed responsible for continued problems. As a result of the new delineation of borders, the Ferghana Valley was parceled out among three national-administrative entities. As a consequence, it disappeared from the political map as an independent economic and cultural whole, turning instead into a peripheral zone connecting the three union republics among which it had been divided.

Table 4.1

Ethnographic Composition of the Rural Population of the Ferghana Province in 1917[a]

	Magidovich-1[b]	Magidovich-2[c]	Zarubin-1[d]	Zarubin-2[e]
Uzbeks-Sarts	1,104,350	1,104,350	1,104,350	1,002,407
Sarts		188,397	—	—
Uzbeks	—	861,316	—	—
Turks	—	7,163	—	21,188
Kara-Kyrgyz	358,470	358,470	359,470	324,827
Kipchaks	42,449	42,449	40,882	42,114
Kara-Kalpaks	10,735	10,735	—	10,298
Kashgaris	—	35,992	—	37,690
Tajiks	148,011	148,011	147,249	143,867
Gypsies	—	429	—	1,000
Juzes	—	86	—	—
Hodjas	—	1,101	—	—
Arabs	—	969	—	—
Kalmyks	—	253	—	—
Kuramas	—	1,324	—	—

Sources: The data in the table are based on *Statisticheskii ezhegodnik, 1917–1923*, vol. 1, Tashkent, 1924, p. 44; *Materialy Vserossiiskikh perepisei. Perepis naseleniia Turkistanskoi Respubliki*, Issue 4: *Selskoe naselenie Ferganskoi oblasti po materialam perepisi 1917*, Tashkent, 1924. pp. 42, 43, 44, 57, 114–115; I.I. Zarubin, *Spisok narodnostei Turkistanskogo kraia*, Leningrad, 1925, pp. 8, 9, 11, 16, 17, 18.

Notes: [a] Excluded are data on Pamiris, included in *Materialy Vserossiiskikh perepisei*.

[b] According to *Statisticheskii ezhegodnik*. Magidovich provides general numbers, including on the urban population: Uzbeks and Sarts: 1,440,168; Kara-Kyrgyz: 362,851; Kipchaks and Kara-Kalpaks; Tajiks: 187,244; Persians: 2,363. Magidovich also presents rounded figures in the text on each nationality, which in the case of the Tajiks turn out to be significantly different: 167,800; Magidovich included other groups, such as Kashgaris, Turks, Kurama, Arabs, Hodjas, and Juzes in the column for "Uzbeks and Sarts" (I.P. Magidovich, *Naselenie TSSR v 1920 g.* Moscow, 1926).

[c] Based on data in *Materialy Vserossiiskikh perepisei*. Again, Magidovich included other groups in the "Uzbeks and Sarts" column; in the same place he presents separate numbers on Sarts, Uzbeks, and other small groups, while in the text number giving the number of Sarts as 116,932, excluding here Sarts of the Osh region. The *Materialy* gives the number of Turks as "not less than 13,000," as Magidovich did not incorporate into the list the Osh region Turks, who, nevertheless appear in his tables, although without any mention of their precise numbers. Magidovich presents an erroneous number for the Kipchaks in the Namangan county: 11,415 instead of the correct figure of 11,475 (*Materialy Vserossiikikh perepisei*, p. 42). The *Materialy* gives the number of Kashgaris as not less than 37,500, but Magidovich did not include the Osh region Kashgaris in the list, although they appear in his tables, albeit without mention of their precise numbers.

[d] According to data from *Spisok narodnostei Turkistanskogo kraiia* (taken from *Materialy Vserossiikikh perepesei*). Although Magidovich included other groups (Kashgaris, Turks, Kurama, Arabs, Hodjas, Juzes in the "Uzbeks and Sarts" column), Zarubin only includes Turks and Kashgaris.

[e] According to data from *Spisok narodnostei Turkistanskogo kraiia* (based on Zarubin's own calculations). Zarubin calls Turks "Turkoman." According to Zarubin, the figures indicating the numbers of Kipchaks and Kara-Kalpaks also include totals for the "Tashkent region"; Zarubin writes that Gypsies numbered "more than 1,000."

Table 4.2

Ethnographic Composition of the Population of the Ferghana Province in 1926

Uzbeks	1,270,368
Turks	23,810
Kyrgyz	408,652
Kipchaks	32,974
Karakalpaks	18,520
Kashgaris	7,920
Dungans	166
Tajiks	161,942
Arabs	2,130
Kalmyks	3
Kurama	2,640
Ferghana and Samarkand Turks	533
Taranchi	1
Uyghurs	31,198
Sart-Kalmyks	233
Persians	675
Irani	43
Turkmen	199
Ottoman Turks	128
Kazakhs	641
Afghans	10
Hindus	2

Sources: The data in the table are based on *Vsesoiuznaia perepis naseleniia 1926 goda,* vol. 15: *Uzbekskaia SSR. Narodnost, rodnoi iazyk, vozrast, gramotnost,* Moscow, 1928, table 6; *Naselenie po narodnosti, rodnomu iazyku i gramotnosti,* pp. 13–14, 38–40; table 10. *Naselenie po polu, narodnosti i rodnomu iazyku po otdelnym gorodskim poseleniiam i volostiam,* pp. 152–153;*Vsesoiuznaia perepis naseleniia 1926 goda,* vol. 8: "*Kazakh ASSR, Kyrgyzskaia ASSR. Narodnost, rodnoi iazyk, vozrast, gramotnost,*" Moscow, 1928, table 10; *Naselenie po polu, narodnosti i rodnomu iazyku po otdelnym gorodskim poseleniiam i volostiam, Kyrgyz ASSR,* pp. 216–219.

Notes

1. Formerly Saint Petersburg.

2. Shokai in Kazakh.

3. *Turkestan v nachale XX veka: k istorii istokov natsionalnoi nezavisimosti,* Tashkent, 2000, p. 74.

4. M. Buttino, *Revoliutsiia naoborot. Srednaia Aziia mezhdu padeniem tsarskoi imperii i obrazovaniem SSSR,* Moscow, 2007, p. 142.

5. Ibid.

6. Cited in P. Alekseenkov, *Kokandskaia avtonomiia: Revoliutsiia v Srednei Azii,* Tashkent, 1928, p. 38.

7. *Svobodnyi Samarkand,* December 2, 1917.

8. Troops under his command at the end of 1917 conquered Orenburg, a city in the southern Urals, and cut communications between Central Russia and Turkestan, having taken regional corn deliveries under his control.

9. At the beginning of March 1918, the Tashkent newspaper *Ulug Turkiston* published a letter by Chokaev, in which he describes the misfortunes that befell him after his government's defeat in February 1918. Captured by Muslim villagers who sought to capture Kokand and expel all non-Sarts (i.e., local natives) and non-Muslims, among whom they numbered the Bolsheviks, Kazakhs (whom they saw as tied with the Bolsheviks, Tatars, etc.). Eventually Chokaev had to strip to prove he had been circumcised. At the end of his ordeal he declared that "My heart bleeds, I considered these people to be my friends but they treated me as an enemy" (*Ulug Turkiston,* March 2, 1918).

10. See Kamil Iarmatov, *Vozvrashchenie. Kniga vospominanii,* Moscow, 1980, p. 50.

11. *Ulug Turkiston,* March 19, 1918.

12. "Basmak" from the Turkic, meaning "oppress" or "press." *Basmach* is a name that had been used since tsarist times to refer to bandits and gangsters in Central Asia.

13. *Turkestan v nachale XX veka,* p. 165.

14. The task of the Turkestan Commission, which included such Bolsheviks as Kobozev, Goloshchekin, and others, was to create a body that could serve as an intermediary between various factions within Turkestan and coordinate the work of local and central bodies. In 1920 such influential Bolsheviks as Rudzutak, Frunze, and Kuibyshev joined the commission.

15. *Turkestan v nachale XX veka,* p. 221.

16. Ibid., p. 227.

17. *Statisticheskii obzor Ferganskoi oblasti za 1914 god,* Skobelev, 1917, p. 9; *Statisticheskii ezhegodnik Rossii, 1914 g.,* Petrograd, 1915, p. 57.

18. This number is calculated based on *Vsesoiuznaia perepis naseleniia 1926 goda,* vol. 15: *Uzbek SSR,* Moscow, 1928, pp. 13–14, 38–40, 152–53; *Vsesoiuznaia perepis naseleniia 1926 goda,* vol. 8: *Kazakh ASSR and Kyrgyz ASSR,* Moscow, 1928, pp. 216–217, 218–219.

19. See N. Pianciola and P. Sartori, "*Waqf* in Turkestan: The Colonial Legacy and the Fate of an Islamic Institution in Early Soviet Central Asia, 1917–1924," *Central Asian Survey.* 2007, vol. 26, no. 4, pp. 484–492.

20. D. Arapov, "Musulmanskoe dukhovenstvo Srednei Azii v 1927 godu," *Rasy i narody,* vol. 32, Moscow, 2006, p. 313.

21. Ibid., p. 318.

22. Ibid., p. 321.

23. L.S. Gatagova and L.P. Kosheleva et al., eds., "Zakrytoe pismo sekretaria ZK KP(b) Turkestana M.S. Epshteina v ZK RKP(b) po itogam poezdki v Ferganu. 17 March 1923," *ZK RKP(b)–VKP(b) i natsionalnyi vopros,* bk. 1: *1918–1933,* Moscow, 2005, p. 102.

24. L.Z. Kunakova, *Zemelno-vodnaia reforma v Ferganskoi doline (1925–1926),* Osh, 1962, pp. 57–58.

25. Ibid., pp. 150–51.

26. Between 1920 and 1925 the Kyrgyz Autonomous Soviet Socialist Republic existed, which was subsequently renamed the Kazakh Autonomous Soviet Socialist Republic or Kazakhstan.

27. V.I. Lenin, *Polnoe sobranie sochinenii,* Moscow, 1981, vol. 41, p. 436.

28. See T.S. Ozhukeeva, *XX vek: vozrozhdenie natsionalnoi gosudarstvennosti v Kyrgyzstane.* Bishkek, 1993.

29. Initially, it was planned to rearrange and then preserve the Khorezm republic, but it was decided in the course of discussions to divide it into national territories as well.

30. Ozhukeeva, *XX vek,* p. 22.

31. Ibid.

32. According to statistical data until 1917—Sarts.

33. The issue of creating such a center in Jalalabad, which was connected to Tashkent by a railway, was discussed for some time.

34. This group lobbied the creation of its own nationality and national institutions on the

county level (A. Haugen, *The Establishment of National Republics in Soviet Central Asia,* New York, 2003, pp. 144–45).

35. Ibid., p. 192.

36. Ibid.

37. See A. Koichiev, *Natsionalno-territorialnoe razmezhevanie v Ferganskoi doline (1924–1927)*, Bishkek, 2001, pp. 32–34, 37–46, 53–67; F. Hirsch, *Empire of Nations: Ethnographic Knowledge and the Making of the Soviet Union,* Ithaca and London, 2005, pp. 168–72.

38. Gosudarstvennyi arkhiv Ferganskoi oblasti Respubliki Uzbekistan (GAFO RU), f. 121. 0.2. d. 594.

39. GAFO RU, f. 121. 0.2. d. 594.

40. GAFO RU, f. 121. 0.2. d. 570. 1.2, 3.

41. D. Abramson, "Identity Counts: The Soviet Legacy and the Census in Uzbekistan," in *Census and Identity: The Politics of Race, Ethnicity, and Language in National Censuses,* ed. D.I. Kertzer and D. Arel, Cambridge, 2001, pp. 187–96.

42. The majority of the settled population was registered as "Sarts" in censuses and local statistics in the imperial Turkestan (see S.N. Abashin, *Natsionalizmy v Srednei Azii: v poiskakh identichnosti,* Saint Petersburg, 2007, pp. 95–176).

43. See Abdudzhabbor Kahhori, *Adzhab Dunee,* Dushanbe, 2003, pp. 37–39.

44. GAFO RU, f. 121. o. 2, d. 595.–1. 140.

45. R. Masov, *Istoriia topornogo razdelenia,* Dushanbe, 1991, p. 149.

46. Ibid. p. 151.

47. Ibid. pp. 115–35.

48. Kazakhstan then gained the status of a union republic.

5

The Ferghana Valley Under Stalin, 1929–1953

*Kamoludin Abdullaev (Tajikistan), with
Ravshan Nazarov (Uzbekistan)*

The so-called Stalin years were a pivotal period in the development of Soviet Central Asia in general and the Ferghana Valley in particular. This was a time when the USSR gained international recognition and when, by the second half of the 1920s, the internal struggle against the *basmachi* in Central Asia concluded. A small number of nationalist émigrés from Turkestan settled in Turkey in the mid-1920s, just at the time when that country was strengthening its relations with the USSR. Apart from running a rudimentary underground network of supporters in the Soviet Union, these Pan-Turkists did not further influence developments in Central Asia. The national delineation of internal borders in Central Asia and the opportunity to carry out creative work in the resulting national entities drew many former Jadids to the side of the Soviet government. On the whole, the government and its major opponents in Central Asia, including bellicose religious radicals and supporters of the *basmachi,* as well as restive idealistic reformers like the Jadids, achieved a modus vivendi.

Soviet Policy Shifts from Tolerance and Growth to Coercion and Exploitation

The process of national development under Soviet rule was uneven. From the establishment of the Soviet government in 1918 until the end of the 1920s the Bolsheviks were in no position to carry out the transformation of Central Asian society, which continued to view itself as Muslim. Throughout those years the government confined itself to neutralizing and eliminating whomever it considered to be the worst "exploiters." It accomplished this by enlisting the support of pro-Soviet Jadids and those Muslim clerics disposed to collaborate with any government, who thereby became the first representatives of the USSR's "official Islam." This allowed Central Asian society in the first decade of Soviet rule to adjust to the new political conditions while not betraying its own fundamental Muslim principles. The tradition of

119

acquiescence with Russian rule reached back to tsarist times, when the majority of mullahs had considered Turkestan to be a kind of Muslim order or "Dar al-Islam."[1] After all, religion was not oppressed, people freely attended mosques, and *qadi* courts continued to implement an order based on sharia law.[2]

Such upper class and privileged groups as the *hodjas, turas, ishans, saiids,* and *mirzas* adjusted to the new realities quicker than others, thanks to the skills they had acquired and maintained through many centuries. Many learned Russian and worked as Soviet teachers, administrators, and accountants. Some of them even managed to keep their pieces of land. Tenant farmers or *choriakkoron* who worked for them gave a fourth (*choriak*) of their crops to their landlords down to the collectivization of land at the end of the 1920s. Members of the Muslim clergy (*ulama*)[3] continued to be the main advisers to local communities, and they served as intermediaries between Muslims and the new authorities. They issued resolutions on what was considered *halal* (allowed) or *haram* (forbidden), including on such matters as the wearing of modern clothing, the use of modern medicines and medical procedures, and the consumption of new products and of alcoholic beverages like vodka and wine. Such ancestral and urban neighborhood groupings as the *avlods*[4] and *mahallas*[5] remained autonomous and detached from politics. Their leaders replaced traditional robes and turbans with suits and skullcaps, and successfully adjusted to the new conditions. In so doing, they assured cultural continuity and stability. Having abandoned their official powers, they managed nonetheless to retain their traditional status and authority in society.

In spite of all the Bolshevik slogans and exhortations, Central Asian settlements did not divide along class lines. Former feudals, officials of the khan, and tsarist administrators sent their young people to study at universities in Tashkent, Moscow, Leningrad, and Baku. Communities continued to support their traditional leaders and take pride in them. They tried to gain their patronage and protection in the event of conflicts or complicated political conditions. Indeed, these traditional leaders came to form the backbone of the new cultural, economic, and bureaucratic elite of the Soviet period.

Thus, Kamil Iarmatov, a Tajik from Kanibadam, became a student at the State Cinematography Training School in Moscow in 1928. Kamil was the son of Iarmuhammad-Mingbashi, a county chief of Kanibadam city, and grandchild of Muhammad Karim-Kurbashi, commandant of Makhram, a fort between Khujand and Kanibadam. Kamil's grandfather, Karim-Kurbashi, had served the Kokand Khan Khudayar and fought against tsarist troops in Makhram in August 1875. His son, Iarmuhammad, worked for the Russian Tsar Nicholas II. At the beginning of 1918, after the defeat of the "Kokand autonomy," Iarmuhammad handed over the administration of the county, which included the best Tajik areas of the Ferghana Valley (Kanibadam, Isfara, Chorkukh, Qarachiqum, Besharyq, and Makhram), to the local soviet. Conjointly, Iarmuhammad also gave his own downtown urban homestead to the Soviet government.[6] In so doing, he saved his own life and the lives of his extended family. The Soviet government did not persecute Iarmuhammad (who died in 1925), even though he was a former tsarist official. Before becoming a famous Soviet film producer and prior to the revolution, his son, Kamil Iarmatov, studied at a local Russian language school for members of the indigenous population. He spent the years between 1919 and 1924 chasing down gangsters, initially as a member of the Muslim cavalry led by Hamdam-kurbashi Qalandarov and then as a district chief of police.[7]

This gradual and evolutionary development of the Soviet government and its adaptation to local conditions changed radically at the end of the 1920s, when Bolshevik doctrine abandoned the goal of spreading the "world revolution" and embraced instead the idea of "socialism in one country." Henceforth, a total political and economic centralization reigned in Central Asia. What was called a system of "command and administrative control" prevailed everywhere, and especially in the cotton production in the Ferghana Valley. The goal was to free the USSR of all dependence on cotton from abroad, especially from the United States. The chosen means to achieve this was to collectivize the ownership of land and to introduce extreme centralization in its management. To fight the inevitable inefficiency and abuses to which this system gave rise, the government resorted increasingly to terror and coercion.

Even during tsarist times the Ferghana Valley had been turned into Russia's largest cotton field. By 1913 it supplied 62 percent of Central Asian cotton and met 37 percent of the needs of Russia's textile industry.[8] Following the civil war of 1918–20, central Russia's textile mills ceased functioning for want of raw materials. No longer able to afford to buy foreign cotton, the Bolsheviks imposed on the toilers of the Ferghana Valley the task of "conquering the heights of cotton independence." Farmers of the region achieved this by devoting all newly irrigated land to cotton and by reducing the area for all other crops. By 1932 investments in irrigation infrastructure constituted a quarter of all new investment in Uzbekistan, while agriculture accounted for 50 percent of the total.[9] In addition to this, the national ("Union") budget devoted still more expenditures to the construction of cross-border irrigation infrastructure, including collectors that discharged water into the Syr Darya River.

The collectivization of land ownership was to be hastened after 1930 by an "offensive against the kulaks." By mid-1931 this had descended into a policy of "liquidating the kulaks as a class." For the crime of using hired labor "kulaks," who were defined in such a way as to include all of the more or less well-off households were charged with "violating Soviet laws." Kulak households were expropriated and expelled from Central Asia and forcefully.[10] Tens of thousands of peasant households were liquidated and incorporated into collective farms that operated on the principle of a "planned socialist economy." On the new collective and cooperative farms, virtually everything became communal property, including land, cattle used for work and offered for sale, the main agricultural machinery, tools and buildings. This said, the collective farms were not equipped with the modern agricultural machinery essential for large-scale agriculture to function even minimally. The Communist Party solved this by creating machine-tractor stations (MTS) under its strict control.

Managing each collective farm, or kolkhoz, was a board headed by a chairman elected by a general meeting of members. Kolkhoz Party committees and the MTS exercised rigorous control over the kolkhoz chairmen. These in turn were controlled by the Party's district committees (raikoms) that reported to the regional committees (obkoms) which, finally, were accountable to the central committee in the union republics that reported to the Central Committee headed by Stalin himself. The web of central committees at the republic, obkom, and raikom levels were responsible for carrying out every task assigned by the Center. The Party also managed the entire system of soviets or councils, beginning in Moscow with the Supreme Soviet, then extending downward through a supreme soviet in each republic to district and village soviets.

In the Ferghana Valley, the aim of this entire system of soviets instituted by the Communist Party was the complete destruction of the class of independent farmers and of private agriculture, to be replaced by gigantic collective farms that would produce cotton. More than half of all cropland was devoted to this one industrial crop. Foodstuffs, including bread, were mainly imported from Siberia along the new Turkestan-Siberia railroad.[11] Forests that long had been home to rare and unique species of animals and birds were hacked down to make cotton fields.

Collectivization in the Ferghana Valley continued from 1927 until 1933. By the end of 1932, some 81 percent of farming households in the valley had been collectivized, and they accounted for 79 percent of all production.[12] Amazingly, collectivization did not disrupt the traditional structure of the typical Ferghana Valley village. Those who traditionally had worked as tenant farmers on feudal lands had, by the early 1930s, become collective farmers who continued to work without rights, but for the state. This was the grand result of all the attention that higher Party authorities lavished on the Ferghana Valley in those years.

Communications

The epochal drawing of internal Soviet borders after 1924 left the Ferghana Valley divided among three republics, each with its own chief executive (chairman of the republic's supreme soviet), council of ministers, flag, anthem, constitution, national language, national Communist Party, academy of sciences, opera and ballet theater, state university, film studio, and radio station—in short, nearly all the domestic features of a modern nation-state. Yet none of the largest Ferghana Valley cities became a republic capital. Prior to the delineation of borders, the Ferghana Valley had been a self-sufficient economic region at the important junction of the Zarafshan Valley, the Tashkent oasis, the Karategin, Alai, and Pamir mountains, and Chinese Kashgaria. The new borders transformed it into a geographically peripheral and economically marginal zone, whose infrastructure, though not lacking development, was relatively backward compared with the republic of which each sector was a part.

The new borders all but guaranteed that the Soviet government would ignore the transport and communications needs of the Ferghana Valley. To cover the 650 kilometers from Osh in the Ferghana to Frunze (now Bishkek), the capital of Kyrgyzia, one had to cross two passes at more than 3,000 meters that were closed during winter. Residents of the Kyrgyz south instead reached their capital via the Uzbek city of Khanabad. A train from Osh to Frunze had to cross the borders of Kazakhstan, Uzbekistan, and Tajikistan several times.

The situation in Tajikistan was no less absurd. To get from the highly developed Ferghana region of Tajikistan to the capital in the south meant a 350-kilometer trip that included crossing passes in the Turkestan and Hisar mountains that were closed half the year. The alternative, 200 kilometers longer, was to go via the Uzbek city of Samarkand. Similarly, the trip from Khujand to Tajikistan's Badakhshan Autonomous Region on the Afghan border took at least two days of driving on a road that ran through Uzbek-owned parts of the Ferghana Valley, then via the now-Kyrgyz city of Osh. As a result, northern and southern Tajiks had only the faintest idea of their newly defined "compatriots" in the other region. Even today there are people in Tajikistan's sector of the Ferghana Valley who have never been to the country's capital of Dushanbe, to the more southern areas of the country, or to Badakhshan.

A similar, albeit less absurd, mismatch of political, cultural, economic, and geographical boundaries can be observed in Uzbekistan. The shortest and most convenient way of reaching Tashkent by car from Andijan and Kokand was, and still is, through the city of Khujand in the Tajik sector of the Ferghana Valley. An alternative road running through the narrow Altynkan corridor and involving the 2,267-meter Kamchik Pass was very inconvenient and closed for winter as well. Similarly, the railway from the Uzbek part of the Ferghana Valley to Tashkent runs for 100 kilometers through the territory of Tajikistan.

The territorial delineation left most of the plains areas of the valley under the control of Uzbekistan. This provided justifications for Uzbekistan to consider the Ferghana Valley as a core Uzbek territory. The foothills, rich in water and opening the way to the Alai and Pamir mountains, fell to Kyrgyzia. Tajikistan got a relatively small but important western part of the valley, through which passed the principal arteries connecting Tashkent with the Uzbek central and eastern parts of the valley. Thus, Uzbekistan controlled the bulk of the valley's territory and population, while Kyrgyzstan controlled the rivers flowing to the valley from the Alai, Tian Shan, and Turkestan peaks, as well as the territory that goods from Badakhshan must cross to reach the nearest railhead, in Uzbek Andijan. As for Tajikistan, it received strategically important sections of the trans-Uzbek railway and motorway. Moreover, with the completion of the Kairakkum reservoir and hydroelectric station in the 1950s,[13] Tajikistan gained a measure of control over the waters of the Syr Darya River. At the time, however, there were no conflicts over water, and all of the three republics had direct access to the upper streams of the Syr Darya.

During the Stalin era Central Asia failed to become a unified economic region. Moscow viewed it as a source of raw materials for the more developed European areas of the USSR. Railways were designed not to promote regional development, but to deliver raw materials in the most direct manner from Central Asia to industrial centers in the Russian Federation. There was minimal investment in the internal development of specific republics or in trade between neighboring republics. Indeed, there was no inherent reason for Soviet policy to look favorably on the development of such inter-republican trade and communications in Central Asia or the Ferghana Valley.

The priority Moscow assigned to the core Russian areas of the USSR assured that the periphery would remain backward and with a weak sense of unity. The Stalin era left Central Asia as a poorly developed, agrarian, and subsidized region dependent on Russia for whatever economic well-being it enjoyed. This is all the more true of the Ferghana Valley, as a periphery of a periphery.

Education and Culture

It is difficult to separate "good" Soviet policies from "bad" during the Stalin years. The Bolsheviks inherited from European Social Democrats certain critically important progressive ideas. Thus, they recognized that mass education was necessary for the industrialization and modernization of society. As such, their policies in this area differed markedly from those of the former tsarist government. By 1938 a network of elementary schools extended throughout all of the USSR. Cities and large villages saw the construction of seven-year schools. Overall, the schools paid special attention to mathematics and the exact sciences, as well as to languages, literature, and history. All this represented stupendous progress when compared with the tsarist and Muslim schools that had taught only basic reading and arithmetic. As early as 1939 three-quarters of Soviet citizens were literate, and by the death of Stalin nearly all were.

Russian colonization brought ideas of modernization to the Ferghana Valley by the end of the nineteenth century. In spite of war, revolution, and civil war, these ideas spread to all social classes and to even the most remote corners of the Ferghana Valley over the following decades. Even though the overall quality of life in the Ferghana Valley in 1953 did not exceed that of 1928, many positive changes occurred nonetheless. Fresh water from the Great Ferghana Canal, dug in six weeks in 1939, replaced water from stagnant domestic wells (*khauzes*). The introduction of potatoes and tomatoes improved diets. Clinics and medical centers opened in all cities and big villages. Preventive medicine made such terrible diseases as malaria, typhus, Aleppo boil, diphtheria, cholera, and trachoma things of the past. By 1953 houses across the valley were lit by electricity; films, including locally made ones, were being shown at public recreation centers; and the radio aired hit songs by such popular local singers as Halima Nasyrova[14] and Tamara Khanum.[15] Men were glad to wear European suits, women boldly unveiled their faces, children went to school, and Soviet police maintained order in the growing cities.

The new borders between Kyrgyzstan, Uzbekistan, and Tajikistan seemed of little consequence. People lived in one country, the USSR, and could move from village to village or republic to republic without being stopped by a border guard or facing an armed gangster. Uzbeks in Kokand could easily marry off their daughters in Osh. Mobile and entrepreneurial Tajiks from Karategin felt comfortable living in the Uzbek quarters of Ferghana Valley cities, or even in Tashkent, as this did not damage their ethno-confessional or cultural identity. Symbols of national identity specific to Kyrgyz, Tajiks, and Uzbeks appeared comfortably on the street, alongside Soviet symbols. Indeed, it was precisely in this period that Ferghana Valley residents, who formerly identified themselves mainly in terms of their place of residence or profession, began realizing that they were also Kyrgyz, Tajiks, and Uzbeks.

Marxists recognized national units and acknowledged nationalism as inevitable, yet considered it an intermediate phase to be overcome as quickly as possible in order to reach a classless and nation-free communist future. For this reason, Bolsheviks took the seemingly paradoxical step of laying the foundation of national states in Central Asia, while at the same time making sure that both the new states and the nationalities on which they were based remained strictly subordinate to the political agenda of Bolshevism.

Islam and Gender

The Soviet government attempted to control all aspects of Muslims' social and political life. Communist ideology declared religion to be the opium of the people and subjected it to large-scale attacks. The atheistic Soviet system's first target was the more intellectual form of Islam, with its powerful financial base and array of educational institutions. The Soviets also sought to undermine the influence of "popular" Islam, which had always existed on the communal level and linked the culture and folklore of people in the Ferghana Valley with their religious identity. The organs of state security were particularly active in the struggle against religion, destroying all influential clerics and getting the survivors under their control. Mosques and madrassas were turned into warehouses and commercial buildings. Sharia courts were abolished in 1927.

Meanwhile, the Soviet government used the loyal and certified mullahs of "official Islam" to create acceptable substitutes for both the intellectual and the popular forms of the faith. The Bolsheviks' use of co-opted "red mullahs" dated back to their struggle against the *basmachi* in the 1920s. Official Islam, which emerged during the height of World War II in 1942, was under firm communist control. Its main body was the Central Asian Clerical Administration of Muslims (SADUM) headed by a mufti. SADUM was based in Tashkent and led by an influential Uzbek clan up until the collapse of the USSR in 1991. Vigilantly controlled by the state, the mufti busied himself with registering an insignificant number of mosques, appointing their imams, and even determining the content for the latter's sermons. However, such religious figures and their institutions did not play a significant role in the lives of the Hanafi Sunni Muslims of the Ferghana Valley. Among those who cared, the majority of Uzbeks, Tajiks, and Kyrgyz preferred official Islam to popular Islam supported by unofficial mullahs and *ishans* at the community level. This "unofficial" or "popular" Islam lacked intellectual depth and operated under the sights of the state security services, which feared the damage it potentially could do to the Soviet government.

In its effort to enlist the sympathies of the "oppressed females of the Orient," the Bolsheviks promised women complete emancipation. With this goal in mind, in 1927 the Bolsheviks organized a *hujum* (offensive, attack) on patriarchal customs, which they claimed led to the oppression of women. The focal points of this *hujum* were the Uzbek and Tajik communities of the Ferghana Valley. They attacked under-age marriage, the paying of a bride price (*kalym*), and especially the wearing of the *farandji* or *chador*, a symbol of female oppression. Ferghana Valley residents, however, considered the wearing of *farandji* to be a necessity in their densely populated and urbanized environment. Most people in the valley, especially males, perceived the *hujum* as an insult to their national and religious identities. True, some women abandoned *farandji* and aspired to take advantage of their newly won opportunity to get an education and master trades. Public acceptance of the anti-religion campaign diminished at the end of the 1920s when the Soviet government began again to resort to violence in its struggle against Islam. The renewed vigor of Soviet policy intensified civil strife. In the Ferghana Valley a number of reactionary clergymen fought back by killing female activists.

Notwithstanding the compulsory nature of the reforms, an increasing number of women found their way into governmental and educational institutions. By 1940 women made up almost half of all students in urban schools. By the mid-1950s almost all Tajik, Uzbek, and Kyrgyz females in the Ferghana Valley stopped wearing veils. However, both females and males in all three republics tried to preserve the old patriarchic traditions at home. Despite all repressions and prohibitions, Islamic customs and traditional habits concerning prayers, weddings, circumcisions, funerals, eating, and hygiene remained omnipresent in the private lives of people across Central Asia. The resulting double standard enabled people in public to put on a show of living according to Soviet practices, but at home to continue adhering to traditional ways of life. These accommodations left women subject to double exploitation: after working all day they were expected to perform all the traditional household chores in the evening. And despite increases in literacy levels among Kyrgyz, Tajik, and Uzbek females, families with five or more children continued to predominate.

Dilemmas of the "Indigenization" Policy and Problems of Leadership

The Soviet government tried to demonstrate that its policies had nothing in common with the tsarist policies that had oppressed the non-Russian peoples. With this goal in mind, Soviet officials pursued a policy of *korenizatsiia* or indigenization. This was an early Soviet notion that supported members of the titular nationalities of recently formed republics and "national minorities." Its objective was to enlist the support of non-Russian peoples and thereby internationalize the communist movement. Minority peoples were called upon to study Russian along with their native languages. Literary works and public documents were being issued in both local languages and in Russian. Clerical correspondence in all three of the Ferghana republics was conducted in at least two languages. Depending on the ethnic composition of a particular area, newspapers in cities across the valley were issued in Russian, Uzbek, Tajik, and Kyrgyz.

A goal of the indigenization policy was to develop competent "national cadres" loyal to the Soviet government. It is during these years that the first Soviet doctors, teachers, writers, actors, and artists emerged from among the Kyrgyz, Tajiks, and Uzbeks. All owed their professional advancement solely to the Bolshevik Party and the Soviet state. Conflict between competence and political loyalty was the major impediment to indigenization. The Soviet government eagerly promoted people from the poorest classes whose educational qualifications were far below those of both Russians and other non-Russians from privileged families. The Bolsheviks treated the latter as unreliable allies and class enemies, in spite of their higher levels of professional training.

The weakness of the indigenization policy began to show immediately. An outstanding figure from among the first Uzbek graduating classes in Uzbekistan that were loyal to the Soviet government was Yuldash Akhunbabaev, a native of Djoi-Bazar village in the Margilan district in the Ferghana province.[16] Loyal and also prominent throughout the Soviet Union were such kolkhoz chairmen as Khamrakul Tursunkulov (1892–1965), from Vuadil village in the Ferghana and thrice a Hero of Socialist Labor, and Saidhodja Urunhodjaev (1901–1967) from the Shaihburhon village in the Khujand district and twice a Hero of Socialist Labor. All three came from poor Ferghana farm families and were only barely literate.[17]

Such leaders were distinguished mainly for their peasant origins, performance of duties, and allegiance to the regime; they were trained collective farmers in the spirit of unconditional subordination to the government. Collective farmers knew that their *rais* (chairman) had influential connections in the state and Party hierarchies, and that the well-being of every kolkhoz member was in his hands. In the case of Tursunkulov and Urunhodjaev, these connections extended to Politburo of the Central Committee. Feared and respected, the *rais* wielded absolute power over kolkhozniki. The entire agricultural system of the Ferghana Valley and of Central Asia rested on these authoritarian and at times charismatic leaders, who suppressed all independent initiative and demanded that tasks assigned from above with no local participation be carried unquestioningly. The figure of the *rais*, loyal to his superiors and unrelenting toward his villagers, came to be the ideal archetype for all Party and soviet-level leaders in the Ferghana Valley and Central Asia.

Their lack of education prevented *rais* from rising in the industrial world. This created a fissure in the economy of the Ferghana Valley, with agriculture and industry developing along parallel but non-intersecting lines. Agrarian Tajik, Uzbek, and Kyrgyz communities, organized into kolkhozes traditionally led by rais-leaders, dominated in the agricultural sector. Locally born and speaking local dialects, *rais* were not familiar with Marxism-Leninism and had only the vaguest notions on how best to promote communism, but did not interfere with internal community affairs. Industry, by contrast, was firmly in the hands of urbanized Russians and not indigenous people. The government dreamed of a merging of city and countryside and of Russian and Kyrgyz, Tajik, or Uzbek; however, no such merging occurred. As in tsarist times, villages and "old towns" populated by indigenous people lived their own lives and showed no interest in the "new towns" growing up alongside them. Conversely, Russians living in the valley's cities and villages continued to identify themselves as Russians, remained oblivious to what was happening in the ethnic communities, and refused to learn local languages or embrace local culture. This ruled out any "merging of peoples" into a single, Soviet community. The little "unity" among the people that existed came from the dictatorship of the Communist Party, and was maintained by the manner in which goods and services were distributed.

The Soviet government worked hard to train young professionals from the local nationalities. By 1930 almost half of the 5,000 workers at cotton mills in the Uzbek sector of the valley were local ethnics.[18] But considering the overwhelming predominance of local peoples in the population of the province, this did not suffice. Moreover, most key leadership positions in industry were filled by Russians and other Slavs, with local workers concentrated in the most low-paying jobs.

Soon the Bolsheviks began damping down the indigenization policy out of fear that the multi-national Soviet empire might collapse if it did not have enough people sharing a single language and culture. Ukrainians and Belorussians, for example, could fall under Polish influence, while Central Asians could link up with Muslims in India, Iran, and Turkey. Indigenization began in the mid-1920s but had faded away by the 1930s, replaced by the time-tested tsarist policy of Russification. True, indigenization did not completely die, but it limped along thereafter in a kind of half-life.

Russification and the Manipulation of Language Policy

Russification, the policy of imposing Russian culture on non-Russian peoples, provoked protests from most of the non-Russian peoples of the USSR. Russians were appointed to key administrative and political positions, and the Russian language became essential for business, Communist Party affairs, industry, science, and engineering. Soon bilingualism prevailed in Central Asia; not the former Turko-Tajik bilingualism of the Ferghana Valley, but Russian-Kyrgyz, Russian-Tajik, and Russian-Uzbek bilingualism. However this pertained only to non-Russians, for while Kyrgyz, Tajiks, and Uzbeks spoke a minimum of two languages, very few

Russians mastered any Turkic or Persian language. Russian soon replaced Turkic and Tajik as the common medium of communication throughout the valley. To be sure, most people became familiar with Russian culture without being forced to do so. But within some strata of society Russification engendered Russophobia, taking the form of passive protests and a quiet withdrawal into "parallel" Islam.

The government's 1927-1940 policy of manipulating language had the further objective of breaking down Muslim unity and isolating Central Asia from the larger Islamic world. Starting from the ninth century, the Tajiks and then other regional peoples had adapted the Arabic alphabet to their languages. The resulting Islamic-Persian-Turkic synthesis formed the basis of the regional culture. Nevertheless, in 1927 the Soviet government abolished what it considered the archaic and inadequate Arabic-based scripts and decreed that the Latin alphabet be adopted instead. By this step the government separated the region from the Muslim world and bound it instead within its own orbit. Latinization broke Islam's monopoly over the publishing industry and pedagogy and compromised the status of both the Arabic and Persian languages, setting against them the younger and predominantly Turkic "popular" languages. It also anticipated the further transition to the Cyrillic alphabet, which helped put an end to the region's Turko-Tajik cultural unity and cleared way for a monolithic Russian-speaking "Soviet culture" and "new Soviet man."

At the end of the 1920s, the Soviet government undertook a large-scale campaign to promote the Cyrillic alphabet and Russian language. It presented this to the outside world as a campaign to "abolish illiteracy," in other words, to introduce culture into a world of absolute illiteracy and a culturally virgin land. Russians presented themselves as the benefactors and bearers of an advanced culture, as opposed to the "backward peoples of Central Asia, who did not even have their own system of writing." This was accompanied by the comprehensive destruction of books in Persian, Arabic, and Turkic languages available in almost every home in the Ferghana Valley. People had to conceal, bury, and often burn their favorite books.

Simultaneously, the Soviets destroyed madrassas across the Ferghana Valley and also many mosques, some dating to the Middle Ages. Thus, the little town of Kanibadam and nearby villages boasted eight madrassas in 1914, most of them built in the seventeenth to nineteenth centuries. Among their founders were great rulers and their families, including women, who left endowments (*waqfs*) for the preparation of teachers at schools in Bukhara and India and for student scholarships. Under the madrassas were some 105 schools for boys and girls in the district, with a total of about 2,500 students.[19] The curriculum, not based solely on theology, included the sciences on the grounds that this would help Muslims in their search for the "right path." These schools taught logic, *adab* (a code of conduct and the appreciation of beauty), the fundamentals of natural science, calligraphy, and Arabic. Alumni of Kanibadam madrassas were considered to be the best calligraphers in the Kokand Khanate, and in the nineteenth century were named to various missions to Kashgar in China.

By the end of the culture war launched in 1927, four of the eight madrassas had disappeared entirely, and three others (namely Mirradjab Dodho, Hodja Rushnoi, and Oim) were being used as a school for tractor drivers, a vocational-technical school, and a prison. Only one of them, the oldest—Mirradjab Dodho—survived in its more or less original form.[20]

The campaign to "abolish illiteracy" was a typical Bolshevik project of social engineering. The price paid for modernization and the introduction of Soviet mass education was the irretrievable loss of culture, subsequent cultural deprivation, and the plunging of whole populations into backwardness. Epistemologically and psychologically this policy was rooted in Islamophobia and a Russian form of "Orientalism," that is in the imperial belief that the Russian people were somehow "chosen" to civilize the more "backward" peoples.

Henceforth, it was all but fatal to admit to having had a "Muslim education." Instead, people in the Ferghana Valley preferred to present themselves in job interviews as the illiterate children of poor peasants. This was quite logical, since the Soviet government considered an illiterate and poor villager dressed in tatters to be more reliable than a neatly dressed and educated mullah. The government projected this rural poverty and illiteracy onto entire peoples, declaring them backward and qualified for generous "domestication" at the price of unconditional political allegiance. To justify this policy the government resolved first to get rid of the educated class, which it did by denouncing it as the bearer of a reactionary religious ideology. The Soviet vernacular considered mullahs strictly in religious terms, whereas Central Asians equated the term with "educated," which, of course, meant well grounded in religion and hence able to read the Arabic-Persian script. Muslims considered such knowledge to be sacred, but the Soviet government considered it a crime and repressed all literate mullahs as supporters of the *basmachi*.[21] Anyone aspiring to advance one's career had to master Russian and, preferably, marry a Russian woman as well.

Turkey followed the USSR in outlawing the Arabic script in November 1928, and then introducing the Latin alphabet. The leader of the Bashkir emigration, Zeki Validi Togan, correctly said that the Latin script "causes deep disgust in Afghanistan, Persia and Turkestan."[22] But when the Soviets then abandoned the Latin script in favor of Cyrillic at the end of the 1930s, it prevented Turkic people in the USSR and Turkey from finding a common language. From this time on Soviet rulers did everything possible to individualize Central Asian languages and deprive them of their common features. As a result, Uzbeks and Kyrgyz in the Ferghana Valley could no longer understand each other's written language, while Tajiks could no longer understand Persian and Afghan texts. Some regional elites, while remaining Kyrgyz, Tajik, and Uzbek in culture, came to prefer the Russian language. This conformed to the policy of replacing Arabic, Persian, and Turkic as the languages of science, culture, and education with Russian. Within a decade Russian had been established as a symbol of dominance, while all indigenous languages were downgraded and Islam stripped of its scientific, literary, and educational bases. But it was not destroyed, as the Bolsheviks wished. Instead it went underground and continued as "popular" Islam sustained by uneducated mullahs and charismatic community leaders. Within families, the women instilled their children with respect for the faith.

The Formation of Identity

When evaluating Soviet policies in the Ferghana Valley, it is worth inquiring into the price the population paid for so sweeping a transformation. The greatest loss was in social capital. For centuries valley residents had maintained a complex irrigation system, collected funds for *waqfs* (religious foundations), built madrassas, maintained schools, and built roads and infrastructure. They prayed in the same way, gave their children similar names, worshiped at common shrines, had a common system of sharia law and, until the mid-1920s, were ruled by the same government. Ferghana Valley residents were also bound together by historical memories of resistance to external enemies. Thus, people remembered the united Kyrgyz-Tajik-Uzbek armed units that charismatic military commanders and supranational religious leaders had led against tsarist forces in the third quarter of the nineteenth century.

Did residents of the Ferghana Valley have their own particular mind-set and common political culture, and do they still? The question does not allow certainty, but is worth asking nonetheless. A good place to begin is their attitude toward the government, on which Ferghana residents of all ethnicities differed markedly from their nearest neighbors, the nomadic Turkic peoples and the mountain Tajiks. Ferghana folk recognized government as such to be legitimate and capable of playing a positive role in their lives. None of the valley residents conceived the possibility of a free existence absent governmental control. Unlike their nomadic or mountain-bound neighbors, Ferghana Valley communities were used to a settled existence and expected to obey laws, pay taxes, and otherwise reckon with the authorities. Their citizens equated authority with justice, and considered a government that defended them from external threats, helped the community to function, and supported religion to be just. Beyond this, as highly urbanized dwellers of irrigated oases they were used to a hierarchical rather than an egalitarian political culture. They were also much more literate and learned than either their mountain or nomadic neighbors. Indeed, the nomads of Central Asia looked on Tajiks and Uzbeks from the oasis cities as their *pirs* or mentors.

Many observers distinguished the diverse inhabitants of the Ferghana Valley's cities and agrarian oases, whom Russian colonial officials called Sarts, from other Central Asians. The Sarts were noted for their peacefulness, solidarity, tolerance, and ability to strike a compromise. Rarely did they raise violent campaigns against the government. Theirs was a highly structured society enriched by professional groups of craftsmen, traders, teachers, mullahs, writers, scientists, bakers, musicians, and others. The urban quarters in which they lived had retained the same appearance over many centuries. Everyone knew each other, had a stable place in society, and practiced professional skills handed down through the generations.

People knew, for example, that anyone named Bakhadurkhan-tura came from the *tura* class, the highest level of officials of the Khan, and that he was to be greeted first among any group. Conversely, someone named Irgash-kuknori was assumed to be a reveler and *kuknori* (opium-smoker). The social hierarchy was considered normal. Poor men, called *omi* (from the word *omma*, or masses), knew their birth excluded them from politics and made no effort to change this condition. In fact, most Ferghana residents accepted the established order and made no effort to change it or to assert their rights. In this respect they differed markedly from the more egalitarian herding communities, whose members practiced a kind of "nomadic democracy" and strongly preferred their semi-independence to any state control.

The population density of cities in the Ferghana Valley was the highest in Central Asia. Cities were surrounded by villages or *kishlaks* and served as points of exchange for goods, services, information, and cultural values. Ferghana cities dominated the agrarian periphery, but without causing antagonism. This may be because the layout of houses and the ways of life of city and village dwellers did not differ sharply. Most organized neighborhoods (*mahallas*) were based on territory rather than kinship or ethno-confessional heritage, and life within them was relatively free of state interference.

With little arable land and few jobs, it was imperative for Ferghana Valley residents to acquire knowledge and skills. Neither the nomadic populations nor the mountaineers lived under this compulsion to diligence. In so densely- populated and ethnically diverse a region as the Ferghana Valley, people also understood that the key to survival was *maslihat* (consensus). Most conflicts were resolved through traditional techniques. Of course, there were conflicts between and within communities, but ethnic hostility was not among their causes. A poor Kyrgyz could work in the home of a rich Uzbek but would still be included within the family circle; the head of the Uzbek family would have felt obligated to take care of the youth as their own son, provide for his education, train him for a profession, and marry him off.

These and other circumstances led to the creation of a distinct Ferghana identity that coexisted with an underlying Muslim selfhood and a weak sense of nationality. A pronounced conservatism lay at the heart of this Ferghana identity. Beginning in the late 1920s, residents of the Ferghana Valley, or *fargonachi*, no longer felt themselves to be a single socio-economic and cultural-religious whole. In fact, the term *fargonachi* fell out of use.[23] The delineation of borders from 1924 to 1936 encouraged the residents to view one another through the prism of nationalism. Hastily drawn borders turned peaceful neighbors into competitors ready to fight over their "national interests." At the same time, Ferghana Valley dwellers were reduced to the status of sub-national groups within the three new Central Asian republics among which their region had been divided. Uzbeks from Namangan, Andijan, and Ferghana City now competed with Uzbeks from Tashkent, Samarkand-Dzhizak, and Khorezm. Tajiks from the Khujand oasis strove to assert their dominance in the fight against southern elites in the capital city of Stalinabad (Dushanbe).

Kyrgyz of the Ferghana Valley, meanwhile, now found themselves in competition with Kyrgyz in the north. All three sectors of the valley had been subordinated to distant republic capitals.

People of the Ferghana Valley embraced the Soviet identity and separate nationalities that had been imposed on them, but these did not replace their older loyalties to family, class, and territory. Their Ferghana Valley identity preserved its major features but shrank to a very local community-based on family clans and a jointly-preserved history. When Ferghana Valley residents moved to the capitals, their devotion to family and clan, and their territorial community, actually intensified. Even in Tashkent, Frunze, or Stalinabad, Ferghana natives retained their traditional mentalities and did not rush to become integrated into their nationalities. Soviet urban culture proved impotent against the more enduring, natural, and emotionally rich indigenous attachments.

Meanwhile, Tashkent continued as the cosmopolitan capital of the entire region, but with a separate "old town" populated by Tashkent Uzbeks. The Tajik capital of Stalinabad from 1929 to 1953 was a large construction site populated by Russians and Tajiks from various regions. Frunze, situated in Kyrgyzia's north, was a Russian-Soviet city *par excellence,* markedly different from the ancient city of Osh, the southern capital. Migration to these capitals did not turn them into melting pots; instead they became the scene of struggles for dominance among the sub-national groups who had moved there.

Overall, Soviet-style modernization did not attain its goal. Soviet rules did not supersede existing norms. Economic development did not lead to the emergence of national economies. At best, as with the emancipation of women, there was a synthesis of the local and the superimposed. In the Ferghana Valley, traditions of harmonious coexistence among ethnic group faded, while Soviet "nation building" disrupted historical memory and social continuities. Yet indigenous identity, grounded on a common culture, mentality, and emotional ties, somehow survived across the valley.

Repression

After adopting the so-called Stalin constitution in 1936, the Soviet government redrafted the republic constitutions to accord with it. The extensive nominal rights specified in this constitution are well known. It also elevated the Kyrgyz Autonomous Region of the Russian Republic (RSFSR) to the status of a full republic. At the republic level, the constitution provided for elections to soviets or councils at every level down to the village, and these in turn elected their own executive committees (ispolkoms). Such was the formal structure of government in the three republics of the Ferghana Valley on the eve of the World War II.

The 1936 constitution was more a sham political act than a legal document. It declared the "victory of socialism" in the USSR and led the next year to millions of "builders of socialism" being sent to prison camps for betraying the Stalinist policy line. No measure since 1917 did more than "Stalin's constitution" to cause citizens to distrust the government and disregard its laws.

The period between 1929 and 1953 marks a tragedy in the history of Central Asia. Under the totalitarian system that crystallized at that time, all power rested with the Communist Party and all non-governmental entities and informal assemblies, including mosques, *madrassas, maktabs,* and *gaps* (male interest forums) were violently suppressed. *Chaikhanas* (teahouses) were turned into communist propaganda centers. Religion was criminalized and believers persecuted. During these years all parts of the Ferghana Valley experienced state terror and the merciless destruction of whole classes of people. The Party, fearing external enemies, violently suppressed the slightest manifestation of dissent within the country. Such fears were of course exaggerated, but they produced a climate in which only a suicidal person would dare say anything critical of the government.

Bolsheviks had instituted their "Red Terror" immediately after they seized power in 1917, with the first concentration camps being instituted by Lenin in order to "reeducate" dissenters. With the onset of collectivization, terror became an essential tool of economic transformation. By 1936 until 1938, when the system of total terror reached its zenith, everyone from Politburo heads down was liable to be sent to the prison camps set up by the Main Administration of Collective Labor Camps (GULAG).[24]

In the Ferghana Valley, as elsewhere in the Soviet Union, many tolerated and even supported these acts of repression. Local leaders tried to save themselves by showing vigilance in hounding down "enemies of the people." Citizens informed on neighbors or colleagues in order to save their own families. Nonetheless, all sections of the population were subject to repression. Party and Soviet leaders and anyone else suspected of ties with such obvious "public enemies" as *bais, khans, emirs, basmachi,* bourgeois nationalists, and pan-Turkists suffered particularly. The central government determined the numbers to be arrested down to the district level and later empowered local officials to draw up their own lists, beyond the quotas. The eagerness they demonstrated at this task did not necessarily save themselves, however.

In the fall of 1937, the secretary of the Central Committee of the All-Union Communist Party (Boshevik [b]), Andrei Andreev, personally "purged" Uzbekistan and Tajikistan. Even though most Uzbek and Tajik Party leaders already had been jailed, the government now organized local "troikas" consisting of a prosecutor, the head of the secret police, and the local chief of police, to consider tens, if not hundreds of, cases a day. From 1937 to 1939 such troikas in Uzbekistan tried 37,000 people and sentenced 6,920 of them to death.[25]

The fall of the first secretary of the Central Committee of the Communist Party of Uzbekistan, Akmal Ikramov, and other senior Uzbek officials was marked by public trials and massive propaganda campaigns against them. In Kyrgyzia a group of the most senior officials,[26] including Torekul Aitmatov, father of the famous writer Chingiz Aitmatov, were executed in November 1938. On October 31, 1937 the former chairman of the Central Executive Committee of the Tajik Republic, Nusratulla Maksum, received a death sentence, with a similar fate suffered a year later by the first secretary of the Central Committee of the Communist Party of Tajikistan. Urunboi Ashurov.[27] A large number of other high officials in Tajikistan also became victims of Stalin's 1937–38 purges.

As a result of these purges, residents of the Ferghana Valley naturally became highly fearful and distrustful of the state and government. Many perceived that Stalinist society rested on lies and intimidation. But in assessing the Stalin period, it is important not to whitewash the situation. Stalin's paranoia was not solely responsible for totalitarianism. National and Party leaders were also involved, as was the public at large. Without all their support the Stalinist regime could never have taken root, let alone survived as long as it did.

World War II: On Whose Side?

On June 22, 1941, Nazi Germany attacked an unprepared USSR. Within four months Hitler's forces had seized 40 percent of the Soviet population and 70 percent of its economy. The remaining 1,500 industrial enterprises were evacuated to the east, including 100 to Uzbekistan, 30 to Kyrgyzia, and 20 to Tajikistan. A million refugees from the war zone were relocated to Kyrgyzia, Tajikistan, and Uzbekistan. This evacuation strengthened the command economy, with people working thirteen-hour days, six days a week.

How did the people of the Ferghana Valley respond to the war? To this day Central Asians hold two contrary views on this period. The first is strictly positive, and dwells on the great construction projects and other achievements that transformed the USSR into a world power. Those who share this view believe that Stalin and the USSR deserve the commendation of all progressive people for winning the "Great Patriotic War," and that the victory proved the superiority of socialism and of Stalin's personal leadership. Many people in the region, including non-communists and the young, still hold this view, one that meshes well with the popularity of authoritarian forms of rule in today's Central Asia.

There are, however, supporters of a contrary approach, who claim that Stalin was a criminal and his policies a chain of monstrous crimes against the people. They believe that the achievements of socialism are a myth, that Soviet policies destroyed the peasantry, ruined manufacturing, engendered servility and a belief in the omnipotence of the state, and inflicted irreversible cultural losses. Indeed, the sufferings of World War II would not have been so huge had Stalin not been in power. Central Asian émigrés cultivated these views in the West during the "Cold War," and they appeared in the USSR particularly during Gorbachev's perestroika.

Today, many equate the "two totalitarian ideologies," Nazism and communism, and increasingly use the term "genocide" with respect to Soviet policy in Central Asia. There is underway an explicit rehabilitation of the *basmachi* of the Ferghana Valley,[28] as well as of anti-Soviet émigré leaders who collaborated with

Nazis during the war, specifically the figures of a Kazakh, Mustafa Chokaev, and an Uzbek, Baimirza Hait. The argument goes that those who fought in the Wehrmacht Turkestan Legion "did not wage war against their native land, but against the Soviet system."[29]

During the first months of the war, expatriate pro-*basmachi* political circles in Afghanistan received funds from Germany to prepare an attack against Soviet Tajikistan. The very distance from the German front and the presence of Allied troops in Iran dimmed prospects for this plan.[30] Its more limited goal was probably to destabilize what had become an important Soviet rear supply base in Central Asia. In October 1941, the USSR and Britain demanded that the Afghans deport all German and Japanese citizens from their soil; the Afghans, fearing a possible attack by those countries from Iran, complied and then declared their neutrality.

Even before its defeat at Stalingrad, fascist Germany had shelved its Asian projects. By 1943 the USSR and Britain forced Afghanistan to make mass arrests of Central Asian immigrants who were working for the Germans, including the notorious Ferghana-based *kurbashi,* Kurshermat, or Sher Muhammad. Meanwhile, back in the Ferghana Valley hundreds of thousands of citizens were conscripted, beginning in September 1939. Some 120,000 soldiers from Uzbekistan, more than 42,000 from Kyrgyzstan, and about 50,000 from Tajikistan would receive medals for bravery. Some 209 ethnic Central Asians became Heroes of the Soviet Union,[31] with more than 100 of them natives of the Ferghana Valley.[32] Many industries and peoples were evacuated to the valley during the war, and after the USSR victory thousands of Tatars, Chechens, Greeks, Bulgarians, Armenians, and other peoples of the Caucasus and Crimea whom the Soviet government suspected of collaborating with the German occupiers of their lands were resettled there.

The Turkestan Legion in the German army had been formed in December 1941, from natives of the Crimea, the Caucasus, Volga river basin, and Central Asia who had been captured or voluntarily had crossed the lines. By early 1942 they had established a training camp in Legionowo, Poland, with other bases elsewhere. When Hitler's forces occupied parts of the North Caucasus and Crimea in the fall of 1942, they had numerous fighters of the Caucasus-Muslim legion in their ranks. The Wehrmacht issued various periodicals for the Central Asian volunteers serving in its ranks, whose numbers are estimated from 70,000[33] to 265,000.[34] Veli Kaiumkhan from Tashkent, Baimirza Hait from Namangan, and others worked on these projects. The Third Reich also relied on such people to serve as colonial administrators in their Central Asian territories.

Clearly, the decision by many from the region to fight against the USSR was a response to the terror, brutality, and injustice of the Stalinist regime. In addition, the defeats the Red Army suffered during the first year of war left their mark on the consciousness of many Soviet servicemen. But whereas the emigrants from the USSR adopted new homelands, the prisoners of war resolved to take up arms against their homeland and fellow soldiers, to whom they had sworn allegiance. Such actions arouse heated debate to this day, and doubtless will continue to do so in the future.[35]

Post-War Developments

Victory in World War II came at a high cost, for the USSR had exhausted nearly all its material and human resources. No less serious, the government attributed its victory to Stalinism, which it argued had proven to be the only correct system and as such certainly needed no reforms. Hence, the economy continued to drag and Central Asia remained mainly a source of raw materials for industries located in Russia. Leaders of the republics had no influence on decision-making, especially in the cotton sector, and depended completely on Moscow. Peasants made a bare thousand a year, with 80 percent of their income being paid in kind.

As if this were not bad enough, 1948 witnessed the start of a fresh purge in Central Asia. In January of that year, the Presidium of the Supreme Soviet of the USSR decreed that any "saboteur" deliberately shirking work on irrigation systems, planting or harvesting was to be sent to Siberia. Soon hundreds of thousands of Central Asians and residents of the Ferghana Valley found themselves in correctional labor camps, prisons, and penal colonies. Such heavy-handed measures gradually restored production and allowed the government to abolish rationing, but agriculture had been plundered and living standards in the Ferghana Valley remained low.

Between 1929 and 1953, residents of the Ferghana Valley endured three periods of starvation: in 1932–33 caused by collectivization; the wartime famine of 1941–45; and the post-war famine of 1946–47. Not only did the horrors of collectivization and Stalin's Great Terror claim tens of thousands of lives, but the repressions continued unabated until the mid-1950s.

Notes

1. Here: "Muslim state."

2. See Hisao Komatsu, "Dar al-Islam Under Russian Rule as Understood by Turkestani Muslim Intellectuals," in *Empire, Islam and Politics in Central Eurasia. Slavic Eurasian Studies,* ed. Uyama Tomohiko, Sapporo, Japan, 2007, p. 5.

3. *Ulama* (s. *alim*), religious experts on Islamic laws who worked as *qadis* (judges), teachers, etc.

4. *Avlod* (plural form of Arabic *valid*): a large family of blood relatives made up of several smaller families. *Avlod*s could live together in the same house, or separately, but they necessarily acknowledged the supremacy of the common grandfather.

5. *Mahalla* (from the Arabic "place of living"): a stable community of neighbors in a city or large settlement. Usually, *mahallas* comprised people sharing a common profession (e.g., blacksmiths) or origins (for, e.g., Kazakhs).

6. Now Kamil Iarmatov city film theater by is located there.

7. Kamil Iarmatov (1903–1978), one of the founding fathers of cinema in Central Asia. His daughter, Gulnora Kamilovna Pulatova, was a minister of health of the Tajik SSR at the end of the 1980s.

8. Michael Thurman, "The 'Command-Administrative System' in Cotton Framing in Uzbekistan, 1920s to Present," in *Papers on Inner Asia,* Bloomington, Indiana, 1999, p. 3.

9. *Ocherki istorii Ferganskoi oblasti v Sovetskii period,* Tashkent, 1980, p. 34.

10. H.N. Drikker, *Formirovanie klassov sotsialisticheskogo obschestva v Tadzhikistane,* Dushanbe, 1983, p. 105.

11. The Turkestan-Siberian railway was built between 1926 and 1931.

12. *Ocherki istorii Ferganskoi oblasti v Sovetskii period,* p. 40.

13. The Kairakkum (Qairoqum) reservoir was created between 1956 and 1958 on the Syr Darya River in the western (Tajik) part of the Ferghana Valley to regulate water flows and provide for stable irrigation of lands covering the area of more than 300,000 hectares. The area of the reservoir is 513 square kilometers.

14. Halima Nasyrova (1913), an Uzbek singer hailing from Taglyk—a village near Kokand. She started her creative activities as a drama actress in 1927 and was a popular artist of the USSR from 1937 on. From 1930 to 1985, she performed at the Uzbek opera and ballet theater and was awarded the USSR State Prize in 1942 and 1951.

15. Tamara Khanum, whose real name was Tamara Artemovna Petrosian (1906–1991), was born in Ferghana and was Armenian by nationality. She was a dancer, singer, and ballet master and participated in the establishment of the Uzbek ballet theater. She reformed the performance style of Uzbek female dances, and was a collector of song and dance folklore of various nations throughout the world. She received the USSR State Prize in 1941.

16. Akhunbabaev (1885–1943), studied in elementary school (*maktab*) and until 1919 he was a day laborer and *arbakesh* (coachman). A communist since 1921 and a chairman of Margilan Koshchi Union (1921–25), from 1925 to 1938 he served as the chairman of the Central Executive Committee of the Soviets of Uzbekistan. From 1938 to 1943 he was the chairman of the Presidium of the Supreme Soviet of Uzbekistan.

17. Tursunkulov participated in the establishment of Soviet rule in the Ferghana Valley in 1918–21 and took pride in being friends with Marshall Semen Budennyi. In 1935 he became chairman of a cotton-growing kolkhoz. Tursunkulov joined the Party only in 1945. Despite his lack of education, he was elected an honorary member of the Academy of Agricultural Sciences of Uzbekistan. Saidhoja Urunkhodjaev, a Tajik from Khujand district, joined the Communist Party in 1929. From 1936 until the end of his life in 1967 he was chairman of a number of kolkhozes in Leninabad district of Leninabad (now Sughd) province. Like Tursunkulov, Urunkhodjaev had friendly connections with the highest ranking officials of the USSR (marshals Budennyi and Voroshilov).

18. M. Rahimov, *Istoriia Fergany,* Tashkent, 1984, p. 42.

19. In the first half of nineteenth century there were 300 *maktabs* and 5,500 students in Kokand.

20. See Abdudjabbor Kahhori, *Adjab Dunee,* Dushanbe, 2003, pp. 31–34, 61. We should add to this that today's Tajiks and Uzbeks have little or no knowledge of calligraphy (*hattoti*).

21. See *Repressiia, 1937–1938 gody. Dokumenty i materialy,* issue 1, Tashkent, 2005.

22. S.M. Ishakov. *Iz istorii Rossiiskoi emigratsii. Pisma A. Z. Validova i M. Chokaeva (1924–1932 gg.),* Moscow, 1999, p. 48.

23. To be more precise, the term continued to be used only by the Uzbek- and Tajik-speaking emigrants (*muhajirs*), who escaped from the Ferghana Valley to Afghanistan in the 1920s and 1930s. They called themselves *fargonachi* until the Soviet invasion of Afghanistan in 1979. The *fargonachi* preferred to marry among themselves rather than their kin Uzbeks and Tajiks from Afghanistan. See Audrey Shalinsky, *Long Years of Exile: Central Asian Refugees in Afghanistan and Pakistan,* Lanham, MD, 1994.

24. From 1917 to 1922 the national security service agency was called the All-Russian Extraordinary Commission for Combating Counter-Revolution and Sabotage (Cheka). In 1922 the Cheka was abolished and its functions transferred to the newly created State Political Directorate (GPU). In 1923 the GPU was reformed into the Joint State Political Directorate (OGPU) under SNK (Council of People's Commissars) of the USSR. In 1934 the OGPU was incorporated into the newly formed NKVD and became the Main Directorate of State Security of the People's Commissariat of Internal Affairs (GUGB of NKVD). In 1941 the NKVD of the USSR was divided into two independent bodies: the NKVD of the USSR and People's Commissariat for State National Security of the USSR.

25. *Repressia, 1937–1938 gody,* p. 8.

26. Chairman of Kyrgyzstan government Iusup Abdrakhmanov was arrested in the fall of 1937, allegedly as a participant of the bourgeoisie-nationalist Alash-Ordyn organization. supreme court charged him with being a member of the anti-Soviet Social-Turan party that planned to overthrow the Soviet government and to secede Kyrgyzia from the USSR. Apart from that, Abdrakhmanov was considered one of the leaders of the fictional Pan-Turkic center and a spy of the "English imperialists."

27. Urunboi Ashurov (1903–1938), a Tajik and native of Skobelev city (Ferghana). He worked in various Soviet and party capacities in Skobelev and Margilan. From 1925 on he worked as a secretary of the Ferghana city committee of the Communist Party (b) of Uzbekistan, and as a secretary of the Andijan Party's district committee in 1927. From 1927 to 1936 he studied and continued holding party positions in Moscow. He became an executive instructor of the Central Committee of the All-Union Communist Party (b) in 1936. From January 1937 he served as the first secretary of the Central Committee of the Communist Party (b) of Tajikistan.

28. See *Turkestan v nachale XX veka: k istorii istokov natsionalnoi nezavisimosti,* Tashkent, 2000.

29. See Bahyt Sydykova, "Istoriia Turkestanskogo legiona v dokumentakh," www.continent.kz/library/turkestan_legions/Glava_4.htm.

30. The USSR and England invaded into Iran on August 25, 1941. The USSR justified its actions based on the terms of the Soviet-Persian Treaty of 1921. According to the treaty, Iran committed itself to prevent the use of its territory as a base for military offensives against Soviet Russia, granting the Soviet government the right to invade Iran should this provision be violated. See Jamil Hasanli, *At the Dawn of the Cold War: The Soviet American Crisis Over Iranian Azerbaijan, 1941–1946,* Harvard Cold War Studies Book Series, Landham, MD, 2006.

31. See K.K. Karakeev, *Vklad trudiashchikhsia Srednei Azii v pobedu. Sovetskii tyl v Velikoi Otechestvennoi voine,* bk. 2, Moscow, 1974, pp. 300–301.

32. N.G. Berezniak, *Geroi Sovetskogo Soiuza—uzbekistantsy,* Tashkent, 1984.

33. Waffen-SS im Einsatz Hitler's Soviet Muslim Legions, http://stosstruppen39-45.tripod.com/id10.html.

34. G. Mendikulova, *Kazakhskaia diaspora: istoriia i sovremennost,* Almaty, 2006, p. 147.

35. The aged leader of the so-called Turkestan National Society, one of the organizers of the Turkestan Legion" a former Grupsturmfuehrer Waffen-SS Baimirza Hait visited Tashkent and his native town Djarkurgan (Namangan) in 1992. He was given the cold shoulder and immediately left Uzbekistan. Hait died in Munich on October 31, 2006 at the age of eighty-eight. Hait's radical views, particularly on the *basmachi* movement and repressive features of the Soviet government, became widespread in Uzbek historiography in the 1990s. See, for instance, G.A. Khidoiatov. "Sto let borby narodov Tsentralnoi Azii za svobodu i nezavisimost," in *Nezavisimost i istoriia: novye podkhody k izucheniiu istorii Uzbekistana,* Tashkent, 1997.

6

The Ferghana Valley in the Eras of Khrushchev and Brezhnev

Ravshan Nazarov (Uzbekistan), with
Pulat Shozimov (Tajikistan)

For the Ferghana Valley, the period of rule by Nikita Khrushchev and then Leonid Brezhnev was the most stable era between the end of the Russian Civil War and suppression of the *basmachi* in 1920–21 and the sending of Soviet troops to Afghanistan in 1979, when radical underground religious networks reappeared in the region.

Social and Political Developments

Central Asia's socio-political development has always included an element of "clan politics" based on tribal, sub-ethnic, and local-territorial groupings.[1] Such politics flourished especially in the Ferghana Valley. Indeed, during Khrushchev's rule the Ferghana political elite controlled virtually all political and economic sectors of the three Ferghana republics: Kyrgyzstan, and Tajikistan, and Uzbekistan.

The prevalence of Ferghana natives in Uzbekistan's politics began in the time of Yuldash Akhunbabaev, who chaired the national government from 1925 to 1943.[2] From 1950 to 1955 Ferghana native Amin Niyazov was first secretary of the Central Committee of the Communist Party of Uzbekistan, having previously served on the Presidium of the Supreme Soviet of Uzbekistan and as speaker of the Uzbek parliament. Between 1953 and 1955 Ferghanan Usman Iusupov, formerly First Secretary of the Uzbek Communist Party and Soviet minister of cotton, chaired Uzbekistan's Council of Ministers.[3] Yadgar Nasridinov from Kokand was vice chairman of Uzbekistan's Council of Ministers (1955–59) and then chaired the Presidium of the Supreme Council of the republic (1959–70). Hadicha Sulaimonova from Andijan served as Uzbekistan's minister of justice (1956–58) and as minister of Uzbekistan's Supreme Court (1964–65).

Until the end of the Soviet period in Uzbekistan, a number of senior Party and governmental posts at the national level were held either by people born in the Ferghana Valley (e.g., I.B. Usmanhodzhaev from Ferghana, P.K. Habibullaev from

Andijan), or by people closely connected with the valley through professional and personal ties (e.g., N.A. Mukhitdinov had worked in Namangan, S.K. Damalov in Margilan and Ferghana).

In these years Ferghana Valley natives exercised similar authority in Tajikistan. From 1946 to 1956 Ferghana native Bobojon Gafurov was First Secretary of the Communist Party of Tajikistan, to be followed by another Ferghana native, Tursun Ulzhabaev, who served from 1956 to 1961. Ulzhabaev's tenure encompassed nearly the entire turbulent period of economic development. However, his career ended when he became a victim of Khrushchev's politically driven program to set and fulfill seemingly impossible goals for the cotton harvest. This strikingly prefigured the so-called Cotton Affair,[4] which rocked Uzbekistan from 1983 to 1987. But it should be noted that it was Ulzhabaev who laid the economic foundations for stable development in the northern (Ferghana) region of Tajikistan. In 1961 Ulzhabaev was replaced by Jabbor Rasulov, also from the Ferghana Valley, who ruled the republic not only during Khrushchev's reign, but also through nearly all of the Brezhnev period, until 1982.

After 1961 Rasulov entered Tajikistan's national political leadership. It is curious to note that even though the Brezhnev period witnessed the modernization of hundreds of existing factories, it began with a decline in factory construction. The new policy probably had its source in the great emphasis that both Moscow and Dushanbe placed at this time on mechanizing cotton production and the agro-industrial complex. In post-Soviet years Rasulov was to be harshly criticized for these policies on the grounds that he shifted Tajikistan's economy from industry to agro-industry, which was by then considered regressive.

The 1960s were a kind of golden age for the Ferghana elites, as they made use of strong support from Moscow to foster development in their region. As one expert pointed out, "Since the 1940s, the key posts in [Tajikistan] have been held by natives of the northern Leninabad region . . . They comprised the substance and leadership of the party apparatus[5] . . . The north supplied Tajikistan's ruling elite."[6] This can be observed in more recent periods as well, when such prominent political figures as R. Nabiev, A. Abdullajanov, J. Karimov, A. Samad, S. Turaev, M. Hudayberdiyev, and others all emerged from Ferghana.

The Tajik scholar S. Olimova called attention to a phenomenon characteristic of all eastern societies, but which is especially pronounced in Tajikistan. Even an influential leader who may have toiled loyally and effectively in the country's sole political party can be readily tarred with the brush of representing not "our" ethno-regional group but "someone else's."[7] This is equally characteristic of Kyrgyzstan and, to some extent, of Uzbekistan.

From 1950 to 1961, the Ferghana Valley native Ishak Razzakov served as First Secretary of the Communist Party of Kyrgyzstan, having served previously as Chairman of the Council of Ministers. In general, the valley was well-represented in the Kyrgyz leadership until the end of the Soviet period. Turabay Kulata, from Kyzyl-Kiya, served as Chairman of the Presidium of the Supreme Soviet of Kyrgyzstan; Abdy Suerkulov from Osh was Second Secretary of the Party from 1949 to 1959 and, concurrently chairman of Kyrgyzstan's Supreme Soviet (1947–50) and minister of trade (1959–69). Ahmatbek Suyumbaev, who was from Kant but had worked for a long time in Osh, held the post of Chairman of the Council of Ministers of Kyrgyzstan from 1968 to 1978. Osh native Absamat Masaliev served as mayor of Kyrgyzstan's capital, Frunze (now Bishkek), from 1970 to the 1980s, and as Secretary and First Secretary of the Kyrgyz Communist Party, as well as Chairman of the Supreme Soviet. Mirza Kaparov from the Uzgen region led the Republic's Komsomol from 1968 to 1972. Dzhumgalbek Amanbaev, who was originally from Naryn but lived and worked for many years in Osh, was the last first Secretary of the Kyrgyz Communist Party. Usen Sydykov, from Jalalabad, was first vice chairman of the Council of Ministers, chair of the State Agricultural Committee, and then state counselor from 1988 to 1990; and Zulumbek Dzhamashev, also from Jalalabad, chaired the republic's Supreme Court from 1974 to 1990. Mamadiyar Isabaev, from Nookat, was a member of the Supreme Court of Kyrgyzstan from 1987 to 1991. Finally, Madan Alymbekov, from Osh served as minister of justice and chaired the republic's Supreme Court.

Kyrgyz scholars A. Ayazbekov and E. Nogoibaeva note that "Until 1991, the Kyrgyz elite was imitative in character, insofar as it developed first under the (partial) influence of Kokand, then of the Russian Empire and, finally, of the Soviet state. . . . For nearly a century the fundamental design of Kyrgyzstan's political culture was Soviet, its main features being the supremacy of one political party and an austere hierarchical system for training elites, which involved recruitment within a closed system."[8] The same can be said of the Tajik elite and, to some extent, of the Uzbek elite.

It is important to point out that under Khrushchev and Brezhnev connections between the Communist Party's first secretaries in Tajikistan and Kyrgyzstan with Moscow were largely mediated by Uzbekistan. This dependence of Tajikistan and Kyrgyzstan on Tashkent, which existed from the final Khrushchev years through the entire Brezhnev period, was due to the strength of Tashkent's voice in Moscow. Out of all the Party first secretaries from Central Asia, only Uzbekistan's sat in the highest councils in Moscow. This person was Sharaf Rashidov, who from 1959 to 1983 was a "candidate member" of the Politburo of the Communist Party of the USSR. As Khrushchev's power eroded and Brezhnev worked to consolidate his rule, Rashidov's powers steadily increased. Rashidov was born in the Dzhizak region but had extensive personal links with the Ferghana Valley.

Rashidov's close personal ties with Brezhnev allowed him to control the Central Asian republics. This led to a situation in which Jabbor Rasulov in Tajikistan and Turdakun Usubaliev, the leader of Kyrgyzstan, undertook many political reshuffles in their own republics under the guidance of Rashidov. At the same time Rashidov served as an advocate and lobbyist for Central Asia's interests in Moscow. This arrangement eventually gave Uzbekistan a dominant position in Central Asia as a whole.

These same years witnessed a planned process of urban development in the Ferghana Valley, which in turn changed nearly all political and administrative structures. The Uzbek sector saw the rise of Kuvasay (1954), Hamza (1974), Kuva (1974), Yaypan (1974), and Rishtan (1977) in Ferghana province; Chust (1969), Uchkurgan (1969), Kasansai (1973), Hakkulabad (1974), Chartak (1975), Pap (1980), and Chartak (1983) in Namangan province; and Shakhrikhan (1970), Markhamat (1974), Kurgantepa (1976), and Karasu (1981) in Andijan province. In 1960, Namangan was divided into the Ferghana and Andijan provinces, an arrangement that was reversed in 1967.[9]

Fundamental changes also took place in the Kyrgyz part of the Ferghana Valley during these years. In 1959, the provinces of Jalalabad and Osh were united and remained so until 1990, forming a single Ferghana Valley province within Kyrgyzstan. Meanwhile, in the Tajik sector of the valley new city centers were formed alongside old cities, including Isfara (1953), Penjikent (1953), Chkalovsk (1956), Kairakkum (1963), and Gafurov (1965).

Border issues that had arisen with the establishment of the Soviet republics remained unresolved and highly controversial. In 1955 the presidiums of the Supreme Soviets of Uzbekistan and Kyrgyzstan reached agreement on how to resolve these disputes. They set up a joint commission that, on the basis of available cartographical materials, came to a joint decision that provided for the transfer to Kyrgyzstan of around 70,000 hectares of land belonging to Uzbekistan, including the Burgandin Massif and northern Sokh.

However, in reaching its decision, the joint commission did not have access to sensitive archival materials assembled during the border demarcation process from 1925 to 1945. Thus, it proceeded from the false premise that certain pasture lands of the Kyrgyz Republic had been given to households in Uzbekistan's Ferghana province for long-term use in 1953. Since these households had not in fact used these pastures, it seemed advisable to transfer them back to Kyrgyzstan.

To gain the force of law, this decision had to be confirmed by the councils of ministers and the presidiums of the supreme soviets of both the Uzbek and Kyrgyz republics, as well as by the Presidium of the Supreme Soviet of the USSR. The joint commission's protocol was reviewed by the governments of both republics and confirmed by the Uzbek and Kyrgyz councils of ministers on August 3, 1955, and October 22, 1956, respectively. Both governments then presented all the materials to their respective supreme soviets for final confirmation. However, when the Presidium of Uzbekistan's Supreme Soviet examined the documents, it rejected the Joint Commission's decision regarding the transfer of several parts of the Sokh region to Kyrgyzstan. As a consequence, the entire protocol was void. But the Presidium of Kyrgyzstan's Supreme Soviet, without waiting for agreement from both sides, ratified the joint commission's proposed boundary line on March 30, 1961. However, since neither the Uzbek nor the USSR-wide supreme soviets had concurred, the new boundary was not legally valid. All this formed the background to the Ferghana crisis that exploded in 1958.

On April 10 of that year, the government of the Kyrgyz Republic had requested the Council of Ministers of the Uzbek Republic to transfer the oil and gas deposits of the north Sokh district to its own jurisdiction. On October 29 the Uzbeks rejected this request. In September, Kyrgyzstan's Council of Ministers petitioned the Council of Ministers of the USSR to approve its proposal. In following up on this petition, the State Planning Committee of the USSR, in a letter dated October 4, 1958, sought the opinion of the government of the Uzbek Republic. On October 18, 1958, the Uzbek government categorically rejected the proposed transfer.

Faced with a standoff over this Ferghana boundary issue, the commission of the Presidium of Council of Ministers of the USSR acted by fiat, instructing the councils of ministers of the Uzbek and Kyrgyz republics to "[take joint actions] to change the state border between these republics." Thus, it settled the issue in Kyrgyzstan's favor.

The Moscow commission's preemptory action raises the question: to what extent can Kyrgyzstan's claims on several heretofore Uzbek parts of the Sokh region be substantiated? The joint commission's protocol of 1955, on which the Kyrgyz side based its subsequent appeals, had no legal standing because it had not been approved by the supreme soviets of the Uzbek Republic and the USSR. Moreover, earlier documents confirm that the oil and gas deposits in the Sokh enclave always had belonged to the Uzbek Republic. On this basis, one may conclude that the deposits of the northern Sokh were, and remain, the property of the Republic of Uzbekistan, Kyrgyzstan's claims to the contrary notwithstanding.

Several further territorial changes affecting Uzbekistan were carried out during the late 1950s and early 1960s. In 1956, the Bostanlik region was transferred from Kazakhstan to Uzbekistan in connection with the construction of the massive Charvak reservoir.[10] In 1956, some 50,500 hectares of irrigated land of the Golodnaya steppe, which was located in the Andijan region of Leninabad (now Sughd) province, were transferred from Uzbekistan to Tajikistan.[11] And in 1963 Uzbekistan received 3.5 million hectares of land from the Golodnaya steppe.[12]

The Soviet government justified these frequent transfers of land from one republic to another on ideological grounds. The "Program of the Communist Party of the USSR" adopted at the Twenty-Second Party Congress in 1962 expressly stated that "In the Soviet republics, people of many nationalities live and work together. Borders between union republics within the borders of the USSR increasingly lose their importance; as all nations are equal, their life is built on a single socialist foundation."[13]

During the second half of the 1950s and extending to the collapse of the USSR, many peoples who had been repressed and deported to Central Asia under Stalin were rehabilitated. This process deeply affected the Ferghana Valley. In 1956, the Kyrgyz provinces of the valley alone had 19,482 Chechens and Ingush, 3,208 Balkars, and 2,819 Meskhetian Turks, Kurds, and Khemshils who had been expelled from the Caucasus.[14]

In March 1958, Crimean Tartars held a protest rally in Kokand, demanding to be allowed to return to their traditional homes in the Crimea following their forced deportation.[15] In October 1996, rallies were organized in honor of the forty-fifth anniversary of the founding of the Crimean Autonomous Region, with groups of 2,000 protestors in Andijan, Bakabad, and Ferghana City. The rallies were harshly suppressed, 65 people were detained, and 17 convicted of participating in riots. Several of these deportees were allowed to return to their historical homelands, but the fate of deported Germans, Koreans, Crimean Tartars, Meskhetian Turks, Kurds, Greeks, and Khemshils remained unresolved until the end of the Soviet period.

The Industrial Sector

New hydroelectric stations in the 1950s greatly improved the supply of energy in the Uzbek part of the Ferghana Valley. Among these were the Kairakkum plant on the Syr Darya and the Uchkurgan plant on the Naryn River. During the same time a gas pipeline was laid from Andijan to Ferghana and Tashkent, an oil-refinery was built in Kokand, and many other new factories were established.[16] The sprawling Andijan factory Andijaniramash, which produced bulldozers, scrapers, trenchers, pumps and other irrigation equipment, was commissioned in 1956.[17]

Dramatic feats of production were achieved through Stakhanovite methods. In Kyrgyzstan's Osh province over ten months in 1953, workers at the Tashkömür coal mines overfilled production goals by 120–130 percent, increasing total coal production by 10 percent.[18] This was matched by similar achievements elsewhere in Ferghana,[19] together with other such campaigns by silk producers,[20] lathe operators in Jalalabad,[21] tunnelers,[22] and cotton cleaners.[23] Such industrial campaigns attracted many workers, with a construction project at the Kairakkum hydroelectric plant alone drawing 3,200 enthusiasts.[24] In Uzbekistan, industries in the Ferghana province out-produced all other provinces except Tashkent.

Of all these mass-organized campaigns, by far the most important in the Ferghana Valley and in all Central Asia was Khrushchev's mobilization to increase cotton production beyond levels achieved in America. In response to this, many industries in the valley switched to meet the cotton industry's needs. In short order new specialized firms arose to repair tractors and combines, and to produce containers to transport bulk cotton. The Kokand super-phosphate plant was completed and other fertilizer mixing facilities were constructed in Andijan, Namangan, and Kokand, all to serve the cotton industry.[25]

In 1959, some 2,280 boys and girls in Ferghana province competed for the title of "shock worker." Parallel with this, a female-led crew at the Kokand Silk Factory managed to do seven hours of work in six hours, churning out a prodigious total of 137,200 garments in one year. Such achievements were rewarded with improvements in health care, education, and social life. Their negative effect was to reduce the number of products for the sake of efficiency, impose a stultifying hyper-specialization on workers, and reduce or eliminate quality controls.[26]

The fifth Five-Year Plan (1951–55) increased capital expenditure in Leninabad from 5 million 1955 rubles to 20.5 million.[27] Over the following half-decade Tajikistan's Ferghana region achieved notable successes, with the construction of many new industrial enterprises, including meat packing plants and garment factories. Thanks to these and such other achievements as the construction of a reinforced concrete bridge over the Syr Darya River, nearly half of workers and public servants in Leninabad were rewarded with a seven-hour work day.[28]

During these years there was still an abundance of semi-skilled jobs, which in 1957 constituted 50 percent of all industrial posts in Tajikistan's Ferghana region[29] and similar percentages in the Ferghana provinces of Uzbekistan and Kyrgyzstan. In 1955, 340 units of uninstalled equipment stood idle in Kyrgyz factories due to a shortage of skilled workers to install them.[30] The opening of a weaving factory, silk plant, auto repair factory, and brewery in Leninabad in 1956, and then the commissioning of the large Kairakkum generating plant the following year, signified a genuine industrial boom in the Ferghana Valley.[31] By the beginning of the 1960s many more factories had begun operating, including a pre-cast panel housing construction factory in Kairakkum, milk and cotton factories in Leninabad, a low-tension hardware factory in Arakman, and an electromagnetic plant in Isfara.[32]

A significant part of the skilled labor force that fueled this boom did not come from local communities, but was attracted to the valley from Russia and Ukraine with the lure of high salaries. Such imported labor was plentiful in the Andijan oil fields,[33] at a pioneering rubber factory in Namangan province, and at the Electro-Apparat factory in Andijan, which opened in 1962.[34] Most of these imported Slavs eventually left the region after independence.

The boom drew attention to the need for specialized training to prepare workers in modern industrial skills. A review of the Uchkurgan butter factory in Namangan province showed that 75 percent of the work force took courses to increase their qualifications, mainly through night classes, correspondence courses, and study groups. Several hundred workers mastered a second trade, and both a Science and Technical Institute and a Society of Inventors and Innovators operated at the plant. As a result, the factory had the lowest rate of injury in Uzbekistan and the lowest rate of absenteeism. Practices at the Uchkurgan butter factory were replicated in all industrial enterprises in the republic.

The "inventors and innovators" movement developed vigorously in the Ferghana Valley. Workers at the Ferghana textile factory presented 371 proposals to improve production, 78 percent of which were introduced at a cost-savings of 25,200 rubles. There were 1,800 such proposals throughout the Ferghana province in 1961, most of which were implemented. Success built on success, with the result that from 1959 to 1965 the number of workers and public servants in Andijan province grew by 51 percent and in Ferghana province by 39 percent.[35] Many found employment at the new shale oil factory in Ferghana or the new truck factory or cellulose plant at Namangan.[36] In 1968 nearly 300 branches, laboratories, construction crews and scientific management groups, comprised of more than 2,000 people, were established in Namangan alone.[37]

Thanks mainly to developments during World War II, the Tajik part of the Ferghana Valley (Leninabad province) already had a strong industrial infrastructure. When 2,420 workers descended on Kairakkum from all over the USSR to build the hydroelectric plant there,[38] they unleashed a fresh boom, especially after the plant opened in the following year.[39] By the 1970s the Leninabad region accounted for more than a third of Tajikistan's industrial production and a significant portion of its agricultural output. Coal mining was carried out at Shurab; oil was developed at Neftabad and Kim; lead and zinc were mined and refined at Altyn-Topkan, Kurusay, and Kansay; tungsten and molybdenum were mined at Chorukh-Dairon; and bitumen and mercury at Ansobskii Mountain. These large enterprises were balanced by a host of light industries producing everything from wine and flour to carpets and knitted wear.

Most of these enterprises could not utilize their full production capacity due to a chronic shortage of skilled labor. To address this problem, the same types of training programs we met in the Uzbek sector were created: industrial and technical courses, schools of progressive labor methods, versatility training. At the Leninabad Silk Combine alone, some 10,260 people went through various forms of re-training.[40]

The Tajik part of the Ferghana Valley enjoyed a significant advantage over the other parts of the republic because most of Tajikistan's elite hailed from there. The fact that the region already had a developed industrial base gave it a further edge over other regions in Central Asia. These factors combined to bring the USSR's new uranium mining industry to Leninabad, even though large deposits of uranium could be found elsewhere. Thanks to this, Tajikistan's Ferghana region played an important role in the USSR's successful creation of its first atomic bomb, which was made from uranium from Leninabad province.

Security concerns dictated that the Soviet uranium industry operate under strict bonds of secrecy. Thus, in Tajikistan's Ferghana region the cities of Taboshar and Chkalovsk and the town of Adrasman were all closed to outsiders. The government maintained a rigorous register of everyone working or living there, and closely controlled all entry and exit. At the same time, these cities were granted a special status that gave them access to financial and other resources unavailable to others.

The mining and refining of uranium in the Ferghana Valley continued unabated from 1945 to 1983. The grave and lasting downside to this otherwise lucrative industry was that the authorities established and operated the uranium mines with little or no concern for their impact on nearby communities or adjacent water resources. Many tailing pits and landfills of waste from the uranium facilities were concentrated in the Leninabad province of Tajikistan and the Jalalabad province of Kyrgyzstan, both in the Ferghana Valley. Nearly 54.8 million tons of radioactive waste accumulated in the above-mentioned closed cities alone.

The uranium-mining town of Gafurov is situated close to the city line of Leninabad (now Khujand). Anyone passing by there today can see 200 meter-long and fifteen-meter-high mounds of uranium tailings right by the road. Even today, many Leninabad residents know nothing about them. Chkalovsk, which once exuded prosperity, is today a dreary place emanating a chill from the past.[41] Chkalovsk has four tailing pits. Like their counterparts in Gafurov and Taboshar, many of them have high gamma-ray levels. Most people avoid walking near Taboshar and consider it a dangerously radioactive zone. None of these pits are protected from wind and water erosion. Worse, they are all located on or near waterways flowing to the Ferghana Valley. This has led to a significant increase in many diseases that are directly related to the province's high levels of radioactivity.

In the Soviet period, uranium was most efficiently mined and refined at Chkalovsk. But once its factory suspended operations, the city seemed to be frozen in a death-like trance. The town has attractive residential areas, but life has fled from it. In many respects it is a microcosm of Tajikistan's Ferghana region. On the one hand, Chkalovsk seemingly has everything: industry, urban infrastructure, transport, and communications. On the other hand, the dynamism that once reverberated there, and without which real life is untenable, has largely vanished. Within these formerly closed cities, one feels the echo of all the successes and failures, the victories and defeats, of Soviet development under Khrushchev and Brezhnev in this part of the Ferghana Valley.

Industrial development in the Kyrgyz sector of the Ferghana Valley flourished at the same time as its counterparts in the Uzbek and Tajik areas. In the 1970s, Osh province (which then included the present Osh, Jalalabad, and Batken provinces) produced a quarter of Kyrgyzstan's industrial output and included 28 percent of Kyrgyzstan's industrial workers. Between 1940 and 1973 industrial production there grew by 9.7 times. All the oil and gas, and 95 percent of the Kyrgyz Republic's coal production, were concentrated in the Ferghana region. Coal was mined at Kyzyl-Kiya, Sylyukta, Kokh-Yangak, Tash-Kumyr, and Almalyk; oil and gas came from the deposits of Mailuu-Suu, Uzbaskent, and Changyr-Tash; mercury came from Haydarken; while antimony came from near Frunze. Metal-working and mechanical engineering thrived in Osh and Jalalabad; the largest light bulb factory in Central Asia operated in Mailuu-Suu, and in Jalalabad there were plants producing construction materials and asphalt. Silk and cotton were processed at Osh, Karasu, Jalalabad, and Aravan. Other plants producing butter, beer, shoes, furniture, processed meat, textiles, foot ware, and furniture were spread across the Kyrgyz sector of the Ferghana Valley. The modern Chukurgan and Toktogul hydroelectric plants functioned on the fast-running Naryn River.[42] With such a technical base, it is no wonder that plants in the Kyrgyz part of the valley were among the first in the region to use electronic data processing machines.[43]

Overall, the development of the Ferghana Valley's industrial potential during the Khrushchev and Brezhnev years is one of the brightest pages in the region's history. With Ferghana natives prominent in the republic-level administrations of Kyrgyzstan, Tajikistan, and Uzbekistan, the budgets of all three Ferghana states assigned major resources to the valley throughout this era.

A negative aspect of this otherwise positive picture is that most of the industrial activity in all three republics was focused in a very few areas. By the 1980s, some 65 percent of Uzbekistan's industrial capacity was concentrated in 5 percent of its territory. Of the 100 small and medium-size cities in Uzbekistan, factories and workshops were nonexistent in 40 of them, while the number of mills and light industries in the other 60 was insignificant.[44] Thus, the entire industrial sector of Kuva in Ferghana province in the early 1980s consisted of small silk and furniture factories, cotton mills, bread combines, and canneries. Many cities had only one or two factories.[45] A similar situation could be observed in the Tajik and Kyrgyz parts of the Ferghana Valley. Industry was poorly developed in such smaller cities in Tajikistan's sector of the valley as Sovetabad, Shurab, and Penjikent, and also in the analogous cities of Kyrgyzstan's Ferghana region, such as Batken, Nookat, Karasu, and Khok-Yangak.

The Agricultural Sector

The death of Stalin in 1953 and the rise of Khrushchev's more liberal administration affected agricultural policy throughout the Ferghana Valley, where investment in agriculture grew more quickly than in the rest of the three countries.[46] As much money was spent on Uzbekistan's agrarian sector in the seven years after 1953 as in the twenty-three years before 1953, with like increases in Kyrgyzstan and Tajikistan. In 1952 there were only 6,224 tractors in all Kyrgyzstan, but five years later the number had grown to 14,247. The level of mechanization in Tajik households was 14 times greater in 1958 than in 1940, while in Uzbekistan the growth was 234 times. For all this, 113 collective farms and 16 state farms in Uzbekistan failed to meet production targets in 1960, while in the same year 600,000 sheep were lost in Kyrgyzstan, more than 8 percent of total livestock.[47] Clearly, there was something lacking in the USSR's emphasis on extensive development, with its ever-increasing inputs of machinery, land, and labor. Yet this *extensive* thrust continued and even increased after Stalin.

As part of the scheme to boost cotton production, plans to cultivate 42,400 acres of virgin or fallow land in the central Ferghana Valley were implemented in the 1950s.[48] This also slowed the shift of labor from farm to factory. Pressure to expand cotton production began to increase by 1953, when many collective and state farms failed to meet production quotas. When 30 percent of Tajik farms failed to meet their quotas,[49] this caused the USSR Council of Ministers in 1965 to adopt a decree "On furthering the development of cotton production in the Tajik Republic from 1954 to 1960." But available workers and equipment fell short of what was required to achieve this objective. In 1953, nearly half of the tractors in Osh province were out of use and 537 of them were simply missing.[50] This led to a massive expansion and modernization of the tractor fleet in the Osh and Jalalabad regions, which was accomplished by 1957.[51] Along with this came a program to enlist urban industries to help upgrade and improve Ferghana Valley collective farms.[52] Thus, the Osh truck fleet took over most transport at the nearby Karl Marx Collective Farm; the Osh cooperative "Metalist" built cotton-drying machinery for the 18th Party Congress Collective Farm;[53] and oil-workers from Mailuu-Suu undertook major construction at yet another collective farm.[54]

By 1953 the government was organizing competitions among Ferghana Valley cotton workers to boost production. M. Jumabaeva from Andijan province won by collecting fifteen tons of raw cotton. Others were rewarded for producing higher yields per hectare.[55] The following harvest saw the first cotton produced on the newly developed virgin lands.[56] This was considered sufficiently promising to devote an additional 25,000 hectares of new land in central Ferghana to cotton by 1956.[57]

The sharp rise in Uzbekistan's cotton production was considered a major achievement.[58] Collective farm workers at the "Ferghana" farm benefited from their high productivity in 1956, when 60 percent of the farm's profits were paid back to them at the rate of 24 rubles per workday.[59] Farms in Andijan gained distinction simply by achieving high production,[60] while others were recognized for reducing per hectare costs of production.[61]

The completion of the Chartak and Iskier reservoirs in Namangan[62] and of the Kairakkum reservoir ("Tajik Sea") and associated pumping stations in Tajikistan[63] enabled yet more land to be brought under cultivation, so as to boost cotton production still further.[64] From the mid-1950s to the mid-1970s water from the "Tajik Sea" irrigated nearly 330,000 hectares of land in Tajikistan, and also in the Ferghana provinces of Uzbekistan and Kyrgyzstan.[65] The new Yangi-Suzak Canal near Jalalabad in Kyrgyzstan made it possible for yet more land to be devoted to cotton.[66]

The cult of production came to infect all other sectors of agriculture. Anyone who could raise 100 kilogram of silk-producing cocoons with one box of silkworm eggs was celebrated.[67] Collective School No. 5 of the Ferghana region took first place for breeding enough rabbits to provide the government with 2.5 tons of rabbit meat and 1,300 rabbit skins. Pig breeders,[68] poultry farmers, and cotton cleaners strove to achieve similarly impressive results.[69] During brief periods, production fell below the officially established norms; this occurred in the Ferghana farms in Tajikistan in the late 1950s and early 1960s. As this happened, many households in the Leninabad region fell into debt to the state[70] and were rescued only by massive efforts by collective farmers in adjacent regions.[71]

During the first half of the 1960s, the realization spread that competitions and campaigns would not suffice to modernize agriculture, and that the human capital had to be upgraded through training. This was the goal of a major effort in Osh province, where industrial training in rural schools was significantly expanded.[72] Hundreds of agriculturalists and machine operators were hired as team leaders,[73] and even cotton harvest drivers received training.[74] At the Janov Aravan Collective Farm 150 young boys and girls received secondary training as tractor or truck drivers, or as combine operators. By the middle of the 1960s a number of women who had been trained as cotton harvest drivers had become household names.[75] However, there were many difficulties. The collective farm leaders resisted change, and there were still few skilled workers. Work stoppages were common and production remained uneven.[76]

No sector of the economy was more directly affected by Khrushchev's fall and the rise of Brezhnev than agriculture. A decree issued by the Communist Party at its 1965 Plenum meeting put a firm stop to Khrushchev's experiments in the agrarian sector. Collective farms moved from payment in kind to cash payments, the prices the state paid for agricultural produce were raised, and the agricultural sector was offered better material and technical support.

By 1972 cotton growers in the Izbaskan region of Andijan province became the first in the valley to fulfill their quota for raw cotton. Mechanized picking, which was now used for more than half of the crop, helped achieve this increase.[77] Soon mechanical cotton harvesters would account for 90 percent of the crop in some areas.[78]

Another change was the growing attention paid to the personal farmsteads of collective farmers. This was especially notable in Leninabad province, where 50 percent of Tajikistan's gardens and vineyards were situated.[79] In the winter months, the Frunze Collective Farm near Leninabad allocated more than 180 tons of alfalfa, hay, and sorghum to families raising cattle on their private plots. The Leninabad Milk and Dairy Combine opened a receiving office for the purchase of milk from private farmsteads, and the province's rural consumer society sold formula feed to private dairy farmers.[80] Such measures marked an important step away from Stalin's tragic collectivization of agriculture and in the direction of privatized farming.

Irrigation developed robustly in the Ferghana Valley under Brezhnev. A trial run of water through the Kyzyl-Tyubin canal, the largest waterway in the new lands of central Ferghana, took place in January 1961. In May of that year construction also commenced on the Kerkidon reservoir and the Frunze pump shelter station, which made possible the cultivation of an additional 5,000 hectares of virgin Ferghana lands. In 1970 water was first released into the Great Andijan Canal, while other canals and irrigation works were commissioned in the following years. It now appeared that the ever-expanding cotton crop's thirst for water might actually be quenched.

After independence, the supplying of water to this ever-expanding irrigation system would become the focus of major international tensions, and the irrigation system itself would be condemned for its profligate wastefulness and gross inefficiency. For now, though, the Ferghana Valley presented itself as the living embodiment of the future of agriculture everywhere. In August and September 1979, Uzbekistan became the venue for an international conference on "Measures to Increase Irrigation Efficiency at the Farm Level." Over the course of two weeks, awestruck representatives from eleven countries studied how the virgin lands of the Ferghana Valley had been transformed into a sea of green.

Social Development

The Khrushchev era saw significant efforts to break down the Ferghana Valley's isolation within Central Asia. In 1956 construction began on the important Tashkent-

Angren-Kokand mountain road, which would improve highway links between Tashkent and the Ferghana Valley. The first cars passed down the highway in November 1959.[81] A few years later the first air routes were opened to the region, including both major centers and towns like Isfara in Tajikistan. Such flights, which made possible new forms of economic and cultural interaction, were later to be suspended after independence due to a shortage of fleets to service them.[82]

Other communications emerged at this time. A relay center built in Andijan in the 1950s improved telephone, radio, and eventually television links with Tashkent.[83] A particularly important event for the Tajik part of Ferghana was the launch of television broadcasting there in 1957. Until this time, most apartments in Leninabad were served only by wired radio. In 1963, the first line of video telephony between Tashkent and Andijan began to operate,[84] and in 1966 a retransmitter was initiated in Uzgen near Osh, through which twenty-seven regions of Kyrgyzstan could access central programming.[85]

Whatever its drawbacks, the prosperity created by the cotton mono-culture brought improvements in daily life. In the late 1950s heating gas lines were installed in Ferghana, Margilan, and Kokand, and a number of rural regions in Ferghana and Andijan provinces, and water systems were constructed in Ura-Tyube, Proletarsk, Sovetabad, and elsewhere. In the late 1950s millions of rubles were spent to build social clubs, stores, teahouses, schools, kindergartens, clinics and hospitals in rural districts of Andijan.[86] A large boarding school was opened in Ura-Tyube, and a health resort was established in Chartak near Namangan. In July 1959, athletes from the Kuva district of Ferghana won top honors in the first national meet for rural athletes.[87] In September 1960, Uzbekistan's first (secular) wedding palace opened its doors in Kokand.

Health concerns in the Ferghana Valley increasingly attracted governmental attention and resources. Following the usual Soviet practice, the initial emphasis was on preventive clinics, which were opened in the Palvantash oil fields, the Andijan hydrolytic factory, and the Kokand superphosphate plant in the mid-1960s.[88]

Later in that decade, large multi-field hospitals began to operate in Andijan, along with maternity clinics in Ferghana and Andijan and polyclinics and dispensaries in all regions of the valley.[89] During the 1970s six new hospitals with 2,300 beds began operating, raising Andijan province's total to 17,880 beds in 1979. Millions were also spent on pediatric and obstetrical institutes. In 1981, a 90-bed maternity hospital began operating in the Andijan province, and the next year a 60-bed branch of a children's hospital opened in Namangan.

A similar expansion of medical services occurred in the Tajik sector of the valley. By the 1970s, there were 96 hospital institutions with 9,800 beds in Leninabad province, which was served by one doctor for every 793 people. In addition, the province built several health sanitariums, including one at Oksukon Lake that provided mud treatments and a spa for climatotherapy at Shakhristan.[90] During the same decade Osh province in Kyrgyzstan focused similar resources on hospital construction. This resulted in 105 hospital institutions with 14,100 beds. The 1,800 doctors who served there provided a ratio of one doctor for every 748 persons. The medicinal baths developed in Jalalabad gained great popularity, as did health spas at Arslanbob, Kyzyl-Ungur, and Sari-Chelek.[91]

Notwithstanding these various initiatives, medical services remained a problem in the Ferghana Valley. It was easier to construct buildings than to train doctors, and most of the medical personnel were poorly prepared.[92] Feldshers frequently did the work of doctors. Many of the newly built hospitals and clinics were merely referral institutions for true hospitals and polyclinic institutes located in Tashkent or Frunze. Indeed, as revealed by studies conducted after the collapse of the USSR, a significant percentage of medical institutions in the Ferghana Valley were unheated and had no hot water. Even in large population centers, medical care fell far short of Soviet norms, let alone international standards.[93] For example, in Tashkent there were 64.6 doctors and 156.2 hospital beds for every 10,000 persons, but in the Ferghana province these respective figures were 13 for doctors and 98.3 for hospital beds.[94] Similarly unfavorable ratios were manifest in both the Tajik and Kyrgyz districts of the valley.

A number of diseases reached the level of epidemics, among them cholera, which in 1970 spread to the Ferghana Valley after initial outbreaks in the Caspian region. Outbreaks of tuberculosis in the 1970s presaged a much larger epidemic of this disease a decade later. When it first spread in Ferghana in 1975, the Andijan Executive Committee discussed the problem at several meetings, which resulted in the arrival in the province of twenty-seven doctors who had completed internships in phthisiology, and twenty-five more who had upgraded their qualifications at institutes of advanced medical study. Moscow-based centers opened branches in the Izbaskent region of Andijan province, but these had to refer all but simplest cases to the national capital.[95] On June 25, 1977 the Council of Ministers of the republic acted to improve efforts to combat tuberculosis among the population.

No less than medicine, the social welfare of Ferghana Valley residents became a major concern in these years. In Ferghana province the Standing Commission of the Kuva State Council on Health and Social Welfare passed legislation to protect mothers and children. In the course of discussing these measures, many shortcomings came to light. The State Ministry required the local social security departments, leaders of industrial enterprises, and state farm directors to eliminate the existing flaws, and the Standing Commission took measures to assure the orders were followed.[96] Pension increases of nearly 10 percent doubtless improved social welfare in all three sectors of the Ferghana Valley in the 1970s.[97] Payments to the disabled were also increased in 1979, thanks to legislation enacted in Moscow.[98]

In the late 1970s there was growing concern over the fate of women throughout the Ferghana Valley. Andijan province was typical of many others, when in May 1976 it carried out a review of pension payments, employment, and maternity-leave benefits for female farm workers. This led to surveys of pension sums offered to female farm workers, which turned out to be a miserly 126 rubles per month. Over the following years pensions for women were increased and extended more broadly, in Ferghana and elsewhere.[99]

These and other measures doubtless improved the lives of many people. However, the official figures record only how much was spent and what the state's intentions were, not what actually happened. The question of what actual impact, if any, these changes had on people's lives is more elusive. However, there are some telling indicators. Regarding the overall health of the population, it is surely relevant that Red Army recruits from the valley were found to be more physically fit than those from the capitals of all the three Ferghana republics, and were comparable to the best nationally.[100]

On the other side, the mounting incidence of self-immolation among Ferghana Valley women in the period from 1950 to 1980 cannot go unmentioned, for it suggests that many younger women not only found their overall welfare unacceptable and their lives miserable, but had given up hope of finding a way out. The Spiritual Administration of the Muslims of Central Asia (SADUM) was one of many official organs to take notice of this tragic but not uncommon phenomenon. In 1950, 1952, and again in 1955 SADUM even issued *fatwas* against self-immolation, but with no appreciable effect.[101] The causes of self-immolation are complex and doubtless include important cultural and psychological elements that go beyond generalized problems of "social welfare." But its existence hints at the possibility of persistent problems in the Khrushchev and Brezhnev periods that went unaddressed at the time and would come to the surface only after independence, and in ways that could be exploited by those wishing to do so.

The Cultural Sector

Throughout its history, and especially in the twentieth century, the Ferghana Valley has been a cultural center and source of artistic and scientific talent for all Central Asia. The list of Ferghana natives who enriched the culture of the three Ferghana republics is impressive by any measure, and includes philosophers, historians, economists, linguists, philologists, orientalists, and film directors. One need only speak of the first president of the Uzbekistan Academy of Sciences, Tashmuhamed Kari-Niyazov, born in Kokand; Tajik philosopher, historian, and academic Zarif Radjanov from Leninabad; literary scholar Izzat Sultanov from Osh; historian and diplomat Sherzod Abdullaev from Ferghana, and his brother, poet Shamshad Abdullaev; or the film director Kamil Iarmatov from Kanibadam, to appreciate the range and depth of the valley's contribution to cultural life. Others who made their name outside the region never lost their Ferghana roots, among them the very successful businessman Alisher Usmanov from Namangan; the world-renowned surgeon Rinat Akchurin from Namangan; and cosmonaut Salidjan Sharipov, from Uzgen, to name but a few.

In the 1950s the Uzbekistan Academy of Sciences organized a multi-disciplinary study on development in the Ferghana Valley.[102] This gave rise to important educational advances, including Uzbekistan's first technical college, established at the Ferghana hydrolysis plant.[103] Other innovative institutions followed in the 1960s, including a textile technical school in Namangan, a reclamation technical school in Markhamat, and a pedagogical institute and conservatory of music in Andijan.[104] Higher education expanded in the 1950s with the opening of the Andijan Medical Institute and a branch of the Tashkent Institute of Irrigation and Agricultural Mechanization in Andijan.[105]

Similar developments took place in the Tajik part of the valley, with the opening of the Kanibadam Institute of Technology in 1959, followed by the Ura-Tyube construction school in 1963.[106] By 1958 Tajiks could acquire specialized training in thirty-two fields, twice the number as three years earlier.[107] A 1955 Plenum of the Communist Party of Tajikistan severely criticized the republic's backward command of technology and its low level of modern skills, but this scarcely applied to the relatively advanced Ferghana region in the north.[108] In the Kyrgyz sector of the valley there was a strong emphasis was on the expansion of primary and secondary education, which made significant strides in the late 1950s,[109] and on training programs for those already employed. This concern pervaded the entire region at the time, with evening classes being opened at nearly all the medical and technical institutions in Namangan, Andijan, Leninabad, and Osh.[110]

By the 1980s the Uzbek part of the valley boasted ten institutes of higher education, including pedagogical, medical, and technical institutes, as well as others devoted to economics and foreign languages. Five of these were established in Andijan, with others in Ferghana, Kokand, and Namangan.[111] Two additional institutions of higher education had by then been set up in Osh, including the Osh Pedagogical Institute (now Osh State University) and a branch of the Frunze Polytechnic Institute, while the Leninabad Pedagogical Institute (now Khujand State University) also by then had opened its doors. Meanwhile, the branch of the Tajikistan Academy of Sciences in Penjikent gained world recognition for the archaeological database it founded and maintained in those years.[112]

During the 1960s and 1970s a dramatic expansion in specialized secondary education occurred in all three sections of the Ferghana Valley, exposing thousands of students for the first time to the achievements and complexities of the modern world. In the Uzbek part fifty secondary schools were now operating.[113] Communist ideology was offered in all of them, of course, but Soviet officials at the time were so deeply concerned over lapses in such training that they rewarded a school in Namangan for the correctness of its curriculum in history and society.[114]

In the Kyrgyz part of the valley, the expansion of specialized secondary education gave rise to six new institutions in the provincial capital of Osh,[115] with others in Jalalabad,[116] Uzgen, and Kyzyl-Kiya. Eleven such institutions, enrolling 10,400 students, operated in the Tajik part of the valley,[117] including such highly regarded institutions as the Pushkin School No. 1 in Leninabad, the Chapaev School in Kanibadam, and School No. 1 in the Nausk region. Those in Leninabad focused on textiles, construction, accounting, pedagogy, medicine, and music.[118]

The arts flourished in parallel with these advances in specialized technical education. The specific arts in question were those supported by the Soviet government in Moscow, which meant that the Ferghana Valley for the first time gained intensive exposure to the arts of Europe, with an important but secondary role for the arts of the region itself. In the 1960s the Uzbek Music and Drama Theater of Andijan and Ferghana was transformed into a theater of Musical Drama and Comedy, where the entire oeuvre of the European and Russian stage was offered for the first time to Central Asian audiences. When the Ferghana Museum opened a "National University of Regional Knowledge," the subject matter was filtered through the prism of European/Russian regional folk studies.

Evidence that works of world culture had found a receptive audience in the Ferghana Valley can be found in the thriving amateur performances in the provincial capitals. In April 1966, Uzbekistan's first amateur choir was created by students from the Margilan pedagogical school.[119] An amateur troupe from the Margilan Silk Weaving Combine prepared a music and dance show on the friendship of peoples, while a group from the Andijan Engineering Plant performed both "European" and national compositions. Other amateur performances were devoted to acceptably Soviet themes like "Glory to the Heroes" and "To the Glory of Labor," and these invariably featured songs and declamations of a type that would have been familiar to any European audience.[120] The fact that several of these troupes performed successfully throughout the Soviet Union attests to their integration into the broader cultural mainstream.[121]

Cultural exchanges within the USSR and Soviet bloc brought European performers to the Ferghana Valley. Typical were a Festival of Belorussian Art and Literature held in Kokand and Margilan,[122] and a visit by Bulgarian literati and filmmakers to Ferghana and Andijan.[123] In October 1968, Ferghana, Kokand, and Andijan celebrated a "Decade of Culture of the German Democratic Republic" with a festival that included performances by the fine Berlin Radio Symphony Orchestra and the GDR State Dance Ensemble. In addition to concerts, exhibitions and film screenings of works from abroad were especially popular.[124]

During the 1960s and 1970s the Soviet government sponsored "youth festivals" that were intended to glorify the achievements of socialism, but which actually became venues for young people to make contact with the latest trends in popular culture worldwide. The Ferghana Valley witnessed a number of these events. In April 1974, the "Days of Soviet Literature" took place in Leninabad and other cities of Tajikistan, in which writers and poets from Azerbaijan, Georgia, Kazakhstan, Russia, Uzbekistan, and Ukraine presented their works.[125] In 1982 the second Youth Festival of the Central Asian Republics and Kazakhstan drew large audiences to Isfara.[126]

The penetration of European culture into the Ferghana Valley reached a new stage with the debut of the Osh Province Symphony Orchestra in February 1966.[127] In May of the same year the Kyrgyz Drama Theater toured to Osh, presenting Chingiz Aitmatov's "Mother Earth" (Materinskoe pole) in the same production that was causing stirs in Moscow and the West.[128] In February 1970, a new Music and Drama Theater opened in Kanibadam in Leninabad province.[129] In January

1973 it presented the play *Ever-Burning Lights* by the Azerbaijani playwright M. Ibragimov, whom the Union of Soviet Writers had once harshly denounced for "serious mistakes." In March of that same year, theater companies from Ferghana, Andijan, Kokand, and Namangan took their most advanced works to a Republic Festival of Drama and Art in Tashkent.[130]

Soviet filmmakers in the 1960s and 1970s stood at the forefront of the cultural avant-garde, their works earning warm praise from the most advanced critics abroad. Not surprisingly, cinema in those years gained a prominent place in the cultural life of the Ferghana Valley as well. In October 1969, the first Republic Festival of Short Films and Television Movies presented Ferghana audiences the latest television, popular science, documentaries, and animated films.[131] This was followed two years later by a second festival, at which twenty-eight films were screened officially and another thirty-four more experimental works from all over the USSR were screened unofficially.[132] Several more such festivals were held in the Ferghana Valley, each of them presenting the liveliest and boldest work by modern filmmakers from across the USSR.[133]

Until the mid-twentieth century, the ancient history of the valley was known through tradition or from the research of outsiders, mainly Russians. The rise of local history museums in the 1950s aroused interest among local residents about their early history. In the early 1950s the Ferghana province's local history museum, founded by Russians in 1894, began to mount archaeological expeditions of its own, which were carried under the direction of Leningrad University graduates N.G. Gorbunova and B.S. Gamburg. Other museums that opened in the 1960s included the Gafur Gulyam Museum of Literature in Kokand; the Museum of Scientific Atheism, the only such museum in the valley, housed in a former mosque in Andijan;[134] and the Usman Iusupov Museum of the History of Construction of the Great Ferghana Canal, opened in the village of Kyigan in Andijan province. In Kyrgyzstan, a memorial museum to Urki Salievoi, the first female Kyrgyz to chair a village council, opened in February 1970 in the Nookat region of Osh province.[135] Also, at Uzgen near Osh, an outdoor museum was created with the restoration in 1976 of an eleventh- century Karakhanid mosque and minaret.[136] In Leninabad province the important Rudaki Museum of Natural History in Penjikent, the Leninabad Province Museum of Natural History, and the Isfara Museum of Natural History[137] all focused on the flora and fauna of the region. In doing so, they prepared the way for a more serious consideration of the environment after independence.

European traditions of monumental art were also introduced to the valley at this time. These culture-changing works included the 1965 sculpture of the great eleventh-century physician, Ibn Sina (Avicenna), in Andijan; the 1967 memorial in Shakhimardan to soldiers who died at the hands of the *basmachi*;[138] a statue honoring the Ferghana-born statesman, Yuldash Akhunbabaev;[139] and a prize-winning statue of Lenin in Leninabad.[140]

Because Soviet culture was based so thoroughly on Russia's participation in European culture, the Ferghana Valley's embrace of Soviet culture during the 1960s and 1970s gave the valley a new window on the wider world. Recognition from abroad validated and celebrated that embrace. At the first All-Union Festival of People's Ensembles in Chisinau, Moldova, in 1968 the Namangan House of Culture received first prize. In 1973 the Andijan Puppet Theater won a second place at the International State Puppet Show, while in 1978 the "Anor" ensemble from the House of Culture in Kuva, Ferghana, took first prize in the International Folklore Festival in Belgium. The next year saw the debut of the Rhythms of Uzbekistan ensemble of the four Khakimov brothers from the Andijan Cotton Mill. Within months they were showcased at the Uzbekistan Folk Art Exhibit in Madrid, along with crafts from across the Ferghana Valley.[141]

All of these many new initiatives were duly celebrated in the Ferghana Valley's media, which mushroomed in these years. *Namangan Pravda* began publication in 1958,[142] with *Andijan Tongi* (Dawn of Andijan) following four years later, and then a third urban paper, *Asaka Hayoti* (Life of Asaka) in 1967.[143] In Leninabad, the urban paper *Hakikati Leninabad* appeared in Tajik while *Leninabadskaia pravda* was issued in Russian. In Osh province the newspapers *Lenin Jolu* (Lenin's Path) was published in Kyrgyz and also in Uzbek (*Lenin Yoli*), in addition to a number of city and district papers published in all three languages.

A number of events and publications in these years celebrated the cultural achievements of Ferghana natives over the centuries. In 1959, the Ferghana-born scientist H.M. Abdullaev, of the Uzbekistan Academy of Science, was inducted into the French Geological Society. More than sixty works by Kokand poets and prose writers of the late-nineteenth and early-twentieth century were honored in a collection titled *Mukimi i Furkat* that was published in Leningrad. A key work by one of Ferghana's greatest writers, Babur, the fifteenth-century founder of the Mughal dynasty in India, was discovered in Hyderabad in 1975. Heretofore available only in a Persian translation, this discovery of the original Chagatai Turkish text of Babur's autobiography, *Babur-Nameh,* was an international sensation and promptly gave rise to many fresh translations, including an English edition.[144]

All these landmark innovations of the 1960s and 1070s brought the culture of the Ferghana more closely into the global mainstream than at any time since the tenth century. However, in the early 1980s anxious questions began to be raised as to whether authorities and cultural institutions in the Ferghana Valley were meeting the religious needs of the region's Muslim faithful. Similar concerns were raised in other traditionally Muslim regions of Central Asia. Particularly noteworthy among such expressions of concern was an informational memo issued by the Chairman of the Council for Religious Matters of the USSR, which was under the Soviet Council of Ministers. Addressed to the Central Committee of the Communist Party of the Soviet Union, the memo stated that:

> In some places, believers are deprived of the opportunity peacefully to meet their religious duties because their organizations do not meet the registration requirements and therefore cannot acquire places for worship. Groups of believers of

various types, in thousands of communities, therefore conduct their religious services illegally. Many of them applied many times over the years to register their associations, but their requests were rejected on unreasonable grounds. This has occurred in the [Soviet] republics of Moldova, Tajikistan, Turkmenistan, Uzbekistan, Georgia, Azerbaijan, and in a number of regions of the Ukraine and Russia. Religious societies that operate legally often prevent [the illegal groups] from repairing places of worship and using electric lighting, and do not permit invitations to priests. There are instances in which people have lost their jobs or been expelled from school for religious reasons, depriving believers of opportunities to find good jobs and impinging on their other rights. . . . In several regions where Islam is traditionally widespread, discontent among the population stems from the fact that they do not have a single registered Muslim association, while many Christian religious societies can function legally.[145]

For the time being, such expressions fell on deaf ears, since by the early 1980s the authorities were already beginning to face the many grave problems that would eventually lead to the collapse of the USSR. However, it was not long after this, in the late 1980s and early 1990s, when these concerns burst into the open and fundamentally transformed the religious and cultural situation in the region.

Notes

1. S.N. Abashin, *Natsionalizmy v Srednei Azii: v poiskakh identichnosti,* Saint Petersburg, 2007; D.V. Mukulskii, "Klany i politika v Tadzhikistane," *Rossiia i musulmanskii mir,* no. 12, 1995; A.Sh. Niazi, "Tadzhikistan: konflikt regionov," *Vostok,* no. 2, 1997; M. Olimov and S. Olimova, "Khudzhand: mezhdu Ferganoi i Tadzhikistanom," *Vestnik Evrazii,* nos. 1–2, pp. 194–211; I. Rotar, "Sredniaia Aziia: etnosotsialnaia perspektiva," in *Islam v Rossii i Srednei Azii,* Moscow, 1993; D.A. Trofimov, "Klanovost kak element politicheskoi kultury Tsentralnoi Azii (na primere Kazakhstana, Uzbekistana i Kyrgyzstana)," in *Politicheskaia kultura stran Azii i Afriki,* Moscow, 1996; idem, *Tsentralnaia Aziia: problemy etno-konfessionalnogo razvitiia,* Moscow, 1994; P. Shozimov, *Tadzhikskaia identichnost i gosudarstvennoe stroitelstvo v Tadzhikistane,* Dushanbe, 2003.

2. K.A. Zalesskii, "Imperiia Stalina," in *Biograficheskii entsiklopedicheskii slovar,* Moscow, 2000.

3. B. Reskov and G. Sedov, *Usman Iusupov,* Moscow, 1976.

4. As has been noted in the literature of this period: "Former Secretaries of the CC Uldzhabaev and Obnosov and Chair of the Council of Ministers, Dodukhov did a poor job managing agriculture. At the same time, they began to deceive the Party and State, admitting to misrepresenting reports on plan implementation and creating the appearance of prosperity. In 1961, the CC CPSU exposed and suppressed the anti-party, anti-state activities of the former republic leaders" (*Istoriia tadzhikskogo naroda,* vol. 3, Moscow, 1965, p. 157).

5. P. Mulladazhnov, "Elity u vlasti: Tadzhikistanskii opyt," *Nezavisimaya Gazeta,* October 25, 2000.

6. "Vnutritadzhikskii konflikt: osnovnaia tochka napriazheniia iuzhnoi dugi nestabilnosti," *Nezavisimaya Gazeta,* December 2, 1997.

7. S. Olimova, "Kommunisticheskaia partiia Tadzhikistana v 1992–1994 gg.," *Vostok,* no. 2, 1996, p. 52.

8. A. Aiazbekov and E. Nogoibaieva, "Politicheskie elity Kyrgyzstana: otsenka i analiz," *Ekonomicheskie strategii—Tsentralnaia Aziia,* no. 3, 2006.

9. E. Akhmedov and M. Teshabaev, *Novye goroda Uzbekistana,* Tashkent, 1984, p. 71.

10. *Istoriia Uzbekskoi SSR,* vol. 4. Tashkent, 1968, p. 248.

11. Ibid.; see also *Istoriia tadzhikskogo naroda,* vol. 3, Moscow, 1965, pp. 156, 212.

12. *Istoriia Uzbekskoi SSR,* vol. 4, p. 230.

13. *KPSS v rezoliutsiiakh,* vol. 10, p. 163, Moscow, 1976.

14. D.Sh. Kyzaeva, T.D. Dotsenko, and S.I. Begaliev, *Arkhivnye dokumenty svidetelst-vuiut: Deportirovannye narody v Kyrgyzstane,* Bishkek, 1995, p. 85.

15. TsKhSD, f. 5, op. 31, d. 56, 1. 178.

16. *Istoriia Uzbekskoi SSR,* vol. 4, pp. 210–111, 222, 226, 252.

17. V. Tiurikov, *Pervyi. Pervaia. Vpervye,* Tashkent, 1996, pp. 64–65.

18. *Istoriia sovetskogo rabochego klassa Kyrgyzstana,* Frunze, 1966, p. 353.

19. *Sovetskaia Kirgiziia,* August 23, 1953, and October 13, 1953.

20. *Sovetskaia Kirgiziia,* January 20, 1954.

21. *Istoriia sovetskogo rabochego klassa Kyrgyzstana,* p. 363.

22. *Sovetskaia Kirgiziia,* September 14, 1943, and November 24, 1943.

23. *Istoriia sovetskogo rabochego klassa Kyrgyzstana,* p. 366.

24. D. Akhatov, "Deiatelnost Kommunisticheskoi Partii Tadzhikistana po osushchest-vleniiu leninskikh idei sploshnoi elektrifikatsii (1956–1965 gg.)," Avtoref. diss., MGU, Moscow, 1967.

25. *Istoriia Uzbekskoi SSR,* vol. 4, p. 253.

26. Ibid. pp. 320–22.

27. "Materialy XIX gorodskoi partiinoi konferentsii," *Leninabadskaia Pravda,* 1956, January 18, 1956.

28. *Istoriia Leninabada,* Dushanbe, 1986, pp. 408, 420.

29. "Materialy XXI gorodskoi partiinoi konferentsii," *Leninabadskaia Pravda,* December 29, 1957.

30. *Istoriia sovetskogo rabochego klassa Kyrgyzstana,* p. 362.

31. *Kommunist Tadzhikistana,* February 28, 1957; Sh. Solomonov, *Promyshlennost Leninabadskoi oblasti v shestoi piatiletke,* Dushanbe, 1957.

32. *Istoriia tadzhiksogo naroda,* Moscow, vol. 1965, pp. 194–95.

33. *Istoriia Uzbeksoi SSR,* vol. 4, p. 321.

34. Tiurikov, *Pervyi. Pervaia. Vpervye,* pp. 68, 69, 71.

35. *Istoriia Uzbekskoi SSR,* vol. 4, pp. 323–25, 328, 331.

36. Tiurikov, *Pervyi. Pervaia. Vpervye,* pp. 75, 80.

37. *Partiinaia zhizn,* no. 9, 1968, p. 78.

38. A. Tursunov and G.Khaidarov, *Ogni Ilicha na Syrdare,* Dushanbe, 1962, p. 15.

39. I. Zorin, "Kairakkumskaia GES," *Druzhba narodov,* Dushanbe, 1967, pp. 21, 43.

40. *Peredovik shelka (gazeta LShK),* March 6, 1981.

41. Iu. Iusupov, *Varorud,* no. 45 (133), November 24, 2004.

42. "Oshskaia oblast: Khoziaistvo," *in Bolshaia Sovetskaia Entsiklopediia (BSE),* 3d ed., vol. 19, Moscow, 1975, p. 55; "Jalalabad," in *BSE,* 3d ed., vol. 8, Moscow, 1972, p. 187.

43. *Pravda Vostoka,* March 25, 1973.

44. A. Khazratkulov, *Sotsialnye problemy Uzbekistana i puti ikh resheniia,* Tashkent, 1992, pp. 57, 60.

45. E. Akhmedov and M. Teshabaev, *Novye goroda Uzbekistana,* pp. 30–31, 73–74, 112.

46. Zh.B. Abylkhozhin, *Khrushchevskii povorot: Istoriia Kazakhstana i Tsentralnoi Azii,* Almaty, 2001, p. 554.

47. Ibid., pp. 554, 558.

48. *Istoriia Uzbekskoi SSR,* vol. 4, pp. 212, 227, 339.

49. P.A. Zhilin, "Istoriia Kommunisticheskoi partii Tadzhikistana za podem khlopko-vodstva (1953–1958 gg)," Avtoref. diss., TajGU, Dushanbe, 1968, pp. 3–4.

50. *Istoriia sovetskogo krestianstva Kirgizstana,* Frunze, 1972, p. 366.

51. V.G. Erorkin, *Mekhanizatsiia i elektrifikatsiia kolkhoznogo proizvodstva Kirgizii,* Frunze, 1959, p. 16.

52. *Sovetskaia Kirgiziia,* October 22, 1953.

53. *Istoriia sovetskogo krestianstva Kirgizstana,* p. 389.

54. *Sovetskaia Kirgiziia,* March 10, 1955.

55. *Istoriia Uzbekskoi SSR,* vol. 4, pp. 230, 237.

56. Tiurikov, *Pervyi. Pervaia. Vpervye,* p. 145.

57. *Ocherki istori: Kommunisticheskoi Partii Uzbekistana,* Tashkent, 1974, p. 532.

58. *Rezoliutsii i resheniia sezdov Kompartii Uzbekistana,* Tashkent, 1957, pp. 462–63.

59. *Istoriia Uzbekskoi SSR,* vol. 4, pp. 239, 271.

60. *Ocherki istorii,* p. 540.

61. *Istoriia tadzhikskogo naroda,* vol. 3, Moscow, 1965, p. 201.

62. Akhmedov and Teshabaev, *Novye goroda Uzbekistana,* p. 72.

63. S.A. Parpiev, "Deiatelnost partiinoi organizatsii Tadzhikistana po orosheniiu i osvoeniiu novykh zemel," Avtoref. diss., TajGU, Dushanbe, 1965.

64. *Voprosy istorii KPSS,* no. 10, 1964, p. 23.

65. *Sovet Tazhikistoni,* November 22, 1974.

66. *Sovetskaia Kirgiziia,* May 19, 1957.

67. *Istoriia Uzbekskoi SSR,* vol. 4, pp. 265, 269, 343, 241.

68. Ibid. p. 351.

69. Tiurikov, *Pervyi. Pervaia. Vpervye,* pp. 69, 146–47.

70. "Materialy respublikanskogo soveshchaniia khlopkorobov," *Kommunist Tadzhikistana,* February 8, 1963.

71. *Pravda,* January 16, 1964.

72. *Istoriia sovetskogo krestianstva Kirgizstana,* p. 535.

73. G. Goldshtein, *Vazhnyi etap v razvitii kolkhoznogo stroia,* Frunze, 1964, p. 30.

74. *Ispolzovanie trudovykh resursov v selskom khoziaistve Kirgizskoi SSR,* Frunze, 1968, p. 40.

75. *Selskoe khoziaistvo Kirgizii,* no. 12, 1965, pp. 3–4.

76. *Istoriia sovetskogo krestianstva Kirgizstana,* pp. 537–38.

77. *Ocherki istorii,* p. 689.

78. *Pravda Vostoka,* November 21, 1973.

79. "Leninabadskaia oblast: Khoziaistvo," in *BSE,* 3d ed., vol. 14, Moscow, 1973, p. 301.

80. *Kommunist Tadzhikistana,* January 25, 1977.

81. Tiurikov, *Pervyi. Pervaia. Vpervye,* pp. 65–68.

82. M. Kurbonov, "Predlagaiu sokratit kolichestvo chinovnikov," *Aziia Plius,* no. 7 (526), February 17, 2010.

83. *Istoriia Uzbekskoi SSR,* vol. 4, p. 297.

84. Tiurikov, p. 73.

85. *Pravda,* September 12, 1966.

86. *Istoriia Uzbekskoi SSR,* vol. 4, pp. 253, 308.

87. Tiurikov, *Pervyi. Pervaia. Vpervye,* p. 378.

88. *Istoriia Uzbekskoi SSR,* vol. 4, p. 377.

89. Ibid., p. 515.

90. "Leninabadskaia oblast: Kulturnoe stroitelstvo i zdravookhranenie," in *BSE,* 3d. ed., vol. 14, Moscow, 1973, p. 301.

91. "Oshskaia oblast: Kulturnoe stroiltelstvo i zdravookhranenie," in *BSE,* 3d ed., vol. 19, Moscow, 1975, p. 55.

92. The reference is to Uzbekistan.

93. A. Khazratkulov, *Sotsialnye problemy Uzbekistana i puti ikh resheniia. Spetsifika, opyt, perspektivy, 1971–1990,* Tashkent, 1992, p. 146.

94. *Narodnoe khoziaistvo Uzbekskoi SSR za 70 let Sovetskoi vlasti,* Tashkent, 1987, pp. 287, 291.

95. TsGA RUz, f. 837. op. 41. d. 3907. l. 155–56.

96. Khazratkulov, *Sotsialnye problemy Uzbekistana i puti ikh resheniia,* pp. 151, 155–56, 159–60, 162.

97. TsGA RUz, f. 96. op. 2. d. 2348. l. 128–29.

98. Khazratkulov, *Sotsialnye problemy Uzbekistana i puti ikh resheniia,* pp. 189, 193.

99. Ibid., pp. 193–94.

100. *Krasnoznamennyi Turkestanskii,* Moscow, 1988, pp. 340–41; also see Tiurikov, *Peryvi. Pervaia, Vpervye,* p. 381.

101. Kh.N. Iskanderov to Kh.G. Guliamov, 20 July, 1954, TsGAUz, f. 2456, 0.1, d. 166, pp. 46–47; cited in Yaakov Ro'i, *Islam and the Soviet Union From the Second World War to Gorbachev,* New York, 2000, pp. 546–47.

102. *Istoriia Uzbekskoi SSR,* vol. 4, p. 285.

103. *Istoriia rabochego klassa Uzbekistana,* vol. 2, Tashkent, 1965, p. 333.

104. Tiurikov, *Pervyi. Pervaia. Vpervye,* p. 209.

105. *Istoriia Uzbekskoi SSR,* vol. 4, pp. 285, 400, 413, 414.

106. P.V. Boiarshinov, "Proizvodstvenno-tekhnicheskaia intelligentsia Tadzhikistana v gody semiletki (1959–1965 gg.)," Aftoref. diss., TajGU, Dushanbe, 1966.

107. "Tekushchii arkhiv Tekhnicheskogo uchilishcha no. 2," *Zhurnal ucheta vypuska spetsialistov,* 1958.

108. TsGA Respubliki Tadzhikistan, f. 1514. op. 1. d. 370. l. 14.

109. *Istoriia sovetskogo krestianstva Kirgizstana,* p. 589.

110. *Istoriia Uzbekskoi SSR,* vol. 4, pp. 415, 418, 419.

111. *Uzbekskaia SSR. Entsiklopediia,* Tashkent, 1981, pp. 520–21.

112. *Istoriia tadzhikskogo naroda,* vol. 3, Moscow, 1965, p. 167.

113. *Uzbekskaia SSR,* pp. 521–23.

114. *Pravda Vostoka,* May 25, 1973.

115. K.O. Otorbaev and Kh.R. Rakhmanov, "Osh," in *BSE,* 3d ed., vol. 19, Moscow, 1975, p. 52.

116. "Jalalabad," in *BSE,* 3d ed., Moscow, 1972, p. 187.

117. "Leninabadskaia oblast," in *BSE,* p. 301.

118. "Leninabadskaia oblast," in *BSE,* p. 300.

119. Tiurikov, *Pervyi. Pervaia. Vpervye,* p. 306.

120. *Istoriia Uzbekskoi SSR.* vol. 4, pp. 451–52.

121. *Istoriia tadzhikskogo naroda,* pp. 170–71.

122. *Pravda Vostoka,* April 19 and 27, 1966.

123. *Pravda Vostoka,* September 10 and 18, 1966.

124. *Pravda Vostoka,* September 29 and October 10, 1968.

125. *Literaturnaia gazeta,* April 17, April 24, and May 1, 1974; *Kommunist Tadzhikistana,* April 19 and 27, 1974.

126. *Komsomoli Tochikiston,* August 25, 1982.

127. *Sovetskaia kultura,* March 1, 1966.

128. *Sovetskaia Kirgiziia,* May 14 and September 4, 1966.

129. *Sovetskaia kultura,* February 5, 1970.

130. *Pravda Vostoka,* March 24, 1973.

131. *Pravda Vostoka,* October 3, 5, 9, 1969.

132. *Pravda Vostoka,* April 30, 1971.

133. *Pravda Vostoka,* June 2, 1977.

134. *Pravda Vostoka,* September 28, 1967.

135. *Sovetskaia Kirgiziia,* February 24, 1970.

136. *Pravda,* January 8, 1976.

137. "Leninabadskaia oblast," in *BSE* p. 301.
138. *Pravda Vostoka,* May 26, 1967.
139. *Pravda Vostoka,* May 11, 1973.
140. *Kommunist Tadzhikistana,* November 26, 1974.
141. Tiurikov, *Pervyi. Pervaia. Vpervye,* pp. 300–301, 311–14, 320, 327–29.
142. *Uzbekskaia SSR,* p. 524.
143. Tiurikov, *Pervyi. Pervaia. Vpervye,* pp. 301, 309.
144. Ibid., pp. 205, 305, 318, 323.
145. GARF, f. 6991, op. 5, d. 3263, l. 52–53.

7

Cultural Life in the Ferghana Valley Under Khrushchev and Brezhnev

Zukhra Madamidzhanova (Tajikistan), with Ildar Mukhtarov (Uzbekistan)

The Transformational Social Role of Cultural and Religious Groups in the Ferghana Valley

Each field views the period from the mid-1950s to the mid-1980s in the USSR through its own lens. Political scientists and historians see this era of Khrushchev and Brezhnev as a time when the top-down administrative system actually worked. Sociologists see it as a time when the state provided a generous safety net to the population. Artists recall the time "of the Thaw," while economists treat these years in terms first of reform and then of stagnation. Whatever one's perspective, the changes that Moscow introduced in these years clearly shaped the cultural life of the Ferghana Valley.

The process of transformation in Central Asia started as soon as Russia annexed it. But the region's communities felt no desire to be modernized or to change; hence they continued as before until the early 1900s and later. Traditional Central Asian communities were slow to come to terms with the changes that came with the establishment of Soviet rule. In the long run this limited the application of the Soviet model of accelerated economic modernization in Central Asia and the Ferghana Valley. This occurred because during the initial stages of Russification and Sovietization, Moscow relied on Russian-speaking migrants from Russia and the western republics. In the end, Soviet-type modernization fostered large-scale urbanization, compulsory secondary education, large-scale changes among elites, and profound changes in the region's way of life. But modernizing values in the Ferghana Valley and elsewhere in Central Asia often clashed with traditions, which undermined popular support for Russification and Sovietization. Yet the Ferghana Valley society did not systematically reject Soviet cultural trends. Instead, it received them but at the same time encapsulated them in a separate cultural space distinct from their own Central Asian customs and rites, which continued to thrive in the bosom of families, neighborhoods (*mahallas*), and local communities.

Soviet policy continued to concentrate industry in Russia and the western regions, and by the end of the 1980s the Ferghana Valley and Central Asia lagged behind the rest of the Soviet Union. Industrial development and urbanization therefore proceeded slowly in the Ferghana Valley. Even though there was some effort in the 1970s to equalize regions, most parts of the Ferghana Valley had far less industry than the republic capitals of Tashkent and Frunze (now Bishkek). Only Tajikistan's part of the Ferghana Valley had strong industrial centers, for example in Khujand and Isfara. The paradox is that the Leninabad (now Khujand) region preserved many traditional institutions and values, including religious networks, until the present, and at the same time it served as the industrial center of Soviet Tajikistan. This is doubtless due to the reality that Ferghana natives exercised far more political influence in Dushanbe than their counterparts from the other two sectors did in their respective capitals.

Internal economic disparities within the USSR began once again to broaden after the 1970s. The clearest manifestation of this in the Ferghana Valley was the reinforcement of the cotton monoculture, which doomed all three sectors of the valley to remain rural, poor, and backwards. As late as 1970, some 34 percent of the population in the Kyrgyz section of the valley, 38 percent in the Uzbek sector, and 42 percent in Tajik parts of the valley remained dependent on agriculture for their livelihoods.[1] The USSR became the world's third largest producer of raw cotton, but neither in the Ferghana Valley nor in Central Asia as a whole did the locals do more than grow the raw material for processing elsewhere. Together, the towns of the valley, including Ferghana, Margilan, Andijan, Leninabad, and others, processed only about 8 percent of the fiber grown locally. Most other local products, including grain, silk, wool, karakul, vegetable oil, fruits, and vegetables, were also processed elsewhere.

By 1970 the valley's population density soared to more than 200 people per square kilometer,[2] with high fertility being the main cause of growth. What urban growth occurred took place in towns of fewer than 50,000 inhabitants, most of them built around new industries. Even though their numbers were few, these communities helped raise the quality of life across the Ferghana Valley.

For all its poverty between 1960 and 1980, the Ferghana Valley populace did not face economic ruin and did not feel compelled by desperation to migrate to the capitals. This preserved many traditional patterns of life even amid the growth of the non-agrarian sectors. The fact that Russians and other migrants filled many industrial jobs further preserved traditional ways among the indigenous people. In 1987, Uzbeks constituted only 53 percent of industrial workers in Uzbekistan, Tajiks comprised 48 percent of the total in Tajikistan, and Kyrgyz only a quarter of those in Kyrgyzia.

Thus isolated from industrial work, the traditional society preserved its rural way of life. This included tribal and kinship links, the perception of individuals in terms of their place in family structure (and hence restrictions on their individual freedom), and the unequal status of women. Though covered with a veil of "official socialism," structures such as the family, clan, village community, or urban *mahalla,* all continued to thrive. This reality emerged from the shadows after the collapse of the USSR, and gave rise to tensions and conflicts across the region.

This is not to deny the many efforts made during Soviet times to promote development in the region. Soviet researchers often noted the many ways in which the population of Central Asia compared favorably to advanced countries in the West and Asia. Thus, by 1989 more than 84 percent of Central Asians over fifteen years of age had a secondary or higher education. During both the Khrushchev-era Thaw and the later decade of Stagnation, similar attention was accorded to women's issues.[3] The many factors contributing to the low status of women in the Ferghana Valley were fully recognized: patriarchal families, ethnic traditions tracing to oases and steppes, polygamy and the resultant rivalry of senior and young wives, and Islamic factors. To neutralize these, the government provided women with jobs in collective farms, labor groups, and industrial enterprises. During these years the organization of specifically female enterprises was common in the Ferghana Valley, as elsewhere in the USSR. These included various collectives that wove carpets, sewed robes and quilts, made skullcaps, and so forth. Women in Namangan, Margilan, Kokand, Leninabad, and other parts of the Ferghana Valley also worked at industrial enterprises that primarily used female labor, such as spinning and weaving mills. *Likbez* (campaign against illiteracy) and cultural-enlightenment work were conducted in women's clubs. Female educational institutions and training colleges were established across all republics, which enabled both urban and village women in the Ferghana Valley to receive an education.

Wherever they worked, women were told of the government's policies and instructed in how to create a socialist way of life. Some analysts argue that by the Khrushchev and Brezhnev eras, women were as important to the local labor force as men. Data from 1984 indicate that women reached 43 percent of all workers in Uzbekistan, 49 percent in Kyrgyzia, and 39 percent in Tajikistan, as compared to an all-Soviet average of 51 percent. In the same republics women constituted from 44-50 percent of all collective farmers.[4]

Women followed many professions in the cities and villages of the Ferghana Valley. In the Uzbek part of the valley they comprised 56 percent of all teachers, 51 percent of cultural workers, and 70 percent of healthcare providers. In the Tajik sector, Tajik and Uzbek women worked in scientific institutions, arts and entertainment, the Communist Party, and public organizations. All this led to important changes in the status of women and to new relationships within the family.

In spite of this, there remained many non-working but able-bodied women from among the indigenous nationalities. During the 1970s nearly a quarter of all Uzbek urban women were not employed,[5] and this percentage did not diminish during the 1980s. This is traceable to the need to care for large families. R.H. Aminova showed that many of those women who did work in these years did so on a seasonal basis. She also noted that "The absence of child-care centers and their slow construction forced many thousands of women to sit at home."[6]

Archival data from Leninabad province collected by Tajik ethnographers[7] show that by the beginning of the 1980s the employment picture for women had changed further. Many women found work at silk farms, as cotton pickers, and as carers for newborn lambs to be extremely demanding. Staying within the law, they tried to find ways to avoid the most backbreaking jobs. Demographers note that by the 1980s birth rates in Uzbek and Tajik families rose, affording women a chance to devote more time to childcare.[8]

In spite of changes in marriage and family life that occurred during the process of Soviet urbanization, many researchers from Uzbekistan and Tajikistan have noted that Tajiks and Uzbeks clung to traditional attitudes supporting early marriage, large families, and strong family ties. It is useful to speak of two phases in family relations in the Ferghana Valley prior to perestroika. During the first, extending through the early Soviet period, females remained fully dependent on husbands, fathers, and brothers. The second, beginning with Khrushchev's Thaw, saw dramatic changes in the fate of women, and especially in health care and education.

By the 1960s and into the 1970s, the Ferghana Valley enjoyed an extensive network of medical treatment and preventive facilities equipped with advanced medical equipment. Indeed, in the Tajik part of the valley alone there were more than 24 doctors per 1,000 inhabitants. Similarly, during this same period one rarely met a person in the Tajik sector who could not read and write. Both the Tajik and Uzbek sectors compared favorably with advanced Western countries in rates of completion of secondary school and other key educational indicators. In the Tajik part of the Ferghana Valley there were nearly 120,000 men and women with higher or vocational secondary education working in economic or cultural institutions, with similarly large intelligentsias in the Uzbek and Kyrgyz sectors. During the Khrushchev and Brezhnev eras this led to interesting developments in such diverse fields of expression as music, art, poetry, belles lettres, and cinematography.

In the Ferghana Valley one can note such famous poets and writers as Ulug-zade, Sator Tursun, Juma Odiana, Aminjon Shukuhi, A'zam Sitky, Ozod Aminzade, Rahim Jalil, Toji Usmon, and Pulat Tolis, all of whom gained distinction both for their poetry and their readings, as did a number of other poets and novelists from the valley, not to mention various actors, popular singers, and artists. All of them originated in the Ferghana region but went on to gain national reputations in the USSR. This rapid development of European-type culture came quickly after the establishment in the 1920s of theaters in all the major cities of the Ferghana Valley, including Andijan, Ferghana, Kokand, Namangan, Leninabad, and Osh. The Leninabad theater of musical comedy became especially popular. Shortly after the establishment of these national theaters a Russian Dramatic Theater was opened in the old tsarist capital of the valley, Ferghana. These new theaters were housed in some of the best buildings in the Ferghana Valley. For example, the provincial theater in Ferghana was housed in the former residence of the colonial governor of the Turkestan region, General M.D. Skobelev. The Andijan Theater was housed in an equally beautiful building in the city center. Thanks to such generous support, theater immediately gained a high social status and came to symbolize the new Soviet culture.

Because the theaters symbolized the emerging secular culture, they came under attack. In the 1920s a new theater in Bukhara was burned, when religious zealots torched it following the performance of a play, by the Azerbaijani playwright H. Dzhavida, which told of the love between a Muslim boy and a Christian girl. During the attempted fundamentalist putsch in Andijan in 2005, religious zealots headed straight to the theater to burn it.

By the 1970s and early 1980s relations between theater and government had sunk into a state of mutual contentment, with the theaters avoiding anything that would engender discontent and the government happy with the results. A few years earlier all theaters in the valley had celebrated their silver anniversary. But the repertoire already had become standardized and unoriginal, repeating whatever was playing in Tashkent. Soon the balance tipped, creating a situation in which the official censors could relax because both writers and producers had internalized the censorship. As George Orwell wrote in *1984,* coercion turned into conviction. Meanwhile, theater was no longer viewed as an important conduit of propaganda, which robbed it of all the ritual significance it previously had enjoyed. Films, literature, and television were pushing theater aside.

Research on the Tajik part of the Ferghana Valley has shown that many residents had no access to theaters or museums in these years due to inadequate transportation. Few rural residents, for example, had the opportunity to enjoy the Pushkin Theater in Leninabad. But this did not mean they were without a vital cultural life. Prior to the rise of European-style theater, the Ferghana Valley boasted its own developed system of entertainment. This included theatrical forms involving the cycle of life, the calendar, and religious holidays, as interpreted through such diverse theatrical forms as various puppet shows and oral folk theaters, called *masharaboz.*[9]

The *masharabozes,* known as *kizikchi* in the Ferghana Valley, were male Tajik and Uzbek folk actors who performed comic and satirical sketches, mummery, dances, and songs. *Kizikchi* theaters drew on both conventionalized subjects and improvisation, and presented their performances in the same cities and towns of the Ferghana Valley where the leading European-type dramatic theaters had been established. With respect to the depth of their repertoire, their originality, and their skills in execution, the *kizikchi* theaters of the Ferghana Valley stood well above other local theaters.[10] If *masharabozes* from other areas of Uzbekistan based their art mainly on mimicry and mummery, the Ferghana Valley *kizikchi* emphasized wit and pointed speech. The same could be said of the unique Ferghana Valley genre of oral folk poetry known as *askiya.* Somewhat resembling the Anglo-Saxon

Limerick, the *askia* tradition survives to the present and gives rise to competitions among local improvisers.

The Soviet government issued endless prohibitions against *masharaboz* performances. As a result, by the 1950s and 1960s researchers had difficulty finding traces of this type of theater even in remote villages of the Ferghana Valley. European-type theaters completely marginalized *masharaboz* theaters and pushed them to the periphery of social and cultural life. At the same time, a traditional musical genre known as *katta ashulla* survived intact in the Ferghana Valley throughout the Khrushchev and Brezhnev eras. This involved musical chanting, and was performed exclusively by men during school and *mahalla* social gatherings. Performers delicately controlled the sound of their voices with Chinaware held to their mouths, which enabled them to perform even the ancient Persian works of so-called *shashmakom.*

Thus, notwithstanding all the Soviet achievements, the Ferghana Valley continued to live its mundane, self-sufficient existence throughout the period under study. However, just under the surface mounting internal strains and tensions existed. These manifested themselves in what might be called a "culture of resistance" that began to form as early as the 1960s. The first signs were brief theatrical sketches that benignly derided Soviet conditions, and poetry that called on people to appreciate their culture and preserve their traditions. These arose not amid conditions of economic decay and "stagnation," as the Brezhnev era later would be termed, but of rapid cultural integration with the Soviet Union as a whole. This occurred despite the ideological pressure on cultural life in those years, and despite the fraudulent statistics that were issued, including the supposed existence of large libraries in the Ferghana Valley. The USSR was closed to the outside world in the 1970s, but in the Ferghana Valley the information space was rapidly expanding.

The combination of extensive official information on cultural events throughout the USSR and of unofficial but readily accessible information on independent trends created a yeasty cultural environment throughout the Ferghana Valley. Talented natives of the valley, such as S. Alibekov, a noted painter and maker of animated films, or M. Churlu, a painter and weaver, sought a fresh cultural synthesis, and in the process gave rise to a new Ferghana school of art. Soon there also arose a distinct "Ferghana School" of poetry, inspired by S. Abdullaev and A. Haidara, both of whom spent their childhood and adolescent years in the Ferghana Valley. Today this informal association of writers and painters enjoys prominence far beyond the borders of Uzbekistan. The play *The Iron Woman* by O. Salimov emerged out of this uniquely Ferghana synthesis, and would become the most famous Uzbek drama in the perestroika era. Full of humor and bitter grievance, it relates the difficulties a typical Ferghana farmer (*dehkan*) undergoes while trying to reclaim his self-esteem. In spite of the different genre and style, the wonderful lines by the Ferghana Valley poet Abdullaev epitomize everything written about the valley in these years, and could serve as the epigraph for Salimov's play:

We believe, and will continue to believe, that the Ferghana Valley, if useless genius is given its due even out of spite, can become, at least for an hour or one dazzling noon, a mesmeric land, where impressions turn into destiny despite the acrimoniousness and swirling uncertainty of our lives.[11]

By the mid-1970s and beginning of the 1980s, institutions of higher learning were firmly established in the main cities of the Ferghana Valley, along with schools and vocational colleges. Also functioning there were polytechnic institutes and a branch of the Tashkent Agricultural Institute, while medical, foreign language, and pedagogical institutes existed in Andijan. Pedagogical institutes also could be found in Leninabad, Osh, and Kokand. Moreover, many young people of the Ferghana Valley traveled to Tashkent, Dushanbe, Frunze, Moscow, and other cities throughout the USSR for higher education.

From the eras of Stalin through Brezhnev, the Ferghana Valley produced many famous figures in the world of modern learning. Prominent among them was the orientalist and diplomat Bobojon Gafurov, from the town of Sovetabad (now Bobojon Gafurov in Sughd province). Besides his scholarship on Tajiks and other peoples of Central Asia, Gafurov had a distinguished diplomatic career. From the career of Gafurov and others, one can see that the traditional society allowed for the spread of "modernity" into politics, economics, and culture, as well everyday life. Industrialization and urbanization were initially successful, and gave rise to an urban intelligentsia that largely accepted Russification and Sovietization. They welcomed the new holidays and various departures from the traditional religion. But this assimilation was superficial and did not lead to a new cultural equilibrium.

The country lived in a world of stereotypes engendered by the top-down system. But beginning immediately after Stalin's death and the Twentieth Party Congress in 1956, these fostered currents of dissent among the intelligentsia, and particularly in the worlds of art and culture. Political controls relaxed and ideological dogmas gradually disintegrated, especially in the arts. During the Thaw, the goal was not to abolish socialist dogmas but somehow to get around them in the arts. This engendered unofficial art, underground presses, recordings on x-ray plates, and new poetry, films, and theatrical performances. Such dissent, however, faded in intensity the further one traveled from Moscow and Leningrad. The Ferghana Valley experienced all this as ripples caused by tossing a stone in the water in Moscow. The government's vigilance flagged, as it closed its eyes to ideological offenses taking place in what it considered the peripheral void of the Ferghana Valley. As a result, the valley continued to live a largely self-sufficient and mundane life, free of political incidents but with the various economic and cultural stresses gradually mounting.

Islamic education was largely banned during the atheistic Soviet era, with Muslim teaching continuing only within families. Tajiks and Uzbeks continued to observe Muslim traditions in private, with the rural population being particularly slow to adopt the new Soviet ideology. At the same time, apathy toward religion was also making headway, especially in urban environments. The result was a certain duality throughout the Ferghana Muslim community, with families living fully in the Soviet world but continuing to mark life-cycle events in the traditional Muslim manner. In the countryside Islam evolved at a snail's pace. Across the Ferghana Valley a kind of spiritual dualism existed, with a correspondingly complex organization. Islam had proved itself not only capable of sanctifying the old order but of maintaining itself under the new political and social conditions. Under these circumstances, it is not surprising that a sort of "underground" piety arose in the Uzbek and Tajik communities of the valley by the end of the 1970s.

As detailed in Chapter 13, the first portents of such an underground appeared in the Ferghana Valley cities of Namangan, Andijan, and Ferghana with the creation of the Islamic Movement of Uzbekistan (IMU) and then the appearance of Hizb ut-Tahrir. Another religious movement, Bayat, operating in Isfara became active in Tajik areas of the valley. This happened not because the government's "all-seeing eye" became less vigilant, but because it considered the Ferghana Valley so peripheral that it could offer no ideological danger. And indeed, under Khrushchev and Brezhnev the valley was relatively free of incidents of this sort. It had no political role of its own and lived a fairly self-sufficient and mundane life, even though internal stress was mounting all the while. By the time a multitude of tough problems arose in the late 1980s Soviet ideology had withered, leaving people to rely on the religious heritage that had managed to survive.

Social Changes and Traditions

Both urban and rural residents of the Ferghana Valley are descendants of the indigenous people known until early Soviet times as Sarts. Some pre-revolutionary Russian Orientalists considered Sarts to be Tajiks, others thought them Uzbeks, and still others considered them a mix of Tajik and Uzbek.[12] Soviet ethnographers tended to consider Sarts as descendents of the settled Iranian population,[13] but many saw them also as the core of the Turkic Uzbek people.[14] While this debate continues, researchers in Kazakhstan recently have amassed new data on such nomadic groups as the Qarluqs and Kipchaks,[15] of whom there were 42,000 in the Ferghana Valley in 1917 and 70,000 today.[16] Divided into four large groups in the early twentieth century,[17] the Kipchaks, or Toza-Kipchaks as they called themselves, began during the Khrushchev era to identify themselves simply as Uzbeks.

Even though the single term Sart died out, Uzbeks and Tajiks in the valley continued to maintain close contact and enrich each other culturally. Even a common Tajik-Uzbek terminology denoted such topics as residence, clothing, and cuisine. During the post-Stalin era both groups accepted certain common features as their own, at the same time as their separate forms of self-awareness grew more pronounced.

During the 1960s and 1970s the population of the Ferghana Valley also included

Russians, Ukrainians, Tatars, Meskhetian Turks and others from the Volga basin and Caucasus. Most were new arrivals who had been exiled there or who had moved there to staff the cotton monoculture or new industries. There were also a few Arabs, Baluchis, Kurds, Gypsies, Central Asian Jews, Uyghurs, Dungans, and Koreans. Russian became the lingua franca of the region, which in turn stimulated efforts at the local level to preserve indigenous languages. As a result, many non-indigenous people learned to speak Uzbek, Tajik, or Kyrgyz. Russification and Sovietization became the norm in the cities. But even while specific national distinctions were less evident in professional life, and had been all but nonexistent in the traditional practice of Islam, they remained important in social structures, consumption patterns, leisure activities, and manners.

At the time of the 1917 Revolution the Ferghana Valley had been extremely backwards, which made its subsequent transformation all the more complex. Large extended families were the rule, and often incorporated non-relatives. In these durable units were preserved many important values, including the primacy of the family, group upbringing of the young, mutual support, and respect for elders. Yet extended families also absorbed innovations. Sovietization, for example, standardized a later age for marriage, even though early marriages remained common in the valley until the 1980s. Interethnic marriages also become more common than formerly, with frequent Tajik-Uzbek unions and also, in the cities, many marriages with Russians and other groups.

Socialism also brought changes in wedding ceremonies. Not only did they more frequently take place in the homes of the bride's family (*choigashtak*)[18] but there were Red weddings (*Kizil-toi*) and Komsomol weddings (*Momsomol-tui*) in all three sectors of the valley. At the same time, the practice of marriage payments continued, with fees up to 10,000 rubles. The mass media attempted to uproot the practice of bride price (*kalym*), but to the extent they succeeded the same money was spent on lavish weddings, gifts, and dowries. These transformed bride payments became measures of prestige and reached enormous sums, forcing common workers into debt for years to come. During the 1960s and 1980s, women's councils and neighborhood committees attempted to propagate more modest weddings that also preserved national traditions, but these efforts largely failed. Similarly unsuccessful were attempts to curtail the tragic inter-family conflicts that often arose over the amount and forms of marriage payments.

Meanwhile, the number of nuclear families in the Ferghana Valley grew, and gradually they supplanted the extended patriarchal families, with all their ancient customs and authoritarian features. The share of extended families including two or more married couples is still high in Uzbekistan and Tajikistan, but many of these were modified during this period, with only part of the salary of the married couple going to the head of the family to pay for joint feasts and other expenses. Nuclear families continued to cooperate, however, with women jointly handling their household gardens and supporting each other in cooking, laundering, and childcare. These close family ties represent the best traditions of the Ferghana

Valley. True nuclear families were also coming into being, not as a result of the breakup of extended families but on their own.

The growing heterogeneity of both urban and rural families was new to the Ferghana Valley. The greater professional diversity of family members enlarged people's contacts and opened them to innovation, and the role of youth expanded. Yet the overall rate of urbanization was low throughout the period, and this limited the spread of these new phenomena, at the same time preserving high birth rates, extended families, and the practice of including non-family members in the circle of complex families.

Interactions Between Traditional and Soviet Forms of Identity amid Social Change

Even when such continuity existed, the heads of households lost some of their absolute control over family budgets, as well as the unquestioning obedience of family members. Education and the growth of professional skills brought financial independence, which in turn modified relations between spouses, parents and children, and with daughters-in-law. The influence of schools on family life grew. Of course, husbands and fathers retained much authority, and household heads still needed to exercise justice and resolve. But when they could not, or when a married son or another family member was more educated and active than the traditional household head, a kind of dual leadership emerged. Yet far from destroying the best traditions of mutual support, attention to the upbringing of children, and care for the elderly, such practices helped preserve these traditions, and enabled them to extend beyond the circle of the family into the world of co-workers and the larger public. Thus, families in the Ferghana Valley experienced various changes during the 1960s and 1970s, even as they preserved in recognizable forms the psychology and ideology of communal solidarity that had existed over the centuries. Whatever the state did not deliberately change tended to keep its earlier forms. This contradicted the beliefs of Soviet scholars, who assumed that old patterns of family life that differed from Socialist ideals were rapidly dying out. But newer research confirms the vigorous survival of the former solidarity in family and kin groups, neighborhood *guzar*s, *mahallas,* and adult associations. L.F. Monogarova has demonstrated the continuing importance of ties of kinship,[19] while A. Kochkunova examines the role of family groups in her thesis on a Kyrgyz family.[20] T. Tashbaeva and M. Savurov consider Uzbek family and kin ties in their book, but not in relation to the continuing tradition patriarchy.[21]

The important organizational and regulatory role of rural and neighborhood groups is reflected in rituals that continue to the present. No wonder that from the late 1950s on, officials tried to engage *mahalla* elders and committees when they invented new holidays or built parks, schools, or amenities—and often abused this practice.

Another old institution common to diverse peoples, the family-kinship group, managed to adapt with little change to contemporary conditions. Earlier, these groups incorporated ten-fifteen related families who shared a common ancestor three-to-five generations back and had taken his name. Each such extended family engaged in a single type of work and practiced mutual support. Only nowadays are the numbers of such groups dwindling. T.H. Tashbaeva reports that in the 1960s and 1970s such groups consisted mainly of the families of uncles and cousins,[22] but much more remote relatives were also included, provided they claimed a common ancestor. During these years such groups became markedly more active, convening family meetings, raising money for *kalym*, dowries, and funerals. L.F. Monogarova showed that Tajik extended families were handled the cost of all traditional ceremonies, but A. Kochkunov has showed that such compulsory payments grew less common among the Kyrgyz. Thus, while such family-kinship groups came to differ in the authority they wielded over constituent families, they remained an institution common to all groups in the valley.

Notwithstanding all the changes that have occurred, family events among all people of the Ferghana Valley still tend to be handled in the traditional manner. Marriages are communal affairs, and all communities have the same traditional offices, beginning with the "white beard" (*aksakal*) or elder. Community-mandated rules continue to define duties in building houses, weaving and quilting, wedding ceremonies, circumcisions, and other activities. Important decisions are reached by the entire community, with elders and mullahs maintaining their influence. Thus, even as they have acquired something of a relic character,[23] archaic traditions continue to manifest themselves most forcefully in the family; for example, through the 1980s there were women whose job was to find wives for marriageable males.

These *khodims* (Tajik) or *kaivonas* (Uzbek) were generally appointed from among the most senior members of poor families. They were also responsible for collecting money from women for wedding ceremonies, for deep-frying the traditional wedding flat breads (*katlama*), and for breaking and distributing them in the manner prescribed by tradition and religion. She (*khodima* or *kaivona*) also would distribute the wedding gifts, sew special shirts for the bride and groom, and would pronounce the blessing (*fotiha*) at the end of the ceremony. On the wedding day the *khodim* was the most active person in the house of the bride, receiving and entertaining guests, passing apricots and sugar, pouring tea, and making jokes. Finally, she embroidered the curtain (*kusha bitish, chimildyk,* or *chodar*) for the wedding night, when the couple slept on one side and female elders on the other to confirm that the bride was a virgin. *Peikals* and *khavarchis* performed a similar range of ceremonial functions for the male half of the house.

As the community's respected fiduciary, the male elder (*aksakal* or *katkuda*) played an even bigger role. He would announce engagements and speak on behalf of the bride's father. The female elder or *kaivoni* fulfilled similar functions for the female half of the house. The *aksakal* or *katkuda* exercised both religious and civil powers, organizing community events and resolving conflicts. Over time their powers narrowed, however, and consisted mainly of organizing events. Adult male associations, called *gaps, gashtaks, dzhuras,* or *ziefats,* helped with the work of husbandry and construction.[24] Female associations[25] (*mushkil-kusho, mavliud,* or *bibi-seshanbe*) did not have the same degree of coherence as male ones but fulfilled a religious role, especially pertaining to the cults of nature and of fertility.[26] The Soviets tried to suppress them, but they lived on. Similarly, the local mullahs read suras from the Qur'an at all family and communal activities, causing these events to be regarded as Muslim even though nearly all had pre-Islamic roots. Higher Muslim leaders—the *saiids, hodjas, turas,* and *ishans*—enjoyed still more respect and continue to do so today, as do their offspring and descendents. Traditional spiritual instructors, or *pirs,* functioned only in the underground during this period, but their adherents, or *murids,* looked to them for guidance on all life questions.

These traditional functionaries and groups, which survived to the late Soviet period, demonstrate the close links between community and family—and the primacy of the former. They played a significant role in managing change at the community level during extremely trying times, and in many respects still do today.

The Relationship of Official and Popular Culture in the Ferghana Valley

Nikita Khrushchev introduced partial decentralization and a more tolerant policy in language and culture, yet he did so unwillingly and inconsistently. He believed in a "merging" (*sliianie*) of nations and cultures, yet still held the Marxist belief that time would solve the national question in the USSR. He put a stop to the repatriation of exiled peoples, and the comparative flexibility and leniency of his early years hardened over time, leading to purges in many republics and to enforced teaching of Russian throughout the USSR.

Khrushchev's reforms also affected education. Instead of higher education reserved just for the middle class and wealthy families, he extended secondary education, lowered university admission standards, and opened more university positions to workers and those with work experience. But because they were poorly planned and financed, these and other reforms virtually collapsed, leading to declining competence among graduates of all but a few elite institutions in the capitals. Social inequalities widened. These developments were reflected in the Ferghana Valley.

Regarding the intelligentsia, Khrushchev and his cohorts relaxed restrictions on contacts with the West, published some heretofore banned works, and allowed some new journals and films. But censorship continued in a weakened form, propaganda still blared, many ideologues continued to wield power, and liberalization was limited to what the Communist Party could accept. At the same time, the supply of goods grew rapidly to meet the huge unsatisfied demand, with a trebling of agricultural production alone.

It was an era of contradictions. Beginning at the end of the 1960s, the Ferghana Valley's cities saw the construction of many new apartment houses, schools, and hospitals. Yet the farming folk who inhabited the new apartments were still denied passports even to travel within the USSR. Religious believers were tolerated, but scores of mosques were closed and a bellicose atheism remained in force. If there were better clothes in the stores, it was at the price of suffering by the sun-scorched women who picked the Ferghana cotton. If some exiled peoples had earlier been allowed to return to their homes, the Meskhetian Turks who had been deported to the Ferghana Valley were not, with fatal consequences.[27] Finally, overall production rose, but at the cost of driving most of the traditional arts and crafts of the Ferghana Valley to the verge of extinction.

The demographic situation in the country also changed. The birth rate among European peoples of the USSR rapidly fell, but continued to rise in the case of Soviet Muslims. After 1967 more Russians and Slavs moved out of the Ferghana Valley than migrated into it, while the indigenous peoples of the Ferghana Valley experienced a "demographic explosion."

The mind-set of the authorities and the endless orders they issued brought them into conflict with local cultural values, which the rulers viewed as outdated anachronisms. Economic and social modernization went forward, but failed utterly to foster a sense of Soviet identity among peoples who spoke more than a hundred languages. Efforts by Khrushchev and Brezhnev to forge a "Soviet people" diluted some aspects of ethnic identity among people in the Ferghana Valley, but at the same time strengthened their defense mechanisms against Russification. Far from being a paradoxical outcome, this result appears to have flowed naturally from the erosion of identity, for the simple reason that so many of the social realities in which individual identity was grounded remained and were there to be embraced.[28] Tajiks and Uzbeks in the Ferghana Valley did particularly well at allowing some Soviet elements into their lives, while still preserving their languages, core traditions, and national identities.

The period of relative calm that prevailed in the Ferghana Valley under Khrushchev and Brezhnev ended with the advent of Gorbachev's policy of perestroika, to which we must now turn.

Notes

1. *Trud v SSSR. Statisticheskii sbornik,* Moscow, 1988, pp. 16–17; *Social Indicators of Development, 1994,* World Bank, Washington, DC, 1994.
2. V. Belova, "Differentsiatsiia mnenii o nailuchshem i ozhidaemom chisle detei v semie," *Vestnik statistiki,* no. 7, 1973, p. 28.
3. See, e.g., R.H. Aminova, "Slavnye docheri Rodiny," *Obschestvennye nauki Uzbekistana,* no. 3, 1986, pp. 14–15; idem, *Oktiabr i reshenie zhenskogo voprosa v Uzbekistane,* Tashkent, 1975; J.S.Tashbekova, *Velikii Oktiabr i zhenschiny Kyrgyzstana,* Frunze, 1975; B.P. Palvanova, *Emansipatsiia musulmanki: Opyt raskreposhcheniia zhenschin Sovetskogo Vostoka,* Moscow, 1982; *Zhenschiny Sovetskogo Uzbekistana,* Tashkent, 1984, p. 6.
4. *Narodnoe khoziaistvo SSSR v 1984: Statisticheskii ezhegodnik,* Moscow, 1985, pp. 414–15.

5. S. Mirhasilov, "Sovremennaia semia selskogo naseleniia Uzbekistana," *ONU*, no. 4, 1977, p. 40; L.V. Monogarova and Mukkhidinnov, I.M., *Tagzhiki*, 2 vols., Moscow, 1992.

6. Aminova, "Slavnye docheri Rodiny," p. 17.

7. G.I. Ishankulov, *Brak i svadba u naseleniia Khujanda v novoe vremia*, Dushanbe, 1972; Monogarova and Mukkhidinnov, *Tadzhiki*.

8. G.A. Bondarenko, "Rozhdaemost u narodov SSSR," in *Sto natsii i narodnostei SSSR*, Moscow, 1985, pp. 19–30.

9. N.H. Nurdjanov, *Traditsionnyi teatr Tadzhikov*, Dushanbe, 2002.

10. M. Kodirov, *Traditsii Uzbekskogo teatra*, Tashkent, 1976, pp. 172–92 (in Uzbek).

11. S. Abdullaev, Foreword to the book *Poety i Ferghana*, Tashkent, 2000, p. 7.

12. N.O. Tursunov, *Slozhenie i puti razvitiia gorodskogo i selskogo naseleniia Severnogo Tadzhikistana 19–20 vv.*, Dushanbe, 1976, p. 82.

13. *Narody Srednei Azii*, vol. 1, 1962, p. 170.

14. M.G. Vakhabov, *Formirovanie uzbekskoi sotsialisticheskoi natsii*, Tashkent, 1961, pp. 44–45.

15. N.N. Masanov, Zh.B. Abylhodzhin et al. *Istoriia Kazahstana. Narody i kultura*, Almaty, 2001, pp. 34–56.

16. *Proekt otcheta turkestanskogo general-gubernatora za 1881*, Sankt-Peterburg, 1885, p. 24; L.F. Kostenko. *Turkestanskii krai: Otchet voenno-statisticheskogo obozreniia Turkestanskogo voennogo okruga. Materialy dlia geographii i statistiki Rossii*, vol. 1, Sankt-Peterburg, 1890, p. 326.

17. K.S. Shaniiazov, *K etnicheskoi istorii uzbekskogo naroda*, Tashkent, 1974, p. 116.

18. M.M. Hamidzhanova, "Devichnik (choigashtak) v Stalinabade," in *Izvestiia otdeleniia obschestvennyh nauk AN Tadzhikskoi SSR*, vols. 10–12, Stalinabad, 1956, pp. 104–8.

19. L.F. Monogarova, "Semia i semeinyi byt," in *Etnografichesckie ocherki uzbekskogo selskogo naseleniia*, Moscow, 1969; Monogarova and Mukhiddinov, *Tadzhiki*.

20. A. Kochkunov, "Novoe i traditsionnoe v structure kirgizskoi selskoi seme," Ph.D. diss., Moscow, 1986.

21. T. Tashbaeva and M. Savurov, *Novoe i traditsionnoe v bytu selskoi semi uzbekov*, Tashkent, 1989, p. 161.

22. Ibid.

23. N.P. Lobacheva, "Drevnie sotsialnye instituty v zhizni sovremennoi semi narodov Srednei Azii," in *Semia, traditsii i sovremennost*, Moscow, 1990, pp. 27–50.

24. N.P. Lobacheva, "Znachenie obshchiny v zhizni semi (po materialam svadebnoi obriadnosti khorezmskih uzbekov)," *Etnicheskaia istoriia i traditsionnaia kultura narodov Srednei Azii i Kazahstana*, 1989. Indigenous terms are given in Russian spelling, G.P. Snesarev, "Materialy o pervobytnoobshchinnykh perezhitkah v obychaiakh i obriadakh uzbekov Khorezma," *Materialy Khorezmskoi ekspeditsii*, Issue 9, 1960, p. 138; idem, "Traditsiia muzhskikh soiuzov i ee pozdneishem variante u narodov Srednei Azii," *Materialy Khorezmskoi ekspeditsii*, Issue 7, Moscow, 1963; R. Rakhimov, "Traditsionnye muzhskie obedineniia i nekotorye voprosy obshchestvenogo byta tadzhikov (konets XIX–nachalo XX v.)," candidate thesis, Leningrad, 1977; N.P. Lobacheva, "Sverstniki i semia," *Sovetskaia ernografiia*, no. 5, 1989.

25. Lobacheva, "Sverstniki i semia."

26. They had more Shamanist than Islamist features, although this issue requires further study.

27. P. Polian, *Ne po svoei vole . . . Istoriia i geografiia prinuditelnykh migratsii v SSSR*, Moscow, 2001, pp. 146–47.

28. K.A. Abulhanova, *O subekte psikhicheskoi deiatelnosti*, Moscow, 1973.

8

The Ferghana Valley During Perestroika, 1985–1991

Pulat Shozimov (Tajikistan), with
Baktybek Beshimov (Kyrgyz Republic) and
Khurshida Yunusova (Uzbekistan)

The era of perestroika, which began with the rise of Mikhail Gorbachev, directly affected the political and economic institutions of the country and, even more so, the thinking of the average Soviet citizen. Perestroika was preceded by such critically important developments as the USSR's 1979 invasion of Afghanistan and the brief rule of Yuri Andropov in 1983. All these events were to have an important impact on the Ferghana Valley.

The Soviet invasion of Afghanistan shocked many people with the sudden realization that profound changes were already under way, if not in the USSR itself then in its immediate region. The Central Asian republics felt this most acutely, because Afghanistan was their immediate neighbor. It was at this time that religious networks were reactivated, especially in the Ferghana Valley. In fact, the process of re-Islamization was launched precisely at that time.

The events in Afghanistan, and the start of Andropov's campaign to carry out a radical reshuffling of personnel within the political apparatus of the USSR, signaled that the Soviet political leadership was prepared to take drastic measures to resolve the urgent problems facing the country. Both reformers and conservatives recognized that without reforming the country's administrative system their own positions eventually would be threatened.

The first reforms of the Party nomenklatura began in 1983. Seeking to revitalize the creaking Soviet system, Andropov attacked corrupt Party officials, whom he accused of using their informal and shadow enclaves within the Central Committee to retard the political, economic, and social life of the Soviet Union. Uzbekistan was among the first republics to come under such attack, with the so-called Cotton Affair in 1983, as discussed below.

Notwithstanding such attacks, on certain levels the perestroika years were a political "golden age" for the Ferghana Valley. The first phase of the perestroika period (1985–88) saw the rise of Ferghana Valley regional political elites in all

178

three countries. Inamdzon Usmankhodzhaev emerged in Uzbekistan in 1983, and Absamat Masaliev in Kyrgyzstan in 1985. In Tajikistan, the leading political figure always had been from the northern region of the country. Borne up by the wave of perestroika, Qahhor Mahkamov from the Ferghana Valley became the first secretary of the Central Committee of the Communist Party in the Tajik Republic.

In 1988 Usmankhodzhaev, charged and convicted in the Cotton Affair, was replaced as first secretary of the Central Committee of the Communist Party of the Uzbek Republic by Rafik Nishanov. In Kyrgyzstan, Masaliev stumbled in 1990 after deciding to run for president of the Kyrgyz republic against the northerner Dzhumgalbek Amanbaev, first secretary of the Issyk Kul Communist Party. The major reason for his fall was the 1990 political crisis in Kyrgyzstan arising from Osh. Askar Akaev was already guiding the final phase of perestroika in the Kyrgyz Republic in 1990–91. Islam Karimov emerged in Uzbekistan on the wave of a political crisis associated with the "Ferghana Events," and he largely managed to keep the republic from sliding into political chaos. However, some members of the international community still question the methods Karimov used to retain political control. Thus, conflicts in the Ferghana Valley were directly responsible for the fall of political leaders in both Kyrgyzstan and Uzbekistan, which once again demonstrates the significance of the Ferghana Valley in the political life of the countries that make up this region.

Tajikistan During Perestroika: The Issue of Political Leadership

Among all Ferghana Valley political leaders, only Qahhor Mahkamov was able to hold onto his office until the end of the perestroika era—August 31, 1991. Mahkamov succeeded in winning a parliamentary election against another Ferghana resident, Rakhmon Nabiev, and was appointed president of the Tajik Republic by a decree of its Supreme Soviet of November 30, 1990.[1] Mahkamov's political fall was connected with his delayed response to the infamous attempted Moscow "putsch" of August 1991, which everywhere accelerated the process of dissolution of the Soviet Union and the formation in its place of a transitional entity, the Commonwealth of Independent States.

On September 5, 1991 the Central Committee of the Tajik Communist Party demanded that Mahkamov step down as First Secretary of the Party and president of the Tajik Republic. At the same time, the name of the Tajik Soviet Socialist Republic was changed to the Republic of Tajikistan. Both events finally took place on August 31, 1991 under the acting president, Qadriddin Aslonov, who hailed from the southern region.[2] Thus, the last representative of the Ferghana Valley quit his high post, as if adumbrating the emergence of new political trends in all three states in the Ferghana Valley.

A month later Aslonov was in turn removed from office on the eve of the national presidential elections. This came about from charges of his plotting with the Chairman of the Dushanbe municipal executive committee (mayor), Maksud Ikromov, to dismantle a monument to Lenin that stood on the central square of the city, and also because his decree banning the Communist Party was judged unconstitutional. At an emergency meeting the Supreme Soviet of the republic passed a motion of no confidence against Aslonov, which led to his resignation. In this way, the political elite of Ferghana delayed, if not stopped, a "southern political putsch" directed against them. Nabiev from the south Leninabad (now Khujand) clan of the Ferghana Valley, replaced Aslonov as acting president. He immediately announced that all decrees by Aslonov had been unconstitutional, and declared a state of emergency throughout the entire republic.[3]

The Tajik part of the Ferghana Valley during perestroika is in many ways distinct from those of Uzbekistan and Kyrgyzstan. In Tajikistan, Ferghana Valley elites from the Leninabad region had occupied all key political and economic posts in the country from the 1950s to 1992. Only following the bloody civil war did they cede their positions to southerners. In spite of his having been in coalition with the Ferghana province of Leninabad during the civil war, Emomali Rakhmonov, of Khatlon's southern province, assumed the presidency, pushing aside the Ferghana elites. After the inter-Tajik peace agreement of 1997, the Ferghana political elites gradually began to lose political and economic power. True, the prime minister still came from Leninabad (now Sughd) province, but he had no real authority. Another partial exception was the Ferghanan Abdumalik Abdulladzhanov, who managed to keep the prime ministership under both the last Soviet government and the new government formed after November 1992.

Fueling the growing coolness in Dushanbe toward the northern (Ferghana) regions was the serious suspicion that members of the Khujand political elite harbored separatist ambitions that would tie the province to Uzbekistan. Moreover, southerners saw the marriage of the daughter of Abdulladzhanov and the son of the chairman of the Leninabad Executive Committee, Abdujalil Khamidov, as part of a political conspiracy against the new order in Tajikistan. These and other factors increasingly excluded the Ferghana Valley political elites from real power at the national level.

Realizing that they could still lose the power they had so recently acquired, southern political elites sought an alliance with the United Tajik Opposition. This led directly to the signing of the inter-Tajik peace accord in 1997. The Ferghana leadership became further marginalized when military units of the former Popular Front colonel Makhmud Khudoberdiev, along with a former Tajik minister of internal affairs, attempted an armed *putches* in Regar city and Khujand with the help of armed fighters from Uzbekistan. The new government put these down by force, but the fight left the new southern leaders all the more distrustful of the Ferghanans and unwilling to share power with them.

The "Cotton Affair" in the Uzbek Sector of the Ferghana Valley

Perestroika radically changed the political situation in the Ferghana Valley by pushing to the foreground leaders who opposed those who had long been in charge in both the Uzbek and Kyrgyz republics.[4] This was no coincidence. The Ferghana Valley had long been dominated by strong informal networks that were not always well connected with the existing political structures. Perestroika destroyed whatever connections existed, moving to the fore the informal networks. Moscow knew of this, and gladly played the various elites off against each other. Perestroika strengthened the local elites and their clans in all spheres of public life, and thrust these leaders from the Ferghana into the echelons of power.

As the social and economic crises intensified in the USSR during the 1970 and 1980s, the first efforts were mounted to address issues of corruption and false reporting in the cotton industry, especially in the Ferghana Valley. The first attempts to investigate cases of corruption and bribery among high-ranking officials in the Uzbek SSR date back to the 1970s. Thus, both the chairman of the Presidium of the Supreme Soviet and the chairman of the Supreme Court of the Uzbek Republic were on the verge of being prosecuted as early as 1975. However, thanks to the influence of an Uzbek woman, I.S. Nasriddinova, then chair of the Soviet of Nationalities of the Supreme Soviet, Leonid Brezhnev dropped both investigations.[5]

The Ferghana economic region of the Uzbek Republic (Ferghana, Andijan, Namangan) occupied only 4.3 percent of the republic's territory and numbered only five million inhabitants.[6] Yet it produced 22.9 percent of all the republic's crops.[7] Although the region also produced silk, fruit, and wine, as well as industrial goods, it was cotton to which 80 percent of the arable land was devoted. Of the twenty-four cities in the Ferghana region, many were rapidly expanding thanks to the rise of the oil and light industry. Since the farmers were otherwise occupied, immigrants flowed in from elsewhere, leading by 1979 to a high population density of 34.4 persons per square kilometer and growing social problems in both the cities and countryside.[8] Even though production of foodstuffs in Ferghana was up to five times greater than in other parts of the Republic of Uzbekistan, it did not suffice to meet local needs. This was partly disguised by false reporting on production which, according to the Academy of Sciences, led to an overstatement of production in all sectors by anywhere from 5 percent to 25 percent.[9]

Strong controls built into the five-year planning process assured that none of these economic problems were adequately examined. Household heads could not institute changes even in such rudimentary areas as weed eradication, watering, and cotton harvesting without first receiving instructions from higher Party organs. Only in 1983 did decisive change begin, when the Central Committee of the Communist Party of the Soviet Union decreed a "cadre revolution" in the country.[10] Under the instructions of the Procurator General of the USSR, a 200-person investigating team was set up under the leadership of one Telman Gdlian. Even though corruption of every sort was rampant across the Soviet Union, the commission began its work in Uzbekistan.[11] This choice was logical, since the government categorically excluded the possibility that the problems might arise from the Soviet system itself and was therefore all the more eager to pin blame on corrupt or incompetent "cadres"—administrators. Investigators assigned to work on the "cotton affair" refused to consider the causes of all the misreporting, which in fact arose from the "top down" system of setting production quotas and its demand for results, with little or no concern for improving the system in order to achieve them. Court records indicate that 198 people were convicted and then acquitted in the Ferghana province alone, with 145 people convicted in the Andijan city court. Gdlian's team indicted twenty executives of the Ministry of Internal Affairs, four secretaries of the Central Committee of the Communist Party of the Republic, eight secretaries of the provincial Party committees, and others—altogether sixty-two senior officials went to trial and were convicted of bribery. Some thirty-five criminal cases reached trial by May 1989. During the previous half-decade the team considered more than 800 criminal cases and brought to trial 600 senior officials and ten Heroes of Socialist Labor.[12] By the time the "Cotton Affair" had ended, charges had been brought against 4,018 people in Uzbekistan, most of them collective farm officials in the Ferghana Valley.

The Results of the "Cotton Affair"

A commission convened in 1989 to review Gdlian's investigation compiled no less than fifty volumes of materials.[13] The review commission found that Gdlian and his team had operated in a chaotic manner, fabricated evidence, and extorted confessions through force. In the course of this "investigation of the investigation," several well-known figures were arrested and convicted, among them Leonid Brezhnev's son-in-law Iurii Churbanov; first secretary of the Central Committee of the Communist Party of Uzbekistan, Usmankhodzhaev; former secretary of the Central Committee of the Communist Party of the republic, A. Salimov; and the first secretaries of the provincial committees in Tashkent, Ferghana, and Namangan. Unofficial evidence indicates that a significant number of those accused committed suicide, including K. Ergashev, G. Davydov, R. Gaipov, and Sh. Rashidov. When Usmankhodzhaev mounted his own defense, he began pointing the finger directly at individual members of the Politburo of the USSR, including E.K. Ligachev, V.V. Grishin, G.V. Romanov, and M.S. Solomentsev. In March 1989, Gdlian and his deputy were both elected People's Deputies of the USSR.[14] But a month later the Plenum of the Supreme Court of the USSR issued a private ruling "on offenses against law committed in the course of the team investigation of the Prosecutor General's Office of the USSR headed by Gdlian."[15] By the following April the Supreme Soviet of the USSR denounced:

> unproven claims of the people's deputies of the USSR T. Gdlian and N.V. Ivanov [his deputy] that discredit the Supreme Soviet of the USSR and individual people's deputies and officials. It warns them that the Supreme Soviet of the USSR will deprive them of their immunity as Deputies should they continue activities leading to the destabilization of the country.

It then went on to fire Gdlian and Ivanov from their jobs as prosecutors and to dismiss their superiors who had failed to supervise the two and thereby allowed massive breaches of the law.[16]

Much later, in a 2008 interview with Radio Liberty, Gdlian admitted that he and Ivanov had at the time written a strictly confidential seventeen-page memo to Mikhail Gorbachev with one purpose: to stop the terror in Uzbekistan.[17] This implied that numerous innocent people had been arrested in order to protect the major offenders in the "Cotton Affair." In his interview Gdlian also wondered why all arrests associated with the "Cotton Affair" had been attributed to him and his team.

To sum up, it cannot be doubted that serious problems existed in the cotton industry, and that these arose mainly from the endless pressure from above to "fulfill and over-fulfill" the Five-Year Plans. It is important to recall that the fulfillment or over-fulfillment of plans brought generous subsidies from the Center. Also, by manipulating reports one could demonstrate one's allegiance to Moscow. Finally, there were those in Moscow who, for their own reasons, actually encouraged various forms of corruption among the peripheral republics and in Russia itself. Beyond this, it appears that Gorbachev and his predecessors had become acutely conscious of their waning control over the republics of Central Asia, especially Uzbekistan, and saw this assault on corruption as a lever by which they could regain lost authority over the region.

Those Ferghana Valley elites whose actions led to their being caught up in the Cotton Affair had been selected by the higher-ups because they could help implement the project at hand. In most cases they began their activities by limiting, and at times even excluding, all prior local political players from elsewhere in Uzbekistan who were not directly associated with the Ferghana group.

Economic and Political Liberalization of the Ferghana Valley During Perestroika: Tajik Perspectives

The policy of perestroika that Gorbachev launched after 1985 found strong support among Soviet citizens, who fully recognized the need for reforms in the economy and the political system. The Soviet leader looked on what he called "the human factor" as the locomotive that would overcome the inertia prevailing in virtually all spheres of Soviet life. Neither he nor anyone else considered what that "human factor" could entail. But by invoking this rather subjective principle, Gorbachev opened the way to projects in the economic and political spheres that differed sharply from the limited initial goals of perestroika.

Thus, the demand for economic modernization led to large state investments that dissipated millions across the huge economic spaces of the Soviet Union. New technologies were purchased from abroad, but people were not trained to use them and most stood idle in big storage yards under open skies. Such failures eventually led to very different proposals to accelerate the country's socio-economic development by fostering economic freedom and entrepreneurship. In the agrarian Ferghana Valley many collective and state farms were shifted to self-accounting and to collective labor contracts. But under the prevailing centralization, these enterprises continued to provide reports to the district governments as formerly, and these in turn reported up the ladder through the republics to the ministries in Moscow. All this put the brakes on economic change, since the further an enterprise was from Moscow the more difficult it was to implement the new economic methods on the ground. Moreover, harsh actions by the central authorities during the Cotton Affair had left a deep residue of mistrust toward Moscow and its reforms. In spite of this, a new business class began gradually to form in the Ferghana Valley, one that eventually would play a significant role in the political arena.

The same mistrust of economic reform existed in the Leninabad province of Tajikistan. Articles in the *Leninabadskaia pravda* newspaper denounced various forms of private trade, for instance, the rare books being sold in various cities throughout the Ferghana Valley. Sellers were branded as speculators, but they were merely building a market for what heretofore had been inexpensive but scarce rare books. This was a market economy in embryo, and it called forth articles demanding stern measures to repress this type of trading.[18] Throughout 1985 attacks on private trade and defenses of socialism persisted.[19] However, private ownership gained momentum and thereby weakened centralized political controls over the economy and strengthened the basis for free expression of ideas at all levels of public life. Meanwhile, every year the authorities in Moscow devised new projects of reform for the provinces. At first the locals lagged in their support for such initiatives, but by the late 1980s people in the Ferghana Valley were themselves setting the patterns and dynamics of these changes.

By 1988 the press in Leninabad province was noting the many economic changes in the province since a year earlier. Such key enterprises as the Isfara hydrometallurgical combine and the Avtozapchast factory in Kanibadam were now self-managed, even as many others feared the effects of freeing themselves from central funding. Falling demand for low-quality products retarded reform, as did the absence of markets for some of the higher-quality goods that had been produced.[20]

While some economic reforms were welcomed, others were problematic. Thus, A. Jalilov, a Tajik vegetable grower and lessee from the Rokhi Lenini kolkhoz near Khujand, reported:

> The introduction of lease-holding was to our liking, since we became something like owners. . . . We await the [further] Law on Land because the new arrangement for leases still did not allow us to manage as we would like. There is still a farm office acting as an intermediary between the government and us that tells us what and how much we can grow. A contract demanded that we produce 400 tons of tomatoes but we could only supply 3 tons. Even then, much produce is left to rot. This is all because the plan comes down to us from above. We increased garden crops by a third. But since we could not deal directly with retailers and instead had to turn over everything to such government agencies as Agrotorg (Agro-Trade), we had trouble selling what we produced.[21]

Gorbachev himself made an uncompromising analysis of the economic situation in the USSR at the time. He saw that by 1989 perestroika was in acute danger because of the rapidly eroding national economy, the rise of large-scale public demonstrations, and sharpened inter-ethnic tensions, with two outbreaks of violence in the Ferghana Valley alone.[22] Gorbachev blamed the crisis on the falling world price for oil, lost revenues from his own ban on the production of alcoholic beverages, the nuclear catastrophe at Chernobyl, an earthquake in Armenia, the war in Afghanistan, and other troubles. He concluded that further economic reform would be impossible without basic changes in the political system.

The Russian scholar Alexander Osipov argues that the "winds of perestroika" did not reach Uzbekistan until as late as 1988. But then perestroika found a strong resonance there, especially among the intelligentsia. Publications on the "Gdlian case" appeared, as did studies of ecological issues, including the Aral Sea tragedy.[23] The first actual conflict occurred in the Uzbek part of the Ferghana Valley beginning in May 1989, and affecting Kuvasay, Margilan, Ferghana, and Kokand. By June 3 to 12, 1989, large-scale clashes were occurring between Uzbeks and Meskhetian Turks. Known nowadays as the "Ferghana Events," these clashes ceased only after the imposition of a curfew. Only a month later, in July 1989, a second ethnic conflict broke out, this time between Tajiks and Kyrgyz. The cause of the conflict was a long-standing dispute over access to land and water in a specific group of fields. As with the "Ferghana Events," this clash ceased only when the military instituted a curfew in the villages of Vorukh, Chorkukh, and Surkh. This in turn was followed in June 1990 by the "Osh events," a sustained conflict between Kyrgyz and Uzbeks in and around the city of Osh.

In February 1990 a plenum of the CPSU Central Committee agreed to the repeal of Article VI of the Constitution, which protected the Communist Party's political monopoly. This opened the way for a multi-party system in the USSR. The Central Committee also tentatively agreed to a restructuring of the USSR as a federal union based on treaties with the constituent republics.[24] Not long after, a conflict over apartment sales broke out in Dushanbe between local Tajiks and Armenian immigrants. Between February 11 and 14 some eleven people were killed, hundreds injured, and many buses, automobiles, and buildings torched. Again, only a curfew quelled the disturbances.

Leninabadskaia pravda covered the ensuing investigation with keen interest. Clearly, other issues came into play besides the conflict over apartments. From these press stories it is clear that the Ferghana political elites already sensed danger. Both that newspaper and the Dushanbe paper *Sadoi mardum* (Voice of the People) blamed the leaders of the Tajik Rastokhez (Sunrise) movement for organizing the crisis. Indeed, they noted that amid the conflict Rastokhez head Tohir Dzhababorov had demanded that the Republic's leaders (mainly from the Ferghana Valley) resign, that a law on language be instituted, and that a general purge be instituted against "charlatans, vermin, traitors, mafia members, and others."[25] At the same time leaders discussed the possibility of returning to Leninabad its traditional name, Khujand. After a month-long debate the issue was put to a national referendum scheduled for the end of the year.

By June 1990, the Supreme Soviet in Moscow decreed the transition to a regulated market economy.[26] But by now events in Central Asia and elsewhere were outstripping the capital. On August 24 the Tajik Republic issued a Declaration of Sovereignty, and on November 30 a Ferghana Valley native, Mahkamov, was named president. It is tempting to contrast him to his counterparts in Kyrgyzstan and Uzbekistan, Masaliev and Usmankhodzhaev, both of whom met with misfortune. But since Mahkamov was the only representative of the Ferghana Valley to retain a senior position in the government of Tajikistan, this contrast is scarcely apt, the less so since the rising elites from the south of Tajikistan already held a Sword of Damocles over his head. Faced with this fundamental challenge, Mahkamov began bringing elites from heretofore underrepresented regions into key administrative posts, naming residents of Kulyab, Garm, and Badakhshan to the chairmanships of the Council of Ministers, State Planning Committee, and Supreme Soviet, respectively. The voice of Ferghana in national affairs was fast being diluted.

The geographical power shift did not end with this. Younger officials from Kulyab in the south, and also officials from Garm and Badakhshan, wanted more than they had been offered. A. Niazi argues that those from Garm were especially active in bringing about the overthrow of Ferghana power in Tajikistan that began during the "hot February" of 1990.[27] But whatever Garm's role in the short-term, more fundamental changes were occurring that favored the further south, for example in Kulyab. To understand the change, one must recall that of the Ferghana Valley political elites in Uzbekistan, Kyrgyzstan, and Tajikistan, only those from Leninabad province in Tajikistan had direct and close ties with Moscow. This enabled them to build and maintain through the decades their preeminent position in the government of the republic. At the same time the Soviet rulers, like their tsarist predecessors, controlled Tajikistan mainly through Tashkent. Hence, the Uzbek Republic had a veto over economic decisions in Tajikistan, and Moscow came to see Leninabad as a link in the chain of control that ended in Dushanbe.

The collapse of the Soviet Union destroyed these "north controls south" arrangements in Tajikistan, as they eventually were to do in Kyrgyzstan as well. In the case of Tajikistan, the southerners could tar the northerners, for example those from Ferghana, as relics of the communist nomenklatura, and claim for themselves the high ground of the national language and culture. As this occurred, the Leninabad leadership reoriented itself away from the ethnic and national identity being promoted in Dushanbe and embraced a more regional and Ferghana-based identity.

This process was clearly articulated in the Leninabad press of the time. Thus, a People's Deputy from Leninabad province discussed the "Complex Facets of Regionalism" in Leninabadskaia pravda. He noted that southern elites were struggling to get candidates from Kulyab and Badakhshan elected to national offices. Having heretofore ignored regional identities, he now detected an alarming trend in Tajikistan's political development. He quotes a statement by a southern politician who asked, "How much longer will the Leninabad people control the republic?" Searching for his own identity, the Deputy now favored Ferghana rather than the national form of identity being promoted by Tajikistan's southerners. In spite of their distinct cultural features, he argued, Ferghana people should not be excluded from the new national form of identity.[28] The Deputy concluded his essay by proclaiming, "YES, WE ARE THE NATIVES OF THE FERGHANA VALLEY."

A related development was the mounting pressure during 1991 to oust the Ferghanan Mahkamov from the presidency of the Tajik Republic and replace him with Rakhmon Nabiev. Everyone understood that both the authorities and opposition forces had far-reaching designs to make this happen. The Central Committee of Tajikistan's Communist Party published a report calling for this, while the Rastokhez party, the Democratic Party of Tajikistan, and the still-illegal Islamic Renaissance Party of Tajikistan (IRPT) were all maneuvering to throw the Ferghana elites from power in Dushanbe. The Central Committee found a pretext for this action in what it considered Mahkamov's slow response to the attempted putsch against Gorbachev on August 19–21.

Mahkamov mounted a most revealing self-defense. He explained that he and a delegation were scheduled to fly to Moscow on August 19 to sign the new union treaty the next day. But on the morning of the nineteenth, a delegation from the Vorukh enclave in the Isfara district of the Ferghana Valley asked him to hold off signing the treaty because border issues had not been resolved. In other words, even at this critical juncture the president championed the interests of the Ferghana Valley and of a Tajik enclave there, and used these to justify his opposition to the union treaty. He went on to indicate that only at 8:30 that evening did the head of the Democratic Party of Tajikistan bring him a letter demanding that he denounce the putsch and call on the Supreme Soviet of the USSR to convene a special session of the Congress of People's Deputies—or they would otherwise appeal to the people of Tajikistan to go on an indefinite strike. On August 21 at 4:00 P.M. he voiced his support for this position.[29]

Mahkamov's response was neutral and ambiguous, except for the idea that the Tajik Republic might in the end assert its sovereignty. This turned out to be insufficient, for the Party nomenklatura wanted a new and stronger person capable of protecting their positions and status. After Mahkamov's resignation, authority temporarily passed to Aslonov from Garm. Later, on September 9, 1991 thousands of protesters from the Democratic Party of Tajikistan, the Rastokhez movement, and the IRPT demanded that the Supreme Soviet of Tajikistan lift the ban on the latter. The Democratic Party, which had split from the Rastokhez movement, had been legalized in June.

The first person nominated for the new presidency was a native of Leninabad, Rakhmon Nabiev, who was followed by the well-known filmmaker, Davlat Khudonazarov from Badakhshan. Everyone knew that the old Soviet nomenklatura would support Nabiev while the Democratic Party, Rastokhez, the IRPT, and a Pamiri group, the Lali Badakhshan, would back Khudonazarov. Elections were set for October. Before they could be held, the Supreme Soviet on September 23 dismissed Aslonov after he had tried to ban the Communist Party and remove a

Lenin statue from a main square in Dushanbe. Concurrently, the new Congress named Nabiev acting president of Tajikistan and declared a state of emergency. Confrontations broke out at once between supporters of the Supreme Soviet and the Congress of People's Deputies. *Leninabadskaia pravda* darkly warned that the situation threatened not only the Leninabad political elites, but the Ferghana region as a whole.

A Leninabad deputy wrote that "[oppositionists] are running the show in Dushanbe." Indeed, he had been told that the crowds there were calling for all politicians from Leninabad to leave the capital.[30] On November 24, 1991 Nabiev emerged as the winner of the presidential elections. On December 8 the heads of now-sovereign Russia, Ukraine, and Belarus met at Belovezhsk in Belarus and effectively dissolved the USSR, forming instead the Commonwealth of Independent States. On December 21, eleven of the former Soviet republics supported these decisions, and four days later Mikhail Gorbachev resigned. Nabiev then came out in support of the Belovezhsk agreement. This should have launched a phase of state-building, but in Tajikistan it was cut short by a civil war in which some 50,000 people perished and twice that number were left homeless or refugees. Only after the signing of an inter-Tajik treaty in 1997 did an independent Tajikistan begin to form.

Causes and Consequences of Ethnic Conflicts in the Ferghana Valley: Uzbek Perspectives on the "Ferghana Events"

The Soviet government's longstanding policy of deporting ethnic groups it considered undesirable had increased the number of ethnic groups in Uzbekistan. Archival records indicate that by 1950 some 184,122 people had been deported to the Uzbek republic, not counting the Crimean Tatars, Turks, Koreans and Greeks deported there during World War II. These included 5,860 "kulaks," 842 Vlasovites, 126,114 Crimean Tatars, 41,885 Georgians, 7,788 Germans, 884 people from the North Caucasus, 746 Kalmyks, and 3 Moldovans.[31] During the war, 110,000 Turks had been forcefully deported from their homeland of Meskhetia in the southwest of Georgia,[32] as were 183,155 Tatars from their homeland in the Crimea.[33] These peoples were resettled mainly in the Ferghana cities of Kokand, Kuvasai, Margilan, as well as other areas of the valley, with a few also in the Tashkent area.

Because Uzbeks and Meskhetian Turks shared similar languages, cultures and religion (both were Sunni Muslims), they related well to each other and even intermarried. Good relations reigned for more than half a century. Even at the height of the confrontation, large numbers of Uzbeks sheltered Meskhetian families in their homes. But when Gorbachev's program of perestroika started instituting sweeping reforms, everyone in the multi-national country began looking to the interests of his own group or nation. Those peoples who had been involuntarily deported began preparing to return to their native lands and restore their national cultures. Crimean Tatars did this, and so did the Meskhetian Turks. They petitioned local officials for permission to return to their homeland, then turned for redress to the newly established Congress of People's Deputies of the USSR,[34] specifying the areas in Georgia to which they laid claim.[35] When both administrative levels ignored their requests, the Meskhetians' leaders Tashtan Aslanov, Obbos Khakhutadze, and Dursun Ismailov ratcheted up their campaign.[36]

Professor Kh. Bobobekov argues that the main cause of the Ferghana conflicts was the region's impoverished economic and social environment.[37] The Meskhetian Turks were primarily involved in relatively prestigious jobs in trade and consumer services, while most local Uzbeks in the Ferghana Valley remained in poorly paid agricultural jobs. As the economy deteriorated, this inevitably engendered resentments. The local populace raised demands of its own for better wages, jobs for youth, and an end to what they considered their subordinate inter-ethnic status. Activist youths were joined by members of the older generation, who combined around the demand to "Raise Cotton Prices!" One demonstrator expressed his discontent by saying that "Many nationalities live in the Ferghana Valley—Turks, Crimean Tatars, Jews, Germans, and others. But they all seem better off than the Uzbeks. Is it our fault that we are forced to live in the countryside and grow cotton?"[38]

Professor Sh. Ziamov explains the conflict very differently. He argues that the KGB encouraged the conflict in order to demonstrate to the public that without strong leadership from Moscow, lawlessness, turmoil and violence would ensue.[39] There is solid evidence that many participants in the turmoil came in from elsewhere,[40] while photographic evidence shows people of other nationalities who had dressed in Uzbek national garb.[41] Ziamov argues that the fact that the mass riots started in Ferghana city, continued in Margilan two days later, and then flared up in Kokand[42] demonstrates that the conflict had been engineered.

The press tended to repeat still another version, namely that "People in cars without license plates came to the homes of Russians and Tatars and showed them photographs of burned corpses, demanding they speedily leave the valley." According to this view, "The Uzbeks wanted to set the Turks against the Russians, and when the Turks refused, the Uzbeks went after the Meskhetians themselves."[43] In yet another vein, the press reported that "it started when a dispute erupted between a Russian lad and a Tatar; when some Uzbeks stood up for the Russian and a few Meskhetian Turks for the Tatar, fighting flared up."[44] Again, they claimed, it was the KGB that wanted to complicate matters for Meskhetian Turks attempting to return to their homeland. On May 23, 1989, fighting in Kuvasai between younger Uzbeks and Meskhetian Turks resulted in the death of 56 people, the burning of more than 400 homes, 116 vehicles, 8 businesses, and several schools, as well as 650 wounded.[45] With their homes in flames and their lives threatened, the Meskhetians gathered in the Provincial Party Committee's building on June 4 and asked for protection. Over the following week troops evacuated 4,981 men and women and 1,765 children to a nearby military base.[46]

On June 4 the Supreme Soviet of the Uzbek Republic in Tashkent imposed a curfew from 10 P.M. to 6 A.M., banned demonstrations and gatherings, and forbade the subletting of houses.[47] Arrests were made and volunteer militias established in many towns. In Kokand, more than a thousand young people assembled from Rishtan, Tashlak, and Uzbekistan districts, many of them armed. When they received no response to their demands for the release of all those arrested and for the immediate repatriation of all Meskhetian Turks, they stormed the building of the Provincial Party Committee and were repulsed by forty armed police. Frustrated, the rioters intensified their protest. Seeing this, the head of the troops from the Ministry of Internal Affairs gave orders to fire on the crowd with sub-machine guns.[48] When the rioters seized various factories and the railroad station, the Ministry of Internal Affairs' troops regrouped around the banks and communication offices. During these "Kokand events" five people died, ninety-three suffered various injuries, and sixty were hospitalized.[49] The young demonstrators eventually released the sixty-nine prisoners they had taken. Three days later, on the seventh, some 3,000 protesters gathered outside the Provincial Executive Committee in Rishtan, demanding the release of all those arrested in Ferghana and Kokand, higher prices for cotton, jobs, and housing. At Kurashkhon near Namangan 400 people took part in a similar demonstration.

In the wake of these conflicts, fully 200 "investigators" who had been studying the inter-ethnic conflicts that had just occurred in Armenia and Azerbaijan arrived from Moscow to carry out a speedy examination of the causes of the Ferghana tragedies.[50] Some fifty-six criminal cases were filed against participants in the June 4 events, and more than forty criminal cases were instituted against participants in the June 21 riots.[51] Thirty murder cases were also resolved,[52] and many small arms confiscated.[53]

The Communist leaders of the republic declared that the conflict had arisen "out of strawberries at a bazaar."[54] The stance of Rafik Nishanov, first secretary of the Central Committee of the Communist Party of Uzbekistan, caused discontent among some deputies at the newly formed Supreme Soviet of the USSR. An Armenian deputy addressed Nishanov directly: "Rafik Nishanovich, I've been fearful for several days and must chastise you. The press reports that the situation in Uzbekistan is perilous but you, the First Secretary . . . are sitting here calmly and telling us 'Don't fear, comrades, everything will work out.' . . . My suggestion to you is immediately to leave for Uzbekistan."[55]

Earlier, Nishanov had reported to a Party group that the young Ferghana rioters, impelled by "nationalism," had engaged "not only in ethnic conflict, but also in acts against the Soviet way of life."[56] Meanwhile, the investigative commission concluded that while the conflicts had started as the accidental result of confrontations among youngsters, they nonetheless had social and economic roots. The commission blamed the fighting on a "fierce nationalistic disposition" among the local population that sought to set group against group.[57] Equally, it noted, the situation had been complicated by official indifference in the Ferghana Valley "to the actions of the Meskhetian Turks, some of whom attempted to fan the situation in order to hasten their return to the southern areas of the Georgian Republic."[58]

Still in June, Nikolai Ryzhkov, chairman of the Council of Ministers of the

USSR, announced that those Meskhetian Turks residing in refugee camps near Ferghana city were free, as a temporary measure, to move to the Black Earth region of Russia, and that "all [other] measures necessary for the resettlement have been started."[59] Ryzhkov's "solution" was disingenuous. Between 1959 and 1979 Russia's rural areas had lost 13 million people. Everything connected with agricultural production was in decay.[60] As farmers departed for the cities and for Central Asia, the number of collapsed houses in the more remote countryside reached 900,000.[61] Now Ryzhkov proposed to revitalize these deserted villages by settling there "an industrious Turkic people, able to restore agriculture."[62] To cover the costs of this ill-advised move, as well as its own expenses, another special commission from Moscow raided the budget of the Ferghana province.[63] By June 10, 1989 thousands of Meskhetian Turks had been settled in places as distant from one another as Belgorod, Kaliningrad, and Orel. Once there, the Meskhetians found that the housing that had been promised them did not exist.[64] But by the end of June, 16,282 people from the Ferghana Valley had been resettled in Smolensk, Orel, Kursk, Belgorod, and Voronezh provinces in Russia.[65]

On July 5, 1989 the Uzbek republic's Council of Ministers granted construction material for rebuilding destroyed homes, as well as compensation for damages inflicted on the Meskhetian Turks. Graduated one-time payments were also made to Meskhetians who lacked insurance, leaving the local government to restore and sell any houses remaining.

The events that took place in Osh and Jalalabad regions of the neighboring Kyrgyzstan doubtless helped aggravate the socio-political conditions in Uzbekistan at the end of the 1980s and the beginning of the 1990s. The bloody strife of the "Osh events" did not spread throughout Kyrgyzstan, although it was Uzbeks who had lived there for many years who were most directly affected. Nor can one view the intense conflicts in the Uzbek cities of Ferghana, Buka, Parkent, and Namangan as separate occurrences. All were integral components of the gathering social and political crisis in the region that found public expression in the unleashing of democratic currents during perestroika.

A View from Without on the "Ferghana Events"

Alexander Osipov has analyzed in detail the various interpretations of the crisis described above. Since his analysis goes beyond those of Bobobekov and Ziamov, cited above, it is useful, by way of summary, to review his findings, and especially the four main interpretations which he detects in the literature: namely, that the conflict arose from an escalation of hooligan acts, from economic factors, from the flowering of competing nationalisms, and from what he calls conspiratorial "political" forces either within or outside the government.[66]

The "hooligan acts" interpretation was voiced first by Rafik Nishanov. It holds that the conflict arose at a bazaar in Kuvasai when a Turk spoke rudely to an Uzbek saleswoman while he was buying "a plate of strawberries." Uzbek bystanders stood up for her, which led to a large-scale scuffle. As we have seen, this rather superficial explanation soon gave way to an economic interpretation, according to which the conflict arose from social and economic competition between impoverished Uzbeks and more prosperous Meskhetian Turks. Osipov argues that the mass media at the time continuously exaggerated the issue of the Uzbeks' supposedly difficult economic plight, their unemployment in rural areas, and other such matters. The local press, he concludes, was enthralled with the narrative of privileged Turk speculators occupying the most profitable places at the markets while the Uzbeks toiled for pennies in hot cotton fields. Beyond journalists, this interpretation was favored by politicians and intellectuals of the Ferghana Valley, among them the leader of the Birlik Party, Mukhammad Salikh,[67] the provost of the Ferghana Pedagogical University, Sherzod Abdullaev,[68] and the writer Alim Mirzaev.[69]

Notwithstanding the rise of national self-awareness and of nationalistic ideas in the popular mind, Osipov does not place much stock in the explanation that turns on nationalism. His argument is simple: while the USSR had numerous conflicting ethnic groups in these years, and while nationalistic thinking was undeniably on the rise at the time of the "Ferghana events," in no instance did this lead to fighting unless a group was targeted with specific liabilities, and unless there were institutional arrangements that restricted the rights and opportunities of such a non-titular group. Violence does not break out on its own, says Osipov. Therefore, while nationalistic thinking may have been a contributing factor, there is no reason to think that it could have *caused* the conflict unless these other factors were present.

Osipov breaks the political interpretation into two components, consisting of conspiracies *against* the government and conspiracies *by* the government. The first version turns on the actions of forces that either opposed perestroika or wanted to go beyond it. All those championing this position acted on the assumption that "the worse, the better." The Turkish association Vatan traces the origins of the conflict to the Meskhetian Turks' rejection of a proposal by the Birlik Party to combine forces against some unspecified enemies. It is possible that this led nationalistic forces to target Meskhetian Turks for attack. The Vatan association traces such suggestions to the leaders of the Birlik movement, specifically the brothers Abdurahim and Abdumanob Pulatov.[70] Articles by these persons published in the Russian journals *Ogonek* and *Novoe vremia* appear to support this view.[71]

Let us now turn to the hypothesis that centers on the KGB. According to this view, the KGB was the architect of the conflict, which it achieved by taking advantage of inter-ethnic problems and of the recalcitrance of the republican leadership. The reason for which the KGB fomented mass rioting was to bind Uzbekistan to Moscow at a time when that link was fast eroding.[72] A related version of this hypothesis was voiced by the Vatan, which argued that the security forces fomented the conflict precisely in order to resettle Russia's depopulated farmland.[73]

Osipov brands as farfetched the interpretation that the conflicts were generated by rogue elements of the KGB. Even if the head of the USSR's internal security forces, Major-General Iurii Shatalin, and the head of Uzbek intelligence in the

Ferghana province, N.G. Leskov,[74] had had the intention of fomenting a fight between Meskhetian Turks and Uzbeks, why would they have chosen the small town of Kuvasai to launch it?

Given the multi-faceted character of the conflict, several of Osipov's hypotheses are probably necessary in order fully to explain the events. However, Osipov's own conclusion is that "the frustration and aggressiveness that were the product of the 'Cotton Affair,' as well as the diminished fear of the government after 1989, when the government began to lose its status as the major target of discontent, led to a situation in which accidentally arising local confrontations, perceived by the public as ethnic conflicts, could create an opening through which aggression could be channeled."[75] This explanation, which might be called a "primordial" hypothesis, is at odds with the hypothesis that the clash was deliberately engineered. Osipov's own title, "The Ferghana Events of 1989 (The Engineering of the Conflict)," leads one to expect him to embrace this view, but he does not. In his interpretation, Osipov considers the economic factor mainly through its absence. Virtually all of the versions, except for the political one, take us back to primordial social issues.

The view that a nationalistic conflict assumed a broader character focusing on the institutional framework is not quite convincing. Many conflicts in the Soviet and post-Soviet space arose spontaneously. Interestingly, it is precisely the political explanation of the conflict that dominates the interpretations of Uzbek intellectuals themselves, while elsewhere the conflict tends to be viewed in terms of primordial conditions on the ground. Yet Osipov is right to remind us that events in the Ferghana Valley have many dimensions, each with its own logic, and these require correspondingly multi-faceted explanations.

Tajik Perspectives on Territorial and Water Dispute During the Perestroika Era

During the curfew on the eve of the Tajik civil war, the First Secretary of the Communist Party of Tajikistan, Mahkamov, held a press conference on a conflict involving three Tajik villages of the Isfara district of the Tajik Republic and some Kyrgyz villages in the Batken district of Kyrgyzia. The conflict, in which several people died and dozens were hospitalized with gunshot wounds, erupted over access to land and water. It started when a collective farm board in the Isfara district responded to a request from the Kyrgyz side of the border by transferring 144 hectares of land to a kolkhoz in the Batken district. Meanwhile a village on the Tajik side had asked for 100 hectares adjacent to its lands, but on the Kyrgyz side. All this should have been simply resolved, as the border never had been clearly defined during the entire Soviet period. When no solution appeared, the Tajik village shut off water flowing in the Matchoi irrigation canal across the border to Kyrgyzstan.

The press conference noted that back in 1958 an agreement had been reached on the border, which the Kyrgyz government ratified but not the Tajik Supreme Soviet. Because of this, the 1958 delineation was now considered illegitimate.[76] Once the curfew was lifted, the Tajiks cleaned the Matchoi canal and resumed the delivery of water to the Lenin state farm on the Batken side of the border. Meanwhile, the leaders of the two republics set up a commission to find a permanent solution to the problem and to assure easy crossing of borders in disputed areas.[77] The Tajiks concluded that the only legitimate map dated not to 1958 but to 1927, and that this left 24,000 hectares of pastureland that now had to be divided between the Tajik and Kyrgyz sides. The two presidents were to have settled this in a meeting in May 1991, but the Kyrgyz president Askar Akaev failed to appear, leaving the issue still unresolved.[78]

The "Osh Events": Kyrgyz-Uzbek Conflict

In May 1990, the economic collapse in Kyrgyzstan reached its nadir, and general political uncertainty prevailed at both the local and national levels. The waning of the Soviet supra-national ideology left people scrambling to protect their rights by affirming their national identities. With neither the imperial center nor national elites able to protect their rights, citizens turned to spontaneous protests to defend themselves.

In June 1990, inter-ethnic strife between Kyrgyz and Uzbeks exploded in Kyrgyzstan's Osh province. The sources of this strife were not dissimilar to those we have explored in the case of the "Ferghana events" between Uzbeks and Meskhetian Turks in June 1989, and in the case of the confrontation between Tajiks from Isfara and Kyrgyz from Batken in July of that year. Once again the question of national identity is at the core of the issue, in this case specifically the revival and preservation of cultural traditions, language especially. The expanding claims of the titular nationalities allowed little room in the typical citizen's worldview for other ethnic groups. In Kyrgyzstan's sector of the Ferghana Valley, many impoverished rural Kyrgyz youths lacked farming skills and, discontented, migrated to the cities in search of jobs and housing. Unable to afford apartments in Osh, they squatted on municipal land on its outskirts, area being used mainly by Uzbek cotton farmers. Soon both there and in similar developments on the fringe of Bishkek one heard political slogans critical of the pace of reform in the waning communist era.

Meanwhile, within Osh city an informal Uzbek cultural association, Adolat (Justice), began calling for the protection of the Uzbek language and Uzbek traditions. Concurrently, the Kyrgyz formed their own national association, Osh Aimagy (Residents of Osh), to defend the national interests of the Kyrgyz living in the Ferghana Valley. Its program called for the granting of land to Kyrgyz to construct houses, and also for the protection of human rights. Adolat leaders leaned toward ethnic separatism, while their counterparts from Osh Aimagy proved unable to engage in dialogue and compromise. In May 1990, Uzbeks from the Ferghana Valley city of Jalalabad appealed to the waning Soviet leadership in Moscow to grant autonomy to Uzbeks throughout the south of Kyrgyzstan.[79] They addressed their plea to the Uzbek Rafik Nishanov, now chairman of the Supreme Soviet's Council of Nationalities, and to the first secretary of the Central Committee of the Communist Party of Kyrgyzia, Masaliev. They argued that the indigenous population of Osh province was in fact Uzbek, and that the 560,000 Uzbeks there constituted half the population of Osh province. Given this, it was unacceptable to them that Kyrgyz had been declared the official language of the new Kyrgyz Republic and Russian the language of inter-ethnic communication, with no place for Uzbek. All the records of Osh now had to be translated into Kyrgyz.

It will be recalled that the Kyrgyz and Uzbek people of the Kyrgyz sector of Ferghana, thanks to centuries of cohabitation, shared a common way of life, traditions, and even dialects, not to mention intertwined households. Understandably, Kyrgyz from the north sneered that their southern Kyrgyz cousins had become Sarts and were indistinguishable from the Uzbeks.

Many Uzbek secondary-school graduates chose to pursue their university studies outside the Kyrgyz Republic. This gradually shifted the ethnic balance in the Osh region in favor of the Kyrgyz. This was reinforced by the fact that, excepting a single hour-long radio broadcast in Uzbek, radio, TV, textbooks, or other publications did not serve Uzbek speakers. Hence the Uzbeks had no recourse but to seek these from across the border in Uzbekistan. Thanks to the indifference of the Kyrgyz leadership, there were few, if any, Uzbek members of the Kyrgyzstan Academy of Sciences, and almost no indigenous Uzbek artists or writers. The Kyrgyz were favored in every sphere, leaving the Uzbeks feeling themselves to be an alien ethnic group within Kyrgyzia. Biased hiring practices meant there was not a single Uzbek first secretary in the Osh or national Party committees, few Uzbeks on district Executive Committees, and few in other major enterprises. In the new language law, Kyrgyz found a tool with which to harass the few Uzbeks in medicine, education, commerce, and agencies of local self-government.

This, in summary, was the Uzbeks' appeal to the higher authorities. Their petition concluded with a plea to create an "Osh Autonomous Soviet Socialist Republic" within the framework of the Kyrgyz Soviet Republic.[80] This statement was issued on March 2, 1990, and by May the situation was slipping out of the government's control. After a series of mass protests by Kyrgyz organized by Osh Aimagy on May 27 in the "Lenin" kolkhoz, a rally of 5,000 people took place near Osh. Following long discussions, it was decided to allocate the collective farm's cotton land for housing construction. The Uzbeks who farmed those lands were furious, and retaliated with a large rally of their own. This ended with the issuance of many new demands, including the designation of Uzbek as a state language in the Republic.[81]

On June 4 more than 12,000 Uzbeks assembled at one end of a field at the Lenin kolkhoz, with 1,500 Kyrgyz on the opposite end. Most of those killed in the ensuing battle were Kyrgyz, but on the following days the situation was reversed. In all, some 600 people were killed, the majority of them Uzbeks, with unofficial estimates of the total as high as 1,500. Thousands of Uzbeks from the Uzbek sector of the valley were marching toward Osh when a strict curfew sent them home. Only the involvement of the army and the pleadings of religious and traditional leaders prevented the outburst from spreading across the entire Ferghana Valley.

A General View of Cultural and Social Processes in the Ferghana Valley, 1985–1991

When Moscow leaders in 1983 thought through their position on tradition, culture, and religion, they concluded that religious habits were among the strongest forces impeding the development of a Soviet way of life. Acknowledging that the three categories are scarcely separable, this conclusion created the context in which perestroika-related cultural and social processes took place across the entire Ferghana Valley. Once more the Ferghana Valley, with its ambivalent mixture of Soviet and religious traditions, was chosen as the laboratory for an experiment from Moscow. The result was less a serious engagement between tradition and modernity than a frontal collision between Soviet and Muslim ways. This forced people to take sides, moving out of the shadowy middle ground that central authorities had long tolerated. Perestroika changed Moscow's strategy in the Ferghana Valley, forcing political elites there to clarify their positions and define their allegiances vis-à-vis the "center."

On the Kyrgyz side of the border, Party officials arriving from Moscow came with a mandate to strengthen anti-religious propaganda in the Ferghana Valley by raising the skills of people working in that field and by expanding relevant programs in schools, technical centers, and institutions of higher learning. As this unfolded, the Central Committee of the Kyrgyz Communist Party grew seriously concerned over the religious involvements of southerners that had been gaining momentum since the 1979 Soviet invasion of Afghanistan.

Similar large-scale measures to expand Soviet atheist propaganda were launched in the Isfara district of the Tajik part of the Ferghana Valley. Religious life in the most traditional villages was closely monitored, while the local administration created cultural centers and other "Soviet spaces" to shift the local culture in the direction of secularism. This initiative from Moscow created new meeting places and secular platforms for people seeking to improve local social and cultural life. During 1985 a number of villages in the Isfara district received new community centers, clubs, libraries, and teahouses (*chaikhanas*) with reading rooms. All of these were created to publicize Soviet traditions and values, and to arm people against the existing religious traditions of the Ferghana Valley.[82] Over time, these facilities lost their original purpose and instead became embodiments of the emerging national culture, acquiring a more official character in the process. Indeed, the maintenance of these facilities, where official functions and *shashmakom* musical competitions are held, has now been entrusted to the government.

Tea-houses, where economic, social, and family issues always have been discussed and where people play chess and prepare the national dish, *plov,* now emerged as the single cultural institution that preserved its traditional function and vitality under the new conditions. The perestroika-era teahouse in the largest village of Chorkukh continues today to function and attract people from nearby villages of Isfara. Now and then the locals invite Kyrgyz from nearby villages in Batken province to come and play chess. Indeed, chess is an important secular ritual that has been preserved from Soviet times, albeit with a very specific Ferghana Valley flavor. It is hard to imagine these teahouses or clubs without chess, the absence of which would shift the old Soviet era dichotomy between secularism and religion in favor of the latter. In the course of mini-tournaments, *plov* and tea are prepared in the traditional manner and tea-drinking goes around the circle, as if joining those who drink in ritual unity centering on conversation and chess. Many a dispute has been solved in the course of this ritual.

Other perestroika-era cultural forces were the cinema, theater, TV, and radio. But the spread of privatization has forced many of these state institutions out of business, terminating the educational and propagandistic functions for which they were created. The director of the cinema center in Isfara, Inomdzhon Ismoilov, reports that in 1990 there were still thirty-eight movie theaters in the region.[83] At the same time, younger and more flexible concert presenters arose, leaving the old cultural behemoths like Goskontsert in the dust. One of them is the flourishing youth center Dilafruz in Leninabad, which quickly marginalized Goskontsert there.[84]

The national languages provided the most vital locus of social and cultural revival in all three republics of the Ferghana Valley. In Tajikistan a decree from the Supreme Soviet in Dushanbe on July 22, 1989, established Tajik (Farsi) as the state language and Russian as the language of inter-ethnic communication.[85] The *Rastokhez* movement that championed this decree had a pan-Iranian rather than a national orientation. Firdausi's Persian-Tajik classic *Shahnama* also came once more to prominence, reflecting the interests of the Tajik intelligentsia. Simultaneously, the patriotic verse of Loik Sherali, Bozor Sobir, Gulrukhsor Safievam, and others came to symbolize the national revival. Through poems that gained popularity as far afield as the Tajik part of the Ferghana Valley, poets hailed the revival of national life and spoke out for democratic change. The intelligentsia of Isfara city and province, including Novoe Matcho, especially welcomed these works.

The large-scale reconstruction of mosques that began during the perestroika era was more a national than a religious development. Thus, the visitor to the mosque at Khodzhai in Isfara is greeted by a patriotic inscription by the poet Bozor Sobir, while the interior is decorated with national texts and *beiits* of Tajik-Persian classical poetry. During perestroika, the celebration of National Language Day in the Ferghana region was more important for residents than officials, who were keenly aware that the national language had become yet another tool that the southern elites were using to seize political power in the republic.

Despite the revival evident in many spheres of culture, other cultural institutions were in crisis during perestroika, especially in the Ferghana region of Tajikistan. The Tajik actress S. Isaeva recalls that the main theaters in Kanibadam and Leninabad were all on the brink of closing.[86] But despite the crises, the dynamic new themes of the day lent vitality to many other developing cultural institutions. It is no exaggeration to say that culture and art were as urgently real as reality itself.

In Kyrgyzstan, TV and radio played the most active role during the perestroika era.[87] Such innovative programs as "The Tribune of Perestroika," "Pulse," "Urgent Talk," "Tele-Arena," "Pace," and "Thorny Screen" openly discussed heretofore taboo issues and presented a sharp contrast to earlier programming. The common theme of the position and role of citizens in society reverberated through television and radio broadcasts across the Kyrgyz Republic of the USSR. In the process, the media grew closer to people's actual needs. As information became more democratized, censorship grew less harsh. Fresh and vital information infused both the large cities and remote population centers of the Ferghana Valley. Diversified programming appealed to a range of tastes and interests. Cable TV also developed rapidly at this time. This information revolution that swept Kyrgyzstan and the Kyrgyz sector of the Ferghana Valley radically changed perceptions about the region, the republic, and the world, exposing long-standing problems in the process.

Criticism of Party and government agencies grew more intense and harsh. Both belles-lettres and journalism came to play an important role in shaping public opinion. Such writers as T. Sydykbekov, M. Baidzhiev, and other poets, publicists, journalists, and teacher took to the pages of such newspapers as *Kyrgyzstan Madaniaty* and *Leninchil Jash* to proclaim the idea of a new Kyrgyzstan. The literary and art journal *Ala-Too* disseminated the works of heretofore banned authors in many fields.

By the 1960s Kyrgyz had ceased to be the state language of Kyrgyzia. Now the struggle to make it the state language became a key focus of independence-minded Kyrgyz. As national self-awareness spread and gained potency, the Supreme Soviet of the Kyrgyz SSR on September 23, 1989 declared Kyrgyz the state language in Kyrgyzstan, at the same time providing for the free development of other languages.

It is a striking to observe that among the three Ferghana states, only in the Kyrgyz Republic did Soviet leaders refrain from unleashing a large-scale assault on religion. The rationale for this was that at the time Soviet officials considered religion to be far less a danger in Kyrgyzia than in Tajikistan and, even more so, in Uzbekistan.

Turning to Uzbekistan, in November 1988 a "visiting session" of the USSR-wide office of language and literature convened at the Academy of Sciences in Tashkent to consider "bilingualism and multilingualism in the multi-national Soviet culture." Professor B. Nazarov, the director of the Institute of Language and Culture at the Uzbek Academy of Sciences, bluntly asked: "How can one explain the fact that in many universities, and even at the Institute of Theater and Art and the Institute of Culture, where future Uzbek actors, artists, and other skilled cultural figures are studying, the Uzbek language chairs have been closed?"[88] Proposals were made to establish Uzbek as the state language of Uzbekistan.[89]

Rather than take action directly, the ideological department of the Central Committee of the Communist Party of Uzbekistan sidestepped the question by setting up a twenty-four-member working group to examine the language issue.[90] The commission included both Uzbeks and members of other ethnic groups living in the republic. It did not initially consider making Uzbek the state language of the Uzbek SSR, and instead focused on elevating the role of Uzbek in society. But from the very outset a sub-group focused on the question of Uzbek as the state language and on the free development of other languages spoken within the borders of Uzbekistan. By February 1989, the Supreme Soviet of Uzbekistan was considering a draft law on making the Uzbek language the state language, which it released for discussion on May 19, 1989.

During the ensuing months the commission received some 4,000 letters and petitions.[91] The commission studied these and alternative drafts from the Union of Writers and from various unofficial organizations,[92] then prepared a new draft it released on October 11. This draft was in turn discussed and adopted by the Supreme Soviet of the Uzbek Soviet Socialist Republic. The Presidium also moved to expand instruction in Tajik, Kazakh, Turkmen, and Kyrgyz in secondary schools, and to open departments of Kazakh, Tajik, and Kyrgyz at the universities in Samarkand, Nukus, and Tashkent. Some 259 secondary schools began instruction in Tajik, 491 schools offered Kazakh, fifty-two Turkmen, forty Kyrgyz, twelve Greek, and seven Korean. Radio programs in Tajik were broadcast each week in Samarkand, Bukhara, Ferghana, Syr Darya, and Surkhandarya provinces, while local newspapers were issued in several districts in Tajik and Kazakh.[93] Nor was Russian neglected, with the Gafur Gulyam publishing house in 1989 issuing twenty-seven works—and a total of two million copies—of literature in Russian.[94]

In these same months the Uzbeks were putting in place a solid footing for fundamentally realigning the country's economic and social life, and ending its domination by Moscow. The key moment came with the change of leadership in June 1989, from which time the process of identifying and pursuing a means of achieving independent progress was launched. Among the long list of problems demanding attention were massive unemployment, declining productivity, poverty-level incomes, lop-sided economic development, a grave housing shortage, and parlous conditions in education, public health, trade, public services, and ecology. All of these were seen as potentially destabilizing.[95]

While all this was taking place, the Soviet propaganda campaign that had been launched in the Ferghana Valley in 1983 continued unabated. Its main target remained the widespread religious rites associated with weddings (*nikokh*). We have seen that such attacks on traditional religious practices occurred also in the Tajik sections of Ferghana and also, to a lesser extent, in the Kyrgyz region, but they were particularly intense in the Uzbek sector of the Ferghana Valley. Salafi and Wahhabi currents were already gaining momentum during these years. The attacks on traditional practices had a paradoxical outcome, however. As the Uzbek scholar Bakhtiyar Babadjanov has noted,[96] the assault on traditional practices opened up space in which nontraditional and even radical religious currents could be considered practically legal. Like the Soviet "agitators," Salafi and Wahhabi propagandists also advanced an ideal of social "purity." To be sure, each defined purity in its own way, with the Soviets championing a communist culture untainted by religion and tradition, and the Salafis and Wahhabis hailing a new faith purged of all false or distorting elements of traditional religious practice. But the Soviet attack on traditional religious ways meshed neatly with the goals of radical Islam and inadvertently facilitated its advance. This process was widespread throughout the Ferghana Valley, but was especially pronounced in Namangan province.

In this connection it is worth noting the changing status of traditional religious authorities and their impact in the Ferghana Valley and beyond. Ferghana figures like Muhammadjon (Hindustani) Rustamov and Qori Abdurashid had taught the majority of mullahs and religious scholars in Tajikistan and Uzbekistan. Muhammadjon (Hindustani) and Qori Abdurashid also played a decisive role in training members of the religious establishment or *ulama*. Abdullo Nuri, a leader of the IRPT, was among their students, as was Mukhammadsharif Khimmatzoda. Nuri often recalled that at the time of his education in the Ferghana Valley there was no division between Uzbeks and Tajiks. But beginning about 1995 he had somehow to accommodate the new national and religious thinking that was fixed in the inter-Tajik negotiations two years later. He advocated a compromise or balance between the religious and the national, something the Soviets had refused to consider. This formed the basis for the peaceful resolution of the civil war and for the stability that has prevailed in Tajikistan since then.

This clearly suggests that the links between the Ferghana Valley and the religious leadership of the entire region that existed in the past are to a large extent still intact today. Equally clear, the resulting connection among the three countries of Kyrgyzstan, Tajikistan, and Uzbekistan took definitive form during the perestroika era.

Conclusion

Conflict in the Ferghana Valley cannot be explained by linear logic. This plainly can be seen in the character and evolution of ethics there. The very dense concentration of people in the Ferghana Valley demanded, as a condition of survival, the formation of an appropriate code of conduct and etiquette—and over the centuries such an ethical code was indeed developed. In many respects this standard of behavior was distinct. Patriots of the valley do not hesitate to claim that their ethics are better than those of neighboring regions. What is not debatable is that without such a widely accepted code of conduct, the delicate social balance could be upset at any time. Thus, ethics became a way by which people could protect themselves from others—and also from their own. To put it another way, these high ethical standards, acknowledged as typical of Ferghana Valley residents of all nationalities, affirm, foster, and help maintain a social balance among the various communities.

Whether in the cultural or religious context, the disruption of such traditional institutions destabilizes the social system. Perestroika introduced a new element of subjectivity into the communal life of the Ferghana Valley, which hastened the upending of existing social and ethical traditions. This inevitably led to conflict. At the same time, societies of the Ferghana Valley also possess a subtle ability to innovate and, failing that, to adapt rather than simply adopt what comes to them from the outside world. Perestroika's goal in the Ferghana Valley was to overcome the prevailing social practices through the introduction of a more subjective principle. The only way to neutralize this tendency, or at least place it in a proper balance with other forces, is through the conferring of legal and political norms or rights implemented and defended by the state. Such norms must protect the rights of individual citizen while also maintaining respect for traditional communal values.

The culture of the Ferghana Valley is rich in the skills of social and cultural mediation, which are manifest in the flexible social qualities that enable them to find compromise. These constitute a form of social capital that, properly invigorated and harnessed, can become an engine of modernization. Translated into the language of contemporary management, they could allow people from the valley to play a key role in Central Asia and beyond. That role could be one of intermediary, moving back and forth among worlds, helping people interpret their cultural and political environments, and serving as living links between peoples, cultures, and values, be they from China, Japan, Europe, Russia, India, or the Muslim world. By adapting such a role to the requirements of modernity, the region will be better able to integrate with the emerging economic, political, and social realities. A law of synergy may be relevant here, one that seeks and discovers the most important truths not within the functioning of one or another system by itself, but in the interactions among all such systems.

Notes

1. *Leninabadskaia pravda,* December 1, 1991.

2. *Leninabadskaia pravda,* September 5, 1991.

3. *Leninabadskaia pravda,* September 24, 1991.

4. The co-author of this chapter from Uzbekistan, Kh. Yunusova, prepared the material on the perestroika period in the Uzbek part of the Ferghana Valley.

5. Vladimir Kalichenko, a former investigator for priority cases under procurator general of the USSR: "The almighty minister of internal affairs of the USSR, Shchelokov, made a decision on my neutralization. In response to this, Andropov ordered 'Alfa' group to protect me" ("V gostiakh u Gordona," Pervyi natsionalnyi kanal [Ukraine], November 7, 2004).

6. *Narodnoe khoziaistvo Uzbekskoi SSR v 1987 g.,* Tashkent, 1988, pp. 143–45.

7. *Sovershenstvovanie struktury narodnogo khoziaistva Uzbekskoi SSR,* p. 73.

8. *Itogi vsesoiuznoi perepisi naseleniia 1979 g., Statisticheskii sbornik,* vol. 1, p. 18.

9. N. Nemelov and V. Popov, *Na perelome ekonomicheskoi perestroiki v SSSR,* Moscow, 1998, p. 44.

10. I.S. Ratkovskii and M.V. Khodiakov, *Istoriia Sovetskoi Rossii,* St. Petersburg, 2001, p. 337.

11. D. Likhanov, "Koma," *Ogonek,* no. 4, 1989, pp. 20–21.

12. *Sovet Uzbekistoni,* December 27, 1989.

13. "Pervyi sezd narodnykh deputatov SSSR," Sten-otchet, vol. 3, Moscow, 1989, pp. 401–2.

14. http://ru.wikipedia.org (search in cyrillic "khlopkovoe delo").

15. *Izvestia,* April 27, 1989.

16. *Postanovlenie VS SSSR ot 18.04.1990 g.* no. 1438–1 "O vyvodakh Komissii dlia proverki materialov, sviazannykh s deiatelnostiu sledstvennoi gruppy Prokuratury Soiuza SSR, vozglavliaemoi T.Kh. Gdlianom."

17. "Uzbekskoe 'khlopkovoe delo' pochti chetvert veka spustia," Interview with Telman Gdlian, Radio Svoboda, June 18, 2008.

18. "Torgovlia: net, Spekuliatsii," *Leninabadskaia Pravda,* July, 1985.

19. "Torgovlia: net, Spekuliatsii," *Leninabadskaia Pravda,* March and June 1985.

20. *Leninabadskaia Pravda,* January, 1988.

21. Ibid.

22. "Novogodnee obrashchenie k sovetskomu narodu Generalnogo sekretaria TsK KPSS, Predsedatelia Verkhovnogo Soveta SSSR, M.S. Gorbacheva," *Leninabadskaia Pravda,* January, 1990.

23. A.G. Osipov, "Ferganskie sobytiia 1989 goda (konstruirovanie etnicheskogo konflikta)," in *Ferganskaia dolina. Etnichnost. Etnicheskie protsessy. Etnicheskie konflikty,* ed. S.N. Abashin and V.I. Bushkov, Moscow, 2004, p. 169.

24. *Leninabadskaia Pravda,* February, 1990.

25. *Sadoi Mardum* (Voice of the People), January 12, 1991; *Leninabadskaia Pravda,* January, 1990.

26. *Leninabadskaia Pravda,* June 19, 1990.

27. A. Niiazi, "Tadzhikistan: regionalnye aspeckty konflikta (1990-e gg.)," http://poli.vub.ac.be/publi/etni-1/niayzi.htm.

28. *Leninabadskaia Pravda,* February 2, 1991.

29. "Doklad Presidenta Tadzhikskoi SSR K. Makhkamova o politicheskoi situatsii v Tadzhikskoi SSR na vneocherednoi sessii Verkhovnogo soveta Tadzhikistana," *Leninabadskaia Pravda,* August 31, 1991.

30. *Leninabadskaia Pravda,* September 25, 1991.

31. P. Murtazaeva, *Uzbekistonda millatlararo muonsabatlar va bagrikenglik,* Tashkent, 2007, p. 98.

32. *Sovet Uzbekistoni,* September 15, 1988.

33. *Nashe Otechestvo,* pt. 4.2, Moscow, 1991, p. 426.

34. Kh. Bobobekov Kh., *Fargona fozhealari, Fan va turmush,* no. 5, 1990.

35. Ibid.

36. Ibid.

37. Ibid., p. 18.

38. *Sovet Uzbekistoni,* June 10, 1989.

39. S. Ziamov, "Mezhnatsionalnye otnosheniia i mezhetnicheskie konflikty v Tsentralnoi Azii," *Central Asian Studies,* vol. 8. 2003, pp. 154–55.

40. *Literaturnaia gazeta,* June 14, 1989.

41. *Sovet Uzbekistoni,* June 10, 1989; Ziamov, "Mezhnatsionalnye otnosheniia," p. 156.

42. *Sovet Uzbekistoni,* June 10, 1989.

43. *Krasnaia zvezda,* June 21, 1989.

44. *Sovet Uzbekistoni,* June 13, 1989.

45. *Sovet Uzbekistoni,* June 8, 1989.

46. Bobobekov, *Fargona fozhealari, Fan va turmush.*

47. *Ferganskaia Pravda,* June 5, 1989.

48. Bobobekov, *Fargona fozhealari, Fan va turmush,* p. 16.

49. *Ferganskaia Pravda,* June 9, 1989.

50. M. Lurie and P. Studenikin, *Zapakh gari i goria: Ferghana, trevozhnyi iiun 1989 goda,* Moscow, 1990, p. 81.

51. Ibid, p. 79.

52. *Sovet Uzbekistoni,* July 6, 1989.

53. *Sovet Uzbekistoni,* June 8, 1989.

54. A.A. Azizhujaev, ed., *Uzbekistonning yangi tarikhi, Ikkinchi kitob, Uzbekiston sovet mustamlakachilig davrida,* Tashkent, 2000, p. 663.

55. "Pervaia sessiia Verkhovnogo Soveta SSSR," Bulletin 2, Moscow, 1989, p. 9.

56. *Tashkentskaia Pravda,* June 16, 1989.

57. *Izvestiia TsK KPSS,* no. 10, 1989, p. 95.

58. *Namangan khakikati,* August 1, 1989.

59. "Khamma uchun zhiddii sabok," *Sovet Uzbekistoni,* June 16, 1989.

60. Z.R. Ishankhodzhaev, *Uchastie Uzbekistana v osvoenii nechernozemnoi zony RSFSR (1975–1985),* Tashkent, 1992, p. 15.

61. D. Bobodzhonova, *Uzbekistonda izhtimoii-iktisodii munosabatlar, (70–80 yillar misolida),* Tashkent, 1999, p. 124.

62. "Khamma uchun zhiddii sabok."

63. *Fargona viloiati,* DA F-1124, ruikhat-15, iifma zhild-374, 84-varazh.

64. *Sovet Uzbekistoni,* June 16, 1990.

65. *Namangan khakikati,* August 1, 1989.

66. Osipov, "Ferganskie sobytiia 1989," pp. 193–207.

67. *Ferganskaia Pravda,* June 8, 1989.

68. *Ferganskaia Pravda,* June 15, 1989.

69. *Sobesednik,* no. 29, 1989.

70. *Vatan Eshki,* no. 1, 1991, p. 3.

71. A. Golovkov, "Ranenie," *Ogonek,* no. 29, 1989; K. Mialo and P. Goncharov, "Zarevo Fergany," *Novoe vremia,* no. 37, 1989.

72. S. Ziamov, "O mezhetnicheskom konflikte 1989 g. v Uzbekistane," *Tsentralnaia Aziia i Kavkaz,* no. 6, 2000.

73. *Vatan Eshki,* no. 3, 1991.

74. Osipov, "Ferganskie sobytiia 1989," p. 197.

75. Ibid., p. 214.

76. "Press-konferentsiia K.M. Mahkamova v Isfare," *Leninabadskaiia Pravda,* July 19, 1989.

77. *Leninabadskaia Pravda,* July 20, 1989.

78. *Leninabadskaia Pravda,* May 22, 1991.

79. www.nlobooks.ru/rus/magazines/nlo/196/328/378/.

80. "Obrashchenie uzbekskogo naseleniia Dzhalalabadskoi oblasti Kirgizskoi SSR k rukovodstvu SSSR" (The original is in Russian. Translated into Kyrgyz in T. Razakov, *Koogalany KGBnyn maalymattary boiuncha,* Bishkek, 1993, pp. 104–8).

81. www.nlobooks.ru/rus/magazines/nlo/196/328/378.

82. *Leninabadskaia Pravda,* October 1985.

83. *Leninabadskaia Pravda,* January 3, 1990.

84. *Leninabadskaia Pravda,* January 5, 1990.

85. *Leninabadskaia Pravda,* August 1, 1989.

86. "Monolog aktrisy. Ne tolko o teatre," *Leninabadskaia Pravda,* January, 1990.

87. The Kyrgyz co-author, B. Beshimov, of this chapter, provided the materials on Kyrgyzstan.

88. "Dvuiazychie i mnogoiazychie v Uzbekistane i ikh rol v kulturnom stroitelstve," *Uzbek tili va adabieti,* no. 2, 1989, p. 69.

89. Ibid.

90. *Sovet Uzbekistoni,* March 23, 1989.

91. A. Ibrokhimov, *Til–takdir demakdir,* Tashkent, 1990, p. 71.

92. *Sovet Uzbekistoni,* October 11, 1989.

93. *Sovet Uzbekistoni,* April 25, 1989.

94. "Millatlararo munosabatlarni takomillashtirailik, khalklar dustligini mustakhkam-lailik," *Inson va siesta,* no. 1, 1991, p. 44.

95. "Iz doklada Pervogo sekretaria TsK KP Uzbekistana I.A. Karimova na plenume TsK KPSS 20 sentiabria 1989 goda," *Sovet Uzbekistoni,* September 23. 1989.

96. B. Babadzhanov, "Ferghana: istochnik ili zhertva islamskogo fundamentalizma?" *Central Asia and the Caucasus Journal,* 1999, No. 4 (5).

9

A New Phase in the History of the Ferghana Valley, 1992–2008

Baktybek Beshimov (Kyrgyz Republic), with
Pulat Shozimov (Tajikistan) and
Murat Bakhadyrov (Uzbekistan)

The Dawning of Independence

The great socialist superpower collapsed amid a deep systemic crisis for which the Communist Party leaders could find no solution. In its place the leaders of Russia, Ukraine, and Belarus created a Slavic union, leaving Central Asians no choice but to define their own fate. The people of Central Asia did not intend to leave the Soviet Union. In a 1991 referendum, 94 percent of voters in Uzbekistan, 95 percent in Kyrgyzstan, 96 percent in Tajikistan, and 70 percent in Turkmenistan favored the preservation of the Soviet Union. The tragic events at the end of the perestroika era frightened the people in the region so much that they looked to the Union to bring order and stability. But events in Moscow surged ahead of the public's consciousness.

The catalysts for the proclamations of independence and the establishment of new states in the Ferghana Valley were to be found not just in the capital cities of Bishkek, Dushanbe, and Tashkent, but in the Ferghana Valley itself. After all, for a century and a half the valley had played an important role in the region's politics. It had been one of the major centers of opposition to Russian colonization,[1] and pockets of resistance to Bolshevik power persisted there until the mid 1930s. The surge of political activity in the valley in the 1980s and early 1990s inevitably influenced what was occurring in the capital cities.

The creation of new states posed formidable challenges: they somehow had to preserve their sovereignty, launch the transition from communism to a new order, form new state institutions and legitimize them, forge ideologies that most people could accept, find a place for the new states in the global community, and preserve order amid general breakdown and a surge of rising expectations. Each set out to the unknown on its own path, posing the further question of whether, and how, they would relate to one other.

For more than a century the population of the Ferghana Valley, like that of all Central Asia, had been accustomed to their elites executing the will of Moscow. The traditions, skills, and instincts required for self-government had all but vanished, and were replaced by whatever was necessary to function under a strictly central-ized Communist government. By 1991 Central Asia had outpaced development in India, China, Iran, Turkey, and Pakistan.[2] Yet if the USSR by then claimed to be a modernized agro-industrial society, that world still had very weak roots in Central Asia and in the Ferghana Valley. Although it had surpassed many other Asian countries, the region remained more traditional and conservative than the western part of the Soviet Union. Thus, the percent of Central Asia's indigenous population employed in industry was the lowest in the USSR (Kyrgyzstan, 34 percent; Uzbekistan, 31 percent; Tajikistan, 28 percent). The percent of the total industrial workforce comprised of native peoples was only 53 percent for Uzbeks in Uzbekistan, 25 percent for Kyrgyz in Kyrgyzstan, and 48 percent for Tajiks in Tajikistan.[3] Military and industrial enterprises and technical institutes were staffed mainly by Russians and Slavs, with Uzbeks, Tajiks, and Kyrgyz relegated to the trades, services, agriculture, health care, teaching, and Party offices. Hence, the new states began with very weak human capital.

Because of the underdeveloped state of indigenous, as opposed to imperial, industry, rural populations played a decisive role in social life, at least at the local level. At the top, former Soviet elites continued on in most cases, forging new relations with an unpredictable Russia, China, and the Muslim world, as well as the West, and working to establish new forms of identity.

Central Asians, and especially residents of the Ferghana Valley, were complete newcomers to the notion of a nation state.[4] The old khanates of the region had absolutely no concept of ethnicity. But as new states, the three countries of the Ferghana Valley were swept up in issues of ethnic identity in a mono-ethnic society, a notion that was not only alien to their heritage but already an obsolete prototype.[5] Yet under the pressure of a collapsing USSR, the notion of a society built according to the principles of unity amid diversity had begun to disintegrate, leaving the field to the ideal of national interest.

This engendered rivalries among countries and weakened regional cooperation. Each country pursued its own path, which meant that in the Ferghana Valley one can trace three separate processes of change.

Kyrgyzstan: From an "Island of Democracy" to the Coup of 2005

After the bloody interethnic conflicts in Osh and Uzgen in 1990, the Supreme Soviet of the Kyrgyz SSR appointed Askar Akaev as the country's president. The demor-alized Communist bureaucracy lost power, and members of a democratic-minded intelligentsia dominated public opinion. As the leader of the new wave, Akaev won the October 1991 presidential election with an overwhelming majority. This opened the first phase of Kyrgyzstan's new history, during which both democratization and a market economy were launched. Between 1995 and 2000, though, democracy was curtailed and corruption became widespread. This led to a third stage, which culminated in the Tulip Revolution and coup of March 2005.

Akaev's main priority throughout his time in office was politics, not economic development. By 1990 he had come under the strong influence of Russian dissident Andrei Sakharov, as a result of which the development of democracy became his main goal. This sharply differentiated Akaev from the other more cautious Central Asian leaders. When he eventually turned to issues of economic development, his views were strongly influenced by foreign experts and international financial institutes. Yet his program was far from clear, as shown in his 1991 comment that "We are moving on a path that is called a third way, based on the values of capitalism and socialism." This curious phrase reflects not only Akaev's ambiguous thinking, but also the complex balance of political and ideological forces within the leadership as a whole.

When the Communist nomenklatura divided into two camps, it left an opening for Akaev. He also needed to gain the support of Kyrgyzstan's south. To this end he forged what he called a "southern policy," the cornerstone of which was to reorganize the administration of the Kyrgyz section of the Ferghana Valley. In the Ferghana region he established three new provinces or *oblast*s: Osh, Jalalabad, and Batken. This allowed the president, at least temporarily, to divide the southern clans in the three provinces and thereby weaken their influence in the capital.

He made Osh Kyrgyzstan's southern capital, and established a presidential residence there to receive the public. In 1991 the government elevated the former Osh Pedagogical Institute to the level of a university. Meanwhile, a southern branch of the Academy of Sciences began to operate in Osh and elsewhere in the south. Fearing a challenge from the old southern elite, Akaev worked to set up a corps of southern administrators and backers exclusively loyal to him. Through these and other measures he managed for ten years to divide and weaken the old southern clans.

During this time, Akaev also focused his attention on Kyrgyzstan's national minorities. The 1990 tragedy in Osh demanded immediate and deliberate actions to address minority interests and issues of interethnic relations. To this end, a Kyrgyz-Russian Slavic University opened in Bishkek in 1992, and shortly thereafter the Kyrgyz-Uzbek University began operations in Osh, while a "University of Friendship among Peoples" opened in Jalalabad, with instruction in Uzbek. Such television and radio channels as Osh TV and Mezon were established to provide Uzbek language programming. As they grew increasingly aware of their own interests, the Uzbek and Tajik populations of the Ferghana Valley strongly supported President Akaev's policies and continued to do so throughout the 1990s.

Overall, the president tried hard to maneuver between the nationalism of the Kyrgyz and the concerns of non-Kyrgyz populations. To this end, he proposed the concept of Kyrgyzstan as a "common home" and actively engaged the UN High

Commission on National Minorities with the country's nationality issues, at the same time craftily using Russian in his dealings with Russia. At his personal initiative, an Assembly of the Kyrgyz Population was established to harmonize interethnic relations throughout the country.

Kyrgyzstan's new political system combined Soviet experience with the new ideology of democratization. De-Sovietization was never carried out in Kyrgyzstan, and symbols of the Soviet era were allowed to remain. State agencies changed their form but remained essentially Soviet; the functions of governors, for example, remained more-or-less identical to those of the first secretaries of regional commit- tees of the Communist Party. Akaev instituted elections at the local level and thus established a degree of self-government, while at the same time mixing appointed offices with elected ones. Because President Akaev spoke of independence, sepa- ration of powers, and checks and balances, U.S. Deputy Secretary of State Strobe Talbott called him "the Jefferson of Central Asia."[6]

A new and genuinely democratic constitution was widely debated and then adopted in 1991. The following year, a progressive law on media was introduced, and censorship was lifted by presidential decree the following year. Addressing the Jogorku Kenesh (parliament) in 1993, Akaev affirmed that "the essence and basis of a genuine democracy is governance through discussion." In his search for a new Kyrgyz identity he turned to the Kyrgyz epic *Manas*, and also to the West. The worldwide media first carefully, then boldly, touted the Kyrgyz president as the hope of democracy not just in Central Asia, but also throughout the CIS.[7]

But within the country, Akaev faced real difficulties. The old clans from the Soviet past and the new regional political groups had no intention of passively ac- cepting his rise and consequently their own demise. Many deputies and politicians considered his privatization of agriculture a hasty and unwise imitation of foreign practices. Moreover, the handing of the country's gold development to a single foreign company gave rise to a scandal that set parliament and president at odds. Akaev seemed willing to make whatever compromises were necessary to maintain his personal power, hiding such cynical deals behind a façade of liberalism. In 1994 he resorted to various forms of bribery to gain control over parliament, falsified two referendums, and curtailed parliament's powers, thereby expanding his own.[8]

The presidential elections of 1995 revealed a country divided into two irreconcil- able camps, with the power of the south and of the Ferghana Valley at the heart of the issue.[9] The southern clans, led by Bekmamat Osmonov and Y. Sidikov, commanded strong support across the Ferghana Valley and beyond. But by fraudulently manipulat- ing the tallies, Akaev received 59 percent of all votes cast. Henceforth, elections were reduced to nothing more than instruments for maintaining Akaev's personal power.

The president's growing effort to monopolize power led to fierce struggles with the parliament. Following his dubious victory in the 1995 presidential elections, Akaev used rigged referendums to concentrate power further in his own hands. Typically, he received more than 90 percent of the votes.[10] He relied on the corrupted Constitutional Court and Supreme Court to ratify each of his actions.

President Akaev skillfully exploited international contacts to further his efforts. The United Nations, Organization for Security and Cooperation in Europe, and World Bank all lent their support, while the World Trade Organization accepted Kyrgyzstan for membership, the first country of the Commonwealth of Independent States to be so honored. Thanks to his good relations with such donor countries as Japan, Germany, and the United States, Akaev received large credits and loans. While these contributed to economic reform in Kyrgyzstan, they also piled up debt and helped entrench corruption.[11]

Despite several positive developments, interethnic relations in the Kyrgyz sector of the Ferghana Valley remained tense, as confirmed by sociological research conducted in Osh and Jalalabad provinces in 1997. The situation became further complicated by a growing population, migration from urban to rural areas, and spreading unemployment, all of which intensified the competition for resources. However, President Akaev partially defused these threats by building a foundation for positive long-term relations with the country's neighbors in the Ferghana Valley. In late 1996 he traveled to Tashkent to sign an "Agreement on Eternal Friendship" between Kyrgyzstan and Uzbekistan. The following year a similar agreement was signed by Kyrgyzstan, Uzbekistan, and Kazakhstan. Akaev also actively supported the agreement ending the Tajik civil war, which Emomali Rakhmonov and Said Nuri signed in Bishkek on May 18, 1997.

At this time Kyrgyzstan also signed the EU's Framework Convention on Minority Rights, extending basic rights to ethnic minorities, in particular the right to preserve and develop their own religions, languages, traditions, and cultural heritage. Given the growing tensions in the valley over water, business, and trade, this affirmation was crucial for improving relations among the Kyrgyz, Uzbeks, and Tajiks. For example, thanks to this agreement, Uzbek youth from Uzbekistan gained access to higher education at the Kyrgyz-Uzbek University in Osh. Such measures laid the foundation for constructive relations during the Batken events, when fighters from the Islamic Movement of Uzbekistan (IMU) attempted to penetrate Uzbek territory through the Kyrgyz border. Yet despite a number of positive developments, the situation on the Uzbek-Kyrgyz border grew tenser. The IMU's ability to penetrate the Kyrgyz border, Uzbekistan's mining of its border with Kyrgyzstan in response, and the ensuing impediments to cross-border trade came henceforth to dominate and define relations between the two countries.

Inside Kyrgyzstan, tensions between the traditionalist Ferghana Valley and the Russified north continued to grow.[12] It did not suffice that Akaev supported a proposal to celebrate Osh's 3,000-year anniversary in 2000. He launched many initiatives, including a new model of social development, a plan to increase agricultural production by 10 percent, and decisive judicial reforms. But all too many of his ideas were stillborn, remaining on paper only. Discontent grew, and in 1998 Akaev responded by launching a campaign to privatize land.

Akaev's typical response to pressure was to change his key ministers. Finally, in early 1998 he decided to form a government staffed with his former academic colleagues. Akaev sought to establish a completely loyal government that also would assent to the further enrichment of his own family. This policy aroused fierce opposition in the Ferghana Valley and across the south, where people already felt cheated by the central government. Akaev responded by naming a southerner and former student Kubanychbek Jumaliyev as prime minister. This proved an utter failure and after only six months, under pressure from parliament and especially from a solid bloc of Ferghana deputies, the president had to dismiss the government.

This led directly to a further escalation of political tensions and eventually to Akaev's fall. Along the way he established a new political party, Alga, completely loyal to him, which further angered the Ferghana and southern regions. He pursued unprecedented measures to strengthen his regime and establish complete control over financial inflows, business, and the media. A 1999 proposal to elect a portion of deputies from party lists had the same effect, as did the establishment of various consultative bodies intended to attract the intelligentsia and tame the opposition. Dubious presidential and parliamentary elections in 2000 gave rise in due course to extreme pressure from the opposition, which focused in the Ferghana Valley.

In 2002 government forces killed six protesters in the Aksy district of Jalalabad province. The remaining Aksy protestors refused to submit to orders from the president or from Bishkek, and instead took all decisions locally. In effect, an entire territory in the Ferghana Valley had declared its independence of the capital. This action, like the Fronde in revolutionary France, instilled in the entire discontented part of the Kyrgyz population the idea of revolution. From this moment Akaev's fall was only a matter of time.

While it is undeniable that Akaev's views helped bring about a more liberal political regime in Kyrgyzstan, they did not play a decisive role. Instead, the determining factors included the various competitions, for example between northern and southern (i.e., Ferghana) regional clans and political groups; between Akaev's bureaucracy and the old Communist nomenklatura; and between the presidential administration and the opposition. All this led to the creation of a de facto system of checks and balances that did not allow any one faction to gain full control. For a time this facilitated the development of civil society, pluralism, and a free press. But the absence of a democratic culture and resistance to pluralism prevented democratic institutions from taking deep root in Kyrgyz society. Foreign assistance, as noted above, both fostered the process of reform and enabled Akaev to strengthen authoritarianism and enrich his friends and family.

The competition between the southern and northern clans played a substantial role in weakening the central power and bringing it to the point of collapse. The northerners, led by Akaev, tried to manipulate those from the Ferghana Valley, who were dissatisfied with the distribution of power within the country.[13] In spite of Akaev's policy of seeking to balance Kyrgyz and Uzbeks in the Ferghana region, the Uzbek diaspora in Jalalabad and elsewhere in the Ferghana Valley wanted more thoroughgoing changes, and gradually turned to the opposition movement for support. The Uzbeks' political stance was fueled by poverty and by their disappointment with developments in neighboring Uzbekistan, which they feared might be replicated in Kyrgyzstan.

The parliamentary elections of February 27, 2005, triggered the final political crisis. Pro- and anti-government parties contended against each other, and even the civil service divided between the "old bureaucracy" comprised of Akaev supporters and the "new bureaucracy" controlled by the president's daughter, Bermet. Akaev's wavering exacerbated the situation.

In this crucial moment, as in 1990, the main catalyst for change arose in the Kyrgyz part of the Ferghana Valley. What was later dubbed the "Kyrgyz mutiny" began to unfold when allies of the losing candidates rioted against the local and central authorities, shutting down roads and seizing administrative buildings. Such riots broke out in Jalalabad, Osh, Naryn, Talas, and other regions. But the best organized were the actions in the Ferghana Valley. At Jalalabad disparate slogans about canceling the elections turned into calls for Akaev's removal. On March 4, 2005, the crowd occupied the district governor's office and declared that within the entire province "Akaev's power has come to an end!" An Eldik Kenesh (People's Council) was elected and a new governor appointed. In Osh events unfolded along the same lines as in Jalalabad. In both of these key Ferghana centers the newly elected governor was Uzbek by nationality. This fact immediately removed all fears of an ethnic conflict between Kyrgyz and Uzbeks in the Ferghana Valley and southern Kyrgyzstan generally.

On March 24, 2005, protesters at a rally in the capital city of Bishkek occupied the house of government. Stores were vandalized and mass looting broke out, while opposition leaders tried vainly to reestablish order in the city. At a meeting of the old parliament, Kurmanbek Bakiyev from Osh was appointed prime minister and Feliks Kulov as head of all law enforcement agencies. Bakiyev and Kulov promptly prorogued the old parliament and forced the new Jogorku Kenesh to go to work, in spite of the corrupt elections by which its members had been chosen. From their first steps, the two new leaders' actions were suffused with Machiavellianism. Indeed, the sudden fall of Akaev and the creation of a so-called tandem between Bakiyev and Kulov revealed clearly that regionalism and clan politics now prevailed in Kyrgyzstan.

From 2005 to 2009 Kyrgyzstan's new rulers manipulated public opinion as needed to establish strict authoritarian rule.[14] In the end, the prolonged effort by leaders and clans from the Ferghana Valley and the south generally to seize power, rather than any movement for democracy, defined Kyrgyzstan's political fate and that of the Kyrgyz part of the Ferghana Valley.

Tajikistan: From Civil War to the Construction of a New State

Tajikistan's path in the post-Soviet era has been highly distinctive and difficult. A first phase extending to April 1992 witnessed unexpected freedom and a steady descent into civil war. A second phase brought the schism among Tajiks into the open and culminated in a fierce conflict lasting to 1997. A third stage brought reconciliation and a fragile peace under the rule of Emomali Rakhmonov. As in Kyrgyzstan, one of the core issues was the weight of the Ferghana Valley's voice in national affairs. But whereas in Kyrgyzstan that process brought a shift in favor of leaders from the valley at the expense of the old elites from the north, in Tajikistan the elites from the Ferghana Valley, many of them Uzbek, ceded power to new forces from the south led by Rakhmonov.

The policies of perestroika and glasnost roused the spirits and emotions of the Tajik people. As the USSR began to collapse, the republic came to life: citizens vigorously debated the history, culture, language, and future of the Tajik people. On September 9, 1991, the Supreme Soviet of Tajikistan declared the country's independence, which accelerated the politicization of civil society in the country. Already by 1991 a range of political forces, chiefly anti-communist, were contending for power, among them the Rastokhez (Sunrise) movement, the Democratic Party of Tajikistan, and the Islamic Renaissance Party of Tajikistan (IRPT).

The main line of fissure in the ensuing conflicts was between the industrialized north, including the Ferghana Valley, and the underdeveloped south. The ethnic component of this split was defined by the numbers of Uzbeks among the northern population. To assert a purely Tajik identity in this situation, the Rastokhez movement, comprised mainly of the Tajik intelligentsia, proposed pan-Iranism, which specified the unification of Tajikistan with the Tajik areas of Bukhara and Samarkand in Uzbekistan and a segment of Afghanistan up to the Iranian border itself. Rastokhez thus proposed nothing less than to redraw the existing political map of large parts of Central Asia.[15]

A distinctive aspect of Tajikistan in these years was the use of Islam in the political struggle. The potential for conflict among the republic's Tajik, Pamiri, and Uzbek populations had been obvious from the time Soviet planners drew the borders. It now burst out when southerners attempted to change the traditional roles of regional and clan groups in their favor. Simultaneously, conflict between the increasingly Islamic society and the secular state began to escalate. According to researcher Viktor Dubovitskii, those who turned to Islam were the least-integrated into the power structure, especially the ethnic-territorial groups. During the Soviet-Afghan war underground groups of Wahhabis had formed among them.[16] Both the historical and cultural preconditions for the Islamization of society were present in Soviet Tajikistan, and the Soviet-Afghan war only intensified this trend. The new period witnessed the revival of traditionalist institutions of society, whose positions in Tajikistan had been strong even during Soviet times.

There was even talk of a complete revival of what were called *avlod* relations. *Avlod* is the Tajik term for an ancestral group "representative of all the living and deceased ancestors along the male bloodline and their wives, tracing back to one single ancestor." In other words, it is the patriarchal clan of blood-relatives or the local community, which can provide "a full range of economic, spiritual, and cultural support systems that make it a kind of micro-state and ensure its independence and flexibility." Whenever people needed substantial assistance in order to survive, they turned to the *avlod* system. Natives of Tajik regions with the keenest awareness of *avlods* became major forces in the civil war of 1992–97. Indeed, the *avlod* structure explains much of the extreme bitterness of the inter-Tajik conflict, with many participants seeking to obliterate an opposing clan. These groups formed the backbone of many armed groups fighting both on the side of the United Tajik Opposition and as government troops.

State building in Tajikistan entailed a major shift in the political elite at the expense of the Ferghana Valley. Since as far back as 1950, the Ferghana elites (Leninabad oblast, now Sughd) controlled the political and economic life of the republic. This was the deliberate result of Soviet policies, which undergirded this arrangement by focusing industrial development in the north as well. The most powerful industrial economic enterprises of Tajikistan were located in or near the Ferghana Valley, which was far more developed economically than the southern and eastern parts of the country. Thanks to the lack of roads and railroads, the economic might of the Tajik sector of the Ferghana Valley was poorly integrated with the rest of the republic, further heightening tensions.

The main ethno-territorial groups include Tajiks from Karategin (Garm), Kulyab (Kulob), and Leninabad (Khujand), who constitute more than 75 percent of the country's population. Then there are the Pamiris (Badakhshani) and Gissaris, who make up a substantially smaller proportion of the population. A root cause of the Tajik conflict was the government's attempt to change the traditional roles of these groupings in Tajik society, roles that were succinctly described in the Soviet proverb, "Leninabad governs, Kulyab guards, the Pamirs dance, and Karategin deals."[17]

Sovereignty brought an abrupt and radical change in this arrangement. Independence stimulated the political and cultural aspirations of the southern elites and clans, who proposed the concepts of pan-Iranism and Islamization. Meanwhile, the Ferghana section of Tajikistan was discredited by its association with the recent Soviet past and with the Communist nomenklatura. Local power struggles during perestroika and the first years of independence gave rise to two opposing ethno-territorial groups. The first, comprised of those from Karategin and the Pamirs, claimed to be democratic; the second was Communist and secular, and was comprised of those from Kulyab, Leninabad, and Gissar, with member of the Uzbek diaspora and other national minorities leaning toward the second group. Because of the political competition between the northern and southern parts of the country, the Tajik part of the Ferghana Valley grew ever more estranged economically and politically from Dushanbe and the underdeveloped south.

Issues of leadership played a key role in the tumultuous events in the country. Such politicians as Qahhor Mahkamov and Rakhmon Nabiev, both former first secretaries of the Communist Party of Tajikistan, proved unable to crystallize a national movement or consolidate Tajiks around any concrete program. Both were eventually removed after mass anti-government protests in Dushanbe.

By 1991 the Islamic opposition had become a parliamentary party, the IRPT, whose aims included the establishment of a national government capable of unifying the major political forces in the country. Hodja Akbar Turajonzoda, the spiritual leader of Tajikistan's Muslims, emerged as the leading figure. Turajonzoda agreed to employ strictly lawful measures, while Nabiev agreed not to prosecute opposition leaders.

Nabiev's government was the first to violate this agreement when the presidential battalion, arbitrarily declaring itself the Popular Front, unleashed terror in several regions of the country, shooting thousands of purported enemies as well as peaceful civilians. This led to a mass persecution of oppositionists and dissidents. The opposition, fearing complete annihilation, responded by mobilizing its own supporters, who united around two parties: the Democratic Party of Tajikistan and the IRPT. Both proclaimed slogans about parliamentary democracy, Islamic statehood, and economic reform. Turajonzoda, who presided over both parties and shared their common goals, led the combined opposition.

The process by which Tajikistan descended into civil war is beyond the scope of this study. Suffice it to say that mass non-violent protests began in Dushanbe's central square in March 1992. After two months the two sides reached a compromise and formed a coalition government. When the extreme diversity of views among the opposition caused the coalition to fracture, Tajikistan descended into armed chaos, which lasted through May. During the first part of that month, when the presidential guard and militias were battling to control strategically important points in the capital, Nabiev agreed to a government of national reconciliation, in which the opposition would receive a third of all positions, including several key posts.

At this point, the confrontation shifted from Dushanbe to the provinces and assumed a purely military form. Islamic forces emerged at the forefront of the armed struggle. On June 28, Islamic troops clashed with forces from Kulyab, the fighting quickly assuming a ruthless and criminal character. Five hundred or more mujahideen fighters crossed into Tajikistan from Afghanistan, bringing with them significant stores of arms. As large numbers of fighters penetrated Tajikistan from the Afghan side of the border, Tajik leaders and Russian border troops charged that fighters for Tajikistan's Islamic party were being trained at ten camps in Afghanistan.[18] Efforts were made to reach an agreement with leading Afghan fighters. All-party talks held in July at the Pamiri border town of Khorog led to what was supposed to have been a ceasefire, lifting of checkpoints, and an exchange of hostages. But this agreement failed to take hold on the ground. Over the summer of 1994, some 15,000 to 20,000 people were killed, many of them civilians.

President Nabiev had no control over the situation and was soon forced to resign. After a long tug-of-war, the Presidium of the Supreme Soviet of Tajikistan met at the Ferghana Valley village of Arbob and elected Emomali Rakhmonov (later Rakhmon) from the southern city of Kulyab as head of parliament, while Abdumalik Abdulladzhanov from Leninabad, was appointed prime minister. This done, the Ferghana and Kulyab clans used the breathing space to form and arm the National Front, a contingent of basic combat troops. The National Front was made up of

Uzbeks, from both Tajikistan and neighboring republics, as well as Tajiks from Kulyab. On September 27, 1992 the National Front occupied the Ferghana city of Kurgan-Tyube, and in December, with the support of Uzbekistan and virtually without a fight, occupied Dushanbe. The country now became divided into two parts, roughly along the border of the river Vakhsh.

Presidential elections were held on November 6, 1994, and Rakhmonov defeated a contender from Leninabad in the Ferghana Valley in what most agreed was a very flawed election. Once elected, Rakhmonov set about consolidating his power, inviting fellow Kulyabi to fill key posts and undermining at every chance the traditional hegemony of the Ferghana or Leninabad forces. He reorganized the National Front into the National Democratic Party, which continues even today to dominate national politics. Henceforth, all politicians from Leninabad in the Ferghana Valley were excluded from the peace negotiations with the opposition, and their leader, whom Rakhmonov had just defeated in November, was prosecuted and banned from politics.[19]

The rise to power of Rakhmonov, a native of Kulyab rather than the Ferghana region, is very relevant to the fate of the Tajik sector of the Ferghana Valley. Some defend him as one of the few politicians acceptable to all groups. Others believe that Moscow played a decisive role in Rakhmonov's rise to power in 1992.[20] A Russian analyst, Arkadii Dubnov, argues instead that it was the Uzbek leader Islam Karimov who brought Rakhmonov to power. "Rakhmonov," writes Dubnov, "was taken from the Uzbek city of Termez, where he was the director of a state farm, only a few weeks earlier. It was then that he was first introduced to Islam Karimov. I should add that, even before 1995, Rakhmonov's personal security personnel included special agents from the Uzbek Ministry of Interior."[21] The prominent Tajik politician Daulata Usmon also asserts that Uzbekistan strongly influenced the balance of political power in Tajikistan at this crucial moment.[22]

Whoever backed him, Rakhmonov's election as leader of the Supreme Soviet and then as president quickly changed the entire balance of power within the government. For the first time in the history of Tajikistan, more than 80 percent of government posts were occupied by representatives of a single region, Kulyab. From 1995 to 1997, the Ferghana elite was almost entirely shut out of political decision-making. This led to discontent even within Rakhmonov's own camp. Colonel Murod Khudoyberdiev, previously an ardent supporter of Rakhmonov and the National Front, now openly opposed him. Rakhmonov responded by sending a joint group of governmental and UTO forces to expel Khudoyberdiev from Khujand. The final attempt by political groups from the Ferghana Valley region to reverse the Kulyabis' coup was the attempted assassination of President Rakhmonov, which ended in failure and led to yet deeper political isolation of the Tajik Ferghana Valley from the rest of Tajikistan. To be sure, the prime minister by tradition still comes from Leninabad. But in reality neither he nor any other native of Ferghana wields real political or economic power in Dushanbe.

The lengthy and difficult Inter-Tajik dialogue that eventually led to peace stretched from April 1994 to June 27, 1997, when the two sides signed an agreement establishing peace and national accord in Tajikistan. Both sides committed themselves to the implementation of all previously signed agreements, and a National Reconciliation Commission was established under the leader of the Islamic party and its leader, Sayid Abdullo Nuri. Iran, Kazakhstan, Kyrgyzstan, Pakistan, Uzbekistan, Turkmenistan, Afghanistan, and Russia, as well as representatives from the UN, OSCE, and the Organization of the Islamic Conference, served as observers and guarantors of the peace. All told, the civil war claimed up to 40,000 lives, cost at least $7 billion, and led to the destruction of 80 percent of the south's economy.

Inter-Tajik reconciliation gave the new government serious political capital, which led to diverse reforms. The peace process, culminating in the formal end of the civil war and the legal registration of the IRPT Party and the Democratic Party of Tajikistan, contributed to the formation of a political system unique in Central Asia, in that it includes a legal Islamic party. The president, although having reconciled with the Islamists in power, unequivocally declared that Tajikistan is a secular state. He emphasized that "every other model of social organization in Tajikistan has led to destabilization and civil war. The vast majority of the population, whose will is enshrined in the constitution, does not want this."[23]

In the aftermath of the civil war, Rakhmonov attempted to focus public attention on the problems associated with building the new Tajik state. Such issues were particularly acute in the north of the country, especially in the Ferghana provinces. In his book *Tajiks in the Mirror of History: From Aryan to Samanid,* Rakhmonov tried to build a foundation of identity for the new Tajik state.[24] Such subsequent national projects as the effort to reclaim the heritage of Zoroastrianism in 1999 and the affirmation of Tajiks' Aryan heritage in 2005 to 2006 were aimed primarily at undercutting the country's growing Islamic religiosity, and also at neutralizing the growing influence of Turkic forms of identity, especially Pan-Turkism. Both projects sought to underscore the differences between the new forms of identity being promoted in Tajik parts of the Ferghana Valley from the Uzbek and Turkic identities taking root in the other two sectors.

Throughout the first decade of the new millennium, President Rakhmonov, now having Persianized his name to Rakhmon, focused on strengthening his political position. In 2002 his People's Democratic Party handily defeated both Communists and the Islamic Rebirth Party of Tajikistan. Then, between 2003 and 2005 the constitution was amended to allow Rakhmon to serve two additional terms, and the law on elections was changed to remove the upper-age limit on candidates for office. Subsequent electoral defeats led the opposition parties to accuse the president and parliament of abandoning democratization and strengthening authoritarian rule in Tajikistan.[25]

The authoritarian model of government in Tajikistan has many sources. National leaders argue that it is a reasonable response to demands created by the effort to advance social and economic development, and that it arises naturally from Tajikistan's cultural and historical circumstances. The political opposition considers it ineffective in addressing the society's basic problems. Defended or attacked, Tajik authoritarianism owes more than a little to the dramatic shift in political and economic power away from the Ferghana provinces of the north in the years after 1991, and the concern of the Kulyabis who dominated Dushanbe thereafter to consolidate their newly won authority.

Tajikistan's political system remains unstable, with a high potential for conflict. However, the country's bloody civil war in the 1990s led directly to the establishment of a coalition government that includes representatives from a legal Islamic party. The success of this arrangement provides the region with a useful model of how Islam and democracy can peacefully and even effectively coexist.[26]

Uzbekistan: Devising Its Own Transformational Model

At the time of independence, Uzbekistan's GDP was one-quarter greater than that of Kazakhstan and 1.8 times higher than the combined total for Turkmenistan, Kyrgyzstan, and Tajikistan. However, with respect to its social conditions, Uzbekistan was one of the Union's most troubled republics. Despite being endowed with huge natural, mineral, and human resources, the republic had one of the lowest standards of living in the entire USSR. Yet Uzbekistan's location, having common borders with all the other new states of Central Asia, made it a natural hub for transport and communications. The American scholar Frederick Starr specifically noted its central geographical position and argued that Uzbekistan could use this to play a catalyzing role for the region as a whole.[27]

The late Soviet policies of perestroika and glasnost did much to prepare Uzbekistan ideologically and psychologically for independence. In March 1990, Uzbekistan's Supreme Soviet elected Islam Karimov president of the Uzbek SSR. Three months later Uzbekistan declared its independence. Then on December 29, 1991, after nearly two years of serving both as head of state and government, Karimov was elected president of the Republic of Uzbekistan by popular vote. The unusual man who now headed the Uzbek state gave rise to conflicting opinions at the time and still does so today, with some seeing him as a despot who held back Uzbekistan's development and sowed uncertainty, and others praising him as the strong leader needed to build and defend the new state.

In a short period of time, Karimov took control of all party-state organs and consolidated his personal authority. He built political support and transformed the Communist Party into the People's National Democratic Party. Russian scholar Yurii Kulchik argues that Karimov prevailed because he focused on the consolidation of the Uzbeks as a nation.[28] The American scholar Nancy Lubin notes that Karimov succeeded by presenting himself as the tough-minded leader striving to bring order, stability, and economic growth to the country.[29] It is undeniable that Karimov chose to move slowly, retaining a large part of the old Soviet system behind a facade of modernization and democratization, all the while maintaining the state's key role in the economy and many other elements of central planning.

Two ideas dominated under Karimov: nationalism and authoritarianism. His goals were to adjust the organs of Soviet power to the needs of an independent Uzbek state and to consolidate his own position at the top of the new political pyramid. He gave the state an all-consuming role, reaffirmed centralization and strict hierarchy. Karimov bluntly acknowledged that "everything comes back to me, and this is not an accident: we went through a very tumultuous period of development and had to respond to many difficult challenges, and I simply had to take everything on myself."[30] Defending what he sees as his country's interests, he has been accused of stoking tensions with neighboring states and interfering in their domestic affairs. The same concern led him to staunchly oppose religious extremism at home and to seek to build links between Uzbek Muslims and the new nationalism.[31]

The new national ideology led to the removal of Soviet and Russian statues and the erection of new monuments to the likes of Amir Timur (Tamerlane), the poet Alisher Navoi, and the ruler-scientist Ulugbek. Books and magazines featuring socialism and other Soviet principles were purged from the country's bookshelves.[32]

In the 1990s the main internal concern was to consolidate an authoritarian political system based both on local Uzbek traditions and on the model of China. Opposing this were a weak democratic movement, Islamist militants, and clandestine regional forces. From the first days of independence, Karimov's new national bureaucracy emerged as the best-organized and most decisive force in the country, eventually enabling it to prevail over all three of its opponents.

Throughout his career Karimov has spoken of threats to the new national state and the need for order and discipline. Some have argued that his nationalism was in part the fruit of his effort to neutralize the nationalism of the opposition. What is clear is that the ideological and armed struggle of the Uzbek Islamists to overthrow him, the bitter underground struggle for power among different political groups and clans, and the need to navigate among competing powers internationally weigh heavily on the president's political consciousness.

In April 1992, President Karimov became the first leader from the region to perform the *hajj* to Saudi Arabia. Using state and academic resources, he worked to inculcate his own understanding of Islam and to suppress alternative views, if necessary with violence. He views the Islamic world as divided into two opposing camps: the traditional "enlightened" Islam, which he aims to support in every way possible; and militant Islam, which would destroy the traditionalists' faith and establish a caliphate in Central Asia.

To maintain power in tumultuous times, Karimov relied on the suppression of discontent and the repression of dissidents. An overwhelming majority of Central Asia experts condemn the repressive policies of the Uzbek president; however, some view them as measures needed to stem "the spread of Islamic fundamentalism in Central Asia," and accordingly they defend his authoritarianism as an essential if regrettable tool against extremists.[33] The Russian analyst Kulchik argues that there was no alternative to Karimov's authoritarianism: "Uzbekistan needs a strongly and sufficiently centralized power. Karimov's conservative, authoritarian regime is fully consistent with established objectives and historical conditions."[34] Yet one might argue that this perspective overlooks the possibility that while repressive policies may keep the Islamists in check for now, they do so at the price of further radicalizing the opposition and thereby clearing a future path for militant Islamism.

State Building in the Name of Nationalism

Like the Communists before him, Karimov skillfully transformed the institutions of traditional society and made them serve new needs. Traditional neighborhood and local structures like *mahallas* and *avlods* were used to consolidate state power at the local, regional, and national levels. Because all these institutions were alive and well in the Ferghana Valley, their transformation to new purposes came about relatively easily there. As Soviet institutions were abolished, these traditional entities came to receive direct financial support from the state and to serve the cause of national independence. They also became local bulwarks against the infiltration of alien ideologies and destructive ideas.[35]

Uzbekistan's 1992 constitution is based on a formal division of powers between the executive, legislative, and judicial, with a bicameral parliament. In practice, Karimov constructed a unitary and strictly vertical system of governance. Representative bodies exist at the provincial, district and city levels, but the governors (*hokims*) are appointed by the president and are directly responsible to him. These *hokims* are the highest authority at all three levels of government, and they wield the same strictly centralized power as their predecessors did in Soviet and tsarist times. As a result, the development of local self-government was thwarted, as was the development of the other branches of government besides the executive.

Communities in the Ferghana Valley responded to this reality just as they earlier had responded to Soviet power, namely, by paying formal respect to the new authorities but otherwise continuing to maintain their traditional lives to the greatest extent possible.

Regions like the Ferghana Valley found themselves with little apparent voice in Tashkent. True, referendums and elections were held, but these occurred at the price of not developing local self-government and the judiciary. This gradually undermined the credibility and efficacy of the Cabinet of Ministers, Majlisi Oli (parliament), non-governmental organizations, law enforcement agencies, and the media. This also threw local communities in the Ferghana Valley and elsewhere back on their own resources. Ineffective parliamentary representation and the vagueness and contradictions of official acts left local officials of the state with seemingly unlimited power over citizens' lives. Inevitably this brought about indiscipline within official ranks and widespread corruption.

Many Uzbek scholars assert that power in their country must be concentrated in the hands of either a political elite or an enlightened leader. Modernization, in their opinion, requires rigidly centralized and essentially total power to guide the gradual evolution from a statist economy to some form of market system. The maintenance of state institutions and services—education, health, and so forth—is more important in the course of this transition than democracy, especially if greater citizen participation leads to the weakening of these social services. Opposing this view are scholars like Karen Dawisha and Bruce Parrott, who decry the Uzbek government's "very limited understanding or interest in democracy or a market economy."[36] Some have seen the Uzbek approach as a manifestation of the strategy employed by the Asian Tigers, but this is discredited by the absence of a vibrant private sector in what, others argue, was an "autocratic wasteland."[37]

Struggles of Regional Groups and Clans

Competition among powerful groupings presents one of the most serious challenges to the Uzbek system. It is convenient to speak of three main regional power group-ings, or clans: those from the Ferghana Valley, including Ferghana City, Andijan, and Namangan; those from the western part of the country, including Samarkand, Dzhizak, and the Syr Darya basin; and those from Tashkent. Even though the latter may be weaker than the others, Tashkent often plays a pivotal role between the oth-ers. All of these groups interact and compete with Uzbekistan's political and business communities. Such competition came to the surface early, when 200 deputies of the Supreme Soviet accused the president of harboring dictatorial ambitions, violating the rights and freedom of the people, and crippling the economy. Karimov responded with a quip that gained renown throughout the country: "In our republic there can either be democracy or order." Uzbekistan chose order. The post of vice president was eliminated and under a series of powerful prime ministers, culminating in the 2003 appointment of the blunt former Samarkand governor, Shavkat Mirziyoyev, the power of the regional power blocs was greatly reduced.

The Uzbek Opposition

Political opposition in Uzbekistan has been split between secularists and radical Islamists. The first never gained much power and eventually succumbed to pressure from the government, while the latter adopted a policy of armed struggle through the IMU and other groupings, as discussed in Chapter 13. Broadly speaking, this history repeated the evolution of many other modernizing Muslim countries, where the state has criminalized most forms of secular opposition and in so doing has created a void filled by extremists.

The precursor to political opposition was the organization Birlik (Unity), which formed during perestroika. Birlik presented itself as the champion of national in-terests, and within a short time attracted many members of the intelligentsia and young people. This alarmed the country's ruling circles. Official statements accused the movement of stoking inter-ethnic conflict in the Ferghana Valley. This led to a schism in the movement: a group supporting compromise with the authorities, led by Muhammad Salikh, announced its departure from Birlik and the foundation of another party, Erk (Freedom).

At the movement's third congress on May 26–27 1990, Birlik adopted a more liberal program aimed at building a secular democratic state on the foundation of national traditions. It actively participated in inter-republic exchanges with other oppositionists, joining the All-Union Democratic Congress, The Democratic Congress of Central Asia and Kazakhstan, and the Assembly of Turkic Peoples. Birlik gradually became a mass movement of more than 400,000 people. It was especially influential in the Ferghana Valley and the Tashkent region. The Birlik Party (as opposed to movement) was established at an organizational conference on June 17, 1990, calling itself by October 1991 the Democratic Party of Uzbekistan.

The nascent secular opposition failed to establish itself as a full-fledged alternative to the former Soviet national bureaucracy, and did not succeed in establishing an attractive model or conception for constructing a national Uzbek state. Constant repression prevented it from openly presenting its views to society.[38] Moreover, inexperience in state and public administration, and limited financial resources, prevented Birlik from turning the tide in its direction during the immediate aftermath of perestroika and independence. The bureaucracy, by contrast, quickly recovered after perestroika and adjusted to the new reality, now calling itself a popular democratic movement. Karimov effectively rode this wave and channeled it to establish his own dominance. He co-opted several influential opposition leaders by giving them prestigious governmental posts. By 1994–95 the government had managed to dismantle the secular opposition by co-opting some of its leaders and repressing the others. Salikh sought refuge in Germany, while Birlik leader Abdurakhman Pulatov left for Turkey. The Erk Party, in effect the liberal wing of the Birlik Party, was banned outright. The authorities firmly suppressed riots by teachers in Ferghana City and Namangan, and demonstrations at a plant in Kattakurgan. This violence by the state served to radicalize what remained of the opposition.

Early on, part of the Uzbek secular opposition participated in the elections. However, as they saw the futility of prevailing in dubious polls, they embraced the goal of overthrowing the president by any means possible. Moreover, part of the democratic opposition joined the radical Islamists' cause on the grounds that the Islamists had from the outset sought the armed overthrow of the Karimov government. In February 1999, Islamic extremists and former members of the Erk Party organized a series of explosions in Tashkent and announced that terrorist attacks would continue until the regime fell and conditions for peaceful negotiations had been established.

The Islamic Opposition

From the first days of independence, the Islamic opposition actively advocated an Islamic path of development for Uzbekistan. The Islamic Renaissance Party of Uzbekistan (IRPU) was established as a branch of the All-Union IRP in 1991, but did not get recognized by the authorities. At this time the Islamic opposition established the organizations Adolat (Justice) and Islom Lashkarlari (Warriors of Islam), and took up arms. The epicenter of Islamic political activity could be found in the traditionally pious Ferghana Valley. In 1991 Islamists in Namangan and Andijan publicly stated their goal of making Uzbekistan an Islamic Republic. The government tried to establish a dialogue with religious segments of the population, and entreated them not to encroach on the established constitutional order or to use Islam for political purposes. When the radical Islamists rejected this request the government responded harshly, prosecuting many Adolat members in 1993. Some of them fled to Tajikistan and Afghanistan, where they took part in the civil wars. In 1998 they created a terrorist organization, the IMU, for the purpose of over-throwing the Uzbek president. The IMU's history can be divided into two phases: first, its activity in the Ferghana Valley before its members fled to Afghanistan and, second, its actions after it united with the Taliban and al Qaeda. During the second stage, under the Taliban's influence, IMU fighters banned music, cigarettes, sex, and alcohol, and generally adopted an anti-American, anti-Western stance. Such puritanism repelled many potential followers in the Ferghana Valley.[39] In 1998 and 1999 IMU fighters twice tried to enter Uzbekistan through Kyrgyzstan, and in 2000 they penetrated into the Saryassiysy and Uzunskoye regions of the Surkhandarya province. However, U.S. military operations in Afghanistan in 2001 effectively destroyed the IMU's resources there.

In 1992 missionaries from Hizb ut-Tahrir emerged in Uzbekistan. This extrem-ist organization openly opposed that country's government, and called for the formation of an Islamic caliphate in the Ferghana Valley and throughout Central Asia. Many of the early leaders of Hizb ut-Tahrir were well-educated people. For example, Farhad Usman, who was killed by the police in 1999, was the son of a well-known religious family from Tashkent; Amin Osman, who died under torture in 2001, had been a prominent Uzbek writer. The authorities' opposition gave this organization an aura of intrigue among many, and the absence of alternative chan-nels of political expression enabled the Hizb ut-Tahrir to attract supporters among those discontented with the government.[40]

Dr. Babadjanov has detailed in Chapter 13 the circumstances surrounding the tragedy of May 2005, in the city of Andijan. The "Andijan events" remain controver-sial, and several versions of what occurred exist.[41] Early reports by the International Crisis Group and Human Rights Watch claiming 700 or 800 deaths[42] have not been upheld by subsequent research, and the Russian organization Memorial's estimation of up to 200 deaths generally has been accepted as correct.[43] A substantial number of these deaths occurred at the hands of the insurgents themselves, who—earlier claims to the contrary notwithstanding—are now known from their own films of the event to have been heavily armed.

What cannot be denied is that a majority of mass demonstrations against the Uz-bek government, and especially those by radical Islamists, occurred in the Ferghana Valley. This can be explained by several developments. Most of the Wahhabi-minded imams arrived in the Ferghana Valley in the late 1980s and early 1990s from the large Uzbek community in Saudi Arabia, which numbers approximately half a million people. They are the descendents of immigrants from tsarist Russia and *basmachi*, mainly from the Ferghana Valley. The Uzbek sector of the valley itself could not help but be affected by Islamist activities in Tajikistan during the civil war there and, via Tajikistan, by Afghanistan. As a result, it was in the valley that two competing visions of state-building came into frontal conflict: that of the prevailing authoritarian nationalism and that of the Islamists' super-national theocracy. Against the Islamists' terrorism the government has brought decisive force of its own, which may have the effect of renewing the cycle of conflict. Sarah Kendzior notes that the Uzbek government also has enlisted mainstream theologians, political scientists, and select experts on Islam in its fight against the fundamentalists.[44] This may have been effective in suppressing calls for immediate violence against the state, but it could have the unintended effect of making Hizb ut-Tahrir more attractive,[45] since the latter nominally opposes violence while embracing the same radical ends as the militants.

Perspectives on the Ferghana Valley After Independence

Glossing over sharp differences within the region, the World Bank has argued that Central Asia is in worse condition today than during the Soviet period. With the exception of oil-rich Kazakhstan, all the countries of the region have experienced a devastating fall in GDP, accompanied by declines in health and education. Among them, Kyrgyzstan and Tajikistan have fared far the worst. Tajikistan's GDP in 2003 was 38 percent of what it was in 1990, while in Kyrgyzstan GDP has fallen by a third since 1990.[46] More than two-thirds of Tajikistan's population and half of Kyrgyzstan's lives on less than $2 a day, while up to a third of Uzbeks fall below the poverty line. Tensions in the Ferghana Valley as a whole have intensified, because population has increased at twice the rate of agricultural production. As for agriculture, with up to 35 percent of arable land devoted to cotton production, the most densely populated areas, including the Ferghana Valley, have had to rely on imported food. In Tajikistan alone fully 40 percent of arable land is devoted to cotton.[47] As a result, large parts of the population of the fertile Ferghana Valley are worse off than those living in the infertile mountain zones. Low payments for raw cotton by state procurement agencies mean that many of the now-privatized farmers must sell their crop at a loss. This has driven down farm incomes to subsistence levels.[48]

After independence, large numbers of unemployed or underemployed residents of all three sectors of the Ferghana Valley sought work in Kazakhstan or Russia. In the 1990s, Tajikistan's Sughd province witnessed particularly high rates of emigration,[49] but these were nearly equaled by those parts of Ferghana under Kyrgyzstan's rule. Suffice it to say that the International Labor Organization (ILO) estimates that more than 80 percent of male ethnic Kyrgyz under 35 are working outside the country. Not all of these all menial workers. In Kyrgyzstan's south and the Ferghana Valley in particular, three-fifths of those leaving to seek work elsewhere are skilled workers—for example, engineers, doctors, professors and teachers.[50] Internal migration within the valley also has grown, as when large numbers of seasonal workers leave Tajikistan for Kyrgyzstan, where it is easier to find land to farm and where taxes are lower. Such conditions have turned male workers into objects to be bought and sold like commodities, and have contributed to growing trafficking in women along the regional borders.[51]

The issue of enclaves, which is a constant source of tension among states, also remains unresolved. The Uzbek territories of Shakhimardan, Sokh, and Kalakh Dzhangayl are located in the Batken region of Kyrgyzstan. The Kyrgyz enclave of Barak and the Tajik enclave of Sarvak are located in Uzbekistan's Ferghana province. There are also two Tajik enclaves in the Batken region, Vorukh and Za-padnaia Kolacha. The three states all seek secure borders, and seek international assistance in creating them, but they must somehow also establish "borders with a human face." Progress on this issue would constitute an important step on the path to regional cooperation.

In terms of geography, economics, and culture, the Ferghana Valley is a single entity, but during the last two decades it has been fragmented into three parts. In spite of the growing differences among them, they share the reality of having become problematic zones for all three states. The Uzbek part of the valley keeps the central government at high alert, lest new manifestations of extremism appear there. Tajikistan's Ferghana province of Sughd is still very uncomfortable over having been excluded from power after almost a century of dominance. The Kyrgyz part of the valley helped bring about regime change in Kyrgyzstan in 2005 and produced a national president in the person of Kurmanbek Bakiyev. But in most respects his rule was disastrous, and the fate of the Kyrgyz part of Ferghana remains altogether unclear as of this writing.

During the twenty years from 1989 to 2009, some twenty dangerous conflicts took place in the Ferghana Valley. Indeed, tensions remain high there today. While the population's traditional conservatism and its capacity to endure prolonged socio-economic and political crises serve as a deterrent for violent conflicts, such patience is not unlimited.[52]

Perspectives on the Ferghana Valley Since Independence

Since independence, three factors have emerged as defining forces in the Ferghana Valley: first, the rate of economic growth in the three states, which requires deft economic policies and the reining in of corruption; second, the degree of cooperation and coordination among the three Ferghana states; and. third, the establishment of a workable relationship with Islam. Martha Brill Olcott argues that the region's authorities have mistakenly assumed that religion can be controlled by the state.[53] True or not, the states need to work out a modus vivendi with Islam, for religion appears to be winning in the competition against current governments. For this reason Charles William Maynes asserts that "The important task today in Central Asia is finding a place in the political structure for the growth of Islam."[54]

The Ferghana Valley faces serious difficulties in relations among neighboring countries, especially regarding water. As Christine Bichsel shows in Chapter 11, it has become increasingly clear since independence that the states themselves cannot resolve this conflict, and must therefore appeal to international organizations and financial institutes. Much the same must be said for the intractable ecological issues, most of which have deep roots in the Soviet era.

Similarly, the situation along the borders has become increasingly tense. The states have not completed the process of demarcation and delineation of borders, and tensions continue over contentious areas and pockets. Between Kyrgyzstan and Uzbekistan alone, there are three dozen disputed plots, the most serious of which are the tracts near Gavasay in Jalalabad, the area of the Andijan reservoir, the Kyrgyz enclave of Barak, and the Uzbek enclave of Sokh.

The political systems of the region's states and public institutions have yet to solve the challenge of dealing with diversity of opinion and political pluralism. During the transition period many considered a "strong arm" to be necessary and desirable, which led to the emergence of authoritarian rule.[55] However, state institutions in the Ferghana Valley are often weak and unresponsive to normal citizens, while presidential parties discourage the kind of interchanges with opponents that could provide a safety valve in difficult times. Elective bodies could fulfill this same function, but for now they are not a factor in local affairs in any of the valley's three sectors. All three governments have long opposed parliamentary democracy on the grounds that it could undermine the implementation of urgently needed changes, that the populations were not ready for it, and that it could become a destabilizing force.

Even when a government championed democracy, as occurred briefly in Kyrgyzstan under Akaev, little attention was paid to such practical issues as rules and procedures, the creation of a responsive civil administration, institutionalization, the responsibilities that must accompany freedom, and the rule of law.[56] The 2005 Tulip Revolution in Kyrgyzstan proved stillborn and elicited bitter hostility in both Tashkent and Dushanbe. As early as April 2000, the Tajik government imposed strict regulations on non-governmental organizations, while Uzbekistan banned 60 percent of such organizations in 2005.[57] This has had the effect of undergirding traditional local institutions throughout the valley.

In later years, the United States and Europe have treated changes in the region with great caution. Many in the West have concluded that democratic processes could bring to the fore the most reactionary forces in Central Asian society, as occurred in Algeria and Iran. Westerners have reasonably asked whether they really want to promote democracy if the triumph of radical Islam is a possible outcome of their efforts. Others respond with equal logic that international passivity could lead to the very same results.

Rivalries among the great powers have had a negative impact on the Ferghana Valley.[58] This has been most dramatically apparent in Russia's successful effort to establish a military base in the Kyrgyz sector of the valley, which both Uzbekistan and Tajikistan perceive as a threat to their territory. The U.S. response of creating a small training facility in the Osh region by no means balances this move. At a deeper level, Russia adopted the view that nefarious designs by Western powers lay behind all Central Asian movements for reform, while Westerners detect illicit Russian money behind every move to defend the status quo. Some claim the aftermath of September 11, 2001, offered an opportunity to use Western assistance to accelerate modernization[59] in ways that would not have led to objections from Moscow or Beijing. Whether this was the case, neither the regional governments nor the United States seized this potential opportunity.[60]

The notable events in Kyrgyzstan in March and Andijan in May 2005 pointedly raised the issue of regime change and its consequences. In both cases it was the Ferghana Valley that posed the issue to the nations affected. Both the successful coup in Kyrgyzstan and the failed coup in Uzbekistan demonstrated clearly that reactionary criminal groups can utilize mass discontent to seize power, and that the Ferghana Valley offered an attractive base for such actions. The reinforcement of authoritarian rule after these events and its popular acceptance in both countries suggest that democratization was not a priority for the majority of the population. Even in Kyrgyzstan, democracy could not take root because it lacked popular support. Across the Ferghana Valley democracy is seen not as an end in itself but as a possible tool for discrediting and eliminating a political rival currently in power. Unsuccessful and tragic in their consequences, the Andijan events and the Kyrgyz coup underscore the increased use of armed action to facilitate regime change in the Ferghana Valley.[61] More recent terrorist acts in all three sectors of the valley suggest that the resort to armed force has not ended.

The Ferghana Valley could yet become the epicenter of a future region-wide conflict. Many abroad continue to regard Central Asia not as a zone of sovereign states but as a kind of artificial formation including Russia, China, Iran, and Turkey.[62] Independence brought together national, religious, and cultural groups that in some cases have little in common with each other. These differences could be exploited in various ways, and even, as a worst-case scenario, as a pretext to redraw existing borders. The greatest danger arises from the possibility of external powers manipulating current rivalries within the region. Arguably, these rivalries are sharpest among the three Ferghana Valley states, and arise in part because the interests of the three countries collide in that region. Uzbekistan, because of its size and determined focus on preserving its security, can readily undertake actions that its two neighbors perceive as detrimental to themselves.[63] A variety of factors have sown mounting distrust, especially between Uzbekistan and Kyrgyzstan. Disagreements over the construction of the Rogun and Kambarata power stations involve all three countries, with each party appealing separately to international agencies and arbiters.

As noted above, the militarization of the Ferghana Valley has stoked tensions between Kyrgyzstan and Uzbekistan. The decision of the Collective Security Treaty Organization (CSTO), of which Uzbekistan is not a member, to open a military base in the Kyrgyz part of the valley met staunch opposition from Tashkent. The agreement between the United States and Kyrgyzstan to set up a training base for special military forces in Batken province near the Uzbek border also arouses suspicions in Tashkent. Clearly, both steps are potentially destabilizing.

The U.S. government is concerned over the Ferghana countries' role in the Afghan drug trade,[64] while the Uzbek government sees a direct connection between narcotics and IMU activity. Afghan drugs helped fund the civil war in Tajikistan, which impacted both of Tajikistan's Ferghana neighbors.[65] The director of Russia's Federal Drug Control Service, V. Ivanov, asserts that $15 billion out of the total $17 billion of Afghan drug revenues are directed through the "northern route," and that significant sums from this cash trove support the Islamic Movement of Uzbekistan and Hizb ut-Tahrir in the Ferghana Valley.[66] Moreover, the drug trade in the Ferghana states feeds corruption and widens the chasm between state and society, which in turn fosters the conditions under which radical Islamists present themselves as a plausible alternative.[67]

A close connection exists between the situation in the Ferghana Valley and the ongoing struggle in Afghanistan. Spillover from the Afghan violence is a constant danger,[68] especially in the densely populated Ferghana Valley. The opening of the United States' Northern Transit Network made Central Asian countries part of the theater of military operations against the Taliban. Moreover, Uzbeks in Mazar-e Sharif and Tajiks from the Panjshir Valley play an important role in Afghan politics. Should a collapse of NATO operations in Afghanistan take place, it could trigger the redrawing of that country's political map, with a division between the Pashtun south and the Tajik and Uzbek (and Turkmen) north.

The end of Soviet-type development strengthened Central Asia's village traditionalism and weakened its urban-based modernization. This led to a collision between the post-Soviet secular Western model of society and an Islamic approach to social development. A victory by the latter would remove from power the national, secular-minded elites who have emerged over decades, and the reconstruction of the region's entire system of socio-economic life. For the time being, religion appears to trump secularism.[69] If in the beginning of the 1990s the number of people performing the *hajj* from moderately religious Kyrgyzstan amounted to only a few dozen, yet reached 3,000 by 1998, 95 percent of them came from the Ferghana Valley. After gaining independence, Kyrgyzstan experienced the construction of more than 1,200 new mosques, the majority of which were built by theological foundations in Iran, Pakistan, and Saudi Arabia.[70] Such penetration of foreign religious organizations into the Uzbek and Tajik parts of the Ferghana Valley was even more intensive.

This occurs because growing numbers of people in the Ferghana Valley doubt whether the secular state truly defends their interests. In frustration they turn to

Islam because no reliable secular alternative exists. This political and ideological mobilization of a traditionalist society is taking place in all sectors of the populous Ferghana Valley, posing obvious dangers for the future. Even now, European secular culture introduced by Russian and Soviet rule is steadily losing ground across the valley, and could in due course disappear entirely. If this happens, the diversity of cultural life that existed in the Soviet period also will cease, and even the most bizarre aspirations of groups like Hizb ut-Tahrir will go unchallenged.[71] This process begins when governments allow Islamist parties and organizations to claim the moral high ground of opposition to perceived widespread corruption. While the remainders of the weak legal political opposition struggle futilely within the secular model, Islamists are proposing radical change. Such a stance is especially appealing to youth;[72] if impoverished Kyrgyzstan and Tajikistan continue to under-invest in education, and if per capita income in all three sectors of the Ferghana Valley does not show marked improvement, the Islamist alternative is bound to grow yet more attractive.

Notes

1. S.I. Lunev, "Ferganskaia Dolina kak odna iz modelei regionalnogo razvitiia," www.ca-c.org/journal/09-1997/st_04_lunev.shtml.

2. S.I. Lunev, *Vyzovy bezopasnosti iuzhnykh granits Rossii,* Moscow, 1999, p. 111.

3. *Trud v SSSR: statisticheskii sbornik,* Moscow, 1988, pp. 22–23.

4. Martha Brill Olcott and Aleksei Malashenko, eds., *Mnogomernye granitsy Tsentralnoi Azii,* Moscow, 2000, pp. 14–26.

5. Iu.G. Kulchik, *Tsentralnaia Aziia posle imperii: etnosy, obshchestva, problemy,* Moscow, 1995.

6. Eugene Huskey, "Askar Akaev," in *The Gorbachev Encyclopedia: The Man and His Times,* ed. J. Wieczyrski, Salt Lake City, 1993, p. 31.

7. "God za godom," *Slovo Kyrgyzstana,* September 1, 1993.

8. M. Sherimkulov, "Stanovlenie zakonodatelnoi vlasti v nezavisimom Kyrgyzstane," *Vestnik mezhparlamentskoi assamblei,* no. 1, St. Petersburg, 1994, 1, pp. 3–9; M. Sheremkulov, "Sekrety stabilnosti," *Narodnyi deputat,* no. 13, 1992, pp. 44–48.

9. A. Elebaeve and N. Omuraliev, "Mezhetnicheskie otnosheniia v Kyrgyzstane: dinamika i tendentsii razvitiia," *Tsentralnaia Aziia i Kavkaz,* 1998, www.ca-c.org/journal/15-1998/st_07_elebaeva.shtml.

10. "Kyrgyzstan za desiat let, 1991–2001 gg.," *Slovo Kyrgyzstana,* September 1, 2001.

11. Eric McGlinchey, "Paying for Patronage: Regime Change in Post-Soviet Central Asia," Ph.D. diss., Princeton University, 2003, p. 221.

12. Eugene Huskey, "Kyrgyzstan's Tulip Revolution," *Demokratizatsiya,* vol. 13, no. 4, 2005, p. 483.

13. A. Kynev, "Kyrgyzstan do i posle 'Tulpanovoi revoliutsii,'" www.igpi.ru/info/people/kynev/1128082583.html and www.stratagema.org/publications/political-technology/item_341.html; A.V. Prokofiev, "Institutsionalnie faktory transformatsii politicheskikh rezhimov v Gruzii, Kyrgyzii i Ukrainy (nachalo 2000-godov)," www.politex.info/content/view/699/30/.

14. Bakiyev was ousted in April 2010 after violent demonstations and a withdrawal of Kremlin support forced him to flee Bishkek.

15. "Sekuliarizm i Islam v sovremennom gosudarstve: chto ikh obediniaet?" Materialy mezhdunarodnogo kruglogo stola (Almaty, 30 Noiabria 2007), Almaty, 2008, pp. 236–37.

16. V. Dubovitskii, "Osobennosti etnicheskoi i konfessionalnoi situatsii v Respublike Tadzhikistan," February, 2003, www.analitika.org/article.php?story=20060307230526550.

17. Iu.G. Kulchik, S.I. Rumiantsev, and N.I. Chicherina, *Grazhdanskie dvizheniia v Tadzhikistane,* Moscow, 1990.

18. Pinar Akcali, "Islam as a 'Common Bond' in Central Asia: Islamic Renaissance Party and the Afghan Mujahidin," *Central Asian Survey,* vol. 17, no. 2, 1998, pp. 267–85.

19. Olivier Roy, "The War in Tajikistan Three Years On," Special Report, U.S. Institute of Peace, Washington, DC, 1995; Shahram Akbarzadeh, "Why Did Nationalism Fail in Tajikistan?" *Europe-Asia Studies,* vol. 48, no. 7, 1996, pp. 1105–29.

20. Shahram Akbarzadeh, "Geopolitics Versus Democracy in Tajikistan," *Demokratizatsiya,* vol. 14, no. 4, 2006, p. 563.

21. A. Dubnov, "Prezident Rakhmon dolzhen dumat kogda vystupaet," December 14, 2009, www.ferghana.ru/article.php?id=6402.

22. M. Kurbanova and R. Mirzobekova, "Khorog-92," February 8, 2007, www.asiaplus.tj/articles/27/1331.html.

23. E. Rakhmonov, *Dostoinoe mesto v mirovom soobshchestve,* Dushanbe, 2002.

24. E. Rakhmomov, *Tadzhiki v zerkale istorii,* vol. 1, Dushanbe, 2002.

25. Christopher Pala, "A Lopsided Victory Is Seen for Tajikistan's Ruling Party," *New York Times,* March 1, 2005.

26. Martha Brill Olcott, "The War on Terrorism in Central Asia and the Cause of Democratic Reform," *Demokratizatsiya,* vol. 11, n. 1, pp. 86–95, 2003.

27. S. Frederick Starr, "Making Eurasia Stable," *Foreign Affairs,* January–February 1996.

28. Iu. Kulchik, "Respublika Uzbekistan v seredine 90-kh godov," www.igpi.ru/info/people/kulchik/uzb.html.

29. Timothy J. Colton and Robert C. Tucker, eds., *Patterns in Post-Soviet Leadership,* Boulder, CO, 1995, pp. 191–234.

30. Islam Karimov, "Pri imperii nas schitali liudmi vtorogo sorta" (interview, in which the president of Uzbekistan declares that a "color revolution" is impossible in his country), *Nezavisimaya gazeta,* January 14, 2005, www.ng.ru/ideas/2005-01-14/1_karimov.html.

31. Sarah Kendzior, "Inventing Akromiya: The Role of Uzbek Propagandists in the Andijon Massacre," *Demokratizatsiya,* vol. 14, no. 4, 2006, p. 545.

32. S.N. Abashin, "Kulturnye protsessy i transkulturnye vlianiia v sovremennoi Tsentralnoi Azii," www.soros.org/initiatives/arts/focus/caucasus/articles_publications/publications/abashin_20090514/russian_20090515.pdf.

33. S. Lunev, "Ferganskaia Dolina kak odna iz modelei regionalnogo razvitiia," *Tsentralnaia Aziia,* no. 3, 1997, pp. 25–30.

34. Kulchik, "Respublika Uzbekistan v seredine 90-kh godov."

35. V. Ia. Belokrenitaskii, V.V. Naumkin et al., eds., *Istoriia Vostoka v 6 tomakh, Vostok v noveishii period (1945–2000),* vol. 6, 2008, p. 439.

36. Thomas Carothers, "Promoting Democracy and Fighting Terror," *Foreign Affairs,* vol. 82, no. 1, 2003, p. 84.

37. Karen Dawisha and Bruce Parrott, *Russia and the New States of Eurasia,* Cambridge, 1994, p. 149.

38. David Lewis, *The Temptations of Tyranny in Central Asia,* New York, 2008, p. 43.

39. Jessica Stern, "The Protean Enemy," *Foreign Affairs,* vol. 82, no. 4, 2003, p. 27.

40. Zeyno Baran, "Fighting the War of Ideas," *Foreign Affairs,* vol. 84, no. 6, 2005, p. 79.

41. Martha Brill Olcott, "The Impact of Current Events in Uzbekistan," speech delivered at the Carnegie Endowment for International Peace discussion, May 17, 2005; Shirin Akinir, "Violence in Andijan, 13 May 2005: An Independent Assessment," Silk Road Paper,

Central Asia-Caucasus Institute and Silk Road Studies Program, July 2005, p. 29; Kendzior, "Inventing Akromiya," p. 545.

42. Alexander Cooley, "Base Politics," *Foreign Affairs,* vol. 84, no. 6, 2005, p. 79.

43. Early reports by the International Crisis Group and Human Rights Watch claiming 700 or 800 deaths have not been upheld by subsequent research, the Russian organization Memorial's estimation of one-third to two-thirds of that number being generally accepted today (Pravozashchitnyi Tsentr "Memorial," "Piket pamiati zhertv Andizhanskoi tragedii," www.memo.ru/2009/05/12/1205091.htm).

44. Kendzior, "Inventing Akromiya," p. 545.

45. "Radical Islam in Central Asia: Responding to Hizb ut-Tahrir," *Asia Report,* no. 58, June 30, 2003, www.crisisgroup.org/en/regions/asia/central-asia/058-radical-islam-in-central-asia-responding-to-hizb-ut-tahrir.aspx.

46. Charles William Maynes, "America Discovers Central Asia," *Foreign Affairs,* vol. 82, no. 2, 2003, p. 120.

47. "Central Asia's Destructive Monoculture: The Curse of Cotton," Report no. 93, February 2005, International Crisis Group, pp. 1, 4, 8, 13.

48. O. Brusina, "Migranty iz Srednei Azii v Rossii: etapy i prichiny priezda, sotsialnye tipy, organizatsii diaspor," *Vestnik Evrazii,* no. 2, 2008, pp. 66–95.

49. N. Zotova, "Vospriiatie migratsii v strane vykhoda: Tadzhikistan," *Vestnnik Evrazii,* no. 23, 2008, pp. 29–30.

50. V.A. Tishkov, ed., *Etnicheskaia situatsiia i konflikty v stranakh SNG i Baltii, Ezhegodnyi doklad za 2006,* Moscow, 2006, pp. 377–78, 386–87.

51. S. Olimova, "Migratsionnye protsessy v sovremennom Tadzhikistane," www.demoscope.ru/weekly/2005/0223/analit05.php.

52. *Okruzhaiushchaia sreda i bezopastnost: transformatsiia riskov v sotrudnichestvo,* UNDP, New York, 2005, http://www.envsec.org/pub/environment-and-security-russian. pdf, p. 43.

53. Martha Brill Olcott, "The War on Terrorism in Central Asia and the Cause of Democratic Reform," p. 86.

54. Maynes, "America Discovers Central Asia," p. 120.

55. Colton and Tucker, *Patterns in Post-Soviet Leadership,* p. 258.

56. Eugene Huskey, "Kyrgyzstan's Tulip Revolution," *Demokratizatsiya,* vol. 13, no. 4, 2005, p. 483.

57. Thomas Carothers, "The Backlash Against Democracy Promotion," *Foreign Affairs,* vol. 85, no. 2, p. 55.

58. Kbarzadeh, "Geopolitics Versus Democracy in Tajikistan," p. 563.

59. Thomas Carruthers, "Promoting Democracy and Fighting Terror," *Foreign Affairs,* vol. 82, no. 1, 2003, p. 84.

60. Martha Brill Olcott, *Central Asia's Second Chance,* Washington, DC, 2005, p. 389.

61. Charles H. Fairbanks, Jr., "Revolution Reconsidered," *Journal of Democracy,* vol. 18, no. 1, 2007, pp. 42–57.

62. "Nations Without a Cause," *Economist,* September 26, 2009, p. 98.

63. R. Grant Smith, "Tajikistan: The Rocky Road to Peace," *Central Asian Survey,* vol. 18, no. 2, 1999, p. 243.

64. S. Frederick Starr, "A Partnership for Central Asia," *Foreign Affairs,* vol. 84, no. 4, 2005, p. 164.

65. Ahmed Rashid, "The Taliban: Exporting Extremism," *Foreign Affairs,* vol. 78, no. 6, 1999, p. 22.

66. Ofitsialnyi sait Federalnoi sluzhby Rossiiskoi Federatsii po kontroliu za oborotom narkotiklov, http://fskn.gov.ru.

67. *Mezhdunarodnaia trevoga.Tsentralnaia Aziia. Strategicheskii podkhod k postroeniiu mira,* London, 2006; Nancy Lubin and and Barnett Rubin, *Calming the Ferghana Valley: Development and Dialogue in the Heart of Central Asia,* New York, 1999, p. 41.

68. Tom Gjelten, "Afghan War Could Spill Over into Central Asia," NPR, December 31, 2010, www.npr.org/templates/story/story.php?storyId=121973427&ft=1&f=3.

69. Kulchik, "Respublika Uzbekistan v seredine 90-kh godov."

70. Olcott and Malashenko, *Mnogomernye granitsy Tsentralnoi Azii,* pp. 14–26.

71. "Radikalnyi Islam v Tsentralnoi Azii: otvet na poiavlenie Khizb ut-Takhrir," Report no. 58, MGPK-Asia, Osh and Brussels, June 30, 2003.

72. Rashid, "The Taliban," p. 22.

10

Economic Development in the Ferghana Valley Since 1991

Sayidfozil Zokirov (Uzbekistan), with
Khojamahmad Umarov (Tajikistan)

The collapse of the communist system led to profound transformations in the economy of the Ferghana Valley. The differing policies pursued by the three Ferghana states meant that land use, ownership of property, and compensation of labor came to differ in the three regions. Underlying all these differences, however, was continuity with respect to natural resources and their exploitation. The Uzbek part of the valley includes major deposits of oil, coal, natural gas, gypsum, iron, copper ore, mercury, salt and silver, bismuth, bauxite, antimony, mercury, and non-metallic building materials.[1] Tajikistan's Konimansur boasts the second-largest silver deposits in the world, with annual production forecasted to reach 50 tons; in addition, Tajikistan has gold at Djilali, Taror, and other sites, along with major deposits of lead, zinc, copper and bismuth, molybdenum and tungsten, strontium, iron, tin, coal, fluorspar, and rock salt.[2] The Kyrgyz part of the Ferghana Valley has significant deposits of mercury and antimony, while Jalalabad province alone possesses 95 percent of the country's generating capacity for electricity.[3]

Major branches of industry are also concentrated in the Ferghana region, including automotive works, chemical and petrochemical firms, food processing plants, and producers of construction materials. Cotton dominates the agricultural sector but sericulture, horticulture, and many forms of truck gardening are also prominent.

The exceptionally high population density throughout the valley means that changes in the economy inevitably affect large numbers of often-impoverished rural people and communities that are very close to one another and intent above all on preserving what they have. Accordingly, all three governments approach economic change in the Ferghana Valley with caution.

Fundamental Trends of the Three Countries'
Economic Development

The Central Asian countries began their independent lives from similar starting points. Per capita annual income in 1990 in the three neighboring republics of the Ferghana

Valley was around 960–1,050 rubles.[4] Since independence, differences in GDP per capita have widened, bringing the 2008 totals for Uzbekistan to $2,660, for Kyrgyzstan to $2,130, and for Tajikistan to $1,860.[5] While resources played an important part in this evolution, the differences in economic development trace significantly to the different economic policies pursued in each country. All were shaped by the practical circumstances, way of life, and culture of their respective societies, but each chose its own means of overcoming the lopsidedness of Soviet development.

Uzbekistan's economic-development strategy from the outset called for gradualism and the preservation of a decisive role for the state. This was not an end in itself but a means of maintaining key social services in health and education, and hence of preventing social unrest.[6] Uzbekistan feared that rapid market reforms could jeopardize macroeconomic stability. While this brought much international criticism in the early 1990s, it also assured a higher degree of social cohesion than might otherwise have existed. As economist Richard Pomfret noted, "the strategy of macroeconomic regulation and reform of the Uzbek economy appears in recent years to be better than, and preferable to, that of Kyrgyzstan, which was oriented toward rapid privatization and liberalization of monetary policy."[7] Through most of the 1990s Uzbekistan's policy of slow reform produced better economic indicators than most other post-Soviet states. More important, the preservation of the state's role created an income stream that enabled the government to maintain the social sector, education, and heath care.[8]

From the first days of independence, Bishkek carefully followed the recommendations of the International Monetary Fund (IMF) and World Bank. President Askar Akaev's economic advisers met with such experts as Daniel Kaeser, Anders Aslund, Aleksandr Agafonoff, Tetsuji Tanaka, Ernst Albrecht, Karl Hahn, and Tatsuo Kaneda. Akaev was the only Central Asian leader to implement all the main provisions of the "Washington consensus," including privatization, deregulation, the protection of property rights, reducing restrictions on foreign direct investment, liberalizing financial markets, and other suggestions.

In 1998 Kyrgyzstan became the first member of the Commonwealth of Independent States to join the World Trade Organization (WTO). Unfortunately, the country did not reap benefits from this, in part because its large neighbor, China, also became a member, leading to the flooding of Kyrgyz markets with Chinese goods. The low import duties prescribed by the WTO also worsened Kyrgyzstan's relations with its other neighbors, who adhered to the Common Customs Tariff. By joining the WTO, Kyrgyzstan committed to binding tariff rates at a relatively low level,[9] opening not just its own domestic market but potentially also those of neighboring states, to goods and services from third countries.[10] To defend themselves, Kyrgyzstan's neighbors imposed trade restrictions and high taxes to protect their manufacturers from an influx of Chinese goods arriving via Kyrgyzstan. Kazakhstan's duties on certain Kyrgyz goods ranged up to 200 percent.[11] Such duties in effect created a Chinese wall of customs through the Ferghana Valley.

Thus weakened, the Kyrgyz economy became dependent on loans and foreign aid, both of which reached high levels relative to other post-Soviet economies. These measures reduced social pressure until 2005, when events in the Ferghana Valley led to the Tulip Revolution.

Tajikistan in 1989 had the USSR's lowest productive capacity and level of economic development, and its per capita income was a mere 39 percent of the level for the USSR as a whole. During 1991 and thereafter, Tajikistan's economy suffered two devastating additional blows from which it has yet to recover. The first was the collapse of the Soviet Union, which severed benefits coming from Moscow, and the second was the outbreak of civil war.

Prices in Tajikistan rose 115 times between 1990 and 1993, while incomes grew by only 36 times; retail trade decreased by two-thirds by 1992 and by a further half in 1993. Living standards fell even further than the decreases in production.

Owing to the republic's precarious socio-economic condition, the United Nations Development Programme (UNDP) Governing Council granted Tajikistan the status of "recipient country" in 1993. By war's end Tajikistan required more than 400 billion rubles to restore its shattered economy. Russia, Kazakhstan, and Uzbekistan extended a twenty-year interest-free loan of 286 billion rubles to pay for oil and petroleum products from Russia.

Since mid-1995 the Tajik government has worked closely with the World Bank and IMF to establish programs for macroeconomic stabilization and structural reform. The government reform program designed for the period from 1995 to 2000 was supported by an IMF agreement that provided a Special Drawing Rights loan of 15 million SDR (1 SDR = US$1.4) and by two World Bank initiatives. In 1996 the World Bank's technical assistance program helped establish a state economic institute, and in September of that year the World Bank extended an additional $55 million loan to reconstruct agriculture and social protection programs.

In 2002, the IMF launched a three-year $87 million project to finance anti-poverty programs and stimulate economic growth. The conclusion of bilateral agreements on debt restructuring, mainly with Russia and Uzbekistan, decreased Tajikistan's external debt to $1 billion (82 percent of GDP), which further strengthened the country's macroeconomic indicators.

High hopes were placed on land reform. In 2002 nearly 50 percent of cooperatively owned land was converted into farms (*dehkans*) as personal allotments. In 2001 a land registry was formed, and in 2002 the land registration fee was decreased, which simplified the process of registering land. That same year forty large state farms were restructured. However, many of these state farms had accumulated large debts, which made them unattractive to private buyers. The privatization process stalled. Even today the Tajik economy remains in a precarious state.

Fundamental Characteristics of Privatization

The motivations, forms, and pace of privatization provide revealing indexes of the overall economic policies of post-Soviet states. The approaches of the three

Ferghana states in this area present a picture of contrasts, each of them worth reviewing in turn.

Professor B. Berkinov observed that privatization in Uzbekistan went through three stages. The first, from 1992 to 1993, was a period of "small privatization," when 29,000 houses, and small- and medium-sized shops and consumer services were converted to private or communal ownership. Workers' collectives received substantial benefits, such as the free transfer of fixed assets that had depreciated by more than 70 percent, and the right to buy small enterprises at a discount. As for the rural population, each family received land adjacent to its home for private use.

In the second stage, from 1994 to 1998, privatization took place among medium- and large-scale enterprises in light industry, machinery, building materials, road transport, and agriculture, as well as other sectors of the economy not deemed strategic by the state. Real estate and securities markets began to form during this period. Small businesses were sold to private owners, while medium- and large-scale enterprises were transformed into joint-stock companies with shares divided among the staff (25 percent), the state (26 percent), enterprises that consume the firm's products (10 percent), foreign investors (10 percent), and open sales (30 percent).[12]

The third stage, which began in 1999 and continues to the present, seeks to attract investments to enterprises that are unprofitable, inefficient, or insolvent. It does this by offering the state's share of such properties at zero redemption cost for investment obligations.[13] This included the privatization of large-scale state-owned enterprises in strategic sectors, such as fuel and energy, metals, and chemicals. In the Uzbek part of the Ferghana Valley, approximately 2,000 government enterprises and agencies in various branches of the economy were privatized from 2000 to 2007. As part of this process, 154 joint stock companies were established, as well as 290 limited liability companies. Another 900 state-owned properties were sold to private ownership.

The privatization process in Kyrgyzstan can be divided into four stages. The first phase, from 1992 to 1993, encouraged citizens to buy shops and household service firms. Progress on privatizing larger firms proceeded slowly, not least because controlling stakes ended up in the hands of the former managers. Thanks to this, the first phase of privatization did not lead to greater efficiency or real management changes. The absence of capital markets posed an additional barrier to privatization, as did the fact that the same administrative organs that heretofore had mismanaged industry were now responsible for drafting the plan for privatization. Consequently, property rights were insufficiently firm to attract investors.

The second stage, which fell in 1994 and 1995, revolved around creating a much broader class of private business owners, so that together they could defend their interests in the marketplace. The introduction of privatization vouchers in 1994 and the establishment of auction centers in every province jump-started this process. Fifty cash auctions were carried out and shares were offered in 547 industries, 283 of which were successfully privatized. Specialized investment funds emerged to accumulate citizens' vouchers and convert them into shares. These coupons had been intended to help Kyrgyz citizens participate in the privatization process, which the government hoped would encourage them to support further economic reform.

The third stage (1996–97) involved the incorporation and privatization of such strategic entities as Kyrgyztelecom, Kyrgyzstan Aba Joldoru, Manas International Airport, and the main power companies, among others. However, an overwhelming portion of shares remained in the hands of the government, with private investors holding only insignificant stakes. For example, electric companies sold only 6.3 percent of their shares to private investors, Kyrgyztelecom 8 percent; the international airport, 12 percent. Investors saw this phase as incomplete and unsuccessful, resulting in large frozen assets.

The fourth stage began in 2000 and continues to the present. This phase again focuses on large, strategic enterprises, including energy companies, hydroelectric projects, Kyrgyztelecom, Kyrgyzgas, the Dastan Electric Works and, again, the international airport. In June 2007, Kyrgyzstan privatized the large Severelectro, Bishkekteploset, and HPP Bishkek electric companies, and also issued a license for the private construction and management of the Kambarata Hydroelectric Stations 1 and 2.

In its privatization, Tajikistan favored the direct sale of industries through public auctions organized by the government, with only a partial application of a voucher system. A first phase, which concluded in 1999, involved the privatization of small- and medium-sized industrial enterprises; the second phase, which lasted until 2003, provided for the auction or sale of medium- and large-scale enterprises; while the third phase, which extended from 2004 to 2007, addressed the privatization of certain important medium and large-scale enterprises in mechanical engineering, chemicals, mining, and construction materials, as well as the restructuring of natural monopolies and extremely large enterprises.

By the start of 2006 only 351 industrial enterprises had been privatized, a mere 4 percent of the country's enterprises. Even today only 31.1 percent of the total have been privatized, with fully 37 percent of them in Sughd province (mainly Ferghana), in Soviet times the country's most developed region.[14] This relatively low number traces to a public fear of destabilization that was the heritage of years of civil war; the fact that 56 percent of the population lived below the poverty level in 2008 and have therefore been excluded from participating in the privatization process. It also was fostered by the absence of a post-privatization support system for new entrepreneurs, and lack of access to loans for renovating facilities, and the corruption of the process, which allowed certain individuals to snap up firms at unreasonably low prices and immediately resell them at 5 to 50 times more than they had paid.[15]

All three Ferghana countries recently have divided large enterprises into smaller firms in order to facilitate privatization. In fact, this has had the effect of splintering organic enterprises into uncoordinated pieces, leaving a multiplicity of owners at a single site, with each making his own arrangements for utilities and raw materials. The resulting fragmentation severely damaged production and all but killed technical progress and innovation.

Banking Sector Development

Slowdowns in the leading OECD economies and rising interest rates have undercut the incentive for investing in new markets such as those of the Ferghana countries. On the positive side, debt/GDP ratios have declined in all three Ferghana states; in Uzbekistan this has been due to an effort to reduce external dependence, and in Kyrgyzstan and Tajikistan there have been agreements with bilateral or multilateral creditors to write off debts.[16] Together, these conditions have subjected the banking systems of all three Ferghana states to heavy strains. Nonetheless, there are significant differences among them that directly affect conditions in the valley.

Uzbekistan claims twenty-nine commercial banks, of which three are state-owned, eleven are joint-stock banks, ten are private, and five are foreign. Together, they maintain some 8,500 branches, mini-banks, and retail offices.[17] Deposits account for most of the banks' assets. To increase their investment in export-oriented and modern production, the government recently allocated them $350 million.[18] A further 2008 measure provided $464 million to increase the capitalization of such leading banks as Uzpromstroibank, Asakabank, People's Bank, Agrobank, Microcreditbank, and Qishloq Kurilishbank, increasing the state's overall role. This is a common anti-crisis measure, of course, and in this case it proved effective because it occurred early.

In the Uzbek sector of the Ferghana Valley, banking activity has been growing steadily. Of the country's twenty-nine commercial banks, two, the JSCB Hamkorbank (Andijan) and Universal Bank (Kokand), are registered there.[19] Since 2000 JSCB Hamkorbank has worked with the International Finance Corporation of the EBRD.[20] Universal Bank, established in 2001, is owned by a group of non-state firms and maintains offices in fourteen Uzbek cities.[21] People's Bank, Agrobank, Microcreditbank, and National Bank of Foreign Trade all have branches throughout the Uzbek Ferghana Valley, while branches of Uzpromstroibank, Alok Bank, Asakabank, Kishlokkurilishbank, Ipotekabanka, Kapitalbank, Savdogarbank, Turonbanka are located only in the large cities.

Kyrgyzstan has a two-tiered banking system. The upper level, represented by the National Bank of the Kyrgyz Republic, licenses and monitors other banking institutions. For many years the Government of Finland assisted Kyrgyzstan in modernizing its National Bank. The second level consists of eighteen commercial banks, the Bishkek branch of the National Bank of Pakistan, and two specialized non-bank financial institutions.[22] In the Ferghana region of southern Kyrgyzstan, the banking sector is weakly developed compared with the other countries in the region. No national banking institution is headquartered there, and only about sixty bank branches function in the region. Similar differentials exist between Osh and lesser Ferghana centers. Thus, while Osh has two-dozen banks, Batken has only four.

As of January 1, 2007, Tajikistan's banking system included eight independent banks, eight loan associations, one foreign branch bank, and 44 non-bank financial organizations.[23] Overall, Tajikistan's banking system suffers from a number of vexing problems. First, credit-risk management remains elementary, in spite of an increased number of loans until mid-2008. Second, a steady increase in the volume of foreign currency, especially dollars, has left Tajikistan vulnerable to foreign-exchange risks, a problem that exists even though the National Bank of Tajikistan has taken measures to assure greater stability. Third, in spite of significant innovations at the National Savings Bank, Tajikistan's banks suffer from a lack of competition, especially from foreign institutions. This curtails the range and quality of services available, which in turn affects capitalization. Fourth, for these and other reasons, credit institutions in Tajikistan are insufficiently capitalized. Total bank capital stands at 5.42 percent of GDP, but the level of authorized capital to GDP is only 3.27 percent. Fifth, the country's legal and regulatory framework lags behind those of its neighbors. Recognizing this, the government is drafting new laws on the National Bank, corporate governance, and oversight. Finally, with few exceptions, Tajik banks have yet to exploit IT technologies to the degree that would make them competitive and hence attractive to investors.[24]

Fiscal Instruments in the Ferghana Valley Region

The formation and use of local budgets have become subjects of reform in most Central Asian countries, including the three Ferghana states. These are being done because the actions of state and local authorities affect national sources of income, and therefore processes should be designed to assure high rates of tax payment without jeopardizing the local economies. As it is, local expenditures are planned without close attention to the sources of the funds to cover them and their impact on local economies. New budgetary frameworks are being designed to correct this, and seek to foster self-sufficiency and stability in local government. To say the least, it is a difficult challenge to improve tax yields without raising taxes, and to do so in an environment of declining transfers from the central government to the regions.

Uzbekistan's local governments derive revenue from local taxes and fees, the rates of which are fixed by national legislation, and from annually budgeted transfers from central revenues. Both the Andijan and Namangan provinces receive subsidies, inasmuch as their expenditures exceed their local revenues. In 2007 this subsidy amounted to 20.8 percent of Andijan's budget and 22.8 percent of Namangan's.[25] Eighty-four percent of these subsidies are focused on social assistance, a significant sum even when nearly half of the state's overall budget is directed toward education and healthcare. Ferghana province receives no subsidies from the national budget.

Kyrgyzstan's new tax code, like that of Uzbekistan, came into effect in 2008. The key innovation was to reduce the number of local taxes from eight to two.

Taxes on advertising, spas, and hotels were not affected by this change. A single sales tax replaced road-use taxes and a host of other levies. Both land and property are taxed locally, the values based on appraisements. Households pay at the rate of 0.35 percent per the value of a square meter, while the rate for industrial real estate is 1 percent.

A striking feature of Tajikistan's national budget is that it does not include subsidies or transfers to the cities and districts of Sughd province in the Ferghana Valley. On the contrary, the Ferghana region is now a net provider of subsidies to other regions, notably to the mountainous regions in the south and in Badakhshan.

In Soviet times Tajikistan, like other republics, levied twelve taxes, which increased to fifteen following independence. Once the civil war ended, Tajikistan instituted a new tax code with seventeen taxes, which was in effect from 1999 to 2004. Problems in the implementation of this legislation led to yet another new code, in 2004, which raised the number of taxes to twenty. Although this new law addressed many of the system's previous shortcomings, important deficiencies remained. Predictably, the increased number of taxes was accompanied by falling rates of collection. Official projections put local tax yields at 1.21 percent of GDP from 1996 to 1998, but between 1999 and 2004 they actually were 0.89 percent, which fell to 0.85 percent in 2006–7. Clearly, the prohibitively high tax burden, as well as the mounting number of separate levies, has led many Tajiks simply to avoid paying taxes. Some economists claim that Tajikistan's tax burden has reached 55–75 percent of the net industrial production.[26] Whether or not this is the case, it can safely be concluded that high rates of taxation put residents of the Tajik sector of the Ferghana Valley at a distinct disadvantage vis-à-vis their Kyrgyz neighbors, and even the Uzbek part of the valley.

Cross-Border Cooperation

The movement of people and trade across borders has everywhere grown in importance. But in the Ferghana Valley after independence, borders that had been porous in Soviet times and nonexistent earlier came to function as barriers to everything but trucks carrying goods essential to the national economies. Cross-border commuting to workplaces, schools, and markets was sharply curtailed. Crises like the incursions of the Islamic Movement of Uzbekistan in 1999 and 2000, and the Andijan events of 2005, called forth security concerns that affected border regimens in all three countries. However, it was Uzbekistan that invariably took the most severe measures, sharply reducing cross-border transit and trade in the process.

Suffice it to say that in 2006 the total foreign trade turnover along Andijan province's border with the Kyrgyz sector of Ferghana was a mere $2.3 million, only 0.5 percent of the province's external trade turnover. In 2007 there were only eleven registered joint ventures between the Uzbek and Kyrgyz sectors of the Ferghana Valley. Evidence of the overall isolation of the Ferghana region by the early 2000s can be seen in the fact that only 232 industries were registered as having any foreign investment.

The economic importance of removing the various impediments to trade cannot be overestimated. On July 7, 2007 the governors of Kyrgyzstan's Ferghana provinces of Batken, Jalalabad, and Osh met for the first time with the *hakims* of Uzbekistan's Andijan, Namangan, and Ferghana provinces. Until common interests are more fully identified and procedures for cross-border commerce brought into harmony with one another, real progress will be impossible.

On no issue is the problem more acute, and the issues more contentious, than the payment for water. In one of many confrontations in this area, both Tajikistan and Uzbekistan rejected a 2001 act by the Kyrgyz parliament on the grounds that it conflicted with normal international water-management practice for transboundary rivers.

Nor has there been progress in the area of border management and customs. In the case of all three Ferghana countries, these are exacerbated by the broadening differences among the basic economic strategies of the three countries. Notwithstanding these many problems, at least one team of international experts is optimistic over the future of trade relations among the Ferghana countries. Klemens Greif, Martin Reiser, and Toshiaki Sakatsume assessed disintegrated data on consumer prices and the prices of nearly thirty export commodities,[27] and figured in estimates on shuttle trade, which is usually understated or ignored. On this basis they denied the existence of a negative "border effect," and concluded that "the Central Asian countries are closely integrated; their borders are quite transparent and represent a much smaller trade barrier than is generally assumed. The shuttle trade is an effective instrument for extracting profits from price spreads on consumer goods."[28]

Foreign Investment

Since 1996 foreign investment in both Uzbekistan and Kyrgyzstan has grown steadily, albeit from very low bases. Instability in Tajikistan and Afghanistan discourages foreign investments nearby, but the negative experiences of earlier investors and persisting fears over the possibility of repatriating profits surely provide the most significant brake on investments from abroad.

A very few major international projects account for most of the foreign investment in the Ferghana Valley. Thus, in 1995 the Daewoo factory in Andijan accounted for 80 percent of foreign direct investment. The TEK complex brought about the reconstruction of the Ferghana NPZ oil refinery, to which 15.7 percent of all capital investment in the Ferghana Valley region was allocated. Many other initiatives also involve foreign investments, which are focused in heavy industry but increasingly include such light industries as sewing factories and food processing. Among these, joint ventures are a common investment vehicle across the valley.

The development of Kyrgyzstan's large Kumtor gold mine accounted for a jump in foreign investment at the national level in the 1990s. Later, investments to reconstruct technology firms rose from 15 percent of the total in 1997 to 48.3 percent in 1999.[29] Regional differentials were large even within the Kyrgyz sector of the valley, with Jalalabad's percent of total investments in the Ferghana Valley rising from 25.9 percent in 2000 to 34.5 percent by 2005. In the Kyrgyz sector foreign investment is directed mainly to mining and electricity, textiles and clothing manufacturing, cotton, and tobacco.[30]

Tajikistan's civil war sharply curtailed all foreign investment throughout the 1990s, and the recovery has been slow thereafter. Foreign investment, significantly from Kazakhstan and Korea, is concentrated mainly in mining, textiles, construction materials, and agro-processing industries. Typical are Tajik-Korean and Tajik-Italian joint ventures being developed to produce fabric and clothing in the city of Khujand.

Several factors have shaped the level of foreign investment in the three sectors of the Ferghana Valley since 1997. The presence of mineral resources is an obvious magnet, but so is the quality of labor. Infrastructure plays a role, but so does the presence of enabling legislation by the national government, the ability to repatriate profits, and the degree of transparency. The interaction of these factors may explain why the Uzbek sector of the Ferghana Valley accounts for more than half of FDI-based industrial production in Uzbekistan and 40 percent of FDI itself, but only 6 percent of joint ventures. Note, too, that while Andijan province accounts for a third of Uzbekistan's FDI, nearby Namangan province claims less than 1 percent of the total.

Whatever the differences among the three sectors of the Ferghana Valley, they all suffer from relatively low absolute levels of foreign investment and hence low levels of transfer of technology and skills. This can be traced in part to inadequate knowledge of the region abroad. But the various factors enumerated above—for example, inadequate infrastructure, poor cross-border contact, insufficient enabling legislation, and the perception of high levels of corruption—also play a part.

Development of the Agricultural Sector

Agriculture accounts for one- to two-fifths of GDP in the three Ferghana countries, and employs 60.3 percent of the work force in Tajikistan, 52 percent in Kyrgyzstan, and 27 percent in Uzbekistan. Agriculture in the Ferghana Valley plays a larger economic role than in the rest of the three countries or in the region as a whole. Moreover, in all three sectors of the valley the area of cultivated land has expanded sharply since independence. In Uzbekistan it has grown from 15 percent of the total area in 1991 to about 41.3 percent in 2006. In Kyrgyzstan, the respective figures are 41.1 percent and 52.8 percent, and in Tajikistan, 13.1 percent and 26.3 percent. The much-criticized cotton culture also has changed its face since independence, with cotton taking up 55.5 percent of the total Ferghana area in 1991 but only 44.3 percent in 2006. However, in the Kyrgyz sector these figures are reversed, with the percentage rising from 6.4 percent to 12.6 percent.

In the Kyrgyz zone, the acreage devoted to tobacco decreased threefold, and the cultivation of fruits and berries declined from 12.8 percent to 8.8 percent, with the rise of oilseed production more than making up for the difference. The end of large-scale meat production for Russia shrank the area devoted to fodder from 19.7 percent to 5.5 percent in Uzbekistan, 44 percent to 7.9 percent in Kyrgyzstan, and from 25.5 percent to 18.8 percent in Tajikistan. However, the rise of private farming in Uzbekistan has somewhat reversed this trend in recent years.

Agrarian reforms have sharply cut back the role of collective farm production from 64.1 percent of the total in the Uzbek sector to only 0.8 percent, with private farms expanding from 0.4 percent to 32.7 percent of the total at the same time. Currently, 100 percent of the raw cotton and grain purchased for state use and all other types of agricultural products are produced on private farms.[31] None of the three Ferghana countries, in contrast to many other developing and developed countries, offers subsidies to their agricultural sectors.

The productivity of agriculture varies considerably across the Ferghana Valley. Farmers in the Tajik section have not received phosphate or potash fertilizers for years, and also lack an adequate supply of organic nitrogen. The productivity of crops and livestock in Kyrgyzstan also was initially very low, nearly 50 percent lower than in the Soviet period that, in turn, was well below international standards. Drought-resistant crops and the production of seedlings were both undeveloped, which undermined yields. Large-scale privatization sharply improved productivity in Kyrgyzstan, to the point that it is able to export substantial amounts of agricultural produce to both Kazakhstan and Russia. Production in the Uzbek part of the region has been steadier, with good yields for raw cotton, wheat, fruits, and garden vegetables.

The unresolved problem of water resources, discussed in detail in Chapter 11, impedes agricultural productivity in all three Ferghana sectors. An agreement among Kyrgyzstan, Uzbekistan, and also Kazakhstan brokered by USAID in 1998 coordinated water flow and electricity production to the benefit of all three. But when the parties could not agree on their annual commitments, the agreement lapsed in favor of simpler bilateral arrangements. Real advances in agricultural productivity will remain hostage to this issue as long as it remains at an impasse.

Development and Distribution of Industry

Since independence, industry in the three sectors of the Ferghana Valley has become increasingly differentiated. The Uzbek part is focused in automotive firms, oil refining, light industry, irrigation engineering, food production, chemical and petrochemical production, and construction. The Kyrgyz sector is dominated by power generation, mining (mercury, antimony, coal), and a variety of light industries. Tajikistan's Sughd province specializes in the production of textiles and sewing firms, as well as a wide variety of mining enterprises.

The Uzbek part of the Ferghana Valley has 204 large enterprises, which employ 123,900 people.[32] Significant increases in output by the giant Asakinsk automotive factory and the oil refinery in Ferghana, as well as improvements elsewhere, have boosted the output of the Uzbek provinces in Ferghana from 1.6 to 6.6 times their counterparts in the other two sectors.

The Kyrgyz provinces meanwhile have experienced a decline in manufacturing, owing mainly to the collapse of Soviet demand for coal from the Sulyukta Komura, Tegenek, and other mines, mercury from the large Haydarken plant, and antimony from the Kadamjai mine. Chinese and other Asian investors recently have turned their attention to these enterprises and may give them new life. If this happens even at only a few of these giant plants, one can expect sudden increases in overall industrial production in the Kyrgyz part of Ferghana.

Kyrgyz output of thermal-power electricity also sharply decreased, since the cost of inputs (oil, coal) soared while the sale price of electricity stagnated. Nearly all the former Kyrgyz production of electricity had been geared to the Moscow-funded USSR power grid. The subsequent decline in output especially damaged the economy of Jalalabad, where the large Kambarata I hydroelectric plant was dedicated mainly to the export of electricity to Russia. Rebuilding this plant, with its reservoir of 10 billion cubic meters, makes good sense, even at a price of $2 billion, but the prospect that this might be owned solely by Russians poses dangers to Uzbek customers, who fear politically motivated power cut-offs. A Kambarata II generating plant is currently under construction, with the first unit scheduled to be commissioned in 2010.

After enjoying a period of flowering during Soviet times, industry in Tajikistan's sector of the Ferghana today is relatively backward. The manufacturing plants of Sughd employed 220,000 people in 1990, but only 86,500 today. The share of the labor force they employed stood at 25.7 percent at the time of independence, but is now only 5.7 percent.[33] These figures reflect the deep crisis into which the economy of Sughd and the Tajik north were plunged by the Tajik civil war, and from which they have yet to extricate themselves. By the end of the civil war, industrial output had decreased to a third of its 1990 level, with the deepest losses in mechanical engineering and metals, chemicals and petrochemicals, and construction materials. The traditionally robust light industries suffered, as did food production, shedding 54,000 and 13,200 jobs, respectively.

However, these stringent cutbacks did not attract fresh capital or lead to the replacement of obsolete equipment or adoption of more progressive technologies. In 2005 industrial production was only 70.7 percent of 1990 levels. Notwithstanding a modest rebound after 1998, the number of industrial jobs continued to fall. Even if the industrial sector were to add 5,500 jobs annually, which was the rate of increase from 1960 to 1985, Tajikistan still will need more than twenty-five years to reach 1990 levels of industrial employment. Worse yet, most of the 133,900 positions in industry lost by 2005 formerly had been filled by highly qualified workers.

Out of 90 products made in Tajikistan's north, the only one that exceeded 1990 levels of production by 2005 was soft drinks, by 46.4 percent. Electricity generation at 97.1 percent came close to 1990 levels. But some 56 items, or 62 percent of the total, stood at barely 10 percent of their pre-civil war production.[34] Tajik power generation today stands at 1985 levels, coal at 1913 levels, oil at 1940 levels, and gas at 1965 levels.

In 1990 industrial production constituted 94.3 percent of Sughd province's total output and 19.0 percent of Tajikistan's. By 2006 these figures had fallen to 58.4 percent and 11.5 percent, respectively. These data provide stark testimony to the process of deindustrialization in the Tajik sector of the Ferghana Valley, which is also accompanied by de-urbanization.

Certain intra-regional shifts in industry can be discerned in the Tajik sector of the valley. In the beginning of the 1990s, industrial production in the towns of Isfara and Kairakkum exceeded that of Khujand, the province's largest city, by 2.8 and 3.5 times, respectively. Today these centers have an extremely low level of capacity utilization. Meanwhile, Khujand has become the province's industrial center, with rapid development in textiles, sewing, and canning, often through joint ventures.

Household Income

According to surveys conducted by Tajikistan's Sharq center in 2004, the main causes of outmigration of labor were low salaries (54 percent) and unemployment (20 percent).[35] With 90 percent of industrial employees nationally working at an average salary of $52 a month, this is scarcely surprising.[36] Wages constituted 58.8 percent of GDP in 1991, but by 2005 they had fallen to 10.9 percent. The comparable figure for Russia is 30 percent and for the European Union (EU) 70 percent. The same surveys indicate that only 22.5 percent of employees can cover their expenses with wages, the gap being filled mainly by activity in the shadow economy,[37] household gardens, informal work, and monetary gifts from relatives abroad.[38]

Data on household incomes in the Kyrgyz sector of the Ferghana Valley is lacking. However, the average income per capita nationally stands at 9,090 som, which means that 48 percent of the republic's population is classified as poor. Four out of five of the 13.4 percent counted as extremely poor live in rural areas. Kyrgyzstan's south being far poorer than the north, it is safe to say that in the Ferghana Valley these national figures must be adjusted downward.

The need to replenish the many thousands of skilled workers who emigrated after 1991 resulted in a sharp increase in the number of institutions of higher education in Kyrgyzstan. Most schools prepared people in the fashionable specialties of business, English, and accounting, leaving a shortfall nationally in the number of technicians and middle managers.

Until recently, wages in the Uzbek sector of the Ferghana Valley were deeply depressed, although not to the same levels as Tajikistan and Kyrgyzstan. With the economic upturn that began in 2006, average monthly wage nationally reached $300 (418,100 som) by the end of 2008.[39] However, these improvements did not suffice to prevent many Uzbeks, including large numbers from the Ferghana Valley, to seek work in Russia and Kazakhstan as migrant laborers, with all the ensuing social dislocations.

Data gathered by the State Committee for Statistics, the EU and UNDP provide a clear picture of the standard of living in the Ferghana provinces.[40] A surprising conclusion of these data is that rates of poverty in the Ferghana Valley, at least in comparison to the rest of the country, are relatively low, 15.8 percent as opposed to 25.8 percent. Only Tashkent has a lower overall average. Poverty rates are higher in the Ferghana cities than in the countryside, where gardens exist, with Andijan and Namangan showing 23.1 percent and 33.4 percent, respectively.

As in other sectors of the valley, poverty correlates with large numbers of children and low educational levels of household heads. Among impoverished families, only 8.8 percent of household heads completed higher education, and 25.2 percent finished secondary vocational training. New vocational-training schools have been built to address this problem. People in small towns where factories have been closed fall easily into poverty, as do those without land. The privatization of agricultural land brought to the surface the degree to which Soviet policy had pinned large numbers of workers to the land to prevent them from migrating to cities and fomenting urban unrest. Some 460,000 redundant farm workers were laid off in 2004 alone, with total farm employment falling by 25 percent. This occurred at a time when the overall workforce was increasing by 250,000 annually.

The fact that fully 60 percent of the poor are employed reflects the abundance of low-paying jobs in the Ferghana Valley and elsewhere.[41] Distorted unemployment statistics sow confusion, however, given that they record only 0.2 percent of the labor force as being officially registered as unemployed.

Migratory Labor and the Problem of Excess Labor

The large-scale migration of Central Asian labor abroad after independence is a consequence of the Soviet system's employment of millions in unnecessary and non-productive jobs. No sooner were these jobs exposed to market realities than they disappeared. Since 1989 Tajikistan has lost about 11 percent of its population. Around 4 percent of the Uzbek population, or one million people, have left the country. Kyrgyzstan has lost more than 7 percent of its population to labor migration.[42] Those leaving have gone mainly to Russia. The most recent data indicate a total out-migration of from 1.7 to 2.7 million workers from the three countries.[43] To be sure, the quarter-million Tajiks who fled during the civil war are included in these statistics.[44] Moreover, the motives of Uzbeks and Tajiks leaving for Kyrgyzstan may be ethnic or political,[45] and not purely economic. But economic causes, rather than local conflicts and issues, account for the decision of most migrants to leave.

A word of caution about the numbers is in order, inasmuch as labor migration in all three countries is largely extra-legal. Existing data on labor migration that is officially organized by the governments grossly underestimate migration as a whole. Thus, while Uzbekistan's Ministry of Labor and Social Welfare reports the number of people working outside the republic in 2005 as 262,900, survey data such as those assembled by S. Olimova suggest a total of between 800,000 and 2 million people.[46] Far more people than this are directly affected by migration, as one realizes from the fact that in 2007 fully 14 percent of households in the Kyrgyz Republic and 37 percent of households in Tajikistan sent one or more members to work abroad.[47]

Research on Tajikistan's Sokh region in 2006 produced vivid evidence of the impact of remittances in the Ferghana Valley. One out of five households in Sokh received payments from family members abroad. As a result, Sokh had the lowest poverty rates in Tajikistan's north, despite the fact that it is an Uzbek enclave within the territory of Tajikistan and suffers economically from the absence of a border agreement between the two countries.[48]

There are significant regional differentials on migration from the Ferghana Valley. For example, the outflow from Osh is far higher than from Jalalabad. Since most migrants work in the shuttle trade and construction, it is natural that urban areas produce more migrants.[49] Whatever their origin, migrant laborers go far afield, with Ferghana migrants traveling as far away as EU countries, the United States and Canada, Japan, South Korea, Turkey, Australia, China, and Afghanistan. It is estimated that 10,000 Kyrgyz citizens are currently working illegally in Britain.[50] However, in recent years the concentration of migrants in Russia has become overwhelming, with 97.6 percent of the total heading there by 2004.[51]

Wherever they are, such migrants, by their absence, help alleviate the problem of surplus labor at home. No wonder that the Tajik government recognizes labor migration as an essential element of the state's employment policy.[52] The possibility that Russia might need to attract as many as 15 million new workers in the next several years[53] suggests that the Ferghana Valley, with its high population density and excess labor, will have a ready outlet for reducing demographic pressures. Such numbers also presage mounting sums coming into the region from remittances, as well as jobs created locally by migrant entrepreneurs based abroad.[54] Arguably the main negative aspect of the migration process is that it denies to the Ferghana area thousands of its most energetic and ambitious young men, which in turn impacts on the character of the unemployed class left behind.

It is appropriate to think of Ferghana workers abroad as overseas extensions of the local economy. In 2008 remittances from migrant workers accounted for 43 percent of GDP in Tajikistan and 28 percent in the Kyrgyz Republic. Uzbekistan gained a solid $3.5 billion from remittances, which went not to the central government but to the local citizenry. The 2008–9 financial crisis was expected to decimate remittances by as much as a third, but the drop, while significant proved less than that.[55] However, an influx of unemployed returning migrants could create instability in the Ferghana region and elsewhere.[56]

Demographic Shifts and the Economy

Demographic changes in the three Ferghana countries inevitably will affect the economy of the valley. Birth rates are down in all three Ferghana countries: between 1998 and 2008 the rate of natural increase (per thousand) in Uzbekistan fell from 28.3 to 16, in Kyrgyzstan from 23.8 to 14, and in Tajikistan from 33 to 22.[57]

Analysis of population changes from 1989 to 2008 in the seven provinces of the Ferghana Valley shows that population growth was strongest in the Uzbek sector, with Namangan province increasing at 148.9. Despite the high birth rate in Tajikistan's Sughd province, population growth there was lower (134.4) than in other areas of the valley due, no doubt, to the impact of civil war.[58]

Whatever the differences among the three sectors, population growth in the Ferghana provinces of all three states far outstripped the rest of their countries. In Uzbekistan as a whole the increase from 1991 to 2008 was 30.6 percent but for the Ferghana provinces it was 36.2 percent,[59] with similar differentials occurring in Kyrgyzstan.

Acknowledging these differences, Ferghana's overall demographic evolution parallels the main trends in Central Asia as a whole. Changing definitions of cities makes it difficult to pinpoint levels of urbanization, but everywhere they have increased except in Tajikistan's Ferghana province of Sughd.[60] Birthrates declined everywhere, but then briefly increased, rising between 2007 and 2008 from 176.7 to 183.1. Since then birthrates have everywhere stabilized at moderate levels.[61] Mortality rates are higher in the Ferghana provinces than in the rest of the three countries (5.1 vs. 5.3), but with normal differences everywhere between urban and rural areas (6.3 vs. 4.6). Mortality is higher for males than females (5.1 vs. 4.5) but this, too, follows national norms. Similarly, increases in life expectancy (from 71 years in 1990 to 72.6 years in 2006) are typical of the region, as is the welcome improvement for men, from 67.9 to 70.7.

The valley's population is very unevenly distributed, with Andijan province in Uzbekistan claiming 582 persons per square kilometer, 9.5 times more than for Uzbekistan as a whole and the densest settlement in all Central Asia. By contrast, the Tajik sector has only 155.9 persons per square kilometer and the Kyrgyz sector a mere 30.9 persons per square kilometer. With respect to the age of the population, intra-Ferghana differences are more significant, with the Kyrgyz population much younger than Tajiks and Uzbeks. This is reflected in the ethnic composition of the valley. The proportion of Kyrgyz in Osh province rose from 56.7 percent in 1989 to 63.8 percent, with the percentage of Uzbeks remaining unchanged and the Russian population declining from 5.4 percent to 1.3 percent of the total. In Jalalabad province the percent of Kyrgyz grew from 60.9 percent to 70 percent during this period.

The most striking anomaly can be found in the Tajik sector of the valley, where population has declined sharply. Between 1991 and 2006 the population of Khujand decreased by 6 percent, Tagoshara by 41.3 percent, Kairakkum by 12.5 percent, and Chkalovsk by 42.8 percent. Only Isfara and Kanibadam experienced growth, but even there the process of de-urbanization advanced steadily, with the percentage of rural residents reaching 35.3 percent in Isfara, 30.1 percent in Kanibadam, and 33 percent in Sughd province as a whole. After the collapse of the Soviet

Union, more than 90 percent of the Russian-speaking population of the Ferghana provinces left the region.

The Ferghana Valley in the Global Financial Crisis

The financial crisis that began in 2008 and enveloped the entire world inevitably affected the Ferghana region, but its impact varied dramatically among the three Valley states. Particularly hard hit were world prices for such important local commodities as cotton, aluminum, and other raw materials, as well as remittances from migrant workers abroad.

Through a combination of good fortune and good planning, Uzbekistan weathered the crisis relatively well,[62] with the UNDP reporting stable growth for 2009,[63] compared to –4.2 percent for the Euro zone,[64] and a strong +7 percent thereafter, according to the IMF[65] On the eve of the crisis Uzbekistan could not have borrowed heavily even had it wished to do so, and its economy was therefore unleveraged when the crisis hit. At the same time, the government prudently insured private savings accounts, thus preventing runs on banks. Thanks to this, the Uzbek sector of the Ferghana Valley continued to experience moderate growth throughout the crisis, with 2009 production in Andijan province growing by 9.6 percent and in Namangan by 9.9 percent.[66]

Tajikistan's finances were also unleveraged on the eve of the crisis, but the economy was fragile and susceptible to external shocks.[67] Even in 2008 its GDP had fallen back to 73 percent of its 1990 level. Disagreements with Uzbekistan over water use at Tajikistan's Nurek hydroelectric plant caused an energy crisis in 2007–9, which cut the flow of electrical power to most of the national economy for all but a few hours a day. As a result, production of Tajikistan's chief export, aluminum, fell at precisely the time that the world price for aluminum was plummeting. This, along with a 30–40 percent decline in remissions from Tajiks working abroad, fomented a crisis that required assistance from the World Bank, IMF, and other international financial institutions and donors.[68]

Kyrgyzstan's external debt on the eve of the crisis amounted to more than 60 percent of GDP. The production of gold from a single mine, Kumtor, accounted for a quarter of GDP, but this source was being rapidly depleted. Russia stepped in with promised loans of $2 billion, aid totaling $150 million, and $180 million of debt forgiveness. But these measures did not counter the finanacial drain caused by large international purchases of grain and natural gas, and decreases in remittances from migrant workers abroad. The resulting crisis was felt particularly in already impoverished mountain areas like Naryn and in the south, notably the Ferghana region.

Prospects

Considering its ample natural resources and large pool of literate and skilled labor, the Ferghana Valley should by now have become a zone of exceptional prosperity. True, it has productive chemical, petrochemical, hydropower, automotive, food processing, and construction materials industries, and the valley is a world-class producer of cotton, silk, and vegetables. But the economies of both the Kyrgyz and Tajik sectors of the Ferghana Valley remain in deep crisis, and while Uzbekistan's Ferghana provinces have fared relatively better since independence, they still suffer from a severe shortage of remunerative jobs and overall are performing far below their potential.

Many factors contribute to these outcomes, but one in particular bears emphasis. Economic ties among the bordering areas in the region are very weak. The number of joint ventures between neighboring sectors of the Ferghana Valley is extremely low, and the region's potential for border trade, let alone transit trade, remains largely untapped. Few if any of the natural intra-regional synergies that could assure the valley's prosperity have been embraced, let alone exploited.

This will not change until the central authorities in all three countries delegate to local authorities sufficient powers of initiative to develop border trade, investment, and joint ventures, and to facilitate the movement of workers across the local borders. There is ample international experience in this area, and several of the most successful cases could serve as models for authorities in Bishkek, Dushanbe, and Tashkent as they seek to build up profitable cross-border economic ties. One of many obvious measures would be to provide citizens of neighboring regions in each country with identification cards that would enable them to trade and work in adjacent Valley areas. Such procedures are entirely compatible with strong sovereignties and the protection of secure borders. Enclave areas such as Chorsu, Vorukh, and Altyn-Topkan in Tajikistan, and Shakhimardan and Sokh in Kyrgyzstan suffer particularly from the absence of such arrangements, but so do citizens of the broader Ferghana provinces of the three countries.

Notes

1. *O'zbekiston milliy entsiklopediyasi*, vol. 9, Tashkent, 2005, p. 199.
2. "Poleznye iskopaemye," www.tajik-gateway.org/index.phtml?lang=ru&id=163.
3. The Jalalabad oblast is home to Toktogul, the region's largest hydroelectric generating reservoir, which has a storage capacity of more than 14 billion cubic meters, allowing for the long-term flow regulation of the Naryn/Syr Darya water system for irrigation in Uzbekistan and Kazakhstan.
4. "Narodnoe khoziaistvo SSSR v 1990 g.," *Finansy i statistika,* 1991, p. 12; *Uzbekistan v tsifrakh v 1990 godu: Kratkii statisticheskii sbornik,* Tashkent, 1991, p. 3.
5. Population Reference Bureau, 2009 World Population Data Sheet, www.prb.org/pdf09/09wpds_eng.pdf.
6. A.Kh. Khikmatova, ed., *Uzbekistan: desiat let po puti formirovaniia rynochnoi ekonomiki,* Tashkent, 2001, p. 23.
7. Richard Pomfret, "Sravnitelnyi analiz natsionalnykh strategii po sokrashcheniiu bednosti: Uzbekistan, Kazakhstan, Kyrgyzstan," *Economicheskoe obozrenie,* 1998.
8. Richard Pomfret, "Tsentralnaia Aziia: rezultaty ekonomicheskogo razvitiia," *Beyond Transition Newsletter,* October–December 2006.
9. According to the report by the Eurasian Economic Community: Economic Pull, www.evrazes.com.

10. Ibid.

11. A. Rakhmanova, *Integratsiia Kyrgyzstana v mezhdunarodnoe ekonomicheskoe soobshchestvo*, Bishkek, 2003, p. 180.

12. *O'zbekiston iqtisodiyoti mustaqillik yillarida: Ilmiy ommabop risola*, Tashkent, 2007, pp. 185–86.

13. Ibid.

14. N. Kh. Khonaliev, "Istoriia razvitiia i razmeshcheniia promyshlennosti Tadzhikistana v 1924–2005 gg.," Avtoreferat diss., Dushanbe, 2009.

15. Ibid.

16. "Doklad EBRR o protsesse perekhoda za 2006 g. Protsess perekhoda i pokazateli stran SNG i Mongolii," www.ebrd.com/downloads/research/transition/TR06r.pdf, p. 15.

17. www.bankir.uz/custom/banks.php.

18. Galina K. Saidova, "Osnovnye mery antikrizisnoi programmy Uzbekistana i ozhidaemyi effekt ot ee realizatsii," in *Mirovoi finansovo-ekonomicheskii krizis, puti i mery po ego preodoleniiu v usloviiakh Uzbekistana (po materialam knigi Prezidenta Respubliki Uzbekistan I. Karimova), Materialy mezhdonarodnoi nauchno-prakticheskoi konferentsii*, Tashkent, 2009, p. 12.

19. Perechen Bankov Respubliki Uzbekistan, www.bankir.uz/custom/banks.

20. Aksionerno-kommercheskii bank Khamkorbank, www.bankir.uz/custom/banks.php?bank=13.

21. Chastnyi Otkrytyi Aktsionerno-Kommercheskii Bank Universal, www.bankir.uz/custom/banks.php?bank=22.

22. "Bankovskaia sistema Kyrgyzstana," www.bankir.kg/ru/adres.

23. Natsionalnyi Bank Tadzhikistara, www.nbt.tj/?c=5&id=211&mode=blank.

24. Mezhgosudarstvennyi bank, *Sbornik tematicheskikh materialov. Po materialam XX zasedaniia Soveta rukovodielei tsentralnykh (natsionalnykh) bankov gosudarstv-uchastnikov EurAsEU*, www.dol.ru/users/isbnk/eaes/TEMA/20/TEMA_203.htm.

25. "2006 yil Qoraqalpog'iston Respublikasi budjeti, viloyatlar va Toshkent shahar mahalliy budjetlari daromadlari va xarajatlari hamda respublika budjetidan ajratiladigan dotatsiyalar cheklangan miqdori," www.mf.uz/?gb_3r=1&n=55.

26. I.R. Ubrokhimov, "Nalogovo-biudzhetnoe regulirovanie ekonomiki Tadzhikistana," Avtoreferat diss., Dushanbe, 2006, p. 12.

27. Klemens Greif, Martin Reiser, and Tashiaki Sakatrsume, "Barery na puti torgovli v Tsentralnoi Azii," www.uisrussia.msu.ru/docs/nov/beytrans/2006/4/all.pdf.

28. Ibid.

29. *Ekonomika Kyrgyzstana*, Bishkek, 2007, p. 303.

30. Ibid., p. 121.

31. Rustam A. Azimov, *Uzbekskaia model reformirovaniia i modernizatsii ekonomiki, ee effektivnost v predolenii posledstvii mirovogo finansovo-ekonomicheskogo krisisa*, Tashkent, 2009, p. 13.

32. Ibid.

33. *Regiony Tadzhikistana: Statisticheskii sbornik*, Dushanbe, 2001, p. 105; *Regiony Tazhikistana: Statisticheskii sbornik*, Dushanbe, 2007, p. 87.

34. Khonaliev, "Istoriia razvitiia i razmeshchenie promyshlennosti Tadzhikistana v 1924–2005 gg."

35. S.V. Golunov, ed., *Regionalnoe izmerenie transgranichnoi migratsii v Rossiiu*, Moscow, 2008, p. 92.

36. Gosudarstvennyi komitet statistiki *Tadzhikistan: 15 let gosudarstvennoi nezavisimosti*, Respubliki Tadzhikistan, Dushanbe, 2006, p. 133.

37. "Obnovlennaia otsenka bednosti v Tadzhikistane. Osnovnoi otchet," World Bank, 2004, p. 14.

38. *Otchet po obsledovaniiu neformalnoi zaniatosti v 4 pilotnykh raionakh Respebliki Tadzhikistan*, Dushanbe, 2002, p. 7.
39. *Dokhody i raskhody naseleniia. Ekonomika Uzbekistana. Informatsionno-analiticheskii obzor za 2008 god*, Tashkent, 2009, p. 73.
40. www.els.uz/index.php/ru/andijan-projekt.
41. *Strategiia povysheniia blagosostaianiia naseleniia Respubliki Uzbekistan. Polnyi dokument strategii na 2008–2010 goda*, Tashkent, 2007, p. 47.
42. *Human Development Report for Central Asia, 2004*, United Nations Development Programme, 2005, p. 161.
43. Ibid.
44. *Otchet po chelovecheskomu razvitiiu, Respublika Tadzhikistan*, United Nations Development Programme, 1995, pp. 49–50.
45. S. V. Golunov, *Regionalnoe izmerenie transgranichnoi migratsii v Rossiiu*, Moscow, 2008, p. 80.
46. S. Olimova, "Adaptatsiia trudovykh migrantov iz stran Tsentralnoi Azii v Rossiiu: rol obrazovaniia," in *Etnicheskaia situatsiia i konflikty v gosudarstvakh CIS i Baltii, Ezhegodnyi doklad Seti Etnologicheskogo monitoringa i rannego preduprezhdeniia konfliktov*, ed. V. Tishkov, E. Filippovoi, Moscow, 2006, p. 47.
47. S.V. Golunov, *Regionalnoe izmerenie*, p. 81.
48. Research on Uzbekistan's Sokh region in 2006 produced vivid evidence of the impact of remittances in the Ferghana Valley. One out of five households in Sokh received payments from family members abroad. As a result, Sokh had the lowest poverty rates, despite the fact that it is an Uzbek enclave within the territory of Kyrgyzstan and suffers economically from the absence of a border agreement between the two countries. See also *Strategiia povysheniia blagosostoianiia naseleniia*, p. 47.
49. "Trudovaia migratsiia v stranakh Tsentralnoi Azii, Rossiiskoi Federatsii, Afganistane i Pakistane," *Analiticheskii obzor*, Almaty, 2005.
50. E. Sadovskaia, "Formirovanie regionalnoi migratsionnoi sistemy," http://migrocenter.ru/publ/konfer/suzdal/m_suzdal02.php.
51. Golunov, *Regionalnoe izmerenie*, p. 83.
52. Ibid., p. 82.
53. "Rossiia budet zasasyvat naselenie Tsentralnoi Azii," www.prim.regnum.ru/news/892119.html.
54. Golunov, *Regionalnoe izmerenie*, p. 39.
55. M. Kakhan, "Sotsyalnye posledstviia globalnogo finansovo-ekonomicheskogo krizisa v Uzbekistane i puti ikh smiagcheniia," in *Mirovoi finansovo-jekonomicheskii krizis*, p. 61.
56. Ibid.
57. Goskomstat SSSR, *Naseleniia SSSR, 1988: Statisticheskii ezhegodnik,*Moscow, 1989, pp. 24–25, 61, 68–69l; www.stat.tj/russian/database1.htm; www.stat.kg/stat.files/tematika/; Population Reference Bureau. "2009 World Population Data Sheet," http://www.prb.org/pdf09/09wpds_eng.pdf.
58. Goskomstat SSSR, *Naseleniia SSSR, 1988*, pp. 24–25; http://www.stat.uz/demographic/; www.stat.tj/russian_database/socio/number_of_constant_population.xls.
59. Decree of the Cabinet of Ministers of Uzbekistan, March 13, 2009, no. 68, "O dopolnitelnykh merakh po sovershenstvovaniiu administrativno-territorialnogo ustroistva naselennykh punktov Respubliki Uzbekistan," *Sobranie zakonodatelstva Respubliki Uzbekistana*, Tashkent, 2009, p. 130.
60. Tug'ilganlar soni, www.stat.uz/STAT/index.php?%ru%&article=131.
61. Ibid.
62. Muhammad Keshavarzade et al., "Druzhba Koreia-Uzbekistan," in *Mirovoi finansovo-ekonomicheskii krizis.*

63. "The economic situation in the Economic Commission for Europe region: Europe, North America and the Commonwealth of Independent States in 2008–2009," United Nations, Geneva, July 6–31, 2009 http://www.un.org/regionalcommissions/crisis/ececis.pdf.

64. "OON: rost v Uzbekistane budet ustoichivym," www.gazeta.uz/2009/06/09/ecosoc/.

65. Materialy mezhdunarodnoi nauchno-prakticheskoi konferentsii, Tashkent, 2009, p. 113.

66. Osnovnye pokazateli sotsialno-ekonomicheskogo razvitiia Respubliki Uzbekistan v 2009 godu, www.stat.uz/STAT/index.php?%ru%&article=27.

67. *Krizis, vyzvannyi glubokimi kachestvennymi izmeneniiami v sisteme pri perekhode ego iz odnogo sostoianiia v drugoe*, Dushanbe, 2009.

68. Nuriddin Kaiumov, "Pervye uroki globalnogo ekonomicheskogo krizisa," in *Mirovoi finansovo-ekonomicheskii krizis*, pp. 143–44.

11

Land, Water, and Ecology

*Christine Bichsel (Switzerland), with
Kholnazar Mukhabbatov (Tajikistan) and
Lenzi Sherfedinov (Uzbekistan)*

As the preceding chapters have shown, the different ecological zones of the Ferghana Valley have been used for agriculture and animal husbandry over many centuries.[1] The lowlands and plains have been the sites of irrigated agriculture for millennia. Their arid, continental climate necessitates the supply of additional water, which always has been drawn from the Syr Darya and its tributaries. Traditionally, the plains were inhabited by sedentary populations, with the foothills and mountain zones devoted to pastures and animal husbandry.

Technical innovation and agricultural expansion during the second half of the twentieth century brought the foothills into the range of irrigated agriculture. Customarily, they were the realm of permanent nomads or of peoples who practiced seasonal migration. However, a long process of converting these peoples to a sedentary way of life, which the policies of the tsarist Russian Empire and the Soviet Union intensified, has changed the lifestyle of these populations. As previous chapters have pointed out, agriculture and animal husbandry never have been mutually exclusive practices in the Ferghana Valley, but frequently were, and are, complementary and closely interrelated strategies for earning a livelihood. Hence, it is useful to focus on the history of irrigated agriculture in the Ferghana Valley, which is central to the region's social, economic, and political development,[2] inasmuch as the valley currently accounts for 45 percent of the total irrigated area within the Syr Darya basin.[3]

A Historical Overview of Irrigation in the Ferghana Valley

Irrigated agriculture may date back as far as the end of the Paleolithic and the beginning of the Neolithic eras. In its early days, it was practiced exclusively in the lowlands in proximity to rivers. At that time, people made use of naturally formed estuaries that were regularly flooded.[4] The building of additional canals may date back as early as the Copper and Bronze ages. This coincided with the emergence of early polities in the Ferghana Valley based on irrigation communities in proximity to rivers (see Chapter 1). For a long time, irrigation techniques involved building radial canals starting out from rivers in order to expand the area irrigated naturally by flooding. A limitation of this technique was that the amount and time of water delivery depended entirely on the flow of water in the river.

During the late eighteenth and early nineteenth centuries irrigation systems were upgraded and refined. This occurred mainly around major urban centers, in particular Kokand and Namangan. As discussed in Chapter 2, the Kokand Khanate also opened up new land for irrigated agriculture in the southeast of the Ferghana Valley, thereby permanently settling formerly nomadic populations there. This was achieved by building the first major canal, the Shakhrikhansai, which remained the biggest one in the Ferghana Valley until the 1940s.[5]

Soviet rule brought about significant changes to the system of irrigated agriculture in the Ferghana Valley. The early Soviet period focused on linking up the manifold but geographically separated irrigation areas and their respective water sources, thereby reducing local dependence on the water flows of any specific river. The capstone of this endeavor was the construction of the Great Ferghana Canal in the late 1930s, to draw water from the Naryn River. Further large canals built during this period were the South Ferghana Canal as an extension of the Shakrikhansai, and the North Ferghana Canal, also drawing water from the Naryn River.[6] Large-scale infrastructure development thus considerably amplified the scale of the irrigation network by regulating the flow and transportation of water over long distances.[7] By means of this technical innovation, the total area of irrigated agriculture in the Ferghana Valley expanded from 530,000 hectares in 1930 to 650,000 in 1950.[8] The primary aim of this expansion was to increase cotton production which, as discussed in Chapter 3, already had been pursued by the tsarist colonizers beginning in the 1860s.

The irrigation network received particularly large financial and technological investments during the rule of Khrushchev (1953–64) and Brezhnev (1964–82). The main aim of these investments was to expand further the area that could be used for cotton. This entailed extending and widening the major canals in order to irrigate such hitherto uncultivated areas as the central Ferghana steppe. To this end, the government enlarged the Great Ferghana Canal between 1953 and 1962 and in 1964, and constructed the Great Andijan Canal from 1966 to 1970.

Starting from this period, irrigated agriculture also expanded upwards and outwards from the plains to the foothills. This was supported by the building between 1970 and 1976 of the Great Namangan Canal.[9] Given the topography of the foothill zone, such expansion required the installation of pumps to supplement those canals operating by gravity.[10] Furthermore, the building of seasonal and multi-year storage reservoirs and dams was undertaken to support this expansion, and at the same time reduce exposure to draught-related seasonal and annual variations in water reserves. This gave rise to the reservoirs at Toktogul in Kyrgyzstan, Kairakkum in Tajikistan, and Andijan in Uzbekistan. As a consequence of these investments, the irrigated area of the Uzbekistan sector of the Ferghana Valley between 1950 and 1985 increased by a third.[11]

Irrigated agriculture in the Ferghana Valley was part and parcel of a complex system of regional economic specialization within the Soviet system. With cotton being a strategic priority, Soviet leaders designated the lion's share of the Syr Darya River's flow for cotton production in downstream areas. The Soviet Union, like the Russian Empire before it, encouraged domestic cotton production because it fostered economic independence from other suppliers and provided a commodity that could be sold on the world market for hard currency. The Soviet Union therefore strongly promoted this seasonally water-intensive crop in the agriculturally and ecologically suitable lowlands of the Uzbek and Tajik republics, and further downstream in the Kazakh republic. Conversely, Soviet planners resolved that the strategic priority in Kyrgyzia was animal husbandry, with a focus on meat and milk products that could be exported to other republics. In addition, Kyrgyz agriculture focused on the growing of rain-fed fodder.

Despite this regional specialization, the Ferghana Valley under Soviet rule maintained close economic relations across the lines of republics. Long-term lease agreements enabled state and collective farms in the Uzbek republic to pasture their animals in neighboring Kyrgyzstan.[12] Conversely, such agreements bestowed usufruct rights to the Kyrgyz SSR to access irrigated land in the plains across the border in the Uzbek SSR.

In the same spirit, water intake and storage facilities were built to serve the irrigation needs of areas beyond republican borders. The most conspicuous example of this in the Ferghana Valley is the Toktogul Reservoir on the Naryn River. Built in the 1970s on the territory of Kyrgyzstan, it was designed to provide seasonal and multi-year water storage to increase the availability of water for irrigation in the Uzbek and Kazakh republics, as well as to regulate the distribution of water downstream in the Syr Darya River basin. Each year the reservoir stored water between October and March, then released it during the agricultural season extending from April to September. As was common with reservoirs in the USSR, a hydroelectric plant was constructed at the same time, enabling Toktogul to generate hydropower as a kind of by-product of its water management function. In exchange, the energy needs of the Kyrgyz Republic were met by importing electricity and/or natural gas, coal, and oil for its thermal power plants from the downstream republics in Central Asia and from more distant Soviet republics.[13] Thanks to these arrangements, the Toktogul reservoir, as part of a highly integrated economic network, became the key element in large-scale cotton growing in Uzbekistan and Tajikistan.[14]

A highly centralized system of management directed the extensive irrigation network in the Ferghana Valley during the late Soviet times. In 1946 the management of water usage was concentrated in the Ministry of Land Reclamation and Water Resources (Minvodkhoz).[15] Working in conjunction with the ministries of Agriculture and Energy, this ministry regulated the distribution of the Syr Darya River's water. Minvodkhoz was also in charge of massive projects to open up new irrigated land, as well as of construction and maintenance of infrastructure in the Ferghana Valley and elsewhere.[16] It enjoyed near-monopoly control over irriga-

256

Figure 11.1 **Irrigation in the Ferghana Valley, 1928**

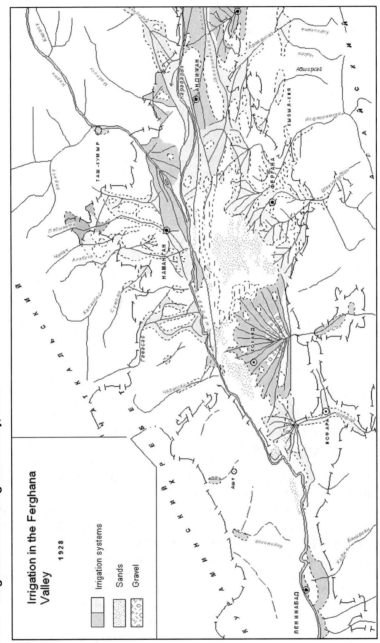

Source: E.M. Beniaminovich and D.K Tersitskii, eds., *Irrigatsiia Uzbekistana*, Tashkent, 1975, vol. 2.

Figure 11.2 **Irrigation in the Ferghana Valley, 1972**

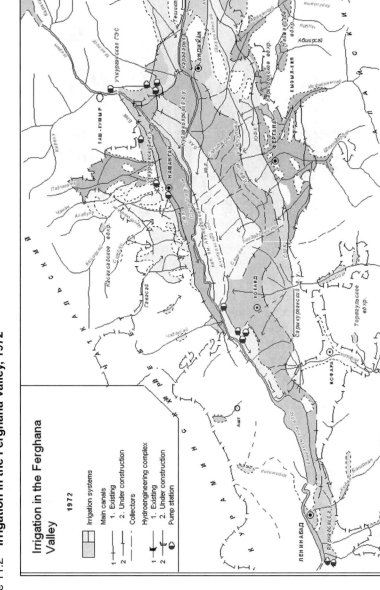

Source: E.M. Beniaminovich and D.K Tersitskii, eds., *Irrigatsiia Uzbekistana*, Tashkent, 1975, vol. 2.

Figure 11.3 **Irrigated Area in Uzbekistan's Sector of the Ferghana Valley Between 1924 and 1990** (in hectares)

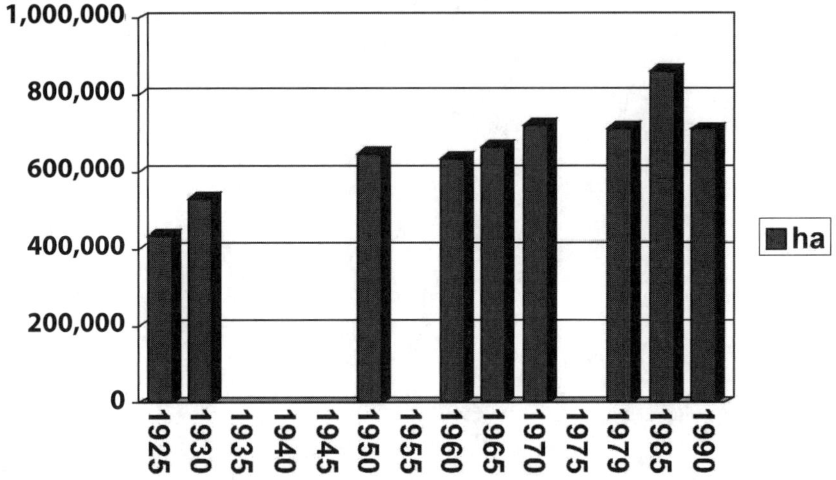

Source: Adapted from Thurman (1999). See note 5.

tion, since the law assigned to it the functions of planner, builder, and consumer. Accordingly, it had at its disposal considerable funds, which naturally bestowed on it substantial political power.

In an effort to address the manifest shortcomings of this centralized and monopolistic management structure, Soviet leaders in 1986 established river basin authorities (RBAs) for both the Syr Darya and Amu Darya rivers, and devolved some responsibilities to these new bodies. The irrigation network in the Ferghana Valley fell under the authority of the Syr Darya RBA based in Tashkent.[17]

Under the aegis of Minvodkhoz, irrigation in the Ferghana Valley took a scientific turn and became the domain of engineering. The Soviet Union invested heavily in data collection, research, and project design. Specialists at the Central Asian Scientific Institute for Irrigation in Tashkent (SANIIRI) greatly advanced irrigation engineering and improved hydrometry in Central Asia. Water distribution began to follow highly standardized schedules set at republic, province and district levels (so-called hydromodules), with each of them depending on local climates and soil types.[18] Minvodkhoz also developed a network of training centers, its own technical schools and, most notably, the Tashkent Institute of Engineers for Irrigation and the Mechanization of Agriculture (TIIIMSKh). By the 1970s, these institutions produced large numbers of irrigation engineers and specialists on water management. Finally, Minvodkhoz invested heavily in the development of technology and advanced the mechanization of irrigation.[19]

The expansion of irrigation and intensified agriculture did not come without costs. Already during the 1970s it became apparent that the huge investments had not increased the efficiency of water use in Central Asia. Water loss from unlined canals was huge, and inappropriate irrigation practices led to the excessive application of water on fields.[20] Moreover, the new Soviet methods of cotton production, which called for considerable mechanical power and large amounts of chemicals, required more water than before. So also did the porous soils of the foothills onto which irrigated agriculture had expanded.[21]

These problems culminated in the well-publicized disaster of the Aral Sea. Owing to the withdrawal of high volumes of water from its tributaries, the Aral Sea rapidly shrank from the 1960s on. By 1989, it had suffered a 41 percent decrease in its surface area and a 67 percent decrease in volume, as compared to 1960.[22] Finally, although ample funds had been devoted to the construction of irrigation infrastructure, almost nothing was spent on maintaining it. It was estimated that by 1985 irrigation networks on over 90 percent of the sown area in the Uzbek part of the Ferghana Valley needed repair. As a consequence, by 1990 the total area of irrigated land had shrunk to levels of the 1970s.[23]

Soviet leaders based their approach to the use of land and water on the slogan, "the great transformation of nature,"[24] refashioning the environment as was deemed necessary to maximize industrial production and enhance national security. It often has been pointed out that this effort to maximize output while ignoring long-term environmental costs had a profoundly negative impact on the ecology of the Ferghana Valley and other regions. It would, however, be wrong to assume that Soviet leaders had no concern for environmental protection or the conservation of natural resources. But more often than not, responsibility for the conservation of resources was assigned to the same institutions responsible for their exploitation, which was the case above all with the monopolistic Minvodkhoz.[25] Moreover, the Soviet Union's top-down approach to water management left users with little or no recourse against errors.

During the Gorbachev era environmentalists pushed for reforms in agriculture. Members of the Uzbek Writers' Union, for example, demanded that Soviet leaders reduce the area devoted to the cultivation of cotton, and seek other sources of water in order to mitigate the shrinking of the Aral Sea.[26] However, the last years before the disintegration of the Soviet Union were a time of deepening economic turmoil that excluded the possibility of such action.[27]

Contested Links Among Water, Energy, and Political Independence

With the disintegration of the Soviet Union in 1991, the formerly integrated system of economic management collapsed. Each of the five newly independent Central Asian states now had to face alone the environmental consequences of Soviet irrigation practices, and was left to its own devices in restructuring the heretofore centralized water management system. The Ferghana Valley's highly integrated network of large irrigation canals and reservoirs now was parceled out among the three successor states that inherited parts of the basin. Kyrgyzstan, Tajikistan, and

Uzbekistan, along with Kazakhstan, somehow had to attend to the management of the Syr Darya's water.

Independence led to the establishment of national water management organizations, with each country establishing its own ministries and departments to supervise water resources. Thus, Kyrgyzstan formed the Ministry of Agriculture, Water Management, and Processing Industries. Within that ministry, a Department of Water Management was placed in charge of irrigation.[28] Here and elsewhere in Central Asia the new ministries retained many of the Soviet organizational structures, and even the USSR's laws governing the allocation of water. Yet the newly independent states faced drastically reduced funding, leaving water management organizations with declining salary pools, shrunken operating budgets, and little money for equipment.[29]

These difficulties, along with concerns over the efficiency of water usage, prompted the new states to introduce cost-recovery measures and "irrigation management transfer," which they did to varying degrees. Cost-recovery measures were built on the new affirmation that water was no longer a free good, as had been the case under the USSR's socialist system, but should be compensated for with an irrigation service fee. "Irrigation management transfers" devolved water management and even the ownership of tertiary irrigation infrastructures to local water users, thereby attempting to increase their rights and responsibilities. This involved the creation of Water User Associations (WUAs),[30] in line with fundamental changes in land ownership, specifically the restructuring or dismantling of the former state and collective farms and the privatization of agricultural production.[31]

The disintegration of the Soviet Union necessitated the establishment of new supra-national institutions for managing the water resources of Central Asia. First, the Almaty Agreement of 1992 established the Interstate Commission for Water Coordination (ICWC) as the highest decision-making body for all matters pertaining to the regulation, efficient use, and protection of interstate watercourses and bodies of water.[32] The ICWC consists of leading water officials from each of the five countries; these officials meet several times annually to set allocations and quotas and to resolve disputes. The ICWC operates through four executive bodies: the Syr Darya River RBA, the Amu Darya RBA, the Scientific Information Center (SIC) and the Secretariat. The RBAs deal with technical aspects of actual water distribution among the states in the respective basin. The SIC prepares analyses for the ICWC and is responsible for conservation issues. A Secretariat facilitates the work of the ICWC.[33]

The end of the centralized Soviet system of water management also necessitated new agreements among the new Central Asian states to regulate the Syr Darya and Amu Darya. The initial Almaty Agreement signed in 1992 by all Central Asian states established joint ownership and management of the region's water resources, while retaining national control over crops, industrial goods, and electric power generated by their use. It also stressed the need for cooperation among the riparian states.[34] A number of additional agreements followed, some of them pertaining to all Central Asia and others to specific rivers. Most relevant for the Ferghana Valley are the annual agreements, reached in 1995 and subsequent years, among Syr Darya River riparian states concerning the allocation of water and energy. These were then folded into the Syr Darya Framework Agreement for 1998–2003, which confirmed the states' commitment to common solutions and involved efforts to balance upstream needs for energy with downstream needs for water.[35] This framework agreement would be extended for a further five years.

It goes without saying that the new states are all complex entities, and their positions on specific issues should neither be personified nor treated in isolation from each other. Neither the processes of domestic reform nor inter-state negotiations have turned out to be smooth or predictable. Thus, the parliamentary debates in Kyrgyzstan which preceded the final passage of the "Law on the Interstate Use of Water Objects, Water Resources, and Water Management Installations" were intense, with experts disagreeing among themselves. This law asserted that water possesses economic value, that it is owned by the state, and that neighbors should compensate the government of Kyrgyzstan for providing it.[36] Similarly, Central Asian water experts have engaged in controversies over water quotas, the responsibilities of inter-state water management institutions, and other issues over the course of many rounds of workshops and conferences.[37] Some experts from Kyrgyzstan charge that the ICWC, owing to its institutional setup and location in Uzbekistan, is biased in favor of downstream countries;[38] these countries in turn respond that their upstream neighbors are preventing reasonable solutions beneficial to everyone. There is also a clash of views between some local and international experts, as shown by the controversy over the role of international law in Central Asian water management addressed in two articles of the *New York University Environmental Law Journal*.[39] These political controversies lie beyond the scope of this chapter; instead it focuses on the three main claims concerning the Syr Darya River, which the new states have advanced, and which continue to persist.

These differing positions pertain to the seasonal distribution and territorial allocation of water in the Syr Darya basin, and the economic value or price to be assigned to it. A first disagreement between upstream and downstream countries concerns the seasonal distribution of water across the Ferghana Valley. The major point of contention is the operation of the Toktogul Reservoir and the related hydroelectric plant. The disintegration of the Soviet Union placed great stress on the existing system of inter-republican compensation for water and energy. The newly independent downstream countries experienced difficulties in regularly providing Kyrgyzstan with cheap gas for its thermal power plants, and later raised prices. Kyrgyzstan, for its part, experienced chronic electrical outages in winter, and in the early 1990s began to release more water from the Toktogul Reservoir during that season to drive its hydroelectric generators.[40] But by providing for its own heating and lighting needs in winter, Kyrgyzstan reduces the quantity of water available to Uzbekistan for irrigating its sector of the Ferghana Valley in the spring and summer. At the same time, Kyrgyzstan's releases of water in wintertime repeatedly have flooded downstream areas, since only a part of the quantity can be held in such facilities as the Kairakkum Reservoir on the border in Tajikistan. Uzbekistan often has complained about the damage caused by winter flooding and demands that water should be released mainly in summer so as to prevent flooding and sustain irrigated crops.[41]

A second dispute concerns the economic value of water provided across national borders. Since independence, Kyrgyzstan has been neither willing nor able to assume the total financial burden of operating and maintaining the Toktogul dam and hydroelectric station and regulating the flow of water into the Naryn River and hence the Syr Darya, especially since it is mainly the downstream countries that benefit from these operations. Kyrgyzstan therefore seeks compensation from the downstream countries. The annual cost to Kyrgyzstan of maintaining the Toktogul reservoir and related infrastructure amounts to an estimated US$15–25 million. Until 2002, Uzbekistan and Kazakhstan did not contribute to the cost of maintaining and operating this facility.

Rising gas prices and the shift to a more market-oriented economy have prompted Kyrgyzstan's lawmakers to re-evaluate the value of water as a resource. As noted above, they argue that the Syr Darya waters flowing from Kyrgyzstan bring considerable economic benefit to the downstream countries, thanks to irrigated agriculture. Therefore, they seek to place a specific value or price on water and to charges users for what they receive from Kyrgyzstan.[42] Uzbekistan to date has been critical of this notion, questioning whether water can be owned by any country and whether it should be treated as an economic good at all. Moreover, Uzbekistan asserts that because Kyrgyzstan provides no "value added" to the water flowing from its territory, it is hardly justified in asking financial compensation for it.[43]

A third point of contention concerns the apportionment of water from the Syr Darya River and the quantity to which the respective riparian countries are entitled. Kyrgyzstan contests the old Soviet inter-republican quotas, which designated the lion's share of the Syr Darya's water to Uzbekistan and Kazakhstan. With the 1992 Almaty Agreement on Water Resources, the new states confirmed that they would continue to observe the existing quotas for the time being, but did not foreclose possible changes later. The Agreement assigned 51.7 percent of the river flow to Uzbekistan, 38.1 percent to Kazakhstan, 9.2 percent to Tajikistan, and only 1 percent to Kyrgyzstan.[44] The Kyrgyz claim that this arrangement effectively barred them from developing irrigated agriculture during the Soviet period, and denied them the economic benefit that would have come from doing so. Kyrgyzstan therefore seeks to correct what it sees as a historical injustice by claiming enough water to develop self-sustaining and market-based irrigated agriculture. However, this runs directly counter to plans by Uzbekistan, Kazakhstan, and Tajikistan, all of which wish to expand and modernize their own irrigated agriculture.

To summarize, the various post-Soviet agreements may have brought into daylight the complex water and energy issues at stake in the Ferghana Valley and in Central Asia as a whole, while giving rise to a more open dialogue about them. However, they have neither resolved these disputes nor foreclosed further controversies. Indeed, public allegations of breaches of the agreements are now a common feature of these disputes. In an acknowledgment of this, actual water and energy transfers between upstream and downstream countries are largely carried out through annual barter agreements for fuel and water that take place prior to each new irrigation and heating season.

Thus far, the focus has been on disputes over water and energy among the successor states following the disintegration of the Soviet Union. However, no less serious tensions over water can arise *within* states, for the distribution of water also strains relations between provinces and districts within all the countries of the Ferghana Valley. For example, Uzbekistan's downstream province of Khorezm has repeatedly blamed the upstream provinces of Surkhandarya and Bukhara for worsening its water shortages.[45] In the specific case of the Ferghana Valley, a number of more local conflicts over water and land have real significance, and as such require our attention.

Inter-Group Conflicts over Water and Land

With regard to conflicts over water, Eric Sievers writes, "As the Syr Darya basin contains the Ferghana Valley, which is the most sensitive part of modern Central Asia in terms of ethnic violence, it presents a special case of conflict."[46] He suggests that scarcity of water and strained inter-ethnic relations could lead to violent conflict in the Ferghana Valley. Indeed, many water users have faced a declining access to water and greater uncertainties over its delivery after independence. The changing seasonal patterns of water distribution and the effects of the always-inefficient and now dilapidated infrastructure, described above, have affected the situation. Moreover, the Ferghana Valley is one the most densely populated areas in all Central Asia. Its population continues to grow rapidly, further increasing pressure on water, land and other natural resources. Finally, along with other areas of Central Asia, parts of the Ferghana Valley experienced a rapid social and economic decline following independence. Further economic deprivation—possibly arising from a scarcity of water—could, for a population overwhelmingly dependent on irrigated agriculture, expose the Ferghana Valley to violence, as Sievers suggests.

Conflicts over the distribution of water are a frequent occurrence in the irrigated sections of the Ferghana Valley. On the southern side of the valley, tensions tend to be focused in springtime, when the flow of the glacier-fed rivers has not yet filled the canals to capacity.[47] At that moment, however, the agricultural season already has begun and demand for water is high. During this time, there may not be enough water available to cover all needs, and thus relationships among water users grow strained. Most of the Ferghana Valley irrigation systems are gravity-operated, which means that nearly all conflicts occur between upstream and downstream users. With independence, more erratic water supply and accentuated differences in access to water between upstream and downstream users appear to have increased competition for water during the springtime. As a result of this spatial arrangement, conflict parties tend to be based on territorial or residential affiliation rather than along ethnic or kinship lines, although these categories may frequently overlap.

Water sources are contested particularly when rivers or canals transect the new international borders and are thus subject to inter-state agreements. Since the early 1990s Kyrgyzstan has claimed a larger share of the Syr Darya water flow in order to expand its agriculture. In the southern part of the Ferghana Valley, this has entailed revising the allocation of water from several rivers and even springs. For example, during the Soviet period 69 percent of the Shakhimardansai River's flow was allocated to the Uzbek SSR, as compared with 21 percent for the Kyrgyz SSR (the remaining 10 percent was attributed to "water losses"). After the disintegration of the Soviet Union Kyrgyzstan claimed, and sometimes simply appropriated, more water. Finally, in 2001 the Departments of Water Resources in Kyrgyzstan and Uzbekistan agreed that the water of the river should be divided equally between them. Similar claims have been made on other rivers and sources, with several of these ending in agreement. In some cases, changed allocations that benefit upstream users have left downstream users discontented over their reduced supply of water. It is tempting to attribute these conflicts to the inevitable disputes arising over the imposition of new inter-state borders where previously they had not existed. However, it is at least as valid to suggest that these disputes should be understood as the fallout from long-term economic shifts occurring in the region, the character and final dimensions of which are not yet fully evident.

As a general rule, Uzbek and Tajik groups in the Ferghana plains have a far longer history of agricultural production and sedentary lifestyles than the Kyrgyz, most of whom practiced animal husbandry and pursued a nomadic or transhumant existence in the foothills and premontane zones. However, as earlier chapters have noted, there were constant interactions between these two modes of production and lifestyles, with no clear-cut boundaries established between them. But with the 1924 Soviet project of national-territorial delimitation, these socio-economic distinctions became territorialized. Thus, they served as a basis for establishing the political-administrative divisions of the Ferghana Valley in the Uzbek, Tajik, and Kyrgyz SSRs. The borderlines of the Ferghana Valley represented not only the territory of newly established Soviet nationalities, but to some extent follow the territorial distinction between different socio-economic practices such as irrigated agriculture and animal husbandry (see Chapter 4).

Soviet regional economic specialization accentuated these territorialized socio-economic distinctions. For example such specialization fostered irrigated agriculture in the form of cotton production in the Uzbek SSR and animal husbandry in the form of meat and milk production in the Kyrgyz SSR. Yet other Soviet actions undermined them. The effort to relocate and permanently resettle nomadic populations and the expansion of the zone of irrigated agriculture into the foothills had precisely this effect. With independence, the disintegration of the big state farms that produced meat and milk in the Kyrgyz sector, and the subsequent privatization of land, led many Kyrgyz to turn to private agriculture for their livelihoods. Today, Kyrgyz, Uzbek, and Tajiks in the foothills all mix animal husbandry and agriculture. This has had the effect of further increasing the demand for both land and water in the foothills of the Ferghana Valley.

But it also has brought about new claims for water and land in the foothills, with the competing interests drawn along geographic and economic lines as much as on the basis of ethnic distinctions. Thus, conflicts over water and land are also driven by territorial claims pertaining to the as yet undelineated borders in the Ferghana Valley. Although the current de facto borderline is unlikely to undergo major changes resulting from the process of delimitation, many sections of the border are still contested among the three countries. Final decisions on the borderline may be influenced by the form of land use and the identities of peoples using specific sections. A consequence of the national-territorial delimitation, of regional economic specialization, and of the overall expansion of irrigated agriculture in the Ferghana Valley is to generate conflicting territorial claims among the new countries. These tensions tend to be concentrated in the irrigation systems in the foothills. While such claims existed throughout the Soviet period,[48] they acquire a new dimension with the nation-building processes post-independence.

In sum, competition over water and land in the Ferghana Valley occurs not just because these are scarce resources. Both are connected with economic and social modes that define people's lives and distinguish them from others, and which become particularly relevant as new nation-states come into being and consolidate these new economic and moral attachments.

Challenges to Livelihoods and the Environment

Soviet agriculture, like the Soviet economy as a whole, was based on an extensive exploitation of resources. In practice, this meant that the way to increase production was to increase all relevant inputs, not to extract more yield from the same inputs. In agriculture this entailed increasing the area of land under cultivation, and the volume of water available to irrigate it. In the Ferghana Valley since 1950, increased agricultural production—mainly of cotton—brought about a degradation of both land and water resources. Independence has not rectified this problem, and some existing irrigation practices are worsening the region's soil and water quality all the more.

Across the Syr Darya basin and in large sections of the Ferghana Valley, soil salinization is a growing problem, resulting from the expansion of irrigation into lands with high salt content and poor drainage. Two types of salinization must be noted. On-site salinization occurs when salts already in the substrata or groundwater are mobilized within the water table; this is particularly common in the Ferghana Valley. Off-site salinization occurs when drainage systems return salts to rivers, from which they are then drawn downstream.[49] Because the drainage system of the Syr Darya basin was designed to lead water back into the rivers, this, too, is common in the Syr Darya, although its impact is particularly felt further downstream.[50] Salinity negatively affects crop yields, as it reduces the ability of plants to absorb water and therefore inhibits their growth. It also may have negative health effects on both humans and livestock.[51] Salinity continues to be high in the central part of the Ferghana Valley, where there is also considerable soil contamination from chemical agents.[52]

The Ferghana Valley is also plagued by waterlogging. This happens when irrigation systems apply excessive amounts of water to inadequately drained land, causing rising groundwater tables. Because waterlogging compacts the subsoil, it may reduce yields. There is a link between salinization and waterlogging, as farmers often apply ever-greater quantities of water to fields with high salinity in order to flush out the salt. Besides wasting water, this practice also leads to further rises in the water tables. Waterlogging also can damage buildings, creating damp conditions that are injurious to human health. By lifting water tables, it also may contaminate drinking water with bacteria, salts, and agrochemicals, and cause polluted runoff water and drainage from irrigation to mix with aquifers from which household drinking water is drawn.[53] Tensions have arisen in the southern part of the Ferghana Valley over alleged waterlogging of downstream areas by upstream users. Tajikistan particularly suffers from high water tables caused by a combination of intensive irrigation, insufficient drainage, and leaking reservoirs.[54]

The use of chemical fertilizers and pesticides has contaminated both water and soil in the Ferghana Valley, as have chemical industries and hazardous waste. Even as the Soviet Union focused on large-scale cotton production in the Ferghana Valley, it established a number of substantial industrial enterprises there. Most were mining or processing industries producing metals, oil, gas, chemicals, and textiles. With the death of the Soviet economy, most of these industries either have drastically reduced their operations or closed their doors. Untreated tailings and accumulated pollutants abounded, some of them near enough to water sourses and towns as to endanger human health. In the northern part of the Ferghana Valley there are a number of plants for mining uranium or processing radioactive waste. At the Mailuu-Suu uranium mine there is a danger of radioactive soils being washed further into the Syr Darya basin, and thus polluting the water and land of large numbers of people. In the southern Kyrgyz part of the Ferghana Valley there are a large antimony plant at Kadamjai, a mercury plant in Aidarken, and the former lead mine at Kant. Tailing dumps and mud storage ponds with leaking protective dams threaten to contaminate water and soil at all three locations.[55]

Even before 1991 most of the irrigation canals and pumps, and nearly the entire drainage systems for the Ferghana Valley, were in need of rehabilitation. The successor states took on this problem as a kind of unpaid debt from the past. While they assumed responsibility for maintaining the primary canals and reservoirs, to a large extent they have parceled out maintenance of the on-farm infrastructure to the water users. In Kyrgyzstan and Tajikistan this was done through a formal process of privatization, which transferred on-farm infrastructure to irrigation communities, or if they existed, to WUAs.[56] While in Uzbekistan this has not been done de jure, the actual practice is that any water user who wants the infrastructure to remain operational must clean and repair it on his own.[57]

Ill-maintained infrastructure thus became a burden not only to the new governments but also to irrigation communities to whose responsibility or even property the infrastructure has been devolved, and who generally have limited funds to carry out repairs. Julia Bucknall suggests that this may create a vicious circle in which a reduced water supply gives rise to falling income, which means fewer funds for repairs and hence even less available water.[58] This is particularly the case for the foothills, which entered the system of irrigated land only with the expenditure of enormous funds from the central government of the USSR. However, the porous soil of the foothills requires more water than do fields on the plains. Because of this, the productivity of water and hence the return on investments in these zones is significantly lower than in the plains, which leaves less money for essential maintenance.

The challenge to maintain somehow the irrigation infrastructure is both a cause and effect of the difficult socio-economic circumstances of many Ferghana Valley residents. Poverty is generally a rural phenomenon in Central Asia, where 80–90 percent of the poor depend on agriculture and animal husbandry for their livelihoods.[59] This is also true for the Ferghana Valley, where rural dwellers constitute roughly 70 percent of the total.[60] This highlights the reality that disputes over the inter-state allocation of water resources, far from being merely dry arguments waged among diplomats, actually determine the economic fate of many people in the Ferghana Valley. Poor households lack the funds to shift to other lines of work and therefore depend all the more on irrigated agriculture to sustain them. This prompts Bucknall, in the same work cited above, to suggest that investments to prevent further deterioration of the irrigation infrastructure benefit the poor even more than larger-scale farmers, so greatly do the former depend on irrigation for their existence.[61] To be sure, poverty is linked as much with soil fertility as with access to water.[62] Yet water remains, as always, the *sine qua non* of agrarian life in the Ferghana Valley.

Post-Soviet institutional changes have highlighted the many and complex power relationships which affect the distribution of water. Processes of redistribution or privatization allowed well-placed individuals and groups to capture the most productive land within irrigation systems. Furthermore, individuals may use their social position to influence, or even bribe, water authorities to upgrade their water supply to the detriment of poorer water users.[63] Such rural inequalities are also institutionalized. Thurman notes that joint stock companies in Uzbekistan are often the first to receive water, followed by private farm enterprises and then individual peasant farms.[64] In all three countries private garden plots are generally the lowest priority when irrigation water is being allocated. However, those same plots are crucial to the welfare of large numbers of families. Since these same poorer families are less able than their wealthier neighbors to lease additional land, the process easily becomes self-reinforcing, especially in the Tajik and Uzbek sectors of the valley. Finally, irrigation is the very foundation of the complex political economy of cotton in Uzbekistan and Tajikistan. Any change in the irrigation system directly affects the lives of the countless subsistence laborers who grow and harvest the cotton, no less than the local or provincial elites who speak publicly in behalf of the industry and benefit handsomely from its successes.[65]

International Involvements and Local Actors

Immediately after the Central Asian countries gained their independence in 1991, a large number of international aid agencies rushed into the region with projects and funding (see Chapter 14). Most such assistance aimed to foster privatization, economic liberalization, and democratization. Such a focus entailed the hope of correcting the "mis-development" wrought by state socialism in many spheres.[66] The goal was not merely to institute discrete projects but to help governments develop and implement comprehensive strategies to reform governance and foster economic growth in specific sectors, among them water management.[67]

A prime concern of early international engagement was to ensure that the new states avoid conflict over water, and instead seek more cooperative modes of engaging with the issue. A further concern was the shrinking of the Aral Sea and its adverse impact on humans and the environment. Efforts were geared to mitigating the disaster and to adopting measures to protect the environment in the future. This meant reducing the draw of water for agriculture from the Amu Darya and Syr Darya rivers by rehabilitating infrastructure and instituting water-saving irrigation practices. It also meant finding more efficient means of using water, including the institution of some sort of pricing mechanism. Finally, international institutions criticized Soviet top-down approaches that had reduced farmers to the status of passive implementers of the decisions of others rather than to entrusting them with responsibility for water use. Instead international groups opted for decentralization in water management, and supported the granting of a high degree of self-governance to water users. These principles were reflected in the international agencies' approach to water management at the inter-state level and to the reform of water management in the Ferghana Valley.[68]

The effort to rectify the Aral Sea environmental disaster led directly to the formulation of inter-state initiatives for the improvement of water management in Central Asia as a whole. This well-publicized disaster generated large funds and a multitude of projects from multilateral agencies, bilateral donors, and private foundations. Spearheading these projects from the outset were the World Bank, the United Nations Development Programme (UNDP), the European Union, and the United States Agency for International Development (USAID).[69] To different degrees, all these organizations conducted scientific assessments, produced management plans, initiated conservation schemes, and conducted inter-state negotiations to improve water regulation and the ecological condition of the Aral Sea.[70]

Opinions differ on what all this work and funding accomplished. Several agreements were reached on the management of water in the Syr Darya basin, and institutions were established to implement them. But the actual allocations of water remain the domain of yearly barter agreements among the states. Moreover, while the ecological condition of the Aral Sea region has been improved, it remains unlikely that this body of water ever will be restored to its pre-1960s level.[71]

Among the many reasons for these outcomes, two warrant special note. One is that nearly all the inter-state negotiations sponsored by international agencies focused on the nexus of water and energy, but devoted insufficient attention to agriculture. As a result, environmental issues in the Syr Darya basin that derived from water-intensive production and other agricultural policies were ignored.[72] A further reason is that many of the international funders and agencies were themselves not organized in such a way as to assure substantial outcomes, while the local actors with whom they interacted lacked commitment to the projects and happily paid them mere lip service. Sievers is equally critical of both sides.[73] These are, however, classic problems of international cooperation and development assistance that also affect other aid-receiving contexts.

A second focus of international involvement in the management of water in Central Asia has been to promote reform along the lines of Integrated Water Resource Management (IWRM),[74] usually coupled with the rehabilitation of infrastructure. Thus, in the Ferghana Valley the Swiss Agency for Development and Cooperation has run an IWRM project in cooperation with the ICWC since 2001.[75] The aim of the project is to improve and reorganize the institutional arrangements for water management. This includes the restructuring of water management on the basis of hydrological rather than administrative boundaries, and increasing farmers' participation in decision-making. The project is coupled with an effort to introduce Canal Automation, which seeks to automate the measurement of water flows and the transmission of data.[76]

More generally, international funders and organizations have been involved to varying degrees in decentralizing irrigation management in the three Ferghana countries along the lines of IWRM, and especially in establishing WUAs. Major projects have promoted this effort, including the World Bank's On-farm Irrigation Project and Asian Development Bank's Building Capacity for the Formation of Water User Associations in Kyrgyzstan, the USAID's Water User Association Support Project in Uzbekistan and Kazakhstan, and the World Bank's Farm Privatization Support Project and Rural Infrastructure Rehabilitation Project in Tajikistan.

Irrigation reform based on IWRM principles has altered the structure of water management in Central Asia. A large number of WUAs have been established, and water service fees have been introduced in the Ferghana Valley and other irrigated areas of Kyrgyzstan, Tajikistan, and Uzbekistan. At first, the collection rate of water fees was low, but considerable progress recently has been achieved. But shortcomings remain. Sehring analyzed irrigation reforms in Kyrgyzstan and Tajikistan and found that the WUA's must bear responsible for their lack of legitimacy and modest impact on the distribution of water.[77] And indeed, IWRM is a prescriptive concept predicated on the belief that democratic governance is good governance. In practice, however, Kipping is right in stating that IWRM is "politically blind" to the actual political economy and power relations that exist in the Ferghana Valley, especially in Tajikistan and Uzbekistan's sectors.[78] One must question whether economic decentralization and self-government ever can be achieved within strongly centralized and governmentalized systems.

Central Asian authors also have expressed discontent with international projects in the area of water management. Valentini et al. reported "that the first series of pilot projects supported by donors' assistance and funding resulted in a mixed feeling of appreciation for the support, inspiration due to additional revenues, and irony [among Central Asian experts] because of the extreme aplomb of some foreign managers and consultants, as well as the substance of the solutions they proposed."[79] They point out that in their earlier stages the internationally funded projects overlapped and duplicated one another, and embraced approaches that local experts considered unsuitable for the political and climatic conditions of Central Asia. However, they report, later projects effectively addressed these shortcomings. In another article, Kemelova and Zhalkubaev question the effort of USAID and other international donors to raise the case of Kyrgyzstan's exclusion from the negotiations over an Amu Darya framework agreement.[80]

Critical Issues for the Future

The Ferghana Valley is and will remain an ecological space that has been fundamentally transformed by human use, above all through the practice of irrigated agriculture. Global warming eventually may alter both the climate and the river regimes essential for such human use. Acknowledging the great complexities involved in predicting climate changes and their impact, studies clearly indicate that the warming trend has caused glaciers in the northern Tian Shan to retreat.[81] Based on a longitudinal study of the Sokuluk basin, Niederer and his colleagues show that after a period of shrinkage that began in the 1980s, glaciers retreated by 28 percent between 1991 and 2000. Should a similar process take place in the mountain ranges adjoining the Ferghana Valley, this eventually could reduce the flow of water to the arid plains and alter the conditions for irrigation in the basin. This would particularly affect the glacier-fed rivers of the southern ranges, but it also would subject water supplies throughout the valley to greater annual variations. Such changes could alter the conditions for inter-state water sharing and irrigated agriculture throughout the Ferghana Valley, and must be taken into account when future water-management plans are being drafted.

Despite this prospect, irrigated agriculture likely will continue to play a major role in the Ferghana Valley. It will remain the source of people's livelihoods and the backbone of the economies of the Uzbek, Tajik, and Kyrgyz sectors, thanks to the water-energy nexus. In coming years this will depend on whether infrastructure is restored and its existing flaws corrected. Micklin cites Dukhovny and Sokolov's estimate that the cost of such repairs throughout the Aral Sea basin would reach US$16 billion,[82] a figure that does not include the cost of applying water-saving technologies or of adding such facilities as the proposed Kambarata hydropower complex.[83] Identifying sources for so large an investment will be a major challenge.

It is all too easy to view the updating of irrigation systems solely as a matter for engineers. However, the physical, economic, and legal configuration of such systems are shaped as much by the character of property rights and user relations as by technical considerations.[84] Any effective steps toward improving and expanding irrigation systems in the Ferghana Valley must address the social and political challenges relating to irrigated agriculture. Decisions on what form of irrigated agriculture is economically viable, environmentally sustainable, and ethically acceptable in the Ferghana Valley should ideally be the result of a process of social negotiation, one that takes into consideration both the existing political economies and the needs of people's livelihoods.

Questions pertaining to the same political economies affect not only the cotton sector in the Ferghana Valley, but also considerably shape the outcomes of interstate negotiations over the Syr Darya water. The yearly barter agreements that remain the central mechanism to determine water and energy transfers between upstream and downstream countries are substantially affected by the domestic politics in the respective states. Kyrgyzstan's is still cash-strapped and only to a limited extent can afford to acquire energy carriers from abroad. Moreover, the Bakiyev government failed to make investments in energy-related infrastructure. The need for heating during cold winters looms large, and the government's inability to provide sufficient electricity for this purpose is more than likely to give rise to public discontent and political unrest.[85] Operating the Toktogul Reservoir to generate hydropower in wintertime—if sufficient water is available—therefore becomes an urgent political and economic concern of the government.

Conversely, political elites in Uzbekistan and to some extent Tajikistan rely on cotton production in the Ferghana Valley to generate foreign currency and to support the existing system of social, political, and economic control.[86] This partly accounts for the leaders' unwillingness to change to less water-intensive crops in the Ferghana Valley, as the related economic changes may no longer sustain the existing political systems based on exploitation and rent-seeking, as is possible with cotton production. In the absence of alternative domestic political visions, the annually recurring ad hoc barter agreements on the use of Syr Darya water may be less the result of inadequate inter-state cooperation, as Western analysts tend to claim, than of the working out of the particular interests of specific domestic political actors in each country.

The Ferghana Valley remains a fragile ecological space for the livelihoods of the large number of people inhabiting the basin. The changing climatic conditions outlined above could exacerbate the risks and uncertainties. Irregular precipitation patterns, the melting of glaciers, and the thawing of permafrost areas have the potential to increase the frequency and scale of the landslides and mudflows in the foothills and premontane zones.[87] Equally, the environmental degradations and hazards resulting from Soviet modernization schemes pose a challenge to the lives of future residents. However, as states in other world regions have shown, it is possible to address even such grave challenges with intelligent policies.

The socio-economic decline in the Ferghana Valley after independence prompted many families to search for additional income outside agriculture in cities or abroad.[88] A large number of labor migrants send back remittances to supplement revenues from agriculture. The influx of these monies is likely to continue to be of central importance to sustaining livelihoods in the Ferghana Valley. Recent research in the valley has show that it is possible for farms themselves to improve livelihoods and even to reverse the degradation of land and water.[89] Yet while such developments are promising, they do not obviate the need to focus as well on more basic political sources of inequalities and injustice.

Water and land are limited in the Ferghana Valley, and might become even scarcer in the Syr Darya basin over time as climates change and populations increase. Moreover, the dilapidated infrastructural heritage of the late Soviet period has left huge problems that must be addressed. These material concerns are at the same time bound up with state territorialization and the construction of new collective identities. Yet the evidence presented above suggests that the core conflicts over land and water do not trace to any inherent ethnic animosities regarding scarce resources, but to the economic and social modes that define the lives of each group and sub-group and set them off from others. This becomes particularly relevant as the ongoing processes of state-building foster new economic and moral attachments. Therefore, the decisions of the bilateral and tripartite border commissions involving Kyrgyzstan, Uzbekistan, and Tajikistan on the final delimitation and demarcation of borders in the Ferghana Valley will have a decisive impact on these conflicts.[90] Of particular importance will be the work of the sub-commissions that address water and land issues. However, the border commissions have made little progress to date, and the process ahead is likely to be a slow one at best.

International agencies have been engaged with water and ecological issues in the Ferghana Valley for fifteen years, and they are likely to continue such work in the future. Large sums have been invested but limited results have been attained. This is doubtless partly the result of the normal constraints on the work of such international aid agencies. However, their involvement largely has taken place within the framework of promoting neo-liberal reforms leading to market economies and democratic politics in the region, as well as, later, the war on terror. In the area of water management, the IWRM model was promoted both for its own sake and also as an indirect means of providing some kind of quid pro quo for broader reforms of governance. This may not always have been the most productive way to resolve pressing water problems; indeed, overly normative or prescriptive approaches may even diverted attention from the stubborn realities on the ground.

At present, international efforts to foster better inter-state agreements on water use in the Syr Darya basin appear to have decreased. This may trace in part to disappointment with the results to date and in part also to the widely accepted assumption that, in the end, states do not go to war over water.[91] The current economic downturn may bring about a rethinking of some of the prevailing normative approaches to water management, and even give rise to new concepts on how best to approach the ancient questions of water, production, and ecology in the Ferghana Valley.

Notes

1. Funding for research on which this chapter is based was provided by the Swiss National Centre of Competence in Research (NCCR) North–South: Research Partnerships for Mitigating Syndromes of Global Change. The NCCR North–South program is co-funded by the Swiss National Science Foundation and the Swiss Agency for Development and Cooperation. This chapter was written during a fellowship for Prospective Researchers granted by the Swiss National Science Foundation as well as during a postdoctoral fellowship at the University Priority Research Program Asia and Europe: Exchanges and Encounters, University of Zurich, Switzerland.

2. There is an ever-expanding literature in Russian and, increasingly, in the Kyrgyz, Tajik, and Uzbek languages on the issues discussed in this chapter. The three contributing authors to this chapter intensively consulted these materials, but space constraints prevent their being listed in detail. For the sake of simplicity, however, some of the more authoritative Russian- and Western-language sources are cited in the notes. Equally significant are the vast number of official documents pertinent to water management in the Ferghana Valley, most of which are still unavailable to scholars. This chapter also draws on Christine Bichsel's interviews in the field.

3. *Environment and Security. Transforming Risks into Cooperation. Central Asia: Ferghana/Osh/Khujand Area,* United Nations Environment Programme (UNEP), Geneva, 2005, p. 15.

4. E.M. Beniaminovich and D.K. Tersitskyi, eds., *Irrigatsiia Uzbekistana,* vol. 2, Tashkent, 1975.

5. Jonathan Michael Thurman, "Modes of Organization in Central Asian Irrigation: The Ferghana Valley, 1876 to Present," Ph.D. diss., University of Indiana, 1999, pp. 31–36.

6. Beniaminovich and Tersitskyi, *Irrigatsiia Uzbekistana.*

7. Sarah L. O'Hara, "Lessons from the Past: Water Management in Central Asia," *Water Policy,* vol. 2, 2000, p. 375.

8. Thurman, *Modes of Organization in Central Asian Irrigation,* p. 265.

9. Ibid., p. 232.

10. Julia Bucknall et al., *Irrigation in Central Asia: Social, Economic and Environmental Considerations,* World Bank, Environmentally and Socially Sustainable Development Sector, Washington, DC, 2003, p. 27.

11. Thurman, *Modes of Organization in Central Asian Irrigation,* p. 265.

12. Julien Thorez, "Fleux et Dynamiques Spatiales en Asie Centrale. Géographie de la Transformation Post-Soviétique," Ph.D. diss., Université de Paris X–Nanterre, 2005, pp. 506–508.

13. E. Antipova et al., "Optimization of Syr Darya Water and Energy Uses," *Water International,* vol. 27, 2002, p. 4.

14. *Skhema kompleksnogo ispolzovaniia vodnykh resursov basseina reki Syrdari. Predvaritelnyi vodnyi balans na perspektivu. Konspektivnaia zapiska,* Sredgazgiprovodkhopok, Tashkent, 1969; *Skhema kompleksnogo ispolzovaniia vodnykh resursov basseina Syrdaria.*

Konspektivnaia zapiska, Sredgazgiprovodkhopok, Tashkent, 1969; *Skhema kompleksnogo ispolzovaniia vodnykh resursov basseina Aralskovo moria. Osnovnye zadachi i napravlennost rabot,* Sredgazgiprovodkhopok, Tashkent, 1970; *Skhema kompleksnogo ispolzovaniia vodnykh resursov basseina Aralskovo moria, Svodnaia zapiska,* Sredgazgiprovodkhopok, Tashkent, 1973; *Utochnenie skhemy kompleksnogo ispolzovaniia i okhrany vodnykh resursov basseina r. Syrdari. Korrektiruiushdaia zapiska,* Sredgazgiprovodkhopok, Tashkent, 1983.

15. O'Hara, "Lessons from the Past: Water Management in Central Asia," p. 376.

16. Thurman, *Modes of Organization in Central Asian Irrigation,* p. 226.

17. E.L. Valentini, E.E. Orolbaev, and A.K. Abylgazieva, *Water Problems of Central Asia,* Bishkek, 2004, p. 53.

18. O'Hara, "Lessons from the Past: Water Management in Central Asia," p. 375.

19. Thurman, *Modes of Organization in Central Asian Irrigation,* pp. 226–228.

20. F.E. Rubinova, *Izmenenie stoka r. Syrdari pod vliianiem vodokhoziaistvennogo stroitelstva v ee basseine,* Gidrometeoizdat, Moscow, 1979; A.S. Khasanov and L.Z. Sherfedinov, *Aridnyi gidrogeologo-meliorativnyi protsess na primerie basseina Syrdaria,* Tashkent, 1987.

21. Thurman, *Modes of Organization in Central Asian Irrigation,* p. 240.

22. Philip Micklin, "The Aral Sea Crisis and Its Future: An Assessment in 2006," *Eurasian Geography and Economics,* vol. 47, no. 5, 2006.

23. Thurman, *Modes of Organization in Central Asian Irrigation,* p. 236; see also A.I. Davydov, *Zemelnyi fond Uzbekskoi SSR i ego ispolzovanie,* Tashkent, 1971; *Generalnaia schema ispolzovaniia oroshaemykh zemel, vodnykh resursov i ikh okhrany v Uzbekskoi SSR na period 1991–2005 gody. Osnovnye polozheniia,* Tashkent, 1990.

24. Natalia Mirovitskaya and Marvin S. Soroos, "Socialism and the Tragedy of the Commons: Reflections on Environmental Practice in the Soviet Union and Russia," *Journal of Environment & Development,* vol. 4, no. 1, 1995, p. 84.

25. Ibid., p. 85.

26. Erika Weinthal, "Sins of Omission: Constructing Negotiating Sets in the Aral Sea Basin," *Journal for Environment & Development,* vol. 10, no. 1, 2001, p. 52.

27. Mirovitskaya and Soroos, "Socialism and the Tragedy of the Commons," p. 103.

28. Mehmood Ul Hassan, Ralf Starkloff, and Nargiza Nizamedinkhodjaeva, *Inadequacies in the Water Reforms in the Kyrgyz Republic: An Institutional Analysis,* International Water Management Institute, Colombo, 2004, p. 9.

29. Mike Thurman, *Irrigation and Poverty in Central Asia: A Field Assessment,* World Bank, Washington, DC, 2002, www-esd.worldbank.org/bnwpp/documents/7/IrrigandPovertyInCAvers2.pdf.

30. WUAs are non-commercial voluntary association of water users, financed by members' payments for water service delivery. Usually established along the boundaries of the former state and collective farms, WUAs are intended to operate, maintain, and rehabilitate the irrigation system, deliver water to the end users, purchase water from the state and collect water fees from the users.

31. See, for example, Jenniver Sehring, "Irrigation Reform in Kyrgyzstan and Tajikistan," *Irrigation and Drainage Systems,* vol. 21, nos. 8–9, 2007; Ul Hassan, Starkloff, and Nizamedinkhodjaeva, "Inadequacies in the Water Reforms in the Kyrgyz Republic"; Kai Wegerich, "Water User Associations in Uzbekistan and Kyrgyzstan: Study on Conditions for Sustainable Development," Water Issue Study Group, School of Oriental and African Studies, University of London, London, 2000.

32. Philip Micklin, "Water in the Aral Sea Basin of Central Asia: Cause of Conflict or Cooperation?" *Eurasian Geography and Economics,* vol. 43, no. 7, 2002, p. 516.

33. Deanne C. McKinney, "Cooperative Management of Trans-Boundary Water Resources in Central Asia," in *In the Track of Tamerlane: Central Asia's Path to the 21st Century,* ed. Daniel L. Burkhart and Theresa Sabonis-Helf, Washington, DC, 2003, p. 195; Hammond

Murray-Rust et al., *Water Productivity in the Syr-Darya River Basin,* International Water Management Institute, Colombo, 2003, p. 5.

34. Sarah O'Hara, *Drop by Drop: Water Management in the Southern Caucasus and Central Asia,* Local Government and Public Service Reform Initiative, Open Society Institute, Budapest, 2003, p. 23.

35. McKinney, "Cooperative Management of Transboundary Water Resources in Central Asia"; Eric W. Sievers, "Water, Conflict, and Regional Security in Central Asia," *New York University Environmental Law Journal,* vol. 10, no. 3, 2002, p. 388.

36. International Crisis Group, *Central Asia: Water and Conflict,* Osh and Brussels, 2002, p. 16.

37. See, for example, Erika Weinthal, "Sins of Omission: Constructing Negotiating Sets in the Aral Sea Basin"; idem, *State Making and Environmental Cooperation: Linking Domestic and International Politics in Central Asia,* Cambridge and London, 2002.

38. Dinara Kemelova and Gennady Zhalkubaev, "Water, Conflict, and Regional Security in Central Asia Revisited," *New York University Environmental Law Journal,* vol. 11, no. 2, 2003, p. 499.

39. Sievers, "Water, Conflict, and Regional Security in Central Asia"; Kemelova and Zhalkubaev, "Water, Conflict, and Regional Security in Central Asia Revisited."

40. D.Iu. Sarsenbekov et al., *Ispolzovanie i okhrana transgranichnykh rek v stranakh Tsentralnoi Azii,* Almaty, 2004.

41. V.E. Chub, "Gidrometeorologicheskie aspekty bezopasnoi ekspluatatsii gidrotekhnicheskikh sooruzhenii," in *Vodokhranilishcha, chrezvychainye situatsii i problemy ustoichivosti,* Tashkent, 2004; L.Z. Sherfedinov and E.L. Pak, "Tsentralnaia Aziia: irrigatsionno-energeticheskoe protivostoianie," in ibid.

42. Valentini, Orolbaev, and Abylgazieva, *Water Problems of Central Asia: Voda i ustoichivoe razvitie Tsentralnoi Azii,* Bishkek, 2001.

43. See also *Voda zhiznenno-vazhnyi resurs dlia budushego Uzbekistana,* Tashkent, 2007.

44. O'Hara, *Drop by Drop,* p. 23.

45. International Crisis Group, *Central Asia: Water and Conflict,* p. 12.

46. Sievers, "Water, Conflict, and Regional Security in Central Asia," p. 375.

47. *Atlas Uzbekskoi SSR,* pt. 1, Moscow and Tashkent, 1982; *Irrigatsiia Uzbekistana.*

48. Francine Hirsch, *Empire of Nations. Ethnographic Knowledge and the Making of the Soviet Union,* Ithaca, 2005, p. 318.

49. Bucknall et al., *Irrigation in Central Asia,* p. 9.

50. Murray-Rust et al., *Water Productivity in the Syr-Darya River Basin,* p. 4.

51. Bucknall et al., *Irrigation in Central Asia,* pp. 10–11.

52. F.E. Rubinova, *Vliianie vodnykh melioratsii na stok i gidrokhimicheskii rezhim rek v basseine Aralskogo moria,* Moscow, 1987; I.S. Aliev, Ia.E. Pulatov, and R. Rakhmatilloev, *Upravlenie vodnymi resursami na urovne khoziaistva. Vodnye resursy Tadzhikistana,* Dushanbe, 2005.

53. Bucknall et al., *Irrigation in Central Asia,* pp. 10–11.

54. See also UNEP, *Environment and Security.*

55. Ibid., 29–34.

56. Sehring, "Irrigation Reform in Kyrgyzstan and Tajikistan."

57. Bucknall et al., *Irrigation in Central Asia,* p. 5.

58. Ibid.

59. In absolute terms, however, the rural poor are only slightly worse off than the urban poor.

60. Bucknall et al., *Irrigation in Central Asia,* pp. 17–18.

61. Ibid., p. iii.

62. Ibid., p. 20.

63. Emma E. Lindberg, "Access to Water for Irrigation in Post-Soviet Agriculture," M.S. thesis, University of Zurich, 2007; Thurman, *Irrigation and Poverty in Central Asia.*

64. Thurman, *Irrigation and Poverty in Central Asia,* p. 20.

65. International Crisis Group, *The Curse of Cotton in Central Asia,* Osh and Brussels, 2005; Deniz Kandiyoti, ed., *The Cotton Sector in Central Asia. Economic Policy and Development Challenges,* School of Oriental and African Studies, London, 2007.

66. Janine R. Wedel, *Collision and Collusion. The Strange Case of Western Aid to Eastern Europe,* New York, 2001.

67. David Mosse, "Global Governance and the Ethnography of International Aid," in *The Aid Effect. Giving and Governing in International Development,* ed. David Mosse and David Lewis, London, 2005, p. 3.

68. *Usilenie regionalnogo sotrudnichestva po ratsionalnomu i effektivnomu ispolzovaniiu vodnykh i energeticheskikh resursov Tsentralnoi Azii,* United Nations, New York, 2003.

69. Sievers, "Water, Conflict, and Regional Security in Central Asia," pp. 393–397.

70. Most prominently is the Aral Sea Basin Program (ASBP), which began in 1994 with the original plan to extend it over a period of fifteen to twenty years, financed jointly by the World Bank, UNDP, and UNEP. The program's aims included 1) rehabilitation and development of the disaster zone, 2) strategic planning and comprehensive management of the Amu Darya and Syr Darya rivers, and 3) building institutions for planning and implementing the two first points. The third point led to the foundation of ICAS and IFAS. After a review of the ASBP in 1996, the World Bank, together with GEF, launched the Water and Environmental Management Project for 1999 to 2003. Between 1993 and 1998 USAID funded the Environmental Policy and Technology project, which supported regional efforts to come to an agreement on the operation of the Toktogul Reservoir. In 2001 it launched the Natural Resource Management Project, the water component of which aimed at improving inter-state cooperation and sharing of the Syr Darya River flow. This project was further expanded in 2002. The European Union ran the Water Resources Management and Agricultural Production (WARMAP) project starting in 1995 for the utilization, management, and allocation of water in Central Asia (Micklin, "Water in the Aral Sea Basin of Central Asia," pp. 518–520).

71. Micklin, "The Aral Sea Crisis and Its Future."

72. Weinthal, "Sins of Omission: Constructing Negotiating Sets in the Aral Sea Basin."

73. Sievers, "Water, Conflict, and Regional Security in Central Asia."

74. IWRM is defined as "a process which promotes the coordinated development and management of water, land, and related resources, in order to maximize the resultant economic and social welfare in an equitable manner without compromising the sustainability of vital ecosystems" (GWP 2000).

75. Jürg Krähenbühl, Johan Gely, and Urs Herren, *Swiss Water Strategy for Central Asia, 2002–2006. Strengthening Regional Water Management Capacities,* Berne, 2002.

76. See also SDC, "Integrated Water Resource Management," www.swisscoop.uz/index.php?navID=22500&langID=1&&officeID=40.

77. Sehring, "Irrigation Reform in Kyrgyzstan and Tajikistan."

78. Martin Kipping, "Can 'Integrated Water Resources Management' Silence Malthusian Concerns? The Case of Central Asia," *Water International,* vol. 33, no. 3, 2008.

79. Valentini, Orolbaev, and Abylgazieva, *Water Problems of Central Asia,* p. 88.

80. Kemelova and Zhalkubaev, "Water, Conflict, and Regional Security in Central Asia Revisited," pp. 496–499.

81. Peter Niederer et al., "Tracing Glacier Wastage in the Northern Tien Shan (Kyrgyzstan, Central Asia) over the Last 40 Years," *Climatic Change,* vol. 86, nos. 1–2, 2008.

82. Micklin, "Water in the Aral Sea Basin of Central Asia: Cause of Conflict or Cooperation?" p. 515.

83. For further reference, see International Crisis Group, *Central Asia: Water and Conflict,* pp. 18–19.

84. Ruth S. Meinzen-Dick and Bryan Randolph Bruns, "Negotiating Water Rights: Introduction," in *Negotiating Water Rights,* ed. Bryan Randolph Bruns and Ruth S. Meinzen-Dick, London, 2000, p. 27.

85. International Crisis Group, *Kyrgyzstan: A Deceptive Calm,* Osh and Brussels, 2008.

86. Weinthal, "Sins of Omission: Constructing Negotiating Sets in the Aral Sea Basin," p. 53.

87. See UNEP, *Environment and Security.*

88. Bucknall et al., *Irrigation in Central Asia.*

89. Andrew Noble, Mehmood ul Hassan, and Jusipbek Kazbekov, *"Bright Spots" in Uzbekistan, Reversing Land and Water Degradation While Improving Livelihoods: Key Developments and Sustaining Ingredients for Transition Economies of the Former Soviet Union,* Colombo, 2005.

90. See for example Alfred Appei and Peter Skorsch, *Central Asia, Border Management, Report of the European Commission Rapid Reaction Mechanism Assessment Mission,* European Commission Conflict Prevention and Crisis Management Unit, Brussels, 2002, http://ec.europa.eu/external_relations/cfsp/cpcm/rrm/cabm.htm.

91. See also Aaron T. Wolf, "Conflict and Cooperation Along International Waterways," *Water Policy,* vol. 1, no. 2, 1998.

12

Culture in the Ferghana Valley Since 1991: The Issue of Identity

Pulat Shozimov (Tajikistan), with
Joomart Sulaimanov (Kyrgyz Republic) and
Shamshad Abdullaev (Uzbekistan)

Informal cultural and religious networks define the social and political processes of the Ferghana Valley. The strength of these networks is assured by the region's powerful informal leaders, who are responsible for preserving and transmitting cultural and religious values to the next generations, and to the valley's geographical isolation from the major external political centers. Thanks to the latter, the region became a natural home to many religious and political figures and intellectuals fleeing persecution. This gave rise to a paradoxical combination of tendencies there: the valley always has been a conserver of cultural and religious traditions and, at the same time, a magnet for new and in some cases dissident ideas. This assured a permanent tension between tradition and innovation, with the full realization of each being constrained by the other. In many respects, the dynamics of this interrelationship in the Ferghana Valley shapes social, political, religious, and cultural processes more broadly in modern Central Asia.

The unexpected breakup of the Soviet Union in 1991 fragmented the Ferghana Valley territorially, with Uzbekistan holding about 60 percent of it, Tajikistan 25 percent, and Kyrgyzstan 15 percent. The unfortunate conflicts that occurred during the first post-independence decades arose in part because the Soviet borders left the new states with both enclaves and "exclaves," where the territory of one state is surrounded by another state and does not have a shared border with its own state. Besides contradicting the basic concept that nation-states adhere to the principle of territorial integrity, such enclaves place firm boundaries between different ethnic groups living in such close proximity to one another that it is impossible to know exactly where one ends and the other begins.

Another source of conflict is the difficulty of fixing cultural borders in the Ferghana Valley, especially between Tajikistan and Uzbekistan. Ethnic indicators there are ambiguous, with many people speaking both Turkic and Tajik-Persian languages. This reality impedes the prospect of building nation-states whose territorial borders coincide with cultural boundaries. It also underscores the fact that all the region's social-political processes inevitably are linked to identity.

Many Ferghana residents identify themselves traditionally as Sarts, with all the cultural ambiguity that that term implies. Sarts lived and worked in the intercultural space along the Silk Road routes, playing the role of cultural mediators between diverse social, political, and economic groups. To an extent, the Sarts also integrated the sedentary and nomadic patterns of life in Central Asia, building cultural commonalities that offset the effects of geographical separation.

The territorial settlement following the break-up of the Soviet Union immediately gave rise to problems of national and cultural sovereignty. Bluntly stated, the Ferghana Valley posed a challenge to all the symbolic and ideological constructs designed to develop a national identity for the states in the region. The response of the intelligentsia of the Ferghana Valley to this issue was ambiguous, as was clearly reflected in the program for the "Ferghana school" of poetry drafted by its leader, Shamshad Abdullaev. This group of poets, he argued, "aspires to keep its distance from all the ideological temptations and various emblems . . . since this environment leads to ethnic withdrawal, even though it also possesses dense and indivisible elements of commonality that constitute its primal if unarticulated spiritual reservoir."[1]

The declarations of independence by the countries of the Ferghana Valley unleashed a struggle over the new territorial borders, and also a search among all three entities for their own cultural identities. Typical of new nation-states, this quest eventually involved all the social, cultural, religious, and political groups in the region. In their search for identity the cultural and political elites looked mainly to the past, resurrecting and reviving traditional symbols. This struggle to create new cultural borders eventually became a distinguishing feature of the first years of independence across Central Asia. Such official political symbols as Timur (Tamerlane) in Uzbekistan, the epic poem *Manas* in Kyrgyzstan, and the ninth-century ruler Ismail Samoni in Tajikistan shed light on the times and circumstances in which they were chosen.

Considering the symbol of Timur in the context of the Ferghana Valley, it is worth noting that in the fifteenth century a major struggle was waged by the Shaybanids in Bukhara against Babur, who not only was from the Ferghana Valley but a descendent of Timur. At the same time, the Kyrgyz, who see themselves as more Mongol and nomadic, consider Timur not as an Uzbek or part of the Ferghana-Pamir people, but as one of their own. The same variability is evident in the issue of the Ferghana people called Sarts, whom Tajik intellectuals consider to be Tajik and Uzbeks view as Uzbeks.[2] An extension of this issue is the clear demarcation between the nomadic culture of the Kyrgyz, the settled agrarian culture of the Tajiks, and the Uzbeks' combination of both nomadic and sedentary cultural patterns. It is worth asking whether and how these different heritages shape interrelationships among these Ferghana ethnic groups in the post-Soviet era and beyond.

Caught in a new crisis of identity, the political and cultural elites of all three countries scour the cultural heritages of their peoples in search of workable models for the present. This process has distinct features in the three countries, reflecting the differing process of state-building in each. Thus, Tajikistan's turn to the ninth- and tenth-century Samanid era is justified not only by the great scientists and poets of that age (among them Abu Ali ibn-Sina, Abulkhasan Rudaki, Abulkosim Firdausi),[3] but also by the tolerance extended then to Christians, Zoroastrians, and Jews, as well as to Muslims. The Samanids' openness to diverse ideas and values, it is argued, gave rise to the dynamism of the age. The Kyrgyz advance analogous arguments in their embrace of the epic *Manas,* while the Uzbeks do the same with Timur.

However, even as all three embraced what they saw as an earlier age of cultural flowering, they also turn to the pre-Soviet model of a traditional society. In the case of Tajikistan, this relatively recent model owed little or nothing to the period of flowering, and much to the centuries of hostility to any form of rational thought and suspicion toward innovation that set in with the collapse of the Samanids' golden age and the rise of the philosopher Abu Khamid Al-Ghazali. What Ghazali rationalized and defended became the foundation of a very different Muslim world that stood squarely against both reason and innovation,[4] and which existed until the early twentieth century. Thus, when one speaks of cultural "revival" in the Ferghana Valley one must ask *what* is being revived: a noble but distant model from the remote past or the traditional society of a century ago that led to a political and cultural dead end? Even that traditional society is greatly weakened today, as are the three great Sufi orders that best embodied it, the Naqshbandiye, Kadiriye, and Yasaviya. This opens the way for Wahhabism and other pan-Islamic extremist tendencies to lay claim to the mantle of traditionalism. Whether and how some type of balance can be struck between moderate or radical forms of traditionalism and a modernization justified in terms of some early "golden age" will determine not only the stability of the region, but also the dynamism of its development in all spheres.

Valuable insights on cultural process in the post-Soviet Ferghana Valley can be gleaned from a study of the causes of conflicts that have occurred there. During the Soviet period most conflicts were inter-ethnic and prompted by such practical issues as water and territory. In the post-Soviet era most conflicts had become ideological, mainly concerning religion. What remains to be seen is whether the valley's cultural resources can be turned into the kind of social capital that can provide for the region's economic and political development.

The Context of Culture in the Ferghana Valley After 1991

Elements of tradition and even pluralism in the Ferghana Valley persisted into the post-1991 era. Traditional practices relating to weddings, funerals, and worship at sacred sites (*mazars*) continued, and neighborhood units (*mahallas*) thrived, even though they were partially governmentalized in the post-independence period. Diverse traditional Islamic rituals attest to the existence of multiple "regimes of truth." At such informal traditional locales as teahouses (*chaikhanas*), bazaars, mosques, and shrines, an awareness of a civil sector began to form. In the absence of solid official institutions, such locales became the setting where new values were formed. Curiously, the new national political symbols adopted by the three Ferghana states did not have much impact in the Ferghana Valley, owing to the marginalization of the formerly influential Ferghana elites from the process of national definition going forward in the distant new capitals. The situation was somewhat different in the Kyrgyz sector, where the many Ferghana Uzbeks defined themselves less in terms of Bishkek than Tashkent, at least until the Tulip Revolution of 2005 shifted power southward from the capital.

Today the Ferghana Valley is emerging as a major locus of political and ideological struggle over identity, not only on the national level of the three countries but also with reference to the external religious actors also involved in the struggle over identity in the Ferghana Valley.

The Uzbek Sector

During the last years of Soviet rule in Uzbekistan the authorities, fearing a revival of religion, launched an offensive against traditional forms of Islam. In 1982 more than half of Ferghana's young people both underwent religious marriage ceremonies and signed the official registries. This led the state to destroy many traditional *mazars*, which threatened religious life and networks, especially around the Uzbek city of Namangan.[5] The Namangan events of 1991–92 were a logical outcome of governmental actions aimed at the destruction of traditional institutions. Other measures to control the selection of imams left religious leadership in the hands of men with little clerical authority and limited ability to engage in serious religious and intellectual discourse with representatives of the radical Hizb ut-Tahrir, Wahhabis, and Salafis.

The Tajik Sector

A similar attack began in Tajikistan, but long after the fall of communism and a decade after the end of the Tajik civil war. Starting in 2007, the government began attacking "archaic" institutions and norms. This assault on tradition began from "above" rather than from "below." What radical Islamists had attempted on the eve of the civil war in 1990–91, and for which they were denounced as Wahhabis, is today being successfully implemented by the Tajik government itself.

Back in 1999 Tajik president Emomali Rakhmon had issued new "regulations in the sphere of rites and traditions,"[6] but they were not implemented. The new regulations of 2007 initially gained the support of the Islamic Renaissance Party of Tajikistan (IRPT),[7] but soon its chairman, Mukhiddin Kabiri, declared that the government had gone too far. The Ministry of Culture's officer on religious affairs, Muradullo Davlatov, pinpointed the difference between the reforms of 1991–92 and 2007: the former was religious in nature while the latter was social, aimed at the modernization of society.[8]

The new reform received an ambivalent response from the Tajik part of the Ferghana Valley. Most residents of the Isfara district reacted positively to the simplification of weddings and funerals, arguing that they themselves had long wanted this. However, many village mullahs opposed the reforms, fearing a loss of their authority in the community. And indeed, the decree prevented many informal mullahs from leading weddings and funerals: in Khujand alone the number of mullahs and *biotins* fell by half, most of them replaced by mullahs who were under the government's control. Older unofficial mullahs became Qur'an readers, the demand for whom did not fall, while those who had become mullahs only since independence generally found work elsewhere. Interviews in Sughd province revealed that many started their own businesses or left to work in Russia.

One cannot help but wonder whether the Rakhmon reforms in Tajikistan will lead to the same consequences as the late Soviet reforms in Uzbekistan; that is, the confrontations in Andijan. It is quite possible that the reforms will provoke a backlash among the Pan-Islamic radicals in the Tajik parts of Ferghana. However, the inter-Tajik negotiations of 1997–99 left Tajikistan considerable political capital. The IRPT to some extent constrains radical trends in Tajik religious life, standing as a champion of national traditions against the Salafis, Wahhabis, and Hizb ut-Tahrir, who would destroy them in the name of Pan-Islamism. The IRPT certainly directs serious criticism against some of the ideas of Tajikistan's religious traditionalists, but in the end it seeks a balance between them and the country's national values. Its aim is to work with the government to modernize both it and religious community, working both from "below" and "above." Participating in presidential and parliamentary elections and with two seats in Majlisi Oli (parliament),[9] the IRPT is a kind of lightning rod providing stability to both the society and religious community of Tajikistan. In spite of tensions with the government over specific issues, the IRPT has found a role testing out various approaches to issues of the day, improving them in the process. In the Ferghana Valley and elsewhere it is important that both the government and IRPT develop proportionally, with each constraining the other.

The IRPT is gradually strengthening its positions among the middle class in the Tajik part of the Ferghana Valley. When 2,500 car owners in the Isfara district sent an open letter to the chairman of the IRPT requesting help in protecting their rights, it was clear that the Party's role in the Ferghana Valley extends beyond religion to economic matters.[10] Indeed, the development of a middle class in Tajik Ferghana is taking place in connection with religious networks largely outside the government's control. Prosperous businessmen donate generously to mosques and religious enterprises, working closely with the IRPT but also with other religious entities. No longer is one surprised at the large number of well-off non-traditional religious groups, which are the IRPT's main rivals in the region. In the Isfara district of Sughd province and Istaravshan, one sees businessmen meeting after work in mosques or teahouses to discuss both economic and religious matters. This seems not to occur on the basis of the ideas of Hizb ut-Tahrir or other radical movements. Rather, it is a means of using religious capital to support one's business, that is of employing local traditions to advance modernization.

Such traditional religious leaders as *saiids, turas, hojas, ishans,* and Sufis are part of this development. Although Soviet rule abolished the privileges and titles of seventy such persons in Isfara alone,[11] their descendents continue to be highly regarded by the populace. Among the best-known Isfara figures is Nugmankhan-tura, who lives in the village of Chorkukh and traces his lineage to Mahdumi A'zam, a sixteenth-century leader of the Naqshbandi Sufi order who formulated the political doctrine of that school. Yet despite their religious heritage, these groups are gradually losing their social status. After the collapse of the USSR, many of them cited ancient documents to affirm their privileges and saw their status rise. But beginning in 2000 the government systematically began undermining them by raising the status of such lower groups as the *fakirs.* Isfara residents report that the standing of *fakirs* has risen significantly, thanks to government support. Heretofore taboo marriages between *fakirs* and other groups are now possible. The same trend can be observed in Tajikistan's Rasht Valley, which has the most immediate connection with the Ferghana Valley despite being located in the southern part of Tajikistan.[12]

The Kyrgyz Sector

The administrative map of the Kyrgyz part of the Ferghana Valley has been redrawn repeatedly.[13] During the last decades before independence the entire southern region—half of Kyrgyzstan—was combined in Osh province. After 1991 Jalalabad emerged as a separate province and then, after 2000, Batken. These changes suited the desire of the politically powerful north to divide the south, and gave new possibilities to local elites in the Ferghana Valley.

The territorial divisions only loosely correspond to the ancient, military-derived division of the Kyrgyz into right and left wings and attendant sub-groups, with the Ichkilik clan constituting the center. A north-south line across Kyrgyzstan through the city of Osh defines the right and left wings, each of them with fifteen kin groups. Together they are called the *Otuz uul,* or "thirty sons." The Ichkiliks include ten kin groups. The division of the Ferghana Valley after 1991 reflects ethnic subgroups defined more by kinship than territory. As result, these ethno-cultural lines cut through the territory of Batken, Jalalabad, and Osh provinces, creating additional cultural enclaves, this time within the south of Kyrgyzstan itself.

Yet even these cultural borders must be further redrawn on the basis of identity. For instance, according to the traditional framework of identification that part of Batken province between the western part of Osh province and the border with Tajikistan belongs to the Ichkiliks, who constitute a majority in the province. However, those Kyrgyz living in the area extending from Osh to Nookat, 40 kilometers away, are not Ichkiliks, leaving the Nookat district with 30 clans or *sons* of the right and left wings who are culturally different.

The complex identity of the Ichkilik kinship group derives from the fact that they adopted a sedentary way of life earlier than the other two groups. Thus, for example, they no longer slay a horse for traditional celebrations, and do not carve sheep into twelve parts, each piece of which has a symbolic meaning. For Ichkiliks this hierarchy no longer has any significance. They do not cook the traditional horsemeat stew (*beshbarmak*), do not drink fermented mare's milk (*kumys*) and are not involved in horse breeding. These disinclinations, along with different styles of clothing and hair dress, set the Ichkilik identity off from that of other Kyrgyz, and in the Ferghana Valley can easily lead to cultural confrontations among the Kyrgyz themselves, quite apart from their relations with Uzbeks and Tajiks.

Once they became sedentary, Ichkilik Kyrgyz adopted many habits from neighboring Tajiks and Uzbeks. Like Tajiks in the nearby Isfara district of Tajikistan's Sughd province, Batken Kyrgyz tend to be farmers who plant fruit trees, process dried apricots, and grow rice—a far cry from their traditional horse-breeding. Especially in areas closest to Tajikistan and Uzbekistan, their dialects also separate them from other Kyrgyz, who can barely understand their speech, with its strong admixture of Tajik and Uzbek words.

Another marker of identity within the Kyrgyz part of the Ferghana Valley is the cultural divide between mountain people and flat-landers. In the Osh district, residents of the mountainous Alai and Karakulzha areas look down upon those inhabiting the plains, considering them Uzbek-ized farmers who are not straightforward and open and who tend to kowtow to officials. What cannot be denied in this is that the Kyrgyz of the plains are to a large extent under the influence of Tajik and Uzbek forms of identity, both in economic and religious terms. Not surprisingly, Islam in general and radical Islam in particular are more pronounced in Batken province than in other Kyrgyz areas of the Ferghana Valley.

Across the entire Kyrgyz sector of the Ferghana Valley, one can observe a revival of a traditional mode of life. This is manifested in the growing importance assigned to clans, tribal ways, and the authority of religious institutions and rituals. The subregions differ from one another only in the pace of this trend, with Batken province leading the way. In Osh province this trend is most clearly evident in the plains rather than the mountains. Related to this development is the pressure to return to traditional weddings and funerals. Evident in Osh, Jalalabad, and Batken, this development is hastened by members of the clergy, many of whom studied in Saudi Arabia, and also by the government, which seeks to enlist the support of religious leaders.

TV and Radio in the Ferghana Valley

Sixty percent of the Ferghana Valley is in Uzbekistan, assuring that that country's informational networks have a powerful impact on the parts of Ferghana located in

Tajikistan and Kyrgyzstan. Residents of the Kyrgyz region of the Ferghana Valley regularly access Uzbek media, especially Uzbek TV channels, including those from Tashkent and those from Ferghana City, Andijan, and other cities. The influence is the more powerful because these stations translate both Russian and foreign television series into the Uzbek language. Another relevant factor in the Kyrgyz sector is that the Uzbek stations are clearer than those from Kyrgyzstan itself, which are all broadcast from the faraway capital in Bishkek. Moreover, Kyrgyz channels offer virtually no drama series or sports programs in the Kyrgyz language, while Russian channels are inaccessible in many parts of southern Kyrgyzstan owing to their weak signal.

Thanks to this, Uzbekistan exerts a powerful influence on virtually all cultural trends in the Kyrgyz part of the Ferghana Valley. Related to this is the overwhelming popularity of Uzbek singers among all residents of southern Kyrgyzstan, with Uzbek singers and their repertoires dominating the music heard in cafes and restaurants, as well as at weddings and other festive occasions.

The same situation exists in Tajikistan. Most Tajik areas of the Ferghana Valley do not have access to national television. For instance, in the city of Kanibadam in Sughd province a local TV station began broadcasting in 1992. After several years it was shut down and only in 2004 resumed broadcasting, and then only for three hours daily. Its programming is largely of an educational nature, and lacks both news reporting and analyses. The same can be said of the two commercial television stations in Kanibadam, Guli Bodom and Anis, where music and educational offerings dominate the programming.

A survey of Kanibadam residents revealed that more than 50 percent of them watch one or more of the three Uzbek television stations that reach Kandibadam: Eshlik, Sport (commercial TV), and Uzbekistan Channel 1. This is due in part to the fact that 35 percent of the local population is Uzbek, but Tajiks also enjoy music and other programs broadcast on Uzbek TV. Those above fifty also listen to Uzbek radio, but youths are switching from TV and radio to DVDs and, increasingly, the Internet. Khujand claims two independent local channels, to which the public is loyal, even though programming is often didactic and lacking in analysis. Uzbek TV, especially its music programs and feature films, is also widely watched here.

The Internet is not well developed in the Tajik part of the Ferghana Valley, mainly because of constant electricity problems in Sughd province. Khujand offers few public Internet centers, and there are fewer yet in the rest of Sughd province. However, the one Internet-café in Isfara attracts the most active and socially oriented youth, and is an island of hope for the future.

Some border areas of Sughd province under the influence of the IRPT appear to be resisting the total domination of the Uzbek TV. In the Novoe Matcho district of Sughd province, residents and the local clergy organize local celebrations on Tajik Language Day without help from local officials, whom they consider indifferent to national culture. Yet Tajik TV remains inaccessible to them. Meanwhile, the Tajik government has become interested in access to information in the Tajik part of the

Ferghana Valley. At an April 2008 meeting the heads of three local TV and radio stations agreed to begin exchanging news of coming events in their neighboring cities.[14] This was in response to the local authorities' growing concern over the strong cross-border impact of Uzbek television.

Education in the Ferghana Valley and the Fate of the Intelligentsia

Educational institutions in many parts of the Ferghana Valley are in crisis today, and religious schools, most of them unofficial, are filling the gap. Thus, in the Tajik sector there are 883 schools, gymnasia and boarding schools with 21,317 students, but there also are a far greater number of regular mosques.[15]

In spite of an adequate number of educational institutions in Sughd, the region has an acute shortage of professional people as a consequence of emigration. The civil war forced a majority of secular intellectuals in the Tajik sector of the Ferghana Valley to leave the country. Those professionals who remained tended to find places in religious institutions or as shuttle traders. The only remaining positions for the intelligentsia were in government, higher education, and in secularized parts of the traditional sector. They met one another at weddings, funerals, and neighborhood (*mahalla*) councils, while music and crafts continued to provide a fragile tie between them and the people.

After 1991 the secular intelligentsia began to cede their spiritual role in society to the clergy. Since the government could no longer adequately support them, their social prestige also waned. With bank staffs and businessmen earning ten times more than academics, directors of research institutes, or teachers, the latter were forced into new roles for which they were unprepared, even as the clergy flourished. Across the Tajik sector of the Ferghana Valley the number of educational and cultural institutions (schools, theaters, and libraries) fell sharply, a decline that still continued in 2008.[16] Meanwhile, the number of folk theaters, dance ensembles, and ancient monuments increased.

For the Kyrgyz sector of the Ferghana Valley we see 221 secular schools in Batken, 664 in Osh, and 444 in Jalalabad, and a total of only ten religious schools. Osh and Jalalabad both have Islamic universities but not Batken, in spite of its religious character. To some extent these figures misrepresent reality, because religious education is thriving in both mosques and homes under the guidance of religious mentors. Moreover, in spite of their number public schools have been gravely weakened by general economic and political crisis, and the social status of all members of the intelligentsia has plummeted.

This has many causes, one of them being the direct heritage of the official atheism of the Soviet era. The strict separation of the secular and religious then causes the public still to assume that all intellectuals are hostile to religion and are even atheists. Conversely, the public also assumes that the keepers of the Muslim community or *ulema* are concerned solely with Islamic religious practice, even though Muslim culture formerly allowed secular knowledge to coexist easily with religion.

Similar issues arise in culture and education. Following independence, schools began gradually replacing Soviet-era textbooks and engaged intellectuals to write new ones. In all three countries the new texts focus on strengthening the new national identity. In the liberal arts and especially history, this opened the door to political manipulation. In the Ferghana Valley, where neither cultural nor territorial borders are fully resolved, this easily might lead to further misunderstandings and conflicts. Uzbekistan's decision to switch to the Latin alphabet had the same short-term effect, even though Kyrgyzstan also plans eventually to make the same change. Tajikistan will not do so, however, nor will it replace Cyrillic with the modified Arabic script used in Iran and Afghanistan. This eventually may isolate Tajikistan within the Ferghana Valley and Central Asia as a whole. Paradoxically, the rise of Latin scripts could have the effect of activating some kind of Pan-Turkic values, which doubtless will push Tajiks more deeply into Persian cultural space. This already has begun in Tajikistan's high-level relations with Afghanistan and Iran. Thanks to these developments, in all three Ferghana countries one can observe the advent of new elites whose views are based on completely different values and cultural foundations.

Social Interactions and the Issue of Identity

In Kyrgyzstan, the tendency to juxtapose national and religious traditions has become widespread. The dominant voice today is of the newly religious, who call for a ban on the performance of all national traditions and rituals. Typically, the mullahs and elders (*aksakals*) of Kyrgyz mountain villages in Ferghana forbid the sacrifice of horses during commemorations. Moreover, where formerly people would wait several days before burying the dead, they are now enjoined to do so immediately. Previously, weddings consisted of a brief ceremony at the registry, but now these are often preceded and followed by the Muslim *nikah,* which takes on a public character, whereas formerly it was done at home.

In spite of these trends, most Kyrgyz in the Ferghana Valley and elsewhere identify themselves as Kyrgyz first and only then as Muslims. Uzbeks in the Kyrgyz sector of the valley exhibit higher levels of religious identity. This is no doubt due to the Uzbeks' low level of integration into Kyrgyz life and to their opposition to the new ethno-nationalism. By affirming a religious identity these Uzbeks in Kyrgyzstan can find common ground with the Kyrgyz on a more universal level. In both cases the ethnic minority embraces religion rather than ethnicity or nationality as the core of its identity. The same can be observed among Tajik ethnics in the Uzbek part of the Ferghana Valley, where the Tajiks identify themselves in terms of religion rather than ethnicity or nationality.

The social fabric of the Tajik sector of the Ferghana Valley shares many elements with that of Uzbekistan, whether in families, *mahallas,* or cultural institutions (*gashtak, gap,* etc.). At the same time it differs considerably from the Kyrgyz pattern, which traces to nomadism. While former nomads stress kin and tribal identities, the sedentary Tajik and Uzbeks focus on territorial *mahallas, avlods,* and *jamaats/jamoats.* Thus, if Kyrgyz (and some Uzbeks) organize traditional events around kin and tribal structures, the Tajiks and most Uzbeks integrate neighbors into their social and cultural space through territorial *mahallas.* The Tajik proverb, "a neighbor can be closer than a relative,"[17] could also be Uzbek, but not Kyrgyz. The basis for this can clearly be seen in the structure of the Vorukh enclave in Kyrgyz Batken. Like towns in Tajikistan's Isfara district, it is comprised of "Big quarters" (Maidon, Guzar, Sari-kurum, and Tiidon); "Small quarters" (Kalacha, Tagi-mahalla, Sari-kanda, Kuchi kozi, Kuchi bolo, Machiti-bolo, and others); as well as "Counties."[18]

Mosques, teahouses, bazaars, and shrines serve an important function as informational space, where people exchange news and ideas on local and international events. The traditional reliance on oral exchanges leaves public opinion subject to rumors. This happens most frequently in isolated areas like Batken in Kyrgyzstan and the Isfara region of Tajikistan, and also in areas underserved by electronic and print media. Thus, the decision by village residents to build a mosque eventually favors traditional over modern media. These decisions get implemented through the volunteer labor (*hashar*) of all able-bodied men. In many villages, including Khodzhai Alo in Isfara district, the work is guided both by local cultural traditions and national ones.[19]

Often the link between national and religious identity is a close one. In 2003 a madrassa teacher at the nearby village of Churkukh, Salmani Forsi, specifically criticized Sufi religious traditions—extremely popular in the Ferghana Valley—for imposing intermediaries between believers and God. Yet he then proceeded to support the connection of national and religious forms of identity in much the way that the IRPT does. Clearly, his view of Islam goes beyond external ritual to include philosophical matters. But even if he can criticize the local practice of Sufism in much the way a Wahhabi or Salafi might do, he finds any Arabic form of the faith unacceptable. Emphasizing the need to strengthen national forms of Islam in Tajikistan, he declares: "We are Tajiks, and not Arabs, therefore we should develop our own understanding of Islam."[20] Forsi's readiness to criticize a deep local tradition yet at the same time to embrace the notion of a national religion should be traced not to confusion on his part but to his desire to adapt to a modernizing world. It is worth noting that Chorkukh is relatively well developed.

Contrasting with Chorkukh is the much poorer village of Surkh. At the same time Forsi was wrestling with tradition and change, the self-trained imam of a mosque in Surkh, Mullah Abdurakhman, expressed his conviction that the changes which more highly educated clergy sought to introduce in traditional rites arose from their desire to diminish the role of traditional religious leaders. Among the "innovations" which he criticized were the inclusion of purely Muslim elements into wedding ceremonies and the rejection of music and dancing. A half-decade later, though, Surkh is moving in the direction of Chorkukh, with both music and dancing disappearing from weddings.

If Chorkukh village exemplifies the new religious-national type of identity with strong modernizing elements, and Surkh the hold of traditionalism, the Tajik village of Khodzhai Alo embodies a national or ethno-national form of identity that transcends political borders and has little or no religious content. Farm chairman Abdukhalil Sharipov, who also chairs the village council, epitomizes this approach. An economist by training, he is an active amateur archaeologist and custodian of local antiquities. He believes that peoples develop only on the basis of cultural continuity extending over eras and generations.[21] For this reason he took a personal role in building a new mosque in Khodzhai Alo, painstakingly painting the ceiling beams with classic national aphorisms, the sayings of sages, and the *Sayings* of Mohammed, ornamenting them all with Tajikistan's national colors. At the entrance he carved verses by the contemporary Tajik poet Bozor Sobir, who helped inspire the national revival in the first years after independence.[22]

For all his Tajik nationalism, the identity of Sharipov and many of his friends from Khodzhai Alo and Vorukh is linked closely with the Ferghana Valley. Sharipov does not at all understand the traditional music of southern Tajikistan (*falak*), yet he is an enthusiast for the traditional *shashmakom,* which is immensely popular in Sughd and the entire Ferghana Valley. Throughout the Soviet era this was performed exclusively in Tajik, but today he listens with pleasure to *shashmakom* in Uzbek.[23]

On the road between Khodzhai Alo and Vorukh there is an inscribed stone from the eleventh to twelfth century indicating that the land was part of the (Turkic) Karakhanid Empire and that the people who lived there were Sarts. Abdukhalil Sharipov[24] views it as part of the local heritage and stresses the importance of the inscription "Sarts live here"—a clear confirmation of the larger Ferghana Valley identity that Sharipov also embraces.

This close view of the Isfara district of Tajikistan could be replicated in studies of any districts in those parts of the Ferghana Valley belonging to Uzbekistan and Kyrgyzstan. All would show clearly, as this look at Isfara district has done, how complex and multi-layered identity is throughout the Ferghana Valley.

Cultural Conflicts over *Shashmakom* in the Ferghana Valley

The traditional music of *shashmakom* can be divided into three main styles: those of Bukhara, Ferghana-Tashkent, and Khujand. The differences among them are not immense, consisting mainly of nuances in vocal performance style. Tajik authorities today are trying to develop national centers for *shashmakom* in Sughd province of Ferghana and in Tajikistan's south. The Tajik academician Mukhammadzhon Shukuri has sharply criticized this governmental initiative for favoring the Ferghana-Tashkent style over the style of Bukhara. According to Shukuri, the *shashmakom* is the very essence of Tajik culture, and the Bukharan style alone is the epitome of *shashmakom*. In this assertion he demotes somewhat the cultural authority of the Ferghana region from which both the Khujand and Ferghana-Tashkent styles arose, and at the same time makes an indirect statement about the political link between the Ferghana Valley and Tashkent, the Uzbek capital. Meanwhile, Uzbeks themselves have de-Persianized the term *shashmakom* in favor of the name *makom,* just as they have changed many Tajik street names in the Ferghana Valley to Uzbek ones. On its side, the Tajik government has virtually canonized *shashmakom* and to some extent ideologized it.

Discussions at a seven-day conference on *shashmakom* held in Dushanbe in April 2008 showed this process in full bloom. Three of the five ensembles that performed came from the Ferghana region, but all had been trained under the new *shashmakom* Academy in Dushanbe. Experts proceeded to debate whether the Khujand and Ferghana-Tashkent styles were indeed independent phenomena or merely altered adaptations of the "canonic" prototype from Bukhara. One speaker implied that the problem with the Ferghana style is that it enjoys too much freedom.[25]

These debates bring to mind the efforts of Abdukhalil Sharipov from the village of Khodzhai Alo to "purify" Islam. They also represent the effort by Tajik nationalist intellectuals to pry Sughd province away from its Ferghana (e.g., Uzbek) identity and link it more closely with the more solidly Tajik world of Bukhara, with its new musical center in the south. The academician Shukuri, who himself hails from Bukhara, has promoted the idea of Dushanbe as the "new Bukhara." The entire project reveals the effort of political elites in Tajikistan to change the vectors of identity in the Tajik part of the Ferghana Valley. By canonizing the Bukharan style of *shashmakom* they are employing the same technique as Muslim fundamentalists who argue that sharia law is not subject to interpretation and must be accepted whole.

The debate over *shashmakom* also reflects concern over the culture and identity of the Ferghana Valley itself, a region to which political, religious, and even cultural dissidents have flocked over the years. *Shashmakom* also thrives in Azerbaijan and Iran itself, both solidly Shiia nations. In both settings the *shashmakom* performance style is more free and emotional than the Bukharan version, the product of a solid Hanafi Sunni culture. Both the Ferghana-Tashkent and Khujand styles share these qualities, which, by analogy, involve *interpretation* rather than *literalism,* and therefore represent a kind of Shiite attitude to the sacred or canonic text. The concerns expressed in Dushanbe trace ultimately to the fact that the entire Ferghana Valley has strong Sufi traditions that recall Shiism, in spite of their having been accepted by orthodox Sunnis as early as Ghazali in the twelfth century.[26]

In the Tajik capital, as in the Uzbek capital, *shashmakom* serves as a powerful cultural symbol and even as a political resource. But in the Ferghana Valley itself, *shashmakom* is nothing less than an elemental spiritual phenomenon. People listen to it everywhere—at weddings, official receptions, bazaars, and even bus stations. In many respects *shashmakom* fulfills a therapeutic role for residents of the Ferghana Valley, easing psychological tensions and restoring spiritual balance to people throughout the region. *Shashmakom* is a state of soul for every Ferghana Valley resident, helping him restore harmony amid the disruptions that prevail everywhere in a region divided by contending ideologies and identities.

In Search of a Lost Identity

Regarding patronage in the Ferghana Valley, foreign institutions often have sponsored cultural organizations there, while domestic businesses (as artists and cultural figures constantly remind us) rarely do so, preferring instead to make large donations to religious projects. Such essentially European cultural forms as ballet, opera, and symphonic music are all in decline in the Ferghana Valley, especially in the Kyrgyz and Tajik sectors but increasingly in Uzbekistan as well.[27] This is due above all to declining interest among the Kyrgyz, Tajiks, and Uzbeks, although this is partially offset by other national groups living there, who supplement the ranks of those who patronize and conserve these art forms. Meanwhile, in all three sectors of the valley the political elites are committed to the preservation of their national cultural identity in an age of globalization, and therefore they pay close attention to the development of the traditional arts.

In a recent session in Uzbekistan involving experts in the fine arts, theatrical producers, and historians, the question arose whether Uzbek theaters were in a state of effervescence or crisis. Ildar Mukhtarov, a well-known Uzbek authority on art, suggested that widely heard concerns over tradition and the social status of the performing arts imply that theater is in crisis and only the decorative and applied arts are flourishing. Another participant, Alimjon Salimov, noted the widespread calls for a return to tradition, but then asked poignantly whether such a tradition exists. "What are we supposed to return to?" he inquired. "We did not gain a mastery of European theater yet in the process of trying we lost our roots."[28]

This is not to say that there are no authentic contemporary arts in the Ferghana Valley. Particularly deserving of mention is the Ferghana School of poetry that emerged in the 1980s and early 1990s in the city of Ferghana. During those years this city gave rise to something reminiscent of a true Hellenistic polis, with a group of poets rising above nationality and race to create a school of poetry espousing universal principles. The group was ethnically diverse but united by this common commitment. Its most prominent members were Sasha Kuprin, who wrote under the pseudonym Abdulla Khaidar (a name he chose in homage to the timeless spirituality of the Ferghana region), Gregory Kohelet, Khamdam Zakirov, Sergei Alibekov, Iusuf Karaev, Daniil Kislov, Enver Izetov, Viacheslav Useinov, Olga Grebennikova, Evgenii Olevskii, Igor Zenkov, Renat Taziev, Khamid Ismailov, Alexander Gutin, and, notably, Shamshad Abdullaev.

The "Ferghana school" began in the 1980s as part of the Russian literary underground and *samizdat* movement. In 1984 the filmmaker Sergei Alibekov completed a prizewinning cartoon based on the works of Ray Bradbury, and then a pointillist and minimalist film titled *Nit* that hypnotically depicts the semi-arid outskirts of Ferghana. The next year Enver Izetov issued a prize-winning volume of illustrations of poems by Rainer Maria Rilke, Ted Hughes, Pier Paolo Pasolini, and Mario Luzi. By 1986 the group established a film society that amassed an ambitious collection of films by French avant-gardists of the 1920s as well as Jean Epstein, Abel Gans, Jean Cocteau, and others.

Over the first half of the 1990s, the Ferghana poets mounted a section on poetry in the journal *Zvezda Vostoka* (Star of the East), which was shortlisted for a Little Booker Prize. Their editorial manifesto declared: "Our work is a useless attempt to express our indecision in the face of the freedom that is steadily slipping away." Their next initiative came in 1997 with the website Ferghana.ru, which also was nominated for the Russian Little Booker Prize.

Beginning in 1989 works by Ferghana writers began appearing in alternative publications in Russia and the West, and in recent years they have received a number of prestigious awards in Russia, including the Andrei Bely Prize and the Globus Award. In 2000 the Open Society Institute in Tashkent sponsored the publication of the *Poetry and Ferghana* almanac, which in turn led to more recognition abroad, notably the British Russian Booker Prize.

Today, unfortunately, the majority of Ferghana authors, like many Renaissance humanists, have left their native city to settle elsewhere, whether in Holland, Israel, Austria, Finland, Russia, Ukraine, or the United States.

The Ferghana poets set forth their program in the following terms:

- To detach oneself from one's roots as far as possible, thereby enriching them by this detachment;
- To stress one's anti-historicism, distaste for social reality, and fear of action;
- To aspire to maintain one's distance from all ideological temptations and emblems;
- To polish fragments rather than the mythic wholeness of artistic memory, with its Manichean duality . . . and comforting offer of emotional survival within a fundamental chaos;
- To avoid explaining reality and instead to make it palpable.

A revealing example of this mental outlook is a paragraph taken from the diary of poet Shamshad Abdullaev:

> Returning home from a Muslim cemetery I met a Tajik from the village of Sokh who was passing along the low brick wall. I immediately recalled a French compilation of Paul Celan translated by Andre de Bussy. This was a jump into the unconscious where, strange as it may seem, there reigns an amazing order, one that can emerge as a thread that can lead us, if we are lucky, to the seeds of other paradigms or at least to sincere references to a hypnotic terrain where one can die.[29]

Taking their work as a whole, the Ferghana poets manifest a steady universalism and at the same time the constant pull of "locality," in this case Ferghana. This induces them to search for the identity they have lost but which is constantly arising anew, like a phoenix, from seemingly inconspicuous fragments of the locality itself, whether a mud brick wall, roof, or tree. In the words of poet Sasha Kuprin, "words like *kishlak* (village), *aryk* (irrigation canal), *chinar* (oriental plane tree), *bazaar, chaikhana* (teahouse), and *plov* (pilaf) are not mere fragments of exotic vocabulary but worlds through which we experience a common time and destiny."[30]

Conclusion

From this overview, we may conclude that the culture of the Ferghana Valley faces the challenge of adapting tradition to modernity, and vice versa. When these become mutually exclusive ideologies, they can become obstacles to development and lead to serious conflict, as has happened repeatedly. Because of this common challenge, the borders of the valley's three states cannot only divide but unite. Yet is no overstatement to say that identity in the Ferghana Valley is in crisis, with each country pointing to threats to its particular identity that it believes are emanating from the other states. Put differently, each country in the Ferghana Valley seeks today to deconstruct and redefine the common Ferghana identity within the confines of its own national identity.

Yet the Ferghana region as a whole must sooner or later confront globalization, and the manner in which it addresses the issues of tradition and modernity will shape its development thereafter. This process today is not helped by the crisis of education in the Ferghana Valley, which is accompanied by a sharp decline in the status of the intelligentsia, whose authority is everywhere being challenged by members of clergy.

The intelligentsia, meanwhile, is finding it difficult to define its own cultural traditions in either spatial or temporal contexts. As a result, the quest for identity in the Ferghana Valley is increasingly perceived as a choice between religion and nationalism, with no third path.

The erosion of traditional networks and institutions in the Ferghana Valley and the still-weak national sovereignties has opened the way to non-traditional religious ideologies of a trans-national and pan-Islamist nature. These currents of political Islam are emerging as primary social forces and have the potential to destabilize the region. This is happening because governments have largely ignored this new Islamist middle class. For the time being this group maintains a balance between its national and religious identities, but this need not last.

In speaking of this, it is useful to distinguish between traditionalism and traditions, modernism and modernization, globalism and globalization, with each of the former being an ideology and the latter a real process in social, economic, religious or cultural spheres. Excessive ideologization leads to polarization and a reduction in the space for dialogue. Social and political space lend themselves more naturally to dialogue, which is particularly important in the context of the Ferghana Valley's cultural and religious situation. However, they play a positive role only when they are grounded on civic principles of coexistence, not on ethnic or national principles.

Special mechanisms are needed today to create the free social space in which key issues affecting the Ferghana Valley can be pondered. This only can be done by drawing on existing social and cultural capital and by developing citizens' ability to present and defend their views calmly, as well as to adapt them to rapidly changing circumstances. This will prevent concern for tradition from descending into an ideology of traditionalism, modernization from becoming a narrow modernism, and globalization from becoming a sterile ideology of globalism. It will foster favorable conditions for people of the Ferghana Valley to adapt traditions to modernity and vice versa. In the end, "free intellectual zones" are as important to such a region of disputed borders as "free economic zones."

The above analysis suggests the need to activate the social capital that inheres in the Ferghana Valley's rich traditions, and use it to mediate among the diverse cultures there and also between those cultures and the modern world. This social capital undeniably derives from an Islamic identity, but it is manifest through locally rooted Muslim traditions that affirm the co-existence of religion with secular and intellectual values. It is possible that many received traditions will be discarded, but others can be restated in a contemporary context and thereby preserved. This process will forge links between tradition and modernity.

The existing infrastructure of the Ferghana Valley limits both cross-border business contacts and the exchange of ideas that is so vital for the region's cultural revival. Poor communications create immense possibilities for radical groups. There is therefore an urgent need not only to expand transport across the Ferghana Valley, but also to open new channels for communication that will help a world of traditions cope with contemporary changes.

Notes

1. Shamshad Abdullaev, "Ob odnom fenomene ferganskoi kultury: genesis i mestnost," unpublished manuscript, 2008.
2. "Arkheologiia uzbekskoi identichnosti," *Etnograficheskoe obozrenie,* no. 1, 2005 (Special Issue).
3. Adam Metz, *Musulmanskii Renessans,* Moscow, 1973, p. 473.
4. See Abu Khamid Al-Gazali, *Krushenie pozitsii filosofov,* translated from Arabic. Moscow, 2007, p. 277; Pulat Shozimov, "Problemy vzaimootnosheniia razuma i very vo vzgliadakh Abu Khamida al-Gazali: sovremennyi kontekst," Izvestiia of the Academy of Sciences of the Republic of Tajikistan, series *Filosofiia i Pravo,* no. 3, 2008, pp. 51–59.
5. See Bakhtior Babadzhanov, "Ferghana: Istochnik ili zhertva islamskogo fundamentalizma?" *Central Asia and the Caucasus,* vol. 4, no. 5, 1999.
6. Order no. 1247 of the president of the Republic of Tajikistan Emomali Rakhmon "On Procedures for the Conduct of Events Related to Customs and Rites of the Republic of Tajikistan."
7. Law of the Republic of Tajikistan "On Regularizing Traditions and Ceremonies in the Republic of Tajikistan," no. 272, July 8, 2007.
8. Pulat Shozimov's interview with Muradullo Davlatov, Dushanbe, 22 July, 2007.
9. At present Muhammadsharif Khimmatzoda, one of the IRPT members of the parlia-

ment, left due to illness. Thus, only one IRPT representative remains—Mukhiddin Kabiri, the chairman of the IRPT.

10. Pulat Shozimov's interview with Mukhiddin Kabiri, Dushanbe, March 2007.

11. Personal archive of the writer Lutfi Said, Sughd Museum of Historical-Regional Studies, Manuscripts Department, Sughd province, Isfara city. Their patents were called *sachara,* which confirmed their genealogical line of descent from the great Sufi leaders.

12. Pulat Shozimov's interview with Abdumanon Raupov, director of the Directorate of Museums of Historical-Regional Studies in Isfara city, Sughd province, 2007, February 20.

13. Joomart Sulaimanov, the Kyrgyz co-author of the present chapter, prepared these materials on Kyrgyzstan.

14. "Teletaip 'AP,'" *Asiia-plius,* April 23, 2008.

15. Data on the number of schools and mosques in Sughd province is from Khudzhand hukumat, "Report of the Ministry of Culture of the Republic of Tajikistan for 2008."

16. Ofitsialnye dannye statistiki Otdela kultury po informatsii pri Ministerstve Kultury Respubliki Tadzhikistan, Dushanbe, 2008.

17. *Khamsoia* (neighbor) from Tajik means "shadow."

18. Valeriy Bushkov, "Osobennosti formirovaniia naseleniia iugo-zapadnoi Fergany (na primere Isfarinskogo raiona Sogdiiskoi oblasti Respubliki Tadzhikistan)," in *Ferganskaia dolina: etnichnost, etnicheskie protsesy, ethnicheskie konflikty,* ed. Sergey Abashin and Valerii Bushkov, Moscow, 2004, p. 109.

19. The information on Isfara city of Isfara province, including on the Tajik part of the Ferghana Valley (Sughd province) is based on anthropological and sociological monitoring from 2003 to 2008 conducted for the Center for Social-Political Research "Korshinos" by Pulat Shozimov, Khairiddin Idiev, and Kurbon Giyev.

20. Pulat Shozimov's interview with a representative of the Salmani Fors Madrassa, Isfara, in village of Chorkukh, 2003; see also Pulat Shozimov, *Tadzhikskaia identichnost i gosudarstvennoe stroitelstvo v Tadzhikistane,* Dushanbe, 2003, p. 209.

21. Khairidin Idiev, *Traditsii i novatsii v kontekste izmeneniia obschestvennoi zhizni sovremennogo Tadzhikistana,* Dushanbe, 2006, p. 96.

22. Ibid.

23. Pulat Shozimov's interview with Adukhalil Sharipov, Isfara, in the village of Khodzhai Alo, 2007.

24. Abdukhalil Sharipov has joined the ranks of labor migrants in Russia. The last cohort of the Isfara intelligentsia, which until the very last moment resisted emigration, finally left its traditional locale in search of better prospects abroad.

25. Pulat Shozimov's interview with Abduvalli Abdurashidov, Dushanbe, April 28, 2008.

26. It is important to note the influence in Ferghana of the "twelve-makom" (*duvozdakh makom*) Uyghur traditions from Kashgaria. Iurii V. Keldysh, Faizulla M. Karomatov, eds., *Professionalnaia muzyka ustnoi traditsii narodov Blizhnego, Srednego Vostoka i sovremennost,* Tashkent, 1981, p. 312.

27. *Iskusstvo Uzbekistana na sovremennom etape sotsialno-kulturnogo razvitiia. Materialy seminarov, dokladov i kollokviuma ekspertov,* Tashkent, 2006, p. 18.

28. Ibid., p. 20.

29. Shamshed Abdullaev, *Iz dnevnika: svobodnaia proza. Poeziia i Ferghana,* Tashkent, 2000, pp. 34–35.

30. Abdullaev, "Ob odnom fenomene ferganskoi kultury."

13

Islam in the Ferghana Valley: Between National Identity and Islamic Alternative

Bakhtiyar Babadjanov (Uzbekistan), with
Kamil Malikov (Kyrgyz Republic) and
Aloviddin Nazarov (Tajikistan)

Each of the three authors who worked on this chapter independently studied the historical, political, and religious processes in that section of the Ferghana Valley that is part of his respective country.[1] Each author's study, while quite distinct, nonetheless has much in common with the others, presenting a neighbors' perspective with a simultaneous view from inside. Exhaustive discussions led the authors to conclude that the current religious situation in each of the three parts of the Ferghana Valley has been shaped by the three countries' specific political circumstances, laws, and policies.

After 1991, the independence of the three countries and the establishment of borders and customs posts increased the mutual isolation of the three zones of the Ferghana Valley. At the same time, age-old ties of friendship, family, and trade did not get lost, even though religious ties were not as intense as they had been. This is particularly true in the western sector of the valley—between Uzbekistan and Tajikistan. Further east, relationships between the Kyrgyz and the Uzbek parts of the valley also became less intense, but not to the same extent as in the west. Personal contacts there remain close, and the religious life in the Kyrgyz and Uzbek sectors is highly interdependent. The intensity of contact reflects the ethnic characteristics of each region—for example, the presence of numerous enclaves of Uzbeks in the territory of southern Kyrgyzstan.

At the same time these borders function as key points for the transfer of the Chinese goods that are so popular in Central Asia. This commerce engages the larger merchants and others associated with trans-valley trade, most of whom happen to be very religious. The customs and other barriers at the borders call forth two very different reactions from the traders. Among older traders they elicit nostalgia for Soviet times, when such impediments did not exist. Curiously, this nostalgia thrives in spite of the fact that the shuttle trade in which these merchants engage did not exist then. Among younger traders these barriers generate interest in transnational parties like Hizb ut-Tahrir (HT; Party of Liberation), which claim that in a single Islamic state such problems would not exist.

The existence of multiple nuances of this sort, many of them based on differences within the valley, prompted the authors to present their findings on each national region as independent studies, at the same time acknowledging the interactions and commonalities among all three sectors, especially in border areas of the Ferghana Valley. All three parts of the valley were once part of a single Kokand Khanate, and later of the Russian colony of Turkestan. In Soviet times the Ferghana Valley, despite being divided among three republics, nonetheless remained a cohesive region in which the suppression of religion and its subsequent revival occurred through region-wide processes. Because of these, the region must be taken as a whole, even while bearing in mind the political, economic, and even ideological circumstances specific to each of the countries.

On this basis, the authors came to appreciate the degree to which the distinctive elements of the religious situation in each of their respective countries have led in two opposite directions. Some tendencies led to the partial disintegration of old relationships among the religious elite of the three countries and in the Ferghana Valley as a whole; others encouraged the assimilation of radical and extremist political parties and Islamist groups whose rhetoric sought to discredit national governments. Members of the religious elites insisted that the leaders who emerged after 1991 were utterly incapable of re-establishing the pre-colonial Muslim integration that they believed once existed in Central Asia.

The authors do not pretend to offer solutions to these pressing problems, or even a definitive analysis of them. Their goal is more modest. They recognize, of course, that the artificial division of the Ferghana Valley and the region as a whole that took place in the Soviet period, and which is now criticized in all countries, had both negative and positive consequences. However, with respect to religion, the new state divisions and borders clearly aggravated the situation by not allowing the populace to address and solve the various challenges they face together. At the same time they make it more difficult to coordinate efforts against religiously motivated terrorism, and they discourage the kinds of rational cooperation among the three regional countries that will in the long run remove the factors that give rise to such terrorism in the first place.

Uzbekistan

Earlier chapters in this volume reminded us that from the early eighteenth century almost all of the Ferghana Valley was part of the Kokand Khanate. Throughout its existence the Kokand Khanate engaged in a perpetual struggle to preserve its territorial integrity. Across the territory ruled from Kokand, border territories frequently changed hands and were settled by diverse tribes and ethnic groups. This created ethnic and linguistic diversity within the khanate and greatly weakened Islamic rules and Islamic institutions there. It is no exaggeration to say that the internal relationships and actual structures of government in Kokand were based more on the traditions and principles of nomadic nations than on Islam.

When Russia invaded Central Asia to colonize it, generals Mikhail G. Cherniaev and, later, Konstantin P. von Kaufman attacked Kokand. The Kokand Khanate lost a significant piece of territory, but inside Kokand a bloody struggle for power continued. Rebellions were raised against Khudayar Khan, who was accused of collaborating with the Russian infidels. These uprisings persisted from 1869 to 1876, and were mounted under the banner of *jihad* (holy war). The succession of revolts prompted the imperial government in February 1876 to eliminate the Kokand Khanate as a state. Thereafter, the territory of Kokand was merged with the already colonized parts of Turkestan, as Russians then referred to the main part of Transoxiana.

Due to their dependence for funds on the government in Kokand, religious institutions, and especially schools, were gravely affected by the destruction of the Kokand state. They lost state funding in the form of *waqf* donations,[2] and that left them fully dependent on donations from private individuals, which often led to abuses. Overall, religious education declined precipitously, even though privately supported religious training increased. As noted in earlier chapters, this private tradition proved very useful during the Soviet era, for when almost all the institutions of religious education (*maktabs* and *madrassas*)[3] were closed, citizens revived teaching in the so-called *hujras* (private religious study groups).

At the same time, the destruction of Kokand's statehood led to a very different phenomenon among Muslims of the Ferghana Valley. The regulations of sharia law had not been closely observed under the Kokand Khanate,[4] but the elimination of the khanate led to an immediate strengthening of the populace's Islamic identity. The frequent calls of theologians for the community to respect sharia law appeared as a natural form of self-defense in the face of invasion by "aliens" and "infidels." The khanate and its officials had been perceived as political symbols and champions of Islam, and their fall had led to confusion among most Muslims, the more so since they had been destroyed by Russians who, of course, were perceived as invaders and infidels.[5] This explains why the local *ummah,* or religious community, whose leaders called increasingly for a return to sharia law in the realm of private life, searched out new ways of emphasizing local identities separate from association with the infidels.

It is no coincidence that one of the most significant Turkestani uprisings against the Russians occurred in May 1898, in the very heart of the Ferghana Valley, Andijan. Its leader, Madali Ishan (Dukchi-Ishan), advocated the re-establishment of an Islamic state. In his secret letters he appealed to the spiritual symbol of a single Islamic Caliphate to be established under the Turkish pasha Abdul Hamid II (1876–1909), who claimed the title of Caliph of the Muslims."[6] Both in the period of the Russian Revolution and in the late-Soviet period and era of independence, this notion of a caliphate, an Islamic state, and other versions of Islamic autonomy were to be reborn again and again. The majority of Muslims in the region did not respond to the calls for jihad, but Dukchi Ishan found strong support locally.

The February Revolution of 1917 gave rise to a transitional government in St. Petersburg that had no desire to lose those territories in the Caucasus and Central Asia that had been incorporated into the Russian Empire. In protest, the notion of Islamic autonomy (*mukhtoriyat*) blossomed once more in the Ferghana Valley. In 1918 in the city of Kokand there was an attempt to establish an autonomous state based on Islamic principles. Even though the Kokand Republic limited its demands to religious and cultural autonomy and did not seek to secede from Russia, the Bolsheviks brutally suppressed it.[7] The episode reminds us that the idea of recovering a lost Islamic state and reaffirming lost Islamic values has been imprinted on the minds of people in the Ferghana Valley for a long time. To the faithful, such diverse events as the declaration of Kokand's autonomy or the Andijan uprising of 1898 appeared as stages in the struggle not only for independence but for Islam as well, and as symbols of the assertion of an Islamic self-identity.

Soviet rule divided the Ferghana Valley among three Soviet republics. The main part of Ferghana (18,044,000 square kilometers) and the major urban centers of Andijan, Ferghana, Kokand, Margilan, and Namangan all went to Uzbekistan. Yet the ethnic and religious structure even within Uzbekistan's sector turned out to be very diverse, with Uzbeks, Tajiks, Kyrgyz, Tatars, Russians, and others.[8]

Such anti-Soviet movements as those of Madamin Bek, Shir-Muhammad-Kurshermat, Rahmankul, and others remind us that the Ferghana Valley offered staunch resistance, both political and military, to the Bolshevik takeover, and that, in the case of the *basmachi*, this resistance lasted until 1930. None of these groups, however, emphasized religious motives in their struggle.[9]

After their final victory, the Bolsheviks instituted a general repression that was particularly harsh in the Ferghana Valley. Organs of the NKVD tried to purge (in other words, physically destroy or exile to the GULAG)[10] nationalist and religious-minded citizens, especially those who had participated in clandestine resistance groups. The most active of these organizations was the religious-national Milliy Ittihad (National Organization), which had maintained especially strong branches in Andijan, Osh, Kokand, and Khujand. Later, in the 1930s, almost all remaining members of this organization were executed or exiled to the GULAG.[11]

The Bolsheviks' bitterly hostile attitude toward religious figures found expression in the most primitive attacks in the official media, with different forms of official persecution and harassment being adopted as circumstances required. The most powerful blow struck against the mosque (as well as Christian churches) was the nationalization of all religious property, including their land and shops. By the end of 1929, nearly all the endowed (*waqf*) property of mosques, *madrassas* and *maktabs* had been confiscated. Sometime later *waqf* committees were disbanded, even as all mosques and religious schools were closed. Their buildings were given

to the newly created collective farms, to be used as storage facilities or as ancil-
lary space for small businesses and the like.[12] Most religious leaders were arrested
and exiled to remote parts of Russia.[13] In the Ferghana Valley the Soviet regime
used special decrees and judicial verdicts to close mosques by 1932.[14] According
to some reports, the main wave of repression against religious leaders occurred as
early as the second half of the twenties, although it was repeatedly re-launched in
subsequent years.[15] Indeed, the repression of religious leaders continued unabated
until the start of World War II in 1941.

The repression of religious life unexpectedly declined during the war. Some
old mullahs in the Ferghana Valley still retell a legend popular at the time, namely
that on the eve of the war the Khazrat (Saint) Khizr (the hero of most Central
Asian legends) appeared to Stalin in a dream. The Saint told Stalin he would soon
have to fight a great and powerful enemy and that he, Khizr, would enable Stalin
to triumph over his enemies if Stalin would reopen at least one mosque. And that
is why Stalin, supposedly after long altercations with other officials, opened not
one but hundreds of mosques. His decision was made easier by the fact that Khizr
presented Stalin with a few victories in advance.

At the time other explanations account for this rapid zigzag in the normally rigid
Soviet policy toward religion. For example, on the first Friday after the German
army attacked the USSR, the Muslims of Tashkent and a number of cities of the
Ferghana Valley assembled at closed mosques and organized Friday prayers under
the open sky. This followed an old and well-remembered tradition that on the first
Friday after an enemy invasion the faithful would recite prayers "for the health and
victory of the country's *padishah*" (Stalin, of course, was called Padishah), and
with pleas for Allah to "rain down death on the heads of the enemy." This, at any
rate, is how one of the oldest members of the Central Asian Spiritual Directorate
for Muslims, Nodir-khon Domla (d. 1976) accounted for these events in his diary.
He was not surprised to learn that Muslims prayed "for the health, power, and victory of the *padishah* (Stalin)," that is of the very person most responsible for their
suffering repression. Nodir-khon Domla was surprised that the Muslims had not
forgotten the old religious traditions, since a full generation had by then grown up
in an environment where religion was anathema and unauthorized prayer could
lead to death. But this did not happen. Many reports, mainly from the NKVD,
expressed similar amazement at the expressions of loyalty to the Soviet authorities
from Muslim as well as Orthodox Christian leaders. Such incidents could not fail
to catch the attention of the "Father of the People" and his faithful servants.

The Soviet Union's improved relations with the Allies also prompted Moscow to
soften its anti-religious and anti-Muslim policies. Winston Churchill, for example,
in his face-to-face contacts with Stalin at the historic meetings and in his correspondence, took note of the fact that he represented a number of Muslim countries allied
with Britain. Nor did he shy away from raising the "Muslim question" with Stalin.
Indeed, it is quite possible that Stalin's rather hasty decision to institute a respite in
the campaign against religion and to establish a Muslim Spiritual Directorate were

both tactical steps that he undertook to foster a better climate at the forthcoming Tehran Conference in December 1943.

The Spiritual Directorate of Muslims of Central Asia and Kazakhstan, better known under the acronym SADUM, was formed in Tashkent in October 1943,[16] by a *kurultai* (council) of representatives of the Muslims of Central Asia and Kazakhstan.[17]

SADUM's goal was to institute centralized control over all religious life in the region. Needless to say, all the directorate's actions and documents were closely censored. Despite the fact that the Soviet government had announced the separation of civil and religious life, the religious directorates were virtually governmental bodies and were perceived as such by the faithful. Inevitably, in implementing the orders of the state bureaucracy SADUM's leader wielded almost limitless power, and imposed strict authoritarian rule on the religious institutions entrusted to his care. Believers perceived SADUM's decrees or *fatwas*[18] as state actions that lacked all religious legitimacy. Nevertheless, the directorate used its power to regulate the number of mosques to provide gradually for the opening of new ones, and in various ways and to differing degrees tried to protect the rights of the faithful.[19]

The heat of repression against religious figures abated somewhat in the post-war years, although the persecution of imams, as well as the spiritual leaders of other faiths, lasted until the period of Leonid Brezhnev (1964–82). SADUM paid particular attention to the Ferghana Valley, for it knew full well that here was the largest concentration of practicing Muslims in Central Asia. Because of this, it appointed special officials (*qadiyats*) to Namangan, Khujand, Ferghana, and Andijan.[20]

Ferghana in the Early Bolshevik Era: The Difficult Path Between Secularization and Religion

Evaluating conditions in the Ferghana Valley today, many experts suggest that the aggressively anti-religious policies of the Soviet regime and then, later, its more balanced policies, both failed. But the policy of atheism, as well as Soviet ideology as a whole, had serious consequences that are reflected in the mentality of ordinary believers as well as religious leaders, including those who either secretly or openly support the idea of a separate Muslim identity. These consequences can be detected in current society across the region, including in the Ferghana Valley. To declare, as some do, that secular elements of the society (which are products of the Soviet era) are totally gone is either to misunderstand the current realities or deliberately to distort them.

To evaluate today's realities one must gain some historical perspective on them. When the Bolsheviks launched their policy of atheism, they were seeking above all to exploit various preexisting conditions that favored what they were trying to achieve. Even prior to Russian colonization the Ferghana Valley community had fallen into a protracted crisis, which was manifested in its spiritual life and religious education.[21] It is true that legislation was based on religious directions from the *qadis* (sharia courts) and the system of appeals under the Shaikh al-Islam, but in reality all this failed to protect the rights of ordinary believers.[22] Reacting against this stagnation, there arose among religious leaders a reform movement—Jadidism—which declared that the true path out of this crisis was through the reform of education and the introduction of secular subjects into the school curriculum.[23]

Meanwhile, the religious leaders themselves became increasingly discredited in the eyes of the religious believers, especially those from the lower classes. In addition to issues of corruption and dishonesty, problems arose from the leaders' higher social class. Further, the prevailing psychology often equated the very fallible interpreters of religion, or those who passed judgments "in behalf of God," with the Faith itself. This made it very easy to advance arguments in support of the Bolshevik idea that "religion is the weapon with which the exploiters enslave the working class."

The Jadids themselves adeptly brought such strong charges against the more conservative religious clerics. Drawing on clichés spread by the Jadids, one could remind workers of the "dark past," when, for example, the religious courts failed to defend their rights, when polygamy prevailed, and when the imams conducted themselves arrogantly. The behavior of religious leaders became a subject for parables, ironical stories, and even special plays that the religious reformers produced and disseminated.[24] Even after the Bolsheviks displayed the utmost intolerance toward these same reformers, and especially those who were proponents of nationalistic ideas, the majority of reformers continued their harsh criticism of conservative theologians, and even used this to ingratiate themselves with the new authorities.[25]

Thanks to this the communist propaganda, with its simplistic paradigms, proletarian ideology, and insistent appeals to "the oppressed," largely succeeded. The primitive and brutal slogans of the Bolsheviks were directed toward an abstract "worker" embittered by past injustices. And that worker adopted them, if not with enthusiasm then at least with tacit approval. He also absorbed the Bolsheviks' overwhelming nihilism. In virtually all publications of that time, we encounter the persistently repeated image of an enemy, whether the bey, mullah, ishan, feudal lord, capitalist, or merchant (*savdogar*), who were all referred to as "class enemies" and worse.[26] The Bolsheviks taught the common citizen that the distinction between "working people" and "exploiters" was the difference between good and evil, and, in the end, between legitimate and illegitimate.[27]

The raw aggressiveness with which the new power struck out at the "class enemies" aroused understandable fear among the majority of the population. The media of the time, and especially the Bolshevik press, emanate this spirit of aggression. Moreover, it effectively exploited the self-criticism of religious leaders from the era of the khanates and colonial rule.

Acknowledging this, we should not lose sight of the spread of basic literacy, especially among women, for which the Bolsheviks so desperately fought. Indeed, the struggle for literacy would appear quite noble were it not for the primitively materialistic motives underlying it, namely, to separate the people from their religions and traditions. The Communists immediately began to forge their "new Soviet man" through the establishment of a new and totally controlled education system, and by destroying religious education, including the so-called new method proposed by the Jadids. Had they not done this their propaganda would have failed with the illiterate populist, and their goal of creating a "new man" would have been called into question. Hence, they closed religious schools and madrassas throughout the Ferghana Valley and other deeply religious regions. The campaign appeared a success, but the story did not end there. Surviving documents from both the pre- and post-World War II eras prove that in most cities of the valley the system of private religious education was rapidly restored.[28] Much the same had occurred in the period of Russian colonization.

It was Lenin who conceived the goal of forming a "new type person," and soon the Communist Party was endlessly repeating the phrase in its propaganda materials. To this end, the Bolsheviks' first task was to struggle against religion, which it saw as an unwanted ideological rival and enemy. But obliterating the influence of religion proved more difficult in Muslim areas and where Islam played a serious role in the life of society. In those places, reality refused to bend to the Bolsheviks' slogans.

A switch to the Latin script in 1927–28 and then, simultaneously in all the republics, to the Cyrillic alphabet in 1932 was conceived as a further move to "pull people from the southern republics of the USSR out from under the dark influence of religion," to quote the resolution of the Nineteenth Party Conference of July 16, 1932, as published in *Izvestia*'s Uzbek edition the next day. The campaign to emancipate women had the same goal, and found expression mainly in sustained efforts to do away with the Central Asian version of the *hijab,* called a *paranja.*[29] This movement was branded Hujum (Attack), expressing the aggressiveness and resoluteness with which the authorities went about their work. However, the Hujum campaign proved particularly difficult in the Ferghana Valley. Only after a full generation under Soviet rule did Ferghana women undergo full emancipation, and then only in a primitive, even vulgar manner. Indeed, until the 1970s one would still encounter women in *hijab*s in Namangan, Osh, Andijan, and even in the more industrialized Khujand. And when Gorbachev reduced anti-religious pressures a decade later, the *hijab* immediately became widespread once more. In the towns and villages of the valley today there exists a balance between the "closed" women and girls (those wearing the *hijab*), and those not wearing it, who are mostly young. In addition, one encounters women who wear a simple kerchief, in the Turkish style, tying its ends at the nape of their necks. These are mainly middle-aged women who did not want to irritate those from traditional families with a more provocatively "open" style.

This diversity of women's dress is now a reality in all the cities of the Ferghana Valley and no longer overtly represents a conflict of values. However, both women and men in the Ferghana Valley who favor the *hijab* do so less as a nod to social convention than as a response to a sacred order. Whether they respond to such an order marks a division between true believers and those for whom faith consists merely of a loosely enforced tradition. This diversity represents the combined product of the Soviet past and of the collapse of the USSR, when new paradigms and ideologies entered the valley, along with re-Islamization.

Most people in the Ferghana Valley despised the Bolsheviks but realized that the old forms of religious life could not be restored. Some embarked on a path of resistance, or emigrated. Most, however, were amenable to compromise, and were prepared to demonstrate their conformity on the pages of the official Soviet press.[30] The Ferghana theologians, however, adopted yet a third position. In their publications at the time they called for Muslims of different persuasions to cease mutual recriminations and disputes and to unite. As the Kokand journal *Kengash* (The Council) expressed it, "Disputes lead to division and division leads to defeat."[31] One can readily understand what kind of "defeat" the writer had in mind.

Local religious leaders had to deal with the theologians, most of whom in one way or another rejected Bolshevik rule. A majority of them concluded that the imbalance between the Bolsheviks' forces and their own was too great, and that they had no other choice than to seek a compromise with the new authorities. For their part the Bolsheviks initially promised "freedom of conscience and religious belief." Those who struck a compromise with the communist leaders were branded with the offensive title of "red mullahs."

Later programs of official atheism and the secularization of all spheres of life put Islam and the community of believers in a very unfavorable position. A significant number of Ferghana theologians resorted to what Muslims always had considered a legitimate means of self-defense, namely *iztirari holat* (in Arabic, *al-idtirar*) or feigning political and even ideological loyalty to the powers that be. Other theologians and ordinary Muslims resorted to another solution considered legitimate, namely *hijrat,* or emigration from the Dar al-Harb territory where a war against Muslims is being waged.[32]

From Stabilization to Religious Revival

The Bolsheviks' primitive formula that "If religion serves the exploiters, then it must die with the exploiters," did not work. Forced secularization and militant atheism failed to crush the Islamic identity of most local people. Moreover, communist ideology failed to offer a vital alternative to the conservative customs, traditions, and ceremonies of everyday life, which remained a living presence. Most of the faithful believed these customs to be based on religion and that they were therefore sacred. This sanctification of customs and even superstitions put religion into a more favorable position with respect to values and beliefs than the secular ideologies, and especially that of the Communists. It cannot be denied that communist ideology found sympathy among many in the lower classes of society, but it never marginalized the religious traditions of the majority of the region's people.

These religious traditions proved most durable in the Ferghana Valley. Even at the height of Soviet repressions and in the face of official atheism, the elders in the valley's traditional families tried to teach the young the basic duties of the faith, sharia law, and Muslim ethics (*adab/odob*). Those theologians who managed to avoid arrest and persecution continued, despite risks to themselves, to teach theology secretly to interested people. Such illegal study was called *hujra*.[33]

The few religious authorities in Soviet times stuck closely to the works of traditional authors, and especially local writers. This reflected the extreme conservatism, local-based traditionalism, and reticence in the face of the new that prevailed in religious circles. In the process, the region's religious authorities became locked into old disputes and confrontations with the theologians from western areas of the Islamic world.

In Ferghana, one of the best known among such theologians was Muhammadjon Rustamov, more commonly known as Hindustani Domla (1892–1989). Under this and other nicknames (Hodja Dada, Mavlavy) he became known as the most authoritative theologian of the Hanafi school of law in the Ferghana Valley and Tajikistan. Rustamov was born near Kokand and studied in Kokand, Bukhara, Balkh in Afghanistan and, after 1921, in Kashmir, from which he got the nickname "Hindustani." In 1928 he undertook a pilgrimage to Mecca. During the purges he was arrested three times and spent eight-and-a-half years in different parts of Siberia. In 1943, Hindustani was recruited into the Red Army, but was promptly wounded and then furloughed out. Between the mid-1950s and his death he served as imam of the Maulana Charkhi Mosque in Dushanbe, where he was buried.

Beginning in the late 1950s, Hindustani organized illegal educational programs (*hujra*), which trained many religious figures who subsequently gained renown in Ferghana and across the region. Hindustani wrote mystical poetry and various treatises, and he authored a six-volume commentary (*Tafsir*) on the Qur'an in Uzbek,[34] completed in 1979 and illegally disseminated thereafter.

Hindustani rejected all violence in the struggle for the Faith, basing his position on Hanafi doctrine. Any opposition to this Hindustani perceived as Wahhabism. He viewed very negatively the notion of a "pure" Islam that religious and political leaders in Arab countries were exporting to the world. In his writings and sermons he tried to show the heresy of such ideas. Hindustani penned two short treatises on Wahhabism, with a brief description of Muhammad Ibn Abd al-Wahhab's (from whom Wahhabism takes its name) dogmas and with strong words of censure for Wahhab's aggressive politics and his religious intolerance. In actuality, Hindustani directed both treatises against some of the younger theologians at home, who were convinced that conditions in the USSR were causing believers to lose faith and that it was therefore necessary to fight for the return of a "pure Islam."

This young generation of theologians had been trained by the "conservatives"—mainly Hindustani—but they became interested in ideas from the rest of the Islamic world, including those concerning politics. They had been influenced to some degree by their Soviet educations, which shaped their idea of the "other world" beyond the Soviet borders. Their disputes with conservatives began timidly and often did not even concern theological issues.

Following World War II and increasingly after the 1950s and early 1960s, various Islamic religious-political parties and movements became established in Muslim countries. But they had no direct impact on the Muslims of the Soviet republics of Central Asia or on the Ferghana Valley. Only with the appearance of a new generation of Muslim theologians in the mid-1970s was their influence felt. Most had been trained in the illegal religious schools or *hujra*, the earliest of which appeared in the Ferghana Valley in late 1970. Its founders were the young theologians Rahmatulla-alloma (who died in 1981 in a car accident) and Abduvali-qori Mirzaev, both of whom were from Andijan; Rafi'uddin Kamolov from Osh; Maruf qori Rahimdzhanov from Ura-Tyube (Istaravshan), Tajikistan; and others. Sometime later members of this group began calling themselves "The Updaters" or, more accurately, the "Renovators" or "Revivers" (Mujaddidiya). The public, however, branded them Wahhabis.

At almost the same time, in 1973, there arose in Tajikistan another movement of young religious reformers. Current members of the Islamic Renaissance Party date the founding of their party to this gathering of young reformers more than thirty-five years ago.

Returning to the new wave of reformers from Uzbekistan's part of the Ferghana Valley, it is revealing that they referred to themselves as Mujaddidiya, from the Arabic word for "update."[35] This refers to the fact that the Muslim calendar marked 1979 as the first year of the fifteenth century. They were consciously following the old belief that at the start of each century there would appear in the Muslim world an Updater who would fight for the restoration of sharia law, especially in those regions where there had been a falling away from Islamic morality and where sharia law had been "trampled."[36]

The Updaters attracted large numbers of supporters across Soviet Central Asia, most of them inspired by their stated intention to "revive" or "correct" Islam. The founders had studied under Hindustani, but also at the famous Ferghana Valley theological *hujra* run by Abdulhakim qori (aka Hakimjonkori Marghiloni; born 1896, lived in Margilan). Their goals were to revive the "true" sharia law as they understood it, "correct" rituals that had long been practiced by the local Hanafis, foster re-Islamization and purge the faith of "innovations"; and gather the faithful under a single religious and political banner. By the early 1980s members of this new generation of theologians, speaking at public meetings, openly began to express views sharply at odds with Islam as it had long been understood locally. Among those who did so were Abduvali-qori Mirzaev and Muhammad-Ali Radzhab (Radzhabov) Kokandi; they, like many other reformers, attracted mass support, especially in the Ferghana Valley and Tashkent. They adopted Salafi positions on many subjects, all of them supposedly grounded in the life of the earliest Muslim communities, which they believed to have been absolutely free of impermissible innovations (*bid'a*) and the influence of "infidels."

As we have seen, local Hanafi traditionalists called those espousing such views Wahhabis or "reformers." The meaning of these terms evolved over time in the local environment. Before the mid-1970s, some local theologians (including Muhammadjon Hindustani) considered any attempts to change the established forms of local Muslim ritual to be Wahhabism. Since then local Hanafis have used the label Wahhabi to signify "someone fighting for the establishment of political Islam." Now the accepted term for both is Wahhabi or Wahhabism, and it is firmly entrenched among local believers, in the media, and in political discourse across the region, in the Caucasus, and in Russia.

What gave rise to the search by the Wahhabi founders of the Updaters for Islam in its pure and correct state? It was stimulated in part by the search for the very opposite during the ongoing Soviet policy of atheism. Beyond this, it was fostered by the clear signs of the beginning of a crisis in communist ideology itself, accompanied by growing interest in the global processes of modernization and its bearing on Islam. In the eyes of members of Mujaddidiya, those Muslims trying to adapt Islam to these global developments were at the same time unacceptably tolerant of the traditional Hanafi rites and rituals. The leaders of the Mujaddidiya believed that those Hanafi-oriented theologians who engaged in this form of tolerance in the face of the atheistic policy of the state and the new forces of globalization were contributing to the decline of Islam and directly threatening the Islamic character of the local community.

Various ideas of "reformers" and "modernists" from elsewhere in the Islamic world had a major influence on the young theologians of Ferghana. Despite the near-total ban on international contacts that prevailed in the Soviet period, legitimate channels existed through which people and ideas could infiltrate the Soviet republics. Thus, a large number of students came from Palestine, Syria, and less frequently, Egypt. Many of them were members of religious-political parties back home, all of which had a powerful influence on young Arabs at the time. Even though their interaction with Soviet students was restricted by special regulations, these students from abroad found a way to communicate with local young people, especially those interested in religious literature.

For example, both Rahmatulla-alloma and Abduvali-qori Mirzaev traveled to Tashkent five or six times a year from the Ferghana Valley, met with Arab students, and ordered religious literature from them, buying at least five or six copies of each book. This religious and political literature from Arab countries became the second source of influence on the ideas of young theologians of the new wave. In the mid-1970s works by the founder of the Egyptian group al-Ikhwan al-Muslimun (Muslim Brotherhood), Hassan al-Banna (1906–1949), reached the Ferghanans, as did writings by the chief ideologist of the fundamentalist reformers of the 1950s, Sayid Qutb (1912–1966),[37] and by the most influential Pakistani fundamentalist reformer, Abul A'ala Maududi (1903–1979). In addition, all sorts of party journals and proclamations (mainly from al-Ikhwan al-Muslimun) found their way into the hands of young theologians in Ferghana.

Another channel of foreign influence on the Muslims of the Soviet Union included the many official delegations from Central Asia to Muslim countries in the Middle East. These were especially numerous at the time of the SADUM mufti[38] Ziyautdin Babakhanov.[39] Invariably such delegations returned with their suitcases bulging with religious and religious-political literature published in the Arabic countries.

A fourth source of external influences on the future local reformers were the radio programs beamed to the USSR from Western Europe, the Middle East, Iran, and Afghanistan. Particularly worthy of mention is Radio Teheran, which devoted much attention to religious themes. These transmissions were very popular, especially in Tajikistan thanks to the common language, and they were discussed at the first illegal meetings of future leaders of the Islamic Renaissance Party of Tajikistan (IRPT). The most senior member of the party, Qalandari Sadriddin, in whose house the first cell of the future party was founded in 1973 (at which time the party was called Nahzat-i Islomi-yi Javonon-i Tojikiston, or Party of Islamic Youth of Tajikistan), writes about those meetings in his memoirs. The same author refers to the religious and political literature that reached Tajikistan from Iran and Afghanistan.

The 1979 revolution in Iran and the armed resistance of the Afghan mujahedeen to the Red Army took on important symbolic meaning for a new generation of theologians, especially for the Mujaddidiya. Perhaps influenced by these events, the Mujaddidiya began to think the only way their ideas could possibly become reality was to make Islam (of course, in its "pure" form) the religion of state in all countries where it prevailed. Such countries would be called Musulmonobod. With this idea in mind, Rahmatulla-alloma penned a utopian essay that in many respects recalled Tommaso Campanella's *The City of the Sun*.[40]

Most conservatives rejected the ideas of the Mujaddidiya, with Muhammadjon Hindustani and his students standing at the head of the opposition. This led to divisions and tensions within local communities, as ordinary believers had difficulty understanding who was right and who was wrong, although of course the question was not really about the "rightness" of any party. In Islam, debates about the existence and nature of "pure Islam" already had dragged on for many hundreds of years. The contending parties invariably appealed to "true Islamic arguments" and above all to the Qur'an and Sunnah. Such debates always started at the level of religious disputations but then descended into confrontations and clashes, with each of the contending parties appealing to its own audience and accusing the opposition of apostasy, if not unbelief.

Thus, the era of perestroika and the beginning of the collapse of the Soviet Union witnessed a split among the Muslims of Central Asia. Heated disputes and scandalous confrontations between the Wahhabis and conservative sects became regular occurrences. Even fiercer were the arguments over the political status of Islam. The Wahhabis maintained that the crisis of communist ideology, the evident signs of the coming collapse of the Soviet Union, and the growing process of re-Islamization in the country opened the possibility for Central Asians to repeat what Iran had done, and thereby "return the country to the path of light and of Islam."

The religious conservatives in Ferghana were distinguished by their high level of religious education and by the quantity and quality of their published works, all of them in a traditional Hanafi spirit but adapted for the modern reader. Their followers tended to be people of the older generation, middle-aged folk, and youths from families that still preserved tradition, as well as others who accepted neither the "Soviet" nor Western way of life. The persistently adverse conditions under which the community of believers had existed and the often-hostile public attitude toward Islam had taught conservatives and their followers to seek any possible form of coexistence with the secular authorities, even with those who denied God in principle.[41]

The conservatives did not have uniform views, and their theologians differed from one another on many points. The main issue over which they divided concerned the appropriate relationship with secular states. Some theologians believed that the secular state should not interfere at all in the affairs of the Muslim community, or at least not on those pertaining to purely religious matters. Others believed that if the secular state did not espouse atheism and allowed Muslims to worship freely and receive education, it had the right and even the duty to manage religious life so as to prevent the Wahhabis from raising their heads. The most striking representatives of this group included students of Hindustani from Andijan: Abdullatif-qori Andijoni; his brother Muhammad-Sodik Andijoni, and others. Those imams who belonged to the Directorate of Muslims and who were incorrectly termed "official mullahs" also shared this position.[42]

Even less homogeneous in their views were members of the so-called new wave, whom conservatives called Wahhabis. Judging by their religious views and their method of interpreting the sacred texts, the term "fundamentalists" may fairly be applied to them. But their time-consuming conflicts with the conservatives and later with the Uzbek government prevented the Wahhabis from developing a consolidated theoretical stance. The one point on which they agreed was that the endless effort "to adapt Islam to the needs of the times" through new interpretations of sacred texts was utterly unacceptable. Eventually the government of Uzbekistan banned the Wahhabis entirely.

It must be acknowledged that the older generation of "fundamentalists" had benefited from a good theological education, and were therefore well oriented in the traditional religious literature from which their opponents drew. Their followers however were either less well educated or completely uneducated. It was they who sincerely called for the universal application, by force if necessary, of sharia law (as they understood it) in all spheres of life. The most radical among them were not squeamish about their choices of means and allies.

During the perestroika era these followers of the "fundamentalists" strove to return to a way of life shaped by sharia law. Their efforts in this line arose from an emotional impulse. The collapse of the Soviet "mono-ideology" led people to rush to embrace their religious origins, which had been repressed in the past. This gave rise to a wave of "re-Islamization." The problem was that very few of those engaged in this pursuit knew anything about the true roots and origins of the Faith. Any genuine "return to Islam" would have required serious intellectual effort over a period of time, and not merely the embrace of it as a dogmatic system of laws. But most "fundamentalists" were not disposed to such an effort, and instead replaced knowledge with emotion.

The generation of Ferghana theologians of the new wave went even further. They called on people to look on themselves as part of the entire Muslim world. Perhaps because of this, those local fundamentalists, most of whom were young, easily fell under the influence of foreign missionaries who brought the view that all local versions of Islam were wrong. Ferghana fundamentalists found it easier to accept this view because they themselves were not strongly associated with any local traditions, nor were they willing to forgive conservatives for having wished, when faced with the most adverse conditions, to conform to tradition.

Significantly, the missionaries who represented religiously based political parties succeeded in strengthening the political aspirations of large numbers of the local fundamentalists, and even of some of the conservatives. Thanks to their efforts, the "fundamentalists" of the Ferghana Valley gradually began to adopt as their own the language of political Islam used by foreign Islamic parties. Those who did so tended to align themselves with such imported religious-political groups as HT.

It has been noted that the "fundamentalists" lacked a well-organized structure.[43] Moreover, as a result of the activity of foreign Muslim missionaries, the new groups and local branches of religious and political parties began distancing themselves from the local "fundamentalist." It bears mention that interviews with HT members and other Islamist groups reveal that they were virtually raised on widely disseminated audio and video tapes of Abduvali-qori Mirzaev and other leading Wahhabis abroad.

Thus, in the last days of the Soviet Union and early years of independence local Muslims of the new (Wahhabi) wave drew heavily on the theological, social, political and other ideas of thinkers from other Muslim countries, especially those who were fundamentalists or extremists. Despite this, however, the former republics of the Soviet Union present noteworthy distinctive features. It is relevant that the forced secularization pursued by Soviet authorities failed in the end to undermine the cultural and religious traditions of local people. Moreover, Gorbachev's perestroika stimulated the rapid revival of national cultural traditions and the beginnings of the re-Islamization of the majority of the population. However, to repeat, the call to "go back to Islam" or "return to the religion of our fathers" did not imply that one either knew or understood the Faith. The break in the transmission of local forms of Islamic life, and especially of traditional religious rituals, could not so quickly be repaired. The renewal of Muslim education had just begun, and lagged far behind the process of "re-Islamization." These circumstances opened divisions among Muslim leaders and enabled Islamic ideologues from abroad to gain influence.

But even here, local circumstances left their imprint on the process. The theologians could heap blame on the communist era, but their own mentality had been formed at that time and under its influence. Even before the impoverishment of the majority of the population in the late 1980s and early 1990s, the "fundamentalists" (Wahhabis) had begun to advance such issues as social justice and economic equality. However, they expressed themselves in clichés familiar to anyone who had been a citizen of the USSR. These terms and phrases obviously had been drawn from textbooks on Russian history, the official history of the Communist Party,[44] and from the controlled television and the press. Among them, no word was more evocative that "equality." Talk of primitive egalitarianism became the order of the day, as local "fundamentalists" (and then, later, political groups based on Islam) rallied on behalf of political equality, economic equality, and social equality. This is the more understandable because at precisely this time economic conditions were rapidly deteriorating, and social differentiation in the Ferghana area were rapidly growing. However, all these ideas of "equality," we repeat, were based on the familiar clichés of Soviet propaganda and Soviet history books.

On the correct political status of Islam and of Muslim political parties and organizations, the fundamentalists have been absolutely clear and categorical; to wit, they believe that Islam can be considered complete only in a state where it is the official religion.[45] Here they differ sharply from the conservatives who, relying a traditional consensus among the *ulama* (religious leaders) and citing many examples, insist that a community of Muslim believers can exist in a non-Islamic or secular state, and coexist with other faiths.

The sources of influence on local Hanafi reformism should be sought both among Islamic authorities of the present era and in religious and ideological currents extant in Soviet times. And of course, there was also the traditional notion of a general Islamic integralism, which on local soil came to connote a struggle for unification among all competing tendencies. Besides this, both the positions of "local Islam" in one form or another and local confessional education drew on the works of mainly local authors of the medieval era.

Precisely because of this, Wahhabi fundamentalists categorically reject all manifestations of a local "confessional Islam" that might legitimize distinctive views or practices. The newest generation of Wahhabi fundamentalists took an even more severe posture by concluding that the individuality of any form of "local Islam" is a major obstacle to the emergence of a "unified Islamic community of believers." And of course both the old and new ideas on dogma and unification had political agendas that, as noted earlier, were set by the leading reformers from the Arab world.

In spite of this, the local Wahhabis had to take into account the mainly conservative religious environment in which they lived. That is why they consistently stressed their commitment to Hanafism, while at the same time proposing to purge it of unacceptable innovations. This religious purism—or nihilism—also can be seen as a reaction to the forms of "Soviet Islam" that still exist among ordinary believers. The majority of Muslims during the Soviet era had struggled to preserve *their* Islam in the same traditional form it had come down to them, including all the ceremonies and rituals, pilgrimages to the graves of saints, and so forth—which the Wahhabis later denounced as inauthentic.

The Battle for the Mosque

The mosque became the main battlefield on which the uncompromising war between Hanafi conservatives and Wahhabi fundamentalists unfolded during the late 1980s. One of the important legacies of Mikhail Gorbachev's reforms had been the increase in the number of religious institutions generally and, above all, of mosques. In the first phase of re-Islamization in Central Asia people wanted to reclaim all the mosques that had been turned into warehouses, museums, and even wine factories during the Soviet era. The most symbolically significant, and also complex, episode in this struggle focused on the Friday Mosque and the Mullah-Kyrgyz Madrassa in Namangan. During the early 1950s the main building had been turned into a winery. Under persistent pressure from the city's entire Muslim community and especially from the conservatives, it was returned to worshippers during the perestroika era. Then, in an unexpected shift, the structure became the main center for the city's Wahhabis, led by Abdulahad ('Abd al-Ahad) Barnaev.

The mosque is the religious and spiritual center of Islam. It is also a center of social life, a place for influencing the community of believers and arousing civic spirit, and even a kind of political center. All these dimensions acquired acute importance during the peak phase of re-Islamization, that is before the collapse of the USSR and in the very early period of independence after 1991. This was a time when the main religious figures of all persuasions were insistently campaigning not only for religious causes, but on behalf of social and even political leaders.[46]

Divisions among the religious leaders intensified the process of re-Islamization itself, and also the struggle to reopen old mosques and build new ones.[47] Conflicts over the reopening of so-called cathedral or Friday mosques were particularly acute, because their return to their traditional function entailed filling the intellectual and spiritual vacuum created by the collapse of the Soviet mono-ideology. This raised the question of what would be the content of the traditional Friday sermon, or *ma'ruza*.

It is necessary to mention the special status of the imam in the mosques, especially in the Friday mosques. During the Middle Ages the position of imam in a mosque became a permanent post, with a fixed income deriving from voluntary contributions and endowments. Once chosen, an imam could count on his position and income for life, assuming that he adapted to the requirements of the community (*qaum*) of the mosque to which he had been named. The establishment of Bolshevik power and the elimination of the endowments of all religious institutions in 1927–29 forced change regarding the funding of mosques. The creation of SADUM in 1943 gave that body authority over the appointing imams, with confirmation by the Committee on Religious Cults of the Cabinet of Ministers of the Republic. The funding of imams' salaries changed. Henceforth the mosques displayed special boxes (*qutucha*) for donations. The sums thus collected were transferred to the Spiritual Directorate of Muslims, which provided imams with a fixed salary.[48] When Muhammad-Sadiq Muhammad-Yusuf became mufti (1989–93), the situation began to change. First, the new mufti tried to end the government's petty control by gaining permission for communities to elect their imams without interference from the state. The unintended consequence of this was to encourage Wahhabis to intensify the struggle over each mosque as a key step toward expanding their influence over the faithful.

Both opposing parties, the conservatives and the Wahhabis, fully understood that the return of the mosques to their former status opened the prospect of their becoming tools of politics. Just as the battle for the control of mosques began to unfold between the Wahhabis and conservatives, the Wahhabis' victory in Andijan established an unexpected precedent. The Wahhabi leader Abduvali-qori Mirzaev and his supporters seized the Cathedral Mosque of Andijan and turned it into a center for the fight against local conservatives. The latter were led by a former student of Hindustani, Abdullatif-qori. The same drama was played out elsewhere in the Ferghana Valley, now divided into three countries, as well as in other cities of Uzbekistan and neighboring countries.

One of the cities where a similar struggle over the Friday or Cathedral Mosque occurred was Kokand, where it was led by the Wahhabi Rajab Ali (Muhammad-Rajab) Kokandi and his followers. As Abduvali-qori Mirzaev had done, the Wahhabis of Kokand defended their position by picking a fight with the older generation. They risked being accused of treason and even of flaunting the sharia, but the game was worth the price. Control of the Friday Mosque would give them legitimate access to a major public podium, which in turn would expand their audience and enhance their political influence in the long run.

Struggles over the control of mosques between the Wahhabis and conservatives often degenerated into brutal confrontations. Wahhabi supporters did not hesitate to assault opponents and their supporters. According to numerous testimonies and memoirs published by the conservatives, the Wahhabis did not respect the venerable age of some of their opponents, nor did they heed calls for compromise and reconciliation. Especially in cities of the Ferghana Valley, there were numerous instances of conservative imams being beaten either by Wahhabis or by people mobilized by them. Over time such aggressive methods became the Wahhabis' customary way of dealing with their opponents. In Kokand, for example, the Wahhabis beat a local supporter of the conservatives, Isma'il qori (another student of Hindustani), so severely that he had to be hospitalized for a month. Other such cases occurred in Namangan, where demands accompanied by open threats were made to the conservative imam to stop the persecution of young members of the new wave of Wahhabi clerics. In cases in the late 1980s and early 1990s when conservative imams refused to cooperate, Wahhabi activists and members of the armed group Adolat resorted to crude pressure and blackmail, including the kidnapping of children and relatives of the conservative imams. Several cases ended with the murder of the kidnapped children. For example, the son of the current Chief Imam Khatib of Namangan, Abd al-Hayy qori, was kidnapped and killed because his father did not agree to cooperate with the Wahhabis.[49]

Thus, the Wahhabis' post-Soviet spiritual nihilism and maximalism degenerated into direct aggression, which had both a religious and social dimension. The movement was evolving in the direction of political radicalism and extremism. Following independence, doctrinal issues began to slip into the background as disputes focused increasingly on politics. A main topic of debates and clashes between the believers and the government was the form of power and its place in the sharia. Even fiercer was the struggle over the position of the mufti of SADUM and, separate from that, over the Directorate of the Muslims. These took the form of demonstrations, which the Wahhabis called *yurish,* a medieval term for a military campaign. Demonstrations by believers became common. The organizations did nothing to hamper the natural aggressiveness of young and inexperienced men—and in fact encouraged them.

Islamic demonstrations of this kind became an integral part of the religious revival and of the struggle among religious leaders for influence and followers. One such demonstration, which occurred in the fall of 1991 on the square in Tashkent near the former Hast Imam Mosque of the Spiritual Directorate of Muslims, reflected the very complex relationships among believers from different regions. The demonstration was actually a test of wills between the faithful from Andijan in Ferghana and the faithful of Tashkent. The latter demanded that the mufti of the Directorate, who was from Andijan, yield his place to the representative from Tashkent. The Tashkent crowd threatened to "rip Muhammad-Sadiq up and stuff his body with straw," all the while chanting *Allahu Akbar* (God is Great). In response, the crowd from the Ferghana Valley seemed out for blood in "mercenary" Kukcha (the old district of Tashkent), and issued various threats accompanied various by its own chants of *Allahu Akbar.* Only the intervention of the police and city elders averted bloodshed.

Similar demonstrations connected with struggles between Wahhabi and conservatives over the control of mosques were common in the cities of the Ferghana Valley, notably Namangan, Andijan, and to a lesser extent Osh. In each case a very aggressive crowd of mostly young people assembled and was encouraged by the religious leaders.

The issue of freedom in general, and of religious freedom in particular, posed a unique and difficult challenge to the unprepared public in the early days of perestroika. Nor is this surprising, in light of the fact that the perestroika movement itself had only a primitive and totally homogenous understanding of religion and religious values and, in fact, possessed a rather anarchistic understanding of freedom. At the same time, the freedom of religion that suddenly appeared had both positive aspects and a negative side, namely a certain socio-political nihilism that arose with the de-legitimation of all authority and quickly degenerated into simple aggression and terrorism. With the first appearance of the radical manifestations of re-Islamization, it was clear that intra-confessional differences, sometimes with a regional dimension, had become a major force for destabilization across the region. In Tajikistan at this time youths, drawn largely from among the religious fundamentalists, tied black scarves on their heads with the words of the faith in one God ("La ilaha illa-1-lah"), and also organized demonstrations, thus contributing to the outbreak of the civil war. In Osh young Wahhabis, encouraged by their leaders, began seizing mosques, mounting demonstrations, and joining in the battle for the mosques in Andijan and Namangan.

Thanks to this, in Kyrgyzstan, Tajikistan, and Uzbekistan the question of regulations to ensure stability arose even before the new governments appeared. About this time the American expert Zbigniew Brzezinski declared that religious conflict in Central Asia would turn the region into something like the Balkans. The situation had indeed become very tense and complicated by the mounting economic difficulties, which brought a humanitarian catastrophe in their wake. Besides this, the success of the Taliban in Afghanistan marked the emergence of a very aggressive Islamic state, ready to intervene in the internal affairs of its neighbors.

The new governments of the region, with no experience in the politics of religion, sought ways to stabilize the situation. Most found means for doing so within their own countries, in their own environments. The most dramatic challenges arose from the very aggressive actions of the fundamentalists in Tajikistan and Uzbekistan. In Tajikistan this eventually led to the legalization of the IRPT, while in Uzbekistan the government mustered enough will and determination to stop all acts of extreme aggression by the new Islamists.

Viewing this situation in hindsight, it seems clear that the collapse of the USSR did not leave Central Asian champions of the new political Islam in a mood to engage in accommodating dialogue. This was especially the case in Tajikistan and not least of all within the IRPT.[50] Quite the contrary, once they gained full freedom of religion, the Islamists of the region charged forward to establish an Islamic state based solely on sharia law, all the while showing extreme intolerance toward the governments, infidels, and apostates. The latter were in fact those Muslims satisfied with the religious freedom they now enjoyed and disinclined to engage in confrontations amid what was already a very fragile political, social, and ethnic situation.

Abduvali-qori Mirzaev: From Critic of Atheism to Religious Radical

The local form of Islam in Central Asia[51] emerged over many centuries, its main features having been shaped by interaction with the nomadic peoples who had long been moving into the region. The manner in which these nomadic peoples received Islam had a very specific impact on many aspects of Islam in Central

Asia. Among these were distinctive forms for the worship of saints and the acceptance of the possibility that *ummahs* could exist in non-Islamic countries. Purist theologians often had railed against this "impure" form of Islam, which some have called "secular" or "steppe" Islam. On this connection one need only mention the famous *fatwas* of Taqi ad-Din Ahmad Ibn Taymiyyah against what he derisively called "Tatar traditions."[52]

Precisely because it had such deep roots among local people, especially in the countryside, this form of Islam proved most tenacious in Soviet times. However, a new generation of local Muslim clerics in the 1980s and 1990s became bothered by the apparent contradiction between this manifestation of the faith and the austere demands of the Qur'an and the Sunnah. These clerics launched their careers by bringing forward a critique of "impure" Islam drawn largely from the arguments of earlier critics like Ibn Tamya.[53]

In Uzbekistan, one of the first young theologians to take a critical look at local Islam was the Ferghana Valley Wahhabi, Abduvali-qori Mirzaev, whom we met earlier. At Friday prayers in the spring of 1990 he delivered his most famous sermon (*khutba*), which his supporters named the *Ghuraba* and disseminated on audio and videotapes. The dictionary definition of the Arabic word *ghuraba* (plural of *gharib*) is "strangers," "aliens," or "the poor." In Uzbek a similar word (*ghariblar*) came to mean "exiles," "rogues," or even "strangers." These are precisely the meanings which Abduvali-qori Mirzaev sought to evoke.

Abduvali-qori's directed his speech squarely against what he termed secular or steppe Islam. He acknowledged that its followers always have recognized the ritual and cultural heritage of religion, but reject those who demand that the sharia control all spheres of life, from the home to the political and legislative spheres and public administration.

Abduvali-qori began his speech with a comment on the famous saying (*hadith*) of the Prophet, "Islam started with an expulsion (*ghariba*) and will return to the same."[54] Abduvali-qori then proceeded to apply this Saying to the Soviet and post-Soviet situations where, in his view, the *ghuraba* in society were those rare Muslims who demanded that all spheres of society "adhere strictly to the demands of the Qur'an and the Sunnah." The other nominal Muslims "came nowhere near to following the directions of Allah and His Messenger." Abduvali-qori often repeated his belief that the "true zealots of Islam" were few and became *ghariblar* not only in societies that call themselves Muslim, but even in their own homes.

Despite its initial popularity, the ideology of *ghuraba* remained the passion of a minority, which was one of the reasons it later could become so radicalized. *Ghuraba* eventually became an ideological reference point for large numbers of radical Muslims, and a de facto recognition of Abduvali-qori's status as the spiritual father of such radical organizations as the Islamic Movement of Uzbekistan (IMU). Indeed, the IMU included Abduvali-qori's *Ghuraba* sermon in its film *Jundullah* (Warriors of God), which both reflected and greatly influenced the IMU's subsequent ideology.

Later ideologues of the IMU, and especially Tohir Yuldosh (born Yuldoshev),[55] interpreted the speech of Abduvali-qori each in their own way, so as to incorporate it entirely within the bounds of their respective political movements.[56] They used the notion of *ghuraba* to legitimize other aspects of their program, and specifically *hijrat,* which meant emigration from Uzbekistan and other countries considered "territories of the infidels" (Dar al-Harb). As indicated in the IMU's publication "*Hijrat,* the first stage of jihad on the path to Allah,"[57] the IMU holds that anyone who commits *hijrat* automatically becomes a *mujahid,* or "warrior of Allah."

IMU: The Beginnings in Namangan

The termination of official atheism under Gorbachev coincided with the collapse of the USSR's entire political and ideological system. But the collapse of communist ideology and the resurgence of religions and nationalism did not mean that all things Soviet were forgotten. On the contrary, old paradigms endured and were even manifested in the rhetoric of the new ideology. The first and most amusing example of this is the charter of the Islamic Renaissance Party[58] that, except for its famous preamble, accorded closely with the charter of the Communist Party of the Soviet Union.

Out in the more "provincial" areas of the Soviet union republics (which included Uzbekistan), perestroika presented a further paradox. Even before the collapse of the USSR, Communist Party secretaries (chairmen) there had been turning to Islam as "the religion of our fathers." The career of the Communist Party's first secretary in Namangan city, Burgutali Rafikov (1990–93; d. 1996), provides a particularly striking example of this. As secretary of the Communist Party's district committee in the town of Pap in the western part of the Ferghana Valley, Rafikov already had been actively involved since 1989 in constructing the district's Friday Mosque (1989–90). At its dedication he stunned the audience by declaring, "I have communism in my head and Islam in my heart." Then Rafikov prayed, albeit in a separate room of the mosque, and admitted that it was the first prayer in his life.[59]

When he was transferred to Namangan as the first secretary of the Communist Party's city committee (and thus, automatically, the city's mayor), Rafikov found himself in an extremely difficult situation. On the one hand, massive numbers of people were embracing an Islamic identity, and everyone realized that the Islamic factor would be of great importance in the future. On the other hand, this was a period of complete economic collapse and social breakdown. Petty racketeers demanded protection money of from 10 percent to 30 percent of their income from the newly legalized small and mid-size businesses. Aided by corrupt police and criminal groups, such rackets flourished across the USSR in 1989–90. Businesses looked for ways to protect themselves against the racketeers. In Namangan, this search led directly to the formation of such illegitimate paramilitary groups as Adolat and Islom militsiyasi/Islom Lashkarlari (Islamic Militia/Islamic Warriors).

The founder of Adolat was Abduhakim (Hakimjon) Sattimov. The basis of his organization was the so-called DND Group,[60] which was established in the summer of 1989 to protect Sattimov's small domestic silk production enterprise. Soon the DND Group had training facilities and people who could teach hand-to-hand combat, supplemented by small-arms manuals. One of those who joined was Tohir Yuldosh, the future leader of the IMU.

By now law enforcement had become completely ineffective, so small and medium-sized businesses from the cities and suburbs began turning to Sattimov for help against the racketeers. Soon Adolat had taken over the security business and even the patrolling of the cities at night. As Adolat developed it attracted funding, which in turn helped it grow.[61] Some money came from grateful entrepreneurs whose shops and workplaces Adolat had protected. Adolat had a general cashier (*bait al-mal*), and its system of charges and accounts went by the absolutely Islamic term '*ushr.*[62] Soon, some of the city's religious leaders (Umar-hon Domla, Obid-hon qori, etc.) took notice of Adolat's growing strength and credibility, and began to make donations from the proceeds of their mosques.

Sattimov himself was completely non-religious,[63] but he began to appreciate the importance of the growing Islamization process. Moreover, members of his fighting squads came from religious families. This is why he assigned Tohir Yuldosh to be his organization's Islamic ideologist. In January 1990 the latter insisted on changing Adolat's name to Islom Adolati (Islamic Justice) and on establishing on the same base the group Islom militsiyasi.

As Islom Adolati expanded, it introduced an oath (*bayat-nomah*) for new members. Candidates had to swear, among other things, to "contribute vigorously to the establishment of an order based on the sharia in Namangan and then in Uzbekistan as a whole."[64] At this time special patrol groups called Islom Adolati were formed, consisting mainly of young people. These vigilantes would appear at the bazaars, catching petty thieves and inflicting physical punishments on them. Other patrols forcibly closed shops selling alcohol, incited brawls at clubs in the old part of the city, and showed up uninvited at weddings to force the organizers to remove alcoholic beverages from the tables.

Thus came into being an Islamic police force in Namangan with a sharia morality. It was an impressive organization, and in fact became a parallel authority in Namangan. Attempts by local authorities to stop the illegal activities of the organization did not succeed. For example, the chief prosecutor of the Namangan region Chori Juraev (d. in 2003) brought thirty-two criminal cases against Islom Adolati members with charges ranging from the murder of pickpockets, illegal beatings, kidnapping, and invasion of privacy. However, the police shied away from serious investigations and did not detain the accused. Islom Adolati groups responded more decisively. They besieged the prosecutors' offices, demanding that cases against them be withdrawn. The guards offered no resistance and handed over their weapons to Islom Adolati commanders. Champions of Islamic Justice then seized the chief prosecutor and beat him, forcing him to apologize to the crowd and publicly renounce his position. Files on the cases were burned in the courtyard of the prosecutor's office while the crowd chanted "Allahu Akbar."[65] Neither the municipal nor regional police, who had brought discredit on themselves from racketeering, dared intervene in such a case, and thereby demonstrated the complete ineffectiveness of law enforcement.

Conversely, after each such action members of the new power felt a growing sense of their own authority and influence. The so-called Yurishlar[66] demonstrations near Namangan's City Hall (Hokimiyat) broke new ground in this regard. This time the fighting groups of Islom Adolati brought forward a series of ultimatums that the city authorities had to meet. Such events showed that Namangan, amid the general crisis of authority, was now ruled by a diarchy, with the Police of Sharia Morality (as Islom Adolati was now called) enjoying greater credibility than the official leaders.

Initially, the names of these groups had a rather Soviet aura: Faollar (Activists), Guruhlar/Jamoalar (Groups), or Islom militsiyasi. Members of the armed groups did not call themselves mujahideen and did not consider their actions as jihad. However, by the end of 1991 the militants began calling themselves Islom Lashkarlari, reflecting their aspiration to attain the status of "parallel power" in the city rather than the true state of affairs.[67]

Management of the organization gradually shifted into the hands of Tohir Yuldosh. He further intensified the work of his fighting groups by organizing 'round-the-clock patrols of the city, increasing the number of groups that controlled access to the city; and setting up still other groups that prevented women and girls from appearing in public without a *hijab* and ensured that everyone went to the mosques for the noon prayers (*peshin/az-zuhr*).

The last and most audacious act by Islom Adolati was its seizure of Namangan's City Hall and the organization of a meeting there on December 19, 1991. Many of Namangan's religious leaders (Umar-hon Domla and Dovud-hon qori among them) supported this action, and some even took part in the meeting. After gaining control of the building, all the young fighters of Islom Adolati assembled in the inner courtyard. At the same time a crowd of ordinary citizens gathered outside on the square. The organizers of the meeting demanded the immediate presence of President Islam Karimov, to whom they wanted to present their petitions in person. Within hours Karimov arrived in the city and proceeded at once to the courtyard of the occupied building. His appearance occasioned shouts of "Allahu Akbar."[68]

Inasmuch as what followed was so important in the overall evolution of the IMU, it should be recounted in detail. Tohir Yuldosh felt himself to be the man of the hour. When President Karimov tried to take the microphone from Yuldosh's hands to address the crowd, Yuldosh literally pushed him away, shouting "No! I am still the master here! Here you will talk, but only when I let you. In the meantime, shut up and listen." With this, the crowd of Islom Adolati fighters began shouting *Takbir* (the Arabic name for the phrase *Allahu Akbar*) so loudly that many simply covered their ears. Yuldosh looked out on the yelling people with the look of a winner; it was evident that he had counted on his actions having the effect they did. By "bringing the president down a peg or two" he expected to make an impression on the crowd and confirm his own image as a fearless leader.[69]

After uttering a few stock phrases, Tohir Yuldosh then began to present the group's demands to the president. These demands, written on scraps of paper, were passed to the podium from the back rows, where the city's religious leaders were sitting. Yuldosh stammered as he read them, obviously seeing the texts for the first time. The demands included the following: first, declare Uzbekistan as Islamic state; second, dissolve parliament; third, nominate a Muslim leader[70] as candidate for president; fourth, turn over the seized building to the protestors so they could create there a sharia center or the headquarters of a new Islamic party; and, fifth, ban males from working in maternity hospitals.

Immediately after Yuldosh presented these demands, several elders who represented the demonstrators gathered outside the building approached Yuldosh and handed him a note on which appeared some additional demands. In contrast to the demands from those within the City Hall, all these demands were purely economic in nature, with calls for the stabilization of prices, indexing of wages to inflation, salary increases, and so forth. Yuldosh quickly read through them and then told the elders that they needed first to establish an Islamic state and institute sharia law, whereupon all these problems would solve themselves. But the protestors staunchly demanded that Yuldosh read their demands to the entire assembly. If he refused, they threatened to leave and organize a separate meeting.[71]

The older man who spoke for the assembled street protestors expressed these points in language rich with significance: "Tohirjon," he told Yuldosh, "those demands that you announced—are *your demands*. Now we demand that you read *ours*."[72] Yuldosh briefly consulted with the religious leaders in the back of the hall, then read out the economic demands brought in by the citizenry.

With this, the contrasting motives and objectives of the two very different groups of demonstrators had been clearly set forth. Significantly, those pursuing economic objectives were in the clear majority, while those putting forth religious and political demands were in the minority. Islam Karimov did not fail to observe this, and he constructed his response to the protesters largely in line with the discussion of economic problems, which were especially acute after the collapse of the Soviet Union. As for the political and religious demands, Karimov said that he could not decide such matters on his own, and that it needed to be done according to the law, which would include a national referendum. Overall, Islam Karimov, a more experienced politician than his opponents, accurately assessed the mood of the meeting and focused the crowd's attention on practical economic concerns, thereby pushing the question of religious and political demands to the background. This tactic paid off, and the protesters soon dispersed.

After the meeting, Yuldosh and his fighters continued to occupy the building for several more days. Members of Islom Adolati, especially their leader Tohir

Yuldosh, felt they had won. Yuldosh emerged as the sole head of the organization. Beginning at this time the fighting groups of Islom Adolati grandly referred to themselves as mujahideen, although as later interviews revealed few if any of the young fighters, including Yuldosh himself, knew the actual meaning of this term. In fact, their understanding of the religious dimension of their new status as mujahideen was rudimentary at best. A former member explained to the author that the young members of the group were simply told that their efforts to revive Islam constituted a jihad. Without offering any explanation of the deeper meaning of this term, their leaders simply reported on the benefits that Allah promised all mujahideen. They learned that their sins would be forgiven and they would enter Paradise without having to pass any tests. Once in Paradise they would enjoy a rich life, beautiful maidens, and on the head of each mujahideen angels would place a jeweled crown. Hence, the "reward from above" promised to rank-and-file members of paramilitary groups appealed to their simplistic and materialistic worldview, which had been shaped primarily by their total absence of educational or economic prospects.[73] Indeed, these were precisely the type of people recruited into the IMU squads.[74]

Returning now to the Namangan of the early 1990s, Yuldosh declared himself Supreme Amir (Bosh Amir) of the Namangan mujahideen and immediately set out to consolidate his new status by expanding and strengthening his organization. New oaths were drafted, identifying members of Islom Adolati as mujahideen for the first time and committing them to the strict fulfillment of all orders from the Supreme Amir, Tohir Yuldosh. The text of this oath, with minor changes, later became the oath sworn by new members of the IMU.

Yuldosh ordered a special throne (*takht*) to be erected in the courtyard of the City Hall, intended to symbolize the new power.[75] Curiously, at first this improvised throne was upholstered with red brocade—a favorite color in rural Central Asia. But Yuldosh objected vehemently, saying that "red was the color of the Communists," and ordered that it be replaced with gold brocade. The episode is revealing, for it reminds one of the "golden throne" promised to each mujahid in Paradise. Yuldosh's order to erect a throne was symbolic in other respects as well, as it reveals his early ambitions and political claims.

Several ex-members of Islom Adolati recall that Tohir Yuldosh happily took his place on this throne and pronounced a brief but quite remarkable "Address from the Throne." Speaking to his fighters, he said, "Now, forget that we were once considered rogues in our own country. Now we will become the owners and proprietors, and all *the infidels and apostates (mal'unlar) will be the rogues.*" But Yuldosh was overly hasty with his Speech from the Throne. The government in Tashkent waited patiently until after the presidential elections in mid-January, 1992. Then, having won a majority, the new administration gradually began to reassert its authority. Many members of Islom Adolati were arrested and later convicted. Tohir Yuldosh and a band of his closest supporters managed to escape Namangan and move to neighboring Tajikistan.

In Tajikistan: The First Lessons of Jihad

Many Muslims in Uzbekistan viewed the civil war in Tajikistan as a war for the Faith. They had only the slightest knowledge of its clan or inter-regional context, and chose instead to believe, at least in the early 1990s, that the Tajik conflict was a jihad against the Communists. The Islom Adolati militants who had fled to Tajikistan were in demand in this war, especially those who had previous military service and training. However, the Uzbek refugees included many with no army background and who thus required training. By early 1993, in areas controlled by the Islamists from the United Tajik Opposition (mainly in Tavildara), special camps were organized, where the training of young mujahideen began.[76] Besides training in armament, topography, and other applied sciences, the young mujahideen learned the basics of religion. The textbook *Lessons of Jihad* (*Johod darsliklari*), written in 1997, played an important role in the curriculum. The *Lesson of Jihad* were by no means limited to abstract theology; they also provided practical instructions on how to conduct diversions, guerrilla wars, and propaganda on enemy territory, which included Uzbekistan and some neighboring countries.

If the *Lessons of Jihad* were in the end quite practical, and its presentation on religion conveyed on a primitive level, the penciled summaries that various mujahideen made of their lessons are even more elemental. Drawing on several such notebooks, one arrives at the following list titled "benefits Allah gives to his martyrs (*shahid*)." Each martyr's specific status would determine which benefits he would actually receive:

1. The pain which a martyr experiences when he dies will be equal to an ant's bite;[77]
2. In Paradise he will have a variety of foods in whatever quantity he desires;
3. In Paradise, each martyr will be married to seventy-two beautiful maidens (*houries*);[78]
4. With his first drop of blood, all of a martyr's sins are forgiven;
5. At the Last Judgment he will not have to worry about himself and will be eligible to stand for seventy of his relatives.

All this suggests that the "benefits for martyrs" had been interpreted in such a way as to respond to the basic physiological needs of young mujahideen. The harsh conditions under which most of them lived in the camps help explain their rather mundane goals in the afterlife promised to them.[79] Hence the first benefit above addresses the natural fear of physical suffering and death that any young militant would feel. Former IMU members insist that these simplistic propaganda tricks were not devoid of psychological effects, and that many young fighters sincerely expected to receive the listed rewards in the next world.

In Afghanistan: From Guerrilla Struggle to a Theological Justification for Jihad

The interpretation of the concept of jihad poses a serious challenge to Muslims in general and to Muslims of Central Asia in particular. Radical and terrorist groups largely ignore spiritual interpretations of the term (as in greater jihad). Conversely, the radicals and terrorists justify and sacralize the religious and military significance of jihad as a war against infidels by referring to the Qur'an and *hadiths* of Mohammed, as well as to certain medieval works. Those theologians who disagree with this limited interpretation defend their position by turning to the same sacred texts. Their argument is endless and futile.

The fact that Islam recognizes no intermediaries between the individual and God exacerbates the polemic. The Qur'an and Sunnah are open to a considerable diversity of views and interpretations,[80] yet no institution or office has the power to define the boundary between orthodoxy and heresy. Few theologians have doubted their own right to do so, however, and many feel it their duty to point out that any position contrary to theirs leads directly to unbelief or delusion.

Even relatively moderate Sunni theologians divided over the meaning of jihad. For example, the famous Sunni theologian al-Baghdadi (d. 1037) defined it as "the fight against the enemies of Islam, until they adopt Islam or pay the *jizya* (the special tax levied on non-Muslims)."[81] Meanwhile, the well-known Shafi'i theologian and Sufi, Abu-Hamid al-Ghazali (d. 1111), emphasized solely the spiritual interpretation of jihad.[82]

In Central Asia it was mainly Sufis and *faqihs* (legal scholars) who addressed the issue of jihad and identified its various interpretations. Clashes with people of other religions and Russian colonization brought to the fore the concept of jihad as a war against infidels. This view arose once more in Central Asia on the eve of the collapse of the USSR, this time in its most aggressive form. It soon drove from the field all other interpretations of the term, and especially the ideal of spiritual self-perfection. This religious and military understanding of jihad had many distinctively Central Asian features, all epitomized by the further development of the IMU.

By emigrating to Afghanistan in 2000, the IMU fighters had moved to what was for them the most favorable environment possible. Their broad ties with the Taliban government and later with al-Qaeda expanded. Both exercised a growing ideological influence over the IMU, with 2000 and 2001 being their most productive years in terms of the issuance of propaganda magazines, proclamations, translations of religious tracts, and videos.[83]

Yuldosh by now realized that their previous defenses of jihad had been random and primitive. He therefore created his own council of religious leaders, which consisted mainly of fellow Uzbek immigrants with good theological educations. The purpose of the council was to devise a religious justification for their jihad and to make theological and legal decisions implementing it, then to introduce

these into the lessons taught by the mujahideen.[84] Yuldosh appealed to the IMU
as follows:

> Soon we will start our jihad, and we must therefore have an understanding what we
> are doing, basing it on the sharia and fearing only Allah. There are some among us
> who know about [jihad] so we must learn from them. The main weapon of our faith
> is to know the true dogmas. If we strengthen our real faith and study the various
> rulings on jihad, we will never lose our path. Therefore, those of our teachers who
> are responsible for lessons on religion should teach with special responsibility and
> effort. And we appeal to everyone, from Chiefs to the cooks and bakers, to master
> all knowledge relating to jihad. If we firmly master these skills, then Allah will
> be satisfied, and that is our goal. We must not be lazy about this, for only through
> such knowledge of jihad do we know our God. Only with this knowledge of jihad
> will we understand dogma (*aqida*) and learn what is allowed and what is forbidden
> (*halal wa haram*). With that knowledge we will make jihad. Let us be ready to go
> to Allah.[85] May Allah make us the true heirs of the Prophet. Amen!

Theologians of the IMU did not take their religious arguments for jihad and
their justification of martyrdom solely from the ideological clichés of the Taliban
or al-Qaeda, but began independently developing their own positions. This process
went forward on two levels. First, the theologians appealed to the Qur'an and
hadiths to legitimize jihad. In doing so the IMU theologians limited themselves
to attempting to relate the texts to the situation in Central Asia and particularly in
Uzbekistan. Second, the IMU theologians took note of the extensive literature on
jihad, translating some of the classics primarily into Uzbek and preparing them for
publication. One such work was by the fourteenth-century Syrian theologian Ibn
Nahhasa, who had closely analyzed the legitimacy of jihad, rules of warfare, the
division of booty, and the treatment of prisoners and infidels.[86]

The man who translated these texts, Abu Mansur Ahmad, included comments
intended to link the document with the present. At the end he appended a small
statement of his own, from which the following is drawn:

> A thousand regrets . . . , but Muslim men and women are losing their conscience
> and religion, and have begun to imitate their enemies. And most of all it is
> regrettable that a community that calls itself "Muslim" has lost its hatred and
> abhorrence of Christians and other infidels. They are mired in sin, and their
> hearts do not ache because of it. We are on our knees, but we think we are hold-
> ing ourselves upright.
>
> O dear brother! You see our current situation well. We do not fulfill what our
> great sharia commands of us. We have forgotten what our attitude toward the
> infidels should be. We do not even remember that we must make our religion the
> supreme value, reclaim the power we have lost, reclaim our rights, and reclaim
> our self-respect. And that we can achieve this only with weapons in our hands.

In their effort to legitimize their actions, IMU ideologists advanced the notion
of "abhorrence of Christians and other infidels." Such passages are obviously

meant to consolidate the image of the enemy on religious grounds and thereby to strengthen the mujahideen's readiness for confrontation. Aggressive militancy also informs the calls for a "return to the power" and "regaining self-respect." Such clichés were drawn from international literature on global jihad readily available in print and via Internet. That Yuldosh could afford to prepare and print the various magazines, translations, pamphlets, and proclamations that embodied these notions, and even to set up his own video studio, attests to the solid funding he was receiving at the time.

Thus supported, IMU ideologues pored over sacred texts in search of additional maximalist arguments to support jihad and the special status of martyrs. This put an end to the rather casual approach to the ideological and spiritual training of earlier militants. Now IMU teachers and theologians brought forward arguments drawn from the Qur'an and *hadiths* and medieval theological literature. They also set forth the requirements for jihad in the general context of Muslim countries and of Uzbekistan in particular. This new trend was particularly evident in lectures and articles by IMU ideologist IMU, Zubayr ibn 'Abd ar-Rahim. The following is typical:

> The Muslim world lives under oppression. Some Muslims live in countries where the infidels rule, while others live in countries under the influence of America, with its anti-Islam policies . . . The belief of these (Muslims) in Allah is therefore far from perfect . . . If the Muslims [of Uzbekistan] can perform the rituals of faith are unable to fulfill its demands in political terms. . . . it means that only some of the commandments the Qur'an orders are being realized, the rest remaining only on paper.
>
> . . . In order to spread Islam to the entire world, we need a state living according to the absolute rule of sharia law. If there is a religious duty for ritual ablution (*tahara*) before prayer, there is also a duty to rid the civil administration of the influence of infidels and reestablish it on the basis of a truly Islamic order! Weakness in fulfilling this cannot be justified in terms of the intrigues of the Jews or that America is helping the CIS countries in the fight against Muslims, or the fact that the infidels have nuclear bombs. Anyone who tries to justify his inaction with that kind of thinking . . . "should beware of the power of God!" (Qur'an, 8:36).
>
> Under the influence of harmful policies, the many millions of Muslims in Uzbekistan are forgetting their religion. The *ulamas* there are well aware of this situation, but act as if they are standing on a hill and calmly watching the Muslim community fall into the abyss of disbelief. Instead of showing the Muslims the right way, they live as if in greenhouses, writing books that seek solutions to minor questions and entering into disputes over them, while the community of believers is heading into the abyss. This is happening all over the world . . . Which is why we must declare that if in a particular Muslim community there is no inspiration for jihad, that community can no longer be called Muslim.[87]

At the end of his article, Zubair writes about the importance of forming a mujahideen worldview that would guarantee victory in any confrontation with a strong opponent. Jihad in the sense of a war against infidels is not only the key to such a worldview but the only legitimate form of Islam and of a correct Islamic community.

Thus, in the Ferghana Valley a radical ideology that included the IMU's militarized program came into being. This deepened the schism with other Muslims of the region, whom, for the sake of convenience, we call "conservatives" on account of their belief that the reopening of mosques, new opportunities to receive religious education, and official recognition of the spiritual values of the religious heritage sufficed to enable the community to thrive. The conservatives were no less intolerant of "aliens" than the radicals,[88] and were quick to pin the Wahhabi label on anyone who advanced a non-traditional understanding of ritual or the status of Islam in Uzbekistan.[89] This further sharpened the religious schism.

The formation of the IMU and similar organizations did not result solely from confrontations between believers and the state, for an intra-confessional conflict was also unfolding. Most believers followed the traditional theologians of Central Asia, whose positions had developed over the many centuries of the community's interactions with non-Muslim political and cultural substrata.[90] This is how the faithful had adapted to the Soviet regime and how they had managed to preserve their religious and cultural identity. No wonder the majority of Hanafi theologians (i.e., conservatives) accepted the coexistence of the community of the faithful and the laicized secular state. In their view, to force the issue of jihad would mean civil war. Moreover, the IMU's calls for jihad to recover the Islamic state got no support from most believers, either in Uzbekistan or in the region as a whole.

The IMU's move to Afghanistan brought about a certain internationalization of the organization, with its ideologues now viewing their call for the "liberation of Islam and of Muslims" as part of a global jihad. Correspondence between the IMU and Taliban officials, directors of madrassas in Pakistan, and heads of training camps for militants all consistently stresses the themes of solidarity and unity of purpose.[91] However, IMU contacts with terrorist organizations further discredited them in the eyes of local Muslims, who viewed the IMU's allies as religiously illegitimate Wahhabis. Yuldosh's leaflets and cassettes try to neutralize this by stressing that the IMU is still Hanafi, and by claiming they oppose only rites and rituals not in accordance with the sharia. But the only method for advancing this struggle, Yuldosh argues, is with weapons in hand, in other words through violence directed against both unbelievers and wrong-thinking Muslims.

In their response, the majority of theologians often resort to clichés: that Islam is a religion of peace, and that there is no compulsion in Islam (based on the assertion, "There is no compulsion in religion" [Qur'an, 2:256]). They also argue that the extremists use religion as a cover for their political ambitions and that they are not Muslims at all, and hence not authorized to speak in behalf of Muslims.[92] All such statements are limited in their effect, however, both because they draw on the same sacred texts as their enemies and because Islam provides no means of adjudicating between opposing views.

The fall of the Taliban in Afghanistan inflicted heavy losses on the IMU and led to the seizure of some of its military bases. Nevertheless, Internet data confirm that the Movement succeeded in maintaining some camps and in reclaiming others. So today, when Afghanistan is once again being reborn as a ground where religious extremists and terrorists can thrive, there is every reason to believe that the heirs of Tohir Yuldosh can revive and flourish there.

Other Religious and Extremist Groups of Ferghana

The opening of Ferghana's borders and the relatively free access to the region by various foreign missionaries brought new groups to the fore and added new political dimensions to the already complex life of the region. Two of the new extremist sects warrant our particular attention because they are at once the most characteristic and most symbolically significant: Hizb ut-Tahrir (HT) and Akromiya, the group that was responsible for the Andijan tragedy of May 13, 2005. The first of these belongs to the group of religious-political organizations that arrived in the Ferghana Valley from abroad, while the second arose locally, albeit under the strong influence of the same HT. Both originated in the late 1980s and early 1990s, amid the revival of Islamic identity, and the intensified social and political activity of the masses of believers.

Hizb ut-Tahrir

Few international writings on the religious situation in Central Asia in the last fifteen years fail to mention the Hizb ut-Tahrir party, mostly in rather mild terms.[93] However, from the moment HT announced itself through illegally produced leaflets, it elicited a very different set of responses within the region. Uzbekistan and Turkmenistan regarded its activities as a direct threat to their own stability, although Kyrgyzstan initially did not think it posed any dangers and hoped that in time it would become a normal part of civil society.

HT's parent party, Hizb ut-Tahrir al-Islami (Islamic Party of Liberation), had been founded in Palestine in 1952–53 as a party of Muslim intellectuals engaged in the Palestinians' struggle against Israel. Its founder, Taqiuddin al-Nabhani (d. 1977), was an active member of another no less well-known religious-political party of Egypt, al-Ikhwan al-Muslimun,[94] the ideas and clandestine methods of which he freely appropriated. The heat of the fight with Israel and what HT members considered the lack of Muslim help for the Palestinians radicalized HT members and strengthened their sectarian fervor. Their core ideas included the following:

> All the troubles of Palestinians and other Muslims are caused by the fact that Muslims since the times of the Prophets had "mortal enemies": e.g., Jews, "polytheists," and Christians.
> Today these enemies are using all means to prevent the political and spiritual unification of the Muslims, which is essential if they are to resist their enemies, manage their resources, and Islamize the world.
> The broader the scope of HT's activities, the more enemies they will have.

> In addition to Jews and Christians they now face American and world imperial-
> ists, communists, "polytheists," etc. The only salvation for Muslims is to restore
> the caliphate as a religious and political entity.[95]

HT was, and is, notably vague on the political and theological nature of the
caliphate it seeks to restore. Leaflets produced by the party leave the impression
that it deliberately keeps it all at a vague mythologized level, avoiding specifics.
This plays on the sacral aura that surrounds early Islam and turns the past into a
kind of magic wand to be used against the abundant economic, social, and cultural
problems of the present, indeed, as an alternative to hard, daily work.

Leaders of Muslim countries who understand that the restoration of the caliphate
is a totally unrealistic idea also appear on HT's list of the enemies of Islam. Unfortunately, this fact collides with what HT claims as its tactics, namely "peaceful
propaganda, the penetration into society, the 'fixing' of the political consciousness
of Muslims, and the creation of conditions under which Muslims will be ready to
transfer power to the caliph."

HT's many statements about its "peaceful methods" of political struggle are, to
put it mildly, questionable, given the known episodes of their activities in Jordan,
where HT organized unsuccessful military coups in 1968, 1969, and 1971. HT
organized another attempted military coup in 1972 in southern Iraq.[96] Prominent
members of the party do not deny these attempts[97] for, as al-Nabhani explained at
the time, "if a society rebels against its regime, then to eliminate the latter, even
by military force, is not an act of violence." The use of violence was considered
acceptable "whenever it was necessary in order to come to power."[98] Such self-
justifications, even when hidden behind modern rhetoric about "noble goals," were
very reminiscent of the early Bolshevik slogans of Vladimir Lenin.[99] They could
not conceal the ultimate goal of HT: political violence. True, it was defined as only
the third phase of the struggle, with the first two being peaceful and non-violent.[100]
But what does this matter if their ultimate goal is a political coup, even through
violence? When HT emissaries attempted to persuade leaders of several Muslim
countries (Libya and Iran, for example) to enlist them to work toward reestablishing the caliphate, they failed.[101]

HT party leaders clearly realize that it is inconceivable that Muslim political
leaders would accept their ideas, with all their ambiguity and questionable religious
status. So if the first two "non-violent" phases are doomed to fail, what does it matter
if violent revolution is only the third phase, when that phase is all but inevitable?[102]
No wonder that HT explicitly demands the overthrow of existing regimes in Muslim
countries.[103] Yet this does not solve anything, because popular opposition to HT
in most Muslim countries, including those in Central Asia, is even stronger than
the government's opposition.[104] Moreover, we know that most theologians find it
unacceptable on religious grounds.[105] Hence, as HT in Central Asia and elsewhere
comes to accept the hopelessness of its struggle, it could abandon its "pacific"
verbiage and end up embracing terror.[106]

Not only politicians but also most ordinary believers in Muslim countries where HT is active oppose both its almost maniacal desire to save Islam and Muslims and its clumsy notion of restoring the obsolete structure of the caliphate. In most of the Muslim countries where HT operates it is banned. The predictable response of HT is to search for new enemies of Islam, this time solely among Muslims. Party ideologists define the new enemy as:

> The lack of political consciousness among the majority of Muslims. This means that Muslims ceased to feel themselves as a united religious community, the sensation of which was lost from the time when the so-called caliphate ceased to exist, e.g., the theocratic state which alone can restore the real rights of Muslims. In the absence of the caliphate (and, consequently, a "voluntarily elected caliph") the current Muslim countries can be Islamic only in name.

Even though most theologians have come to accept the diverse forms of established Islam as natural and theologically legitimate,[107] HT considers them to be both utterly illegitimate and the chief obstacle to the future unification of modern Muslims against the common enemies.

HT's conflicts with Muslims in its region of origin and with the entire Muslim world do much to radicalize the party. Sociologists might call this an attitude of "contentiousness," a condition where the potential for social and political conflict can be sustained regardless of the positions of the contending groups or countries.

In 1989 Abdurashid Kosimov (b. 1960) formed a local branch of HT in Andijan, the largest city in the Ferghana Valley.[108] It is said that he came to the attention of HT during one of the first mass pilgrimages to Mecca, and was immediately named head of the first branch of HT in Uzbekistan. Kosimov studied for some time in the home of the father of Wahhabism in the Ferghana, Abduvali-qori Mirzaev, and gained a solid knowledge of Arabic. He translated and published an Uzbek edition of Taqiuddin al-Nabhani's *Nizam al-Islam* (The System of Islam).[109]

Not until 1993 did the local HT group stabilize and issue a charter to the public.[110] It then took steps to form branches elsewhere in the region, although its main centers of activity remained the Ferghana Valley and Tashkent. Far from seeking to legalize itself, HT promptly denounced officials of the government as the "henchmen of Jews and Communists" (or of Americans and Russians), and called on all "Muslims who serve them" to "turn away from such rulers and choose a true caliph from their own world."[111] The overwhelming majority of local clerics rejected this, however.

HT's structure in Central Asia is simple. A representative of the region (*mu'tamad*)[112] is appointed by the *qiyadat* (political council or politbureau), headed by the Supreme Amir of the party. The *mu'tamad* (sometimes called also *amir*) appoints his assistants (*mas'ul*) as leaders in the districts and large cities; these in turn appoint their assistants, the *mas'ul yordamchisi*.[113] Under the *mu'tamad* is a regional council (*shuro*), which convenes at times and venues set by the *mu'tamad*. The council includes *mas'ul*s and the collector of donations or treasurer, and the person responsible for publications.

At the mid-level is a *musa'id* and his assistant (*naqib*), appointed by the *ma'sul* to head a district or large neighborhood (*mahalla*). The *naqib* actually administers the locality, along with a treasurer reporting to him, who is also responsible for distributing literature. The *naqib* also works through assistants to oversee small groups of four or five people (*khalq*) working with a teacher or *mushrif*. From such groups are elected reliable messengers (*choparlar*) who link the middle and lower ranks of the organization. Only the senior management has the power to initiate communications between the top and middle ranks, while the various persons at the lower and middle ranks typically do not know one another. This atomization and its accompanying communication barriers serve as an obvious precaution against arrests.

It is tempting to evaluate the activities of HT in the Ferghana Valley on the basis of interviews that local amirs have given to journalists. But over the past half-decade members of HT have come to view such interviews as part of their informational campaign and hence as propaganda, which leaves published litera-ture, leaflets, and articles in party journals as the best source of evidence on HT's activities. Yet even this source must be treated with caution, because it is known that certain leaflets that exude moderation were written and issued for the explicit purpose of supporting human-rights organizations that were denying the extremism of HT and related groups.

In 2003 a local branch of HT released a brochure titled "The Caliphs" (Khali-falar). Here the anonymous author seeks to refute the reasoning of a medieval theologian from the region, Najm ad-Din Abu Khafs 'Umar an-Nasafi (d. 1142), who had used the *Sayings* to back his argument that the caliphate had existed only for thirty years and that Muslims thereafter had been ruled by padishahs and amirs—in other words, by secular rulers. This conception, which accurately reflects the realities of governance in the Islamic world, was adopted by a majority of local Hanafi theologians and helps account for the political peculiarity of the local form of Islam. It is therefore no accident that local theologians and officials alike quote Nasafi when disputing HT claims. To refute Nasafi, the unknown local author of "The Caliphs" invokes comments by a fourteenth-century writer, at-Taftazani.

Over time, HT's regional (mainly Uzbek) adherents found themselves in con-flict both with the local conservative Muslims and with the government.[114] All three governments in the Ferghana Valley, and especially the Uzbeks and Tajiks, had no desire to see a repetition of the clashes with the Wahhabis and therefore instituted tough measures against HT. This produced a loud outcry from certain international human-rights organizations that believed that just because HT had been banned by several European countries was no reason to consider it extrem-ist. Typically, these defenses of HT and similar parties were based on a complete ignorance of their history and international and regional activities, and a limited or non-existent knowledge of their published literature. Often their only knowledge of the voluminous literature is the few leaflets created specifically for consumption by these groups and therefore placed in their hands by HT. The absence of radical anti-Semitic or anti-Christian slogans in these sheets differs sharply from those distributed among the ordinary believers in the local languages. These leaflets addressed to ordinary members of the party and local audiences provide a far more reliable index of HT's true views and activities than its statements regarding its commitment to peaceful methods.

These brochures and leaflets initiate the reader into a very private and mysterious world, one that possesses the secret to the "liberation of Islam," the "purification of the faith," and a "return to true Islam." Even though other groups may have similar goals, HT seems deliberately to have isolated itself from all other groups of believers, not just the conservatives. In the end, whenever a religious-political party or movement is driven by a spirit of alienation, secret knowledge, privacy, and conflict with the larger community, it moves inexorably toward even greater isolation and radicalization. Such a transformation of HT is already evident, even as we hear repeated assertions of its peaceful intentions.

To be sure, the activities of HT in England, where it is headquartered, are peaceful, for the simple reason that they have no alternative but to bring their activities into line with local laws.[115] Indeed, favorable economic conditions in Europe allow many party members to engage in profitable businesses that in turn feed HT's treasury. But if any Central Asian country were to legalize HT (which most Muslim countries have resolutely refused to do), then it would perforce have to yield to its rules, which means abandoning a policy of tolerance and interfaith harmony, becoming mono-confessional, and breaking off diplomatic relations with all "infidel" states. It also would mean adopting as national policy sharia law and the militarized form of jihad expounded in party literature.

The contrast between HT's purported tactic of peaceful methods and the reality of its strategy is vividly evident in HT's English-language updated regulations and articles in its local language publication al-Wa'y (June, 2001). The former, delivered as a report at an international conference of Muslim students held in December 1989 in the United States,[116] extols democracy and related values. The latter features a discourse on contemporary suicide bombers, and soberly champions the use of a suicide bomber belt (a waistband with bombs) in peaceful crowds, on buses, and other targets. Never mind that modern theologians unambiguously denounce this as suicide, which is anathema in Islam. The anonymous author of the article in al-Wa'y denounces such fatwas and reiterates HT's conviction that in waging jihad against infidels all means are acceptable. The article laconically concludes that "the Muslim who blows himself up to destroy the enemy is, by Allah's command, a martyr."[117] Another article in the same publication idealizes a female suicide bomber in Palestine who killed or wounded fifteen people.[118] The author concludes that her martyrdom was "an expression of love" for her two now-orphaned children. Similar tracts focus on jihad against American operations in Afghanistan and further attest to the extreme radicalization of HT.

Some have argued that the radicalization of HT occurred only when it was rejected by the majority of Muslims in Central Asia and suppressed by the governments of that region. But the very first HT emissaries in the region arrived with an uncompromising commitment to confrontation.[119] From the start they were branding conservative local Muslims as "the henchmen of Islam's enemies" and denouncing the Americans, Russians, and other "infidels." It is therefore no surprise to discover that the first HT emissaries in Central Asia made absolutely no effort to legalize their party. Instead, they have focused on organizing branches across Central Asia, as well as in Azerbaijan, Russia, Ukraine, and Belarus, and on upgrading their presence on the Internet. Meanwhile, their self-proclaimed successes have been limited to generating some vague sympathy toward the party, while their active support among the faithful seems to have waned. This does not mean that HT will quit any time soon, since the problems that foster sympathy for them remain: a continuing crisis of identity in the region, the weakness of religious counter-arguments, inexperience on the part of organs of government, and conflicting legislation in the various countries.[120] Because of this, the number of those who view HT with sympathy is large, even though the number of active member is insignificant.[121]

Despite their primitive style, HT leaflets continue to find a response among believers in the Ferghana Valley.[122] Indeed, HT tends to respond faster and more openly to socio-economic problems than do most journalists. HT skillfully and successfully plays on the unwillingness of journalists to say anything critical of government. HT presents the greatest danger in societies where official ideologies are weak or unconvincing, and where official bodies do not openly discuss, analyze, and thus eliminate problems facing the communities. In the face of increasing social differentiation and the decline of social protection, HT calls for social and economic equality, which finds a receptive audience among youth and the unemployed. The fact that society is long exposed to Soviet slogans about the "equality of workers" and "fair and equal distribution of public goods" makes people the more receptive to ideas about the "natural equality in Islam."

Akromiya

The post-communist return to the "religion of our fathers" did not bring deepened knowledge of the complex ideas and history of the faith. This gap between an intellectual and purely emotional embrace of religion gave rise to a number of small religious communities, above all in the Ferghana Valley. One of these is called Akromiya, after its founder Akrom Yo'ldoshev (b. 1963). After attending high school in Andijan and serving in the Red Army, Yo'ldoshev worked at a textile mill. From 1985 to 1990, he studied at the cotton institute in Andijan, served as a leader of the local Komsomol Committee, and was appointed a candidate member of the Communist Party. His classmates recall that Yo'ldoshev was particularly interested in elective courses on such perestroika-era topics as social studies, history, and literature. After reading the Qur'an in translation, he shared his newfound interest in religion with his classmate, Abdurashid Kosimov, whom we have discussed as a local founder of HT. Yo'ldoshev joined HT in 1991 after reading al-Nabhani's *Nizam al-Islam*. For his part Kosimov was attracted by Yo'ldoshev's speaking abilities, his ability to lead provincial intellectuals, and his businesslike handling of local party funds.[123]

After more than a year, Yo'ldoshev withdrew from HT in 1995 and founded his own group along lines similar to HT. From the outset Yo'ldoshev focused on business, engaging in cross-border trade and establishing small and medium-sized enterprises, including a network of bakeries that became well known in Andijan. Small businesses became the kernel of the organization, offering lessons for members on the basis of Yo'ldoshev's work. Part of the income went to a general fund (*umumy jamgharma/bayt al-mal*) that provided aid to needy members and recruits. Appeals to the egalitarianism of the first Muslims gained Akromiya many followers, even though former members report that this principle existed more in rhetoric than reality.

Information turned up in official investigations confirms that money from the general fund regularly went to bribe law-enforcement officials and prison guards.[124] A few months before the May 13, 2005 armed uprising in Andijan, the general fund purchased more than fifty firearms and transported them to Andijan for use by those planning the attack.[125] Another branch of Akromiya was Ijody Khalqa (the Creative Group), which organized classes on the works of Yo'ldoshev.

The government of Uzbekistan issued warnings to Yo'ldoshev that Akromiya's activities were illegal, but Akromiya's only response was to go underground, in 1997. That year Yo'ldoshev was sentenced to two and a half years but was released early as part of an amnesty; he was reconvicted in 1999. However, its leader's arrest did not slow the activities of Akromiya.

Initially, Yo'ldoshev found it acceptable to pray only twice a day (as in the earliest Muslim community) instead of five times, and to pass over other commandments imposed after the death of the Prophet.[126] In his *Yimonga Yul* (The Path to Faith) he proposed that since God had sent the Qur'an over a period of twenty-three years, the first Muslim community only gradually could study Islam. Modern societies therefore need not hurry in mastering the Holy Book. Yo'ldoshev was well aware that religious scholars in Uzbekistan and the region, as well as ordinary believers, staunchly opposed such notions.[127] However, Wahhabi literature published prior to the Andijan tragedy indicates that they, too, opposed Akromiya's ideas. Yo'ldoshev's plan for overcoming the schism was vague, consisting mainly of arguments against "logical reasoning" on issues of dogma.

Akromiya's inability to shape traditional religious arguments reinforced the conflict between the group and the government and with the main body of Muslims. This condition of "conflict with everyone" further isolated Akromiya and contributed to its further radicalization.

This trend was evident in two commentaries that Yo'ldoshev wrote on the Qur'anic Sura "Al-Saff," the first of which he penned in late March 2005, the second in late April. Both, it should be stressed, preceded Akromiya's May 13 armed assaults in Andijan. In his commentary, reinforced by further Qur'anic citations, Yo'ldoshev called directly for jihad, which he interprets purely in terms of armed action.[128] For security reasons Yo'ldoshev at first shared his political objectives only with a small group of Akromiya members, and even then only gradually. His notion of the caliphate, for example, was largely an abstraction,[129] and in *Yimonga Yul* even jihad was somewhat of an insinuation.[130] On the social and political front he was more concrete, asserting that economic problems greatly increased the potential for conflict in Uzbek society. In the words of an Akromiya leader, "Light a match and all will blaze up." Events in neighboring Kyrgyzstan seemed to prove this, for they had led relatively easily to regime change, albeit with much looting. Yet in the end, Akromiya grounded its hopes more in religious arguments that defended armed conflict than in theories about the power of the "discontented masses."

Chronology of the Tragedy in Andijan

At 12:43 A.M. and 12:46 A.M. on the night of May 13, 2005, armed militants from Akromiya attacked a police sub-station and military units, killing several officers and soldiers and seizing more than 250 firearms, as well as grenades, vehicles, and other materiel.[131]

A few hours later, the now well-armed Akromiya band attacked the prison and freed more than 500 prisoners, whom the militants forced to take up arms and join them. Around 5:00 A.M., the enlarged group launched a two-hour siege of the Andijan headquarters of the National Security Service (SNB), killing or injuring several officers and soldiers. Around 6:00 A.M. the Akromists set fire to the city's main theater and cinema, which stand opposite to the Andijan City Hall on Babur Square. The Akromists meanwhile used all types of maneuvers, including the fires, to lure large numbers of spectators, including many women, to the square, where they were joined by still more armed militants.

But although they had "lit a match," no blaze followed. When this outcome became clear, almost all the Akromiya militants who were inside the City Hall or on the square poured out through the crowd, some of them running through yards and throwing down their weapons. Within a couple of hours they had crossed the border with Kyrgyzstan and entered refugee camps there. Most of the fighters (especially the combat team leader T. Khodjiev) declared that they had had no weapons. However, Akromiya itself had filmed its own actions with video cameras, and their films all confirmed that the attackers had been heavily armed. When this information was passed to the Kyrgyz prosecutor general and reviewed by his staff, the Kyrgyz sent the accused back across the border to law-enforcement offices in Uzbekistan.

Akromiya's own videotapes of the events in Andijan ended up in the hands of Uzbek law enforcement bodies and became a key argument for the prosecution.[132] Akromiya's eager video cameramen had not only filmed the militants' actions in Andijan, but also some of their meetings. One long sequence shows the burning of the movie and drama theaters. During the scene, the photographer himself was distinctly heard exclaiming, "It's great, awesome! . . . Now everyone will come" (*Zo'r bolayapti, a, dahshat! . . . Ana endi hamma [odamlar] kelishadi!*]. As noted, the goal was to assemble a crowd, including relatives, friends, and fellow members of Akromiya. Using landlines from the City Hall and cell phones, they called everyone they knew.

One of the videos includes the following snippet from a cell phone conversation: "Come, come here . . . here, everyone here! Even if someone doesn't have courage, bring him here anyway . . . Our women are already here" (*Kelinglar, kelinglar, mana bu yoqqa . . . hamma shu erda! . . . Duhi bolmasayam olib kel! . . . Ayollarimiz shu erda turibti*). Later, a frustrated Akromiya member says, "The crowd is not gathering, that's why we have to shout 'Allahu Akbar'" (*Talpa bo'lmayapti, ashinchin "Allahu Akbar" diysh kerak*).[133] The videos include scenes of activists, especially women, being pushed onto the square. There an Akromiya member lines them up and commands them to wave their hands and shout "Allahu Akbar," so as to draw others to the spot. On a second film (21st minute) an Akromiya organizer admonishes the women, "Don't be afraid! Line up in a row . . . If you're killed, we will take full responsibility for it" (*Qo'rqmanglar, qator turinglar . . . O'ldirsa biz javob beramiz*).

Soon a large crowd of the curious did assemble, many arriving by bicycle. There were large numbers of teenagers and even children, who are shown in the videotapes walking idly near the City Hall and on the square. At one point the operator of one of the video cameras is heard to say, "Thank God, a crowd is gathering . . . This is what we needed" (*Talpa boshlanayapti, Khudoga shkur, ashinisi kerak edi bizga*). Note that several of these speakers use a variation of the Russian word for crowd, *tolpa,* which almost means "mob," and that Akromiya was working hard to mobilize the curious or disgruntled for its own ends.

Traditional religious leaders who were drawn to Babur Square posed a problem for Akromiya. One was filmed calling on everyone to disperse. The Akromiya fighter immediately interrupted him and forced him to look directly at the camera. As he did so he yelled, "Your intentions are different from ours. Where is the second one of [the mullahs]? Drive them out of here" (*Bitta niyatingiz bo'lay [bo'lak] yuribsiz . . . Qani haligi ikkinchisi? Chikarib yuboring mana shularni*). Akromiya activists were eager to remove such voluntary "anti-agitators" from the square.

The three extant videos leave the clear impression that most of the people who gathered in the square and at the City Hall wanted to leave as soon as they saw guns everywhere. But Akromiya activists would not let them disperse, as proven by the cordons set up at the exit points. One of Akromiya's videos actually records one of the armed insurgents telling someone on Babur Square, "You can enter . . . but you cannot leave" (*Kirish bor . . . chiqish yo'q*).[134]

Beyond this, the Akromiya's camera operators recorded scenes of large numbers of armed militants among the crowd, Akromiya snipers on rooftops, armed men in positions around the City Hall, banks being seized on nearby Fitrat Street, and other indications of violent intention. Some militants even pose before the cameras, grandly holding their guns at the ready. One video sequence shows young fighters in front of the City Hall preparing Molotov cocktails. Overall, the films recorded more than a hundred young men with rifles in front of City Hall and on Babur Square. They show terrorists leading into the City Hall columns of hostages, among them ordinary soldiers, City Hall guards, militia officers and troops, and a number of civilians. One of the insurgents commands a captive police officer to "Look at the camera" (*Kameraga qara*). Of the seventy hostages identified, nearly half were civilians.

What was Akromiya's purpose in so deliberately filming its actions? Why did its members film armed hostage-taking, including of civilians, and force them, with guns pointed at their heads, to look into the camera? Obviously, they intentionally created a large body of highly compromising evidence that could be used against them.

The camera operators themselves provide some answers. Thus, when the lens catches a group of Akromiya militants armed with AK-47s sitting on the edge of Babur Square, the operator calls out for them to "Come closer, let me film you for history" (*Kelinglar, sizlarniyam tarix uchun olib qo'yay*). When a crowd of women saw they were being filmed, one of them asked, "Why are you filming us?" (*Nima uchun bizlarni videoga olayapsizlar?*), to which the cameraman replied, "For a new government" (*Yangi hokimiyat uchun*).

However differently the Andijan events might be interpreted, it is clear that the Akromists confidently believed they would triumph, that they themselves would constitute the new government, and that their films would therefore become important documents in forging a new and revolutionary history.

Reflecting on developments in the Uzbek sector of the Ferghana Valley, one should not be surprised that Yo'ldoshev and similar leaders of informal religious communities would have produced an often contradictory body of writing, or that many of their views would have come into conflict with those of the bearers of traditional religious knowledge. In spite of their ambition to become "connoisseurs of truth," they suffered from their lack of having had any systematic religious education. The dramatic increase in the number of translated sacred texts and theological works freed them from dependence on traditional theologians, yet caused them to turn to "experts" who in most cases already were thoroughly radicalized and who harbored their own leadership ambitions.[135] This set the stage for mutual hostility and recriminations between the traditionalists and the new Wahhabis.

In spite of strict government controls, the signs of emerging re-Islamization had been evident even in Soviet times. Calls to purify Islam and Muslims found a particularly receptive audience in post-Soviet Uzbekistan and gave rise to many new groups, including extremist and terrorist ones. From the outset, all manifestations of this process of re-Islamization found their focus in the Ferghana Valley, and it was there that Wahhabi ideology first took root.[136] Re-Islamization brought many positive gains, including freedom of worship and a revival of spiritual values. However, it had a negative side as well, in the form of aggression, violence, and even terrorism, much of it directed against the government but just as much aimed at the conservative majority of believers, who were seen as political conformists and followers of the "wrong" Islam. The majority applied the popular label Wahhabi to all those whom they considered strangers,[137] including HT and Akromiya, while the new groups acted on the principle that "Whoever is not with us is against us." Thus, intolerance bred intolerance.

Law-enforcement bodies were entirely unprepared for this explosion of religion, ideological ferment, and political-religious aspirations. Naturally they took the side of the conformist majority, or conservatives, who were the bearers of the ancient regional tradition of political loyalty. Accordingly, official bodies adopted the positions and approaches of the conservatives with respect to all those who were non-conformists, and in doing so fostered an environment conducive to further dissent.

Some of the resulting groups, like Tablighi Jamaat and HT, became branches of Muslim parties elsewhere, while others, like Ahli Hadith and Ahli Qur'an, were more locally grounded but pursued the same goals with the same slogans. Nearly all of them appeared in the Ferghana Valley, mainly in those parts belonging to Uzbekistan. Underlying these many currents was certainly an attempt, if only in embryonic form, to bring about some sort of Reformation within Islam. However, this effort could not make headway among the population at large, and so descended increasingly into aggression and terror.

Jadidism, the first reformist and modernist religious movement in the former Russian Empire, arose under the direct influence of similar undertakings in Egypt and Turkey. Bolshevism interrupted this movement but did not kill it. With the religious revival that began in the late 1970s a reformist movement once more slowly emerged, again under the influence of reformers from the eastern (Maududi from India) and western parts (Muhammad Abdo/Abduh, Sayid Qutb, and others) of the Muslim world. It is fair to say that almost all branches and currents of this religious-political reformism in the Ferghana Valley, as in Central Asia as a whole, are fundamentally imitative, adapting the most extreme manifestations of foreign currents to local conditions. Yet in the end the Wahhabis and their radical or Salafi successors failed to launch real political and economic programs, or even to create a body of ideas that could thrive locally.

The future of Hizb ut-Tahrir in Ferghana and the region appears more promising. Recent interviews with members suggest a far smaller increase in HT membership than the organization itself claims. At the same time, many ordinary believers now view HT more calmly, and some imams who disagree with their ideas openly call for the party to be legalized.[138] But the head offices in London have cut off funding for HT publications in the Ferghana Valley, and those that are issued no longer attract much attention, especially among young people. Increased activity on their websites, however, suggests that local leaders may be trying to reverse this.[139]

Besides such formal entities, the Uzbek sector of the Ferghana Valley teems with self-proclaimed messengers of God, and with new prophets. While their activity is mainly limited to a single village or urban district, their very appearance and popularity attest to the crisis of identity that persists even in the face of official propaganda about Islamic values.

The core of nearly all radical groups and parties are young people between the ages sixteen and thirty. With no religious education at all, they have at best a secondary schooling, during which they were poorly indoctrinated in "correct political thinking"[140] in a very simple, primitive form. Such people, most of them unemployed or impoverished farmers and small businessmen who have been sidelined by economic reform, can readily accept as immutable truth that the only just system of government is a caliphate. Faced with seemingly insurmountable difficulties in their personal and economic lives, such young people easily embrace the notion of an ideal realm on behalf of which they can struggle.[141] Theirs is an ideology of the Muslim "lumpenproletariat," defined in terms of jihad in its militaristic sense, so long as it is "on God's path" and "against infidels."[142]

Meanwhile, even so-called moderate Islamists fill their publications and sermons with retrograde talk about the hostility of the "infidels" toward the faithful, and the need for Muslims to join forces against their common enemies. We have explained this in terms of the suppression or failure of earlier reform movements (for example Jadids), which denied to Islam in the Ferghana a natural evolution and left it, at the start of perestroika, in a very conservative and highly defensive condition, constantly expecting treachery from infidels and dissenters, but with only the most primitive means of responding to such perceived threats.

The most dangerous potential threat to the security of the region remains the IMU, which recently re-named itself the Islamic Movement of Turkestan (IMT). According to former members,[143] the Movement, working from its camps in Pakistan, is seeking new funding, mainly from Saudi Arabia.[144] But since the fall of the Taliban in 2001 and the arrival in Afghanistan of coalition forces, IMT's prospects have diminished sharply.

In conclusion, it is important to review the main factors shaping re-Islamization in the Uzbek part of the Ferghana Valley today. These include the enduring economic problems that cause inter-group tensions, the identity crisis of a large part of the population, the related embrace of religious identities, the absence of a coherent national ideology and of an official strategy for dealing with the issue of religious extremism, the decline of secular education and the control of religious education by radicals (i.e., the "Salafization" of religious education), the dissemination of publications by Muslim extremist groups fostering hatred toward domestic and foreign infidels, the absence of a cadre of trained specialists in the area who are not themselves under the sway of one or another religious group, and the lack of coordination of policies for dealing with such issues among the three Ferghana states.[145] The future of religious extremism in the Uzbek sector of the Ferghana Valley will be shaped by these elements, and by the responses to them by official bodies.

Islamic Political Movements in the Ferghana Valley of Kyrgyzstan

From the time of Russia's colonization of Central Asia, the status and condition of Islam in what is now Kyrgyzstan's part of the Ferghana Valley has been shaped by governmental policies.[146] Tsarist Russia's approach did not have much consistency. Initially, the colonial authorities interfered little, if at all, in the religious life of the population, under the expectation that loyal local Muslim clerics would help keep the local populace under control. Events in the 1860s reinforced this approach.

Under the influence of the Taiping Rebellion, the Uyghurs, Kazakhs, Dungans, and other Muslim people in the Chinese territory of Xinjiang mounted an uprising against the Chinese feudal lords. Many Uyghurs and Dungans (ethnic Chinese Muslims), fearing persecution, fled to Central Asia, mainly to the eastern part of the Ferghana Valley. They arrived with ancient and settled farming traditions that strengthened the position of Islam in what is now northern Kyrgyzstan and southern Kazakhstan. To escape what they regarded as China's dangerously foreign culture and alien religious environment, they accepted Russian citizenship.[147]

Meanwhile, Russian authorities were concerned by the replenishment of the Muslim population in the strategically important Semireche (Seven Rivers) region, which strengthened Islam there. The 1914 Russian census indicated that by that year there were 8.5 million Muslims in the territories of the empire east of the Urals.[148] Russia therefore imposed restrictions on further immigration by Uyghurs and Kazakhs.

Dissatisfied with their socio-economic status, Turkic subjects of the Russian Empire waged frequent rebellions based on jihadist notions of war against infidels. During the 1916 national uprising in Talas, it was rumored that the Turkish sultan was sending troops to support the rebels; and in the south of the region the entire Muslim population rose against the "White King." Certain mullahs interested in fomenting hostility helped turn this into an inter-faith conflict by focusing their wrath against prisoners of war who had been shipped there, including Austro-Hungarian and German military officers and some Catholic and Protestant clergy. Russian imperial forces brutally suppressed these efforts by religious zealots.[149]

Following the overthrow of the tsar in 1917, the indigenous inhabitants of Central Asia, employing Islamic rhetoric, established their own authorities, including the Council of Muslim Representatives in Osh and the Kyrgyz People's Committee in Pishpek (later Frunze, now Bishkek).[150] Various national and religious parties appeared and grew active, most of them affirming Pan-Islamic and Pan-Turkic programs. Once the Soviet regime was established it branded them all as reactionary and suppressed them.

Islam Today, Between Ideology and Politics

The emergence of Islam as a significant factor in the political life of Central Asia following the collapse of the Soviet Union was in no sense a surprise, even where religion had declined to the status of a cultural artifact. In responding to it, the new elites in the three Ferghana countries reverted to Soviet approaches and failed to develop flexible policies toward religion. Far from solving the problem, they obfuscated it. Meanwhile, the opening of the external borders and the nominal return of Central Asia to the lap of Islamic civilization led to increased public interest in Islam and to its politicization. At the same time, after the collapse of the USSR Central Asian countries benefited from major investments made by the Muslim world, mainly from the Gulf states. Central Asian leaders strengthened their links with the Muslim world by making pilgrimages to Mecca. However, the response came not from Muslim governments but from religious-political parties, most of which were committed to radical Islamist ideologies.

Thanks to these developments, Islam in Kyrgyzstan is not only reclaiming the societal role it lost ninety years ago, but is acquiring new forms of influence that cannot be ignored. Broadly speaking, the goal of the new currents is to integrate all Muslim countries into one cultural-confessional space, and to ensure that Central Asia, including Kyrgyzstan and the Ferghana Valley, are part of it. One might refer to this as Islamic globalization, taking place in the context of authoritarian regimes. In this sense, events in the Ferghana Valley must be seen as part of a larger development.

This Islamic mobilization arose as a political protest against the powerful impact of external forces on the Arab-Muslim world.[151] Events in recent years in Palestine, Lebanon, and elsewhere show that despite its inability to solve basic social and political problems, and its tendency to experience internal schisms, political Islam can still mobilize huge masses of sympathetic people and legitimize its actions in the eyes of society. This obviously would not pass unnoticed in Central Asia.

Initially the new authorities in Kyrgyzstan and elsewhere endeavored to show their commitment to Islamic tradition as a part of national culture. Later they came to treat the Islamic resurgence with more caution, seeking to submit Muslim organizations and movements to state control. Even though these measures were by no means successful, the question remains as to what extent re-Islamization can actually be achieved. After all, the consolidation of micro-communities in the Ferghana Valley, including the Kyrgyz part, came about more by national, ethnic, tribal, political, and economic forces than by Islam. Indeed, it is the regional and ethnic divisions that define the ideologically disparate groups that comprise the Muslim communities (*jamaats*) of Kyrgyzstan's part of the Ferghana Valley.

A 2005 study that included the two Ferghana districts of Jalalabad and Osh, as well as northern Kyrgyzstan, revealed that 82 percent of respondents believed in God, and among them a similar percent had received higher educations. Fully a quarter observe religious laws and perform Muslim rites, while half said they did so but only irregularly.[152] Every year the Muslims of Kyrgyzstan become more a part of the political process, especially after the democratizing new constitution of 2007 made it advantageous for political parties to recruit Muslims into their lists. Today Kyrgyzstan stands on the threshold of a struggle among the various political forces to determine who will succeed in bringing Muslims to their side. This is quite interesting, as it raises the question whether the Muslim community, a patchwork of ethnic groups and clans, can speak in one voice in politics.[153]

More than a half of the population of the Kyrgyz Republic (54 percent) lives in the southern region, which includes the Ferghana Valley and Batken province, which directly adjoins it. Three-quarters of the total consists of ethnic Kyrgyz. At the moment, there is a massive outflow of Kyrgyz north to the capital of Bishkek, to the Chui Valley, and especially to Russia. Between 2005 and 2008, nearly 650,000 Kyrgyz left the Ferghana region, while as many as a million (officially only 600,000) Uzbeks and Tajiks entered, largely on account of the more liberal economic environment in Kyrgyzstan. Thus, the region is now dominated by only two groups—Kyrgyz and Uzbeks. The rise of Kyrgyz nationalism has had the effect of pitting these two groups against each other. However, it should be noted that a region-wide mobilization of an Islamic alliance would have the reverse effect, putting them all on one side against infidel forces, whether domestic or foreign.

Most authorities long considered the formerly nomadic Kyrgyz, with their shamanist traditions, to be inherently less religious than the settled inhabitants of the ancient oasis. To be sure, the Kyrgyz, while part of the conservative majority, always followed rather strange and even bizarre forms of the faith. But whatever the situation in the past, it cannot be denied that the process of Islamist revival over the past two decades has enabled the faith to steadily expand its influence on social relations among Ferghana Kyrgyz. Increasingly, Kyrgyz from all regions resort to Islam as the highest court of appeal in addressing their daily concerns. In spite of this, Islam still has been unable to fulfill the important integrative function in society. In spite of Soviet efforts to destroy them, Kyrgyz tribal structures and their replication within the government have proven very stable and entirely relevant to present-day realities. Acknowledging this, the division of north and south appears to be a more decisive factor in domestic affairs than the much smaller differences among the clans of each region.

A 2008 survey of students at secular universities in Osh and Bishkek sheds light on their views on religion. Barely a quarter attend Friday prayers even irregularly, but this is from two to three times more than the figure from a 2003 study. Also, while 53 percent identify themselves as "not religious," 63 percent regard themselves as primarily Muslim and only secondarily Kyrgyz. These positions clearly contradict the stereotype of the irreligious Kyrgyz, as opposed to the pious Uzbeks. Today's youth are undergoing an ideological transformation, shifting from a traditional and passive understanding of Islam to an active commitment to Muslim values. This heightens the possibilities for religious-political perspectives and parties, and indeed 67 percent thought that believers should be free to form political parties, which is about the same percent who believe that Islam and democracy are compatible under certain conditions. It is not surprising that just over half of the students polled see Kyrgyzstan's future as a secular state informed by Muslim values (like Turkey or Malaysia), while 14 percent see it as a purely Islamic state and a mere 1.26 percent of those from rural areas see it following a Western model.

Thus, we can observe at least the beginnings of a purely Islamic mode of identity that crosses borders, although this remains a minority position among members of the Muslim community in Kyrgyzstan. By contrast, the majority of Kyrgyz Muslims from thirty to sixty-four-years old aspire to more self-determination within a nationally oriented form of Islam. This stress on the national or tribal character of Muslim identity is a distinctive feature of all nationalities in Kyrgyzstan. Of course, regional mistrust and tensions are not openly expressed, much less in the press, but they definitely give rise to a division of authority based on regionalism within all Muslim organization.

The monopoly on religious power of the Ferghana Valley regional group in Kyrgyzstan has existed since far back in Soviet times. A consequence of this has been that, with the exception of Talas province, the heads of Muslim communities throughout Kyrgyzstan were all drawn from either Osh or Batken. Since the southerners emphasized tradition over formal theology, this became the emphasis of the top religious administration everywhere. But when southern clerics began propagating their traditionalist views and culturally specific approaches and mentality in the north, many Muslims there simply did not accept them. The view that women should not go to mosques, the special status of the imam as holy man, and many more non-Islamic practices that are deeply ingrained among Kyrgyz in the Ferghana Valley were rejected in Kyrgyzstan's north.

Another feature of so-called southern Islam is its commercialization of ritual services. An example of this is the widespread southern phenomenon of *davran*. The term, probably of Tajik origin, derives from late Sufism, and is from an Arabic root (*dau'r*) which means to circle or turn. In traditional Ferghana Islam this means counting up the five-times daily prayers (*salah*) that one has missed throughout one's life and making a payment in grain that translates into money.[154] Ferghana clerics explain that this is a demand of the sharia, but there is no evidence for this. *Davran* is in reality a burdensome death tax, imposed in the name of Islam but having absolutely no basis in the Faith.

Another consequence of the monopolistic control wielded by Ferghana Kyrgyz over Islam in Kyrgyzstan is that students from the Ferghana Valley are disproportionately represented among those sent to study at Muslim institutions abroad, leaving few positions to northerners. All these practices arising from the Ferghana Valley's domination of Kyrgyz Islam represent a serious problem in inter-regional relations that confronts the government.

With the strengthening of religious identities in Kyrgyzstan, meaningful study of Islam has grown, contact with centers of Islamic learning has expanded, and overall the educational level of typical Muslims has significantly increased. As this more conscious approach to the Faith takes hold, people seek to apply religious precepts to everyday life and, in so doing, broaden the role of Islam beyond its traditional ceremonial functions. That this reinforces the regionalization of Muslim life in the Kyrgyz Republic is scarcely surprising, given the existing north-south division of the country's life.

Uzbek inhabitants of the Kyrgyz sector of the Ferghana Valley constitute the second-largest group of Muslims in the country. The stereotypical view is that Uzbeks are more religious than their Kyrgyz neighbors, but this refers mainly to the role of traditional ritual rather than to inner spiritual life. During the post-Soviet revival of Islam this led to the opening of more mosques in the Uzbek communities than in Kyrgyz ones, and to more open manifestations of religious ritual in public life. This was accompanied by a continuation of the old habit of identifying a specific mosque by the ethnicity of its parishioners, as for instance, the Uyghurs' mosque or the Uzbeks' mosque. All this fostered a spirit of national Islam among each of the two main groups in the Ferghana Valley.

The size and compact character of the Uzbek population in Kyrgyzstan's part of the Ferghana Valley gives urgency to the question of its integration into the national society. Its identity is based above all on ethnicity, which in the minds of many Uzbeks in Kyrgyzstan is identical with religious affiliation, and only secondarily with religion. Any spirit of religious unity that might arise will be based not on the secular state, but on the Muslim community of Kyrgyzstan. The same issue arises with other ethnic groups in the Ferghana Valley.

During the Soviet period, Muslims were placed under the authority of four *muftiyat,* or Spiritual Directorates, one of them covering Central Asia from its headquarters in Tashkent.[155] For forty years after its founding in 1943 this agency, SADUM, managed the affairs of Kyrgyzstan's Muslims through a local office or *qazyat.* Beginning in the late 1980s the republican offices started to separate themselves from SADUM,[156] and in 1993 the new government in Bishkek established a Spiritual Administration of Muslims of Kyrgyzstan (DUMK) with responsibility for religious organizations, institutions for religious education, and mosques. Within that entity is a council of religious leaders (*ulama*), which has generally been dominated by an absolute majority of imams and madrassa teachers from the Ferghana Valley. Nearly all of them adhere to the traditionalist or conservative theology associated with the so-called Bukharan school, and they are advocates of the Ferghana Valley system of individual learning called *hujra.* Widely recognized spiritual mentors and theologians from the Ferghana region are such figures as Moldogazy Ajy, Kudratulla Ajy, Sabyr Moldo, and Sheikh Abdusattar Ajy (Hajji) from Uzgen. Another is the former mufti and director of the madrassa at Bukhara, the University of Jordan graduate Kimsambay Ajy Abdrakhmanov, from the Batken region. Nearly all such leaders are staunch traditionalists/conservatives and are direct disciples of, or have a relationship with, the Babakhanov family of muftis from Uzbekistan.

Meanwhile, the traditional religious life of Kyrgyz households—the so-called popular Islam, with its blend of pre-Islamic practices and Islam—is still very much alive in both villages and cities. Indeed, this domestic or "folk" Islam is firmly entrenched and widely considered an essential component of the traditions and mentality of the Kyrgyz people.

The failure of the official or conservative clergy to help believers respond to the needs of a changing life has led many Muslims to switch their loyalty to others. As a result, Salafi or Wahhabi theologians are well represented in the Kyrgyz sector of the Ferghana Valley. Among those who have gained popular followings are the late imam of the Karasu Mosque, Muhammad-Rafiq Kamalov (killed in August 2006), his brother Sadykjan Kamalov, and Iliyas-Ajy. Many if not most of these support radical changes in society, based on a politicized concept of Islam. It is appropriate that the term parallel Islam has come into use to describe this new religious and political reality.

Political Islam in Kyrgyzstan's part of the Ferghana Valley, as in Kyrgyzstan as a whole, is represented by such non-traditional movements as Hizb ut-Tahrir and the Wahhabi (or Salafi) communities. These movements are all characterized by a flexible, "bottom up" strategy of Islamization leading to evolutionary changes in society. Brought to Kyrgyzstan from other countries, such Islamist movements as Ahl Sunnah wal Jama'a Al-Salafiya and Hizb ut-Tahrir passed through similar processes of development that can be divided into four main periods: first, a period of direct penetration from abroad and rapid spread of the movement at the local level due to the absence of alternative points of organization; second, a period of conceptual and methodological adaptation, during which the level of activity diminishes somewhat; third, application of the new principles and methods focusing now at the national level; fourth, a shift of ideology and activity to the regional and transnational level, along with a reunification of the ideology with the broader political currents of Islamic protest.

According to their widely disseminated leaflets, the initial penetration into Kyrgyzstan of Wahhabi groups and the Hizb ut-Tahrir was confined mainly to the Uzbek population of the Ferghana Valley, and was directed against the political leadership of neighboring Uzbekistan.[157] After the transnational ideologies of the Wahhabi communities (*jamaats*) and Hizb ut-Tahrir were adapted to the socio-political environment of Kyrgyzstan, a long period of transformation began, which is still underway. The return in the 1990s of Kyrgyz nationals from periods of study at Muslim institutions in the Middle East brought the often-radicalized ideologies of political Islam to the south of Kyrgyzstan and the Ferghana Valley. Initially, their dependence on instructions (and money) from the religious centers of Saudi Arabia and on the Arabic language, in which all their materials were written, undermined their credibility among the population. As in neighboring Uzbekistan, their radical beliefs led to conflict between the Wahhabis and the traditionally oriented majority, and also with the government, which supported the latter. Until the appearance of Hizb ut-Tahrir, radical Islamists acted impulsively and gained adherents almost exclusively among the Uzbek population of Kyrgyzstan's Ferghana Valley. The continuing dependence of Kyrgyz Wahhabis on ideology and money coming from Arab religious centers all but guarantees that while their organization structures may adapt to local circumstances, their ideology will not. The Wahhabis' radicalism and intransigence toward the traditionalists or conservatives are therefore likely to alienate them from most believers and render them irrelevant.

It is tempting to trace the rise of Hizb ut-Tahrir to the spreading poverty in the Kyrgyz sector of the Ferghana Valley. But the causes are more complex, and include at a minimum the decline of political freedoms in all the regional countries as well as the continued deterioration of economic prospects and social services there. These factors have enabled HT to win widespread support among the masses, and have encouraged it to continue to promote its anti-secular, anti-Western, and anti-corruption ideas. HT's supporters in Kyrgyzstan are geographically more diffused than the Ferghana-focused Wahhabis, and hence the party must address a wider range of socio-political issues, which it does by issuing its own commands or *fatwas* and engaging in advocacy both within the Muslim community and before the authorities.[158]

HT aims its program of ideological protest at a broad spectrum of both religious and secular people. That program, which has remained virtually unchanged since HT first appeared in the region, includes the de-legitimization of the constitutional order and existing secular authorities in Kyrgyzstan; establishing an Islamic caliphate to include the territories of modern Uzbekistan, Tajikistan, and Kyrgyzstan;[159] the establishment in Kyrgyzstan of a new constitution based on sharia law;[160] and ideological loyalty to foreign centers. As to means, HT in Kyrgyzstan, as elsewhere, states its commitment to peaceful methods but does not preclude the use of armed power.[161] In recent years HT, in an effort to win over ordinary people, proclaimed a new goal of "fighting corruption and the illegal actions of local officials."[162] Unlike the Wahhabis, HT recognizes other Muslim organizations as brothers in the faith, despite their broad and fundamental differences.

Without abandoning what many see as the party's utopian goal of a global Muslim caliphate, HT has proposed to pursue its transnational project in phases, thus slowly forming in the minds of believers a new perception of "geopolitical space" in the Islamic commonwealth. Of course, Hizb ut-Tahrir is not interested in Kyrgyzstan as a country. The party seeks to merge it first conceptually and then in reality into a region-wide political and economic entity under Islamic rule.

To date, efforts by mainstream religious leaders and civil authorities to check the growing influence of Hizb ut-Tahrir have been without effect. Young people especially see in it a more authoritative voice of religious leadership than that provided by the religious hierarchy supported by the state. The government's response began with tolerance and then moved to repression, including HT among other terrorist organizations like the IMU. Today there is agreement that HT is potentially destabilizing, but some favor further repression while others call for it to be legalized.

HT views its proposed caliphate as a form of government in which all power belongs to Allah[163] but both secular and religious authority is entrusted to the caliph, who is appointed by the community of believers. It dismisses the existing governments of Muslim countries as non-Islamic. Infidels, including the existing governments of Central Asia, Americans, Russians, Jews, and others, rule the world, and the very name of Hizb ut-Tahrir—Party of Liberation—stresses its commitment to free the world of domination by infidels.[164] The strategy for achieving this calls for gradually shifting the political balance in each country in favor of

HT's supporters and then, whether by legal processes or by an illegal coup d'état, overturn the system in favor of an Islamic caliphate.[165] The fact that Muslim jurists fundamentally disagree among themselves on so many aspects of the application of sharia law leaves one wondering whether such a state of future harmony as HT envisions is more than a utopian dream.[166]

Yet the HT party remains in a strong position. Its powerful centers in the Ferghana Valley at Osh and Jalalabad are paired with centers in Khujand, Kurgan-Tyube, Tursunzadin, and Dushanbe in Tajikistan, all the major cities of the Uzbek sector of the Ferghana Valley, and in many centers in neighboring Xinjiang in China— indeed, there are said to be more than twenty cells just in the capital, Urumchi. With its effective use of the printing press and Internet and its rejection of ethnic enmity, HT can bring together masses of people and concentrate their efforts in a unique manner, employing both internal and external resources.[167]

HT cells in the Kyrgyz sector of the Ferghana Valley are directly subordinated to the *mu'tamad*, or currently *mas'ul*, of Hizb ut-Tahrir in Uzbekistan, as are other cells in the Kyrgyz Republic. All are in close contact with one another. Thus, the reorganization of cells in the Ferghana Valley in 1999 caused the transfer of computer equipment from Uzbek to Tajik centers, and literature and leaflets from Uzbekistan to Kyrgyz groups. The Uzbek leaders of Hizb ut-Tahrir not only appoint the leaders of cells elsewhere in the region but receive reports from them and occasionally meet to offer them guidance. HT offices in Xinjiang regularly e-mail Uzbekistan reports on their projects and sometimes ask for help. The Uzbek offices in turn summarize and analyze the reports from neighboring countries, as well as from Uzbekistan itself, and forward them, along with their own recommendations, to HT's central office in Jordan.[168]

Kyrgyz areas of the Ferghana Valley close to the Uzbek border play an additional role in the life of HT regionally. Thus, the thoroughgoing corruption of law-enforcement officials in Kyrgyzstan makes it far safer to print books and leaflets in the Kyrgyz town of Karasu or at Osh than across the border in Uzbekistan. Such publications can then easily be spirited into Uzbekistan.

In spite of smooth operations in some spheres, HT in Kyrgyzstan has been torn by serious internal disagreements. Several of the most senior and influential members of the Kyrgyz organization reject the shift from purely underground to partially open activity, including the organization of mass actions, distribution of leaflets, and public sermons. When members left public-service jobs to do this and then promoted publicly their way of life, they exposed the organization to massive arrests at the secondary and tertiary levels, caused an overall loss of momentum, and fostered the discrediting of HT's ideology in the eyes of mainstream believers. These dissidents split with HT and formed a new party under the name Hizbun Nursa (Party of Victory). This new party, still young and small, bases itself on a simplified version of the HT ideology and program.[169] Such developments are inevitable. HT's aim today is apparently to develop well-trained members who can operate independently, completely outside the organization but in accordance with its goals and directives. Small cells would be bound only by their commitment to HT's ideology of jihad but would otherwise enjoy tactical independence. Such an approach will depend heavily on the rigorous military-style training of members that is to be carried out through a process of self-education via the Internet. By this means, the jihadist training that was earlier available only in special camps in Afghanistan or Pakistan will be available in every home.

It is now clear that the crisis of power at the national level has become permanent.[170] A feature of this condition is that increasing numbers of Kyrgyz voters are supporting religious candidates. In the campaign leading to the July 10, 2005, early presidential elections, HT activists for the first time campaigned in behalf of the Muslim candidate, Tursunbay Bakir Uluu, who at the time was Kyrgyzstan's official ombudsman and also a lay prayer reader. HT campaigned mainly outside mosques, promoting the idea that now voters could support a true Muslim. This would appear to bode well for HT's future were it not for two problems. First are the serious internal disagreements over tactics discussed above. The second problem, is that corruption within Hizb ut-Tahrir undermines not only the organization's ability to serve as a model for a future Islamic order but its legitimacy within the movement of political Islam generally. Predictably, some former party members trace this problem to the efforts of Western secret services to discredit Islam.[171]

These difficulties led HT to shift its strategy in Kyrgyzstan, which now included supporting social projects and introducing its activists into state agencies, including law enforcement. The new strategy also focused more on recruiting mid-sized businessmen, who could help fund the party through a tax (*zakat*). The party remains most prevalent in southern Kyrgyzstan, especially in the densely populated areas of the Jalalabad and Osh provinces. Membership there continues to be drawn mainly from among the poor and especially those with low levels of education. But the liberal attitude of authorities there toward religious influences from abroad, the region's many social and religious problems, and the migration there of many Islamist oppositionists from neighboring Uzbekistan, have created exceptionally favorable conditions for radical Islamists. Indeed, many of them now see this region of Kyrgyzstan as the best possible base from which to organize their activities throughout the Ferghana Valley, including in Uzbekistan and Tajikistan.

Such an environment makes this region well suited to serve as a test-case of HT's aspiration to become a legal party. In this effort they are organizing legal charitable NGOs through which they can advance their cause; also, they have cut back their production and dissemination of illegal extremist literature. Recently confiscated HT leaflets confirm that their most current publications have changed drastically. Previously, these leaflets contained direct appeals to overthrow the existing constitutional order, thus providing grounds for the government to institute criminal charges against the organization. The leaflets' new content makes it all but impossible to bring criminal charges against the sponsors, as no crime has been committed.

Paradoxically, just as HT is taking steps to enter the mainstream in Kyrgyzstan's sector of the Ferghana Valley, HT missionaries abroad have become more visible. They aim their appeal directly at the unemployed and uneducated youth, whose numbers have grown significantly amid the deteriorating social conditions, spreading corruption, and breakdown of the court system that followed the Tulip Revolution in Kyrgyzstan of March 24, 2005. With all other avenues closed, many turn to religion for a solution.

This makes it entirely possible that secular but definitely pro-religious political forces will emerge in the region and country, championing the right of Muslims to participate in politics as Muslims. One should expect such a party to make its debut in the south of Kyrgyzstan, and specifically in Kyrgyzstan's sector of the Ferghana Valley. Tursunbay Bakir Uluu is playing a significant part in this development. He now leads the political party Erk (Freedom), which claims to oppose the involvement of Islam in politics, but which in practice does precisely that, presenting itself as a secular party that happens to protect the rights of Muslims.[172] Such a party could easily involve former HT members.

Other possible lines of future development are even more problematic. After the religious-ethnic conflict in Nookat on December 12, 2008, the authorities stepped up their efforts to combat religious extremism. They launched a huge purge in the Osh and Jalalabad areas of the Ferghana Valley, focusing on the imams of certain mosques and ordinary believers in the Nookat area, as well as the cities of Jalalabad and Uzgen. Most of those arrested were Uzbeks. Drugs were planted on members of Hizb ut-Tahrir to discredit them. Many went into deep hiding following the Nookat events. The independent press attacked the Bakiyev government as anti-national and anti-Islamic, and compared it to the most repressive regimes in the region. This episode, rooted squarely in the Ferghana Valley, indicates how the religious-secular controversy can easily metamorphose into an ethnic conflict, with HT and the Wahhabis nonetheless at the center.

As the HT seeks to reposition itself, the other wing of the radical Islamists, represented by the Wahhabis or Salafis (Ahl Sunnah wal Jama'a al-Salafia), is still concentrating its efforts on rectifying the views of the official clergy, which it sees as "unacceptable innovations."[173] It seeks to accomplish this mainly through preaching. However, several problems have arisen as they grapple with the realities on the ground in the Kyrgyz sector of the Ferghana Valley. For one thing, other groups present themselves as competitors, among them the Tablighi Dawat, which has taken root in many parts of Kyrgyzstan. Currently, the number of dawatists is estimated at from 20,000 to 35,000 people, mostly Kyrgyz rural youth.

This movement, unlike the Salafi and HT, shuns the sphere of practical life and politics, concentrating instead, like the Wahhabis, on devastating criticism of the conservative majority. Research has shown that many members eventually defect from Tablighi Dawat and join more socially activist movements. Through this process, which occurs in other countries as well, Tablighi Dawat unwittingly fulfills a recruiting function for more radicalized groups, including HT and the Salafis.

Despite its political self-isolation, the Tablighi Dawat movement in the Ferghana and Kyrgyzstan as a whole has a clear organizational structure and program of action. *Mashwaras* or councils of ordinary citizens exist at the neighborhood, district, and national levels. Commitment to advocacy rather than education or religious training is the main criterion for membership in these bodies, which gather monthly in mosques in Kara-Balta city and Bishkek. At each meeting, members of the *mashwara* elect by open ballot an *amir-sapa* (captain), who is responsible for conducting the event. Clerics and non-members may express their views at such meetings, to which local government or law enforcement officers are often invited. It is strictly forbidden to discuss politics at cell meetings, however.

A further challenge to the Wahhabis' future in Kyrgyzstan arises from the fact that in their first period they appealed mainly to such ethnic minorities as the Uzbeks, Uyghurs, and other small indigenous communities, all, of course, mainly in the Ferghana Valley. Kyrgyz meanwhile favored mono-ethnic communities (*jamaats*) comprised of Kyrgyz, mainly in the northern provinces. The deeper problem facing the various Salafi groups in Kyrgyzstan stems from what appears as their political passivity and refusal to participate in public life. This arises, of course, from their conviction that society as such is in a state of ignorance (*jahiliya*) that extends to the political system and political parties, including those that call themselves Islamic. As such, they are fundamentally illegitimate. To be sure, the Wahhabis differ among themselves on this, with moderates seeking to connect with, as well as correct, other Muslims, and the radicals refusing to extend any hand to the deluded. Neither faction, however, has any political project for the existing nation-state, as does HT.

Beyond these groups, the Ferghana Valley of Kyrgyzstan has a host of sectarian groups such as the Ahmadiya, Isma'ilia, and Bahaiyya. Each has its own distinct history and position, but their marginal scale and minimal social impact place them beyond the scope of the present study. Many of these groups derive from inward-looking Sufi traditions. However, as with the Tablighi Dawat, with its neo-Sufi posture tracing to Pakistani origins, these groups may be so critical of the main body of conservative believers and their public activities that they want nothing to do with them. Yet at the same time, they consider themselves within the main body of Sunni Islam traditional in Central Asia.

Many students from the Kyrgyz sector of the Ferghana Valley, as from Kyrgyzstan as whole, pursue their religious education abroad. Thus, in Egypt one finds at least three different groups: Wahhabis, who reject the method of teaching at the famed Al-Azhar University and usually move on to institutions in Saudi Arabia; Kyrgyz, who are so named because they stick together on the basis of their strong patriotic stance; and Nurcilar, followers of the Turkish cleric Fethullah Gülen. At present fully eighty-five percent of all Kyrgyz religious students in Egypt are funded by the Gülen movement, receiving free rent and a monthly allowance in addition to free tuition.

The Nurcilar organization parallels a Sufi order, with a leader (*amir* or *hodja*) to whom members owe obedience. Despite its clear religious orientation and solid financial resources, the Nurcilar organization is nowhere actually registered as a religious group.[174] It has successfully penetrated the Kyrgyz sector of the Ferghana Valley through the work of member Turkish businessmen. Establishing several nominally secular lycées in the region, they also founded a full university in Bishkek. All these institutions are staffed mainly by members. Like the Tablighi Dawat, the Nurcilar pursue a long-term program of Islamization through evolutionary means, working through bottom-to-top tactics. As such, they are in sharp opposition to those Islamists who advocate violent tactics, even though their strategic goal of thoroughgoing Islamization may be similar.

Islamic movements in Kyrgyzstan may have come initially from beyond the borders, but they have now taken root and adapted to local conditions, in the process becoming an essential element of both individual and social life. Already they have gone far toward creating in the country, and especially in the Ferghana Valley, an Islamic ideological space. What remains unclear is whether this will evolve peacefully or follow a radical scenario as in Chechnya or Afghanistan. Many mainstream conservative local clerics insist that they are in the best position to prevent a radical future, thanks to their many opportunities to educate people in the dogmas and theology of Islam, as opposed to simply downloading information from Wahhabi and other extreme sources. Whether or not this is true, it accurately reflects the general concern in the Kyrgyz part of the Ferghana Valley, and even in the country as a whole, that rising Islamic radicalization now threatens social stability there. While it is true that in the initial stages radical Islamists from Tajikistan and especially Uzbekistan played a catalyzing role there, the extreme currents are now thoroughly indigenized in Kyrgyzstan. Similarly, during the early years after independence any influence of religion on politics was considered a threat to the secular regime and to social stability. Especially since the shift in power in Kyrgyzstan that occurred in March 2005, a very different approach has emerged. Instead of seeing Muslims and even Muslim activists as a threat, most parties now court them. In a society still divided by tribal and regional tensions, religion is seen increasingly not as the problem but as part of the solution. Because in Kyrgyzstan the most active religious movements and currents are to be found in the Ferghana Valley, this shifts the national balance of power in favor of that region.

Less-positive possibilities also abound. It may be that the government, in the name of protecting secularism, will use repressive measures against religious groups, especially in the southern region—Ferghana. This in turn would lead to the radicalization of what are now moderate voices in the Muslim community, and to Middle Eastern forms of protest and politics. The government has sought to avert this by demonstrating its good will toward the Muslim community through new initiatives favorable to "Muslim life" and the further development of Islam in the country. But for the time being Muslim activists have received these as empty rhetoric and as a mere flirtation, rather than as the start of serious engagement with them. In any case, it is clear that Islam can now be used as a mobilizing factor, particularly in the south and in Ferghana, and that a new game on the Islamic field already has begun, even though none of the players have yet figured out which rules of play are appropriate in a country that remains multi-cultural in character.

Serious destabilization remains an active possibility in the Ferghana Valley, and even in Kyrgyzstan as a whole. Interethnic relations in the Ferghana region remain difficult, and current developments are not bettering them. Authoritarian power now supports a fragile stability there, but inter-clan and inter-regional tensions could easily lead to political turmoil, especially if there is uncertainty at the leadership level. All this is going forward amid a two-fold process of de-secularization of the society and the politicization of religion. In Kyrgyzstan, both are hastened by the ongoing systemic crisis and the volatility of governmental institutions. Indeed, it is no overstatement to say that developments that began in the Ferghana Valley are creating a crisis of secular power in the country as a whole. Under such circumstances, it is likely that the number and scale of protests will continue to increase, and that the role of religious elements in them will expand.

Nor is it likely that the traditional or conservative clergy will be able to resist this, for as a group they are in crisis, as well. The government has been satisfied to exercise its control over and through the clergy, but at the same time new clergy have appeared beyond the control of the Spiritual Directorate, and it is these who would figure in any future protests.

At least as problematic as the clergy's role is the position of the government itself. With respect even to the religiously moderate institutions, the government's role is unclear. All in all, there are neither boundaries nor rules governing the government's interaction with religion in all its forms. Lacking such definition, the authorities are not ready to accept religious organizations as legitimate political actors. Needless to say, this situation means that the rights of believers remain quite unclear, and believers respond to this condition by casting doubt on the legitimacy of the post-2005 government and Constitution.

Religious Revival and Emerging Political Paradigms in Tajikistan's Sector of the Ferghana Valley

Today, a process of re-Islamization is taking place in all the post-Soviet republics of Central Asia, and particularly in northern Tajikistan, most of which belongs geographically to the Ferghana Valley. Governments of the region have preferred to speak of this in more politically correct terms as a revival of Islamic values and the Islamic heritage. The religious situation and direction of evolution in the region as a whole, and consequently in the valley as well, has changed, as have the positions of the various theological and legal schools. For a millennium the dominant theological and legal school has been that of the Hanafis, named for al-Nu'man Sabit al-Imam al-A'zama Abu Hanifa (699–767). Over the centuries, Hanafi Islam in Central Asia absorbed many local traditions, customs, and ceremonies, which created the conditions necessary for the formation of an independent center of Muslim culture in the region.[175]

After the liberalization of religious life that started in the mid-1990s, religion began to emerge from under the onslaught of Soviet official atheism. It turned out that Islam not only had not lost its place in the worldview of the Tajik people, but was reviving with a new vigor that enabled it to encompass all areas of life, including the political. Today, extremist religious organizations in the various areas of Sughd province (i.e., Ferghana Valley)[176] are working under the guise of various parties,[177] movements,[178] and groups.[179] Their programs and stated goals confirm that they are indeed extremists, and that they were introduced from abroad in order to bring about a reformation in the religious sphere and transformation in the political order.

Divided among three countries, it is no surprise that the Ferghana Valley recently should have become the object of influence and pressures from beyond its borders. These arise from the intense competition for influence in the region, and result in efforts by outside groups to impose by various means their own religious, political, and ideological agendas. Inevitably, this has led to mounting tensions.

Local conditions also contribute significantly to the increase in tensions. Specifically, prevalent social and economic hardships, ethnic diversity, and unresolved territorial disputes all give rise to destructive passions. The fact that there exists a high level of religious consciousness among the general population also becomes to some degree a factor of alienation and even conflict; individuals and communities seeking solutions to their problems are readily subjected to the ideological influence of radical and extremist religious and political groups.

The goal of such extremist groups is to replace the public's traditional notions of Islam with radical approaches that call for the overthrow of secular governments and the establishment of a modern version of a theocratic state. Curiously, they are agents of the process of globalization in religion, shaking up seemingly immutable theological and legal schools within Islam and causing turmoil in the collective consciousness of Muslims of the region.

In Soviet times, the role of religion for the bulk of Muslims in the province of Sughd was as a regulator of relations within families, kinship groups, and among neighbors. Knowledge of the finer principles of the faith remained weak, as one would expect in an environment filled with anti-religious propaganda pouring forth from an atheistic state. When in the 1920s the Soviet government abolished the Arabic-Persian script in favor first of Latin and then the Cyrillic alphabet, it distanced Muslims from the written sources of religious knowledge. The destruction of religious literature, the closing of religious schools, the hounding of Islam by the media, and the struggle against holdovers of religion led to the complete transformation of Islam internally and externally. Nevertheless, to repeat, religious norms continued to influence families, sometimes *mahallas*, and relationships between people, as well as their ethics and collective memory.

Efforts to strengthen religious consciousness in Tajikistan began in the late 1970s when study groups in the private sector, such as *hujras,*[180] began responding to a groundswell of interest in religious literature. Such groups focused on intensive readings on the Muslim credo (*aqida*), religious law (*fiqh*), politics, history, and religion. Students in these groups learned about the recent developments in the Middle East and the views and activities of Islamic scholars and theologians intended to resolve these and other issues.

This renewal of religious consciousness among Tajiks is associated with the name of Muhammadjon Hindustani,[181] as well as with his pupil Sayid Abdullo Nuri (1947–2006), who founded the Islamic reform movement in the country. It was under Nuri's leadership that on April 20, 1973 a reformist Muslim society was founded in Kurgan-Tyube under the name Islamic Renaissance of the Youth of Tajikistan (Nahzati Islom chavononi Tojikiston).[182] This group immediately began introducing into the curriculum of educational circles the study of Muslim origins. It tried to introduce reforms and develop training programs based, so they claimed, on Hanafi principles.[183] In the second half of the 1980s they launched the clandestine religious periodical *Truth of Islam* (Haqiqati Islom).[184]

Following the collapse of the Soviet Union, the Islamic Renaissance became an influential political movement, the IRPT. Many Islamic clergymen and Muslim women joined the party, which at this time worked to promote Islam among Tajik youth and did not seek to create or oppose enemies. Its literature paid particular attention to bringing about a return to Islamic values through the education of young people. One section of the organization carried out advocacy (*da'wah*); a second oversaw the party's internal security; the third dealt with finance and property management; and the fourth organized trainings and workshops.

Its creators claimed that the organization had been formed without any foreign involvement.[185] However, the indirect influence on the IRPT of religious and political ideas from elsewhere in the Islamic world is obvious. To take one example, the Tajik religious elite and young people had carefully listened to radio broadcasts in Persian from Iran and Afghanistan. Through these they became acquainted with reformist currents in Islam that influenced their worldview and contributed to the rather hazy political credo that they developed. Even during Soviet times the IRPT was setting up many new groups to study the new religious literature, establishing relations with Islamic intellectuals and representatives of the intelligentsia, and organizing discussions, debates, and meetings.[186] The education program for youths was based on such books as *Tawhid* (Monotheism), *Al-Madd wa al-Jazr* (Flux and Reflux), and a summary of the *Tarikh al-Bidayah wa'an Nihaya* (History of the Beginning and the End) by Ismail Ibn Kathir.[187] All such study of religious literature in Tajikistan was strictly illegal. Nonetheless, authoritative Islamic scholars contributed enormously to the effort, even training people from other republics. Tajikistan's system of illegal Muslim education became widely known throughout the USSR.

Of course, such educational groups as *hujra* operated in the Ferghana Valley. Its founders there were Solim-Domullo from Khujand, Kamol-Gori from Ura-Tyube, and others. Although not all of them were linked to the new clandestine organization, they nevertheless contributed to the support of Islamic education and the preservation of religious identity against a background of total ideological pressure from the atheist authorities. Today the old clandestine group has greatly changed since Soviet and immediate post-Soviet times. The IRPT developed its political strategy in conformity with the Basic Law, or Constitution, and other relevant legislation. Its program seeks the creation of a democratic and progressive civil society that protects Tajikistan's sovereignty and culture. The IRPT calls on all political and social groups to maintain an atmosphere of peace, brotherhood, and love. Moreover, it seeks economic development in accordance with relevant domestic and international law, while supporting a multi-party democracy, media freedom, and protection of the rights of journalists.[188]

The IRPT is associated with the traditional Islam to which a significant number of its members adhere. The IRPT acknowledges the extremism of such "imported" Islamic parties as HT, and operates on the principle of reform, not revolution. To this end, the IRPT publishes the newspaper *Najot,* magazines, books and brochures, and holds meetings around the country. Yet neither the majority of the Tajik population nor all Muslim leaders support the formation of religious parties, believing that this politicizes religion and therefore harms it, and will lead to internal conflicts. This negative attitude only increased during the Tajik civil war of the 1990s, when the population divided into two camps comprised of believers and non-believers. Today, the IRPT claims over 23,000 members, with representatives working actively in almost every town and district and with extensive links with parties and parliaments abroad. It enjoys considerable support in the Sughd region of the Ferghana Valley.[189]

In the parliamentary elections of February 27, 2005 the IRPT won two seats in the lower house of the parliament. Some experts[190] argue that these modest results show that the party remains inexperienced and has yet to establish itself. Uninformed promises by the IRPT have certainly damaged it in the eyes of many in the electorate, who believe it incapable of meeting their expectations. Divisions within the IRPT are also damaging, especially the rift between modernists led by deputy chairman Mukhiddin Kabiri and conservatives consolidating around Mohammad Nuri, the son of the late president of the party, Sayyid Abdullo Nuri.[191] Kabiri's followers support a westernized orientation, like the Iranian reformer, Khatami, seeking to impart a veneer of liberalism to Islam. European-educated and with extensive connections in the West, Kabiri strikes some as a new type spiritual leader, but the conservative wing of the party that opposes him is clearly far stronger. No wonder, then, that he and his followers lost out to conservatives in the 2008 parliamentary elections.

The conservatives predominate in the rural provinces and account for fully 70 percent of the IRPT's support. They are especially strong in Rasht and Garm, but also in Tajikistan's part of the Ferghana Valley.[192] In addition to responding to these rural voters on most domestic issues, Nuri and the IRPT's conservative leaders follow Iran's lead on foreign policy. However, they are extremely careful not to give rise to charges that they favor a Shiia orientation, which would, of course, be very damaging.

Long and difficult negotiations at the end of Tajikistan's five-year civil war seemed to put an end to the confrontation between state and religion. However, it soon became apparent that various currents of radical Islam, mainly imported from abroad, posed new dangers, not least to the IRPT. New Islamic forces in active opposition to the government are particularly active in the Ferghana Valley. They have few links, if any, to the IRPT.

One of these newly imported movements is Salafism.[193] This extremely conservative and puritanical ideology was brought back to Tajikistan by students returning from religious centers in the Middle East, mainly the Gulf states. The Tajik government is wary of Salafism because it could lead to a schism among Muslims in Tajikistan, and especially in the Sughd region of the Ferghana Valley. Here the Salafis have issued a call for the re-creation of the pure Muslim faith that purportedly existed in the early years after the Prophet and his immediate successors, bitterly opposing all changes not explicitly approved by the Qur'an and the traditions (Sunnah and *hadith*).[194] They are especially hostile to Sufism, which has always been popular in the Ferghana Valley and Central Asia generally, and which they accuse of distorting Islam with unacceptable national and regional rites and customs. They also oppose Ismailis, whom they do not consider Muslims at all. The Salafis take as their spiritual guides such theologians as Ibn Hanbali,[195] al-Shafi'i,[196] Ibn Taymiyyah,[197] and Muhammad Ibn 'Abd al-Wahhab. Adherents of the movement argue that they favor only peaceful tactics, but the armed Salafi attacks in Algeria in 2007 remind us that tactics can quickly change, and for the worse.

The first acknowledgement of Salafis in Tajikistan came from the former minister of internal affairs, Husniddin Sharipov, in January 2006, when he told the press that "Proponents of this movement have already been recorded in the north of the country Ferghana,"[198] and then linked them with Osama bin Laden's terrorist network.[199] Leaders of the Salafis in Tajikistan are young men; the average age of those in Sughd province (Ferghana) is thirty years. Most received generous scholarships to study at the Faisal International University in Islamabad or at universities in Yemen and Saudi Arabia.[200] Through such studies they developed their hatred of Sufis, Ismailis, and also the cult of saints or holy men (*awliya*), which has been a main feature of Central Asian Islam for a millennium, especially in the Ferghana Valley.[201]

There is reason to think that after their return from studying in the Gulf, the young Salafi leaders of Sughd and elsewhere continue to receive financial assistance from abroad. Having enjoyed stipends of $300–$400 a month during their student days,[202] it is unlikely that they would settle for less back home, even though many are semi-literate.

In the summer of 2008 the prosecutor's office in Sughd announced that law-enforcement authorities would tighten their control over the Salafis of the province. Prosecutor Khayrullo Saidov admitted to the news service "Kazakhstan Today" that for the time being "no illegal actions by supporters of the movement have been recorded." However, he defended his preventive action on the grounds that the

Salafis had first presented their activities as innocuous, but that they later "acquired threatening forms."[203] The prosecutor also reminded his interviewer of the terrorist attacks that Salafis had mounted in Algiers the year before.

Whether or not potential danger provides sufficient legal basis for such strict controls over citizens, the general prosecutor demanded still-sterner measures. Accordingly, the Supreme Court of Tajikistan on January 9, 2009, outlawed the Salafi movement. Tajik authorities charged with enforcing the ban argue that they are "defending the constitutional order and preventing inter-religious strife." Among other stipulations, the ban covers the dissemination of any religious literature that presents the movement's ideas. Clearly, the government in Dushanbe believes the Salafis of distant Ferghana constitute a genuine danger. It may not be irrelevant that about the same time as the court decision in early 2008, Tajikistan's "special services" concluded that there were also several thousand Salafis in the capital itself.[204]

Another Islamist political party imported into Tajikistan is the Hizb ut-Tahrir al-Islami, better known in the local form of the name, Hizb ut-Tahrir. The first units of the party appeared in Andijan, Tashkent, and Ferghana City in the 1990s,[205] and in a short time it significantly expanded its influence within Uzbekistan and then across the region. HT first appeared in Tajikistan in 1998. Beginning in areas of the Ferghana Valley adjoining Tajikistan's border with Uzbekistan, it then spread to the central and southern parts of the country, the city of Dushanbe and its suburbs, and even to the Pamirs. When Uzbek authorities took drastic measures against the party, many of its leaders crossed into adjoining countries, seeking to take advantage of more liberal laws on religion there. HT launched its Tajik efforts in the Sughd region of the Ferghana Valley. Thus, Abdudzhalil Iusupov and Abduholik Mulloev, both residents of the Gafur district in Sughd province, had been recruited by their fellow students and had trained in HT's Andijan branch. Utilizing young men aged eighteen-to-twenty who were traders at local markets, Iusupov and Mulloev established HT branches in several towns in Sughd province.[206]

Prosecutors in Sughd presented HT literature that openly calls for the incitement of ethnic and religious strife and the overthrow of the constitutional order. The sources of financing HT's activities in Sughd turn out to be very similar to the usual means of financing political parties: membership dues, the sale of party literature, the creation of legal party-owned commercial and financial enterprises, and money channeled to the leadership from abroad.[207] Needless to say, HT's adherents are irreconcilable enemies of the IRPT and of its decision to work within the framework of the Constitution.

In the Sughd region of the Ferghana Valley, HT has grown at a rampant pace. It has succeeded by focusing primarily on young people, who are alienated from the political system and are inspired by the party's directives to liberate Islamic territories from the rule of "infidels" and create a worldwide caliphate.[208] The parent organization in London, unable to find sufficient support among the Muslims in the Middle East and Arab countries, sees Central Asia and especially Sughd as fertile ground. Its translations of Qur'anic studies into Tajik and Uzbek are of high quality, and its leaflets appeal effectively to the many problem areas in the religious, social, and political life of the region.

In 2001 the prosecutor' office of Tajikistan reviewed the activities of HT and judged them both extremist and destructive, and on this basis banned the party throughout the country. After the ban HT activities either went even deeper underground or fled to neighboring Kyrgyzstan.[209] Since the party conducts its activities in secret and its structure is deliberately atomized, law-enforcement agencies have difficulty identifying its members and leaders. However, reasonably reliable media reports affirm that HT still has several thousand members in the Sughd region, with only a few dozen of them having been arrested and sentenced to terms of varying lengths. Among the convicted are very few significant leaders of the party.

It should be noted that in the Sughd region the bulk of HT members are Uzbeks, who comprise only 40 percent of the total population of the province. The involvement of Uzbek-speaking people into this type of organization probably traces to the fact that Uzbeks and other Turkic-speaking Muslim ethnic groups, including Kyrgyz, Lokayts, Marka, Kungurat, and Barlas, constitute only a very insignificant percent of the members of the IRPT, not only in Sughd but across Tajikistan. Even if the IRPT did not largely ignore Turkic speakers, it is doubtful that it could draw members away from HT, since their goals are antithetical and the goals for joining one rather than the other mutually exclusive. Moreover, Uzbeks of Tajikistan who participate in HT can feel themselves part of a network of Uzbeks who exchange information and disseminate leaflets and brochures across the entire Ferghana Valley.

A further reason for the heavy focus of HT activities in Sughd is that some activists from the Uzbekistan party who were being hounded by the authorities in Uzbekistan found it convenient to hide in the adjacent Sughd province of Tajikistan. Thus, in 2003 law-enforcement agencies of the area detained a large group of HT members from Uzbekistan who had merely resumed their activities in the city of Khujand. The leader of this group was Saidkamoliddin Nosirov, a native of the Kasansai district of Namangan province in Uzbekistan.[210] Not only had Nosirov's group carried out the translation, publication, and dissemination of extremist literature and leaflets, but also recruited young people from Sughd into its ranks. The investigation disclosed that the group had a channel through the Aibek border checkpoint (on the border of Uzbekistan and Kyrgyzstan), through which money in U.S. dollars flowed from Uzbek Ferghana to support the printing house in Khujand and equip it with computers and other office technologies, and to maintain a house for the staff.

Not all the funds for the Khujand operation came from Uzbekistan, however. A member of the Khujand group, Z. Abduvahhobov, on December 20, 2002, received $5,995 in cash to support the work of the group. These funds originated with a U.S. national, Imamuddin Muhti, who apparently transferred them from the bank of J.P. Morgan in New York to the Alpha Bank in Moscow and thence to the Eskhata Bank in Khujand, which then paid Abduvahhobov. A planned second transfer of money did not take place because by then the mufti had been arrested. These cases of remittances show that religious extremist movements are financed in part from abroad.[211] Other similar cases confirm the extent and method of HT's foreign support.

Most extremist organizations, including HT, also receive significant funds from domestic sources, especially contributions from members. Thus, each HT member is required to make a fixed donation from his salary or other resources, the amount for ordinary members typically ranging from five to twenty percent of income.[212]

The reality of domestic financing compels local political and religious leaders to underscore again and again what they argue are Hizb ut-Tahrir's foreign funding sources. The well-known theologian and political figure Hodja Akbar Turajonzoda calls this party a special organization sponsored from the West in order to "undermine the states of Central Asia." Turajonzoda goes on to argue that "a detailed analysis of the program and ideology of HT and of specific examples of its activities indicates clearly that it was created [not by Muslims but] by anti-Islamic forces." If this were not the case, he asks, how could HT survive so comfortably in the West, maintaining offices in London and other cities, where HT leaders developed the concept of an Islamic caliphate?[213]

Turajonzoda is an authoritative representative of traditional Islam in Tajikistan. He traces the growth of Islamic extremism to ignorance of the true principles of the faith. He believes that "imported" religious parties, movements, and groups are destabilizing the country and threaten its existence as a nation and as a state. He misses no opportunity to fault such groups on theological grounds, arguing, for example, that by denying any role in public life to the traditional advisory councils or shura, HT contradicts the Qur'an itself.[214]

This kind of approach to the problem of radical Islamic organizations on the part of Tajik authorities is based on the false assumption that problems can be solved by force. Since 1999 more than 5,000 members of HT have been sentenced to prison terms of varying lengths. This not only frustrates and angers the families of the convicted, but further radicalizes the behavior of the remaining party members who are still free. Moreover, the fact that many incarcerated party members lose their health in prison earns Tajikistan the opprobrium of international human rights organizations. Turajonzoda's solution to all of these problems is to upgrade the skills of the Muslim clergy, improve the technical base of the Islamic Institute in Dushanbe, make better use of the media, and finance scholarly research on theology—none of which is possible without government support.[215]

In the meanwhile, all of Tajikistan's neighbors have drawn the same conclusions about HT as Tajikistan itself, labeling it an extremist group with the potential to threaten social harmony and stability, the rights of citizens, and even the continued existence of the state. Not only have its web sites been banned, but also the importation and distribution of its audio and video productions and printed matter.

Yet another active extremist organization in the Tajik part of the Ferghana Valley is Bayat (the Oath). The main goal of supporters of this group in the Sughd region is to resist the incursions into the area of all non-traditional religions and sects. To this end, Bayat members in 2004 killed a Baptist clergyman. Members of Bayat also fought alongside the Taliban in Afghanistan. Indeed, in 2007 three Bayat members, all Tajik citizens from the city of Isfara, were transferred to the authority of Tajikistan's Ministry of Internal Affairs from the Guantanamo prison.[216]

Law-enforcement officials report that the first crimes committed by members of the group were recorded in 1997. Since then investigators have indicted members for burning their enemies' mosques, robbery, extortion, and contract killings of members of other religious groups. The Office of Internal Affairs of the Sughd region believes that Bayat was formed by opposition fighters who fled the country after the civil war and moved to Afghanistan. According to a source at the Office of the Ministry of Security, the Bayat organization has close ties with, and is financed by, the Islamic Movement of Uzbekistan/Turkestan. In early February 2008, Tajik police arrested two IMU fighters near Isfara who previously had undergone military training in Afghanistan and taken part in campaigns there.

In January 2009 the head of the Department of Internal Affairs of the Sughd region, Abdurahim Kahhorov, announced that as a result of coordinated law-enforcement activities with other states, Anwar Kayumov, head of the IMU's group in the city of Isfara, Sughd province, was arrested in Kabul. The prosecution charged Kayumov, a resident of the city of Isfara, with the "organization of criminal gangs" and "terrorism." In 1997, after special military training under the guidance of the head of the IMU, Jumma Kasimov, aka Juma Namangani, and after taking the special oath (*bayat*), Kayumov had been sent to Isfara to recruit for the IMU.

So far nineteen associates of Anwar Kayumov have been identified and arrested for perpetrating "particularly serious crimes," including murder, attempted murder, and the killing of two police officers, an armed attack on the Ministry of Internal Affairs' holding facility in the city of Kairakkum, murdering the lieutenant who headed the local office of the Ministry of Internal Affairs, the organization of a prison escape by IMU member Fathullo Rahmatov, and more. Prosecutor A. Kahhorov also noted that in 2008 eleven members of HT were arrested in Sughd province, and 156 Salafi supporters were placed under "special control."[217]

As we have noted, several of the religious groups involved with terrorism have close links abroad. HT and the IMU both have been mentioned in this context. The Bayat group is in all likelihood a branch of the international terrorist organization Bayat al-Imam.[218] Of these, the IMU warrants further comment. Back in mid-January 2004, a few armed men attacked the holding jail in Kairakkum, killing the officer on duty and releasing their comrades before fleeing to Kyrgyzstan. The Tajik prosecutor's office confirmed that the IMU was actively functioning at the time in northern Tajikistan, especially in the Isfara region.[219] Later, in the summer of 2005, we find the IMU once again active in Tajikistan, this time bombing the gates of the Emergency Situations Ministry in Dushanbe. It later turned out that the IMU planned this attack to avenge the minister of internal affairs' assistance in the transfer of IMU militants across the territory of Tajikistan to Kyrgyzstan, from which they were to be sent to Uzbekistan.[220]

IMU activities in Tajikistan continued in 2006. Late in the night of August 20, 2006, officers of the criminal-investigation department of Tajikistan's Ministry of Internal Affairs detained IMU activist Orif Dzhalolov in the village of Navgilem near Isfara. Dzhalolov activated a grenade during the arrest, which resulted in the death of two police officers and the wounding of several others. An ally of Dzhalolov managed to escape but was later arrested in the north of the country. According to the Tajik Ministry of Internal Affairs, twenty active IMU members and forty HT members were arrested in Tajikistan's sector of the Ferghana Valley in 2006.[221]

A number of Tajik officials have been killed in the course of confrontations with members of extremist groups. For example, on May 12, 2006 a group of IMU militants attacked the Lyakan border post in the province of Isfara and the Kyrgyz customs post at Ak-Turpak in the Batken region of Kyrgyzstan's sector of the Ferghana Valley. This same group is also accused of the murder of eight militiamen in the Sughd region.[222]

The appearance of Islamic extremist movements and parties in Tajikistan has forced society there to reflect on the preservation of national unity and stability in the country once again. The government has outlawed several groups labeled as extremist, among them HT, the Islamic Party of Turkestan, Harakati Tablighot, Sozmoni Tablighot, Todzhikistoni Ozod, and the Islamic Movement of Uzbekistan/Turkestan. In a very different spirit, it also declared 2009 "The Year of Imam A'zam Abu Hanifa," founder of the moderate school of Muslim law that prevails in Central Asia. In the coming period many other conferences will consider the status of religion in Tajikistan, which may help build public consensus on the best future directions. An official of the IRPT, Hikmatullo Sayfuyllozoda, thinks this will all make it less likely that extremist groups will develop further.[223] But it is far too early to tell whether or not such activities will prove effective.

In conclusion, one might suggest that the involvement of people from the Ferghana Valley province of Sughd in extremist movements may have less to do with their desire to establish a vague theocratic state than with their desire to address their own very real socio-economic and political problems. In doing so, supporters of these organizations still seek their religious identity within the Muslim community of faith as it exists in the emerging world order. However, it bears emphasis that the main tradition of society in Sughd, namely Hanafi Islam and widespread Sufi currents, were suppressed by atheist rule for nearly seventy years. In spite of this, the overwhelming majority of society remains devoted to the long-established and moderate local form of Islam that has evolved there over the centuries.

This suggests that religion, in its traditionally balanced form, far from representing a threat to national integrity, can be a force for consolidating society and protecting national and state interests. Whether or not religion grows and evolves in such a harmonious manner will in turn be significantly determined by the manner in which principles of democracy are implemented. If this is carried out in a moderate yet thoroughgoing manner, Islamic values can serve as a healthy counterweight to the kinds of destructive trans-national Islamist ideologies that we have commented on in Tajikistan's sector of the Ferghana Valley and in the Ferghana Valley as a whole.

Notes

1. The section of this chapter on Kyrgyzstan was written by Kamil Malikov, that on Tajikistan by Aloviddin Nazarov, and on Uzbekistan by Bakhtiyar Babadjanov. The latter served as general editor and proofreader of the chapter.

2. *Waqf*: a legal term means the suspension ("stopping") of the right to private property in favor of the acceptance of facilities, or other charitable cause.

3. *Maktab*: a religious school. The highest religious school is the madrassa. However, in the Khanate of Kokand the level of religious education declined, with a focus on scholasticism without support from rational interpretations.

4. See B.M. Babadjanov, "Russian Colonial Power in Central Asia as Seen by Local Muslim Intellectuals," in *Looking at the Colonizer. Cross-Cultural Perceptions in Central Asia and the Caucasus, Bengal, and Related Areas,* ed. B. Eschment and H. Harder, Berlin, 2004, pp. 75–90.

5. However, the colonial authorities took into account the management experience of "foreigners" and "infidels" in other territories of the empire (especially in the Caucasus), and tried to control the majority of Islamic institutions, including *qadi*, the municipal mosques, madrassas.

6. Beatriss F. Manz, "Central Asian Uprisings in the Nineteenth Century: Ferghana Under the Russians," *Russian Review,* vol. 46, 1987, pp. 267–281; B.M. Babadzhanov, "Dukchi Ishan i Andizhanskoe vosstanie 1898 goda," in *Podvizhniki islama. Kult sviatykh i sufizm v Sredney Azii i na Kavkaze,* ed. S.N. Abashin and V.O. Bobrovnikov, Moscow, 2003, pp. 251–277.

7. A. Agzamkhodzhaev, *Istoriia Turkestanskoi avtonomii (Turkiston mukhtoriyati),* Tashkent, 2006, pp. 37ff.

8. In 2004, the Uzbek part of Ferghana Valley consisted of more than 7.5 million people, of whom 6.5 million are Uzbeks, 400,000 are Tajiks, and 180,000 are Kyrgyz and other ethnic groups. See Z. Khusnutdinov, A. Achildiev et al., *Etno-konfessionalnyi atlas Uzbekistana,* Tashkent, 2005.

9. See Marwat Fazal Ur-Rahim Khan, *The Basmachi Movement in Soviet Central Asia,* Peshawar, 1985, p. 164. Note also that some of the Jadids (including former Buharskaya Narodnaya Sovetskaya Respublika (BNSR) or the People's Soviet Republic of Bukhara president Usmanhodzhaev asked the Afghan governor Amanullah Khan (1919–29) to help Enver Pasha, whom some Jadids of Bukhara had already joined.

10. In the Party documents of that time, all kinds of repressions and persecutions on ideological grounds were called "purging" or "cleansing."

11. R.T. Shamsutdinov, E. Iu. Iusupov et al., *Repressiia 1937–38,* Tashkent, 2007, pp. 67ff.

12. See, for example, the "rational uses" of mosques and madrassas in the Ferghana Valley (especially in Namangan and Osh) enumerated in the secret document "Protokol soveshchaniia upolnomochennykh Soveta po delam religioznykh kultov" (July 1951). TsGA RUz, f. 2456, op. 1, no. 134, 11. 61–79.

13. Ibid.

14. See R. Shigabatdinov, "Dokumenty repressirovannykh religioznykh deiatelei

('dukhovnikov') kontsa 20-kh–nachala 30-kh gg," in *Uzbekistan v gody stalinskikh repressii.* ed., A. Sagdullaev, Tashkent: Yangi asr avlodi, 2010, pp. 236–267.

15. *Repressiia 1937–38,* p. 7. See also the memoirs of a well-known theologians of the Soviet period, Muhammadjon (Hindustani) Rustamov, who was involved in this wave of persecution of religious leaders. Bakhtiyar Babadzhanov and Muzaffar Kamilov, "Domulla Hindustani and the Beginning of the 'Great Schism' Among the Muslims of Uzbekistan," in *Politics and Islam in Russia and Central Asia,* ed. Stéphanie Doudoignon and Hisao Komatsu, London and Bahrain, 2001, pp. 195–220.

16. The name and, consequently, abbreviation has changed over time. For example, in 1976–77 the establishment was called "Dukhovnoe upravlenie musulman Srednei Azii i Kazakhstana." In addition, SADUM was known under such simplified names as Upravlenie (Boshqarma), Muftiyat, Khast-Imom (following the name of a complex in the old city of Tashkent, where it was located).

17. The heads of delegations of the republics were Abdulgaffar Shamsutdinov (Kazakhstan), Solih Bobokalonov (Tajikistan), Olimkhon-tura Shokirov (Kyrgyzstan), Shaykh Anna-Ishan (Turkmenistan).

18. *Fatwa:* a theological document with a decision on any question of one or more theologians.

19. B. Babadjanov, "O fetvakh SADUM protiv 'neislamskikh' obychaev," in *Islam v Tsentralnoi Azii. Vzglyad iznutri,* ed. M.B. Olcott and A. Malashenko, Analiticheskaia seriia Moskovskogo otd. Fonda Karnegi, no. 6, Moscow, 2001, pp. 65–78.

20. Ibid., p. 70.

21. Starting from the early eighteenth century, education in the Ferghana Valley assumed a strictly confessional (Hanafi) and narrow character. Because of an extremely weak demand for deep religious knowledge, the majority of madrassa students had an only one incentive, namely, to gain enough education to secure a position, whether imam or qadi, that did not require knowledge beyond the limited training programs in most madrassas. See Bakhtiyar M. Babadzhanov, Ashirbek K. Muminov, and Anke von Kügelgen, "Disputes on Muslim Authority in Central Asia (20th Century)," in *Critical Editions and Source Studies,* Almaty, 2007, pp. 10–20.

22. See TsGA RUz, f. 1, op. 12, delo 963, 1. 56–69. Many historians of the time wrote about similar defects in the judiciary system of qadi courts (i.e., its obvious class nature and mass corruption). For example, Muhammad-'Aziz ibn Muhammad-Riza (Rida) Margilani in his famous history, talks with unconcealed regret about the open corruption of *qadis,* which intensified after the Russian colonization (Sh. Vokhidov and D. Sangirova, eds., *Tarikhi Azizi. Nashrga tayorlovchilar, sozboshi mualliflari,* Tashkent, 1999, pp. 68–70).

23. Adeeb Khalid, *The Politics of Muslim Cultural Reform-Jadidism in Central Asia,* Berkeley, 1998.

24. On the theatrical activities of Jadids (primarily Avlani), see A. Samoilovich, *Dramaticheskaia literatura sartov,* Petrograd, 1917; M. Rakhmonov, *Uzbek teatri tarikhi,* Tashkent, 1968, pp. 320–360; and Sh. Rizaev, *Jadid dramasi,* Tashkent, 1997.

25. This is very vividly described by Munavvar kori Abdurashidkhonov in *Tanlangan asarlar,* Tashkent, 2003, pp. 218ff.

26. In this regard, the journal *Mushtum/Kulak* (Tashkent, first published in 1922) is particularly interesting. See also the journal *Mullo Mushfiqi* (Khujand, published since 1924).

27. Many famous poets and writers contributed their talent to aggressive propaganda (e.g., Hamza Hakim-zada Niyazi, Gafur Gulyam).

28. See the special memorandum on this issue in TsGA RUz, f. R-2456, op. 1, delo 134. 50–79.

29. A burqa (*chachvan,* local name: *paranja*) almost completely covers the women's body.

30. This mainly concerned theologians of Tashkent. See Bakhtiyar M. Babadzhanov, "The Journal *'Haqiqat'* as a mirror of the religious dimension of the Jadids ideology," *Islamic Area Studies,* 2007, pp. 54–56. See also *Kengash,* "Islomning khozirgi kholati," no. 2, 1924, p. 2.

31. "Islomning khozirgi kholati," p. 2.

32. These directions were not valid at the time of Russian colonization, because the majority of local intellectuals (especially theologians) concluded that during the Russian reign the territory of Turkestan remained as Dar al-Islam (Land of Islam) or Dar al-Ahd (Land of Unity). Moreover, the colonial administration did not impede the management of religion and maintained the sharia courts, however dividing their proceedings into "sharia" and "empire" crimes. Nor did it directly interfere in the system of denominational education. See Babadzhanov, "Russian Colonial Power," p. 78.

33. In the early Soviet period, religious education in the Ferghana Valley was maintained only inside families for security reasons. The organizers of such "classes" were called *Qori-pochcho khujralari* ("Qori-pochcho" means "relative reading the Qur'an"). However, the study was limited to reading prayers and selected chapters of the Qur'an. Usually, this was the first sura al-Fatiha, and the last four ayats of the Qur'an, Ayat ul-Kursi (Qur'an, 2:251), and some prayers (*du'a*). These "domestic *hujra*" have survived until now in towns and villages of the Ferghana Valley.

34. See Babadzhanov et al., "Disputes on Muslim Authority," pp. 10–16, as well as the texts published in the volume of treatises by Hindustani.

35. Other meanings of the term *mudjaddid* in modern Arabic are restoration, rebirth, and renewal.

36. Recall, for example, that followers of the spiritual leader of the 1979 Iranian Revolution, Ayatollah Ruhollah Khomeini, referred to him as the "reviver of the fifteenth Millennium."

37. In a private library in Andijan we discovered the famous commentary on the Qur'an by Sayid Qutb (*Fi zilal il-Qur'an* [Under the shadow of the Qur'an] with a gift inscription to Rahmatullaha-allam on behalf of Faysal al-Filastini.

38. Spiritual Administration of the Muslims of Central Asia (SADUM).

39. According to verbal communications from 1997 to 2004 with a number of theologians in Tashkent and in the Ferghana Valley.

40. From Bakhtiyar Babadjanov's archive (one of the authors of this chapter.)

41. These forms increase the adaptability and survival of *mazhab.*

42. Scholarly studies, especially in the West, often use such terms as "official Islam" and "parallel Islam, or "official mullah" [clergy] and "parallel mullah." The first definition means to the circle of imams and theologians who served in the system approved by authorities—organizations like SADUM and its mosques. At the dawn of Soviet power they were also called "red" or "public" mullahs. "Parallel Islam," according to the Soviet scholar of Islam Alexander Bennigsen and his followers, was represented by those theologians who covertly opposed the Soviet power. However, this characterization of Islam and the positions of theologians in the Soviet period seemed too simplistic, and certainly did not reflect the substance of debates that took place among religious scholars.

43. The exceptions are those religious and political groups that became part of the well-known foreign organizations as Hizb ut-Tahrir and Tablighi Jaamat, as well as local organizations (e.g., Ma'rifatchilar, Akromiya).

44. Courses on the history of the Communist Party of the USSR were mandatory in all secondary schools and higher educational institutions, including religious institutions.

45. These and similar views appeared not without certain influence of the Muslim religious and political literature.

46. Ibid.

47. During the entire period of re-Islamization, the majority of new mosques or madrassas in Central Asian cities were built on the remains of old ones. This can be seen as a desire

not only for spiritual but also for physical (tangible) continuity and the revival of public religious symbols and paradigms of the past.

48. However, under this system, a constant problem was and remains to be the desire of the majority of imams to hide a part of the donations, which are not monitored. In addition, imams tend to have, so to say, "their own income," i.e., voluntary donations from the organizers of various ritual meetings and ceremonies (*dzhanaza, amr-i ma'ruf,* etc.).

49. In total, we discovered fourteen cases of kidnapping in Namangan on purportedly religious grounds.

50. On the one hand, it can be seen as a reaction against the Soviet policy of atheism. On the other hand, one should recall that in the late 1980s the liberalization of religious policy led to the actual freedom of religious belief. But this fact did not stop the politicization of Islam and, consequently, its radicalization.

51. The theory of interaction of Muslim principles and its regional forms received its most complete justification in the works of Russian Islam scholar Stanislav M. Prozorov. See his *Islam kak ideologicheskaia sistema,* Moscow, 2004, esp. pp. 78–88, 375–380.

52. Ahmad ibn Taymiyyah. Madzhmu'a fatava shaykh al-islam Akhmad ibn Taymiyya. Madzhmu' bi-'Abd ar-Rakhman b. Mukhammad b. Kasim. Rabat: Maktaba al-ma'rif, dzhuz' 28. Ibn Taymiyyah (1263–1328) was an Arab-Muslim theologian, prominent representative of the traditionalist wing of Muslim religious and legal thought—Hanbali. The sole sources of religious truth he considered the Qur'an) and prophetic traditions (Sunnah), based on which a true doctrine was created, expressing the unanimous opinion of the Prophet's associates. In his later studies, Ibn Taymiyya qualifies them as "deplored innovations." See V.E. Makari, *Ibn Taymiyyah's Ethics,* Berkeley, 1983.

53. It is interesting that in the library of the oldest theologian in Ferghana, Marghiloni, we saw several volumes of works by Ibn Taymiyyah that were brought to Margiloni by pilgrims in 1974. Abdulhakim Qori was teaching most of the Ferghana theologians of the new wave, which is why he is sometimes called "the father of neo-Wahhabism" of the valley.

54. In the *hadith,* it means the relocation ("exile," "alienation") of the Prophet from Mecca, when he settled in Medina, in 622.

55. Tohir Yuldosh was born in Namangan in 1960. After high school he worked as a baker. He received primary religious training from Qori-pochcho, then from Umar-khon domulla. Together with Juma Namangani established the Islamic Movement of Uzbekistan in 1991.

56. This is especially evident from the IMU video "Ular" (They). The main idea of this movie is to expose the official position of the Uzbek government and of theologians who sharply criticized IMU actions. Abduvali-qori's speeches were used to justify the jihad against the "unfaithful" government of Uzbekistan and those who supported it.

57. Publication of *Dar ul-Khidzhrat (IMU),* no. 25, *Zu-1-ka'da,* 1421/January 2001.

58. It was adopted at the first Congress of the party in Astrakhan, in 1989. This statute was copied by the party branches, including the one in Uzbekistan (Chairman A. Utaev).

59. Hereafter, we rely on our interviews with participants of the Namangan eventsWe I assume that this was the first time in Uzbekistan (and perhaps in the whole Soviet Central Asia), when the secretary of a Regional Committee participated in a prayer with other communists. In this episode, I also see the beginning of the Islamization of former members of the Communist Party. This meeting was recoded on videotape and is in the author's possession (Bakhtiyar Babadjanov's personal archive).

60. Voluntary People's Druzhina (DND): a group of volunteers who helped the police, established in the days of Stalin. DND orcibly recruited among the workers in enterprises and other Soviet agencies, and in the evenings it patrolled the most populated parts of towns and villages, helped to arrest drunks, petty thieves, pickpocketers, etc.

61. According to our information, Adolat members did not work anywhere and received wages from Hakim Sattimov and later from Tohir Yuldosh.

62. Literally it means one-tenth of any income from different types of property or wage.

See A. Grohmann. "Ushr," in *Encyclopedia of Islam,* vol. 4, Leiden Leipzig, 1934, pp. 1137–1139.

63. Almost all of our respondents said that Sattimov could not even perform prayers correctly.

64. From the text of *bayat-namah,* which was rewritten by an ex-member of *Islom militsiyasi* into his notebook.

65. Based on the eyewitness account.

66. *Yurish* is a medieval term for "military campaign," "hostage." In general, the demonstrations of this kind became part of the religious revival and struggle for power among religious leaders.

67. According to R. Akramov's estimates, the maximum number of Tohir Yuldosh's fighters was 2,000. Namangan's population in 1989 was about half a million people.

68. This meeting was recorded on videotape, which is in the author's possession (personal archive of Bakhtiyar Babadjanov).

69. Almost all of our interviewees, former IMU fighters, commented ironically on Yuldosh's notorious courage. The most frequently repeated and very illustrative story is that once he heard the sounds of shots he became severely scared; not even concealing his animal fear, he rushed to his Jeep, and took off. Later it was found out that these shots came from a training camp. When the young fighters found out that the topic of his planned speech was to be fearlessness of "real mujahideen," this story—quickly spreading among the IMU militants from Tavildara to the Afghan camps—severely damaged the credibility of the hapless leader of the movement.

70. According to R. Akramov, this requirement was made under the undeclared order of Muhammad-Sadiq Muhammad-Yusuf, who was also in Namangan at that time but did not take part in the rally for reasons of safety. Muhammad-Sadiq Muhammad-Yusuf insists that this information is incorrect.

71. Ordinary citizens comprised approximately 92 percent to 95 percent of the approximately 20,000 people who assembled.

72. From an interview with rally participants.

73. By the early 1990s, according to former employees of the regional hokimiyat, the rate of youth unemployment in Namangan ranged from 35 percent to 50 percent.

74. Based on our interviews with former members of the organization.

75. From an interview with a former member of Islom Adolati. This story was confirmed by R. Akramov.

76. Here and below we use interviews with former members of the IMU collected together with M.B. Olcott.

77. In another version: "as if he is scraped by fingers without nails."

78. The Qur'an refers to the "70 rooms" and "70 *houries* in them" (9: 36, 38, 72).

79. This confirmed by all the former IMU fighters we interviewed.

80. Stanislav M. Prozorov, *"Pravoverie" i "zabluzhdenie" v rannem islame: Islam kak ideologicheskaia sistema,* Moscow, 2004, pp. 7–22.

81. Ibid., p. 212.

82. A. Morabia, *La notion de gihad dans l'Islam médiéval: Dès origines à al-Gazali,* Lille, 1975.

83. A major part of this material came from the archives of the Carnegie Endowment for International Peace in Washington, DC.

84. The text appears on one of the IMU's leaflets. The top of the page shows the IMU emblem, andthe inscription is set in capital letters.

85. That is, "we will be ready to become suicide bombers."

86. Abi Zakariya Ahmad ibn Ibrahim *ad-Dimashqi thumma ad-Dimyati* (Ibn an-Nahhas), *Mashari' al-ashwaq ila masari' al-'ushshaq (fi-1-jihad wa fada'iliha).* Beirut, 1410/1989. We have fragments of the Uzbek translation done by one of the IMU theologians who had

left his signature at the end of the translation: "With the help of Allah the translation of this book was completed in 1422 AH, the 10th Muharram. 03.26.2001 by the hand of Abu Mansur Ahmad [Arabic script signature]." We do not know whether the translation was published. However, we found that in the abstracts of *Mujahideen* (from the archives of the Carnegie Endowment, Washington, DC) the fragments of this book were also used. It is safe to assume Abu Mansur Ahmad's lectures to mujahideen were based on this book.

87. Zubayr b. 'Abd ar-Rakhim. *Dar ul-khidzhrat "Islom ummati,"* no. 1, 1999, May 7.05.07.

88. For more see Bakhtiyar Babadzhanov, "Debates over Islam in Contemporary Uzbekistan: A View from Within," in *Devout Societies vs. Impious States? Transmissing Islamic Learning in Russia, Central Asia and China, Through the Twentieth Century,* ed. Stephane A. Dudoingon, Berlin 2004, pp. 39–60.

89. A typical example is the activity of the Ma'rifatchilar group (Margilan). Its leader, Mamajanov Bakhodir (b. 1950), concluded that the usual five prayers should be read by local Muslims in Uzbek (or Tajik), because a praying person not knowing Arabic should understand the words with which he appeals to Allah. This attitude soon gave birth to a conflict with the conservatives, who immediately labeled the group Wahhabi. After the conservatives rejected thr group, pressure followed from the state authorities, which sided with the conservatives and suspiciously treated any "non-standard" display of religious identity. As a result of this pressure, many members of the Ma'rifatchilar decided to leave the country and join the IMU. However, even here their ritual and theological positions were not accepted. As a result, most Ma'rifatchilar members left the IMU and returned to Margilan. Currently, the attitude of others toward them is more tolerant.

90. On this see Bakhtiyar M. Babadzhanov, Ashirbek K. Muminov, and Martha B. Olcott, "Muhammadjon Hindustani i religioznaia sreda ego epokhi," *Vostok,* no. 5, 2005, pp. 19–33.

91. From the Carnegie Endowment archive.

92. Babadjanov concludes this based on the speeches by local theologians at many international conferences and numerous publications on this topic.

93. Here, we use Nizom—the name of the Central Asian branch of the used in its statute, leaflets, and party literature published in Central Asia, Caucasus, and Ukraine.

94. For details, see Suah Taji-Farouqi, *A Fundamental Quest: Hizb al-Tahrir and the Search for the Islamic Caliphate,* London, 1996.

95. Most theologians affirm that there was a true caliphate thirty0 (twenty-nine solar) years after the death of the Prophet. Perhaps, then the community was able to maintain a certain level of social justice known as "pure religion." We must not forget that three of the first four successors (caliphs) of the Prophet were killed in the course of governmental coups. That alone casts doubt onto the effort to idealize early Muslim history. Succeeding dynasties of caliphs were not elected but rather crowned.

96. Taji-Farouqi. *A Fundamental Quest,* pp. 27–28.

97. "Radikalnyi islam v Tsentralnoi Azii," Analiticheskaia zapiska "International Crisis Research Group," Bishkek, 2000, p. 10.

98. Taji-Farouqi, *A Fundamental Quest,* p. 104. See also "Radikalnyi islam v Tsentralnoi Azii," p. 8.

99. However, Lenin and his followers, unlike the HT ideologues, indicated more clearly the need for extremely violent methods to deal with the tsar's regime.

100. The education and nurturing of ideological party members; *da'va,* meaning propaganda (verbal and printed) to the members of the Ummah Party regarding their ideas and "mass education."

101. "Radikalnyi islam v Tsentralnoi Azii," p. 7.

102. Taji-Farouqi, *A Fundamental Quest,* p. 104; "Radikalnyi islam v Tsentralnoi Azii," pp. 10–11.

103. Ibid., p. 8.

104. This is based on many interviews with the region's religious leaders.

105. An interview of Bakhtiar M. Babadjanov with Muhammad-Sadiq Muhammad-Yusuf, the famous theologian of Central Asia.

106. For example, Narodnaya Volya (People's Will) orginization in Russia went on a similar path, starting their activities in the middle of the nineteenth century with a number of attempts to participate in educating Russian people politically. The movement, as is known, was later transformed into political nihilism and afterward resorted to become individual terror against government officials.

107. More often, theologians appeal to the famous *hadith*, in which the Prophet foresaw the division of his community into seventy-three communities (*firqa*). Only one of those would be placed in paradise. As a reaction to such a division, some purist theologians have long been struggling to impose the removal of inter-community (*mazhab*) variations. However, as some theologians noted, those who fought against the separation of communities created their own communities, parties, and other groups, further contributing to the divisions among Muslims. It happened so with the followers of Ahmad ibn Hanbal. The followers of Ibn 'Abd al-Wahhab went down the same path and in the heat of the struggle against *mazhabs* in general created a new *mazhab*, shocking the Muslim world with their intolerance to all forms of legitimate existence of Islam in other regions.

108. Around the same time, Kosimov attracts a prominent leader of another religious group into the ranks of HT, Akrom Yo'ldoshev. Quitting the HT, Y'oldoshev founded his own group—Akromiya, which is responsible for the events in Andijan on May 13, 2005.

109. In 1999, Kosimov was arrested and sentenced to twelve years of imprisonment on the charge of forming an illegal religious organization. He was released in January 2004 based on the act of amnesty and penitential letter to the president. From an interview with A. Kosimov, July 2006.

110. New edition published in 2002.

111. From undated HT leaflets.

112. *Mu'tamad*—literally, "helper."

113. *Mas'ul yordamchisi* translate party literature from the Arabic language, compiling and distributing leaflets to the lower layers of the party structure.

114. By the way, the ideas of HT were not supported and still are not supported by the IRPT.

115. Recently the party has created many problems in a number European countries, including England—the location of its main office. Excessive zeal in the promotion of assistance to Iraq in resisting the allied forces, direct calls for jihad among the Muslim youth of Europe, and other activities predetermined a number of repressive actions against the Hizb ut-Tahrir al-Islami in Germany, England, Spain, and other countries.

116. This report, known as the "method of updating the Hizb ut-Tahrir," was subsequently published and translated into many languages, including Uzbek.

117. See www.al-waie.org.

118. *al-Wa'y,* no. 204, February 2004, p. 40.

119. This was confirmed in the interview by A. Kosimov, who, referring to the instructions received from the management of the parent party, insisted that HT did not try to legitimize its legal status in any of the countries in the region, even though in some of them (for instance, in Kyrgyzstan) in the early 1990s this could have been done. Conversely, the instruction on behavior of the young party members at a time of arrest was developed by Kosimov, who taught them that from the moment they were in jihad and had to "without any fear condemn the satrapy [the police—B.B.] and unfaithful tyrants, explicitly telling them that they served Jews and infidels." In other words, the provocative behavior of inexperienced young people was stimulated with instructions to intentionally flaunt the principle "anything you say will be used against you." Moreover, it suggested to the young members of HT that violence during the jihad automatically converted the

arrested into suicide bombers and guaranteed them a place in paradise. Of course, such suggestions often stimulated irrational and openly provocative behavior on the part of young HT members during interrogations.

120. For example, relatively liberal laws related to this kind of religious organizations in Kyrgyzstan led to the activation of HT leadership in the south of the country (especially in the Osh and Jalalabad districts), moving there its clandestine printing, management of Web sites, and other party propaganda.

121. Given that the number of Muslims in the region is approximately 40 million, and the number of HT members, according to different estimates, is between 15,000 and 20,000, relative figures counting those involved in HT would be a number with many zeros—in other words the number of HT members is insignificant I regard to the Muslims in the region.

122. According to some experts, the current regional leadership of HT mainly resides in southern Kyrgyzstan, taking advantage of its liberal laws.

123. See two leaflets of the local branch of HT dated May 15 and 20, 2005 (personal archive of Bakhtiyar Babadjanov). In them, among other things, the local leadership of HT acknowledges that Akrom Yo'ldoshev was a former member of their organization, and talks with sympathy about the failed final attempt of armed rebellion in Andijan but still denies HT's involvement in the actions of Akromiya.

124. Members of the organization were able to bribe officials and guards at the prison where A. Yo'ldoshev was under detention. The latter, thanks to generous bribes, remained in constant communication with his organization via cell phone and could write and send instructions to the members.

125. From the criminal cases based on the testimony of organizers of Akromiya's operation, among whom were citizens of Kyrgyzstan.

126. According to former members of Akromiya, Yo'ldoshev has recently renounced these ideas, claiming that he was misunderstood.

127. For translation and detailed analysis of *Yimonga Yul*, see Bakhtiyar Babadjanov's publication: "Kto po tu storonu barrikad? (O sekte Akromiya i ey podobnykh)," *Rasy i narody,* no. 32, 2006, pp. 82–100.

128. Ibid, 80–106.

129. The idea of a single Islamic state—in the form of a caliphate or a Union of Islamic States—is considered by many Islamists as itself a product of Western ideological influence.

130. See the detailed analysis in Bakhtiyar Babadjanov, "Kto po tu storonu barrikad"? (see note 128). Incidentally, A. Yo'ldoshev in his compositions often resorted to allegory, omissions, or direct abridgement of quotations from the Qur'an, in order to camouflage the calls to jihad. For example, in one place the author calls upon his followers to overcome their fear of "rendering charitable cause." He justifies this with a reference to the Qur'an: "(truly) you can hate what you benefit from and love what is evil. Allah knows you do not" ("al-Baqara," 216). This misty rationale becomes clear when we look into the beginning of a passage deliberately skipped by the author: "a struggle/Jihad is ordered for you (al-qattalu/qattal), but you hate it."

131. Half of these weapons are still being sought.

132. The videotapes seized from Akromiya are not filmed complete, with the total time in the recorded video being approximately 1 hour and 24 minutes. Here and below we used the materials assembled for the criminal cases by the general prosecutor of Uzbekistan.

133. In the translation of those statements we have preserved the original (Andijan) dialect and slang.

134. According to the recorded telephone conversations between the terrorists and the headquarters for settlement of the conflict, around noon it was agreed that all the terrorists would be given buses and they would be allowed to go to camps prepared for them on the territory of Kyrgyzstan. The condition was that the hostages would be released at the neutral border post. However, K. Parpiev, after consulting with some *hodja-aka,* refused to accept

his offer, which led to the solution of the issue by force. Interestingly enough, that unknown *hodja-aka,* according to the decoded evidence of Parpiev's conversations, was in Kabul.

135. In this case, the opposition of Muhammad-Sadiq Muhammad-Yusuf to some of the theologians in Andijan and Kokand is particularly true.

136. Since the republics of this region gained independence, Tashkent increasingly became the center of religious life in Uzbekistan. In Tajikistan, Dushanbe became the center of political Islam. In Kyrgyzstan, the main center of Islam (including political activity) is still in the south of the country, that is the eastern part of the Ferghana Valley.

137. For more information see Babadzhanov, *Debates over Islam.*

138. The most symbolic figure in the process of calling for tolerance toward HT was Rafi'zhon Kamolov (killed in August 2006), who told us in an interview on July 20, 2006 that he treated the members of this party in the same way he would treat other Muslims. That is why HT members prayed at his mosque, including young people from local jamaats.

139. It appears that southern districts of Kyrgyzstan has become the regional center of HT.

140. We noted during the interviews we conducted in July–August 2006 that the members of regional HT divisions had very low level of education. For example, one of our interlocutors (Aravan village, Osh district) said that Shiites originated from Shafi'i madhhab, and thought Israel is one of the states of the United States of America.

141. Babadzhanov, *Debates over Islam,* pp. 39–60.

142. Incidentally, recently Hizb al-Tahrir al-Islami demonstrated the same militaristic interpretation of jihad, which gives us reason to include it into the list of radical parties. For details see M. Olcott and B. Babadzhanov, "Hizb ut-Tahrir in Uzbekistan: Non-Violent Methods of Struggle or Instigation to Terror?" in *State and Religion in Countries with a Muslim Population,* ed. Z. Munaviarov and R. Krumm, Tashkent, 2004, pp. 163–172.

143. Our interviews in the cities of the Ferghana Valley, July 2006.

144. Special thanks to my colleague from Osh, I. Mirsaidov, for providing the detailed contents of the movie. Currently, he is preparing a special article with a description and commentary on this film, to be published on Ferghana.ru's section on terrorist organizations.

145. According to what we know, this coordination is willingly exercised only by the authorities. However, in fact, this is a "struggle with the consequences" and not with the causes of religiously motivated terrorism.

146. In section of the article, especially in the conclusion, the works of other expert colleagues were used, in particular, the work of V.N. Ushakov, *Politicheskii islam v Tsentralnoi Azii,* Moscow and Bishkek, 2005.

147. F. Poiarkov, *Poslednii epizod dunganskogo vosstaniia (Malenkaia stranitsa iz proshloi zhizni Semirechia),* Frunze [1901] 1983, p. 54.

148. *Kyrgyzstan-Rossiia. Istoriia vzaimootnoshenii (XVIII–XIX vv.). Sbornik dokumentov i materialov,* Bishkek, 1998, p. 45.

149. A.V. Piaskovskii, *Vosstanie 1916 goda v Srednei Azii i Kazakhstane. Sbornik dokumentov,* Moscow, 1960, p. 74.

150. Ibid., p. 80.

151. Abu Zakhra, *Nazariat ul-kharb fi-1-islam,* Cairo, 1958, p. 12.

152. *Sotsiologicheskii opros. Institut strategicheskogo analiza i prognoza KR//Otchet za 2005,* Bishkek, 2006.

153. *Dannye perepisi statisticheskogo Komiteta Kyrgyzstana za 2000–2001 god,* Bishkek, pp. 260–261.

154. Currently, the fine is 8 som per one missed prayer.

155. For more details on this organization, see above on the Uzbek part of the Ferghana Valley.

156. B. Babadzhanov, "Sredneaziatskoe dukhovnoe upravlenie (SADUM): predystoriia i

posledstviia raspada," in *Mnogomernye granitsy Tsentralnoi Azii,* vol. 2, ed. M.B. Olcott and A. Malashenko, Moscow, 1999; B. Babadzhanov, "O fetvakh SADUM protiv 'neislamskikh' obychaev," pp. 65–78.

157. Representatives of the radical approaches emerged in the early 1990s in southern Kyrgyzstan, under the influence of Uzbeks living in the Ferghana Valley and related by blood to the Uzbek diaspora of Saudi Arabia, which used them as agents of the ideas of Wahhabism.

158. The ideological work of Hizb ut-Tahrir consists of two dimensions: a purely religious one based on political-legal *fatwas,* which delegitimize the constitutional order and laws of the secular state of political Islam; and recruitment, which involves promoting and attracting new members of Hizb ut-Tahrir, consisting mainly of practicing Muslims. The permanent religious source is the Muslim community in Kyrgyzstan.

159. The transnational project aims to build a global Islamic state.

160. Islamization based on the administrative and legislative framework is to be preferred.

161. This includes political terror as a method of struggle, but terror (*irkhab*) is considered the most extreme measure, beyond the permission (*ruhsa*) to use mental or other kinds of pressure.

162. As an example of the active implementation of this program over the past few years, we can cite the speech of one of HT activists on protecting the rights of consumers of electricity, assistance to young families in the new buildings, and organization of large-scale meals during the holidays of Qurban and Orozo Ayt/Uraza 'Id in the south of Kyrgyzstan. See www.24.kg/community/2008/11/05/97189.html.

163. The first publications of *Taki al-Dina Nabhani* were issued with the slogan from the *hadith Al-khukmu li-Llakh:* "All power belongs to Allah."

164. A. Alisheva, *Religioznaia situatsiia v Kyrgyzstane, Tsentr. Aziia i Kavkaz,* Bishkek, 1999.

165. Hizb ut-Tahrir document "Partiinoe splochenie" (n.p., n.d.).

166. Michael C. Hudson, "Islam and Political Development," in *Islam and Development,* ed. John Esposito, Syracuse, 1980, p. 134.

167. Ibid.

168. Here and below, we use the results of surveys and studies by an independent group led by the author Bakhtiyar Babadjanov.

169. From an interview with a member of Hizb ut-Tahrir with fifteen years' experience, Khatamzhan from Nookat.

170. A. Kniazev, "Afganskii uzel: vyzovy i ugrozy dlia Tsentralnoi Azii" (Doklad na nauchnoi konferentsii po vneshnemu vektoru politiki stran Tsentralnoi Azii)," Issyk Kul, October 25, 2008.

171. From a 2007 interview with the former HT emir of Talas district.

172. From a personal interview with Tursunbay Bakir Uluu on December 15, 2008.

173. A. Ignatenko correctly points out that the term Wahhabism currently is not used in its original sense (as the name-eponym of Ibn 'Abd al-Wahhab, the founder of the religious-political movement that emerged in the eighteenth century in Arabia), but in its second, well-established meaning: a political current, the followers of which, basing themselves on a specific and subjective interpretation of Islam, carry out activities (mainly with the use of violence) aimed at changing the socio-political system, primarily in countries where Islam is spreading. Ignatenko also believes that the radicalization of Muslim societies in such cases does not follow the scheme: an increase in social and economic problems leads to the search for ideological expression and to the Islamic radicalism in the form of Salafism, (See A.A. Ignatenko, *Khalify bez khalifata,* Moscow, 1988, p. 33).

174. Interview with the leaders of the Foundation of Adep Bashat and the adviser to mufti in Kyrgyzstan, Iusuf Loma Ajy.

175. Especially in its centers of theological studies such as Samarkand, Kokand, and Tashkent, theologians of other schools (e.g., Shafi'i) traditionally coexisted with those who

did not recognize separate communities. In general, such diversity was evolving into a collision between the different leaders, which was typical for the Soviet and post-independece periods. See Babadjanov et al., "Disputes on Muslim Authority in Central Asia."

176. The territory of Sughd region is 26 thousand square kilometers, the population—1,900,000 people. There are fourteen districts and seven towns in the region.

177. Islamic Renaissance Party of Tajikistan, Hizb ut-Tahrir.

178. Salafi, Islamskoe Dvijenie Turkestana.

179. Bayat, Tablighi Jaamat, Islam Jihad.

180. More on this method of illegal education see the Uzbekistan section of this chapter.

181. Ibid.

182. Sadriddin Kalandari, *Shodam, ki KhNIT dar manzili kamina ba dunyo omad,* Dushanbe, 2003, pp. 127–139.

183. *KhNIT. 30 sol. Zodai ormoni mardum,* Dushanbe, 2003, p. 141.

184. This newspaper isnow called *Najot* (Salvation).

185. Kalandari, *Shodam,* pp. 127–139.

186. *KhNIT. 30 sol,* pp. 142–144.

187. Ibid., p. 141; Ibn Kathir-Abu al-Fida, Imad ad-Din, Isma'il ibn 'Umar ibn Kathir al'-Qurayshi al-Bursawi (1326–ca. 1370), a well-known scientist, *faqih,* Qur'an interpreter (*mufassir*), and the author of many books of commentaries on the Qur'an.

188. Regulations of PIVT (Partiya Islamskogo Vozrojdeniya Tadjikistana).

189. *Vechernii Dushanbe,* September 24–30, 2007.

190. From Bakhtiyar Babadjanov's interviews.

191. Aleksandr Kniazev, "Grozit li Tadzhikistanu 'makovaia' revoliutsiia?" August 20, 2006, www.centrasia.ru/newsA.php?st=1156048860.

192. Ibid.

193. Salafiya, from the Arabic *salafi* (be original), is a fundamentalist religious-ethical line within Sunnism, created in the fourteenth century and based on the works of Ibn Taymiyyah. It hailed the era of the Medina communities (622–630) as the "golden age" of Islam. The most prominent Salafi preacher is Muhammad Ibn 'Abd al-Wahhab. Currently, Saudi Arabia is considered the center of Salafism.

194. *Hadiths* were collected mainly by early scholars from Central Asia such as the Imam al-Bukhari.

195. Imam Ibn Hanbal—the founder of Hanbali mazhab.

196. The founder of Shafi'i madhhab.

197. See V.E. Makari, *Ibn Taymiyyah's Ethics,* Berkeley, 1983.

198. In other words, their activities are monitored by the special organs of internal security.

199. Parvina Khamidova, "Vokrug dvizheniia 'Salafiia,' aktivizirovavshegosia v poslednee vremia v Tadzhikistane tsirkuliruet mnogo slukhov, vedutsia spory i diskussii. Kto oni? K chemu stremiatsia? K chemu mozhet privesti rost ikh vliianiia?" Radio Liberty, July 24, 2008.

200. Daler Gufronov, "Interviu s Akbar Turadzhonzoda," *Asia-Plus,* July 24 2008, www.centrasia.ru/newsA.php?st=1216929960.

201. Ibid.

202. Ibid.

203. "V Tadzhikistane zapretili fundamentalistskoe dvizhenie 'Salafiia,' " *Asia-Plus,* January, December 8, 2004.

204. Unofficial sources claim the movement has between 20,000 and 40,000 adherents.

205. See the section in this chapter on Uzbekistan for more details.

206. "Hizb ut-Tahrir s tochki zreniia prokratury." Interviu korrespondenta IAA "Varorud" K. Komilova so starshim pomoshchnikom prokurora Sogdiiskoi oblasti, sovetnikom iustitsii pervogo klassa Urunovym Asadullo Urunovichem,www.varorud.org/old/analitics/security/security161105.html.

207. Ibid.

208. Taji-Farouki, *A Fundamental Quest,* pp. 153–87.

209. See the section on Kyrgyzstan in this chapter.

210. According to the information service "Novosti," the trial of Saidkamoliddin Nosirov was concluded and he was sentenced to imprisonment for fourten years. Forty-two-year-old Saidkamoliddin Nosirov was charged under six articles of the Criminal Code of Tajikistan, although he did not plead guilty. Nosirov is the first citizen of Uzbekistan convicted of being memebr of Hizb ut-Tahrir in Tajikistan.

211. T. Turaev, "Kak vedetsia borba s religioznymi ekstremistami v Sogdiiskoi oblasti? (rasskaz spetsialista)," *Varorud,* no. 47, December 8, 2004.

212. Zurah Todua, "'Khizb ut-Takhrir' v Tsentralnoi Azii," www.i-r-p.ru/page/stream-trends/index-8725.html.

213. Akbar Turadzhonzoda, "Islam, protivorechashchii Koranu," *Aziia-Plius,* February 12, 2004.

214. Ibid.

215. Ibid.

216. *Daydzhest-press,* no. 46, November 13, 1997.

217. Sanobar Maksudova, "V Kabule arestovan glava isfarinskoi (Tadzhikistan) iacheiki, 'Islamskogo dvizheniia Uzbekistana' A. Kaiumov," *Khovar,* January 16, 2009, www.centrasia.ru/newsA.php?st=1232140200.

218. Erkin Yurt, "Ugroza stabilnosti Tsentr. Azii—religioznyi terrorizm?" July 29, 2004, www.centrasia.ru/newsA.php?st=1091070000.

219. "Spetsifika proiavlenii terrorizma i ekstremizma v Tsentralnoi Azii: osnovnye tendentsii i itogi 2005–2006," Doklad tsentra antiterroristicheskih programm proiavleniia terrorizma i ekstremizma v stranakh Tsentralnoi Azii v 2000–2006, http://studies.agentura.ru/centres/cap/itogi2005–2006/.

220. Ibid.

221. Ibid.

222. Aleksandr Tikhonov, "Alfa kyrgyzskoi proby," February 7, 2007, www.i-r-p.ru/page/stream-trends/index-8725.html.

223. Nigora Bukhari-zade, Khanafiti protiv salafitov, December 23, 2008, www.ariana.su/?S=2.08122306262.

14

The Ferghana Valley and the International Community

Inomjon I. Bobokulov (Uzbekistan)

The International Community Discovers the Ferghana Valley as a "Tinder Box"

With the collapse of the USSR, the former Soviet republics of Central Asia gained independence and, in doing so became factors in the foreign policies of many countries and subjects of concern for international organizations.[1] The concerns that defined the region's place on the international agenda included religious extremism, instability in Afghanistan, hydrocarbon resources, regional transit capacity that could serve as a connecting link between Europe and Asia, and international terrorism. The Ferghana Valley, as the region's geopolitical core, came to play a special role in all these discussions.

Having been divided among three republics by Soviet decisions of the 1920s and 1930s, each of the national sectors of the valley now gained distinct advantages with respect to the others. Uzbekistan's sector dominates the valley's plains and therefore controls most of the agricultural land. Kyrgyzstan's sector leads up to the mountains, whence the major hydroenergy resources arise. The Sughd province of Tajikistan, serving as a gateway to the Ferghana Valley, controls major existing transportation lines connecting the valley with the outside world. All of these factors affect both economic interdependence and security in the valley as a whole, and define the nature of inter-state cooperation and competition there. By virtue of its geographic position and ethnic makeup, the Ferghana Valley is also a particularly vulnerable entity, affected equally during the 1990s by the civil war in Tajikistan, the ongoing conflict in Afghanistan, and the complex internal situation in China's Xinjiang Uyghur Autonomous Region.

These circumstances account for the interest of foreign governments and international organizations in the Ferghana Valley, as manifested in a series of studies, projects, and reports following their implementation.[2] Notable is the fact that both Western and Russian publications on the Ferghana Valley focus on the issue of regional conflict. They have viewed the valley as a breeding ground of instability and a source of inter-ethnic and inter-state conflicts. Such analyses variously describe it as a "tinder box"[3] or "cradle of Islamism"[4] in Central Asia. Indeed, inter-ethnic conflicts in the late 1980s and early 1990s, and the Batken events of 1999–2001, in which members of the Islamic Movement of Uzbekistan (IMU) attacked the valley from the south, did much to shape Western opinion about the Ferghana Valley. In this regard, the UN Ferghana Valley Development Programme argued that "The Ferghana Valley reemerged on the international scene as the site of two particularly unfortunate ethnic clashes."[5]

Undeniably, such extremist groups as the IMU, Akromiya, and others are directly or indirectly linked with the valley. High population density,[6] widespread unemployment, scarce land resources, and the incomplete process of defining national borders make the valley a hotbed of potential and real regional security challenges, many of which have engaged the attention of the international community. Concerning that involvement, let us therefore ask what issues and projects have been identified as international priorities, what assumptions about the nature of conflict in the valley are these based on, and to what extent have they affected regional development there?

Positive Potentials of the Ferghana Valley and the International Community

Perceptions of the Ferghana Valley's potential for conflict define many, if not most, initiatives there; yet, its "potential for peace" should by no means be discounted as a factor in shaping developments there, especially in an age of growing economic interdependence and globalization. The valley has the potential to become an important alternative transport corridor, a hub of regional trade, and a key element of regional hydroenergy systems. Security challenges can have the welcome effect of engaging the international community in realizing these positive potentials and thereby strengthening the valley's economic viability. Such engagement would be particularly useful in developing mechanisms to address cross-border ecological issues.

There are a number of positive features of the Ferghana Valley potentially important to the international community. First, its population of thirteen million includes one out of five Central Asians, and is the largest consumer market in the region, even though it occupies only 5 percent of the territory.

Second, about 6 percent of Uzbekistan's arable land, 16 percent of Tajikistan's, and 50 percent of Kyrgyzstan's lies in the Ferghana Valley.[7] In all three countries more than three-fifths of their populations live in rural areas, with the figure as high as 70 percent in some provinces. The improvement of farming, the development of processing industries, and the creation of "value-added" for agricultural products all present attractive possibilities for foreign investors and international programs.[8]

Third, the valley has a substantial industrial potential. Ferghana, Kokand, Kuvasay, Andijan, and Khujand are important industrial centers that also play a crucial role in the national economies of their respective republics. Roughly half of Kyrgyzstan's industrial profits come from its three provinces in the south.[9] Ferghana city hosts the region's largest oil refinery, and Andijan is home to Central Asia's only automobile factory, developed by Koreans and now owned by General Motors.

Fourth, important transport lines connecting Tajikistan, Uzbekistan, and Kyrgyzstan with adjacent states and the rest of Eurasia traverse the Ferghana Valley.

Northern routes through Uzbekistan reach Kazakhstan, Russia and other members of the Commonwealth of Independent States (CIS), while southern routes through Termez and through Tajikistan connect with ports on the Persian Gulf and Arabian Sea, as well as to Pakistan, India and beyond. Routes through Kyrgyzstan link to China and via the Karakoram Highway to Pakistan, India, and Southeast Asia.

Fifth, the Ferghana Valley has a single, integrated hydroenergy system fed by the water and electrical energy resources of Naryn Darya and Kara Darya and supported by storage reservoirs at Andijan, Kasansai, Kairakkum, Karkidon, and Papansk, and by hydroelectric stations at Uchkurgan and Kampyrabad.

These and other attributes of the valley endow it with great potential for future development, and warrant the attention of international bodies and investors. To be sure, they do not negate the reality of vexing problems that have brought international notoriety to the Ferghana Valley in recent years. But they do provide a positive context for the solution of those problems, and beckon to future prospects that can be realized if today's concerns can be successfully addressed.

Studies and Projects of International Organizations and Foreign Governments

The Ferghana Valley needs the international community's presence, especially on those issues that require joint decisions by two or more of the valley's adjacent republics. Such involvement will be most effective and contribute most to security if it is cast as a supplement to national and regional efforts to resolve problems, rather than as an alternative to them.

At present the main countries engaged in economic and social development work in the Ferghana Valley are China, Russia, and the United States. International organizations functioning there include the United Nations (UN), European Union (EU), Organization for Security and Cooperation in Europe (OSCE), Shanghai Cooperation Organization (SCO), North American Treaty Organization (NATO), and others, while international development agencies such as the World Bank, European Bank for Reconstruction and Development (EBRD), and the Asian Development Bank (ADB) are also active in the region. The special studies and programs implemented under their auspices address a broad range of issues, from support for local non-governmental organizations (NGOs) to disaster management, ecological initiatives and business development. Initially, most programs focused on conflict management and prevention. Today the focus is on a more positive agenda that serves as both an end in itself and as the best means of preventing conflict. Typical of such projects is the effort to create a financial basis for cross-border cooperation and economic growth. At the same time, older programs have undergone qualitative changes that increase the number and skills of local participants and broaden the scope and scale of their activities. Programs are also more focused, with typical emerging themes being primary and secondary education,[10] entrepreneurship, the management of borders and water resources, and counter-narcotics.

The Ferghana Valley Development Programme of the UNDP (United Nations Development Programme) was the first international project to seek to develop a comprehensive approach to conflict-prevention in the Ferghana Valley.[11] To its credit, the project took what might be called a "preventive" approach to conflict, building conditions that make growth and development possible rather than dwelling on a host of separate issues and points of contention. The project focused on maintaining inter-ethnic peace and good community relations, promoting regional dialogue and cooperation, and regional institutional building. The UN took the general approach that the official actions of the three Ferghana countries did not provide an adequate response to the problems before them, nor did the separate actions of civil society organizations in the three countries. The only path forward, so the UN asserted, was a cooperative one involving both government and civil society groups in all three countries.

The project translated its major foci into initiatives dealing with growth and equity concerns, inter-ethnic tolerance, transparent boundaries, language and education, and the revival of what was assumed to be a common cultural heritage. Among proposals put forward were plans to establish tax-free zones, develop crafts and tourism, and engage local governments and even neighborhoods (*mahallas*) in peace-building. Because the three governments viewed the UN Ferghana Valley Development Programme as impartial, it successfully extended its work into all three republics of the Ferghana Valley.

In 1994 the privately funded U.S.-based Council on Foreign Relations set up a Center for Preventive Action to conduct research on conflict-prevention in Nigeria, the Great Lakes area of Central Africa, the South Balkans, and the Ferghana Valley, which many regarded as one of the most important conflict zones in the world.[12] Scholars, NGO leaders, and governmental experts visited all three parts of the Ferghana Valley throughout 1997 and 1998.

The Center's belief that "conflict-resolution must be a job for U.S. policy in the region"[13] gave it a political cast corresponding to the position of the U.S. Department of State at the time. The recommendations that arose from the project were explicitly directed to the U.S. government; these included the creation of cross-border institutions to promote economic development and interethnic cooperation, support to civil society institutions and human rights groups, support to efforts seeking intercultural dialogue, the concentration of foreign assistance on cross-border regional programs while at the same time maintaining country-to-country aid, and support to foreign direct investment in the valley.

The results of both the UN and the Council on Foreign Relations programs were modest at best. This was due, above all, to their refusal to give governmental institutions any role in implementing the programs. Also, other civil society groups and traditional social mechanisms in the valley were far weaker than the projects believed, while the governments proved far less susceptible to pressure from the outside.[14] Given this, a better course would have been to engage directly with the three governments, giving them a role in carrying out the projects. But this was not done. In spite of this, the UNDP and Council on Foreign Relations projects pioneered the comprehensive study of conflict prevention in this Central Asian flashpoint, and significantly influenced the international community to take realities on the ground as the basis for launching future programs in the region.

Indeed, a number of other projects aimed at conflict prevention in the Ferghana Valley were undertaken. Most were bilateral in character rather than regional, and focused mainly on the south of Kyrgyzstan and to some extent the north of Tajikistan.[15] The IMU's 1999 attack on Batken spurred both the Soros Foundation and the UNDP (Preventive Development Project) to mount projects there, while also stimulating the International Crisis Group to begin a Central Asia Project with headquarters in Osh city.

Also notable are the ten projects in all three adjacent Ferghana countries of the Swiss Agency for Development and Cooperation (SDC) and Swiss State Secretariat for Economic Affairs (SECO). In Kyrgyzstan Swiss projects provide support for forest management,[16] the power sector, and agriculture; in Tajikistan they focus on energy, water and agriculture; and in Uzbekistan they work on water use and the supply of electric power. Regional projects of the SDC mainly included the cross-border Integrated Management of Water Resources Management in the Ferghana Valley (IWMR), Automatization of Channels in the Ferghana Valley, and Regional Information Base of the Water Sector in Central Asia (CAREWIB).

The major goal of the IWMR project was to engage farming households directly, not with the issue of how much water is available but with its effective management as a resource through inter-state cooperation. The IWMR project stretched from 2001 until 2008 and covered three experimental zones along "pilot channels" and "cross-border small rivers" crossing all three countries. Through public participation and cross-border water management, the project hoped to foster social stability in a way that could be applied elsewhere in the region.[17] For the first time in Central Asia it succeeded in forging a common, integrated system of long-distance supply channel management. It was implemented in close contact with the important region-based Scientific-informational Center of the Interstate Commission for Water Management and International Water Management Institute (IWMI).[18]

The international community also quickly engaged with issues of ecology in the Ferghana Valley. In Soviet times some fifty uranium mines had been opened there, mainly in Kyrgyzstan's Jalalabad province and near Khujand in Tajikistan's Sughd province.[19] After 1991 mining ceased, but the vast areas where these mines and mountains of tailings were situated were left virtually unguarded. Many of these sites are in close proximity to cross-border rivers (Syr Darya, Zarafshan, Mailuu-Suu, and others), threatening them—and ground waters as well—with radioactive contamination in times of floods and landslides. Huge piles of radioactive waste along the Mailuu-Suu River in Kyrgyzstan some 30 kilometers upstream from the Uzbek border threaten the environment and population of the entire Ferghana Valley. For years, ore from as far away as the German Democratic Republic, Czechoslovakia, the People's Republic of China, and Mongolia were sent there for processing: 23 tailing ponds and 13 dumps contain 3 million cubic meters of radioactive waste.

Under the auspices of the Kyrgyz government, together with experts from the OSCE, Potsdam Land Institute, and the Lawrence-Livermore Laboratory (United States), the World Bank since 2004 has been rehabilitating the ponds and tailings at Mailuu-Suu at a cost of US$12 million. A German project on "The Prevention of Emergencies in the Mailuu-Suu City," which began functioning there in 2005, has been devoted to the same ends. Another effective program in this field has been the initiative of the OSCE, carried out since 2003 with help from the UN's Environment Programme and Development Programme, and with NATO's participation beginning in 2004. The priorities of this program include the development of early warning systems, emergency preparedness, and the reduction of risks to the affected populations of Kyrgyzstan, Tajikistan, and Uzbekistan, and both land and water resource management in the upper Syr Darya Valley. Overall, the program seeks to address proactively those environmental problems that can become the source of conflict between countries, regions, or districts.[20]

NATO's activities in the Ferghana Valley are not restricted to this project. NATO held international exercises of rescuers and rapid-response forces in the Ferghana village of Vuadil under the Partnership for Peace's program "Ferghana 2003."[21] This was the first time that NATO and UN crisis centers conducted joint exercises in Central Asia. The Euro-Atlantic Emergency Response Center and the UN's department for coordinating humanitarian programs managed the exercise, in which more than a thousand military personnel and rescuers from Uzbekistan and 200 of their counterparts from twenty-eight countries participated.[22]

All major United States government programs and projects in Central Asia are implemented under the auspices of the U.S. Agency for International Development (USAID)—the major conduit of the government's international aid and development policy. USAID has been actively operating in the region on the basis of bilateral agreements with Central Asian states since the early 1990s, and is considered one of the leading national donors. Today USAID's annual expenditure in the three Ferghana countries totals more than US$1 billion, of which $300 million goes to Uzbekistan, $400 million to Kyrgyzstan and a like amount to Tajikistan.[23] USAID focuses its assistance in three areas: economic growth, human development, and "just and democratic governance." Tajikistan also benefits from a "Food for Peace" program.[24] Projects carried out under these rubrics include the rebuilding of health care at the village level,[25] water-resource issues, support for small- and middle-sized businesses, farming, bank and tax reform, and the development of civil society. Most of such projects—some thirty in all—have a regional character and are carried out in all three Ferghana countries.[26] Those active in the Ferghana Valley foster linkages among the region's farmers and agricultural businesses, ties between communities, support for associations of water users, and assistance to regional energy markets.

All these projects promote long-term stability at the sub-regional level. USAID also has sought to address trans-border challenges and the issue of enclaves in the Ferghana Valley. Because of its geographical location, the valley is attractive to drug traffickers and those engaged in human trafficking. To reduce these, USAID sponsors various programs in all three countries,[27] many of them directed toward reducing the demand for drugs among youths.[28] One program in Tajikistan and Uzbekistan seeks to combat trafficking in persons across Central Asia as a whole. The phenomenon of enclaves is a major factor in inter-governmental relations in the Ferghana Valley. Besides the undeveloped nature of international law in this area, the existence of enclaves gives rise to many social and economic issues that are the subject of other USAID projects. Typical was a 2003 initiative to provide drinking water to the Kyrgyz village of Charbak near Batken and to Khushiar village in Sokh district of Uzbekistan.[29] A similar project, which involved Swiss aid as well, addressed the issue of water supplies to neighboring villages on either side of the border in the Ferghana Valley. At the initiative of several communities, this project also improved water supplies to the Uzbek enclave of Vorukh and the nearby Rabot village in Tajikistan.[30]

The EU's projects in Central Asia also take a regional approach. Among these are a program for improving border management, another for reducing the spread of narcotics, an intergovernmental commission promoting the development of transport links from Europe to China (Transit Corridor Europe-Caucasus-Asia, TRACECA), a program for energy transport, and general humanitarian assistance. From 2003 to 2005 the EU funded a regional project on emergency preparedness in the Ferghana Valley that worked with local authorities to train the population to deal with natural disasters. Some forty-eight villages in all three countries were selected on the basis of their exposure to potential disasters, with special emphasis on cross-border situations and enclaves.[31] Governmental institutions and both civil and business groups all participated.

The EU's 2007 Central Asia strategy notes that "the Ferghana Valley best reflects both the problems and prospects of Central Asia. In this connection, the EU is ready to assist the Central Asian countries sharing joint borders in the Ferghana Valley with projects aimed at stability, prosperity, and sustainable development in the region."[32] Under the framework of the Technical Assistance for the CIS program (TACIS) the EU has engaged regional states in programs in a variety of areas,[33] but for the Ferghana Valley the main foci have been border management, environment, transport, and drug control.[34]

Since 1992 the EU has carried out programs aimed at reducing both drug trafficking and consumption in the Ferghana Valley. It has equipped border posts along major drug routes, especially in the areas of Osh and Isfara-Batken,[35] and with the Uzbek government now expanding the effort to include such Uzbek towns as Sokh, Vuadil, and Madaniiat. These initiatives form part of a larger EU-funded program of the UN that has worked since 1992 to upgrade all aspects of border management in the region, so as to facilitate the movement of goods and people and to reduce illicit trade and border tensions. (Border Management Programme in Central Asia; BOMCA). Three of the four posts on which it has concentrated are located in the Ferghana Valley: the Tajik-Kyrgyz border on the road from Isfara to Batken, the Uzbek-Kyrgyz border, and the Tajik-Kyrgyz border in Osh, with Kokand on the Uzbek-Tajik border and Karasu on the Kyrgyz-Uzbek border added later. To encourage the Uzbek government to remove mines on border areas with Tajikistan, the program built a further border post at the enclave in Sokh in 2007.[36] Such integrated border posts reduce the duplication of procedures and allow frontier guards and customs officials of both countries to be housed in the same building. Thanks to these efforts, the Committee on the Protection of State Borders in Uzbekistan could remove mines in the Ferghana Valley and provide modern training and equipment to border troops.[37]

It is worth noting that EU programs seek to strengthen stability within Central Asia and at the same time neutralize various challenges to the EU itself. Several of the projects enumerated above strive to reduce threats to the EU that might arise from Central Asia.

For all their good intentions, most of these many projects have fallen short in terms of their long-term impact. Projects funded by separate donor countries are often poorly coordinated, regional governments sometimes have lacked the political will to push the efforts forward, and many projects get dropped after a few years for lack of sustained support. Thus, for example, much has been learned about preventing the spread of radioactive waste, but little actually has been done to prevent it.

The Major Powers in the Ferghana Valley

The Ferghana Valley is an integral part of the Central Asia strategies of all the great powers. At present, two immediate regional neighbors, the Russian Federation and the People's Republic of China, and one non-regional actor, the United States, are directly involved in the region. All three are driven by what they see as their security concerns and interests. Russia and the United States have both a political and military presence in Central Asia, while China's emphasis is on economic ties—sales and resources. Each utilizes regional collective-security institutions to pursue its goals, whether the CIS, Collective Security Treaty Organization (CSTO), and Eurasian Economic Community (EurAsEC) in the case of Russia; the Shanghai Cooperation Organization (SCO) in the case of China and Russia; and NATO's Partnership for Peace programs and Trade Infrastructure Framework Agreements (TIFAs) in the case of the United States.

Russia's presence in Central Asia can be explained first and foremost by geopolitics. Existing transport networks, ethnic links, ties with the energy sector, and other economic and military relationships benefit the region as well as its large northern neighbor.[38] All Central Asian states participate in the Russia-dominated CIS, CSTO,[39] and EurAsEC.[40] CSTO sponsors drug-control initiatives and also joint military exercise under the "Commonwealth Southern Shield" program. All three Ferghana states participate on CSTO's Coordination Council.

At the heyday of the civil war in Tajikistan and conflict in Afghanistan, Russia stationed border troops on the Kyrgyz-Chinese and Tajik-Kyrgyz borders and patrolled the trans-Pamir highway. These initiatives coincided with an increase of drug trafficking through the Ferghana Valley. The IMU's 1999 incursion into the Ferghana Valley via Batken in Kyrgyzstan was directly connected with its efforts to gain control of drug routes along the Osh-Khorog road and the Sary-Tash nodal point, where China, Tajikistan, and Kyrgyzstan come together.[41]

As a component of the CSTO's Rapid Response Force at Kant, Russia since 2003 has maintained a military base at Kant, 30 kilometers from Bishkek. In March 2008 the Kyrgyz parliament approved an "Agreement between the Kyrgyz Republic and Russian Federation on the Use of Russian Military Objects on the Territory of the Kyrgyz Republic and Status of Military Personnel of the Armed Forces of the Russian Federation in the Kyrgyz Republic." This agreement gave Russia the use of three military resources in Kyrgyzstan—in Chaldovar, Karakol, and Mailuu-Suu—over a period of fifteen years.[42] In addition, Russia proposed to establish yet another base, near Osh.[43] While some defend this as a stabilizing force in the region, others see it as a means by which Russia can dominate the entire Ferghana Valley and position itself for future activities in Afghanistan.[44]

Uzbekistan has strongly objected to the establishment of any Russian military base in the Ferghana Valley. Its position, as disseminated by the Foreign Ministry's Zhakhon press agency, is that: "Uzbekistan sees no need or sense for establishing a further contingent of Russian troops in the south of Kyrgyzstan. The realization of any such project on so complex and problem-fraught a territory, where the borders of three Central Asian states come together, can only further the processes of militarization and arouse various forms of nationalistic protests; equally, it can lead to the introduction of the forces of radical extremists, which could seriously destabilize the broader region."[45]

Whatever claims are advanced to the contrary, it is hard to conceive how the militarization of the Ferghana Valley by outside states can serve the real interests of any Central Asian country. A foreign military presence in this area, regardless of intentions, will escalate inter-state tensions, disrupt military and political balances, and lead to the deterioration of security and economic conditions in the region, further complicating the settlement of cross-border issues. The only reasonable solution is to exclude all foreign military from the Ferghana region.

Migratory labor is an important link between Russia and the Ferghana Valley. The Tajik expert K. Umarov reports that from the Tajik sector alone (Sughd province) more than 400 thousand workers have gone to Russia. In some parts of the province more than 70 percent of working-age males work in the Russian Federation, Kazakhstan and other countries, producing annual remittances of US$720 million, which equals the province's entire annual budget.[46] The social cost is high, however, both when thousands of families have no male household head for years at a time and when, during the financial crisis, jobs and incomes are lost.

Russia also has moved actively into the hydroelectric power field in the Ferghana Valley. In 2009 Prime Minister Putin proposed US$1.7 billion to fund the construction of the Kambarata Hydroelectric Power Stations I and II on the upper reaches of the Syr Darya River. Although Kyrgyz investors are nominally part of this project, it is likely that the power plant will end up entirely in Russian hands, thus further changing the political dynamics of electric power in all three sectors of the Ferghana Valley.

China's comparative advantage among major external powers is that it is the only one with a direct outlet to the Ferghana states of Kyrgyzstan and Tajikistan, via a 1,400-kilometer common border with the two.[47] Kyrgyzstan's Osh province at the eastern end of the Ferghana Valley has direct access to the China's Xinjiang-Uyghur Autonomous Region via the high but easily crossed Tian Shan range. The reality of Uyghur and Xinjiang Kazakh ties of ethnicity, religion, and culture with the former Soviet states of Central Asia defines China's concerns in the region and in the Ferghana Valley particularly. It could not help but perceive the rise of sovereign states among the Turkic peoples to its west as a harbinger of separatist currents in Xinjiang, and the appearance of extremist religious groups in the Ferghana Valley as a threat to its own security. The presence of some 600,000 Uyghurs in the Central Asian states only deepened China's anxiety.

Because of this, China came to see its own security and that of Central Asia as interdependent. Its key objective came to be to neutralize religious radicalism, terrorism, and separatism within the Ferghana Valley and nearby regions of Central Asia. In defense of this view, it is worth noting that analysts have brought to light the plans of Uyghur separatists who took refuge in Afghanistan to work their way back to Xinjiang via the Ferghana Valley in order to carry out terrorist acts in China itself.[48]

China's main policy instrument in Central Asia is the SCO. Initially it arose as a mechanism for resolving border disputes with the new Central Asian states and Russia. Because much of the relevant documentation and information remained in Russia, China engaged the Russians in the effort. In due course both countries signed agreements that legally fixed the borders with the new Central Asian states. Following the IMU's 1999 incursion into the Ferghana Valley at Batken, Russia responded slowly, but China moved quickly to send arms to the Kyrgyz Army and aid to frontier guards at Batken.[49] These events in the Ferghana Valley directly gave rise to a new framework agreement, signed in Shanghai on June 15, 2001, that established the SCO for the purpose of "combating terrorism, extremism, and separatism." Soon the SCO moved beyond these concerns to engage the Central Asians on long-distance transport issues. Chinese investments followed, an early one being to develop small oil fields in the Uzbek part of the Ferghana Valley.[50]

Unlike the CSTO, the SCO's charter and other documents do not include any reference to the duty of collective self-defense, which is a mechanism of repelling an armed attack in accordance with article 51 of the UN Charter. At the same time, SCO member-states accept the possibility of joint use of their armed forces to counter terrorism, extremism, and separatism.[51] Joint SCO military exercises in 2007 developed common techniques for crisis management and maintaining security. Some Russian politicians pointedly spoke of Central Asia as a potential flash point where armed forces might be required.[52]

The interests of the United States in Central Asia focus on security issues, western access to hydrocarbon resources, and concern with strengthening the sovereignty and independence of the new regional states. During the first decade of the twenty-first century, the United States' main concern was to pursue successfully its campaign in Afghanistan, to neutralize terrorist and extremist forces there, and turn that country into a responsible regional player in Central Asia.

The U.S. presence in the Ferghana Valley dates to the early 1940s, when the Soviet government invited Americans to extract uranium from the Mailuu-Suu River Valley.[53] After independence, U.S.-Uzbekistan relations witnessed ups and also downs caused by the IMU's 1999–2001 incursions into Batken, the events of September 11, 2001, and the 2005 "Andijan events." Each of these events provided the impulse either to intensify relations with the region or to lower their tempo. Following Andijan the tempo definitely fell, but it bears mentioning that after the "Batken events" the Pentagon reassigned the Central Asian region to the Central Command and launched the Central Asian Initiative for Secure Borders (2000). Also, the United States Senate set up a special subcommittee on Central Asian affairs (2001), and the U.S. State Department created a new Deputy Directorate for Central and South Asian Affairs.

The United States always has been skeptical of what it considers Uzbekistan's slow progress (or, in Uzbekistan's view, deliberate pace) toward a market economy and a more participatory system of government. However, a Strategic Partnership Declaration[54] signed in 2002 laid the basis for more stable relations, as did the TIFAs, noted above, and the Northern Distribution Network for transporting goods to Afghanistan. By contrast, U.S. relations with the Kyrgyz Republic were consistently positive until the eve of the so-called Tulip Revolution. A proliferation of USAID-funded projects in the Kyrgyz sector of the Ferghana Valley touched many economic and social issues. More recently, the U.S. reliance on the Manas Air Base has caused it to remain silent on the decline of democratic institutions in Kyrgyzstan and on the proposed Russian base in the Ferghana Valley at Osh. With respect to Tajikistan, the United States figured actively in the mediation that led to the end of the civil war but otherwise has not pursued an active development program in the Tajik sector of the Ferghana Valley.

The very different strategies of the three Ferghana countries toward economic and political development led to clear differences in U.S. policies toward them. Moreover, much of that was disseminated through NGOs, which enjoyed a different status in each of the three Ferghana countries and hence achieved different levels of effectiveness. This caused complications, particularly with Uzbekistan, and led one U.S. expert to complain that "the United States had *programs* affecting Uzbekistan but not an overall *policy*, let alone a *strategy*."[55] That said, as early as 1997 the United States held four-day joint military exercises with Uzbekistan in the Ferghana Valley.[56] The United States responded positively to Tashkent's request to list the Islamic Movement of Uzbekistan as a terrorist organization, and continues to honor and build upon the terms of the important March 2003 Declaration on Strategic Partnership.

The NGO Factor in the Ferghana Valley

During the 1990s the international community generally favored non-governmental organizations (NGOs) as instruments for promoting change and development. Because the state had previously dominated society and voluntarist institutions had atrophied, it seemed natural to correct the balance by supporting NGOs. The legal and social conditions for NGO development differed in the three Ferghana countries, with the most favorable circumstances prevailing in Kyrgyzstan. As a result, some 500 NGOs currently operate there, with a high percentage of them present in the Ferghana Valley.[57] Many of these call on mutual associations among citizens to resolve common problems. Others do not. As the German analyst Beate Eschment noted, "many [people] established NGOs not for idealistic purposes but as a source of income."[58]

By contrast, the number and activity of foreign-sponsored NGOs in the Tajik sector of the Ferghana Valley is less than in Kyrgyzstan, while they are all but nonexistent in Uzbekistan's sector and in Uzbekistan generally. While some trace this to Uzbekistan's unwillingness to participate in cross-border projects,[59] a truer explanation lies in that government's determination to maintain internal stability in the face of organizations whose purposes and directions are defined abroad. The belief that foreign-funded NGOs had played a role in the so-called color revolutions in Georgia, Ukraine, and Kyrgyzstan has reinforced Tashkent's distrust. Instead, Uzbekistan has sought to foster non-governmental activity by supporting and partially funding the revival of traditional neighborhood organizations, which thrive across the Uzbek parts of the Ferghana Valley.

Kyrgyzstan's Tulip Revolution of March 2005, which arose first in the Ferghana Valley, gave rise to a certain reaction against NGOs among all the governments of Central Asia, and to demands that foreign sponsors engage more directly with official institutions. Some came to view NGOs simply as agents of foreign states. But in the Ferghana Valley this concern is less compelling because in fact most NGOs have shied away from some of the most urgent social issues. For example, the NGOs have created no mechanisms for the resolution or prevention of intercommunal conflicts.[60] While NGOs working to promote the rights of religious dissenters, women, and other marginalized groups have achieved progress, as have NGOs working in the area of democratic institutions,[61] the problems that have given rise to actual violence remain largely unaddressed by NGOs.

More serious still is the fact that there is no effective dialogue between nongovernmental organizations and governmental authorities. Both sides doubtless deserve blame for this, but the results of this situation benefit neither. What Frederick Starr wrote of the activities of NGOs in Uzbekistan might be extended to all three Ferghana countries: "some international NGOs made major mistakes in their work . . . and allowed excessive politicization of their activities. . . . NGOs should develop a more patient and long-term approach, and spend more time understanding the cultural environment in which they intend to operate."[62] In the fractious conditions of the Ferghana Valley their effectiveness would surely increase if they were to view themselves as a less-confrontational part of the normal political process while simultaneously working patiently but tenaciously for the long term.[63]

International Involvement in the Development of Transport in the Ferghana Valley

The transport sector stands out as a high point of international involvement in the Ferghana Valley. Regional and non-regional states, international organizations, and international financial institutions have all participated in this development. The very difficulty of the situation has turned it into a challenge. Not only is the Ferghana Valley double-landlocked, it is divided into national enclaves,[64] surrounded by mountains, and with often very narrow mountain passes—Kamchik, Rezak, Teo-Ashuu, Anzob, Shakhristan, and Khujand—providing entry and egress. Notwithstanding this, the valley's central position demands that it be reconnected with China, Europe, Afghanistan, and the Indian sub-continent as it was centuries ago. This is being accomplished thanks to the United Nations Economic and Social Commission for Asia and the Pacific (UN ESCAP), the United Nations Special Program for the Economies of Central Asia (SPECA), Central Asian Regional Economic Cooperation (CAREC) program of the Asian Development Bank (ADB), and the EU's Transport Corridor Europe-Caucasus-Asia (TRACECA).

The TRACECA project was conceived in the early 1990s, subsequently languished for many years, and is now being revived.[65] The program of the European Union aims to revive one of the Silk Road routes. All of the Central Asian states, including the adjoining republics of the Ferghana Valley, participate in this project. Stretching some 10,800 kilometers between China and Europe, it will serve the Ferghana Valley mainly through spurs and connectors. More immediately relevant is the Uzbekistan-Kyrgyzstan-China highway launched in 1998 when the governments of China, Kyrgyzstan, and Uzbekistan agreed to construct a 600 kilometer-long road connecting Andijan, Osh, Sary-Tash, Irkeshtam, and Kashgar.[66] The next year China, Iran, Kyrgyzstan, Turkmenistan, and Uzbekistan signed a protocol to speedily construct a further link to Tashkent and thence to Turkmenbashi, Baku, Poti, Batumi, and Constanta. The Government of Japan also took an interest in this route, signing with China a joint declaration on creating a transcontinental Asia-Europe link.

The significance of this transcontinental route is that it runs directly across the Ferghana Valley from Osh to Tashkent. As such, it will compete with, supplement, and be supplemented by more northerly east-west routes through Kazakhstan and through Russia.

However, for the time being this project is far from a reality. The 258-kilometer Kyrgyz section of the route to Kashgar is in poor condition and requires major repairs and upgrading. The four passes along this route—Chigirchik (2,406 meters), Taldyk (3,615 meters), Kurpaktor (3,541 meters), and Taunmurun (3,536 meters)—

all require attention as well, especially during winter. Thanks to US$328 million from the Asian Development Bank and lesser amounts of assistance from the Islamic Development Bank and from China, it will be possible to complete all these tasks.[67] A particularly important feature of the project is the redevelopment of the Kamchik and Rezak passes, completed in 2002, which greatly improve the transport links between the Ferghana Valley and the rest of Uzbekistan. That same year the Ferghana Valley benefited from the new China-Kyrgyzstan border point at Irkeshtam, with a capacity of 300,000–500,000 tons of cargo and 100,000–200,000 people annually. The opening of the road through Irkeshtam reduced the distance between China and the Central Asian states by 700 kilometers and connected them with the Karakoram Highway that provides the shortest way to Pakistan, the new Arabian Sea port at Gwadar, and the countries of Southeast Asia.[68]

Still more ambitious is the new railroad being constructed from Andijan to Osh and then to Irkeshtam and Kashgar, a length of 577 kilometers. Thanks to the further connections from Kashgar to Urumchi, and from Andijan west to the Caspian, 25 million tons of freight will be able to pass through the Ferghana Valley annually.[69] TRACECA has meanwhile carried out a technical study of a promising railroad linking the Ferghana Valley to Kashgar via Bishkek.

Because these lines enable goods to pass from the Ferghana Valley to Kashgar, they open a route via the Karakoram Highway to the south. Other routes heading directly south from Tajikistan and Uzbekistan to Afghanistan will have the same result, and will open what may be an even faster alternative. The chairman of the ADB, Jin Liqun, rightly observed that "Outlets to the sea will not only fulfill the Central Asian states' hope for economic diversification, but will turn the region into a land bridge between East Asia, South Asia, Russia and Europe."[70] China is the main supporter of railway construction projects, which it sees as essential to its "Develop the West" strategy.[71] Whether and how these ultimately will contribute to stability in the volatile region of Xinjiang remain to be seen. Some observers, fearing they could have the opposite effect, point to the impact of the newly opened Urumchi-Kashgar on the Uyghur population as evidence for their view. What cannot be doubted is that these projects will have a profound impact not only on Xinjiang but on the Ferghana Valley.

A priority for Tajikistan is to develop transport links between Sughd province in the Ferghana Valley and the rest of the country. The Khujand-Dushanbe road will link both Tajikistan and Uzbekistan with Iranian ports on the Persian Gulf via Afghanistan (Dushanbe-Termez, Dushanbe-Nizhnii Panj-Kunduz), and thence to Pakistani ports on the Arabian Sea. This route requires the surmounting of formidable natural barriers, which is being accomplished with financial assistance from the United States, China, Iran, and the ADB. In the summer of 2007, a 672-meter bridge, costing US$28 million, went into operation on the Panj River at the Tajikistan-Afghanistan border. Built by the United States, it is the fourth bridge in the area constructed with American technical assistance and funding. Tajikistan is also building two tunnels through the Zarafshan Mountains, with financial assistance from Iran and the ADB.[72]

The role of international financial institutions in building and rehabilitating transport corridors has been significant. As noted above, the ADB designated this as its special focus.[73] Thanks to the CAREC transportation sector development initiative, the World Bank and Islamic Development Bank were also heavily involved, specifically in projects (rehabilitation of the Osh-Irkeshtam road, and construction of the Osh-Batken-Isfara road)[74] affecting the Ferghana Valley. Related to all these is the upgrading of the Karakoram Highway and other automobile roads in Central Asia in the framework of the "Asian Highway" project of the United Nations Economic and Social Commission for Asia and the Pacific.

These many transport projects have attracted much foreign investment to the region, and they promise to reap important economic, social, and security benefits. Besides promoting trade within the region, they will connect or reconnect the Ferghana Valley and Central Asia as a whole with three of the world's most dynamic economies, those of China, Europe, and India.[75]

Conclusion

The Ferghana Valley is a key element in the evolving regional security system in Central Asia, which might be characterized as "a complex of security"—a group of states whose major security interests are so closely interlinked that the national security of individual states cannot be considered outside the context of their intraregional relations.[76] This notion of "a complex of security" suggests the importance of the valley's role in shaping stable inter-state relations in the region as a whole.

A fundamental aspect of many of the most vexing problems involving the Ferghana Valley is their cross-border character, which embodies and reflects both historic tensions and equally historic links and interdependencies. It is precisely in this area of cross-border relations where the international community can make the most effective contribution to the stability and security of the Ferghana Valley and the region of which it is the heart.

The international community has a record of resolving common problems and identifying and building upon common interests. Other countries and financial institutions would do well to continue to expand their focus on these cross-border concerns, and NGOs should also engage with them more directly, since they constitute the very core of current political and social-economic realities in the Ferghana Valley. The existing sub-regional integrated transport network is a particularly important guarantor of regional stability, for it facilitates ties among local communities, governmental bodies, and businesses. Further international assistance in developing this resource and linking it to continental trade routes can only benefit the cause of regional stability. To the extent that international groups can also assist in improving the system of managing national borders, this will help reduce the number and severity of cross-border problems.

Notes

1. Specifically, in May 2007 the EU adopted a "European Union and Central Asia: A Strategy for New Partnership." The strategy serves as a basis of the EU's policies in the region. The United States National Security Strategy (as of March 16, 2006) introduced a new section on "South and Central Asia," confirming a growing significance of this region for U.S. foreign policy. Russia's foreign policy concept identifies cooperation with the Central Asian states as a priority goal.

2. Nancy Lubin and Barnett R. Rubin, *Calming the Ferghana Valley: Development and Dialogue in the Heart of Central Asia,* New York, 1999; Anara Tabyshalieva, *The Challenges of Regional Cooperation in Central Asia: Preventing Ethnic Conflict in the Ferghana Valley,* Peaceworks 28, United States Institute of Peace, June 1999; Randa M. Slim, "The Ferghana Valley: In the Midst of a Host of Crises," in *Searching for Peace in Central Asia and South Asia,* London, 2002.

3. Murat Laumulin, "The Shanghai Cooperation Organization as 'Geopolitical Bluff'? A View from Astana," Institut Français des Relations Internationales, Russie.Nei.Visions, no. 12, 2006, p. 9.

4. Anna Matveeva, "EU Stakes in Central Asia," Chaillot Paper no. 91, Institute for Security Studies, European Union, Paris, July 2006, p. 37.

5. The UNDP Ferghana Valley Development Program. Lubin and Rubin, *Calming the Ferghana Valley,* p. 142.

6. The population density is especially high in the Uzbek part of the valley—277 persons per square kilometer, compared to 69 in the Tajik part and 18 in the Kyrgyz part. "Okruzhaiushchaia sreda i bezopasnost: Transformatsiia riskov i sotrudnichestvo. Tsentralnaia Aziia: Ferghana-Osh-Khujand, Otchet po realizatsii programmy," 2004, www. envsec.org/centasia/pub/ENVSEC%20FV%20DeskA%20rus.doc.

7. *Uzbekiston Respublikasi Er Resurslari Davlat Qo'mtasi, Atlas, Uzbekiston Respublikasining Er Resurslari, Birinchi nashri,* Tashkent, 2001, pp. 12–13; Olimjon Abdullaev, *Fargona vodiisi: izhtimoii-iktisodii rivozhlanish zharaenlari,* Namangan, 2000, p. 148.

8. In this light it is important to note that the EU identifies increases of living standards in the rural areas as "key priorities of bilateral aid" to Central Asia. Bilateral aid programs will make 70 percent of the EU's €750 million budget appropriated for support to Central Asia in 2007–13. Council of the European Union, "The EU and Central Asia: Strategy for a New Partnership," Brussels, May 31, 2007.

9. Kenneth Weisbrode, "Ferghana and Central Asia," in *Central Eurasia: Prize or Quicksand?* Adelphi Series, New York, 2001, p. 47.

10. Specifically, the Japanese government, starting in 1995, implemented more than 240 projects in Uzbekistan over the course of thirteen years. Of them, more than 100 projects were carried out in the provinces of the Ferghana Valley. For 2008 alone the valley saw the implementation of seventeen projects. They mainly aim at equipping medical institutions, secondary schools, and providing necessary equipment to educational centers. Based on the speech of ambassador extraordinary and plenipotentiary of Japan to the Republic of Uzbekistan, japan.go.jp/cooperation/grants/social/openingfergana.html.

11. Slim, "The Ferghana Valley," p. 155.

12. Lubin and Rubin, *Calming the Ferghana Valley,* p. xi.

13. Strobe Talbott, "A Farewell to Flashman: American Policy in the Caucasus and Central Asia," speech delivered at the Central Asia–Caucasus Institute, Johns Hopkins University School of Advanced International Studies, Washington, DC, 1997, www.state.gov/www/regions/nis/970721talbott.html.

14. Lubin and Rubin, *Calming the Ferghana Valley,* p. xviii.

15. According to the data of the state committee on investments and regulation of state

property of the Republic of Tajikistan, about thirty various projects under the auspices of international organizations, international NGOs, and foreign governments were implemented in the Sughd province in 2007. "Partnery po razvittiu—2007," www.caftar.com/clientzone/gki/images/stories/pr_rus.pdf, pp. 144–145.

16. Specifically, five stages of the Kyrgyz-Swiss Forestry Support Program (KIRFOR) were implemented between 1995 and 2007 in Kyrgyzstan's Jalalabad and Osh provinces.

17. O khode vypolneniia proekta "IUVR-FERGHANA," Seminar "Mezhdunarodnoe i natsionalnoe vodnoe pravo v kontekste ispolzovaniia transgranichnykh vodnykh resursov," September, 2007, http://sic.icwc-aral.uz/releases/rus/143.htm.

18. IWMI, headquartered in Colombo, Sri Lanka, carries out projects in twenty-one countries of Asia and Africa. Its sub-regional Central Asian office is in Tashkent. It is one of the fifteen institutes of the Consultative Group on International Agricultural Research (CGIAR). It is primarily funded by governments, private foundations, as well as international and regional organizations.

19. "Tsentralnaia Aziia: Ferghana-Osh-Khudzhand," Vspomogatelnyi otchet, 2004, www.envsec.org/centasia/pub/ENVSEC%20FV%20DeskA%20rus.doc.

20. Ibid.

21. Currently all Central Asian states participate in the Partnership for Peace Program. Tajikistan was the last state in the region to become a member in 2002.

22. "Central Asia: Civil Emergency Exercise Opens in Ferghana Valley," April 28, 2003, www.reliefweb.int/rw/rwb.nsf/db900sid/OCHA-64CP3B?OpenDocument.

23. See http://centralasia.usaid.gov.

24. It is worth noting that two-thirds of the aid given by USAID in the 1990s was directed to dealing with the consequences of the humanitarian crisis that resulted from the civil war of 1992–97. On USAID in Tajikistan see http://centralasia.usaid.gov/page.php?page=article-90.

25. In the sphere of public health the following USAID projects bear mention: "Improving Mother and Child Health" (carried out in the Ferghana provinces with the minister of health of Uzbekistan); "Improving Health at the Community Level," which strengthened interconnections between village residents and rural medical institutions, public health offices and NGOs. See the biweekly summary of the USAID work, March 3, 2006, http://centralasia.usaid.gov/datafiles/_upload/biweekly-Rus_March_03-06.pdf.

26. For details see http://centralasia.usaid.gov.

27. It should be noted that ministries and local governmental offices, as well as Central Asian NGOs were involved in carrying out work with American partner organizations.

28. This project was carried in the Kyrgyz sector of the Ferghana Valley from 2002 to 2007. See International Narcotics Control Strategy Report, 2008, http://bishkek.usembassy.gov/uploads/images/W6qzW0z2gzzjjhnJj0PoYg/2008_International_Narcotics_Control_Strategy_Report.pdf.

29. "Ferganskaia dolina: v Sokhskom raione razreshen eshche odin vodnyi konflikt," September 16, 2003, http://news.ferghana.ru/detail.php?id=476771918016902.

30. United Nationa, "Obzor rezultativnosti ekonomicheskoi deiatelnosti: Tadzhikistan," New York and Geneva, 2004, www.unece.org/env/epr/epr_studies/Tajikistan%20r.pdf, pp. 140–150.

31. V.Huraliev. "Chtoby ne stat zalozhnikami ChS," http://www.osce.org/uzbekistan/71086.

32. Council of the European Union, "The EU and Central Asia."

33. From 1991 to 2006 the states of Central Asia received some €636 million of aid within the TACIS framework. "TACIS in tables," April 2007, http://tacis.uz/docs/Tacis_tables_EN.pdf.

34. As a result of reforms of the EU Commission external assistance program and

development of new regulations for 2007–2013, the Central Asian countries, starting from 2007, are under the purview of Development Cooperation and Economic Cooperation program, which replaced the TACIS program. The new program provides for more flexible use of financial means across priority areas of assistance, simplification of budget approval processes, retargeting of funds, and expansion of assistance beyond technical aid.

35. "Programma Evropeiskogo Soiuza po predotvrashcheniiu rasprostraneniia narkotikov v Tsentralnoi Azii," May 2009, www.bomca.eu/upload/docs/pr/BOMCA_7_Inceptio_ Report_May_2009_rus.pdf.

36. "Border management in Central Asia" Progress Report, August 2007, http://bomca. eu/upload/docs/pr/5%20BOMCA%205%20PR%20June-August%202007_ENG.pdf.

37. "Pogransluzhba Uzbekistana raziasniaet: 'Minirovaniiu podverglis tolko te gornye i trudnodostupnye . . . ,'" January 28, 2006, www.centrasia.ru/news2.php?st=1138436700.

38. Inomjon I. Bobokulov, "Central Asia: Is There an Alternative to Regional Integration?" *Central Asian Survey,* vol. 25, nos. 1–2, March–June 2006, p. 87.

39. Of the Central Asian states, only Turkmenistan is not a member of the Collective Security Treaty Organization. Moreover, the country's new military doctrine, adopted in January 2009, prohibits Turkmenistan to enter any politico-military alliances.

40. Turkmenistan does not participate in the activities of the EurAsEC. In October 2008 Uzbekistan submitted an official statement on suspension of its membership in this organization.

41. M.B. Olcott and A. Malashenko, eds., *Mnogomernye granitsy Tsentralnoi Azii,* Moscow, 2000, p. 52.

42. "Protokol o vnesenii izmenenii v soglashenie mezhdu Rossiiskoi Federatsiei i Kyrgyzskoi Respublikoi," www.bestpravo.ru/fed2000/data02/tex13300.htm.

43. The agreement was reached between the leaders of Russia and Kyrgyzstan in August 2009, during the informal summit of CSTO member states.

44. "Rossiiskii voennyi faktor v Oshe: 'Za' i 'Protiv,' Obschestvennyi reiting," May 30, 2005, www.centrasia.ru/newsA.php?st=1117410360.

45. Informational announcement of the agency Zhakhon, "Uzbekistan demonstriruet priverzhennost vibrannomu kursu," www.press-uz.info/index.php?title=home&nid=36& my=082009&st=1&date=20090825&ctry=1000.

46. Khojamakhmad Umarov, "Kak razvivaetsia tadzhikskaia chast Ferganskoi doliny?" November 25, 2008, www.easttime.ru/analitic/1/1/528.html.

47. "Turdakun Usubaliev vystupil protiv oppozitsii i za territorialnye ustupki Kitaiu," *Slovo Kyrgyzstana,* May 16, 2002, www.centrasia.ru/newsA.php?st=1021585200.

48. "China's Growing Problem with Xinjiang," http://freerepublic.com/focus/f-news/542180/posts.

49. Orozbek A. Moldaliev, *Sovremennye vyzovy bezopasnosti Kyrgyzstana i Tsentralnoy Azii,* Bishkek, 2001, pp. 30–31.

50. "Doklad o chelovecheskom razvitii v Tsentralnoi Azii. V budushchee bez barerov: regionalnoe sotrudnichestvo v oblasti chelovecheskogo razvitiia i obespecheniia chelovecheskoi bezopasnosti," Regionalnoe biuro PROON po stranam Evropy i Sodruzhestva Nezavisimykh Gosudarstv, 2005, http://europeandcis.undp.org/home/show/FCADD38D-F203-1EE9-BBAD4D358FDD375D, p. 218.

51. "Shankhaiskaia organizatsiia sotrudnichestva i sovremennyi mir," Analiticheskie doklady, Moskva, MGIMO (U) MID Rossii, no. 3, May 2007, p. 49.

52. Vladimir Ryzhkov, "Rossiia i Kitai—eto 'iadro' ShOS," http://shanhai.rfn.ru/interviews/doc.html?id=394.

53. "Sudba uranovykh khvostokhranilisch v Kirgizii volnuet i Uzbekistan," *Nemetskaia volna,* April 27, 2005, http://www.dw-world.de/dw/article/0,,1565886,00.html.

54. United States–Uzbekistan Declaration on the Strategic Partnership and Cooperation Framework, March 12, 2002, http://uzbekistan.usembassy.gov/pr031203.html.

55. S. Frederick Starr, "Introduction," in *Anatomy of a Crisis: U.S.-Uzbekistan Relations, 2001–2005,* ed. John C.K. Daly, Kurt H.Meppen, Vladimir Socor, and Frederick S. Starr, Central Asia–Caucasus Institute Silk Road Studies Program, February 2006, p.v8.

56. "U.S.–Uzbek Military Exercises Finish," *RFE/RL Newsline,* June 10, 1997.

57. "O kirgizskikh NPO i 'metrvykh dushakh," *Nemetskaia volna,* June 27, 2007, www. centrasia.ru/newsA.php?st=1182889380.

58. Ibid.

59. Slim, "The Ferghana Valley," p. 155.

60. Valentin Bogatirev, "Grazhdanskoze obshechstvo v stranakh Tsentralnoi Azii: povestka sotrudnichestva ili missiia preduprejdeniia konfliktov, http://lgi.osi.hu/cimg/0/1/3/6/3/.doc

61. Sheradil Baktygulov, "Problemy i perspektivy uchastiia NPO Kyrgyzstana v priniatii gosudarstvennykh reshenii," Tsentr sotsialnykh issledovanii, Amerikanskii universitet Tsentralnoi Azii, http://src.auca.kg/images/stories/files/Sheradil_rus.pdf.

62. "Frederick Starr: Priatno potriasen politikoi Uzbekistana," *Uzbekistan Today,* no. 2, September 15, 2006, http://www.iscs.uz/rus/intervyu/frederik_starr_priyatno_potryasen_politikoy_uzbekistana.mgr.

63. S. Frederick Starr, "Clans, Authoritarian Rulers, and Parliaments in Central Asia," Central Asia–Caucasus Institute Silk Road Studies Program, June 2006, http://www.silkroadstudies.org/new/docs/Silkroadpapers/0605Starr_Clans.pdf, p. 5.

64. This fact has been noted by the United Nations. In this connection the UN General Assembly adopted resolution in 1994: "Tranzitnye transportnye sistemy v gosudarstvakh Tsentralnoi Azii, ne imeiushchikh vykhoda k moriu, i sosednikh stranakh transita," www. un.int/kazakhstan/170101pr.pdf.

65. In 1998 Uzbekistan signed a framework agreement on Transport Corridor Europe-Caucasus-Asia. Since then the republic has taken part in thirty-two projects of TRACECA costing €50 million. These projects aimed at further development of transport complex and infrastructure in Uzbekistan. The country's active participation in the program contributed to implementation of institutional changes, improvement of professional skills for hundreds of specialists, provision of necessary information on the EU legislation to government agencies, and so on. Moreover, with the TRACECA support Uzbekistan joined and ratified twenty-two multi-lateral conventions on air transport and thirteen agreements on auto and railway transport.

66. Azerbaijan also announced that it joined the agreement, "Central Asia Regional Economic Cooperation: Harmonization and Simplification of Transport Agreements, Cross Border Documents and Transport Regulations," Asia Development Bank, October 28, 2005, http://www.adb.org/Documents/Reports/CAREC/Transport-Sector-Reports/CAREC-harmonization.pdf, p. 44.

67. Materialy Gosudarstvennoi aktsionernoi kompanii "Uzavtoiul."

68. Speech of the first deputy of the minister of foreign affairs of Uzbekistan, Isan Murtazaev, in *Mezhdunarodnyi politicheskii dialog. Novye perspektivy economicheskogo dialoga v Tsentralnoi Azii,"* Materiali konferentsii, Berlin, May 8–19, 2006, p. 41.

69. Rustam Mirzaev, "Kommunikatsionnye vygody dlia mirovogo soobshchestva," in *Velikii Shelkoviy Put: Realii XXI veka,* Moscow, 2005, www.rustammirzaev.com/book4/4.pdf.

70. Speech of Jin Liqun of Asian Development Bank in *Mezhdunarodnyi politicheskii dialog,* p. 41.

71. Oleg Sidrov, "Novyi staryi Shelkovyi put," July 4, 2007, http://articles.gazeta.kz/ art.asp?aid=93202.

72. Official documents of the Central Asian regional economic cooperation program of the Asian Development Bank define it as a steadily evolving partnership of countries and institutions cooperating to achieve a common goal. The program provides direct assistance to the Central Asian states in the areas of transport, energy, and trade through cooperation with international financial institutions. Therefore, it is also characterized as an alliance of multi-lateral programs and international organizations seeking to promote economic cooperation in

Central Asia. Transport is a priority area in the ADB's strategy and regional cooperation program for the CAREC countries. "Central Asia Regional Economic Cooperation: Harmonization and Simplification of Transport Agreements, Cross Border Documents and Transport Regulations," Asia Development Bank, October 28, 2005, http://www.adb.org/Documents/Reports/CAREC/Transport-Sector-Reports/CAREC-harmonization.pdf, p. 7.

73. "Central Asia: Increasing Gains from Trade Through Regional Cooperation in Trade Policy, Transport, and Customs Transit," Asia Development Bank, Manila, 2006, www.adb.org/Documents/Reports/ca-trade-policy/, pp. 52–53.

74. "Tsentralnoaziatskoe regionalnoe ekonomicheskoe sotrudnichestvo," Asia Development Bank, September 2008, http://www.adb.org/Documents/Translations/Russian/Regional-Energy-Coop-Strategy-ru.pdf.

75. Bobokulov, "Central Asia," p. 83.

76. Barry Buzan and Ole Waever, *Regions and Powers: The Structure of International Security*, Cambridge, 2003.

Conclusion

S. Frederick Starr

By this point the reader may well be wondering, "What does it all mean?" Does this large volume somehow "explain" the terrible bloodshed in Osh and Jalalabad in the summer of 2010, or the "Andijan Events" of 2005, or the IMU's incursions into Batken a half-decade earlier, or the bloodshed in Osh in the summer of 1990? Probably not, if one is looking for simple answers to questions about complex events. But it surely identifies most, if not all, of the factors in play at the time of each of these very different moments of conflict. It speaks both to the "global" changes that have taken place over the past generation, and to the often-trivial triggering events that could transform a peaceful day into a time of horror. The summary below also enumerates some of the general themes that link these points in the present or recent past to the deeper history of the region under study. Several of these themes have been evident in the Ferghana Valley for decades, even centuries. Among them, none is more important than the question of identity as it is understood by three very distinctive communities, all of which have more in common with each other than with *anyone* else further afield. We shall return to this theme shortly.

The task the editors set for themselves was to present a portrait of the Ferghana Valley over time, a rich mosaic of the many overlapping realities that define a region which can, with justice, be considered "the Heart of Central Asia." Thanks to the international team of experts whom they assembled, and who toiled alone and together over some four years, they largely succeeded. Within the space of a few hundred pages a topic that may earlier have lent itself to clichés and stereotypes has emerged in its true richness and complexity. Of course, what is offered above is little more than a telegraphic overview, with many lacunae remaining. Such issues as communications within the valley, and between it and the outer world, remain largely untouched here, as do such diverse topics as labor markets, capital flows into and out of the valley, popular culture, and the evolution of family life. Given this, it is all the more important to draw whatever conclusions the evidence at hand allows, to advance hypotheses in other areas and, finally, to venture a look into the alternative futures that may unfold for this pivotal region.

Beginning at the most general level, it is pertinent to ask what "silver thread," if such exists, runs through the entire story presented here? This question, posed to the lead authors as they concluded their work, produced a surprising unanimity of views. These experts, drawn from all three countries of the valley, Europe, and Russia, agree that the underlying theme of their collective enquiry revolves around identity. By this, they mean identity at the level of individual citizens of the three countries that comprise the valley, of communities and, finally, of the valley as a whole. Three aspects of this issue emerged. First, the authors accepted that the Ferghana Valley has always been a zone of social diversity and pluralism, with multiple identities existing side by side over the centuries. In this respect, the present represents a high degree of continuity with the past. Second, it was felt that identities, whether personal or collective, are all in an extraordinary state of flux today. It is no exaggeration to say that across the length and breadth of the Ferghana Valley there is today a kind of "crisis of identity" that imparts a high degree of precariousness to all social life. Third, as of this writing, it is simply impossible to predict whether and when new and more stable identities might emerge, or whether they will come into being through an evolutionary process or as a result of further crises.

A significant realization that emerged from the research is that we know much more about identity issues as they exist within the framework of individual states than we do about identities that overlap two or more states. Both forms of identity exist in the Ferghana Valley today, with such diverse forces as traders and Sufi groupings figuring among the valley-wide communicators. Beyond these, of course, there are other and more radical religious groups that exist on a transnational basis and oppose all other forms of identity, civic and national as well as religious. The challenge of the present is to create institutions that can embrace the various identities prevalent today and provide safety valves that can reduce the attraction of extremist approaches.

The three states that divide the valley are all seeking to identify the social capital that can be productively engaged to further the region's economic modernization. Each must be credited with forging new forms of national identity, but the price of this success has been to increase the psychological distance among physically adjacent groups. Just how great that distance has become became cruelly manifest in April 2010, when Kyrgyz and Uzbeks in the Kyrgyzstan sector brutally attacked each other, driving from their homes hundreds of thousands of residents, mainly Uzbeks. In the end, if the benefits of economic modernization are to be secured, these diverse national groups must somehow work together. It is impossible to predict which traditions in the Ferghana Valley will survive, and how they will, or will not, be able to contribute to the region's social capital. Clearly, it will be important to monitor this issue in the coming years, and to seek institutional solutions as necessary.

On this somewhat precarious basis, let us now turn once more to the series of questions we posed at the beginning. First, is there in some sense a "Ferghana" history and culture, and what is the role of localism within the Ferghana region? The picture that has emerged is one of a highly developed sense of localism, with identities and loyalties focused on where one's family and community is based.

Yet a larger sense of region always has been present as well. Islam fostered this, of course, but so did a common way of life, art, music, customs, and even languages in what was a multi-lingual but integrated culture. The centuries of rule by Kokand united the urban populations through common tax and administrative structures, although this was not shared by parts of the valley's Kyrgyz population. Soviet rule also imposed a common history on the valley that endured for nearly a century. The process of collectivization, the transformation of education, and the emancipation of women were all common experiences, as were forms of resistance. Especially important was the massive expansion of irrigation and of the related cotton culture during the 1970s, which can be compared in its depth of impact on the Ferghana Valley with the Virgin Lands program of the 1960s in Kazakhstan.

Today, our authors agree, these commonalities are breaking down as the valley's population divides into three national states and is drawn towards three distant and very different capitals. This process is comparable to what occurred in early modern Europe, when national states arose out of the wreckage of the Holy Roman Empire. The decision by many ethnic Uzbeks in the Kyrgyz and Tajik sectors to learn the language of their new titular state reflects this development, even as they maintain their use of Uzbek. Yet the process is very different from early state development in the West in one fundamental respect, namely, that powerful forces of market-based development and globalization are everywhere present today.

What is by no means clear to our experts is how far this centrifugal process will go, and when its apogee will be reached. As it has been through the centuries, trade is seen as the most likely determining force. The fact that the Ferghana Valley is the single largest and most densely populated potential market in all Central Asia carries enormous importance for the future. This market cannot be developed without economic and human bridges between the constituent national zones of the valley, and between the Ferghana area as a whole and the surrounding region.

A further question the Ferghana Project posed concerns the interplay between isolation and contact in the life of the valley, past and present. At important periods stretching sometimes for several centuries, a rich culture of trade and contact prevailed in the region. At such times populous and rich cities like Kasansai and Aksikent arose. Archaeological evidence has established that these great centers maintained close contact with China, India, the Middle East and Europe—in short, all of the Eurasian land mass.

In his memoirs, the Mughal emperor Babur waxes lyrical over the incomparably delicious fruits of his native Ferghana Valley. Writing in India, Babur notes gratefully that his beloved pears and melons were available in Agra at the local market! Besides confirming the existence of trade ties in the sixteenth century that cannot be matched today, Babur's statement underscores an important truth: namely, that the periods of greatest effervescence of life and culture in the Ferghana Valley coincided with the great ages of overland trade along what we misleadingly call the "Silk Road(s)." Reduced to a formula, one can state that trade and contact always have enriched Ferghana life and culture, while isolation impoverishes it.

Against this background one can only hope that the apogee of centrifugal forces will soon be reached, and that new forces of coordination and integration will come to the fore.

Closely related to this issue is the question of whether change in the Ferghana Valley has characteristically been driven from within or without. It is probably no surprise that our enquiry seems to confirm the prevalence over the centuries of external forces. True, there have been important periods, such as the era of the Kokand Khanate (1709–1876), when indigenous factors dominated. At such times, one may speak of the Ferghana Valley as a *subject* of political and economic life, rather than an *object* acted upon by outsiders. But throughout the subsequent era and extending until the present, the Ferghana Valley has been shaped and defined largely from without.

However, this is not to say that its population has been passive or lacking in re-sourcefulness. Subjected to massive external influences, residents of the valley have exhibited extraordinary *adaptive* skills. Rather than merely *adopt* new procedures, practices, and norms which the outside world has presented to them, these people generally have endeavored to *adapt* them to their preexistent mores. This has had the effect of preserving many features of Ferghana life that otherwise might have disappeared. At a deeper level, the process of making such adaptations was itself an exercise of independence, and doubtless reinforced the notion that there was a local or regional "we" distinct from the power-wielding "they" from beyond the valley. The obvious question arises over whether this juxtaposition will long survive into the post-independence world, or will instead be replaced by new senses of national identity so strong as to integrate what earlier was separate.

A related and urgent question is where to place non-standard Muslim religious movements within this spectrum. Surely this is the most urgent issue facing the Ferghana Valley today (as well as all three governments that rule there), and the international community as it addresses the problem of social stability in the valley. Should they be seen as an important though alien presence, or as a local adaptation of tradition to reckon with new and disorienting circumstances being imposed from without—or in some sense both?

The few articles that have appeared on the Ferghana Valley in the international press tend to assume that the worst social problems in the region today arise from thwarted economic development, that is from stagnation. At some common sense level this is doubtless true. Our researchers have underscored how economic stag-nation and poverty, and such related phenomena as the emigration of labor, have generated social instability. Whenever large swaths of the working-age population become frustrated with the inability of government to address their needs, they are ripe for recruitment by extremist religious movements.

Acknowledging this, an important conclusion of this study is that the main force fueling social unrest in all three sectors of the Ferghana Valley is less stag-nation than it is rapid, unsettling change. Beginning with a thoroughly traditional rural existence four generations ago, Ferghana Valley residents have endured the replacement of old governing institutions, the collectivization of private property, the emancipation of women, the massive growth of irrigation and industrial agriculture, the fragmentation of local life into three national sectors, and varying degrees of re-privatization. In the process of this whirlwind of change, the single national ideology of communism arose suddenly, served as a battering ram against Islam and many traditional values, was inculcated into several generations, and then disappeared as abruptly as it came. To a Ferghana resident, the world has long been in profound flux.

Yet however numerous and radical, these upheavals proved less than thoroughgoing, in that they still left an extremely high percentage of the population remaining on the land. What could be more paradoxical than the fact that collective farms, introduced by Stalin amid great dissension and bloodshed, could, in the Ferghana Valley, serve as safe zones where many aspects of traditional life and values could be preserved? This perpetuation of important elements of traditional rural life and culture may be a boon to ethnographers and collectors of *makam*. Beyond this, it may provide the basis of something to fall back on when everything else is in flux; yet at the same time, this perpetuation doubtless creates tensions that outsiders can scarcely understand. These take the form of a clash of fundamental values, of identities, and of expectations. This fracturing can occur in communities and families, among and within generations, and within individuals, especially younger men and women.

The terrifying pictures of scores of Ferghana Valley women immolating themselves in the 1970s and early 1980s attest to the grave economic and health crises of that time. No less, it shows that the crisis of identities between modernity and tradition, and between globalization and localism, was already in full flowering in late Soviet times—and that it particularly affected the lives of women. Thus, the withering of the age-old art of village needlepoint, or *suzane* (Persian for needle), coincided exactly with the rise of television. But thanks to Soviet controls on urbanization, the life portrayed on television remained inaccessible to the rural folk of the Ferghana. Most dealt with this by engaging in the normal practice of adaptation, but tragically some could not endure the tension between the conflicting worlds they faced.

These same tensions exist today, but in yet more acute form. It cannot be denied that there have been important signs of economic progress in large sections of the Ferghana Valley, most recently in Uzbekistan's sector. Yet Ferghanans everywhere understand that, whatever economic gains they may (or may not) have achieved, they are modest in comparison with the prosperity and cosmopolitanism that seems to be flowering in the mushrooming distant capitals.

The obvious conclusion to which these developments point is that religious extremism has arisen and spread in an environment that combines relative economic deprivation with disorienting and even dizzying changes occurring simultaneously at many levels. This gives rise to a kind of psychological dislocation, one prolonged and deepened by the fact that few, if any, of the normal pillars on which stable lives might be built are sufficiently strong to sustain people.

This brings us to a related question raised at the outset of this study: should the Ferghana Valley be seen today as a *center* or a *periphery*. The answer is not simple. In all three countries, and especially in Uzbekistan, the Ferghana region is considered a center. Uzbeks note that their literary language took form there, and it was the site of many other central events in their culture. Acknowledging that the valley region has at important points in its history been a *center* in its own right, all three sectors today are at some distance from their national capitals. Yet in terms of much decision-making and administration, the Ferghana Valley today is a *periphery*. Lacking a single center, it can claim no clear institutional identity, whether at the national or regional level. True, all three national sectors of the valley have their regional centers, whether Khujand, Osh, or Andijan and Namangan. But the highly centralized character of all three countries renders ambiguous the role of these provincial capitals not only with respect to the territories subordinate to them but, even more, with respect to the national capitals. This in turn means that the intra-regional affairs of the Ferghana Valley are managed not within the region itself but in the national capitals. An important question is whether it is possible to attain the region's economic and social potential without some sort of locally based body to coordinate the affairs of the three national territories that comprise Valley. The experts participating in this project agree that such a body is very much needed.

As we touch upon questions of public administration in the Ferghana Valley, we return to another question raised at the outset of this study: has the Ferghana characteristically been "over-governed" or "under-governed"? The spontaneous response of many residents, and still more so of foreign observers, would be that the region generally has suffered from "over-government." By this they mean that during Soviet times, if not earlier under Kokand, the state exercised its authority with a heavy and sometimes ruthless hand. Some extend this complaint to the present. Indeed, many foreign analysts and more than a few local critics argue that social problems in all three sectors of the valley arise mainly from what they see as the clumsy acts of authoritarian governments operating from the distant capitals. Yet without denying this, such an approach may misstate the issue of over- versus under-governance. To get at this question, one must ask whether government, at the level of its actual contact with the citizenry—that is, the most local level—is effective. In other words, can it address people's real needs, assure and protect the vigor of economic and social life locally, and manage crises?

A major hypothesis arising from this study is that, beginning at some point in the 1970s, the effectiveness of governance in the valley has steadily declined, and remains at a low level today. To be sure, there are notable exceptions to the rule: the hard-working *hakim,* the civic-minded district administrator, the dedicated and competent head of a new vocational college, and so forth. But centralization in general and now the centralization of administrative decision-making in three distant capitals has left the Ferghana region progressively less well-governed. Both Soviet and post-colonial elites have been concentrated in the republic/national capitals of Dushanbe, Bishkek, and Tashkent. The issues that preoccupy them may be far removed from the realities of daily life in the valley. This can lead to a steady breakdown of services, whether absolute or relative, even as the claims of a nominally strong government increase.

It seems to most of our authors that such a progressive breakdown of government services has indeed occurred, extending over more than a generation. In late Soviet times this left political and social space in the valley for someone like the late criminal master-organizer, Ahmadjon Adilov, to run a virtual state within a state. Following the collapse of the USSR, the new national leadership was understandably concerned above all to protect their fragile new sovereignties and assure that their countries would survive as independent states. Such a focus naturally left less energy for addressing the myriad of local issues that constitute the warp and weft of actual lives across the Ferghana Valley.

Development assistance from abroad, including that provided under the UN Ferghana Valley initiative in the early 1990s, appears to have exacerbated the problem. Rather than build up the competence of local administrators, this assistance focused instead on "civil society." Foreign funding provided big salaries, Land Cruisers, and radio telephones to the young staffs of independent organizations, while older administrators in virtually every area of life across the entire Valley had to fend for themselves, without training, equipment, or adequate salaries. Inevitably, many turned to corruption to survive, thus further alienating a populace already in the throes of a crisis wrought by the many head-spinning changes occurring around them.

This, too, forms an important part of the context for the rise of radical religious currents at various points in the Ferghana region. No longer able to adapt to disorienting change, some valley residents embraced philosophies that promised a direct and simple answer to all the problems they faced. Yet, as the reader has seen, this is only part of the story of religion in the Ferghana Valley today. To be sure, various currents of radical Islam thrive there. Some of them are so well-organized, deeply entrenched, and well-funded that they now define the struggle with Muslim extremism at the national level in each of the three countries.

Careful research on the ground has left many of our authors doubting the ability of the three countries, Kyrgyzstan, Tajikistan, and Uzbekistan, to reckon effectively with the phenomenon of radical Islam. Yet this theme of deepening polarization and crisis is only one of several narratives that arise from the Ferghana experience. Another focuses on the fact that the region always has been a land of religious diversity and hence of tolerance. This, it is claimed, is undergirded by the fact that the Hanafi school of Muslim jurisprudence that has prevailed there for a millennium is the most worldly and practical-minded of all the four schools of Muslim law. It is therefore natural that this doctrine should have been codified there and spread thence to Afghanistan, Pakistan and on to India. That Babur's fifteenth-century upbringing occurred in a Ferghana city, Aksikent, where Muslims and Christians shared the same cemetery, finds a contemporary parallel in the periodic and cordial meetings today of Muslim and Christian leaders in nearby Namangan. Ferghana, then, is the tolerant heart of the Muslim heartland, not a peripheral zone in need of instruction or inspiration by any radical new philosophies imported from abroad.

A third narrative stresses the deep history of secular education in the valley, and its vitality in many sectors of society today. This version stresses the importance of the Jadid tradition of the early twentieth century, which fed into Soviet secularism even as its adherents were eventually liquidated by the Communists. In today's world it emphasizes the important role for secular education in all three sectors of the valley, the new vocational high-schools and academic lycées established in the main cities of the Uzbek sector, the new or expanded institutions of higher education in Osh and Khujand, and the prevalence of secular values in such diverse areas as popular entertainment, dress, communications, and sport.

These alternative narratives might lead one to doubt that religious fundamentalism will take permanent root in the Ferghana Valley, however vigorous it may be in some quarters today. Yet the strength of countervailing forces cannot be denied. The region is certainly contributing talented young men and women to the national elites of all three countries, but far larger segments of the population are still contending with the difficult realities of daily life in the *qishloq* or village where they grew up, and where their forefathers lived. Many young men and women in the valley feel at home in the emerging global monoculture. Any evening they can be seen strolling in town or sipping wine together, their ears pressed to cell phones as they plan the next party or rendezvous. But many more have yet to enter this world. They might enjoy sports but the main competitions they see are national, not regional; purely local television is poorly developed or nonexistent, hence "news" pertains mainly to a larger world of which they do not feel a part. Most of the best jobs would take them out of their familiar worlds, but they are as yet too unsure of themselves to leave.

The message to them, then, is that there is indeed a big world out there, yet their own domain seems stuck on the distant periphery of that world. In the environment with which they are familiar, threatening centrifugal forces seem to rule, and the reassuring world of their family's courtyard, where three generations still live under one roof, is shrinking.

To what conclusions do the findings of our exploration point, and do our conclusions provide any insights into the future? The experts who have lent their skills to this study evince a wide range of views, some of them mutually incompatible. There are optimists among them, but perhaps more pessimists. Significantly, their adherence to one view or the other corresponds to neither nationality nor citizenship. However, after examining the trends of the past half-century, no one in the group denies the possibility of a dark outcome. All express concern over the existing interplay of centrifugal and centripetal forces, of coordination and un-coordination, of localism and globalism and of competing brands of globalism, of integration and disintegration. And all acknowledge that the drama being played out within the three national sectors that exist within the historic boundaries of the valley will go far toward defining the future of each of the three countries as a whole.

Our experts affirm that the complex economic and social realities of the Ferghana Valley will constrain and challenge the elected leaders of Tajikistan, Kyrgyzstan, and Uzbekistan, and will go far towards prescribing the terms in which leaders in Tashkent, Dushanbe, and Bishkek will set the agendas for both national and international policy.

The editors and authors of this volume set themselves the task of better understanding the past and present of the Ferghana Valley. They have no crystal ball, and do not pretend to be able to foresee the future. Still less do they claim the right or ability to set down policy proposals for their national governments or the international community. However, their discussions have led them to a few general thoughts that might profitably be shared.

The great defining event of recent times in the Ferghana Valley has been the collapse of the Soviet imperial system and its replacement by national states. Inevitably, the new governments have focused on the monumental task of affirming their existence as independent states. As in so many post-imperial situations worldwide, this caused all three countries to look inward and to distance themselves from their neighbors. All three nations focused on forming crucial ties with major external powers, at the price of partially ignoring their relations with immediate neighbors. None of the three—Kyrgyzstan, Tajikistan, Uzbekistan—can be said yet to have fully consolidated its sovereignty and the new institutions in which it is embodied. Yet all three appear to have passed successfully through their difficult birth process.

Like all countries, the three states that share the valley still face grave challenges. But the majority of our participating scholars believe that the most dangerous period of their formation may have passed, or that this might soon be the case. As these countries reach this important marker, it may be possible to focus on Ferghana issues in a way that has not been readily possible heretofore.

Among these issues, none poses more formidable challenges than the management of borders and border posts and of the water and hydroelectric power of the rivers in the Naryn Darya–Kara Darya–Syr Darya basin. For more than a decade, pessimists have predicted the outbreak of armed conflict over those issues. But in spite of the sharpest differences, and of many pointed threats, this has not happened. Perhaps this is due to the fact that the national leaders understand the dangers that an utter breakdown would pose. Perhaps it is due to the fact that the three peoples know each other far better than outsiders think they do. But for nearly two decades they have always stopped short of the brink, finally pulling back after periods of great tension.

To move beyond the mere absence of war to a climate in which enduring solutions might be found will require immense political, diplomatic, technical, and human skills. Above all, it will call for higher levels of cooperation across national borders. Members of the international community have repeatedly offered their services in building a structure in which such cooperation can occur. Some have moved beyond lofty rhetoric to deal more practically with the core issues of security and money. All three regional governments, including their technical experts, diplomats, and elected leaders, should welcome such help. But in the end, these are matters for the three countries themselves to decide. International players can provide mediation, technical assistance, and financial aid. But the will to move towards practical solutions must come from the regional states themselves. This will arise only after some foundation of trust has been established.

Trust arises not from ringing declarations but from successfully working together on less vexing issues. At present, no institutional setting exists for such collaboration beyond rare meetings at the highest levels. A more practical approach might be to establish some kind of "Ferghana Valley Coordination Council." Comprised of regional governors, relevant ministers, and a few public representatives, such a council should meet frequently and without undue publicity. Its sessions should rotate among venues located within the three national sectors of the valley. Its task should be to serve as a low-keyed clearinghouse for trilateral issues affecting the valley, identifying matters of concern, assembling relevant information, and framing alternative solutions for governmental action.

Such a Ferghana Valley Coordination Council should concentrate on issues affecting daily life, excluding nothing as too trivial for its attention: athletic competitions, joint cultural endeavors, family contacts, educational exchanges, and the like. In the larger scheme of things such matters may seem modest, but they are far from insignificant. Our study suggests that in recent decades the Ferghana Valley region has suffered from marginalization (as a peripheral zone) and isolation. This has contributed to a certain atomization in society, and the sense that real life is somehow to be found elsewhere. The kind of initiatives suggested here may create a counterweight to these trends, and in a manner that would dilute the sense of alienation that has been the seed-ground for extremism. It is entirely compatible with the emergence of strong national states and normal international borders.

If it proves successful in these endeavors, the Ferghana Valley Coordination Council might then consider questions concerning the improvement of local services, regional transport and trade, and eventually even more complex issues such as foreign investment. With no pretense of being a legislative body, the Council would be a sensor of public concerns and, to repeat, a clearinghouse for trilateral issues. Its goal would be to foster not *integration* but *coordination*. Secure modern borders, far from being enemies of coordination, should be seen as prerequisites for its attainment.

Since 1991, the international community has poured millions of dollars into projects in the Ferghana Valley. Some of these have been successful but a far larger number have not, and for a simple reason: too often projects have arisen not from local perceptions of need but from the judgments of outside experts. Disabled by this birth defect, these projects often have been undertaken not *with* local authorities but *on, around,* or even *against* them. To their credit, international donors sometimes have sought the advice and collaboration of local "society." But in the absence of a more legitimately constituted entity such as the Ferghana Valley Coordinating

Council proposed here, they have turned to self-appointed representatives of society and even to local interest groups. Unfortunately, self-designated "representatives of civil society" often pursue their own narrow interests at the expense of the whole, and have fallen prey to the very corruption that they decry in the governments. Besides addressing this issue, the proposed Council could facilitate projects that embrace more than one of the valley's national sectors.

Whether or not this specific suggestion proves useful, it will be necessary for the three countries involved in the Ferghana Valley to build somehow a basis for mutual cooperation. Many observers, sobered by the inter-communal and international tensions that have proven so costly during the first years of independence, question whether such cooperation is possible.

There are good reasons for such skepticism. However, among the factors that might challenge the skeptics is the book now before you. The twenty-seven experts who collaborated in its preparation are as different from one another as anyone in the Ferghana Valley. They are as capable of pointing fingers of blame as anyone who lives in the three Ferghana countries. These "outsiders" brought to bear yet another range of perspectives drawn from their backgrounds in Russia, Europe, and the United States. Yet in the end they coordinated their efforts with persistence and immense good will. At its conclusion, the Ferghana Project and this book that resulted from its four years of work stand as proof that the kind of cooperation envisioned here is not only possible today, but highly productive and, no less important, deeply rewarding for all who choose to engage in it.

About the Editors, Authors, and Contributing Authors

Editors

Baktybek Beshimov (Kyrgyz Republic) was a national manager of the United Nations Ferghana Valley Development Programme and of the UNDP Local Initiative Facility for Urban Environment Programme. He served as president of Osh State University, vice president and provost of the American University of Central Asia, and as Kyrgyzstan's ambassador to India, Sri Lanka, Nepal, and Bangladesh. He was MP and leader of the opposition in Kyrgyzstan's parliament from 1998 to 2000 and from 2007 and 2010. He is a visiting scholar at the Massachusetts Institute of Technology, after which he will be a visiting scholar at Harvard's Davis Center for Russian and Eurasian Studies.

Inomjon I. Bobokulov (Uzbekistan) holds a Ph.D. in International Law and is associate professor at the University of the World Economy and Diplomacy in Tashkent. He is the author of thirty papers published in Germany, Malaysia, the United Kingdom, the United States, and Uzbekistan. In 2005 he was a visiting scholar at the Central Asia–Caucasus Institute, Johns Hopkins University School of Advanced International Studies in Washington, DC. His current research is on the international legal aspects of regional security and boundary issues in Central Asia.

Pulat Shozimov (Tajikistan), Ph.D., heads the Department of Western Philosophy at the Institute of Philosophy of the Tajikistan Academy of Sciences. He is the author of *Tajik Identity and State Building in Tajikistan* and more than seventy articles. In 2005, Shozimov was Fulbright Scholar at the Central Asia–Caucasus Institute at Johns Hopkins University School of Advanced International Studies in Washington, DC. He was a visiting scholar of the Watson Institute for International Studies at Brown University in 2001, and a visiting scholar of the Catholic University of America in 2008.

S. Frederick Starr (USA) is founding chairman of the Central Asia–Caucasus Institute at Johns Hopkins University School of Advanced International Studies in Washington, DC. He is currently writing a book on the "Golden Age" of Central Asia. Trained as an archeologist, classicist, and historian, he earlier served as founding director of the Kennan Institute for Advanced Russian Studies, and president of Oberlin College. He has published numerous books and articles on political and cultural history, architecture, and music.

Authors and Contributing Authors

Sergey Abashin (Russia) holds a Ph.D. in history from Moscow State University. He has worked as a lead scholar at the Institute of Ethnology and Anthropology at the Russian Academy of Sciences, specializing in history and anthropology of Central Asia. He is the author of *Nationalisms in Central Asia: The Search for Identity* (2007).

Kamoludin Abdullaev (Tajikistan) is an independent historian from Dushanbe, Tajikistan. A two-time Fulbright Scholar, Abdullaev is among the most active Central Asian participants of the U.S. government-sponsored research exchange programs in the field of history and political science. From 2001 to 2010, he regularly taught modern Central Asian subjects at Yale University and at Ohio State University. His most recent publications include *Ot Sintsiana do Khorasana. Iz istorii Sredneaziatskoi emigratsii XX veka* (From Xinjiang to Khurasan. From the History of the Twentieth-Century Central Asian Emigration; 2009) and with Shahram Akbarzadeh, *Historical Dictionary of Tajikistan* (2010).

Ravshan Abdullaev (Uzbekistan), Ph.D., is a senior research fellow at the Department of History of the Colonial Period at the Institute of History of the Uzbekistan Academy of Sciences. He has published more than forty works on national issues and political movements in Central Asia in the twentieth century.

Shamshad Abdullaev (Uzbekistan), a native of Ferghana City, is a founder and leader of the Ferghana School of Russian poetry. He is the author of several collections of poems. In 1994 he received the coveted Andrei Bely Prize for poetry and in 1998 his work was featured in the journal *Znamia*. He has been a distinguished guest at many Western cultural institutions and his work has appeared in many languages.

Abdulkhamid Anarbaev (Uzbekistan) holds a Ph.D. in archeology and is the head of the Archeology Department at the Institute of Archeology in Samarkand. He is the author of more than ninety publications in Uzbek and Russian.

Khaydarbek Bababekov (Uzbekistan), Ph.D., is a professor of history at Tashkent State Pedagogical University. He is the editor-in-chief of the journal *History of Turan,* published in Russian and Uzbek. He is also the author of more than 30 monographs and 300 articles. His main research interest has been the history of the Kokand Khanate.

Bakhtiyar Babadjanov (Uzbekistan) holds a Ph.D. in religion. He is a senior research fellow at the Institute of Oriental Studies at the Uzbekistan Academy of Sciences. His research interests include the history of Sufi brotherhoods in Mawarannahr, the political activities of Sufi leaders, the interactions between Sufism and politics, and the Soviet (and post-Soviet) re-Islamization in Central Asia. He is the author of more than 100 publications in Russian, Uzbek, English, French, and German. He is also the coauthor of *Schaibanidische Grabinschriften* (1997) and *Les inscription persanes de Char Bakr, necropole familiale des khwaja Juybary pres de Boukhara* (2002).

Murat Bakhadyrov (Uzbekistan) holds a Ph.D. in political sciences and heads the Department of International Relations at the University of World Economy and Diplomacy in Tashkent His current research focuses on environmental issues and their relation to the geopolitics of Central Asia.

Christine Bichsel (Switzerland), Ph.D., is a senior researcher at the Department of Geosciences at the University of Fribourg, Switzerland. She is the author of *Conflict Transformation in Central Asia: Irrigation Disputes in the Ferghana Valley* (2009). Her main research interests include political geography, historical geography, developmental studies, and issues of peace and conflict.

Victor Dubovitskii (Tajikistan) is vice director of the Institute of History, Archeology and Ethnography of the Tajikistan Academy of Sciences. In addition to his Ph.D. dissertation, "A History of the System of Geopolitical Relations Between Russia and Middle Asia, 1700–2002," he is the author of two monographs and more than seventy articles published in Tajikistan and abroad.

Valentina Goriyacheva (Kyrgyz Republic), a graduate of Tashkent State University, is a Member of the Philosophy of Science Department at the Kyrgyz-Russian Slavic University. She is the author of 11 monographs and more than 100 scholarly articles on the history of Kyrgyzstan, cultural anthropology, and religious studies on Central Asia.

Tashmanbet Kenensariev (Kyrgyz Republic) is the rector of Jalalabad State University in Kyrgyzstan. A graduate of the Kyrgyz National University and Moscow State University, he holds a Ph.D. in history. He is the author of 300 scholarly articles in Kyrgyz, Russian, Uzbek, Turkish, English, Farsi, Chinese, German, and Polish, as well as 17 monographs, and 3 textbooks.

Namoz Khotamov (Tajikistan) is the head of the Department of Philosophy and Enterprise at the Institute of Enterprise and Service in Dushanbe. He is the author of 12 books and more than 200 articles, as well as a contributor to the six-volume *Istoriia Tadzhikskogo naroda* (A History of the Tajik Nation) published by the

Tajikistan Academy of Sciences. He is currently researching the history of banks, banking, and enterprises in Middle Asia.

Arslan Koichiev (Kyrgyz Republic) holds a Ph.D. in history and specializes in the history of Soviet Central Asia. He is the author of books and articles on border issues in the Ferghana Valley, crises in water and energy, and inter-ethnic relations. Currently he is a correspondent for the Central Asia and Caucasus BBC Service in London.

Zukhra Madamidzhanova (Tajikistan), Ph.D., is the head of the Department of Political Studies at the Institute of Strategic Studies Under the President of the Republic of Tajikistan. Her published monograph and more than fifty articles focus on themes of culture, tradition, ceremony, and ritual among the peoples of Tajikistan.

Kamil Malikov (Kyrgyz Republic) earned a Ph.D. in political and Islamic studies from the Department of Arabic, Islamic and Central Asian Studies of the Madrid Autonomous University in Spain. He also holds a a Certificate on Conflict Studies from the Center for International Security and Cooperation, Complutense University of Madrid, Spain. At present, Malikov is the director of the Analytical Research Center for Religion, Law, and Politics at the OSCE Academy, where he reads lectures on political Islam.

Kholnazar Mukhabbatov (Tajikistan) is a professor of geography at Tajik State University and head of the Department of Regional Economics at the Institute of Ecological Studies in Dushanbe. Dr. Mukhabbatov holds a doctorate in geography and is the author of 250 scholarly articles and 15 books. He has participated in many international research projects, including that on the Aral Sea.

Ildar Mukhtarov (Uzbekistan), Ph.D., is a leading art critic in Uzbekistan. He is the chairman of the Department of Cultural Studies at the Institute of Scholarly Research on the Fine Arts at the Academy of Arts of Uzbekistan. He is also a professor of the history of theater at the State Institute of Art in Tashkent. He has authored more than ninety papers and books.

Aloviddin Nazarov (Tajikistan) is a research fellow at the Donish Institute of History, Archeology, and Ethnography of the Academy Sciences in Dushanbe. In addition to his Ph.D. dissertation, "The History of the Religious Life of Muslims in Tajikistan During the Soviet Period (1941–1991)," he has published more than thirty articles. During the 2006 spring semester, Nazarov taught at the Department of Philosophy and Religious Studies at the University of Wisconsin-Whitewater.

Ravshan Nazarov (Uzbekistan), Ph.D., is the head of the Department of the History of Independence and International Relations at the Institute of History of the Uzbekistan Academy of Sciences. He is a member of the Council of Coordination of Dissertation Topics on History at the Institute and the author of 100 publications issued in Uzbekistan, Kazakhstan, Ukraine, Russia, Belarus, Germany, and the United States.

Abdukakhor Saidov (Tajikistan) is senior researcher of the Donish Institute of History, Archeology, and Ethnography of the Academy of Sciences of Tajikistan. He has authored 7 monographs and some 100 articles. His Ph.D. dissertation was on the "Political, Social and Economic History of the Bukhara Khanate in the Seventeenth and the First Half of the Eighteenth Centuries." He has presented at international conferences and symposia in China, India, South Korea, Iran, and Turkey.

Lenzi Sherfedinov (Uzbekistan) holds a Ph.D. in geology and is the head of the laboratory on the Methodology of Complex Use and Protection of Water Resources at the Institute of Water Problems of the Uzbekistan Academy of Sciences. He is the author of 140 papers on water resource management, hydrology and hydrogeology, nature preservation, and on the quality of water resources.

Joomart Sulaimanov (Kyrgyz Republic) holds a Ph.D. in anthropology and ethnography. He is an assistant professor of history at Osh State University and publishes widely on interethnic relations in Kyrgyzstan and the Ferghana Valley.

Khojamahmad Umarov (Tajikistan) is a professor at Tajik State University and the head of the Department of Macro-Economic Studies of the Institute of Economic Studies of Tajikistan's Ministry of Economy and Trade. He regularly lectures at the universities of Moscow, Tel-Aviv, Stockholm, Prague, Cairo, London, Delhi, Bombay, and Sweden. He had published 28 books and 230 articles in Tajik, Russian, and English.

Khurshida Yunusova (Uzbekistan), Ph.D., is an associate professor at the Department of History of Uzbekistan at the National University of Uzbekistan. She is the author of *The Nationality Policy of the Soviet Government and Its Consequences* (2005; in Uzbek). Her postdoctoral research focuses on the "Cotton Affair" and the late period of Soviet rule in Uzbekistan.

Sayidfozil Zokirov (Uzbekistan) holds a Ph.D. in economics. He is the chair of the Department of Economics at the National University of Uzbekistan. In the past, he has served in the Ministry of Economy of Uzbekistan.

Index